IDA B. WELLS-BARNETT AND AMERICAN REFORM, 1880–1930

Gender and
American Culture

Ida B. Wells-Barnett

and American Reform,

1880–1930

PATRICIA A. SCHECHTER

The University of North Carolina Press

Chapel Hill and London

Publication of this work was aided by a generous grant from the Z. Smith Reynolds Foundation.

The poem "weaponed woman," by Gwendolyn Brooks, is reprinted from Gwendolyn Brooks, *Selected Poems* (New York: Harper & Row, 1963), 125. Reprinted with permission of the estate of Gwendolyn Brooks.

Library of Congress Cataloging-in-Publication Data. Schechter, Patricia Ann, 1964–   Ida B. Wells-Barnett and American reform, 1880–1930 / by Patricia A. Schechter. p. cm. Includes bibliographical references (p.) and index.
ISBN 0-8078-2633-2 (cloth: alk. paper)—ISBN 0-8078-4965-0 (pbk.: alk. paper)
1. Wells-Barnett, Ida B., 1862–1931. 2. African American women civil rights workers—Biography. 3. Civil rights workers—United States—Biography. 4. African American women social reformers—Biography. 5. African American women political activists—Biography. 6. African American women journalists—Biography. 7. Lynching—United States—History. 8. United States—Race relations. 9. Afro-Americans—Politics and government. 10. Women's rights—United States—History. I. Title.   E185.97.W55 S34 2001   323'.092—dc21 [B]   00-068313

05 04 03   5 4 3 2

To my family, Nicholas and Maria Fish,
to my parents, Carmen and Alan Schechter,
and to all my teachers.

CONTENTS

ILLUSTRATIONS

A book about a well-known person raises certain expectations in readers, and a word is in order about what this book is and is not. It is not a definitive biography of Ida B. Wells-Barnett. There is, to my knowledge, one biography already published and at least one more on the way. My interest is primarily in Wells-Barnett's ideas and in her social activism. My goal is to present both in as rich an historical context as possible in order to understand more fully the history of women, racism, and reform in the United States. The many interpretive puzzles and mysteries of Wells-Barnett's life will continue to provoke historians for a long time, and I look forward to reading the work of others whose treatments are sure to follow, and perhaps dispute, mine.

This book cuts against what by now is an old saw in feminist writing about women: that the private and public aspects of life are intimately connected and shape each other. In Wells-Barnett's case, however, intimate matters—the deeper recesses of her religious faith, her feelings for her husband and children, her relationship with her parents and siblings, her friendships—are almost absent from the historical record, and for good reason. As historian Darlene Clark Hine reminds us, the African American women of Wells-Barnett's generation were very circumspect, secretive even, about expressing their personal feelings. Black women lived in an extremely hostile world, and any information disclosed to the wrong hands, even something as simple as marital status, could be and was used against them. In such a context, African American women who assumed positions of leadership in their communities took special care with their public image. Wells-Barnett was no exception, and I have paid special attention to the politics of self-representation over a fifty-year period. Finally, even relatively advantaged African American women like Wells-Barnett were often cut off from the institutions where a more complete record of her work and social relations might have been kept. Wells-Barnett was, among many things, a professional journalist and a skilled publicist, but she kept her letters and papers at home in a trunk that was destroyed in a fire sometime around 1920. After ten years of tracing her legacy in the United States and abroad, I have no doubt that there is more material on her life to be found, and I hope the search for it will continue.

A note on usage. In this study, the phrase "club women" refers to female members of voluntary associations, most of whom could be described as middle class according to their educational level or church standing. Following the scholarship of historian Kevin Gaines, the term "racial uplift" as used in this book describes an ideology that endorsed thrift, sobriety, Christian morality, education, service, and bourgeois family norms as a blueprint for African American advancement. I use the words "African American" and "black" somewhat interchangeably, as has become customary in academia when referring to people of African descent in the time period under consideration. I refer to Americans of European ancestry as "white people," a shorthand that evokes the racially polarized climate of the era. Similarly, this book occasionally refers to the "black press" and "white press" or "black leadership" and "white leadership" as a shorthand, not to reify nineteenth-century racial constructs. Finally, in quoting from historical sources I have retained words like "colored people," "Afro-American," "Negro," and occasionally more disparaging terminology in order to recapture the world of Ida B. Wells-Barnett.

That world and Wells-Barnett's struggle in it have taught me much. I began the serious study of U.S. history in order to figure out what it means to belong, in my own case almost by accident, to this country. As the daughter and granddaughter of European immigrants, I frequently feel like an interloper in my travels through the American past. While in graduate school during the mid-1980s, I found myself wondering at another gap: the distance between contemporary educated American women and those of the nineteenth century. As the following pages will show, a significant number of Victorian literary and activist women believed that women could be a unique force for racial healing in this country, more so than is usually sounded out today. With a need to explore what happened to this belief, I turned to the study of Ida B. Wells-Barnett. Pondering the record of her ideas and experience has been a most privileged aspect of my education. I hope the care and respect I brought to tracing her legacy comes through in the pages that follow.

ACKNOWLEDGMENTS

This book would not exist without the institutional and personal support I have been so fortunate to receive. A year-long fellowship from the Pew Program for the Study of Religion in American History in 1997–98 afforded me precious writing time. Grants from the North Caroliniana Society, Portland State University, and the City University of New York's Research Foundation underwrote major pieces of my research. An article from my dissertation, "Unsettled Business: Ida B. Wells Against Lynching or, How Antilynching Got Its Gender," received the 1998 Judith Lee Ridge Article Prize from the Western Association of Women Historians. Special appreciation is due to those people who shared their personal archives and family histories with me. I am extremely grateful to M. V. Blatchford, the late Roberta Church, Benjamin C. Duster, Frances D. Hooks, Dr. Clementine McConico Skinner, and Albert Lee Kreiling. Paul Lee's astounding generosity and meticulous research vastly enriched this project. Spotting my interest in the Chicago Municipal Court on the internet, Michael Willrich graciously offered guidance and citations for the Daley Center records.

I must thank those scholars who helped create a sense of community and shared purpose despite our dispersed academic lives. Several pieces of this book benefited from feedback at conferences. I am grateful to Rosalyn Terborg-Penn for inviting me to participate in the 1994 American History Association (AHA) panel "New Graduate Work on African American Women's History" and for encouragement from Ellen

DuBois and Evelyn Brooks Higginbotham during that session. Robert Engs provided excellent commentary at an AHA panel on Southern biography that we shared in 1998. Feedback from my presentation at Princeton University's Afro-American Studies graduate colloquium in the spring of 1998 was most helpful, especially the comments received from Cheryl Hicks, Crystal Feimster, and Kenneth Mack. The Pew Fellows Conference at Yale that same spring, convened by two outstanding historians of religion, Jon Butler and Harry Stout, provided an extremely stimulating weekend of study. Comments from Colleen McDannell and conversations with Amanda Badgett, Joel Dinnerstein, Sarah Gordon, Eric Grant, Jacqueline M. W. Robinson, and Lillian Taiz at the conference were edifying and great fun.

I am especially indebted to colleagues and mentors who read sections, chapters, or the entire manuscript at various stages. Kevin Gaines offered insight and encouragement early on and I hope he is pleased that I accepted his challenge to "do the intellectual history." His work blazed a magnificent trail. Fitzhugh Brundage helped me clarify my thinking on lynching and black resistance at a critical phase. Gail Bederman cheered me on at the beginning of my dissertation research, read (on ridiculously short notice) drafts of Chapters 3 and 4 of this book, and taught me much along the way. David Tucker reviewed my work on Memphis with an expert eye. Glenda Gilmore has been a most generous colleague. Her thoughtful and passionate readings of the entire manuscript were a gift. Claudia Tate took time out of her busy schedule to read a late draft of Chapter 1. Jill Bellrose gave the manuscript a much-needed going over at a key juncture, as did David A. Horowitz. Linda Kerber read a late draft and guided me more than she knows. Working with Kate Douglas Torrey and Kathy Malin at the University of North Carolina Press has been a delightful professional experience, and I owe them and Barbara Sicherman a large debt of thanks for greatly improving the manuscript by their insights.

In Oregon, Sue Danielson took the lead in fostering a shared intellectual life at Portland State University; her welcome into the American Studies faculty reading group was a boon. Francesca Sawaya has been an invaluable colleague. Jan Haaken and Carl Abbott gave me feedback at a particularly worrisome moment, as did the Women's Studies Faculty Colloquium and Ann Mussey. Karen Carr has been an incredible ally on the job and off, as have David Johnson, Gordon Dodds, Johanna Brenner, Melissa Gilbert, Susan Wladever-Morgan, and Melody Rose. Cyril Oberlander, head of the interlibrary loan department at Portland State's Millar Library, made long-distance research a possibility. Corinna Buchholz, Sam Byers, Anthony Granados, Tracy Pomaro, Kate Scott, and particularly Anne Shewring provided superb research assistance. Thank you, one and all. My students at Portland State deserve special tribute, such that I hesitate to single out only a few. I count them among my teachers, to whom this book is dedicated.

From my undergraduate years at Mount Holyoke College, I have to thank Carolyn Collette, Marjorie Kaufman, Mary McHenry, Andrea Sununu, John Faragher, Daniel Czitrom, and especially William S. McFeely for opening up the world of learning to a starveling from the suburbs. Studying with them changed my life. I would not have come back to graduate school at Princeton after dropping out without Christine Stansell, and I would not have finished my dissertation without Nell Irvin Painter. Professor Stansell put me on to Ida B. Wells-Barnett when I needed direction in my studies. Professor Painter then showed me the way. As all her graduate students attest, Nell Painter sets a standard of excellence in historical scholarship that inspires. Her path-breaking work on Sojourner Truth is a point of departure for my treatment of Wells-Barnett, and her guidance and mentoring have made all the difference in my career. I was also fortunate to study with Elizabeth Lunbeck, Valerie Smith, and Cornel West at Princeton; they made a major impression on me. James McPherson, Sean Wilentz, and Daniel Rodgers played important roles in seeing me through the graduate program and taught me a great deal of history. Finally, I am indebted to those upon whose scholarship on Ida B. Wells-Barnett my book depends: Paula Giddings, Wanda Hendricks, Thomas Holt, Mary M. B. Hutton, Linda O. McMurry, Dorothy Sterling, Mildred I. Thompson, Emilie M. Townes, David Tucker, Miriam DeCosta-Willis, and Jacquelyn Jones Royster. I would also like to recognize the work of Elsa Barkley Brown, Hazel Carby, Ann duCille, Mae Gwendolyn Henderson, bell hooks, Deborah McDowell, Carla L. Peterson, Hortense V. Spillers, and Mary Helen Washington. Their vision lights the way for students in the field; any stumbling in these pages is my responsibility.

I must thank several friends for their love and encouragement. Katharine Moon is my sister in the struggle; Heather Thompson knows not just history but the "whole story." The ordeal of graduate school was sweetened by comradeship with Ben Alpers, Jane Dailey, Vincent Digirolamo, Steve Kantrowitz, Phil Katz, Jerry Podair, and Susan Whyman. Barbara Gershen is in a category all by herself. The brilliance of Arthur Holmburg, Antonio Cao, and Edward Hochman remains irreplaceable. Jessica and Michael Marlitt, Sherri and Ralph Austin, Corey Bowey, Kim Cuyler, Marianne Koch, and Howard Shorr heard more about this book—or, rather, my feelings about it—than I'm sure they ever cared to. I'm grateful for their patience and senses of humor. Finally, this book is dedicated to my family. To my parents I can only say that I love you; to Nick and Maria, that I live for you.

Portland, Oregon
July 2000

IDA B. WELLS-BARNETT AND AMERICAN REFORM, 1880–1930

weaponed woman

Well, life has been a baffled vehicle

And baffling. But she fights, and

Has fought, according to her lights and

The lenience of her whirling-place.

She fights with semi-folded arms,

Her strong bag, and the stiff

Frost of her face (that challenges "When" and "If.")

And altogether she does Rather Well.

—Gwendolyn Brooks

All womanhood is hampered today because the world on which it is

emerging is a world that tries to worship both virgins and mothers

and in the end despises motherhood and despoils virgins.

—W. E. B. Du Bois, *Darkwater* (1920)

Introduction

Between 1880 and 1930, a sweeping transformation of political rights and social privileges took place in the United States. Following three decades of rapid and dramatic increases in women's access to education, wage labor, and public activism, all female citizens secured the right to full suffrage in 1919. At the same time, African American men and women endured lynching,[1] Southern disfranchisement, and Jim Crow segregation. African American women were caught in both of these whipsawing trends. Educated and urban black women took advantage of the expanded opportunities in civic life that accrued generally to middle-class women in this period; across class lines, however, black women faced violence and exclusion from many quarters. African American women simultaneously tapped the promise of this "Woman's Era" of female achievement and endured the nadir of U.S. race relations, trends that seemed, at first glance at the newspapers, to involve only white women and black men.

This book is about the accomplishments and frustrations of one extraordinary African American woman, Ida B. Wells-Barnett (1862–1931). It examines how she moved to the center of organized resistance to lynching in the 1890s and seeks to explain why her leadership waned over time. It analyzes the conflicts she experienced as a wage-earning woman, as a social critic, and as a political organizer of women and men. It explores her role in a distinctive tradition of African American women's protest activity and community building, a tradition often concealed within the discourses and practices of female reform and black politics in the United States. Finally, this book probes the irony articulated by Du Bois that femininity posed irresolvable contradictions for women in American culture.

Du Bois was on to something, but women like Wells-Barnett could not submit to these contradictions and expect to survive. Literary critic Mary Helen Washington once described turn-of-the-century black women writers as "suspended" figures, caught in the period's fierce turmoil over race, sex, and place in American life.[2] This book traces Wells-Barnett's efforts to confront and transform this turmoil and reveals a life that embodied not suspension but movement, not inhibition but "talking back."[3] In the area of gender expectations especially, Wells-Barnett's refusal either to be confined as a proper lady or to be lightly dismissed as a rebel girl claimed a wider latitude for African American women's intellectual and social engagement than was possible ever before. Claiming this freedom was both life-preserving and provocative, liberating and threatening, a source of her power and a political liability for her. People closest to Wells-Barnett sometimes voiced the sharpest criticisms or simply turned away, Du Bois among them.

We remember Du Bois primarily by his writing, but in her day Wells-Barnett was noted as much for what she said and did in public as for what she wrote down and published. She is due the reckoning of a Du Bois or a Jane Addams, but she was not only—or even primarily—a writer. Like African American women evangelicals Maria Stewart, Sojourner Truth, and Amanda Smith before her, Wells-Barnett was a well-known public speaker and trusted teacher in her community for quite a few years before she took to the podium to denounce lynching in the 1890s. She also kept up her work as a teacher and community organizer after the demand for her platform speeches tapered off in the 1920s. Wells-Barnett thus fits in a tradition of African American women "doers of the word"—especially God's word—who engaged the power of language spoken and written and lived as faith.[4] No simple Western calculus of meaning, like "knowledge equals power" or "beauty equals truth," could be relied upon by Wells-Barnett. Indeed, these very formulations were often used against her; as we shall see, she was repeatedly deemed to be an incompetent knower, incapable of beauty. For Wells-Barnett's generation of African American women, the meaning of life and freedom inhered not in Western abstractions but in, as historian Elsa Barkley Brown recently phrased it, "a notion of community wherein all—men, women, and children; freeborn and formerly slave; native and migrant—had inherent rights and responsibilities requiring no higher authority than their commitment to each other."[5] This book argues that Wells-Barnett's social commitments took profound inspiration from religious faith and gave rise to a "visionary pragmatism" that sustained a lifetime of agitation for social justice.

Like other strands of American pragmatism, visionary pragmatism describes not a European "school" of philosophy but rather a style of thought and activism. "Visionary" links Wells-Barnett to the prophetic traditions in African American religion documented by Cornel West and others. "Pragmatism" locates her in both the intellectual ferment of turn-of-the-century Chicago as well as in black women's legacy of "making a way out of no way" for themselves, their families, and communities forged under slavery.[6] Wells-Barnett's dual impulse to faith and politics developed in a context of Southern African American religion, a set of beliefs, institutions, and practices for salvation and community betterment that shaped and was shaped by an ongoing concern with political power and suffrage rights.[7]

Building on a heritage of resistance to slavery, the middle-class African American women of Wells-Barnett's generation sustained their intense religious and political commitments at the same time they, like educated white women, moved into teaching, journalism, social work, nursing, and civil service.[8] While it was not uncommon for intellectually driven white Protestant women in the North to struggle with or resist converting to Christianity—Jane Addams and Sophonisba Breckinridge provide salient examples—religious faith was much less problematic for Southerners and for educated African American women of all regions.[9] In Wells-Barnett's hands, visionary pragmatism entailed a distinctive view of self and service designed for personal survival and social contestation, for God and for community, and for rights and responsibilities for all U.S. citizens.

Chapter 1 establishes the contours of Wells-Barnett's visionary pragmatism by examining her autobiography *Crusade for Justice*. This chapter explores how she constructed her social authority in a range of public venues, focusing especially on the idea of exile. Through the metaphor of exile, Wells-Barnett crafted a writer's persona (the pen name "Exiled") and commented on black women's and black peoples' political situation in the late-nineteenth-century United States. For generations, the biblical Exodus story made theological sense of African Americans' predicament as slaves in North America. In the generation after slavery, Wells-Barnett put the idea of exile to new uses in order to forge a critique of lynching. Chapter 2 examines how this new cluster of meanings around "exile" took shape. While living in Memphis in the 1880s, Wells-Barnett found herself, as a self-supporting woman in that nascent urban Southern black community, tugged by clashing trends of female equality and gender conservatism, of new social freedom and racial proscription. These trends created social and political tensions that peaked in 1892, the height of lynching and of the populist upsurge. For Wells-Barnett, these severe social crises translated into an intense period of personal dislocation and political movement—a series of exiles and removes—which culminated in her transatlantic campaign against lynching.

Chapters 3 and 4 follow Wells-Barnett's trajectory as an "exile" from the South in a career that made her an internationally known figure. Chapter 3 examines her pioneering antilynching work, accomplished during the 1890s after she left Memphis. Her writings in this period, especially the pamphlet *Southern Horrors* (1892), updated the protest traditions of antebellum black agitators Maria Stewart and David Walker with a similar blend of spiritual angst, political insight, and a rousing call to armed self-defense. Although she was initially celebrated as a religious heroine—a "modern Joan of the race"—negative reactions to a black woman moving so out of her "place" soon precipitated a shift in gender expectations for African American women in organized reform. By 1900, the space for black women in national leadership had shrunk, and Wells-Barnett's vision of a broad-based social movement to end lynching failed to materialize. Chapter 4 continues the story of antilynching reform, tracing the pressures that further transformed the movement. By 1910, the heroic, biblical model of black womanhood in leadership became marginalized. By then, theoretically anyone with the "facts"—but especially men with college degrees working in the new National Association for the Advancement of Colored People (NAACP)—could make a compelling case to be heard as an expert on lynching. Wells-Barnett found herself and her vision of agitation out of favor among the NAACP's professional reformers who led the fight against lynching in the World War I era.

Chapter 5 steps back in time to situate Wells-Barnett in her adopted home of Chicago, Illinois, where she settled in 1895 and ended her exiles. There, she married and had four children and engaged in innovative efforts to deliver social justice and social services to a growing African American population on the city's South Side. Most notable among her many undertakings in Chicago was the creation of the Negro Fellowship League (NFL), a social settlement she established in 1910. The League grew directly out of Wells-Barnett's Sunday school teaching and represents a vivid example of southern black women's community-building strategies transplanted to a northern urban context. Several distinct variables shaped the work of the League. First was a mission statement that clearly focused on boys and men in a period in which "woman's work for woman" (and children) was the keynote of most female activism. Second, electoral politics figured prominently in the life of the settlement, much more so either than in the South, where disfranchisement was the rule, or among reforming white women in the North, who edged more gradually into partisan life after 1900. Wells-Barnett's need for funds motivated her to join electoral politics in the hopes of securing support for her settlement. All of her plans for community improvement had female equality at heart, as demonstrated by her active and steadfast support of suffrage rights and voting power for black women throughout her Chicago years.

Two pillars of Wells-Barnett's work in reform—a faith-centered focus on community that affirmed women's equality and the constant struggle for resources, which pointed her to party politics—frame this study's final chapter on the 1920s. As historians Glenda Gilmore and Laura Edwards have demonstrated for the South, citizenship rights created new opportunities for social influence among black women by making them clients of the state. In Chicago, African American women claimed a place of their own in public life as *agents* of the state, as shapers rather than recipients of political power, and not just as voters but as party activists and candidates for elective and appointive office. The passage of the Nineteenth Amendment and a reenergized women's club movement underwrote Wells-Barnett's own ambition for elected office in 1930. Though she lost her bid, few in black Chicago would have denied that Ida B. Wells-Barnett had been a vitally important figure in the life of the community, state, and nation for two generations.

CHAPTER ONE

Talking through Tears

I n 1886, while living in Memphis, Tennessee, a twenty-four-year-old Ida B. Wells copied an incident into her diary, "for fear I will not remember it when I write my 'novel.' " She noted that a "colored girl" was convicted of assault and sentenced in a local court after getting "the best of a fight" with a white girl. The brawl capped a series of confrontations in which the white girl had refused to "give half of the walk" when the two passed daily on a "wooded path up the country." At one point, the white girl's brother also came along to the woods and "abused" the colored girl. When again attacked on the next day, the colored girl successfully defended herself. In court, however, the judge "carried [the sentence] to the utmost of his power by giving her 11 mos. 29 days & ½ in the workhouse!"[1] The case outraged Wells and highlighted the dilemmas of resistance for black women. If self-possession and self-defense had criminal consequences, writing a "novel" about it seemed to invite disregard, misunderstanding, or even punishment.[2] Wells never wrote her novel, but she never forgot the lessons of the colored girl on the wooded path. The issues of racial violence, bias in the legal system, and the dilemmas of resistance for black women would be central to her work against lynching for the next four decades. Musing in a later diary

FIGURE I. "Campaign News from Republican Headquarters." This cartoon from a northern newspaper (probably in Illinois) negatively portrays African American women according to the plantation and minstrel imagery typical of U.S. popular culture in the 1890s. The figures are unfeminine and unfashionable, striking masculine poses in garish clothing and outlandish headgear. The original caption, "The Thompson Street Influence Club is now fully organized," pokes fun at the Republican Party at black women's expense, painting their political aspiration as gender deviance and their presence in the public sphere as a kind of minstrel show. Clipping from unidentified source, September 1892, in Temperance and Prohibition Papers, copy from 1977 microform edition, Ohio Historical Society, Columbus, Ohio

in 1930, Wells wrote that she had been "reading from Carter Woodson's book [*The Negro in Our History*] in which is no mention of my anti-lynching contribution."[3] Still determined not to forget, Wells finally wrote a book—not a novel, but her autobiography, *Crusade for Justice*.

Crusade for Justice maps Wells's engagement with the dilemmas of resistance for black women and documents her response to these dilemmas.[4] As suggested by the case of the colored girl from Memphis, black women had little enforceable claim to rights and respect in American society during Wells's lifetime. When visible at all, their image typically served as a foil or negative counterpoint for the dominant order. As one southern white woman put it in 1904: "the negro woman is the Frankenstein product of civilization. . . . a sinister figure behind the black man, forever dragging him downward" (see Figure 1).[5] To escape marginality, ridicule, and the workhouse or worse, Ida B. Wells relied on visionary pragmatism, a distinctive blend of religious and political commitments involving African American Christianity and a particular understanding of Reconstruction's unfinished business in the United States. These commitments often found expression in literary and practical projects of family recuperation and community education in resistance to racism, of which her autobiography is an example.

Ida B. Wells engaged in a strategic and religiously inspired self-fashioning to meet the demands of life in New South Memphis, fin-de-siècle London, and Progressive-era and Jazz-age Chicago.[6] Among the most vivid of these personae are found in Wells's use of testifying and parable telling in her autobiography, her use of pen names like "Iola" and "Exiled" in journalism, and the use of honorific titles like "Joan of Arc" and the "Mother of Clubs" by black communities who supported her political initiatives. Each of these self-identifications was rich with religious meaning and critically engaged the pervasive negative stereotypes about black women in U.S. culture. Taken together, they trace out a politics of the possible, a visionary pragmatism, for African American womanhood between the end of Reconstruction and the beginning of the Great Depression, a path charted by an orphan who, in the mid-1880s, picked up a pen and renamed herself "Iola."

Crusade for Justice

The problematics of authority, identity, and resistance are central to Wells's personal narrative, *Crusade for Justice: The Autobiography of Ida B. Wells*, published by her youngest daughter, Alfreda M. Duster, in 1970. Wells complained in her diary of 1930 about impediments to finishing the work—"Tried to get on to the last chapter of my book, so many interruptions"—and, lacking a formal end, readers are denied the closure that critics find so important to evaluating stories of origins.[7] Though she died before its completion, the narrative's unfinished state and the author's grumbling about it offer their own richness. Alfreda altered her mother's story but little, and the published book, like the manuscript, stops midsentence, midword even, suggesting the drama and movement that characterized Ida B. Wells's life.[8]

Crusade for Justice tells the story of how Wells came to her antilynching calling, carried out that calling as best she could, and maintained the work in the face of increasing political isolation. The narrative is a frustrated American success story as well as a portrait of an unusually brave and heroic woman. Its drama of physical movement and personal transformation draws on themes found in American slave narratives and Christian conversion narratives. In a critical departure from these traditions, however, Wells's narrative dispenses with the key organizing plots of both genres as developed by African American women—namely, finding freedom, finding God, and finding one's mother.[9] Although Wells does not worry out loud about her soul or her mother in *Crusade for Justice*, the narrative takes on full meaning only in relationship to God and to the legacy of slavery, especially to her slave mother. Wells's process of self-discovery and self-fashioning was rooted in family, faith, and the connection between slavery and freedom, a set of concerns that weighed heavily on her and the women of her generation.

The autobiography divides roughly into three parts: birth, youth, and early womanhood in the South (1862–1892); travels in England and across the United States during the early antilynching campaign (1892–1895); and her long and productive, if unevenly successful, years in Chicago, 1895 to approximately 1919. Rather than claim authority over slavery, the archetypal "black experience" of the nineteenth century, Wells's preface instead stakes out a special claim to the Reconstruction era, to "the facts of race history which only the participants can give" from the "time of storm" immediately after the Civil War.[10] As the story of this child of Reconstruction unfolds, it appears that her mother's legacy is assured and that the challenge is finding surrogate fathers.[11] In Wells's particular case, orphanhood, marriage resistance, and personal fame created unusual opportunities and challenges for working out her destiny as a freed woman. The lack of a living father created special burdens and uneasy freedoms in her life; self-naming and self-protection emerge as the key markers in her struggle for safety and security, especially during her Memphis years.

When Wells wrote, in the late 1920s, the freedwoman's story was not a full-blown literary convention, and she used at least three different narrative voices—those of testifying, speaking as "Exiled," and parable telling—to articulate its complexity.[12] These voices correspond to sections in *Crusade for Justice*. In the opening eight chapters, Wells testifies to the southern conditions that led her to oppose lynching in the African American Christian tradition of personal witnessing. The second section—nearly half the book but covering barely three years of her life—describes Wells's early antilynching work, especially her time in Great Britain, as a phase of "exile" from the South and the United States. In this middle section, the author's contemporary voice is literally exiled from the text, and the story is told largely through reprinted newspaper articles from the 1890s. Seven entire chapters and numerous inserts consist of reprinted letters, press clips, and travelogues written some thirty-five years earlier. This part-documentary, part-scrapbook approach suggests that Wells's voice from the 1920s needed bolstering; the narrative's concluding chapters explain why. This final section describes her years in Chicago in parables—brief vignettes with a moral attached—of personal frustration, political betrayal, and only occasional success, in which God or fate vindicate her efforts. Together, these voices articulate the multilayered struggle of a dynamic black woman to be both heard and whole during one of the most violent and promising periods of American history.

Toward Visionary Pragmatism

Ida B. Wells was born to slave parents in 1862 in Holly Springs, Mississippi, a town located fifty miles to the southeast of Memphis. Her father, Jim Wells, was the son of his white master and a slave woman named Peggy. Raised as a relatively privileged slave on a plantation in Tippah County in northeastern Mississippi, Jim was trained as a carpenter and, as Wells tells it, was spared stoop labor and severe discipline in his youth. While apprenticed to a contractor in nearby Holly Springs, Jim met Elizabeth "Lizzie" Warrenton, who worked as a cook for the contractor, and the two married according to slave custom. Lizzie's skilled labor in the kitchen also gave her high status among slave workers, and she enjoyed a fine reputation in the neighborhood. Born in Virginia, Lizzie's father was "half Indian," and her connections to eastern kin remained important to her. Like many freedpeople, she tried to contact them after the war by letter, but without success. After emancipation, Lizzie and Jim Wells legally remarried and had a family of eight children: Eugenia, Ida Belle, James, George, Eddie, Annie, Lily, and Stanley. Their partnership was economically successful enough to allow the Wells family to break with their white employer over political differences in the 1870s and establish a home of their own in Holly Springs. Unfortunately, only six children—and neither parent—survived the fatal yellow fever epidemic that struck the Mississippi valley in 1878.[13]

Wells's autobiography identifies her parents' deaths as the moment "when life became a reality to me," a loss of innocence through tragedy common to both slave narratives and working-class autobiographies. Jim Wells's fellow Masons placed five of the children in apprenticeships, adoptive families, and the "poor house" (for the severely crippled Eugenia), leaving the sixteen-year-old Wells, in her words, "to fend for myself." The narrative notes Wells's protest to her father's associates at the breakup of the family: "I said that it would make my father and mother turn over in their graves to know their children had been scattered like that and that we owned the house and if the Masons would help me find work, I would take care of them."[14] As a devoted daughter, honor to parents rather than solitary heroism shaped Wells's sense of right, and she determined to teach school to earn income for the family. Aware of Frederick Douglass's famous autobiography and familiar, too, since childhood with the work of Louisa May Alcott and the Alger-like *Stories for Boys* by Oliver Optic, Wells portrayed herself as a resourceful orphan in the American tradition, but one neither alone in the world nor lost. Echoing African tradition, the connection to kin and the honoring of ancestors' wishes was central to her moral universe.[15]

The threads of Wells's values and worldview were spun in childhood. The autobiography highlights Jim Wells's role as a trustee of Shaw University, later called Rust College, the local Methodist Freedmen's Aid Society school in Holly Springs, as well as his interest in politics.[16] Home discussions of news and of the Ku Klux Klan as well as Jim's late-night political meetings (which worried her mother) made a lasting impression. So did her mother's devotion to God and family. Lizzie Wells was a "deeply religious woman" who attended school with her children "until she learned to read the Bible." With children in tow, she attended Sunday school without fail, winning a prize for attendance and the respect of her daughter. "I often compare her work in training her children to that of other women who had not her handicaps," Wells later wrote. "She was not forty when she died, but she had borne eight children and brought us up with a strict discipline that many mothers who have had educational advantages have not exceeded."[17] Commenting briefly in the press about her own religious training, Wells credited both of her parents. She noted that "my father and mother were Methodists and reared me in the Methodist faith," and she received baptism at the age of twelve in Holly Springs.[18]

While some scholars of the post–Civil War South note African American women and men's complementary activities in politics and community life, Wells's narrative hints at a gender division of responsibilities between her parents.[19] Such a division did not remain fixed, however. Her father's involvement with school and politics and her mother's devotion to learning, church, and parenting melded in their daughter as she matured into the head of the Wells household in her late teens. Wells wove the threads of her parents' talents and commitments to meet her changing needs and circumstances. In this process she was strengthened by Methodist precept and teaching: personal piety, a stress on human agency in the work of salvation, and a stringent but hopeful moral code designed for the practical improvement of daily life. From these fibers, Wells created a life's pattern unique to her generation of black women, one linked in texture and design to the legacy of slavery. The resulting fabric of belief was inseparable from faith in God but not reducible to formal religion.[20]

In contrast to the transcendent ideals found in much of Christian thought, Wells linked religious principles to worldly social relationships and faith in God to everyday needs.[21] This connection is evident in the prayers she recorded in a diary she kept in the mid-1880s. "Today I write these lines with a heart overflowing with thankfulness to My Heavenly Father for His wonderful love & kindness; for His bountiful goodness to me, in that He has not caused me to want, & that I have always been provided with the means to make an honest livelihood."[22] For Wells and the southern black women of her generation, life and death, politics and religion, and responsibilities to self, community, and God were deeply interconnected. After writing a "dynamitic" newspaper article "almost advising murder!" in retaliation for the brutal lynching of a black woman in Jackson, Tennessee, in 1886, Wells's diary echoed the dilemma of the colored girl on the wooded path and placed an accent on faith. "It may be unwise to express myself so strongly but I cannot help it & I know not if capital may not be made of it against me but I trust in God."[23] Wells prayed for personal needs in a context of service to God and community. "Thou knowest I hunger & thirst after righteousness & knowledge," she prayed in her diary. "O, give me the steadiness of purpose, the will to acquire both."[24] This prayer echoed and revised Jesus' Sermon on the Mount: "Blessed are those who hunger and thirst for righteousness, for they shall be satisfied." Wells added a practical need for "knowledge" to the visionary's desire for connection to God ("righteousness"), as promised to the faithful by the Beatitudes. Though in this instance she positioned herself among the hungry and "the meek, who shall inherit the earth," she was no meek spirit.[25] "Yet I do not fear," Wells affirmed in her diary. "God is over all & He will, so long as I am in the right, fight my battles, and give me what is my right."[26]

The determined quality of Wells's prayers and the "dynamitic," angry tone of her journalism deserve further comment. Wells's anger distinguishes her visionary standpoint from the calculus of business and politics characteristic of her secularizing age. African American poet Audre Lorde reminds us that anger is "loaded with information and energy" crucial for survival, even as racists and other opponents use its expression to discredit, dismiss, or punish black women. "Anger is a grief of distortions between peers," Lorde explains, "and its object is change." Such was the thrust of Wells's visionary pragmatism. Wells raised pointed, often angry questions about racism and inequality in the United States. She demanded practical answers to questions posed in the spirit of Isaiah and Jeremiah, biblical prophets whose exhortations sometimes began with a sardonic "Ha!" Like the prophets' passion for Zion, Wells's visionary pragmatism was shaped by a righteous rage that was also part of the work of love.[27]

In *Crusade for Justice*, Wells labeled her "temper" a "besetting sin," even as her faith that God was on the side of justice earned her a right to that temper.[28] She often expressed anger as sarcasm, most famously in her pamphlet against lynching, *Southern Horrors*, whose title and arguments mocked "Southern honor." The pamphlet's concluding line tweaked archetypal Christian meekness with the grim, vaguely pagan aphorism: " 'The gods help those who help themselves.' "[29] "Many of our contemporaries locate hell in the South," stated a typically scornful squib of Wells's from the early 1890s. "We protest that it is a reflection on hell. Only those upon whom judgement is passed, are sent to hell for punishment. Here we are punished and murdered without judgement."[30] She also trained sarcasm on herself. "The stupendous idea of writing a work of fiction causes me to smile in derision of myself at daring to dream such a thing," she wrote in her diary in 1886.[31] Wells fretted over expressing anger and derided her literary ambition because anger and ambition were transgressive and stigmatized emotions for middle-class women in her era.[32] Later, readers would scratch their heads at her "forcible pen, her caustic oddness" in journalism and wonder at "an entire absence of the witty and humorous in what she writes."[33] These tin ears aside, Wells's anger and mocking sense of humor derived from a rich religious sensibility and provided potent sources of personal creativity and political purpose. American society often denied black women their "right," but *Crusade for Justice* demonstrates how God and Wells's slave parents, especially her mother, taught her better.

Testifying

The drama of the narrative's first section turns on achieving control over language, personal reputation, and physical safety, issues of prime historical moment to postbellum African American women. These issues, in turn, are linked to the legacy of slavery. The most vivid details of slavery concern the violent treatment of Wells's female kin, specifically her mother and paternal grandmother. Her mother "used to tell us how she had been beaten by slave owners and the hard times she had as a slave."[34] Jim Wells never forgave his former mistress for abusing his own mother—"stripped and whipped" as Wells quoted him—upon her husband's death. "I have never forgotten those words," wrote Wells, "I cannot help but feel what an insight into slavery they give."[35] From this history of violence toward slave women, Wells built her own story toward a powerful statement of identification for women of the next generation.

Like their enslaved foremothers, freedwomen evinced a deep concern with personal safety and bodily integrity. While living at a degree of remove from former masters, women like Wells still needed to deflect physical danger as well as the charge of immorality that could jeopardize her social standing and her access to the "honest livelihood" that Wells thanked God for. The scene emblematic of these issues occurs in chapter 5 of *Crusade for Justice*. In 1891, an African Methodist Episcopal (AME) church minister in Vicksburg, Mississippi, labeled Wells's loss of her teaching job in Memphis as "very suspicious" and he shared his disparaging views with her acquaintances in town. Wells relates the incident "because of its bearing on an important question," namely, the widely held assumption that "morally there were no virtuous southern girls." Her response to the slander was dramatic. Wells went to Vicksburg and gathered together her "friends"—including a local town father, postmaster James Hill (a former friend of Jim Wells's)—to serve as "witnesses" and "bodyguards" in a confrontation with the minister.

She charged him with "having tried to injure my character." The clergyman admitted as much then "begged pardon and stood ready to make amends." Wells then handed him a note she wrote to be read publicly to his congregation, to which he agreed. She quoted herself in the narrative. "I told him that my good name was all that I had in the world, that I was bound to protect it from attack by those who felt that they could do so with impunity because I had no brother or father to protect it for me. I also wanted him to know that virtue was not at all a matter of the section in which one lived; that many a slave woman had fought and died rather than yield to the pressure and temptations to which she was subjected. I had heard many tales of such and I wanted him to know at least one southern girl, born and bred, who had tried to keep herself spotless and morally clean as my slave mother had taught me."[36] Feeling the minister had been "punished enough," she "let the matter drop." The narrative then takes stock of her available weapons for self-vindication, like exposure through the press, legal action for slander, and an appeal to AME church superiors, in this case, Bishop Henry M. Turner.[37] By defending her name and her slave mother's memory, Wells "vindicated the honor of the many southern girls who had been traduced by lying tongues."[38] In confronting the minister, she not only defended herself but all the African American women of her region and generation.[39]

The path to this confrontation was fraught with the legacy of slavery and with the fragile social status of unmarried black women. Her mother's moral example centers Wells's resistance to slander, but *Crusade for Justice* also indicates that the lack of a living father (or other male protector) required careful management in language and social relations. One of the autobiography's opening scenes describes the painful disempowerment of a child reduced to speechlessness. When people in Holly Springs saw Wells speaking to the family doctor about the money Jim Wells had left his children upon his death, gossips saw only a young black woman asking a white man for money and suspected the worst. Others speculated that her brothers and sisters were actually her own children and wondered why Wells lived in a house "by herself" (that is, without an adult male). A solitary "colored girl" was especially vulnerable to misunderstanding. "I am quite sure that never in all my life have I suffered such a shock as I did when I heard this misconstruction that had been placed upon my determination to keep my brothers and sisters together," stated Wells.[40] The negative rumors surrounding Wells in Holly Springs trailed her to Memphis, where she moved in 1882. Her diary referred to the "base slanderous lie that had blackened my life" in Mississippi and to her aching desire "to cast the dark shadows out and exorcise the spirit that haunts me."[41]

Like her slave mother's fertility and sexuality, a freedwoman's reputation was an intimate yet public matter over which she had at best only partial control. And like the autobiography's telling of events in Holly Springs, Wells's Memphis diary also recorded a debilitated wordlessness over matters of reputation. When confronted by a male acquaintance with some "bad things" he had heard about her, Wells became "so angry I foamed at the mouth, bit my lips & then *realizing my impotence—* ended in a fit of crying" (emphasis added).[42] The frothing anger, the biting back of words, and the dissolving into tears portray a woman— and a gifted and confident talker, at that—silenced by severe social and emotional constraints. Volubility threatened a woman's dignity as much as anything else. In matters of reputation, as one etiquette book put it at the time, "explanations are bad things" for women.[43] But the survival of women like Wells or the colored girl on the wooded path demanded self-possession, self-defense, and "talking back."[44] Wells's diary noted her determined reaction to a male friend's suggestion that she simply forget the old slander from Holly Springs: "I . . . clenched my hands darkly and proudly declared I would never forget!"[45] Given the importance of her slave mother's legacy and the serious business of reputation for black women, Wells could not afford to forget.[46]

Crusade for Justice further suggests that writing was a key component of not forgetting. The autobiography describes newspaper writing—especially her work at the *Free Speech*, an African-American-owned newspaper in Memphis—as an outlet for Wells to "express the real 'me.'"[47] This "real 'me'" emerged under the pen name "Iola." Pen names were fairly common among black women journalists of the period, offering a shield against the prejudice so easily flung at them. As journalist Gertrude Mossell points out, in newspaper work "sex and race are no bar, often they need not be known."[48] Pen names were somewhat favored by single women who moved into the public sphere without the legitimizing status of marriage. As "Iola," Wells renamed herself exclusively in feminine terms, without the validating surname of either husband or father. For a country girl making her way in the city, the rural twang of "Iola" offered a light-hearted counterpoint to journalistic prose that showed "plenty of nerve" and a mind "sharp as a steel trap."[49] The use of "Iola" also indicates the cultivation of a writer's identity, one Wells enjoyed so much that she even signed personal letters with it, for which at least one correspondent chided her.[50] The blurring of her private and public identities suggests a powerful experiment with identity, a "real 'me'" under construction.

Capped by the confrontation in Vicksburg, the autobiography's first section portrays the movement of a "southern girl, born and bred" from the silent shock of childhood loss to the effective, wage-earning words of a mature adult. Wells's private diary from her Memphis years reveals an added layer to this movement, a prayerful struggle to be "glad because my Father saw fit to send these trials & so fit me for His kingdom." Since public explanations were bad things for individual women, Wells turned to God: "O my Father, forgive me, forgive me.... Humble the pride exhibited [by the vow not to forget the slander] and make me Thy child."[51] The autobiography testifies less about God's saving grace or to heaven-sent trials and more about public struggles and practical strategies for survival—like speaking out, having powerful friends, and even carrying a weapon. Stressing the public spheres of press, court, and pulpit, *Crusade for Justice* was written to "fire the race pride of all our young people."[52] The diary records Wells's private struggle with God; the narrative provides a survival guide for making freedom real for African Americans, particularly for women.

Having established command over language and over her reputation, Wells reaches the major turning point of the autobiography: the lynching of three black male shopkeepers in Memphis in March 1892 functions as a conversion experience. The event, wrote Wells, "changed the whole course of my life."[53] The Memphis lynching sealed her turn to protest much as the hanging of the Haymarket anarchists in 1886 moved a young Emma Goldman to a lifelong commitment to radicalism.[54] The event pushed Wells's thinking about lynching, confirming that the cry of rape of white women, used to justify lynching, was an "excuse" to "keep the race terrorized and 'keep the nigger down.'"[55] The triple lynching and subsequent attack on the *Free Speech* office for a critical editorial Wells wrote on lynching also prompted her to leave the South permanently.[56] Finally, the lynching gave the aspiring writer in Ida B. Wells a story to tell.

Talking through Tears

Telling that story outside the South posed another set of challenges related to the dilemmas of resistance for black women, especially concerning reputation and the tenuous social status of unmarried females. The middle section of *Crusade for Justice* highlights the moral support and funds Wells received from African American women in the North as well as the guiding, fatherly protection delivered by that elder statesman among African Americans, Frederick Douglass. The delicate means by which Wells secured their support is symbolized in the narrative by talking through tears, tears that once immobilized her. By talking through tears, Wells carried out a demanding and highly political public performance while keeping femininity visibly in play.

After denouncing lynching in the *Free Speech* in May 1892, Wells left Tennessee for the relative safety of the North, first in Philadelphia and then in New York. She found and embraced a welcoming African American community in Brooklyn, whose organized women seemed particularly eager to adopt her and the cause of antilynching. School teacher Maritcha Lyons and journalist Victoria Earle Mathews likely saw in Wells and in the possibility of restarting the *Free Speech* in the North a way to expand their ongoing community work, efforts that included public school desegregation and relief of needy children.[57] In the narrative's words, the members of New York women's clubs, led by Lyons and Mathews, formed "a solid array behind a lonely, homesick girl who was an exile" for speaking out against lynching.[58] The dedication of *Southern Horrors* to the "Afro-American women of New York and Brooklyn" cited their "race love, earnest zeal and unselfish effort," shown especially at a testimonial dinner for Wells in October 1892, which raised the funds for the pamphlet's publication.[59]

FIGURE 2. "Mizpah." This portrait of Ida B. Wells, possibly taken in England, shows her wearing the brooch inscribed with the name "Mizpah," bestowed upon her by African American club women in 1892. From Charles F. Aked, "A Blot on a Free Republic," *Review of the Churches* 9 (May–October 1894): 97

The women's testimonial blended gestures from religion, theater, and politics into a ritual naming ceremony and a great show. Wells's name literally was in lights, with "Iola" illuminated on the dais by gas jets. The event was a grand affair that attracted African American women from Boston and Philadelphia. Down South, Wells defended the name of "the many southern girls traduced by lying tongues." Up North, club women adopted Wells's name and her cause. "Iola" was printed on silk badges worn by the ushers and organizing committee members; the printed program was a facsimile of the *Free Speech*. In addition to a cash purse of two hundred dollars, Wells was presented with a "gold brooch in the shape of a pen, an emblem of my chosen profession" and a symbol of the power of words to create conditions for survival. The pin was inscribed with the word "Mizpah," a place name from the Hebrew bible meaning "lookout," christening Wells with a new identity and mission from scripture. Wells proudly wore the brooch at public events in the coming years (see Figure 2).[60]

Although Wells was a veteran of toasts and public recitations in Memphis, *Crusade for Justice* identifies the Brooklyn testimonial as the occasion for her first "honest-to-goodness" address, a signal moment in her life. She cried during her presentation, but despite her "streaming face," she continued to speak with a steady voice. The narrative attributed her tears to feelings of "loneliness and homesickness" summoned by recounting the Memphis lynching and called these tears an uncharacteristic "exhibition" of "woman's weakness." "Whatever my feelings, I am not given to public demonstrations," she wrote. For their part, the women in the audience assured Wells that she had not "spoiled things" by the "breakdown," but quite the opposite. The tears, Wells reported, "made an impression. . . . *favorable to the cause and me.*"[61] A man in the audience, a relative of Frederick Douglass, told Wells she "could not have done anything more effective" than cry to win over that New York crowd.

Wells's confession at this point—"I had no knowledge of stage business"—was not quite the case. While living in Memphis, she had performed public readings, organized and acted in a dramatic club, and even been scouted by New York talent agents. The northern press had already noted her ambition to be a "full-fledged journalist, a physician, or an actress."[62] And a newspaper account of a journalists' gathering a few months after the Brooklyn testimonial noted how Wells, the "star of the convention," was again "moved to grief" during her address.[63] Tears probably signaled Wells's comfort to express emotion with her African American audiences. The image of tears moving silently down her face without interrupting her speech is also rich with other meanings. Tears could be an intuitive, "natural" expression of right feminine feeling, proof of her status as female victim (and survivor) in her community. The image of Wells talking through tears also conveys verbal competence hard-won and tested by faith. Tears were much more acceptable for a proper lady than anger or its cousin, sarcasm. And tears worked.

In the shared context of Christian faith and racist violence, Wells's tears marked both the promise and fragility of community among African Americans. Two years after the Brooklyn testimonial, Wells bitterly denounced in print any "cowards" who "hurt" the cause of racial justice by failing to rally to the antilynching effort. Noting that "bitter tears" were "coursing themselves down my cheeks," Wells wrote in the press: "I weep because the manhood of the race knows itself slandered, its women and children slaughtered, its mothers, wives, sisters, and daughters insulted and despoiled and traduced and still fails to assert its strength or extend its protection to those who have a right to claim it." This forceful admonition to racial solidarity, figured here as proper family relations, was accompanied by womanly weeping, feminine sacrifice, and an expression of love. "I would be willing to suffer all that I have and more, if thereby might be brought about a healthier moral tone, and stronger physical stamina among our men, if they would unite their forces and present a solid front for self defense to the world. Then I could not only love my race with a love which passes my own understanding, but admire and respect it with all the intensity of my nature for its courage, honor and true manhood."[64] Tears signaled proper femininity as her words took the "manhood of the race" to task. In this public plea, Wells foregrounded the Christian values of suffering and submission to God's will. She also revisioned scripture, specifically the letters of Paul, by evoking the "love of Christ that surpasses knowledge" to describe the bond of community.[65] Rather than let suffering or victimization immobilize her, Wells directed her feelings toward fostering the love, respect, and solidarity that she expected to be shared and acted upon by those who opposed lynching.

Talking through tears captures the particularly fraught quality of middle-class black women's participation in the public sphere. The autobiography further highlights Frederick Douglass's role in this difficult task. Wells and he first crossed paths at lectures in Washington, D.C., in mid-1892, began a correspondence, and eventually collaborated on several projects. Douglass anointed Wells's lecture tour to England in fatherly terms: " 'You go my child,' " she recalled him saying, " 'you are the one to go, for you have the story to tell.' "[66] *Crusade for Justice* carefully distinguishes Douglass's role as an "orator" with Wells's own role as a "mouthpiece." " 'With me it is different,' " she explained to Douglass. " 'I am only a mouthpiece through which to tell the story of lynching and I have told it so often that I know it by heart. I do not have to embellish; it makes its own way.' "[67]

By comparing Douglass as an artist and interpreter of reality to herself as a feminine vessel, cipher for fact, and pure heart, Wells gained much. Douglass was the best known and most respected African American of the nineteenth century. A letter of endorsement that Wells requested and received from Douglass became the preface to her pamphlet *Southern Horrors*. "Brave woman!" Douglass declared. "You give us what you know and testify from actual knowledge. You have dealt with the facts with cool, painstaking fidelity and left those naked and uncontradicted facts to speak for themselves."[68] In another legitimizing gesture, Wells distributed Douglass's *Lessons of the Hour* pamphlet, which included his speech "Why is the Negro Lynched?," at her speaking engagements on lynching. "It is, as you say, the argument," Wells demurred to him in a letter, "and should be published along with my facts."[69] Deference to the authoritative Douglass bolstered Wells's feminine gender credentials, credentials severely questioned in the dominant culture, while reinforcing her junior status in agitation. Douglass pronounced, Wells implored, and audiences expected as much. British Quaker, educator, and former abolitionist Ellen Richardson (who had raised funds to purchase Douglass's freedom while he was abroad in 1846) explained this expectation to him in a letter, comparing his manly high style and learning to Wells's womanly moral fervor: "The same protests in the course [of] which made you an *orator* makes her an efficient *Pleader*."[70]

In her role as critic, Wells relied on Douglass to vouch for both her facts and her virtue, the status of one being inextricable from the other. As in the incident at Vicksburg, she needed public verification.[71] "Thank you a thousand times for so strengthening my hands," wrote Wells to black club women in Boston during her British speaking tour in 1894. "It is the first word of support which has come to me from across the Atlantic from my own race and it helps the cause so much," she explained, signing herself "Yours lovingly."[72] But British reformers directly prevailed upon Douglass for a public letter bearing "testimony to the character of Miss Wells and to the truth of her statements."[73] Wells carried Douglass's letter around England and used it regularly, like a weapon. For example, when an English reporter asked, "Do you really mean all that your article implies [about the South]?" Wells responded, "Frederick Douglass knows that what I say is true," and handed the man the letter.[74] Douglass's letter bolstered her reputation, and club women shored up her spirit, but, like the colored girl on the wooded path, neither could completely protect her from bodily harm. Back in New York, Wells was assaulted on the Fulton Ferry in the summer of 1894. A pair of white toughs had heard "about the crusader and her alleged traducing of Southern women" and decided that she was a legitimate target for violence.[75]

No single individual in *Crusade for Justice* receives more personal appreciation than Douglass, whose death scene Wells recounts in detail and whom she praises as "the greatest man that the Negro race ever produced on the American continent."[76] Wells was in Kansas City when she learned of his passing in early February 1895 and wrote a letter of acknowledgement in the press. Declaring "I have no heart to write," she confessed. "It was to me the saddest hour of my life, save that when I knew I was an orphan, when I realized that not only the noblest man of our race was gone, but my best friend and strongest supporter. I have no words at command to express my sense of personal loss; the blinding tears will not let me . . . narrate a tenth part of his personal goodness to me and his help to the cause."[77] The passing of Douglass was another occasion for talking through tears, for exhibiting strength amidst adversity, and for a public demonstration of feminine bona fides, in this case,

the vocation of grieving. The letter claimed both a useful political genealogy and a unique emotional bond, linking private feeling with public
service, religious duty with practical politics. That Douglass's death created for Wells a virtual second orphaning was scarcely an exaggeration.
In the preceding three years, with the support of Douglass and black
club women, Wells accomplished the most creative and daring work of
her life, work that would seal her reputation for the next century.

Exiled

The period between May 1892, when Wells left Memphis, and June
1895, when she settled permanently in Chicago, receives more attention
than any other in *Crusade for Justice*. Throughout the historical record,
these years, especially the part of them devoted to her British lecture
tours, echo as the high point of her life. Her travel abroad involved two
visits to England and Scotland, one in 1893 and one in 1894, for three
and six months respectively. Before her second trip, Wells secured an
opportunity to publish letters written from Britain in a widely read
Chicago newspaper, the *Inter-Ocean*, and a series of these appear in the
autobiography. As much as the letters, Wells's pen name from this
period, "Exiled," captured the peripatetic quality of her life and her
visionary pragmatism in action.

Wells first used the name "Exiled" when she wrote an article describing the Memphis lynching and subsequent mob attack on the *Free Speech*
for the *New York Age* newspaper in June 1892. Over the next few years,
she continued to refer to herself as an exile in her antilynching speeches
and pamphlets. Identifying herself as outcast or fugitive from the
United States, the " 'land of liberty' " in Wells's sarcastic phrasing, provided theatrical bite to her stage presence abroad and an ironic counterpoint to her otherwise chirpy press accounts reporting on "Afternoon
Tea at Lady Jeune's" or "Ladies in Parliament" in the *Inter-Ocean*.[78]
Between 1892 and 1895, "Exiled" and Wells's lecture personae drew
partly on the authority of testifying and partly on the more mediated
mode of ciphering, of letting the facts "speak for themselves," as Douglass put it. "Exiled" testified to what Wells herself saw in the South
while insisting that the details documented by others were the best
evidence for her arguments. Culled from newspapers like the *Chicago
Tribune*, Wells claimed transparency for her facts and figures about
lynching with the scathing declaration: "Out of their own mouths shall
the murderers be condemned."[79] Whether addressing the rational "student of American sociology" or, more grandly, "Nineteenth Century
civilization," Wells's empirical approach relied in part on already ac-

cepted facts and, central to my concerns here, underscored the limited social authority available to her as a critic.[80]

"Exiled" artfully revisioned historical subjectivity for southern freedwomen by linking their contemporary political dilemmas with the predicament of their slave foremothers who also endured and survived violence.[81] Exiled-as-victim made for acceptably feminine politics by deflecting individual heroics and identifying the actions of wrongdoers. Exiled-as-survivor (like orphanhood) allowed Wells to claim unusual amounts of both autonomy and support from her community. Unlike the accident of orphanhood, however, exile was not random. It was the result of conscious, potentially unfeminine political activity that Wells was taking to new heights of visibility and controversy as an opponent of lynching. In the context of African American Christianity, "Exiled" also connected Wells to the larger African American community, for whom a key metaphor of self-identification was the biblical Exodus story and the continuing "exile" in America of people of African descent.[82] As an example of visionary pragmatism, "Exiled" expressed black women's and the black community's spiritual and political situation in the United States in 1892 and, by naming it, created a space for its transformation.

Of particularly liberating potential was the ability of "Exiled" to depart from the bodily aspects of race and sex that ordered Victorian identity and labeled black women deviant. The meaning of "Exiled" derived from politics and place, not nature; the symbolics of "Exiled" concerned citizenship and religion and deflected attention from the body.[83] "Exiled" could appear in print as an androgyne critic of indeterminate race and gender, affording Wells a degree of literary license.[84] However, the space opened up on paper by "Exiled" contracted before live audiences. As was the case for black abolitionist women, Anglo-American audiences expected to discern or "read" Wells's authority, identity, and to some extent, her argument, through her body, in "the skin and sex," as Elizabeth Cady Stanton once put it, "the badge of degradation—the 'scarlet letter' so sadly worn upon the breast."[85] Such readings by whites relied on the plantation slave stereotypes of black woman as "mammy" or "Sapphire," as asexual menial or supersexed wench.[86] When Wells moved from the press to the podium, she encountered a politics of authenticity once rooted in the slave experience but now, in freedom, also linked to skin color.[87]

Crusade for Justice suggests that despite her facts, her press clips, and her exile, Ida B. Wells's body became an exhibit for her arguments about the South. The British keyed skin color to credibility. A London hostess succinctly stated that Wells's success abroad would have been much greater had she been a "few shades blacker."[88] This comment appears in *Crusade for Justice* within a few paragraphs of the author's noting what "an absolutely new thing" it was to be in England where people did not seem to notice "the color of the skin."[89] Wells was trying to impress her readers in the 1920s with the social freedom she found abroad, but in the 1890s, color consciousness and commentary on her "odd racial composition" or her "mixed Anglo-Saxon, Negro, and Red Indian descent" figured regularly in British publications.[90] Wells was announced in London as "A Coloured Woman in the Pulpit," and the charge that her mixed heritage somehow tainted her point of view caused Wells to bristle in an interview. "Taint, indeed! I tell you, if I have any taint to be ashamed of in myself, it is the taint of *white* blood!"[91] "Exiled" resisted the negative or even *non*subjectivity assigned to black women in American culture. England offered, alternately, a chance to play up "blackness" or to straddle the color line, sometimes uncomfortably.[92]

In the context of sexual objectification and skin color consciousness, Wells's platform personae before white audiences in England suggests a muting of her body language that was consistent with the physical displacement evoked by "Exiled." British listeners remarked repeatedly on Wells's composure at the podium, familiar as many were with the comic and rough flamboyance of blackface minstrelsy then popular in English music halls.[93] Rather than risk teary declamations while under visual scrutiny, Wells masked passion and feeling in order to avoid the charge of unrestraint or immorality that so easily attached to African American women. As someone interested in the theater, Wells was probably aware of and perhaps played to the "sculptural" feminine ideal for actresses, derived from Greek art, which dominated the London stage in those years.[94] One British supporter vividly described Wells's speaking style: "She spoke with a cultivated manner with great simplicity & directness & with a burning intensity of feeling well-controlled. It was the most convincing kind of speaking—it sounded intensely genuine & real. There was no attempt at oratories, no straining after effects."[95] Kindly English commentators consistently noted Wells's powerful restraint and its effectiveness. "Her indictment is all the more telling from the absence of rhetoric," concluded the *Manchester Guardian*.[96] Audiences remarked on her "quiet and unimpassioned but earnest and forcible" delivery as well as her "avoidance of all oratorical tricks, and her dependence upon the simple eloquence of facts."[97] Her style won rave reviews: "She spoke with singular refinement, dignity, and self-restraint; nor have I ever met any other 'agitator' so cautious and unimpassioned in speech," noted London's *Christian Register*. "But by this marvelous self-restraint itself she moved us all the more profoundly."[98] Wells herself highlighted the effectiveness rather than the cost of such restraint. If at this moment the theatrical ideal for women was a kind of frozen beauty, her powerful stage presence held audiences fast. "I spoke an hour and a half" in Bristol, Wells wrote to the *Inter-Ocean* in 1894, "and not a person in that vast audience moved."[99]

Parables

Slave narratives end with freedom. Spiritual autobiographies climax with salvation and the doing of God's work. Anglo-American Victorian life stories typically close with marriage for women or with public success for men. Striking a much more modern, even postmodern note, *Crusade for Justice* ends—or, rather, fails to properly end—with a series of redundant, unresolved parables of crisis in Wells's authority. The final section of the autobiography contrasts the international success and visibility of the antilynching years with the local, usually unrecognized, and sometimes thwarted struggles of the Chicago decades. This denouement points back to the spiritual autobiographers, since Wells's inability to fulfill her calling at home alludes to Jesus' saying in Luke that "no prophet is acceptable in his own country."[100] The parable-like stories of the final section contain another religious reference, since Jesus taught in parables. Wells also describes drawing strength for her Chicago community work from the example of Jesus' ministry among "sinners."[101] This usage resonates with theologian Delores S. Williams's identification of Jesus' ministry rather than his crucifixion as empowering for black women.[102] The parables' message of frustration and disappointment further implicate faith, since misunderstanding is the portion of prophets in Christian tradition.

The parables, probably written in 1929–30, encompass a range of rhetorical styles and moral lessons, some of which catch the signature sarcasm of Wells's early writing. A few offer homely, even clichéd, bits of folk wisdom. Echoing ideals from the American Revolution, Wells admonishes her readers that "eternal vigilance is the price of liberty." As befit someone likened to Joan of Arc, she mixed religious and military metaphors, urging African Americans to be "alert as the watchman on the wall" for the "preservation of our rights."[103] A few parables describe scenes of triumph, as in Wells's confrontation with the white sheriff of Cairo, Illinois, after a lynching there in 1909. At times, the stories border on melodrama. In one chapter, a Chicago minister who opposed Wells in 1906 over the advisability of a black-owned theater with a reputation as a dive operating on the South Side gets his comeuppance years later.

After vowing may his "tongue cleave to the roof of his mouth and his right hand forget its cunning" should he ever set foot in that establishment, the clergyman is struck down with paralysis at a political gathering at the ill-fated theater years later.[104] When God thus smites Wells's opponents, the scene approaches the carnivalesque, in which the mighty are brought low and the meek triumph, if only momentarily.[105]

Chicago put Wells-Barnett's visionary pragmatism to the severest test, and the parables highlight a troublesome aspect of community organizing. The last section brings into sharp relief the ways in which efforts to mount social struggles sometimes turn on the attitude of individuals closest by. This tendency, while true to some extent in any political project, carried special significance for African American women who, since the early nineteenth century, risked the charge of "betraying the race" for turning criticism toward the community, especially toward men.[106] Three parables in the narrative's final section especially capture Wells's complex story of loyalty and betrayal, endurance and frustration, self-possession and social embeddedness, all of which touch back on the narrative's founding parable, the Vicksburg incident. One concerns Wells's marriage in 1895 to Ferdinand Lee Barnett. The other two parables involve clergy who reject her initiative in political protest, first in 1894 upon her return from England and again in 1919 in the wake of the Chicago race riot.

The chapter bridging Wells's return to the United States from abroad describes a gathering of AME church ministers in Philadelphia, the founding city of the denomination. During the summer of 1894, she visited many churches, spoke against lynching, collected antilynching resolutions, and helped organize local committees to keep up the fight. In Philadelphia, however, clergy raised a note of protest. After her address to the group, a minister objected "on the ground that they ought to be careful about endorsing young women of whom they knew nothing—that the AME church had representative women who ought to be put before the public and whom they could endorse unhesitatingly." After a moment of "amazement" and stunned silence that again points to the immobilizing potential of male moral judgment, Wells found her words. She dispensed entirely with the idea that she needed the clergy, relying directly on God instead. "Why gentlemen," Wells recalled saying, "I cannot see why I need your endorsement. Under God I have done work without any assistance from my own people. And when I think that I have been able to do the work with his assistance that you could not do, if you would, and you would not do if you could, I think I have a right to feeling of strong indignation. I feel very deeply the insult which you have offered and I have the honor to wish you a very good morning."[107] Like the evangelical Maria Stewart, Wells cited God as empowering despite the world's dithering or opposition.[108] Setting the tone for the entire final section of the narrative, she described the ministers' response in this scenario as emblematic, as "the beginning of a great deal of the same sort that I received at the hands of my own people" and which inhibited the fight against lynching.[109]

About a year after the Philadelphia incident, Wells found herself exhausted, "physically and financially bankrupt" from the antilynching crusade. "Thus it seemed to me that I had done my duty," she explained, and, unable to return to the South for fear of violence, she settled down in Chicago.[110] There, in June 1895, she married Ferdinand Lee Barnett, a lawyer and editor of the *Chicago Conservator* newspaper. Antilynching as exile proved extremely taxing both politically and emotionally. Wells wrote to Helen Pitts Douglass (second wife of Frederick) from England in the spring of 1894: "I . . . will be coming home again. Home did I say? I forget that I have no home."[111] The autobiography does not discuss the marriage proposal or engagement but tellingly refers only to "the offer of a home of my own" from Barnett.[112] Nearing age thirty-three, Wells perhaps could depend less comfortably on surrogate fathers for protection. As noted above, Frederick Douglass's death in February of that year eliminated a major source of emotional and political support.

In the autobiography's parable of her marriage, Wells highlights her community's negative reaction to her engagement, using irony and a bit of sarcasm to explore the politics of work and marriage for black women. She described the public as "more outspoken because of the loss to the cause than they had been in holding up my hands when I was trying to carry a banner," alluding again to the idea of exile, specifically Moses' leadership of the Israelites in battle in the book of Exodus.[113] "Strange as it may seem," she continued, "my people . . . seemed to feel that I had deserted the cause, and some of them censured me rather severely in their newspapers for [marrying]."[114] Chicago club woman Fannie Barrier Williams archly noted Wells's "unique career" and her "determination to marry a man while still married to a cause," figuring her ambition as a kind of odd bigamy.[115] Susan B. Anthony also delivered a "rebuke" to Wells concerning her "divided duty" between home life and a "special call" for "special work."[116]

As contemporary black feminist scholars have argued, women like Wells viewed marriage and family as compatible with both wage labor and public efforts for community benefit. *Crusade for Justice* suggests that this view found critics within black communities as well as among white suffragists.[117] The parable also implies, however, that Ferdinand Barnett supported such a politically engaged partnership. Because one person—or one couple—could not end lynching, Wells continued her political work as a married woman and mother and strongly backed a protest organization, the Afro-American Council, which was revitalized in 1899. "So despite my best intentions," Wells wryly concludes this parable on marriage, "when I got back home to my family [after the first Council meeting in Rochester, New York] I was again launched in public movements."[118]

After a quarter century of "public movements" in Chicago, the penultimate chapter of the autobiography describes an emotional climax in a series of challenges to Wells's leadership. The scene is her resignation from the newly formed local Protective Association, organized to sort out the aftermath of the Chicago race riot of July 1919, a conflict in which thirty-eight people died and hundreds were injured or left homeless. In the wake of the riot, Wells took testimony from riot victims at her home and planned to assist state's attorney Maclay Hoyne with grand jury proceedings against the perpetrators of violence. In taking this initiative, Wells was motivated by the court conviction in March (later overturned) of a dentist named Leroy Bundy of East St. Louis, Illinois, for his role as a supposed ring leader in that city's riot—racial massacre, really—back in 1917. Since prosecutor Hoyne did not follow up on the information Wells helped provide, she published a letter of protest in the press, hoping to have him removed from his post.

Nor was Wells a fan of Illinois state's attorney general Edward Brundage, who was slated to handle the Chicago proceedings, given his similarly poor performance after East St. Louis. The Protective Association, which was led mainly by black clergy, supported Brundage over Hoyne, weighing their partisan fortunes and favoring a Republican over a Democrat. At the deciding meeting, Wells made an "impassioned speech" whose premise echoed the predicament of the colored girl from Memphis sent to the workhouse for the "crime" of self-defense. "I oppose [Brundage] in the name of Dr. L. N. Bundy who is now serving a life sentence in the penitentiary because he was a leader among his people."[119] The motion in support of Brundage prevailed. When Wells put her membership card on the table and turned to leave, the words "Good-bye" and "Good riddance" followed her out.[120] Back in 1894, she had left the Philadelphia ministers sitting "with their mouths open" as she proudly walked out of their meeting. In 1919, it was Wells-Barnett who left the room silenced with "tears streaming down" her face. Unable to talk through her tears this time, the scene points to a severe crisis of authority and intense personal suffering. In this scenario, partisan calculation trumped visionary pragmatism. The autobiography offered a justification after the fact. "I never went back to a meeting of the so-called Protective Association," Wells explained, "and very soon it became a thing of the past."[121]

The chapter describing this rejection and other jarring events of 1919 culminates in high Christian drama, in a kind of resurrection from death. In late 1920, Wells's social settlement, the Negro Fellowship League, closed due to a lack of funds and support. The closure marked an end to a decade of consuming, difficult work—Wells called it "my burden"—and precipitated a physical crisis. Shortly after the League's folding, she was hospitalized for gallstones, noting in her narrative that "for weeks my life was despaired of." She took a year to recuperate fully, during which time she "did more serious thinking from a personal point of view than ever before" in her life. "All at once the realization came to me that I had nothing to show for all those years of toil and labor." From this realization came another turning point: "It seemed to me that I should now begin to make some preparation of a personal nature for the future, and this I set about to accomplish."[122] With only four pages remaining to the narrative, however, the reader is deprived of a full sense of what Wells meant by this change of heart and this new chance at life.

The Chicago parables suggest, however, that the access to audiences and publication that Wells garnered through witnessing as a "southern girl, born and bred" or through testifying as "Exiled" eroded in the years after 1895. Once a special place, the South, and her exile from it, offered a unique public persona and a distinctive, if tenuous, kind of social authority. Wells was an exotic specimen to the British; foreign news that "our Iola" brought back from abroad was exciting to African Americans, many of whom never left their hometowns of St. Paul, Denver, East St. Louis, or Brooklyn. In Chicago, by contrast, Wells became one among many contending for the crumbs of white patronage, the loyalty of African American voters, and an economic foothold in the black neighborhoods emerging on the city's South Side. Wells's community-building efforts, her continued investigative reporting into lynching and race riots, and her party politicking in Chicago were all important resistance work. The final section of her narrative stresses political reversals and economic problems that were difficult, if not impossible, to answer either with the facts of lynching, personal testimony about political conditions, or the invocation of God's authority. Solving social problems required money and votes, both of which were withheld from American women until late in Ida B. Wells's lifetime.

Two honorary titles bestowed on Wells, "Joan of Arc" and the "Mother of Clubs," capture the ongoing dilemmas of resistance for African American women into the 1920s. Each title points to the resources—God and kin—relied upon by black women in a context of political disfranchisement and relative poverty compared to whites. By referring to legitimate spheres of female activity—religion and family—each title attempted to contain and defuse the tensions surrounding African American women's public roles in reform and protest. The historical record beyond *Crusade for Justice* hints at the ways in which Wells continued to play upon these tensions to make herself heard and create social change.

In September of 1929, the *Chicago Defender* newspaper carried a photo of Wells (see Figure 3), explaining that she was "Mrs. Ida B. Wells-Barnett, mother of clubdom . . . [who] first gained distinction when she mounted platforms and made appealing speeches against lynch law in the South. She is an outstanding national character."[123] Wells had been dubbed the "Mother of Clubs" in 1927, at a testimonial dinner given by local black club women in honor of her service, an event reminiscent of the Brooklyn women's gathering some thirty-five years earlier. At this testimonial, Wells, described in the *Defender* as "gracious, gentle and genial" in her manner, remarked with a touch of her famous sarcasm (apparently lost on the reporter) that she was "proud to receive her flowers while she was able to enjoy them," instead, of course, after she was dead.[124]

The title "Mother of Clubs" evokes a redemptive, founding maternal figure. In contrast to the symbolics of place evoked by "Exiled," "Mother" implicated the body. "Mother" also resonated with Christian faith, as in the expression "mother church" and the image of "Mother Mary," through whose body came Jesus and salvation. Perhaps the title "Mother of Clubs" echoed in Wells's mind during the writing of her autobiography. Her diary of 1930 refers to the narrative's uncompleted chapter as "the last," and this chapter opens with events from the year 1927.[125] Possibly, she planned to end the story of her life by proudly recounting recognition by the community of her role as a social "mother." Yet the other feminine figures associated with her work—especially Joan of Arc or Biblical heroines Deborah, Esther, and Jael—were women who took on traditionally male roles like soldier or judge on an emergency basis when the men were disabled.[126] In the 1920s, the first decade of political equality for women citizens, the use of the term "mother" suggests a tidying, domesticated sensibility that at first glance

Who Is She?

—Photo by R. D. Jones.

Her face is familiar. She is well known all over the United States. She is the mother of clubdom. If you cannot identify her, turn to page 22 and you will find her name.

FIGURE 3. "Who Is She?" This photo appeared in the *Chicago Defender* newspaper in 1929, showing how in the closing years of her life Wells-Barnett could still command front-page coverage in one of the most important African American media venues of the day. However, the quiz format here suggests that many readers might have known the woman but not the deeds or words behind the face. *Chicago Defender*, 21 September 1929

does not completely square with Wells's ambition and style but which actually links her to the honor due mothers, especially slave mothers, in black women's history.

In this context, the association of Wells with Joan of Arc merits special attention. Wells chose the image of Joan of Arc to frame the writing of her autobiography. Her preface to the narrative opens with a description of a Young Women's Christian Association (YWCA) gathering at which a young woman identifies Wells with Joan of Arc but cannot say why.[127] The image—itself multivalent as virgin, child, martyr, soldier, and witch—clung to Wells in the public's imagination long after her marriage and the birth of her children and long after the headline-grabbing days of the early antilynching crusade. It was apt because it captured Wells's ability to transgress gender norms to make a religious and political point. Yet the same preface to the narrative closes with the parent-like dedication of the narrative to "our youth." "It is therefore for the young people who have so little of our race's history recorded that I am for the first time in my life writing about myself."[128] Captured in the preface and reinforced throughout the text, *Crusade for Justice* refuses to simply settle or choose between the religious heroine or devoted mother, affirming instead the freedom to be either or both.[129]

Conclusion

The Vicksburg incident, the Brooklyn testimonial, the antilynching crusade, her mourning of Frederick Douglass, her marriage, and the writing of her autobiography depict a range of public venues that contained shifting, uncertain opportunities for political connection or social alienation, for personal triumph or even physical injury for Ida B. Wells. *Crusade for Justice* records her at first faltering then deft engagements with stereotypes and expectations about black women and her bold, sometimes angry conflicts with these expectations. In middle-class African American settings, gender expectations often were most salient and made serious demands on the body, as in talking through tears. Security in her slave mother's legacy as well as father-daughter mentoring relationships, epitomized by that with Frederick Douglass, were crucial to securing Wells's public presence. For their part, white people in the North, South, and abroad offered their own stage cues and trip wires. In nearly all settings, however, negative presumptions about black women created nearly impassible barriers for those who did not position themselves as a wife, a mother, or a daughter.

Crusade for Justice further suggests how nearly impossible it was for Ida B. Wells to escape the cultural "drag of the body" in social discourse.[130] Theories and fears and hopes about the world were inescapably projected onto her. In the 1890s, people looked: "If her pleasant face is not an absolute guarantee of absolute truthfulness," crowed an English newspaper reporter in 1894, "there is no truth in existence."[131] By 1910, however, Wells could be overlooked all too easily. The autobiography describes a white Chicago club woman who dismisses Wells's perspective on lynching with a laugh: "My dear, your mouth is no more a prayer book than that of any other of my friends who have talked with me about this subject." These words felt to Wells like a "slap in the face," and the oral and facial imagery here is suggestive. Neither "the facts" nor Christian bona fides—here figured tellingly through the body—guaranteed Wells's social authority. Such circumstances, so typical of her Chicago years, entailed a genuine political and personal crisis.[132]

Ida B. Wells's embrace of writing and public life as paths to self-making and social change demanded critical, creative engagement with a world that persistently associated black women with the monstrous or unintelligible body. Like her peers in literature and reform, Wells remained invested in the value of freedom, in the power of language—if not in protest novels then in political theater—to create meaning, and in heroic human potential, all capacities that were denied to slaves and doubted among freedpeople by white Americans. The authenticating strategies in Wells's autobiography and in her antilynching agitation suggest two further historical insights. First, she needed unimpeachable, selfless reasons to call attention to her life or her intellectual abilities, indeed, to "talk back" to power at all.[133] And second, Wells relied fundamentally on religious faith for her sense of self and vision of service. Antilynching's dual quality as religious vocation and political career derived not from Wells's status as a "transitional" figure in American reform but from the integrity of southern black women's protest traditions and a visionary pragmatism that blended the imperatives to faith and politics. Epitomized by the figure "Exiled," Ida B. Wells's visionary pragmatism took shape at the crossroad of slavery's memory, African American Christianity, and the promise and crises of the 1890s, comprising the unique inheritance of the post-Reconstruction generation of black women.

Ida B. Wells did not just exemplify the Christian ideals taught by the Bible but "revisioned" or "theologized" them as she determined necessary. In the Beatitudes, Jesus identifies the meek and persecuted as specially blessed by God, but Wells went one better, praying for righteousness *and* knowledge as she saw fit. This religiously directed sense of her own possibility was neither merely meek nor only heroic, and it allowed Wells to be a rebellious "Joan of Arc" who was also a nurturing "Mother of Clubs." As "Exiled," Wells did not just play upon the world as a stage but rewrote the script, grounding her sense of self and service in religious tradition and communal understanding. More than any other of her public identifications, "Exiled" abandoned the dominant culture's racist demand for bodily fixity around the coordinates of sex, race, and place. Some black critics obliged the demand for fixity, even celebrated it, as in Anna Julia Cooper's proud identification as "A Black Woman from the South" in her well-known collected essays *A Voice from the South*. In that text, Cooper memorably figured the honor of the "whole *Negro race*" in the "quiet, undisputed dignity" of black womanhood.[134] Cooper turned on its head the stereotype of "the black woman bringing down the black man," but as "Exiled," Wells remapped social possibilities by abandoning her "place," be it the repressive South or ladylike "quiet," and by challenging others to join her.

Crusade for Justice describes how as the southern girl "Iola," as "Exiled," as a "modern Joan," or the "Mother of Clubs," Ida B. Wells engaged the theatricality of modern life and politics, marked then, as now, by struggle around sex, race, and place in American society. Like the colored girl who wound up in the workhouse, Ida B. Wells was also a fighter who risked misunderstanding and punishment for assertive conduct. By challenging the stories of her day about how the world worked as well as the assumptions about who she could be in that world, Wells unsettled nearly all of her audiences, eliciting tears in some settings, cheers or taunts in others, and violence and vengeful fantasies in still others. Indeed, death threats attempted to enforce her staying in her "place." Official Memphis threatened "a surgical operation with a pair of tailor's shears" to the author of the *Free Speech's* editorial against lynching—Wells's article (they assumed the author was male).[135] The next chapter suggests that Wells in fact plotted and staged her "exile" from the South by provoking the white mob in Memphis with a flair that would not be outdone by African American activists until the 1960s. How Ida B. Wells crafted and enacted her vision of self and service and how her work was read, criticized, and transformed are what this book is all about.

CHAPTER TWO

Coming of Age in Memphis

Between 1883 and 1892, Ida B. Wells became the most accomplished African American woman journalist of her generation. In these years, she transformed, as one editor put it, from "a mere, insignificant, country-bred lass into one of the foremost among the female thinkers of the race to-day."[1] Wells came of age in Memphis, Tennessee, in a growing urban and middle-class African American community. By century's end, cities like Memphis, Atlanta, and Washington, D.C., would be the southern homes of black leaders in the United States, a group dubbed the "talented tenth" by the scholar W. E. B. Du Bois in 1903.[2] In his now-famous collection of essays published that year, *The Souls of Black Folk*, Du Bois described the "talented tenth" as both reason for and result of "the training of black men." His book overlooked the fact that this period also produced a "Female Talented Tenth," a "renaissance" in African American women's intellectual production, and an upsurge in social organizing led briefly by Ida B. Wells.[3] On the literary front, this wave of female accomplishment crested in 1892 with the publication of Anna Julia Cooper's collected essays, *A Voice from the South*, Frances E. W. Harper's novel *Iola Leroy*, and Wells's antilynching pamphlet, *Southern Horrors*.

New books by and about black women proliferated in the decade before Du Bois's *Souls* was published. Amanda Smith's *Autobiography* (1893), Gertrude Mossell's *The Work of the Afro-American Woman* (1894), Lawson V. Scruggs's *Women of Distinction: Remarkable in Works and Invincible in Character* (1893), and Monroe Majors's *Noted Negro Women: Their Triumphs and Activities* (1893) tapped new reading markets and fresh optimism about the future of African Americans in the United States. Each of these texts grappled with a changing set of regional, generational, and political relationships within an increasingly diverse and far-flung "talented tenth." In such a dynamic context, what did it mean, exactly, for Ida B. Wells to become a leading "female thinker of the race"?

African American women played the dual and sometimes ambivalent role of both agent and symbol of racial progress. As historian Wilson Moses points out, the post-Reconstruction era was a period of "breathless social advancement for black people," one that brought new insecurity along with new confidence, uncertainty amidst the brightest dreams of success.[4] Educated African American women traced out a hopeful, even heroic response to this historic juncture. "Aha, I can rival that! I can aspire to that!" proclaimed Cooper. "I can honor my name and vindicate my race!"[5] The "work of the Afro-American woman" that Mossell described was similarly ambitious; the endeavors she celebrated encompassed both public and private life, paid and unpaid labor. But some leading men were scarcely prepared or simply uninformed. On the eve of African American women's literary renaissance, Frederick Douglass responded to Monroe Majors's inquiry for *Noted Negro Women* as follows: "I have thus far seen no book of importance written by a negro woman and I know of no one among us who can appropriately be called famous."[6]

As Ida B. Wells and her peers quickly changed this situation, there was chiding—some good natured, some less so—about black women having "outdistanced our great men" in various spheres of American life.[7] A source of both pride and anxiety, African American women's contributions to community life were desperately needed, yet worried over; their talents elicited uneven measures of praise, surprise, unease, or silence.[8] Cooper herself admitted that "the average man of our race is less frequently ready to admit the actual need among the sturdier forces of the world for woman's help or influence."[9] "The work of women is greater in this country than man is willing to concede," noted the *African Methodist Episcopal (AME) Zion Church Quarterly* in 1893. "They are so far his superior, he is ashamed to give them an equal chance."[10] This typically ambivalent Victorian attitude toward women—worshipful, yet somehow disdaining—could be found across the color line, too, but it presented African American women with a particularly demanding set of practical and ideological negotiations in their lives, hemmed in as they already were by racial proscription and economic disadvantages.

Evidence of gender tension rarely entered the public record of middle-class black community life, where optimistic expressions of unity in the work of "uplift" were at a premium. "Our progress depends on the united strength of both men and women," went a typical declaration. "This is indeed the woman's era, and we are coming."[11] Such language inspired action and harmony while muting, even waving away, potential gender conflict. Private, personal sources like Ida B. Wells's diary, however, reveal significant struggle over African American women's "place" in both southern society in general and in new, middle-class black communities in particular. These conflicts smoldered in and around Wells until 1892, when racial violence in Memphis ignited a crisis and demanded a dramatic response. "Woman's place" was deeply implicated in the New South's evolving class relations and in the emerging politics of racial identity; lynching was both an expression of and reaction to these dynamics.[12] And in Memphis during the 1880s, Ida B. Wells was at the center of them all.

A View to Memphis

Wells's adopted home of Memphis was a growing and modernizing city, touted by local boosters as the "Chicago of the South."[13] Memphis's location on the Mississippi River fostered its role as a commercial center for the surrounding cotton-producing region and as a major railroad connecting point for the South. After the yellow fever epidemic of 1878–79, which took the lives of Wells's parents, business elites moved to clean up the city, supporting a special tax to build a new sewage and drainage system.[14] By 1890, modern electric streetcars and telephone lines also were in place. Pre-epidemic Memphis had had a thriving population of about 40,000, made up of white commercial and planter families, German (including some Jewish) shopkeepers, Irish laborers, and an African American population numbering about 13,000. The fever reduced the city's inhabitants by one-third, and during the 1880s the city's population was dramatically remade in "black" and "white." By 1890, the population had climbed to about 65,000, with the proportion of foreign-born residents falling to 8 percent, down from 36 percent in 1860.[15] Country people poured in, inaugurating a period of social mobility and social conflict.[16]

The deadly yellow fever epidemic left another legacy: it broke the city's budget. Coming on the heels of a decade of graft and speculation in government finances, the epidemic's demands on local resources emptied the city's coffers. Bankruptcy, in turn, cost Memphis its charter, and the city became a taxing district in 1879. Until 1893, Memphis received its budget from the state legislature and was governed by a three-person commission made up of representatives of the fire, police, and public works departments.[17] As would be the case in numerous reformed city governments in the coming decades, the replacement of Memphis's ward-based electoral system with an appointive commission-style government threatened to reduce democratic representation of African Americans and working-class whites, none of whom served as city commissioners between 1879 and 1893. But in 1882, the popularly elected commission president, David P. Hadden, set an inclusive, nonpartisan tone for city politics. "Pap" Hadden, a native Kentuckian and cotton factor who came to Memphis in 1864 by way of New York City, was eager to profit from improving the city's political, financial, and sanitary conditions. He courted the now sizable black vote by hiring black policemen and by including a black representative on the board of public works.[18] African Americans also served on the Memphis school board. In 1885, two new schoolhouses were built for black students, for which Ida B. Wells felt the Board of Education deserved "great praise."[19]

Due to lingering controversy over the state debt incurred during the Civil War, two-party politics in Tennessee—including black suffrage—remained viable, even lively, for most of the 1880s. In Memphis's surrounding Shelby County, African Americans constituted 56 percent of the population, with an edge of nearly 500 black voters over white in 1880. Memphis's black politicians, led by the freeborn Union army veteran Edward Shaw, made a serious if unsuccessful attempt at fusion politics, similar to those occurring in Virginia. Under Democratic governors, conservatives' willingness to bargain with black voters at the local level helped elect eleven African American legislators to the state house between 1882 and 1886. Though one of the bloodiest race riots of the century occurred in Memphis in 1866, a spirit of reconciliation characterized the 1880s.[20] "The relations of the two races are and have been kind and cordial," stated the local voice of the New South, the *Memphis Appeal*, in 1886, "and the mutual respect for each other's rights and regard for each other's welfare increases as time, with gentle fingers, erases the asperities of the past."[21]

The city's public health and financial disasters created unusual opportunities for the fortunate and enterprising. An outstanding African American citizen, Robert R. Church, for example, turned the small legacy left by his white, slave-owning father into real estate investments that made him one of the wealthiest men in Memphis. Another native of Holly Springs, Church was by 1890 the most conspicuous economic success in a vibrant African American community numbering about 30,000. At the center of the community was a network of Baptist and Methodist churches, seven public schools attended and staffed by African Americans, Le Moyne Normal and Industrial Institute (a missionary-run college), three military organizations, and a web of lodges, fraternal orders, burial associations, and social clubs, including the so-called secret societies.[22] A small but active and self-conscious middle class was made up of professionals, clergy, small business operators, and politicians (see Figure 4). By 1890, black Memphians supported three newspapers—the *Watchman*, *The Living Way*, and the *Free Speech*—as well as an assortment of smaller church and club newsletters.[23] African Americans' hopes for peace and prosperity echoed those of official Memphis boosters. "Almost every profession and all avocations are here represented by Negroes," wrote a visiting reporter in 1890. "Efforts on the part of the Negroes to improvement of their condition morally, intellectually and physically will move away the cloud [of racial prejudice] now overshadowing [them], as the sun removes the morning dew."[24]

In this context of relative political openness, demographic change, and economic development, women initiated quiet challenges to sex roles. Though such efforts dotted southern cities in this period, members of Memphis's white female elite were vanguard advocates of woman suffrage as well as promoters of educational reform, of raising the legal age of consent for girls (from ten to sixteen in 1873), and temperance.[25] Supported by church and kin networks, they opened new girls' schools in the 1870s, a mission home called "The Refuge" for "erring women" in 1876, and a "Young Women's Boarding Home" for factory workers in 1887—all for whites only. By 1892, a new Association for the Advancement of Women met in convention in Memphis and sponsored lecturers on social purity and woman suffrage.[26] Frances E. Willard, president of the Woman's Christian Temperance Union (WCTU), visited Memphis several times during her southern tours of the 1880s, and during that decade the city's white and black women organized into separate temperance locals.[27]

The city was also home to two of the South's earliest white woman suffragists, Elizabeth Avery Meriwether and Lide Meriwether, sisters-in-law of aristocratic slaveholding background.[28] In an 1886 address to the local Knights of Labor, Lide Meriwether impressed Ida B. Wells as a "grand woman," her suffrage message as one of "truth and justice." Even more remarkable to Wells was the way in which African Ameri-

MISS IDA B. WELLS (IOLA)
Editress of Free Speech & Headlight.
Memphis, Tenn.

BEN J. FARNANDIS.
Merchant and Jewelerist. Memphis.
Tenn.

W. A. WADE.
Of the Tennessee Grocery Co., Memphis. Tenn.

MISS LUCILE O. WASHINGTON.
Memphis, Tenn.,

FIGURE 4. Prominent members of Memphis's black middle class. *Indianapolis Freeman*, 5 April 1890

cans were seated with "courtesy" and without discrimination at this meeting.[29] The meeting marked for Wells "the first assembly of this sort in this town where color was not the criterion to recognition as ladies and gentlemen."[30] The Knights were known for their cross-race and gender-inclusive organizing, but Wells still had reason for surprise. As a fan of the theater, she was aware that de facto racial segregation usually prevailed in public accommodations in Memphis. Given her father's political interests in the area, she also may have known that the Ku Klux Klan had been founded in Elizabeth Meriwether's drawing room twenty years earlier.[31] For the moment, at least, racial tolerance and female advancement boded well in New South Memphis, especially among the "ladies and gentlemen" of the city.

As Wells's presence at the Knights' lecture indicates, African American women also moved into new areas of public visibility in the 1880s. Their initiatives against racism especially stand out in the record. In 1880, a Miss Jane Brown sued and won damages from the Memphis C & R Railroad Company for removing her from the first-class car of a train.[32] Equally dramatic and well publicized was the arrest of Mrs. Julia Britton Hooks, an accomplished musician and schoolteacher. Hooks went to a matinee at the downtown Jefferson Theater in March 1881. She sat in the newly segregated family circle and was forcibly removed by police. Hooks was jailed, fined, and ridiculed in the *Appeal* as a "cheeky wench" for her efforts.[33] An esteemed member of Memphis's black elite, Julia Hooks set an important example of female accomplishment in teaching and the arts as well as in civil rights agitation. So did Virginia Broughton, a Fisk graduate, outstanding local schoolteacher, and prominent Baptist churchwoman. Broughton attempted to organize black Baptist women into all-female "Bible bands" in this period, but clergy objected strongly. "[C]hurch houses were locked against our Bible women," she later wrote, "and violent hands were laid upon some."[34] Despite resistance from many quarters, hope for social influence and personal achievement still ran high among African American women in Memphis, notably among the younger generation. Ida B. Wells was "very much enthused" to make the acquaintance of Mary Church, the daughter of Robert Church, since Church shared her own "desires, hopes, & ambitions" for community service and literary success.[35]

Arriving in Memphis around 1882, Wells took a page out of these women's books. While traveling into town from the countryside in the fall of 1883, she physically resisted removal from a first-class "ladies'" railroad car, even biting the conductor's hand to get free of his grip. Wells suffered rough handling and the tearing of her jacket as train officials put her off while white passengers stood on their seats to watch and applaud. Undaunted, she refused the smoking car on the same line again in 1884.[36] In accordance with Tennessee's separate car law of 1881, which required a separate first-class car for each "race," Wells sued the company for discrimination and won both of her cases. In court, she testified with no little sarcasm that the conductor "said to me that he would treat me like a lady but that I must go into the other car, and I replied, that if he wished to treat me like a lady, he would leave me alone."[37] Like Broughton and Hooks, Wells met resistance to her expectation of safety and respect in the public sphere. The railroad company fought back, appealing Wells's cases to the state supreme court. For their part, black Memphis did not rally. "None of my people had ever seemed to feel that it was a race matter and that they should help me with the fight," she later wrote.[38] But Beale St. Baptist Church pastor Rev. R. N. Countee thought the lawsuit important enough to write about. Wells did so under the pen name "Iola" in the pages of his church weekly, *The Living Way*, marking her formal entrance into journalism in 1883.[39] For all the optimism about making Memphis a prosperous and racially harmonious city, the examples of Hooks, Broughton, and Wells suggest that there was little consensus across or within the color line about the proper place of black women in the New South.

Black Women in the Public Sphere

Confusion over social place in the Gilded Age derived in part from the mobility and social dislocation brought by industrialization, urbanization, and new transportation technology. All of these forces plus kinship ties drew Wells from small-town Holly Springs to big-city Memphis. She accepted an invitation from Fannie Butler—an aunt by marriage and a widow with children of her own—to move into her home in town. Taking in kin to board allowed the women to pool childcare, share income, and enjoy companionship. Wells managed to have her crippled sister Eugenia placed with a relative and found local apprenticeships for her brothers. Bringing along sisters Annie and Lily, Wells joined Aunt Fannie's household. She continued to teach in the countryside and commuted by train until 1884, when she received an appointment in the Memphis school system.[40] Wells shared head-of-household responsibilities for income producing and child rearing with her aunt until 1886, when Butler moved west to California. Wells then boarded with other black families in town until she, too, left Memphis in 1892, for the North.

School teaching was the only regular employment available to educated African American women beyond domestic service, and that opportunity was tied to politics. In the 1870s, a desire for autonomy among black Memphians combined with ex-Confederate antagonism toward northern missionaries to force out Yankee teachers from the city's schools. By 1875, Memphis's "colored" schools were entirely staffed, if not controlled, by African Americans. Black women became teachers in increasing numbers, and they excelled. In 1885, Virginia Broughton became the head teacher of Memphis's Kortrecht school, the most advanced public school for black students.[41] Perhaps inspired by Broughton's example and goaded by the need for better pay among notoriously undercompensated women teachers, Wells contemplated what it would take to "study up & get a principal's certificate" in these years.[42] By 1890, surrounding Shelby County's nine schools for black children employed sixty-seven women and fifty-five men teachers; by 1908, seventy-three of ninety black school teachers in Memphis proper were female.[43]

A social institution mingling public and private elements—namely, taxes and children—schools epitomized the kind of institution through which "new women," black and white, secured a foothold in civic life in the late nineteenth century. Yet the politics of access to public institutions hardly stood still. The feminization of school teaching in Memphis was itself caught up in the gender bias entailed in cost-cutting measures taken during the 1870s, when school budgets were slashed during the city's financial woes. In 1873, Elizabeth Meriwether led a fight for equal pay for female teachers, who were being paid less than half as much as men. Her efforts included a petition to the Board of Education signed by all the women schoolteachers in the city, black and white. The women's initiative was soundly defeated by the Board, leading Meriwether to her pro-woman suffrage views. Eventually the old wage scale that paid men more than women was eliminated in favor of a single graded system; all salaries were lowered and as a result, many men left the field.[44] School teaching made African American women like Wells visible and political in the civic life of Memphis. They worked amidst the tensions of city politics, the birth pangs of the woman suffrage movement, and the internal class and gender dynamics of an emerging black elite eager to affirm a place in the city.[45]

School life for African American teachers meant much more than earning a livelihood. Schools were cherished spaces, vested with hopes of achievement for individuals and the larger community. Equal education in black schools, given a running start by missionary patterns during Reconstruction, now took fresh impulse from an inclusive spirit of self-improvement. "The co-education of the sexes has given to [the black woman's] life a strong impetus in the line of literary effort," commended Gertrude Mossell.[46] In a constellation of student and faculty clubs, lyceums, and societies, men and women sought mutual improvement, sociability, and, not infrequently, political engagement. Wells associated with a literary lyceum whose members were mainly teachers like herself. This group's tone was set by school principal and Republican Party activist Benjamin K. Sampson. Sampson was a native of

Vicksburg, Mississippi, and an Oberlin College graduate, lauded in the press as "the triple embodiment and rare combination of the scholar, orator and educator."[47] The fluid, multiple roles of teachers and schools in the community in this period uniquely shaped a generation of educated African Americans for accomplishment and service.[48]

Because schooling was infused with personal, social, and political meanings, it is no surprise that Ida B. Wells's lack of a college degree caused her pain to the point of tears. Upon visiting commencement exercises at her would-be alma mater, Shaw University in Holly Springs, (see Figure 5), her diary noted that "a great sob arose in my throat and I yearned with unutterable longing for the 'might have been.'" When a male acquaintance later raised the issue of her finishing up school and graduating, Wells explained: "I could not restrain my tears at the sense of injustice I felt, and begged him not to ask me why I said 'I could not.'"[49] Here Wells's tears may have been tied to the matter of reputation, the archetypal Victorian trigger for female wordlessness. Reputation was critical because only proper feminine behavior—girls Wells described as "easily controlled"—garnered the educational rewards and intellectual recognition she craved for herself. Wells claimed that she failed to meet the standard of "extreme tractableness" expected of female students at Shaw. She blamed her lack of success at school on her "tempestuous, rebellious, hard headed willfulness," on the "trouble" she gave, and her "disposition to question [the principal's] authority."[50] Victorian taboos of female desire—among them, knowledge and money—mingled everywhere in Ida B. Wells's surroundings, not as abstract temptations but as necessities for survival.

In this context, reading was critical to Wells's social and professional life as well as to her regime of self-improvement, particularly if she wanted to advance in the teaching profession. Whenever possible she spent entire afternoons poring over novels like Evans's *Vashti* (borrowed from a teacher friend, Mrs. Fannie Thompson), Victor Hugo's *Les Misérables*, or, with a story line located closer to home, Albion Tourgée's *A Fool's Errand*, a novel about Reconstruction. Plot, characterization, and admiration for "cutting, witty" dialogue caught her attention and were noted in her diary.[51] Reading, like writing, often took place in reflective, dialogic settings—either in her diary or at lyceum gatherings and especially in letters. Whenever possible, Wells devoted the better part of whole days to carefully writing and rewriting long missives to her valued correspondents, most of whom were teachers who she met at work, social functions, conferences, and church. Great care went into these productions, as letters could be shared and circulated

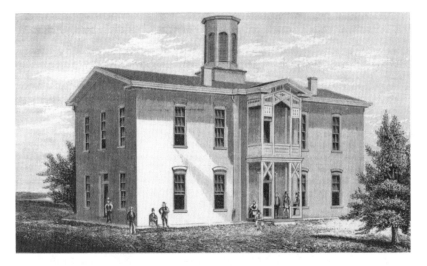

FIGURE 5. Shaw University, Holly Springs, Mississippi. From Matthew Simpson, *Cyclopedia of Methodism* (Philadelphia, 1878), 796

among friends, colleagues, and family in town and across the region. In time, these drafts were developed into articles and news columns. Among the intellectual exchanges most noted in her diary were those with local teachers, Mr. and Mrs. Theodore Lott and Josiah and Theresa Settle, and, through correspondence, with Charles Morris and Louis M. Brown (both of Louisville). Through these relationships and formal or informal tutorials, Wells explored topics ranging from literature and science to courtship and family.[52]

For poorer or self-supporting women like Wells, opportunities in and around school life were crucial for economic and social well-being. A "voracious reader" as a child, Wells found the adult lyceum gatherings to be the "breath of life."[53] In contrast to the stifling conditions at Shaw, a welcoming intellectual atmosphere for black women flourished in Memphis. In October of 1886, Wells's diary noted: "Was elected editress of the Evening Star," the teacher lyceum's newsletter. The entry implied a rather matter-of-fact, if gendered, event. Wells's autobiography later noted her "great surprise" at the appointment.[54] Both sentiments ring true. Wells was the novel yet logical result of conditions almost unthinkable for her own mother at a similar age. Within a year of taking over the *Evening Star*, Wells became the first woman to address the national Afro-American Press Association at their annual convention and soon became its first female elected officer. Some observers characterized Wells in these years as having an "ambition . . . not found in most girls, or women either."[55] Yet there she was.

Words, Meanings, Money

Part of what colleagues responded to in Ida B. Wells was her gift with language, especially the spoken word. In the rich oral culture of school, club, and church life, Wells developed a flair for public speaking. Over the course of the 1880s, black Memphians came to know and appreciate Wells's essays, dramatic and literary recitations, toasts, and impromptu wit. By decade's end, she was known as far away as New York as "the Anna Dickinson of the race," as a women whose verbal "brilliance is dazzling."[56] When the schoolteachers hosted a welcome reception for friends returning from the World's Fair at New Orleans in 1885, Wells was chosen to offer "the toast of the occasion."[57] In addition to hosting occasional dinnertime "entertainments" for her friends, Wells gave formal papers, like the address "What Lack We Yet?" at the LeMoyne Institute in 1887.[58] In settings like the Golden Star Club or the salon of Julia Hooks, Wells was not above reciting amusing verse for her audiences.[59] One of her selections at the Golden Star, "Widder Bud," indicates fluency with southern dialect. Elocution lessons dearly paid for and public recitations of Lady Macbeth's soliloquy, "Le Marriage de Convenience," and "The Doom of Claudius and Cynthia" depict another range of carefully cultivated verbal skills.[60] The subject matter of these passages—female ambition, marriage, and tragedy in love—hint at the period's preoccupation with femininity and destiny. Figures and themes from *Macbeth* would echo across Wells's career through to the writing of her autobiography.

Ida B. Wells came of age in a setting in which the use of language, voice, and gesture were matters of great social value and artistry. In her diary, Wells reacted against pretension and emotionalism in public address—what she called "mannerisms" and "spouting"—and preferred the use of "words weighted with the eloquence of meaning rather than sound."[61] Evident, too, is her disdain for those who could not command standard English. For example, Wells's diary gently mocked a newspaper man's compliment to her as a " 'powfull writer.' "[62] She publicly took Memphis teachers to task for failing the examinations required for school appointments. "Every year the same disgraceful result over an ordinary English examination," she stated in the press. "Colored applicants fall out on the first test—that of spelling."[63]

Wells was among a generation of educated Americans for whom

mastery of English, symbolized by the mastery of the words of William Shakespeare, marked a new standard of cultural competence and class identification. Caught up in the nineteenth-century transformation of Shakespeare from broadly popular performance into "classical" art, Wells and her peers in Memphis dutifully spooned and chewed their cultural spinach. Wells found a reading of *Macbeth* at LeMoyne "exceedingly dull & tiresome & some of the pronunciation . . . execrable in the extreme."[64] Language was especially serious business for teachers, charged as they were with fostering and maintaining cultural standards. A correspondent of Wells, a teacher, thought that her choice words to describe Lady Macbeth in a letter to him exceeded propriety; he felt she "could have found [words] less objectionable." Wells likely found in Lady Macbeth a fascinating horror who, as Victorian middle-class women could appreciate, worked out her ambition through her husband's career and lost her self in the process. When Wells rehearsed Shakespeare or sought out Edwin Booth's theatrical productions, she also connected with a tradition which, like her own native traditions across and within the color line, "enshrined oratory" and released the magic of words.[65]

Wells's theatrical interests and literary pursuits were closely linked to her social, professional, and financial fortunes. Tight monetary circumstances motivated Wells to blend creativity, sociability, and enterprise. In 1887, she organized a "Dramatic Club" with some friends and colleagues, and the group performed public "Concerts." One Concert's "artistic & financial success" netted "clear nearly $60." "Thank the Lord for His blessing!" Wells exulted.[66] Expected as a teacher to uphold standards, however, Wells was discouraged from attending the theater, long considered the domain of professional liars and loose women. A group of male teachers gave her a "severe lecture on going to the theater" warning that it was dangerous to her morals and set a poor example for her elementary school students. Wells agreed so as not to "be the cause of one soul's being led astray"—a promise she had trouble keeping.[67]

Like theater, writing offered links to financial opportunity, personal recognition, and socially conscious uplift. The novel she planned to write with her friend Charles Morris was to be "classical, representative, and standard," suggesting a disinterest in the dialect and local color methods that aspiring American writers, black and white, experimented with in these years. Throughout her career, Wells disdained the vernacular in print.[68] Literary success held out a means for Wells to make herself "loved, honored & respected," but developing as a writer proved difficult, expensive, and frustrating. Poor finances in 1886 prevented

Wells from attending summer courses at Fisk University in Nashville. After finishing a piece she had written for the AME *Church Review* and sending it off "to get the opinion of others," she lamented: "I think sometimes I can write a readable article and then again I wonder how I could have been so mistaken . . . and yet—what is it that keeps urging me to write notwithstanding all?"[69] Wells declined an offer to publish and edit an edition of the *Little Rock Sun* newspaper in Memphis because she "could not make it pay."[70] The novel-writing project foundered on related matters. After exchanging notes with Charles Morris, Wells found herself "not much attracted" to the outline. His concepts were "rather sensational," she thought, driven, no doubt, by the need to make it pay.[71]

Wells's literary and theatrical efforts offer tantalizing glimpses into her experiments with language, performance, and enterprise in her Memphis years. The stakes in such endeavors were complex, however, and she fretted and prayed over the strained links between relationships, money, and employment. When she asked a suitor, Mr. I. J. Graham (another schoolteacher), for a loan, she "hated very badly to do it— but was compelled."[72] Struggling to pay for rent, clothing, and school supplies for herself and her sisters, Wells groused in her diary: "I wish I could feel that my money was not so persistently sought after." Straining to catch a secure direction for her talents, Wells looked to God. "I wonder if I shall ever reach satisfaction in this world. My Father prepare me in my undertaking I pray Thee."[73] When she gave a pair of "severe" whippings to her sister Lily for stealing money from her purse in 1887, perhaps she actually used the rather stilted words recorded in her diary—"felonious offence" and "peculation"—during the sisters' "pitched battle."[74] To mitigate these strains and outbursts, Wells cultivated a stinging wit with which to relieve tension and express herself, finding good company in the "fine humor & sarcasm" of her bubbly correspondent Charles Morris.[75] She honed her literary and verbal skills in a world fraught with "pitched battles" at home and at the rough edges of boomtown Memphis, where a "colored girl" could wind up in the work house for defending herself.

Balance and self-possession were not easily achieved amid the irritations, insults, and dangers of being black and female in the New South. Furthermore, the intimate world of Memphis's aspiring black middle class placed its own demands on female composure and comportment. Wells's diary notes unceasing efforts "to be more calm & philosophical" in her dealings with the world.[76] Religion provided the deepest framework for her to assimilate the contradiction of freedom and proscription in her life. "May I be a better Christian with more of the strength to overcome, the wisdom to avoid & have the meekness & humility that becometh a follower of Thee," she prayed.[77] Wells struggled to maintain her "womanly equipoise & dignity" in social settings; her diary laments having "lost my temper & acted in an unladylike way" at a public event. She beseeched God: "O, help me to better control my temper!"[78]

Though she practiced deflecting rage in prayer and containing insult in repartee, Wells also fought back. In the spring of 1887, she visited Holly Springs by train with three female friends. "Of course we had the usual trouble about the first-class coach," she noted in her diary, "but we conquered."[79] Other African American women were less successful. When a Miss Hattie Manley resisted police removal from a Memphis public park in the summer of 1885, she wound up in jail, the black community "greatly indignant" over her treatment. That Pap Hadden "discharged the case with a smile" at the hustings points to the kindly, condescending attitude facing African Americans from white allies.[80] In January 1886, Wells rushed to a teaching colleague's home after school in order to borrow a copy of the AME *Church Review* that she was "anxious" to read.[81] She was looking for T. Thomas Fortune's article on race in politics. In the very next issue of the *Review*, controversy stirred the church over the recent ordination of North Carolinian Sarah Ann Hughes as a deacon by Bishop Henry McNeal Turner—a decision soon reversed by AME leadership.[82] The conquering attitude and promise for high achievement among African American women was impossible to miss either in the local neighborhood or the national press.

Southern Black Womanhood after Reconstruction

While Ida B. Wells struggled at school, on trains, in court, with her friends, and with God, the figure of "the Southern black woman" became newly visible and argued about in the work of post-Reconstruction African American writers. Leading thinkers took stock of her past and predicted her future, mainly with an eye toward her recruitment to the work of race uplift. Wells contributed to the debate about "the Southern black woman" in the 1880s at the same time as Dr. Alexander Crummell and Anna Julia Cooper engaged the discussion in Washington, D.C. Students of African American women's history are familiar with Cooper's collected works *A Voice from the South; by a Black Woman of the South*, but few have touched on the regional dimensions of the text or the date of 1884, in which the opening and often-cited essay "Womanhood a Vital Element in the Regeneration and Progress of a Race" was first written. Also mostly overlooked are Cooper's references to

Crummell's essay "The Black Woman of the South: Her Neglects and Her Needs," a pioneering address he delivered in 1883. Together with Wells's short pieces on women written between 1885 and 1888—"Our Women," "A Story of 1900," "Woman's Mission," and "The Model Woman: A Pen Picture of the Typical Southern Girl"—these writings comprise an early phase of the "reconstruction" of African American womanhood after emancipation. This was a hopeful, uncertain, exploratory phase, less freighted with the grisly racist backlash of the century's end and very revealing of the context for Wells's developing insights about sex, race, and place in southern society.[83]

Born free in New York City in 1819, Crummell was a highly influential Cambridge-educated cleric and leading black nationalist figure of the period. In his 1883 lecture, he sounded a despairing note. Among those of "the African race in this country," Crummell identified "the black woman of the South" as among the least fortunate. Isolated, poor, and uneducated, he offered statistics to highlight the "*vastness* of this degradation," especially her educational deprivation. "The black woman is the Pariah woman of this land!" Never one shy of provocative statements, Crummell affirmed: "She is still the crude, rude, ignorant mother." Crummell reflected the objectifying tendencies of the day, which keyed the body to social condition, noting that "eighteen years of freedom have not obliterated all [of slavery's] deadly marks from either the souls or bodies of the black woman." Breaking with racist assumptions, however, Crummell praised her in her "natural state," holding up native African and West Indian feminine ideals of "tenderness, modesty, and sweetness," drawn from his missionary work abroad. Crummell insisted that "humble and benighted as she is, the black woman of the South is one of the queens of womanhood." Rather than hamper black men, she actually held a distinct advantage, since she rarely suffered the "bitter gibe, sneer, contempt" of racists. Such were "never [uttered] against the black woman!" Crummell declared. "On the contrary," he claimed, "she has almost everywhere been extolled and eulogized." While certain that the black woman could naturally benefit rather than hinder African American progress, he argued that she still needed to be "uplifted . . . from a state of brutality and degradation." Crummell thought uplift could be accomplished through missionary sisterhoods for home visiting as well as through industrial schools for girls and young women.[84]

Reading Cooper's essay against Crummell's brings a number of elements into focus. First, Cooper admired Crummell's work, dubbing him "Moses" and a "Prophet" on the subject of black womanhood. Her essay worked a gentle critique framed through a strategic bit of deference that legitimized and bolstered her own points. Cooper noted that Crummell masterfully treated "the Black Woman"; she respectfully added her "plea for the Colored Girls of the South," as a proper female would tend to the children. By positioning herself as "*a Black woman of the South*" (she was born to a slave mother in North Carolina around 1859) and by displaying her own great erudition, Cooper refuted Crummell's image of a singularly rude and unlettered type. An Oberlin graduate, she echoed and expanded Crummell's case for female education by stressing not black women's historic degradation under slavery but their present-day need for equal education as well as for protection by male kin, who should "defend their honor with his life's blood." Finally, she charged the church with letting Crummell's proposals languish, complaining that his "pamphlet fell still born from the press." She challenged wealthy northern Methodist denominations to move quickly in the South, lest the Baptists completely capture the region. Cooper and Crummell shared a central assumption, in her words: "That the race cannot be effectually lifted up till its women are truly elevated we take as proven." And domestic competence, education, and moral training in practical Christianity would be the pillars of any such program.[85]

Ida B. Wells's writings about women projected a more ambivalent terrain. In "Woman's Mission" (1885), Wells took little as "proven" and instead stepped back and posed a question to her reader: "What is, or should be woman?" Bracketing for the moment the particular needs of rural or uneducated women, Wells began an answer by describing a person of strength and moral purpose: "[a] strong, bright presence, thoroughly imbued with a sense of her mission on earth and a desire to fill it." What that mission was exactly she did not spell out. The article identified a few coordinates for shaping that mission, like college, the professions, the writing of good and useful books, and service in "positions of trust" in community life. Rather than touch on the woman suffrage issue, Wells stressed women's family roles as key components of her mission. Not as voter but as daughter, wife, and especially as mother, woman was most "potent to move men's hearts."[86]

Crummell and Cooper were sure that Christian history was on the side of African Americans and that Jesus' redemption would usher in equality, peace, and justice for all. Wells expressed a more mixed assessment of historical Christianity as she cast about to frame woman's mission. Adam was better off with a helpmate in the Garden of Eden, but because of Eve, wrote Wells, "the world labored under a curse of four thousand years." Turning to the Gospels, she found more hopeful signs in two of the Marys. Mother Mary brought Jesus and redemption into the world; the prostitute Mary Magdalene was especially pitied by and faithful to Jesus. By singling out a "Jewish virgin" and a fallen woman in her discussion, Wells highlighted Jesus' special connection to low-status or outcast women in a way that might have resonated with southern black women. After this less than triumphalist treatment of Christian history, she closed by suggesting a religiously imbued standard by which women would "warm, comfort and command with something of an angel's light." There is, perhaps, as much plaintiveness as affirmation in Wells's declaration: "O woman, woman! Thine is a noble heritage!"[87]

In her subsequent essays on women, Wells pieced together more bits of a response to the question she laid out in "Woman's Mission." In "A Story of 1900," she offered a history of the future featuring a devoted, southern-born, black woman schoolteacher's impact on her students and neighbors. The successful teacher "exhorted them to cultivate honest, moral habits, to lay a foundation for a noble character that would convince the world that worth not color made the man." Wells presented a less strictly domestic vision than Crummell's hoped for "thrifty wives" and "worthy matrons," favoring a community-based standard of general health and progress, one critically shaped by women educators who bridged the public and private spheres. Though like Crummell and Cooper she championed a "practical Christianity," Wells's teacher also encouraged her pupils "to be self-respecting so they might be respected" by their community. Written no doubt to ease the tedium of teaching in the underfunded schools that she and so many of her peers faced every day, Wells made this vision of the near future a dream of success, closing with the shared hope for her "gentle reader" that "you and I 'may go and do likewise.'"[88]

In sharp contrast to Crummell's assertion that black women were less ridiculed than black men, in "Our Women" (1886), Wells pointed to "the wholesale contemptuous defamation of women" as among the most debilitating "accusations" that so "dishearten[ed]" African Americans. She also affirmed that African American women had, in fact, achieved a "true, noble, and refining womanhood." As opposed to Crummell's census statistics and archetypes, Wells offered local knowledge: "There are many such all over this Southland of course, and in our own city they abound."[89] In "The Model Woman: A Pen Picture of the Typical Southern Girl" (1888), Wells further argued against the negative presumption against African American women. The "'typical Southern girl' of today is not without refinement, is not coarse and rude in her manner," contended Wells, nor was she "loud and fast in her deportment." Wells balanced this argument against the economic disadvantages that she herself knew firsthand. The southern girl's "only wealth, in most cases, is her character," wrote Wells, and her "first consideration is to preserve that character in spotless purity." Unlike Cooper's plea to male kin for protection, however, Wells stressed strength of character—chastity, to be sure, but not only that—as well as the importance of wage labor and domestic skills for the integrity of African American womanhood. The southern girl "regards all honest toil as noble," proclaimed Wells, "and esteems it among her best accomplishments that she can cook, wash, iron, sew and 'keep house' thoroughly and well." A sense of yearning appeared again in her closing hope that the southern girl could rise above the many obstacles of everyday life. This she might do by imitating the moon, sailing serenely in the night sky. Wells the theater fan also appended to this essay a few lines of inspirational verse in which "the model woman" played upon the world as a stage. The last line of the poem encouraged her to "be a star!"—an image that evokes both spiritual transcendence and worldly celebrity, precisely the tension in Wells's own life in Memphis.[90]

Gender Protection and Marriage

The debate and stigma surrounding "the Southern girl" derived in part from the concerns over employed women and working "girls" in the late nineteenth century and the necessity, overlooked by Crummell, for most adult African American women to work for wages.[91] Though increasing numbers of young women and girls entered the paid labor force in this period, marriage and attachment to family still defined female social maturity.[92] In Memphis, elite white women built institutions like the Boarding Home to extend the shelter of "home" around employed or dislocated girls and women until marriage brought them male protection and homes of their own. As in the North, career wage-earning or reforming white women in Memphis were expected to forfeit marriage for lives of "single blessedness."[93] African American women, however, faced more complex expectations. Wage labor was necessary for individual and family survival, but self-sufficiency led more quickly to suspicion, stigma, or isolation. North and South, white "school ma'ms" were expected to leave teaching upon marriage. Black women's wage work relieved them neither from the pressure to marry nor from the stigma of singleness. At age twenty-five, Wells felt uncomfortably conspicuous at school as the "only lady teacher left in the building who is unmarried."[94]

In contrast to the relatively unencumbered "model woman" and "southern girl" projected in Wells's journalism in these years, her diary stresses the centrality of marriage to female social standing in her community. Either one was a wife, a former wife, or a wife-to-be—all else was strange or irregular. "I am an anomaly to my self as well as to others," she mused. "I do not wish to be married but I do wish for the society of the gentlemen."[95] Frustrated by a lack of "middle ground" in social relations with men her own age, Wells complained that it was "either love or nothing."[96] As with Wells's own parents and other freed-people who quickly remarried legally after emancipation, the social ritual and official contract of marriage offered legitimacy and status in a society that promised little to African Americans. In New South Memphis, marriage also symbolized adulthood for young people like Wells whose futures were bright but highly uncertain.[97] Matrimony was a key component of gender protection, the idea that husbands and fathers could insure the safety of women and dependents in exchange for a wife's sexual exclusivity, domestic labor, and fertility.[98] Short of marriage, Wells's relationships with men in Memphis—like shopkeeper and former politician Alfred Fromans, whom she called "my dad"[99]—indicate a felt need for social fathers and protection by men, especially given her orphan status.

A restless spirit, Wells struggled with the expectation of marriage. She enjoyed male friends and company but resisted marriage and the "inevitable baby" that followed.[100] A gregarious soul by nature, she never made even an uneasy peace with being alone, as did her younger contemporaries like poet Angelina Weld Grimké or immigrant writer Anzia Yezierska. In the novel *Bread Givers*, Yezierska's protagonist vows of her loneliness: "if it does not kill you, it will be the making of you."[101] Committed as she was to maintaining her family ties, Wells found neither solitude nor "single blessedness" appealing. Her commentary on her Aunt Fannie's friend Lutie Rice was a thoroughly classic cut at spinsters. She described Lutie's face as "hard," her manner as overly "precise" and with an "unconscious tone of superiority and pride in a fact she often repeats; of living within herself and on her own resources."[102] Being an "old maid" held no charm for Wells, but marriage and domesticity entailed unappealing maternity and confinement. Concerned with her own financial security and the erratic fortunes of her brothers, she determined at one point in her diary to "go to house-keeping"—a chicken farm was one idea—and pursue domesticity with her siblings rather than through marriage.[103] This plan never materialized. There was simply not enough cash or secure social space outside of marriage for African American women to reconstitute "homes without men," as did wealthy white women in this period. In Memphis's African American community, households, rather than separate female institutions, sheltered orphans and the elderly as well as working people and travelers through the early twentieth century.[104]

Given the limited social space for unmarried black women, one recent scholar labeled Wells's bid for social autonomy in her Memphis years as "male-identified" behavior. That Wells's own daughter Alfreda, in a fictional biography of her mother, imagined that Jim Wells wished for a son at Ida's birth furthers this impression.[105] The idea evokes a Victorian pattern of female rebellion in which a daughter's identification with her father and his world in the public sphere leads to a critique of inequitable gender arrangements. The vivid autobiographical image of Wells as a child "reading the newspaper to my father and an admiring group of his friends" fits this pattern, much as does one from Elizabeth Cady Stanton's memoir, that of her reading casebooks in her father's law office, bantering with his male clerks and students.[106] When Wells explored the theme of female destiny in her one work of published fiction, however, she did not elaborate on the fictive kin in Memphis who sustained her quest for autonomy or on her father's pride in a precocious daughter. Instead, she worked within the period's dominant social convention for women: marriage. In "Two Christmas Days" (1894), Wells's protagonist Emily Minton triply converts her suitor to temperance, the work of racial uplift, and wedded domesticity. At the story's end, the two go off equitably enough—arm in arm and married— into the sunset. Emily Minton knew what she would do about social conditions "if [she] were a man": leave the South. But as a woman, she focused on men's morals and steering them toward an obligation to the race consecrated through marriage.[107]

This short story and the joint novel-writing project with Morris suggest that Wells valued mutual respect and warmth between men and women in a partnership around work, particularly in service to racial progress.[108] When Louis Brown began seriously courting Wells in late 1886, she expressed the hope that if they married, they could "show the world what love in its purity can do."[109] This construction of their union muted the reproductive burden on wives in favor of "pure" transcendent or spiritual love and foregrounded shared service ("show the world") rather than the political and economic dependence that Victorian marriage entailed for women. Brown loved Wells, but she kept warning him off. Her diary suggests that though he was well positioned in his field, she did not completely respect his mind or enjoy his rather fussy personality; he was a too self-satisfied "blase man of the world."[110] In the 1880s, Wells looked for sturdy friends and reliable colleagues in men rather than a husband. Of her suitors Graham and

Brown she wrote: "I don't think I want either for a husband but I would miss them sadly as friends—and of course that would be an intermission of friendship if I said nay [to marriage]."[111]

Ideally, marriage protected women from bodily harm and financial hardship. Physical safety and economic security were important issues in cities like Memphis, where the safety of black women was a daily contest. Marriage also enmeshed women more firmly in social relations, making them accountable to community authorities, like clergy. Protection had its costs; it was men's and not women's words and gestures that ultimately confirmed or denied female respectability. Were this not the case, Wells would not have needed a public apology from the Vicksburg minister, since presumably her "friends" and "bodyguards" already knew he was a liar. Nor would her diary record the persistent use of rumor, innuendo, and sexual slander to extract female loyalty to particular men or their general deployment against unacceptable female behavior. I. J. Graham tried to get Wells to "submit to 'conditions'" in exchange for his exclusive friendship, perchance to lead to marriage.[112] When Wells refused such manipulation, Graham engaged in what she felt to be retaliatory moves, instigating rifts with her other friends and spreading rumors. Her boiling anger at such "deliberate insults" made Wells "burn . . . for revenge." These feelings she buried in her diary and lifted up as prayer to "My Father" both for Graham's soul and for strength for herself to "bear it meekly, patiently."[113] When Wells poorly handled a job offer in Kansas City in 1886 (she accepted a teaching position there and abruptly left it after one day of work), male teachers punished her. They cast suspicion on her morality by writing letters to Memphis school officials in a move that not only "angered" Wells but could have cost her job and livelihood.[114]

When Wells identified unfairness to women in her diary, she ascribed it mainly to the failings of "weak, deceitful" individual men who themselves were vulnerable to exploitation by racism. She was aware of the institutional workings of power, noting but not elaborating on a "painful fact": that "white men choose men of the race to accomplish the ruin of any young girl."[115] She regarded racism as a systematic evil and unfairness to women as a function and property of that system. That men within the African American community held significant advantages in the pulpit, politics, and press was neither particularly unjust on its face nor, for that matter, particularly fixed or exclusive. For example, under Wells's editorship, the *Free Speech* took a stand against a Memphis "preachers' alliance" which sought to shield the sexual indiscretions of a local minister by publishing the names of alliance members who were willing to "uphold immoral conduct."[116] Black women certainly had a hand in forging and sometimes enforcing community standards; individually, however, they had limited recourse in matters of personal reputation.

During the 1880s, Ida B. Wells negotiated, avoided, and sometimes flouted gender expectations according to her own evolving theology of self and service. This process led to a maturing sense of personal right and public justice, a process especially visible during her sojourn to the Far West in 1886. When Fannie Butler moved to Visalia, California, that year, she took her own children as well as Annie and Lily Wells with her. Ida sent money to help with the girls' support, but Butler pressured her to join them. Departing from a teachers' convention in Missouri in late summer, Wells went on a trip across country to at least visit Visalia. Butler convinced her to stay. "I know I owe her a debt of gratitude" for the care of her sisters, Wells admitted in her diary, but she quickly became miserable when faced with curfews and restrictions in Butler's household and with poor schools for black children in the neighborhood.[117] After considerable personal struggle—and a crucial loan of $150 for travel costs from Robert Church back in Memphis—she decided to leave in late September, taking Lily with her. "I know not if I will ever have another chance yet I try not to be rebellious but extract consolation out of the thought that My Heavenly Father will reward and bless me for doing what is right and just and if I did nothing, sacrificed nothing in return for all that has been done for me, I could not expect his blessing and sanction. Help me & bring success to my efforts I pray."[118] Her prayer casts the opportunity to leave California as a "chance," perhaps from her "Heavenly Father," to demonstrate a willingness to "sacrifice" home ties even as Wells confesses to inappropriate "rebellious" feelings against the family claim on her. To distinguish God's will from one's own willfulness demanded the intense personal reflection and self-criticism that prayer and diary keeping afforded. A sense of God at work in her life helped Wells act on her desire for autonomy, a desire stigmatized for women in her community. In such a context, work on behalf of others had more weight and legitimacy than efforts for self.

Gender and Journalism

Tensions around self-assertion and service characterized Wells's work in journalism in these same years. Newspaper work's informality, its ubiquity given the technologies of printing, paper making, and telegraphy, and the availability of part-time work at home with little apprenticing made the field inviting for women writers across the color line.[119]

Enterprising clergy like Rev. William J. Simmons of Louisville, eager to spread Baptist influence in the region, cultivated rather than put off female talent. He established the journal *Our Women and Children* in 1888, a publication later credited with having accomplished "more than all the Afro-American papers together in bringing to the front the latent talent of our lady writers."[120] He recruited Wells to edit the Home Department. Kentuckians Mary Virginia Cook and Lucy Wilmot Smith also wrote for Simmons and later became among the first female office holders in the National Baptist Convention.[121] According to Smith, women found that the "doors are opened before we knock" in journalism because "brother" reporters were familiar with having their "sisters" beside them in the fields during slavery.[122] "The men of the race, in most instances, have been generous," agreed Gertrude Mossell, "doing all in their power to allow the women of the race to rise with them."[123] *Washington Bee* editor Calvin Chase noted in 1887: "There is no question but intelligent colored women of our race should become adepts in journalism as much so as white women."[124]

In a refrain that echoed across the discourse on race uplift, Chase upheld the idea of equality between black and white women while bracketing equality of the sexes. "We do not mean to compare her with man," went a similar appeal from clergy, "but compare woman with woman."[125] Journalism, like teaching and social life, was marked by a gender divide, however shifting and uncertain. Many women, including Mossell herself, wrote in the "Woman's Corner" or "Hearthside" sections of newspapers. Wells attributed her own early success in the field in part to her "novelty" status as a woman who reported on party politics and elections, typically male preserves.[126] Mentoring from men like Simmons could legitimize such boundary crossing, but it also exacted a price. "Dr. S[immons] has placed me on the program of the Press Convention against my consent," complained Wells in her diary in 1887. "[O]f course [I] will have to prepare, and *preparation* takes money."[127] Despite these difficulties, Wells credited Rev. Simmons's "influence and encouragement" as essential to "whatever fame" she achieved as a "newspaper woman."[128]

Her evolving political interests and literary ambition took other editors aback. Calvin Chase was a difficult gatekeeper who publicly reproved Wells for sending out long articles and expecting to be paid for them. Razzing Wells as a vain and attention-seeking "star-eyed goddess" in 1886, Chase likened her to the pretentious "literary cranks and essay hawkers" whom he felt contributed little to the serious field of political journalism.[129] Keeping her own criticisms private in her diary, Wells bristled at his condescension, calling him "contemptible & juvenile in the extreme" and vowing to "write something someday that will make him wince." Yet this same entry recorded her shyness and inexperience in dealing with editors who were disposed to pay money for her writing. Wells found one request to "state my price" to be "an embarrassing thing to do." "I have no idea of [my work's] worth & shall tell [the editor] so when I answer."[130]

The mix of welcome and surprise, ambition and deference around women in journalism points to the fractured, transitional quality of gender expectations in Wells's world. For example, at a banquet of the prestigious all-male Live Oak Club in Memphis in 1889, toasts included a tribute to "Our Ladies" and another to "Our Men and Women of Letters," capturing both the traditional chivalry of gentlemen to ladies as well as more modern-sounding intellectual comradeship among women and men.[131] When in doubt, however, the body provided a quick way to sort out confusion. Commentators often tagged appraisals of beauty and marriageability on to evaluations of female intellectual worth. For example, when a columnist praised Wells and Fannie J. Thompson as the "most prominent" figures in Memphis's black literary circles, talk of courtship was not far behind. "These ladies," explained the writer, "though they have a host of loving admirers, keep so busy that they have no time to devote in emulation of those who woo and win." The men in the group were simply described as "champion debaters."[132]

Attention to the body encumbered women's participation in public life and raised the emotional stakes. During her first press convention at Louisville in 1887, Wells noted in her diary: "My picture (God save the mark) in yesterday's *Courier Journal* and I am still here."[133] When an unflattering etching of Wells appeared in a newspaper during the 1889 press convention, the *New York Age* jibed, "Iola will never get a husband so long as she lets these editors make her so hideous."[134] When Wells complained in print that more care should be taken with pictures of women in the papers, she only brought on more ridicule. "Iola makes the mistake of trying to be pretty as well as smart," quipped the *Indianapolis Freeman*. "Beauty and genius are not always companions."[135] Wells tested the Victorian convention that intellectual and sexual power could not properly exist in the same female. "She handles her subjects more as man than as a woman," later noted T. Thomas Fortune of the *Age*, lightly describing Wells as a kind of throwback to "the great women of the past who believed that they could still be womanly while being more than ciphers in 'the world's broad field of battle.'"[136]

At times, participation in the mostly male world of journalism required Wells to relinquish claims to male protection—precisely what

Anna Julia Cooper felt was in already short supply for the "colored girls of the South." A cartoon in the *Freeman* depicting Wells and Fortune as a pair of yapping dogs set off another round of debate about gender expectations in public life (see Figure 6). The *Freeman* concluded that "Iola" could not be "petted and spoiled" in newspaper work but "must sometimes take a man's fare."[137] For her part, Wells sometimes sought to maintain a gendered sensibility and endorsed the use of feminine nouns like "editress" and "journalistess" in reporting.[138] Many men also upheld a chivalric model of gender relations. "Miss Wells is a lady, the brightest and most energetic of the race ladies who have taken much interest in journalism," noted the *Cleveland Gazette*, adding that she "has as protectors every gentleman journalist of color in the country."[139] Aware as she was of the powerful negative presumptions about black womanhood lurking in the dominant culture, Wells took protection where she could find it.

Journalism neatly captured the new freedoms and constraints facing educated African American women in the 1880s. Men often set the tone, but the field also offered a climate in which it was possible to forget about sex or dispense with gender deference, at least for a moment.[140] When asked to speak spontaneously on the topic "Woman in Journalism" in 1887, uppermost in Wells's mind was the "favorable opportunity to urge the young women to study & think with a view to taking places in the world of thought & action."[141] In the coming years, she developed a less rather than more gendered model of intellectual and political life, stressing the shared responsibility of men and women to confront deteriorating social conditions in the South. A major address in 1892, "The Requirements of Southern Journalism," contained neither paeans to the special gifts or needs of woman—à la Mossell, Harper, or Crummell—nor any claims on the duty of fathers or chivalry of brothers, such as Cooper endorsed. Instead, Wells issued a call to educate and agitate through the press in the interest of ending racism. "A prosecution of this work requires men and women who are willing to sacrifice time, pleasure and property to a realization of it; who are above bribes and demagoguery; who seek not political preferment nor personal aggrandizement; whose moral courage is strong enough to tell the race plainly yet kindly of its failings and maintain a stand for truth, honor and virtue." She ended her talk with a flourish characteristic of her visionary pragmatism, an urgent question meant for answering: "Can you longer stand in comparative idleness [and] wrangling, when there is earnest, practical, united work to be done?"[142] By stressing race and community in her public writing, Wells muted the gender expectations that she personally found limiting and told to her diary. "A proper

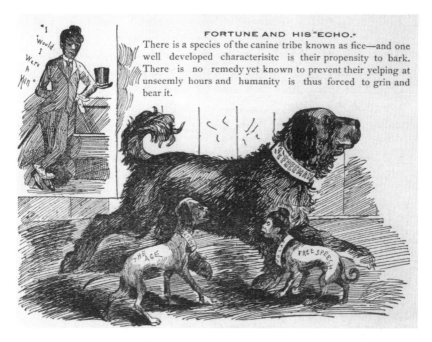

FIGURE 6. "Fortune and His Echo." *Indianapolis Freeman*, 19 April 1890

self-respect is as expected of races as of individuals," Wells explained in an article entitled "Race Pride." "We need more race love; the tie of racehood should bind us as the tie of brotherhood, beget a tenderness and helpfulness for the weaknesses and failings, and a more hearty appreciation of each other." "Backed by the support of each other," Wells proclaimed, "we can demand what we will."[143]

Church Life

Wells's appeal to race love touched back on her fundamentally religious understanding of self, community, and politics. Individuals' treatment of one another determined the quality of community life and, by extension, shaped political possibilities and general progress. In this framework, religious work was sometimes indistinguishable from education or even politics. At the same time, however, new patterns of social organization tended to push these spheres apart through increasingly specialized training, institutions, and official practice in ways that deeply implicated gender relations and sex roles. African Americans across the

South generally shared the cluster of hopes that Wells expressed as "race pride." They expressed that sentiment, however, through a growing array of forums, including electoral politics, the Knights of Labor, fraternal orders and female societies, the Colored Farmers Alliance, and churches, to name just a few. These groups shared the goal of mutual benefit and the spirit of racial uplift; as a result, they often competed for followers, resources, and status.[144] In this context of competition, the public scrutiny of ministers often marked the class and cultural aspirations of nascent secular elites in a bid for influence during a moment of rapid social development. African American women's comments on clergy underscored their commitment to insuring that the church remained central to the work of race uplift. The stakes were particularly high for black women, because church was often the major resource and training ground in their lives. At the same time, their abilities and needs sometimes exceeded the categories the church held out for them.

Through a series of articles on the clergy in 1888, Ida B. Wells staked out her own claim to authority in the areas of church life, education, religion, and race progress. In three articles for the *Christian Index*—newspaper of the elite Colored Methodist Episcopal (CME) church, published in Jackson, Tennessee—Wells made a critique of the ministry in 1888. Any "intellectually and—alas! too often morally—unfit" clergyman injured the interests of the "masses," the "cause of religion," and "the race" in general. A weak, uneducated, and undisciplined person lacked real respect for God, self, and community, and as such betrayed the principles of "truth, honesty, and virtue" that Wells endorsed in her article "Race Pride." She offered explicit criteria: a minister should be "cultivated in intellect, dignified and earnest in manner, noble of purpose and consecrated to his work." Because clergy had more access to the "rank and file" than either teachers or journalists, Wells insisted that they "can and must be, in and out of the pulpit, a teacher to the people in temporal and racial matters." Finally, she demanded community accountability, implying a strong role for women. "Our efforts toward a purer ministry must be more energetic, our refusals to support and uphold one who is not worthy must be more decisive," Wells argued, "if we would have the world believe in our efforts to build the race."[145] She took this role very seriously throughout her life.

Wells joined her peers Anna Cooper and Fannie Williams in making a critique of clergy in these years.[146] Williams called outright for a "new and better ministry." "With due regard to the highly capable colored ministers of the country," she explained, "I feel no hesitancy in saying that the advancement of our condition is more hindered by a large part of the ministry entrusted with leadership than by any other single cause."[147] Wells's *Christian Index* articles similarly advocated "much-needed reform in our manner of public worship," condemning any minister who would "enact . . . the monkey" in the pulpit or preach merely with a "view to raising a shout" or getting people " 'happy.' "[148] In the mid-1880s, Wells had kept such commentary to her diary, but by decade's end she actively sought out others with her criticisms, identifying herself as a like-minded colleague.[149]

In 1890, she wrote to Booker T. Washington at his recently opened school, Tuskegee Institute, in Alabama, praising his "manly criticism of our corrupt and ignorant ministry." This gendered bit of flattery was followed by a complement in one breath—"I know no one more fitted for the task than yourself"—and in the next, a demure reference to her own "numerous scribbling[s]" in which she "long ago took the same ground" on the ministry. In case he missed the *Christian Index*, she enclosed copies of her articles for good measure.[150] Wells did not, however, endorse the criticism of black clergy that Washington offered to whites while on a fundraising trip to Boston around this time, preferring that he "tell them about it at home rather than [to] our enemies abroad."[151] Differing only in tactics in 1890, Wells and Washington parted ways politically by 1900. Fannie Williams, however, embraced Washington's conservatism. As a result, Washington included Williams's writing on black women's clubs in his anthology *A New Negro for a New Century*. A major statement on black leadership, this volume devoted seven of its eighteen chapters to military history and the rest to achievements in business, politics, and education—with scarcely one word about the church.[152]

As the case of Tuskegee demonstrated, proliferating social institutions and the high premium on black women's community betterment work raised the stakes in church and denominational life in the late nineteenth century. Wells's choices suggest the ways in which some women leveraged more social space and authority for themselves than might ordinarily be allowed by church custom. For example, Wells engaged a range of connections in religious journalism, contributing to AME, AME Zion, CME, and Baptist publications.[153] As a congregant in Memphis, she and her friends regularly spent all day Sunday in church. "[W]ent to church 4 times yesterday," she noted in one diary entry; in another, "went to Cong[regational] S[unday] S[chool], to Countee's [Beale Street Baptist] church for morning service . . . and to Collins Chapel [CME] at night."[154] To raise interest in the Dramatic Club, she visited Congregational Tabernacle, Beale Street Baptist, Avery Chapel AME, and Immanuel Episcopal Church.[155] She distinguished all of these churches from "my own church" (which she never actually named in the diary) and taught Sunday school at Avery Chapel to a class of "young men or rather youths."[156] These linked religious associations allowed women to focus broadly on God's work in the community, region, and nation. Joining an influential extradenominational organization like the WCTU similarly provided a venue for African American women to pray and think grandly in a period that otherwise hemmed them in all around.[157] By voting with their feet in matters of church and organizational membership, black women exercised influence in spheres that limited if not denied them a voice or a vote.

Temperance reform offers a good index to this approach by black women as well as to the distinctiveness of Wells's evolving thought. An evangelical women's group, the WCTU outpaced any other female association in organizing across the color line. President Frances E. Willard's "Do Everything" policy and the WCTU's motto, "For God, Home, and Native Land," comported well with notions of race uplift among African American women. Frances E. W. Harper, who served as Superintendent for Colored Work in the WCTU in the 1890s, extolled temperance as "one of the grandest opportunities that God ever placed in the hands of the womanhood of any country." In a temperance symposium of women writers in the AME *Church Review*, she advised her readers to "Consecrate, educate, agitate, and legislate" around this issue. By contrast, Wells's contribution to this symposium relied on neither God nor abstract polarities of gender to make the case against alcohol use. Like her arguments for a less sex-typed journalism profession, she argued her temperance case "from a race and economic standpoint."[158] According to Wells, alcohol was linked to the oppression of southern African Americans in at least three ways. First, intoxication provided an excuse for law enforcement officials to arrest blacks and fill the jails with potential convict laborers. Second, for sharecroppers already "at dead level, without money," the expense of liquor only placed them further at the "mercy of landowners." Finally, the liquor trade preyed on peoples' weakness, tempting "our young men" to enter the "nefarious traffic" for profit. Intemperance, like racism, was "general and organized" and required the concerted efforts of church, press, and school to oppose it.[159] The contrast between Wells and Harper's arguments, in this instance, at least, was partly generational. Harper was born in 1825 and came of age during the evangelical fervor of the Second Great Awakening. Wells lived in a more secular, yet still religiously consecrated context.

The details of that religious context in Memphis remain obscure. Memphis historian David Tucker notes that shouting and ring dances took place at Avery Chapel in the 1870s and 1880s; Wells's writings on religion indicate her disapproval of such expressiveness.[160] "When his soul overflows with remembrance of the loving kindness of the Savior," she wrote in an essay critical of shouting in church, the believer "rejoices . . . as a leaf stirred by a summer breeze." Like many educated, freeborn African Americans who sought to break with so-called backward slave religion, Wells preferred restraint in worship, favoring practical "good works" over emotion.[161] This sensibility puts some distance between her religious experience and that of evangelicals Harper, Virginia Broughton, and Amanda Smith, these last two well-known for lively teaching, vigorous exhorting, and powerful singing.

A former slave from Maryland, Amanda Smith was enormously popular in the northeast's revival circuit in the 1870s. While Wells drafted her letters and essays in Memphis, Smith was off to England and India for more than a decade of highly acclaimed missionary and temperance work. By the late 1880s, "Sister Smith" was called famous in religious circles (if not by Frederick Douglass), and her life story circulated in tracts and pamphlets for missionary and church fund-raising purposes.[162] Smith's autobiography vividly details her preaching and singing in camp meetings, as well as her experience in prayer groups, describing, for example, how she, her daughter, and church sisters would fall asleep together on their knees in prayer after their long days spent as laundresses at the wash tub.[163] Wells's diary records curling up with a novel and sending out her washing whenever she could afford it.[164]

Smith and Wells would later become firm allies in social betterment work in Chicago, and, not so unlike Smith, Wells also made a personal commitment to spreading the gospel. Her lifelong devotion to Sunday school teaching began in Memphis out of a renewed commitment to God and Christian living in her New Year's resolution of 1887. As the anniversary of Lincoln's Emancipation Proclamation, New Year's Day had special import for former slaves and their children and was celebrated, usually in church, by African American communities well into the twentieth century. On this particular day, Wells confessed to her diary, "I am so overwhelmed with the little I have done for one who has done so much for me, & I resolved to . . . work for the master." "The bible & its truths are dealt with too flippantly to suit me," she concluded, determined to try her hand at religious teaching. "God help me to try," she prayed. "God help me to be a Christian!"[165] This commitment to Sunday school teaching functions as closely as anything in the written record to a religious conversion in Wells's life.

Ida B. Wells noted shedding tears at a college graduation ceremony but seems not to have written about the personal trials or joys of receiving salvation. Her conversion was perhaps so taken for granted that it needed no written commentary. In the spring of 1886, her diary notes in passing that a "Mrs. Ragland" had "professed religion."[166] A few months later, Wells "went to confirmation" one evening with her friends Mrs. Theresa Settle (a schoolteacher with whom she boarded briefly) and Mrs. Fannie Bradshaw (another schoolteacher). Perhaps this ceremony made them full members in good standing in their church. After this event, Wells noted in her diary, "Mrs. B. stayed all night and we had a long confab & came nearer being acquainted than ever before."[167] The spontaneity and intensity of this encounter perhaps hints at a new spiritual bond shared by the women. Even though she counted Theresa Settle a dear friend and to at least one other woman in town she felt "as near to as to a mother," Wells turned not to religious sisterhood or the consolation of church when she experienced "fits of loneliness." It was romance, the "temptation of a lover" that she found, in her words, "irresistible."[168]

Wells's fascination with and practical need for men touched her religious life. It was in Memphis that she "first heard of the AME Church and saw a Negro Bishop, Bishop Turner," who befriended her.[169] She was also drawn to the politics and ideals of local Baptist clergy. Wells's praise for Louisville's Baptists as "a bright example for other denominations as well as their own to follow" no doubt reflected Rev. Simmons's patronage.[170] It would have been difficult, however, not to be impressed with the success of the Baptists in the region. In Memphis by 1890, Baptists had three times the number of congregations as the AME (twelve as opposed to four) and more than twice the membership (4,200 compared to 1,500)—though they enjoyed only two-thirds of the AME's wealth.[171] In the 1870s, it was not unusual for Beale Street Baptist Church, Memphis's oldest black Baptist congregation, to attract 2,500 parishioners to Sunday services.[172] After Reconstruction—or rather, in order to survive it—African American churches in Memphis eschewed politics. Partisan matters went underground, into the lodges, fraternal orders, and secret societies. In the mid-1880s, however, a few young, educated Baptist ministers embraced a new politics and style. The Reverends R. N. Countee, W. A. Brinkley, and Taylor Nightingale appealed to black Memphians like Wells who were growing restless with the apolitical posture of the clergy.[173] Countee, Brinkley, and five other Baptist ministers sought political goals—for example, petitioning President Garfield on behalf of Robert R. Church for a patronage position in the post office—by identifying themselves "not as politicians but as leaders of our race."[174]

Like Rev. William Simmons, these younger, politically minded Baptist clergymen were drawn to Wells and she to them as each searched out their needs for social access, status, and credibility in Memphis. Rev. Countee's well-regarded *Living Way* newspaper first circulated the column "Iola's Letter" throughout Tennessee. His start-up religious school, the Baptist Bible and Normal Institute, founded in 1888, opened rather than locked its doors to Virginia Broughton, hiring her to organize women, fund-raise, and teach.[175] After a divisive and public church scandal involving Countee and the church's relationship to secret societies—for which the white press in Memphis ridiculed him— Rev. Taylor Nightingale took over at Beale Street around 1886.[176] To shore up new support and bind together his congregation, Nightingale extended the church's publishing work by giving a home to J. L. Fleming, a recently exiled newspaper editor from nearby Marion, Arkansas. Fleming had edited the *Free Speech and Headlight* in Marion until he was run out of state by a white mob in 1888. Nightingale's gesture of solidarity probably appealed to Wells's sense of "race pride," and having already proven herself in Baptist religious publications, she joined the *Free Speech* in June 1889.[177]

The hardening racial climate of the late 1880s created incentives for reconsecrated church work; for closing ranks amid generational, gender, and denominational divisions in the black community; and for healing what Wells called "our remaining peculiarity—the disunion that has characterized us from the beginning and is our bane to this day."[178] In 1887, the leadership of Memphis black churches and fraternal orders, usually in competition for members and dollars, came together in the Negro Mutual Protective Association. Wells called this group "the best thing out," noting with pride, "The Negro is beginning to think for himself and find out that strength for his people and consequently for him is to be found only in unity." She further explained that "the men of the race who do think are endeavoring to put their thoughts in action for those . . . who do not think."[179] Such dichotomous assumptions about the world were typical of the Victorian era and could be found elsewhere in the record of racial uplift, as in Fannie Barrier Williams's characterization of women's club work as efforts by the "few competent in behalf of the many incompetent."[180] The parallel belief in "race love," however, created imperatives for solidarity, not separation. Together, these ideas generated space for talented women to align themselves with the "thinking" male leadership in order to be heard. Strategic alliances with Baptist clergy in journalism provided precisely this opportunity for Ida B. Wells.

With Fleming and Wells on the staff of the *Free Speech*, the paper began criticizing creeping racism in Memphis, especially lynching and disfranchisement, and earned Rev. Nightingale a reputation as an "incendiary." In September 1891, Nightingale was convicted of assault and battery in criminal court through, one local historian argues, the manipulation of another church feud by city authorities.[181] To avoid his prison sentence, Nightingale fled Memphis for Oklahoma, leaving Fleming and Wells to carry on at the *Free Speech*. These two had their own growing objections to Nightingale's use of the paper as a sounding board. Wells's autobiography explained that when Nightingale "abus[ed] his enemies" in print, he alienated "our supporters," that is, the Beale Street congregants and others who bought the *Free Speech*. With Nightingale gone, Wells and Fleming seized the opportunity to grasp full control. They bought out Nightingale's interest in the paper and then "moved the office from church grounds," only half aware, perhaps, that they traveled out of church controversy and into more direct confrontation with the growing forces of white supremacy in Memphis.[182]

Newer South Memphis

Rebukes and intrigue against African American leaders in Memphis became an established pattern in the late 1880s. As the city became more sanitary and solvent, the coalition government under Pap Hadden unraveled. In 1886–87, conservative Democrats reversed their earlier, post–yellow fever position on city redevelopment and asserted themselves against taxes for public works. Businessmen now resented the exclusive power of the police and fire commissioners over city contracts and greedily eyed a new streetcar franchise. For their part, Ida B. Wells and her friends could financially afford the first-class coach and felt that as citizens they could "conquer" or sue for public access. Because market forces and existing laws no longer could maintain segregation in Tennessee, calls for an official "white man's government" were heard at the Democratic nominating convention. As historian Edward Ayers points out, a younger generation of southern whites was becoming frustrated with contending with blacks in politics and commerce and equally impatient with the paternalism of the "older men." According to one writer in the *Memphis Weekly Avalanche*: "The young men of today say, 'We are going to work this [racial situation] out, and do it right now,'" adding defiantly, "the North can do all the howling it wants to."[183] In 1888, Memphis Democrats styled themselves the party of Home Rule and ousted the hybrid carpetbagger Hadden and his People's Ticket with charges of corruption and black rule. The Democrats also won the governorship. Congressional consideration of the Lodge Federal Elections Bill in Washington prompted the Tennessee legislature to act. Voting restrictions quickly went into place, singling out Memphis and other cities with larger black populations for regulation.[184]

These changes made a strong impact on African Americans in Memphis. The black community lost its representative on the local school board in 1886, the last year until 1964 that an African American served in Memphis city government. Wells recorded her frustration over this loss in her diary, noting that of the two black candidates who lost the election, one was a "toady and could unknowingly be used by the white men."[185] At the same time, ridicule, harassment, and threats plagued independent leaders. Ministers like Countee and Nightingale were not spared; neither were politicians such as Edward Shaw. When Shaw's name was floated as a candidate for appointive federal office in 1885, racists libeled him extensively in the press as a "wholly dishonest, treacherous, thoroughly bad, morally rotten and corrupt" individual.[186] Though the black community rallied around Shaw in a mass meeting, their refutation of the libel and a positive character endorsement did little good. The white press shot back with another public smear campaign intended to kill his career. A teacher in the local "colored schools" named Mary Burton was married to a white man named George Battier. A troublemaker accused Mary of being "black" and brought a lawsuit under a local anti-miscegenation statute. The court found her "not guilty" (!), thus saving the marriage from invalidation. After this ruling, however, Shaw's testimony to the grand jury was manipulated into an indictment for perjury; apparently he had testified that Burton was "colored" (she was rumored to have some Mexican ancestry). Ida Wells likened Burton's treatment to that of the colored girl sent to the work house for defending herself, that is, as more evidence of institutional racism. She was furious that Memphis officials "tried to send them to the penitentiary for legally doing what had been illegally suffered and nothing said or done about it." Shaw was eventually exonerated but lost the appointment.[187]

The next year, 1887, the state supreme court overturned on appeal Wells's civil rights claims against the Memphis C & O Railroad. The judges ruled that compliance with the law was not at issue. Instead, they argued that Wells's claims were "not in good faith" and that she intended to unfairly "harass" the company; the previous rulings were reversed and the plaintiff found "in error."[188] "I feel so disappointed," Wells wrote in her diary, "because I had hoped such great things from my suit for my people generally. I have firmly believed all along that the law was on our side and would, when we appealed to it, give us justice. I feel shorn of that belief and utterly discouraged, and just now if it were possible I would gather my race in my arms and fly far away with them."

She prayed, "O God is there no redress, no peace, no justice in this land for us?"[189]

The decision against Wells crystallized important new political currents. First was growing sentiment among whites against black assertiveness. Second was the end of the paternalistic politics that had buffered African American initiative in the preceding decade. The arguments of Wells's white lawyer neatly summarized this shift. "Though we may share the prejudice of Southern *men* who were born slaveholders, never can we permit out sense of justice to so yield to our passion that . . . a court should judicially determine [that] a prejudice is a reasonable rule."[190] In this construction, real "Southern *men*" historically valued white supremacy but were still responsible to uphold duly constituted laws like the equal car statute. The judges' disingenuous attribution of bad faith to Wells allowed them, as "new men," to bracket the law requiring separate first-class cars for each "race" and to rule strictly on prejudice against Ida B. Wells. As more of these new men entered political life, they would assemble a Jim Crow regime of "racial" separation in law that would last the better part of a century.

The sharp turn against the rights of black citizens, especially of black women, came together powerfully for Wells over Memphis school conditions. In a *Free Speech* article she wrote in the summer of 1891, Wells targeted inadequate funding and facilities for black children and the poor quality of the teachers. Black schools received less funding than white schools, and some lacked basic equipment, including desks. Many black teachers were overworked. In the 1880s, 30 percent taught split-sessions, compared to only 5 percent of white teachers; Wells herself handled classes of seventy children. Poor building conditions endangered the safety of students and teachers. Faulty ventilation sparked a fire in the Seventh Street School, where only Julia Hooks's quick action prevented disaster.[191]

Wells also likely spoke out in frustration after the sensational suicide of a black woman schoolteacher in town. Miss Hattie Britton, aged twenty-three, lived with her sister Julia Hooks; her classroom abutted Wells's at the Clay Street School. In June, a brief squib in the black press tersely reported that Julia's husband Charles "accused [Hattie] of immorality" on her way to church one Sunday morning, at which point she turned around, went upstairs to her room, and, in Wells's words, "blew her brains out" with a pistol. While much more must have been operating in Britton's life to prompt this desperate act, it was known in the community that she had been involved with a white man, a lawyer for the Board of Education. Wells's *Free Speech* article discussed Britton's situation as an abusive pattern with damaging effect. The Memphis school board, now composed exclusively of white men, gave positions to black women in exchange for "illicit friendship," she argued. Wells wanted to expose such corruption because if wrongdoing was believed true of one teacher, it "put all forty of our public school teachers under suspicion."[192] Through the press, Wells tried to protect black women as well as expose the ill-gotten privilege of official Memphis. If the talented and capable Ida B. Wells still felt the need to ask Rev. Nightingale (before he left town) to "father"—that is, sign—that newspaper article, she still determined to "let it ride" after he refused to do so. "I thought it was right to strike a blow against a glaring evil," she later wrote in her autobiography, "and I did not regret it." She paid for her outspokenness with her job.[193]

Given the inclination of Memphis white leadership to discipline initiative from African Americans, Wells and Nightingale had to know that the article could backfire. She probably was prepared for the "sensation" that ensued; the word out in the African American press was that Wells already had plans to "resign" as a teacher that summer.[194] Success in journalism likely added sparks to the embers of frustration with teaching. Her autobiography noted the "confinement and monotony of primary work"; her diary, that the students could be "trying."[195] Moreover, Wells was spreading herself thin by teaching regular school and Sunday school, coediting the *Free Speech*, keeping up with correspondence and her studies, and taking care of her sister Lily. The press noted she was sick in the summer of 1890 "from an illness superinduced by overwork."[196]

By striking out at the Memphis Board of Education, Wells moved away from blaming individual male weakness to analyzing institutional dynamics that harmed black women. She also confronted the declining political power of African Americans in Memphis, testing the clergy's and her own authority along the way. After the school board declined her reappointment in 1891, Wells was further dismayed that her students' parents did not appreciate her efforts at school reform. "Up to that time I had felt that any fight made in the interest of the race would have its support," she explained in her autobiography. "I learned then that I could not count on that."[197] Nor, it seems, was she satisfied with established black leadership. Wells publicly took Mississippi politician Isaiah Montgomery to task for "acquiescing" to black disfranchisement in that state's new constitution of 1890. She also criticized Mississippi's ex-senator Blanche K. Bruce in the press, suggesting that neither the profits from his Delta plantation nor his lingering patronage power in the region were sufficiently serving the needs of African American citizens.[198]

These challenges to white racism and to local and regional black leadership took place in the context of rural discontent and in an increasingly polarized racial climate. In 1891–92, the cotton-growing Delta region boiled with populist and agrarian unrest. The Colored Farmer's Alliance announced a strike in September 1891, effective from Texas to North Carolina, unless demands for a pay raise were met. Conditions in the Memphis area pushed the farmers to the brink. Ambitious planters had been hustling into undeveloped lands around the city for years; in the competition for labor and profits they agreed among themselves to set wages, paying pickers not more than fifty cents per 100 pounds. As the restiveness of pickers and croppers grew, planter control was politically reinforced. Historian William Holmes notes that "planters even asked the Memphis police to drive all the 'idle and vagrant negroes' into the cotton fields and the police agreed to cooperate." The strike failed to materialize except in nearby Lee County, Arkansas. Another politicized black Memphian, thirty-year-old Ben Patterson, traveled west to organize pickers in Lee County and push for a strike. When conflict among the pickers and strikers broke out, a white posse formed to catch Patterson and end the initiative. Ten days of violent chase left at least twenty-seven African Americans dead and another half dozen in jail. Patterson was shot and killed near Marianna.[199]

For elites, the actions of such "sore-headed, skin-flint, communistic, third-party Alliance fellows" signaled long-feared rural organizing across the color line, slyly likened to alien political forms like the Paris commune. "This puts a very serious color on the connection between the white and black Alliances," warned the *Memphis Commercial*, "and makes it very evident that the settlement of the race question . . . is likely to be attained at the expense of the peace of the South and the safety and welfare of the white people."[200] This rhetoric was meant to scare whites into line, but as the Lee County murders and lynching statistics bear out, black people were in the gravest danger. In 1892, Tennessee ranked second in the nation's lynching statistics, with twenty-eight killings that year.[201]

As they warily eyed the agrarians, Memphis whites also anxiously witnessed expressions of African American pride, like celebrations of West Indian Emancipation Day during that same summer of 1891. These festivities included parades and armed displays by "colored military companies," including Memphis's own Tennessee Rifles.[202] In the context of countryside violence, whites feared retaliation by imagined "Black Caps" against the Klan-like terrorism of groups known as "White Caps."[203] As if to justify the crackdowns on African American protest and leadership, the white Memphis press began to chant about black criminality with headlines like "Bad Negro Robber," "He May Be Lynched," and now a new "Old, Old Story: A Brutal Negro, A White Lady, an Assault, and a Lynching."[204] Wells's angry sarcasm was piqued. "Unfortunately for the Negro he is imitating the white man too much with different results," she wrote in the press in November 1891. "If a white man steals he often times goes to the legislature, and the Negro goes to the jail or the penitentiary."[205]

Tensions continued to run high in Memphis in early 1892. Confronted with a spring drought and continued agrarian unrest, the city faced heavy inmigration from the countryside, and racial clashes intensified. On 6 March, a black man named John Mosby was shot in a scuffle at a white-owned store.[206] Whites like the store clerk who killed Mosby had been arming themselves in the wake of a so-called riot that occurred a few days earlier in a neighborhood at the edge of the city. In the course of five days, this "riot" culminated in a brutal triple lynching, which permanently changed the life of Ida B. Wells.

The Lynching at the Curve

It began with child's play. Some boys were shooting marbles in the street when a disagreement broke out. A black boy bested a white boy in the ensuing fight. The scrape brought out the white boy's father, a man named Hurst, who struck the black boy. Accounts conflict at this point, but some black men in the vicinity then gathered and either threatened violence in retaliation or, as Wells remembered it, actually beat up Hurst.[207] Next, a white man named Barett, the owner of a nearby grocery store, intervened, "rescued" Hurst, and then lodged a complaint against several of the black men, among whom were the three owners of another local business—Thomas Moss, Calvin McDowell, and Henry Stewart. Wells recalled that the dispute over the street fight was settled in court with nominal fines; however, local criminal court Judge Julius J. DuBose issued a warrant for Tom Moss's arrest for assault and battery.

Barett then escalated the situation by swearing revenge, threatening to "clean out the negro store."[208] McDowell and his associates consulted a lawyer about their rights to protect the store and prepared themselves for Barett's retaliation. When a half-dozen white, armed "deputy sheriffs" arrived at the grocery at 10 P.M. on Saturday, 5 March, supposedly to arrest Moss, those inside assumed that Barett's threatened attack had begun. They opened fire. Three whites and two blacks were wounded in the shootout. Official Memphis quickly dubbed the incident an "ambush" and a black conspiracy. A "veritable dragnet" followed, lasting over two days and resulting in the arrest of some thirty-six African Americans, including at least two women.[209]

Three years before, in early 1889, the opening of the People's Co-operative Grocery Store in the Memphis neighborhood known as the Curve (named for a bend in the streetcar line) had offered an economic challenge to local businessmen. The new, black-owned store competed directly for customers with Barett's grocery.[210] Moss, a letter carrier; McDowell, the full-time store manager; and Stewart, an expressman, were its part-owners.[211] Shaken no doubt by the bloody events in Lee County, McDowell and Moss's willingness to defend their store roused the ire of official Memphis. "They Bought Guns," announced headlines in the *Memphis Commercial* with newly characteristic overkill. "The Negroes Had Prepared for a Regular Race War."[212] McDowell, identified as the so-called conspiracy's "ringleader," reportedly "boast[ed]" that he did not fear the criminal court. Moss also was described as "boast[ing] on several occasions" that he was not afraid to stand up against a policeman because as a postal employee he was under the protection of the federal government, raising a red flag from Reconstruction. The press further alleged that in the initial confrontation with police at the Curve, Moss had wished out loud that all the white deputies had been killed in the shootout.[213] For those in Memphis bent on limiting African American political and economic power, the incident at the Curve allowed a venting of new and old fears in the interest of reestablishing racial hierarchy.

During the dragnet, local whites began a frenzy of gun buying; a mounted patrol of newly deputized "police" enforced a strict curfew on black Curve residents. On Monday and Tuesday, African Americans concentrated on protecting the prisoners in custody by stationing the Tennessee Rifles at the jail. Tensions mounted in the neighborhood of the Curve. Armed white mobs roamed the street, and violence nearly exploded on Tuesday. After it was announced that the white officers who had been injured at the grocery store shootout would live, some believed the situation would calm down. But that same day Judge Du-Bose fined and sent to the rock pile a local white gun merchant found "guilty" of selling firearms to blacks. He also ordered the Tennessee Rifles disarmed, ending their protection of the jail.[214] Whites believed the disarming and policing of Memphis's black population to be justified; the judge "intended to keep down the impending riot," concluded the self-serving *Memphis Commercial*.[215] The opposite proved true. That night, about a dozen white men, one with "his face blackened" and the others disguised with handkerchiefs, entered the jail. They removed

Moss, McDowell, and Stewart, drove them to an empty field about a mile away, and shot all three several times in the head and neck.

The triple lynching marked the climax but not the end of the crackdown on Memphis's black community, especially on its leadership. In March and April, Rev. Countee, who still published the *Living Way* at his new church in town, Tabernacle Baptist, was stoned and threatened with lynching by a mob.[216] In June, seven of the so-called black Curve "rioters" were tried for charges ranging from conspiracy to assault and attempted murder. Six were found guilty and sentenced.[217] Ida B. Wells was near the center of both the black community's response to the crackdown and the white violence itself. It was reported in the black press that Thomas Moss's dying words were "Turn our faces to the west."[218] From her editor's desk at the *Free Speech*, Wells encouraged the emigration of black Memphians to newly opened territory in Oklahoma. In April, she investigated conditions there and wrote reports to counteract negative accounts in the white press designed to discourage the exodus of black workers from the city. The Reverends Countee and Brinkley eventually led their entire congregations out of Memphis to the West.[219]

Wells also aided a boycott of the city streetcars, an effort organized to protest the triple lynching and to generate savings to fund the Oklahoma migration. Her articles praised local ministers who exhorted their church members to "keep off the cars," and she rebuffed the streetcar company representatives who appeared in her office to pressure her to lift the boycott.[220] Democratic business leaders who had linked the creation of a "white man's government" to personal profits from city service contracts must have been galled by this turn of events. The economic tensions behind the triple lynching lend credence to Wells's later claim that her support of black migration and the streetcar boycott made the *Free Speech* a target for violence. She bought a pistol out of fear of "cowardly retaliation from the lynchers."[221] In her "Southern Journalism" address in April, she stressed the *Free Speech*'s success in this effort. "Our paper showed the character of these men to be unblemished . . . and so in part has countered the libel on these foully murdered men."[222]

Several thousand people gathered for the funeral services for the lynched men at Avery Chapel, where Tom Moss had been a member. The street procession was a somber affair.[223] Sadness and defeat pervaded the community long after the victims were buried. "The lynching at Memphis has had a most disparaging effect upon the Afro-Americans of that city," reported the press in April. "Many are coming North as fast as they can pack up their belongings."[224] Over a period of months, an estimated 4,000 African Americans left Memphis. The remains of the People's Grocery was auctioned off by creditors. "The sad taking away of Calvin, Tom and Will has told dreadfully upon the quiet peaceful spirit of the once proud Southern Negro Mecca," remarked an observer in September.[225]

Wells, too, considered the idea of leaving and relocating the *Free Speech*.[226] She spent considerable time away from Memphis between March and May 1892, selling newspaper subscriptions in the Delta and reporting on the migrants' progress in Oklahoma. Perhaps the pioneering spirit of the migrants heightened her own restlessness and anger about conditions in Memphis. Her newspaper was doing well; she felt she had "found [her] vocation" and was earning nearly as much money as she had from teaching.[227] The lynching also touched Wells personally; she was godmother to Tom Moss's daughter. After a series of violent outbreaks in the area in May, Wells likely felt both frustrated and bold enough to write another "dynamitic" article about lynching. In the *Free Speech* of 21 May 1892, the following appeared: "Eight Negroes lynched since last issue of the *Free Speech*. Three were charged with killing white men and five with raping white women. Nobody in this section believes the old thread-bare lie that Negro men assault white women. If Southern white men are not careful they will over-reach themselves and a conclusion will be reached which will be very damaging to the moral reputations of their women."[228] Wells's anger at the mistreatment of Mary Burton, Julia Hooks, Hattie Britton, and the nameless other black women whose fates she agonized over in her diary likely seethed beneath the editorial's sarcastic identification of southern white women's "moral reputations" as problematic.

Dispensing with any byline and with the type set and gone to press, Wells left Memphis on a visit North, perhaps not so naïve as to the consequences of her words as she suggested in her autobiography's version of events. In *Crusade for Justice*, she recalled her fear of retaliation for "harping" on the lynching in the press yet claimed that "fate" decreed that punishment would happen when she was away.[229] Seasoned by her school board experience, it seems much more likely that Wells followed the example of newspaperman Jesse Chisolm Duke. After a mob chased him from Montgomery, Alabama, in 1888 for penning a very similar editorial about "white Juliets" and "colored Romeos" in his newspaper, the *Herald*, Duke ran to Memphis, where undoubtedly his story circulated among journalists.[230] Wells publicly acknowledged that an antiracist, pro–free speech editor "might have to be on the hop, skip and jump" in the South.[231] Angry and frustrated, confident and armed, Wells now ran to Philadelphia. Within one week, a white mob attacked the *Free Speech* office, and Wells's partner J. L. Fleming barely escaped with his life to Chicago.

From Memphis, Wells stopped to visit the AME Church's 1892 General Conference in session at Philadelphia and then made her way to New York City. There, T. Thomas Fortune met her at the train station and informed her of the attack on the *Free Speech*.[232] "Iola, the dauntless, has been warned not to come home for the present and she is now in the East," noted the press in mid-June.[233] Likely prepared for such an outcome, Wells now shrewdly latched on to the mobbing as a highly symbolic denouement to the racial crisis in Memphis and a neat précis of the southern political situation. As she had forecast in her address on "Southern Journalism," the mob literally and figuratively ended "free speech," creating a vivid parable of political and economic repression in the South. Joining the staff at Fortune's *New York Age*, Wells wrote her first version of events in Memphis under the byline "Exiled" on 25 June 1892. Some 10,000 copies were printed and distributed throughout the country.[234]

In becoming an outstanding "female thinker of the race," Ida B. Wells negotiated an increasingly hair-trigger political situation in New South Memphis, one that nearly cost her life. During the 1880s, she staked a claim to both autonomy and protection within the black community through a skillful blend of marriage resistance, the support of female friends and male fictive kin, and the practical patronage of clergy, notably Baptist churchmen. By dint of hard work, prayer, and the inspiration of black women activists in Memphis, Wells developed a distinctive voice that she put to the service of community building and advocacy as a teacher, writer, and speaker. Finally, through her faith in God, Wells caught a vision of social change and the courage to press for justice, acting on her belief that "backed by the support of each other," African Americans "can demand what we will." Her struggle to fulfill that vision in a campaign against lynching follows in the next two chapters.

CHAPTER THREE

The Body in Question

I n 1892, the year Ida B. Wells wrote her account of events in Memphis in the *New York Age*, lynching reached its all-time peak. Some 241 people, 66 percent of whom were African American, lost their lives to mobs. Pressure mounted on black leaders for solutions. In July, Frederick Douglass published an essay titled "Lynch Law in the South" in the prestigious, Boston-based *North American Review*.[1] Douglass was still the most prominent black leader in the country, yet earlier in the year a press survey on the proposition, "the old leaders of the race must go, because they do not lead," found African American opinion split. Some mocked "our leaders" for fattening on government jobs without demanding rights or protection for the masses.[2] With Douglass aging and conditions worsening, new voices demanded a hearing, prominent among them women and clergy. In addition to Wells, Cooper, and Harper, there was the indomitable Bishop Crummell as well as J. C. Price, president of Livingstone College in Salisbury, North Carolina, widely thought to be Douglass's heir apparent.[3] The secularism and reactionary politics of the turn of the century gave the advantage to Booker T. Washington, but the question of women's roles hardly dissolved in his wake. As Cooper phrased it, African American women were "confronted by a woman question and a race problem and [were] as yet an unknown or an unacknowledged factor in both."[4] Shedding her country girl's tag "Iola," Wells's new pen name, "Exiled," captured black women's sense of being doubly singled out yet invisible. Upon leaving the South, she played upon this dual identity to forge a movement against lynching.

The confrontation Ida B. Wells had in mind took shape in a period of intense social conflict in U.S. history. Wells personally experienced politics as a kind of exile, but in this larger sense she was not alone. Barely a month before the triple lynching in Memphis, Homère-Adolph Plessy sat in the "white" section of a Louisiana train to test the state's equal car law in what became a landmark case of the Supreme Court. Oppositional voices also could be heard in the Populist Party; in the "nationalist" clubs inspired by Edward Bellamy's futurist novel *Looking Backward: 2000–1887*; in the "decade of economic discussion" and socialist debate underway at Hull-House, a new social settlement in Chicago; and in the bitter labor strikes at Homestead and Pullman. The litany of social issues in the 1890s—the money question, the woman question, the "Negro Problem," the trust question, the tramp question, and the labor question—marked a crisis of national identity, values, and authenticity in the United States, creating what Hull-House founder Jane Addams called a "between-age mood" unique to the end of the century.[5] Labor strikes and civil rights contestation, the late Indian wars, and the newly consolidated woman suffrage movement also posed urgent questions as to what bodies—by sex, "race," nativity, or corporate status— were full social persons in U.S. society. Exactly what or who was a rights-bearing "body" entitled to full citizenship and the authority to make claims on the state?[6]

Wells understood the lynching of African Americans as an ugly instance of the struggles over social boundaries and bodies that were characteristic of her era. Optimists like Douglass hoped that "discriminations" based on "color and sex" were "passing away" in the interest of democratic progress in American life, but lynching in the South precisely highlighted matters of "color and sex."[7] Traveling rapidly through the Associated Press wire service, newspaper stories justified lynching as punishment for black men's sexual attacks on white women. Incantatory headlines like "More Rapes, More Lynchings" made this association a cultural reflex. Circulated in cheap postcards, doggerel verse, and other lynching "souvenirs" produced at public executions, the resulting "folk pornography of the South" was serious business (see Figure 7).[8] Not only were thousands of people killed by lynch mobs between 1880 and 1930, but lynching implicated the moral and legal

SCENE IN SABINE COUNTY, TEXAS, JUNE 15, 1908.

The Dogwood Tree.

This is only the branch of a Dogwood tree;
　　An emblem of WHITE SUPREMACY.
A lesson once taught in the Pioneer's school,
　　That this is a land of WHITE MAN'S RULE.
The Red Man once in an early day,
　　Was told by the White's, to mend his way.

The negro, now, by eternal grace,
　　Must learn to stay in the negro's place.
In the Sunny South, the Land of the Free,
　　Let the WHITE SUPREME forever be.
Let this a warning to all negroes be,
　　Or they'll suffer the fate of the DOGWOOD TREE.
　　　　　—*Pub. by Harkrider Drug Co., Center, Tex.*

FIGURE 7. "The Dogwood Tree," a lynching souvenir. From NAACP Papers, Library of Congress; copy courtesy of Library of Congress foundations of the nation at its deepest levels. In the 1890s, the black body became American culture's primary object of fears about social disruption and disintegration.[9]

Ida B. Wells thus undertook criticism of racism and lynching at a moment of intense anxiety about authentic personhood in general and about race, gender, and black bodies in particular. In order to launch resistance to lynching, Wells had to prove African Americans to be victims worthy of sympathy and citizens deserving of protection. At the same time, she needed to present herself—an educated, middle-class Southern woman of mixed racial ancestry—as a credible dispenser of truth, a "representative" public figure who was, as Cooper reminds us, still an unassimilated factor in American life. Wells's efforts against lynching shed light on the ways in which black bodies became the site of a shifting contest over civil rights and physical integrity, over human dignity and social power.[10] The body in question, whether that of the lynching victim or the African American woman critic, was impossible to represent as a state of biological fixity demanded by Americans to bring order to an uncertain world. And much more was at stake than symbolic integrity. Wells personally carried a gun and advised her readers that a "Winchester rifle should have a place of honor in every black home, and it should be used for that protection which the law refuses to give."[11]

Southern Horrors

In this context of danger and dislocation, Wells relied more than ever on her connections to African American women and the church to establish her bearings. In her visit to Philadelphia in May she mingled with "all the big guns of the African Methodist Episcopal church," like Bishops Payne and Turner. She was also the house guest of Frances Harper and "sat at the feet" of educator Fannie Jackson Coppin and her husband, Bishop Levi Coppin, adding their wisdom to the lessons taught to her by Memphis women.[12] It was among the African American women of the North rather than among clergy, the Populist Party, or Bellamy clubs, however, that Wells found a ready audience for her antilynching message and a receptive community for herself.

Consistent with her thinking about journalism, church life, and the prospects of "southern girls, born and bred" honed in Memphis, Wells located black women at the center of both her developing analysis of racial conflict and her strategies for social organizing.[13] The New York Age article written under the name "Exiled" eventually became the core of her pamphlet Southern Horrors and her basic antilynching address.

These treatments situated racial inequality in the context of sexual politics and terroristic harm to black peoples' bodies, male and female. By so framing the lynching issue, Wells extended the antislavery tradition of protest that placed the abuse of rights-bearing, ensouled bodies at its center. Like Sojourner Truth and Frances Harper before her, Wells did not parse out rights and responsibilities differently between men and women nor, of course, along the color line.[14] Instead, she made a broad appeal for united action, a sweeping claim to freedom and equality under the law for all citizens, and a call to armed resistance for self-protection by African Americans.

Though not recognized by scholars until recently, Wells's pamphlet, *Southern Horrors: Lynch Law in All Its Phases*, is a point of origin in American critical thought on lynching and racism.[15] The pamphlet's refutation of the idea that lynching punished rape—Wells's finding that less than 30 percent of all lynchings involved even the *charge* of rape—became the cornerstone of all subsequent arguments against mob rule well into the twentieth century. Her insight was quickly taken for granted by like-minded critics, and the point soon needed neither argumentation nor citation of its author.[16] Beyond statistics, *Southern Horrors* also offered a wide-ranging critique of southern society as a "white man's country" in which free speech and fair treatment were systematically denied to African Americans. Wells further debunked the rationalization of lynching as punishment for rape by documenting consensual and sometimes illicit sexual contacts between white women and black men as well as the role of white women in abetting mobs. Finally, she stressed that black women were the victims of sexual assault and lynching by white individuals and mobs.

A call to resistance that echoed the antebellum jeremiads of evangelist Maria Stewart and self-taught pamphleteer David Walker, *Southern Horrors* was a kindred statement of angst, an apocalyptic vision "that justice be done though the heavens fall."[17] The pamphlet was an incitement to action in the tradition of Stewart, Walker, and even Tom Paine. Like these agitators, Wells peppered her writing with wilting sarcasm and theatrical asides designed to provoke.[18] She questioned how America "legally (?) disfranchised the Afro-American" and whether black men "always (?) rape white women."[19] Instead of the neat closure of genteel fiction, *Southern Horrors* is full of questions and commands in a call-and-response-like dialogue with the reader.[20] The pamphlet instructed readers to "note the wording" of newspaper reports of lynchings and if the press was "singularly silent" on key issues, people were urged to demand answers. "Has it a motive?" Wells asked. "We owe it to ourselves to find out."[21] Rather than exhibiting ladylike tact, *Southern Horrors* has an unbounded quality, combining the features of a sociological study, exposé journalism, and sermonizing. In a key chapter entitled "The Black and White of It," Wells read newspaper reports of lynching with a critical eye, playing on the supposedly self-evident truth of newspaper texts and skin colors. Wells showed that the "facts," moral certainties, and even racial divides portrayed in the mainstream press were not at all what they seemed.

Wells insisted that the so-called black rapist was in reality the innocent victim of both the mob's blood lust and, highlighting a previously suppressed element in the lynching-for-rape scenario, white women's sexual lust.[22] *Southern Horrors* provided "a defense for the Afro-American Sampsons who suffer themselves to be betrayed by white Delilahs."[23] Through the acknowledgment—even tacit endorsement—of the activities of "white Juliets [and] colored Romeos," Wells countered white supremacists' dread of race mixing with a story of potential racial equality. Instead of marking the beginning of the end of Anglo-Saxon civilization, Wells read sex across the color line as evidence of shared culture and common humanity. At the "bottom of this [lynching] business," argued Wells in England, lies "the fact that coloured men, advancing as they are in intelligence and position, have become attractive to certain classes of white women."[24] *Southern Horrors* suggested that there were "many white women in the South who would marry colored men" if it were socially and legally permitted. Wells had "no disclaimer to enter" concerning "slandering Southern white women" on this point, for given her vindication of black men, "such need not be said."[25]

Wells understood lynching as terrorism against an entire social group as well as a particular assault on men and "manhood." A "race's manhood" evoked, on one level, an evolutionary understanding of the development of human "races" in which each passed from infancy/barbarism to manhood/civilization.[26] On another level, a "race's manhood" symbolized a "peoples' peoplehood," the full humanity and prestige of a group, usually measured by the ability to deliver an historically specific set of male social functions like political power, economic security, and protection of dependents.[27] As Wells saw it, the rape charge and lynching together were designed for the "subjugation of . . . the young manhood of the race" in both an individual and collective sense.[28] "This cry [of rape] has had its effect," noted Wells bitterly. "It has closed the heart, stifled the conscience, warped the judgement and hushed the voice of press and public on the subject of lynch law throughout this 'land of liberty.' "[29]

In addition to a vindication of black manhood, *Southern Horrors* made African American women visible in the dynamics of southern lynching and sexualized racism. Wells documented not sideline suffering but attacks—lynching and rape—on black women and girls. In so doing, Wells staked a claim of outraged womanhood for African American women, a claim first articulated by opponents of slavery but becoming unthinkable under white supremacist ideology at century's end. She stressed the general public's ignorance of black women's experiences of sexual attack and declared that even if the facts were known, "when the victim is a colored woman it is different."[30] Americans knew "nothing of assaults by white men on black women, for which nobody is lynched and no notice is taken." Wells identified the white South as a hypocritical "apologist for lynchers of the rapists of *white* women only."[31]

Southern Horrors refigured the links between private and public social facts and thereby created new space for its author's critical perspective on power relationships across the color line. To make plain to readers the racist underpinning of the lynching-for-rape myth, Wells described both the "private" crime of rape and the more "public" crime of lynching as systematic wrongs perpetrated by whites against blacks.[32] The press portrayed lynching as something men did to other men in public. It was publicized aggressively and its victims made into a spectacle. By contrast, rape was mundane, usually unnamed, and "private." It happened to women, often in domestic spaces, and was typically surrounded by silence rather than fanfare. Many of Wells's peers shared these general assumptions. In *A Voice from the South*, for example, Cooper discreetly identified the problem of sexual assault on black women as a force of nature, as action by "tempestuous elements" against "delicate plantlets," and kept its solution in the family with a plea for protection from fathers and brothers.[33] Frederick Douglass's essay "Lynch Law in the South" framed lynching in more masculine terms, as a matter of law and order and the breakdown of public authority. He thought that press and pulpit could "easily" effect popular sentiment to end the crime.[34]

By contrast, Wells described the "legal (?)" attacks on black women as neither fate nor nature but politics, of a piece with the assault on black men through lynching. And in documenting the sexual liaisons and personal betrayals that sometimes occurred between white women and black men and led to lynchings, Wells articulated the "private" origins of an issue that Douglass understood as a failure of public institutions. According to *Southern Horrors*, lynching and rape formed a web of racist sexual politics designed to subjugate all African Americans. By analyzing, not just decrying, the treatment of black women and girls, Wells broke down the distinction between public and private crimes against African Americans and in so doing moved beyond the gendered critiques of race and power produced by her peers Cooper and Douglass.

As in Wells's earlier arguments about journalism and temperance, *Southern Horrors* muted gender difference and privileged race in order to make the case for unequal power across the color line. Yet at moments she tweaked the concept of "race" itself, mocking the very notion of fixed racial boundaries and the supposed "black and white of it." She pointed to ongoing sexual contact across the color line, to the population of southerners of mixed racial ancestry, and to cases in which white men committed crimes with "their faces blackened" in a kind of perverse racial theater performed to thwart the law.[35] In other words, Ida B. Wells exposed how taken-for-granted concepts like "race" and "rape" were socially constructed and politically deployed. In so doing, she challenged readers to examine the assumptions that held their personal identities and sense of the social order together. It was a challenge few joined and many resisted, even to the point of violence. The *Memphis Commercial* later regretted "not having lynched the saffron-colored speakeress" before she left town with her facts on lynching.[36] The New South that produced but could not contain Ida B. Wells sought to destroy her. *Southern Horrors* was a powerful text, but assuming and maintaining the power to name proved much more difficult than the literary persona and political condition of "Exile" could sustain.

In the Balance

The antilynching cause was off to a violent and uncertain start. In the summer of 1892, negative reaction set in back in Memphis. Clergy and teachers, among them B. K. Sampson, wrote conciliatory letters to the white press distancing themselves from Wells's antilynching editorial and going on record against black migration out of town. When Wells in turn criticized her former colleagues, she came under fire for unfairness and even for a feminine "love of notoriety" in what was becoming a national debate over southern conditions.[37] Under the sponsorship of T. Thomas Fortune and the *Age*, Wells's antilynching lectures met with better, if still mixed, reactions in the North during the summer and fall of 1892. In late October, a meeting at the Metropolitan African Methodist Episcopal (AME) Church in Washington, D.C., one of the city's most prominent and prosperous congregations, was an unexpected failure. Despite substantial publicity in the *Bee* (see Figure 8) and editor Calvin Chase's challenge to outdo "the ladies of Brooklyn," the meeting

"RIGHTEOUSNESS EXALTETH A NATION; BUT SIN IS A REPROACH TO ANY PEOPLE."

ALL EYES WERE TURNED ON IDA B. WELLS, FOR IT WAS SHE, HERSELF A VICTIM OF THE PORTRAYED OUTRAGES AND SHE WAS MOVED TO GRIEF. MISS WELLS WAS THE STAR OF THE CONVENTION; THOUGH MODEST IN APPEARANCE SHE SHONE WITH INTELLECTUAL BRILLIANCY.—PROVIDENCE(R. I.) TORCHLIGHT, OCT. 8, 1892.

The way to Right Wrongs is to turn the Light of Truth upon Them.

Yours for Justice,
IDA B. WELLS.

"SOUTHERN MOB RULE;" The Simple Story of an Eloquent Woman.

Miss Ida B. Wells

(of the Editorial Staff of THE NEW YORK AGE)

WILL DELIVER

A LECTURE

AT

Metropolitan A. M. E. Church

M Street betwen 15th and 16th Streets.

MONDAY EVENING OCT. 31st, 1892.

Mrs. Robert H. Terrell will preside.

Admission   **25cents**

DOORS open at 7 o'clock   Exercises will begin at 8 o'clock.

Subject:—"SOUTHERN MOB RULE."

T. THOMAS FORTUNE

Will introduce the Lecturer.

Miss Wells made a National Reputation as Editor of the Memphis Free Speech, the publication of which she was compelled to suspend because of her Bold, Fearless and Intelligent Denunciation of Mob Violence and the enactment and enforcement of malicious and degrading class laws.

As a platform orator Miss Wells takes high and commanding rank as an earnest and eloquent speaker. No woman of the Race has greater power than she possesses to hold the attention of an audience. In a public address before the Afro-American League at Knoxville, in July, 1891, she astonished her hearers by her impassioned denunciation of the Separate Car Law and Mob Rule. In her lecture on "The Afro-American in Literature," delivered before the Concord Literary Circle of Brooklyn, New York September 15, 1892, she completely captivated the large and cultivated audience; and at the Testimonial tendered her by the women of New York City and Brooklyn, at Lyric Hall, New York, October 5, 1892, she moved the vast assemblage to tears by the pathetic recital of the terrible lynching of three of her friends at Memphis, in March, 1892, and the forced suspension of her newspaper.

(Fortune and Peterson, Managers.)
Col. Geo. M. Arnold, Manager of the Washington Engagement.

FIGURE 8. "A Lecture," an advertisement for one of Wells's public speeches. *Washington Bee*, 22 October 1892 was poorly attended.[38] Frederick Douglass, who recently had become familiar with Wells's work, apologized for the poor showing. He personally guaranteed a more successful return visit for her. Douglass kept his word, encouraged, perhaps, by Wells's subsequent success in Boston—a success she made sure he knew about by sending him a note and a favorable press clipping.[39]

In the years preceding the federation of black women's club and reform networks, the influence of men like Douglass and Fortune was critical for Wells's access to audiences and publication in the North. It was Fortune's press at the *Age* that published *Southern Horrors* in October 1892. In January 1893, Douglass himself invited the "leading women" of Washington—including Anna Cooper and Lucy Moten, head of the nearby Miner Normal School—to assemble again at the Metropolitan Church.[40] Wells remembered this audience as her biggest up to that point. Mary Church Terrell, formerly of Memphis but now married to lawyer Robert H. Terrell and living in Washington, introduced Wells. Terrell praised Wells, the "exile," for her "undaunted courage" and "zeal" and cited not the support of the ladies from Brooklyn but that of T. Thomas Fortune, who "espoused her cause and made it possible for her to continue the work so nobly begun."[41] "The meeting ended in a blaze of glory," recalled Wells, with "a donation of nearly $200 to aid the cause."[42]

Wells learned the next day that during her lecture a brutal lynching had taken place in Paris, Texas. A black man charged with the rape and murder of a five-year-old white girl had been burned alive before an audience of thousands. Newspapers advertised the event and school children were released from school as if on holiday. Special trains carried people to the scene of the spectacle. Sickened by news of the atrocity, Wells took the money she collected the night before and hired a Pinkerton detective to conduct an investigation, hoping to assemble a legal case against the Texas authorities. Believing that a northerner might be more objective or sympathetic, Wells requested a Chicago agent, but the company dispatched a man from St. Louis. In the end, the investigation produced only news clippings about the incident from white papers in Texas. The agency failed to take the situation seriously and Wells learned a lesson in northern indifference to lynching.[43]

Within a year of leaving Memphis, then, the main barriers to an antilynching movement were evident to Ida B. Wells. There was little hope of freedom of speech in the South, and she likened northern opinion to a "stone wall."[44] Regional, gender, and generational considerations over leadership simmered just below the consensus in black communities that something had to be done about lynching. Also of pressing concern was the physical and social insecurity Wells faced in this new public venture. The *Memphis Commercial* still goaded her. Upon discovering Wells's female identity at the end of 1892, the *Commercial* proceeded with libel to discredit her. The paper denounced Wells by raising the specter of miscegenation and charging her with immorality: only the "effete civilization" of Boston made up of "thin-legged scholars" and "glass-eyed females" could have so mistakenly elevated "this Wells wench" to "martyr" status. The *Commercial* disputed that Wells even wrote the offending *Free Speech* editorial about southern white women, asserting instead that "she was the mistress of the scoundrel" who did. The paper impugned her motives for raising money from the lynching in Memphis by claiming she was really a "black harlot" in search of a "white husband."[45]

Wells decided to file a libel suit. Not only was her fragile public reputation at stake, but, as she argued in *Southern Horrors*, including black women under a single standard of legal protection went hand-in-hand with ending the lynching of black men. Wells recognized both the substantive and the symbolic importance to her movement should a court rule that she, a black woman, had been defamed.[46] She contacted two powerful men for help, Frederick Douglass and Albion Tourgée. It was probably Douglass who suggested Tourgée, a well-known writer and lawyer who was defending Homère Plessy. Wells wrote to Tourgée hoping that he would either represent her in court or pen a "vindication" of her character in his "Bystander" column in the *Inter-Ocean*, the widely read Chicago newspaper.[47] Pleading financial constraints, Tourgée declined the case but suggested that she would have a better chance of a fair trial in Chicago. Reflecting the heavy burden of proof on women in such cases, he counseled Wells that she needed to "deny and sustain a denial of impropriety *with any man*" in addition to disproving the specific charge of being Taylor Nightingale's mistress. He thought she could obtain a *"very large verdict"* if she assembled the requisite proof.[48] Tourgée recommended African American lawyer and newspaper editor Ferdinand L. Barnett of Chicago to assist her, but Wells abandoned her claim. A win was far too unlikely and a loss far too devastating for her cause and reputation to sustain at this moment.[49]

The combination of support without real momentum among African American audiences, the frustration of the *Commercial*'s libel, and the new friendship and sympathy of Frederick Douglass created incentives for Wells to embark on a trip to Great Britain in early 1893. The decisive factor was Wells's introduction to Catherine Impey, a well-off Quaker reformer from Street, England. Impey published a small journal called *Anti-Caste* which she "devoted to the interests of coloured races" and to cultivating anti-imperialist sentiment.[50] On a visit to the United States around 1890, Impey attended an Afro-American Press convention, where she pledged to publicize the evils of lynching in her journal to inspire sentiment *"against Caste."*[51] This work and her friendship with Frederick Douglass gave Impey a reputation among African Americans as "one of the best and most tireless friends of the dark races in the world."[52]

On another visit to the United States in 1892, Impey heard a lecture by Wells in Philadelphia, and the two women were introduced at the home of William Still, well-known former "conductor" on the abolitionist Underground Railroad.[53] Impey found publicity of American racism to be useful for launching criticism about British foreign exploits, and she filled her journal with sensational, eye-grabbing copy. "Our English press has been getting hold of some of those Texas lynchings," Impey wrote to Wells in mid-March 1893, "and our people are beginning to feel that there is something very wrong somewhere. . . . Can you come soon? Almost at once?"[54] *Anti-Caste* had caught the attention of Isabelle Fyvie Mayo, a Scottish reformer. Mayo contacted Impey about the reports on lynching in the United States and expressed interest in "arousing public sentiment" on the issue. Impey suggested Wells as a speaker and Mayo agreed to finance a trip.[55] Less than three weeks later, Wells sailed for Liverpool on a ship named, with splendid irony, the *Teutonic*.[56]

Wells's lecture tour inaugurated a new organization formed by Mayo and Impey called the Society for the Recognition of the Brotherhood of Man (SRBM). Impey and Wells were both looking to jumpstart a movement and found in each other lively sparks. Impey had been casting about for ideas and personalities for years in correspondence with Douglass, having invited educators Fannie Jackson Coppin and Hallie Quinn Brown to England back in 1889. "In fact Mrs. Coppin's meetings & possibly 'Anti-Caste' & other things combined serve already to have made an opening and I should like to see it well followed up," Impey explained to Douglass.[57] Wells was perhaps a more desirable candidate for Impey's purposes, entirely lacking as she was in institutional ties. Coppin and Brown were affiliated with black schools—the Institute for Colored Youth and Wilberforce University, respectively—which were always in need of funds and support. Impey had confided to Douglass about her "fear" that "coloured men and women" were "tainted" by an "American tendency" to "serve [their] pocket" rather than practice Christian "self forgetfulness" in agitation.[58] By dismissing the social and financial context of black activists' work, Impey here took a dubious moral high ground underwritten by her wealth, political insularity, and self-absorption, a position repeatedly assumed by white women and one that undercut Wells's antilynching and reform efforts.

As an "exile," Wells could make few major demands on her British hosts; she went abroad with assurances only of meeting her expenses, and she received no payment for her services.[59] Boding further ill was the bugbear issue of sexual relations across the color line that cropped up during her trip. A few weeks into the work, Impey disclosed her affections for a houseguest of Mayo's, a dentist named George Ferdinands from Ceylon, who was affiliated with the Society.[60] She was shunned by Mayo for this action and, threatened with public exposure in the press, eventually resigned from the SRBM. The potential scandal—notorious as much for the female initiative it showcased as for its "interracial" quality—could, ironically enough, discredit the nascent movement "against caste."[61] Impey once blithely described herself to Frederick Douglass as a person with a "somewhat erratic personality"; now her behavior caused people like Mrs. Mayo to deem her to be "failing mentally" or, as Wells remembered it, to dub her a "nymphomaniac."[62] Like the charges of free love and sexual decadence used to discredit earlier advocates of abolition and woman's rights, the taint of immorality could jeopardize this new cohort of women activists because a female's social authority was only as secure as her reputation for chastity.[63] Wells found herself caught in a drama scripted to play into the hands of white supremacists, and she aborted her trip.

It had still been a success. Wells gained valuable experience in front of British audiences, including the Young Men's Christian Association (YMCA) and the Society of Friends, and tasted a relatively liberal racial environment. She recalled that the "most enjoyable feature" of her association with British reformers was the "absolute courtesy" with which she was treated as their guest.[64] Wells's sojourn abroad also lifted her status and credibility in the eyes of American audiences, as had similar trips for the Fisk Jubilee Singers in the 1870s and Amanda Smith in the 1880s.[65] Smith returned to the United States just as Wells left, bringing home $10,000 in savings after a decade of missionary work abroad. Wells returned from England no richer financially, but the sheaf of positive press clips she carried became another kind of currency for her antilynching crusade.

The Impey scandal, however, threatened to overshadow her newspaper notices, and it irritated her patrons Fortune, Douglass, and Tourgée. Wells told them the "unvarnished truth" about Impey and Ferdinands, and the men agreed to say no more about the matter; offering explanations would be a bad thing for both the antilynching cause and Wells's fragile reputation. Later, in her autobiography, Wells defended

Impey. She had hardly "committed a crime by falling in love and confessing it," and Impey genuinely wanted to marry Dr. Ferdinands. This position is consistent with arguments Wells made in Memphis and in *Southern Horrors* for destigmatizing legitimate sexuality across the color line. For good measure, Wells's autobiography also defended Douglass's own 1884 marriage to a white woman, Helen Pitts.[66] Such views were very advanced for the 1890s. African American leaders consistently opposed state level "anti-miscegenation" laws, but few publicly condoned sexual contact of any sort across the color line. Much more common was opposition to "racial" restrictions on legal marriage coupled with strict policing of the color line by African American communities. As the Ladies Home Circle of St. Paul's AME Church put it in their endorsement of Wells's antilynching message in 1895: "Be that as it may [concerning revelations about consensual sex across the color line]: *The Afro-American shall be taught, that whatever folly a white woman may commit the suspicion of participation in that folly means torture and death for him.*"[67]

The Fair and Fallout

Upon returning to the United States in May 1893, Wells walked into another nationwide controversy over race and racism: the exclusion of African Americans from the World's Columbian Exposition in Chicago.[68] In a sharp break with American expositions of the preceding decades, the event contained no spaces for black exhibitors, employees, or managers, making the Fair, in Ferdinand Barnett's words, "literally and figuratively a White City." Across the country, Barnett noted, there was an "honest difference of opinion" among African Americans about how to remedy exclusion.[69] Those differences turned on the same issues that Wells faced in speaking out against lynching, especially regional and generational tensions over leadership as well as ambivalence over female initiative in reform. Options included a request for separate exhibits, attacking employment discrimination, and the appointment of "colored" commissioners to the Fair's governing board.[70] Around the time that Wells left for Scotland, Frederick Douglass proposed writing and distributing a pamphlet at the Fair to publicize the achievements of African Americans since emancipation.[71] Black women mobilized some of the most effective protests, notably for inclusion in the Woman's Building, which was under the governance of the Fair's Board of Lady Managers.[72] Fair organizers in Washington, D.C., and in the Chicago-based Lady Managers used the diversity of proposed solutions as an excuse to throw up their hands and ignore all requests.[73]

Wells, energized by her trip abroad and inspired by the efforts of

Chicagoans like Ferdinand Barnett, threw her energy into the pamphlet project. Capitalizing on frustration in the community as well as anger at another horrific lynching of a black man at Bardwell, Kentucky, on 7 July, Wells began a series of meetings in Chicago's black churches.[74] She joined Douglass on a platform addressing a Colored Peoples' Protective Association to develop strategies for protest and endorsed the pamphlet idea. Here again black women—Wells, Lucy Thurman, Frances Harper, Fannie Jackson Coppin, and Sarah Earley—figured prominently as speakers and supporters.[75] Across the country, however, there was concern that a pamphlet would highlight rather than remedy black exclusion and thereby waste time, energy, and hard-earned dollars.[76]

In addition, gender politics in protest remained unresolved. Harper, Coppin, and Earley broke the color line at the Fair by addressing a meeting of the World's Congress of Representative Women. Wells took a different tack, supporting the pamphlet idea as well as a boycott of the Fair Commission's late concession to black protest, a "Colored People's Day" slated for 25 August and featuring special train excursions and a watermelon sale for the occasion.[77] In the process, however, she stirred the gender pot. A black sharecropper in Bolivar County, Mississippi, sent Wells one dollar for the pamphlet fund. The man's letter conveyed the appreciation of southerners—"the words 'God bless her' is written here on every acre of ground"—and hinted at the gender and generational strains over leadership. He wrote: "To note that you are a woman (I might say a girl) and I a great big man and you are doing what I ought to do and have not the courage to do it, I think sometimes it's a pity that I am in existence."[78] Those expecting only "womanly influence" instead of aggressive organizing from females censured her. One editor complained that Wells's tactics brought "a matter of high race importance down to the level of a washer-woman's collection."[79] A Kansas City critic insisted that the pamphlet should address issues within the black community, especially women's primary duty as mothers; rather than stir up controversy, "single women [ought] to get husbands and give birth to male children."[80] According to this writer, women had no place in the world of politics and official leadership. Their proper role was supporting, not leading, in matters of "high race importance," not forging political equality with whites, but rearing boys.[81]

Wells's initiative even strained her relationship with some organized black women, whom she counted as her earliest and most devoted supporters in the North. A Boston group felt that Wells's opposition to Colored People's Day—she had refused their request to put her name on their circular in support of the idea—betrayed their personal loyalty to her over the preceding year.[82] In Chicago, however, a network of black women rallied around Wells in the churches and in "ladies' day" programs she initiated at the all-male Tourgée Club (the club was founded as a social meeting place for black dignitaries and visitors to the Fair). By the Fair's end, black women incorporated the "Ida B. Wells Woman's Club of Chicago," a club known as the first such organization in the city.[83]

During the World's Columbian Exposition, Ida B. Wells moved at the center of generational, regional, and gender tensions in the work of confronting Jim Crow. When a group of African Americans was refused service at the Fair's Kentucky Building, Wells "rejoice[d] with all my soul" that one of the young men in the group "resented the manager's insulting refusal by breaking his nose and otherwise battering up his face."[84] Anna Cooper also might have cheered such gallantry but she was less comfortable herself with confronting personal insult. Cooper poignantly described the "feeling of slighted womanhood" in such cases: "Its first impulse of wrathful protest and proud self-vindication is checked and shamed by the consciousness that self assertion would outrage still further that same delicate instinct."[85] By contrast, Wells had a history of physically striking out when attacked, and she turned her fearlessness into energy for the cause. Her autobiography describes how she and Douglass managed to be served lunch at the Boston Oyster House restaurant during the Fair. Wells appreciated Douglass's "vigorous way" and she described how the two "sauntered" into the restaurant "as if it were an everyday occurrence, cocked and primed for a fight if necessary."[86] Certainly having Douglass at her side bolstered Wells's courage. About the question of confronting racism at the Fair—as in Wells's own tussle with the Memphis trainman back in 1883—there was little consensus.

To the end, Wells viewed Colored People's Day as a cynical attempt to add black dollars to the till, and she boycotted the event. "The self-respect of the race is sold for a mess of pottage," she insisted, "and the spectacle of the class of our people which will come on that excursion roaming around the grounds munching watermelons will do more to lower the race in the estimation of the world than anything else."[87] With essays written by Douglass, Barnett, publicist I. Garland Penn, and herself, Wells published *The Reason Why the Colored American Is Not in the Columbian Exposition: The Afro-American's Contribution to Columbian Literature* and distributed thousands of copies gratis by hand with Douglass during the summer. As feared, however, Colored People's Day was mocked by media cartoonists, replete with watermelon jokes. Douglass keynoted a small, formal program at the Haitian Pavilion, his official post at the Fair as former U.S. minister to that country.[88] Wells and a few unnamed "hotheads" (her word) stayed away in protest. But there was some positive newspaper coverage of Douglass's speech the next day and after reading it, Wells went to the Pavilion and "begged his pardon for presuming in my youth and inexperience to criticize him."[89]

Wells could hardly do without Douglass. To be sure, she created important new ties of support and friendship in Chicago, especially with Ferdinand Barnett and her new associates at the Ida B. Wells Woman's Club. These ties would last a lifetime. But launching a national protest against either segregation or lynching required the imprimatur of the nation's single most influential and recognized African American leader, aging though Frederick Douglass was. In the months after the Fair, Wells relied upon Douglass to mediate and legitimate her role, especially as her growing reputation in the North brought out tensions among those competing for place and attention. Striking where she was most vulnerable, some joined in the attack of her character, the surest way to silence and discredit a female, especially an unmarried black woman.

In December 1893, C. H. J. Taylor of Kansas City declared that some-one should "put a muzzle on that animal from Memphis," because Wells's writing "ruined" any "clean paper worthy of entering any home."[90] A libel suit against a black man only would have trivialized her cause in the eyes of whites; she therefore appealed to gender protection and turned to Douglass. "I submit to you if this is not too much to bear," she wrote. "It is very hard to have to stand such insult from white and black men too." Though well established among African American journalists, Wells felt, in her words, "utterly unable" to defend herself when her personal reputation was at stake. "Can you not do something to aid & defend me?" she implored. As life in Memphis had taught, Wells's claim to worthy womanhood was only as secure as the word of the nearest authoritative male. Wells asked Douglass to punish Tay-lor, specifically to block his aspirations for a political appointment in Washington. Douglass did not.[91] Instead, newspapermen spoke up and shifted the blame away from the Kansas City editor to an office boy, whose "splutterings," Wells's chivalric defenders noted, deserved only "the contempt of every man who has a spark of honor or manhood in him."[92]

Perhaps feeling spent by the World's Fair wrangling and dismayed by this new libel in early 1894, Wells leaped at the chance to go back to England in March. Though the Society for the Recognition of the Brotherhood of Man was weak financially and its leadership still reeled under the fallout of the Impey scandal, Wells was determined to make a go of it. She was encouraged by the prospect of contributing letters from her trip to the *Inter-Ocean*, one of the few mainstream newspapers that denounced lynching in this period.[93] From Liverpool, she tersely announced her situation to Douglass: "I have come abroad to give 3 months of my time to the work and I'm going to do it."[94] It was a matter of public record that Wells would not be welcome in the SRBM's Scottish outposts, in accordance with the wishes of Isabelle Mayo, but the invitation came from Catherine Impey and Charles F. Aked, a white Liverpool Baptist minister. [95] Wells was again "compelled to depend on myself somewhat" financially on this visit, having agreed to travel for expense money only.[96] Eventually, she secured a loan from Douglass and a crucial letter of support for this trip. By its end, however, Wells felt that she owed Rev. Aked "a debt of the strongest gratitude, a debt which can never be paid."[97] Aked took Wells into his home and his church when Impey's connections with the SRBM began to crumble soon after her arrival. Wells named her firstborn son for him.

England, Again

The quality of Ida Wells and Charles Aked's relationship remains difficult to assess. In 1894, Aked was the ambitious thirty-year-old minister of Pembroke Baptist Chapel, credited with saving a dying congregation. Aked grew the church with preaching in the "style of a 'barn-stormer,' or 'barn-door actor'" and by taking "any cause célèbre which had caught the public mind and [making] that his gospel of the day." Pious Liverpool sniffed at building renovations at Pembroke—new doors, expanded seating, and a platform—which turned the church rather more into a theater than a chapel. But Aked's Social Gospel—comprising antimonopolist, anti-imperialist, and pro-temperance views—found an eager audience among reform-minded, dissenting Christians.[98] Already on his way to influence as a critic of the city's Tory establishment, Aked had a place ready for Ida B. Wells. Her this-world religiosity and her stage presence fit right in with the new Pembroke style. Her stories of politically and economically driven violence against African Americans likely resonated in Liverpool where striking laborers and Irish nationalists were regularly suppressed, jailed, and even bloodied in the streets by authorities in those years.[99]

Like most political alliances, Wells and Aked's relationship was probably both genuine and instrumental. Aked made good use of Wells's presence, featuring her work serially in his house organ, *The Liverpool Pulpit*. Drawing freely on her work, Aked also penned his own articles on lynching and U.S. race relations, publishing them in prominent national and international journals of opinion.[100] Whatever the exact balance of their relationship, Wells was poorly positioned to dictate terms. "The South will not listen to me nor to anyone of my race," she contended while abroad. "Where Frederic [*sic*] Douglass has failed you may be very sure that an unknown negro will not succeed."[101] Yet Wells's "unknown," homeless, and "exile" status also garnered her sympathy and allies. She wrote in May to the liberal editor of the *Manchester Guardian*, William Axon, that her visit with him "will be one of the most delightful memories I shall take back with me to my—country. I was about to say my home, but I remember that I have no home."[102]

In England, Wells effectively dramatized herself as an exile from democracy, but she still encountered significant challenges to her message. During what turned into a six-month stay, Wells spoke at many gatherings in parlors and drawing rooms or to groups assembled by the London-based branch of the SRBM. A typical audience was made up of "several ministers, members of the Society of Friends, and ladies and gentlemen interested in local philanthropic work."[103] In her letters to the *Inter-Ocean*, Wells carefully recorded the endorsements of her work by the Baptist and Congregational Unions, the British and Foreign Unitarian Association, the Aborigines Protection Society, the British Women's Temperance Association, and the "women members of the Society of Friends."[104] It remained difficult, however, to obtain substantive endorsements for action against lynching by organized groups. The churches did not rally. "I find the Christian bodies here less responsive by far than the Press has been to the cry of the oppressed," Wells asserted in London.[105]

To cope with this limitation, she made general press coverage of her lynching facts a primary goal. She republished *Southern Horrors* in London as *United States Atrocities* and sold this pamphlet at lectures (see Figure 9). The press was, after all, her area of expertise. "When the American Press and pulpit take up this matter as the British Press and pulpit have taken it up, lynching will be a thing impossible," she contended. "That is all I can say."[106] The SRBM could not pay her, but it could publicize her work. Their organ, *Fraternity*, was glad to feature her articles in hopes of generating momentum for the Society and its cause. "Her greatest success has been with the London newspapers," noted that journal in July. "[L]ynching has never been so strongly condemned by the Press in England as during her visit this year."[107] Even so, Wells's autobiography claimed that while in England, "hardly a day passed without letters in the daily papers attacking and discrediting my assertions."[108]

At issue was Wells's claim that U.S. churches failed to rebuke and in

FIGURE 9. Title page of Wells's *United States Atrocities: Lynch Law* (London: Lux Publishing, 1894).

some cases actually abetted lynching. Big-city newspapers in London and Liverpool, as well as the religious press, reported criticism of Wells on this point. Most of these accounts repeated the complaint heard at the National Conference of Unitarians in April, which refused to pass an antilynching resolution. Delegates there called Wells's claim about the complicity of the church in lynching a "terrible misrepresentation" and "unjust" to their Unitarian brethren in America.[109]

"I am very disappointed at the failure of the resolution and angry at the charges of misrepresentation," Wells wrote to William Axon. "I cannot recover from the set-back given the work in this public manner and by so large and representative body of those whose professions are so broad. It will neutralize & paralyze further effort in other bodies, taking this as a precedent."[110] The Unitarians' reaction deprived Wells of allies and, more critically, cast doubt on her veracity, thereby potentially undermining all of her propaganda efforts.

Antilynching made better press than politics. In such a context, the symbolic aspects of Wells's tour moved to the forefront. The fresh sheaf of clippings she collected in England and the lists of dignitaries who signed on to a new London antilynching committee generated credibility for her efforts. By paying honorary visits to past associates of Douglass, like Ellen Richardson, and to former British antislavery leaders Canon Wilberforce and the Clark family, Wells positioned herself and her movement as a rightful heir to their legacy. When British commentators favorably compared her work's impact to that of Harriet Beecher Stowe's *Uncle Tom's Cabin* (1852), Wells wisely did not quibble.[111] She tapped the Beecher family legacy in her own way, writing an article in New York's *The Independent* that made an analogy between her work and that of Henry Ward Beecher's controversial antislavery lectures in Liverpool before the Civil War.[112] Wells was grateful to the African students and visitors who sought her out in London and lent their personal and financial support to the cause, but apparently she did not pursue any African networks in reform.[113] Instead, she banked on antislavery's moral legacy and Charles Aked's rising star among the dissenting churches to help her discredit lynching in the eyes of the world.[114] Both failed her.

Wells's supporters tried to intercede with critics on her behalf. Speaking for Boston's Woman's Era Club, African American club leader Florida Ruffin Ridley wrote an open letter in the press to Mrs. Ormistan Chant. Chant was a wealthy and prominent Unitarian also of that city who had heard Wells's lectures abroad and had taken issue with her. Ridley tried to persuade Chant to "hear 'the other side' " of the lynching story. For the sake of mob victims, she implored, "[W]orkers of humanity everywhere, if [you] can do nothing for us, in mercy's name do not raise [your] voices against us."[115] "I shall make no 'reply' in the *Inquirer!*" huffed Manchester critic Brooke Hereford at Axon's prodding to patch things up with Wells. "Let her statement go for what it is worth." Hereford believed that U.S. churches were simply uninformed about lynching, and he resented the analogy to tolerance of slavery. He eventually softened his opposition but not before ridiculing Wells's antiquated, David-and-Goliath approach. "Miss W. says she has sent them [northern clergy] her pamphlet &c," he wrote to Axon. "What do *pamphlets* amount to in these busy days?"[116]

The question neatly caught the dilemma of the individual on the eve of mass society, but, like Catherine Impey with her sanctimoniousness about money, Hereford was equally blind to the urgency and risks that historically surrounded radical African American protest. David Walker's pamphlet was so controversial in the 1830s that there was a price on his head. Wells's words also jeopardized her safety, and given lynching's lethalness, she could not afford to be ignored. This fact perhaps inspired her to ratchet up her gadfly approach during her May crisis with the Unitarians. She needed to prove that the forces of American Protestantism were racist and complicit in lynching. Wells seized upon the reputation of the so-called Queen of American Democracy, WCTU president Frances Willard, to prove her point.

Willard lived in England during these years as the guest of Lady Henry Somerset, president of the British Women's Temperance Association (BWTA). Lady Henry had welcomed Amanda Smith during her visits through England in the 1880s and had also extended courtesies to Wells in 1893. The temperance ranks were attractive for Wells's purposes for several reasons. Unlike nascent anti-imperialist organizations like the struggling and underfinanced SRBM, the temperance movement was never stronger, counting hundreds of thousands of dues-paying female members in the Anglophone world under the aegis of the new World's Woman's Christian Temperance Union (WWCTU).[117] Faced with British disbelief at the indifference of American churches to lynching and racism, Wells set out to prove her point among the evangelicals who dominated the Anglo-American temperance movement.

In mid-May, Wells published a critique of Willard in *Fraternity*. She pointed to racial segregation in the WCTU and targeted Willard's acceptance of southern whites' descriptions of sexual predation by African American men that were used to justify lynching. Wells quoted a New York interview of Willard's from 1890 in which she stated that "the colored race multiplies like the locusts of Egypt" and "the safety of womanhood, of childhood, of the home, is menaced in a thousand localities at this moment, so that the men dare not go beyond the sight of their own roof tree."[118] In a published interview with Lady Henry, Willard in turn rebuked Wells for this exposure, noting she was "sorry to have my words thus construed," especially since she had "tried to help" Wells while she was in England.[119] For her part, Lady Henry went straight to Frederick Douglass, complaining of Wells's "vituperation, bitterness, and unfairness" toward her friend.[120] Yet Wells skillfully turned the incident into a public relations coup. Willard and Somerset's actions made it seem like powerful white leaders intended to "crush an insignificant colored woman."[121] Helped by editorial praise for her "almost single handed" antilynching work in the London *Daily Chronicle*, Wells wrote to Douglass that she and the cause were saved from the equivocating temperance leaders. "No other save Divine strength could have helped me so wonderfully," she wrote to him, "and to God I give all the praise and glory."[122]

Wells praised God with good reason. In the course of a few weeks, her earthly supporters nearly deserted her. Douglass already felt put out by public announcements that she had his personal endorsement and by new requests from Charles Aked for letters of support. "I had not supposed that, being invited to England, you needed my endorsement," wrote Douglass to Wells. "Will you oblige me by telling me frankly who invited you to spend three months in England and what assurances they gave you of support while on this mission?"[123] This doubting and critical letter "hurt" Wells "cruelly"; she was pained at the thought of being classed with those self-promoters who "imposed upon" Douglass's confidence for their own ends.[124] She needed the letter from Douglass very much, planning for it to perform triple duty: vouch for her facts, confirm her character, and tip the Unitarians into line in time for their next conference in mid-June.[125] Douglass came through.[126] "I thank you for it," wrote Wells, "and the race which already loves and honors you for your words and works in its behalf—cannot but more highly venerate you for your work in your old age."[127] Wells never forgot her debt to Douglass, honoring him annually at "Douglass Day" celebrations in Chicago for the rest of her life.

Launching the American Crusade

Fortunately, strife in the British crusade never reached the bulk of Wells's readers in the United States. They were proud of "Iola's" achievements abroad.[128] A parliamentary dinner at the end of June 1894, sponsored by William Woodall, a liberal MP and supporter of woman suffrage, was a particular point of pride for her and a fitting close to a personally exhilarating though demanding trip.[129] "Miss Wells should be royally greeted and lionized by all concerned in the triumph of justice and rights, but by no class more than her own people, who are notoriously denied both," enthused the AME Church's newspaper, the *Philadelphia Christian Recorder*.[130] Wells's success offered her readers a renewed sense of pride and hope, especially to black women.[131] "What Miss Wells has accomplished in England," wrote Fannie Barrier Williams, "strongly suggests the importance of a greater sense of conscious dignity and self-respect among colored women."[132] An exultant poem from Katherine Davis Tillman highlighted Wells's impact on black women's sense of heroic possibility:

> Charlotte Corday for the English,
> Joan of Arc for the French,
> And Ida B. Wells for the Negro,
> His life from the lynchers to wrench. . . .

And the wise Afro-American mother,
Who her children of heroines tells,
Shall speak in tones of gratitude,
The Name of Ida B. Wells![133]

Hailed as the "modern Joan of the race," Wells became "the most noted race woman of her day."[134] Her acknowledgement by the British as a "lady of culture and refinement" made her the "peer of any in the land," regardless of skin color.[135] Black Floridians planned to have a new town named "Wellsford" in her honor.[136] The *Freeman* stated simply: "She is making history."[137]

Returning to an inspired and mobilized African American readership, Wells embraced political organizing back in the United States and committed herself to a year of lectures and agitation. She had described her English lectures as "a moral rather than political agitation," since the laws against lynching meant nothing without "strong public sentiment to back them."[138] Now she advocated education and active resistance, echoing the call of radical black abolitionists. "I said a while ago that it was impossible for hereditary bondmen to be free unless they struck the first blow themselves," stated Wells to a Brooklyn homecoming audience at Bethel AME church. "We are not organized now, and therein lies the great trouble."[139] The plan she announced was ambitious; it involved getting out the facts of lynching, urging churches and all "Christian forces" to take a stand against mob violence, demanding the right to a fair trial for accused criminals, and petitioning the government for redress from mob rule.[140] Antilynching demanded financial and political support to be effective, but over the coming year neither materialized. The awful legacy of the Memphis lynching deterred many southern blacks from protest out of fear of retaliation. In addition, some leaders and editors resented female initiative and leadership. Moreover, American racism made it extremely difficult for Wells to parlay her gender credentials as a lady reformer in England into a credible vehicle for agitation in the United States. Unlike the British, white American audiences did not see in Wells a fascinating exotic. She was just another "negro," a "problem," and, as a black woman, a favorite scapegoat.

Southern whites blamed Wells's publicity about relations between white women and black men for inflaming prejudice and thereby putting blacks further at risk; others claimed she "aroused prejudice and passion among the negroes" for revolt or revenge.[141] "It is impossible to measure the extent to which Ida Wells has retarded [the fight against lynching] by her outrageous attacks on the Southern women," insisted the *Louisville Courier-Journal*. "She is a mischievous agitator who can do the negroes of the South no possible good."[142] According to Wells's old foe, the *Memphis Commercial*, her campaign had "done more to intensify the bitterness of race-prejudice" among whites than any other event in the past ten years.[143] Retaliation was swift and violent. Near Jackson, Mississippi, a protest meeting, reportedly inspired by a "negro agitator" who had "carried the news of the recent antilynching meeting in New York," was broken up by authorities; arrests were made and "the men were tied and whipped severely by whites."[144] Southern whites associated Wells with "slandering white ladies" and punished local blacks who supported her crusade.[145]

Southern white supremacists questioned Wells's authority through her body. For them, Wells's indeterminate "racial" biology entailed ambiguous or divided political loyalties. Memphis opponents attacked her by claiming that "this sharp yellow woman" was "not altogether of the race which she claims to represent."[146] By figuring Wells's body as tainted, marked by and capable of further race mixing, white critics identified her as an advocate of miscegenation, as one seeking "to blend the blood of the two races."[147] They also likened her to radical women who were tainted by murder, like Haymarket widow Lucy Parsons and the French revolution's Charlotte Corday, or described her as a menacing "saddle-colored Sapphira," a sexual hazard to family, "race," and nation.[148] Expanding the association between skin color, transgressive femininity, and negative sexuality, racists cast Wells's initiative against lynching as prostitution, activity directed by her personal financial and sexual desires. Critics in the North and South asserted that Wells was an "enterprising missionary" bent more on an "income rather than an outcome."[149] As someone labeled racially corrupted, Wells was assumed to be morally corrupting. The critical *New York Times* described her as being of "very light complexion," "coffee-colored," "octoroon," and, making the link to lying and immorality, called her a "slanderous and nasty-minded mulattress."[150] By contrast, the sympathetic *New York Tribune* identified Wells as a "coal-black negro girl" (at age thirty-two). "Girl" evoked a more docile, less sexualized female figure, and "coal-black negro" indexed skin color to racial purity and thereby implied credibility.[151]

Wells's analysis of lynching was rejected wholesale by southern whites. Editors boomed that only when rape ceased would lynching stop. "The moment the colored criminal of the South gives up his favorite crime, that moment 99% of the Southern lynchings will cease," went the typical argument; the "true and only solution" to the lynching evil was to "induce the negroes not to commit crime, to cease their

ravishing, and live peaceful, honest lives."[152] Southern conspiracy theorists linked Wells with "northern capitalists" and "western bondhold-
ers" bent on sabotaging economic investment and foreign immigration
to their region.[153] The publicity and outcry about lynching put very few
white leaders on the defensive. The value of a Memphis trial convicting
a new group of lynchers or the denunciations of mob law by Alabama
and Ohio's governors were overwhelmed by the vehement defiance of
most white southerners.[154] Hopes of Populist support against lynching
also dissolved during 1894.[155] The few antilynching laws passed in these
years were generally ignored in practice, symbolizing only southern
resolve against interference by outsiders.[156]

Southern African Americans depended for survival on amicable relations with whites. Conditions there did not permit the kind of confrontation Wells advocated. A state Colored Teachers Association in
Georgia voted down a resolution endorsing Wells; southern members
of the Colored Teachers National Association declined to support a
similar resolution at their annual convention in Chicago because "it
would make matters hard for them when they returned to their Southern fields."[157] Some rejected her tactics outright. J. L. Fleming still
fumed about the *Free Speech*'s destruction in Memphis, and in the press
he bitingly described Wells's "fire eating speeches" as hopelessly ineffec-
tive.[158] A black minister from Birmingham proclaimed her methods
"questionable" and publicly offered himself as better able to present a
"calm and dispassionate appeal" to southern whites, which would do
much more, in his mind, to promote the demise of lynching.[159] "Colored Democrats" dubbed Wells a "fraud" and sensationalist; some lobbied for antilynching planks in their party's platform but identified
Wells's agitation as "unwise and uncalled for."[160] Faced with the hazards
of confronting whites with the falsehood of the rape charge, many
instead stressed the less controversial idea of law enforcement to curb
mob action.

Northerners also took exception to Wells's work. In New York, she
was approached by a "delegation of men of my own race" who requested that she "put the soft pedal on charges against white women
and their relations with black men" in an upcoming interview. She
"indignantly refused" their request, arguing that her silence would "tac-
itly admit" the "false charge against Negro manhood."[161] The delegation may have felt that raising the question of sex across the color line
complicated an already difficult situation. Others, supporters of the
chivalric tradition in gender relations, were offended by Wells's defense
of black men at the "expense" of white women's moral reputation. Two
African American men from Philadelphia complained that it was "dis-

honorable in the extreme to attempt any defense based upon an attack on the virtue of any class of women."[162] While few African Americans went so far as to attack Wells personally, there was little consensus, North or South, about how to best confront lynching. "All colored people do not sanction Miss Wells [*sic*] fiery flings at the South," commented Kelly Miller from his post at Howard University.[163] Another Washington, D.C., critic, C. C. Astwood, outright denied "that decent colored women were outraged of their virtue by white men, as stated by Miss Wells." He advised readers to "repudiate the association with debauched women and look upon Miss Wells's crusade with disgust."[164]

Issues of gender further complicated the development of a consensus on tactics in black communities. Wells had launched her crusade in part by defending black manhood. As her celebrity grew, however, she encountered resistance on the grounds that such agitation was not womanly. Julia Coston of Cleveland, Ohio, editor of *Ringwood's Afro-American Journal of Fashion*, reflected this view when she declared that "essentially feminine" women were "not troubled with affairs of State," nor were they "agents of reform." When Coston criticized those women who would "throw off the veil of modesty, and . . . in the name of reform, pose as martyrs, sacrificing themselves to a great work," she could easily have been referring to Wells.[165] Ironically, supporters also relied on gender, especially femininity, to justify Wells's actions. For them, Wells's womanliness was never questioned, and her alleged appetite for praise was marshaled as proof of femininity. "To our mind, therein lies one of the chief charms of Miss Wells's crusade," the *Freeman* explained, "in that she has not permitted the cares and labors of the same to unsex her. The full blown rose of a blameless womanhood abideth with her."[166] Monroe Majors agreed. Wells taught the nation "that sublime lesson of *modesty unchanged* even at the severest test."[167] These images of purity, modesty, and selfless service defused anxiety that Wells violated precepts of femininity.

Ambivalence about female leadership and her own visionary pragmatism likely fanned Wells's commitment to a grassroots movement. She insisted that her exuberant black audiences not merely adopt her as heroine, but take up the charge themselves. "I only ask in return that they give of their means to sustain the work in the future. That will be the surest test of appreciation for the past and greatest guarantee of gratitude. I could ask no higher reward."[168] Wells envisioned a community-based confrontation with the lynching problem. When a black Texas Republican proposed a "national collection day" to raise money for the fight, Wells praised these efforts and channeled them through the press.[169] Such funds could fuel local efforts to investigate, publicize, and agitate against lynching, she wrote, and "thus the race would furnish the sinews of war to carry on the work which has been begun."[170]

Given the violence of white reaction and her vulnerability as a public figure, Wells had to be extra careful about bringing attention to herself rather than the cause. In *Crusade for Justice*, she described herself an "instrument" for justice in the 1890s and noted her refusal to accept a job as a paid speaker for a lyceum bureau, a job that otherwise would have been a natural fit. She refused on the grounds that to accept money was "sacrilegious" to the goal of ending lynching, a position that wealthy Christians like Catherine Impey would have supported. Though Memphis taught Wells the importance of capital in any literary or political undertaking, the fragility of her claim to public authority as a black woman undercut her ability to act on this insight. The bureau that approached her was not interested in lectures on lynching, more evidence that white Americans did not care to hear her views even though they appreciated her speaking talents as a potential money-maker. With the benefit of hindsight, the autobiography reports Wells's regret at having been "too inexperienced and unappreciative of the great opportunity . . . to make some money for myself" at the height of her crusade.[171]

When the Brooklyn faithful—now joined by interested whites—convened at the end of 1894 to hear Wells summarize her progress, they heard a disturbing report. Lynchings were "not only on the increase" but were becoming "intensified in their barbarism and boldness," illustrated by broad-daylight lynching "bees" where photographs were sold as "souvenirs."[172] The funds and commitment for the propaganda war were hard to come by. Ally T. Thomas Fortune and others looked to black elected officials to lead in donations, since they owed their positions and paychecks to black constituents, but the politicians contributed little.[173] The AME church declined to put its imprimatur on Wells. By April 1895, the press reported that her "tour of this country has been a financial failure . . . her views are too radical."[174] In June, the *Freeman* noted that Wells was "becoming discouraged with the most unappreciative Negro race."[175]

Despite these mixed reviews, African American women remained Wells's strongest supporters. They sustained her work with personal letters and endorsements and supported her candor on the rape charge and her criticisms of Frances Willard.[176] During the Atlanta Cotton Exposition in 1895, a Woman's Congress composed of black women rejected a resolution that linked a condemnation of lynching to a denunciation of rape, a position Wilson Moses rightly calls an "act of defiance," given the hostility of southern whites to such criticism.[177] Yet after Booker T. Washington's address at the Exposition, which disavowed politics—the so-called Atlanta Compromise speech—many of Wells's old supporters retreated, even the stalwart *Freeman*, which now expressed the hope that "discretion and moderation may mark all future utterances" on lynching.[178] Criticism in the black community became a growing chorus, and Wells's crusade was pronounced "a failure."[179]

The British could not help. English support of antilynching protest remained warm but inadequate. The Society for the Recognition of the Brotherhood of Man made a small flap in the newspapers when its investigating committee eventually arrived in the United States in September 1895, but British sentiment did not translate into American reaction.[180] Though the Society invited the outspoken Hallie Q. Brown to follow Wells on a speaking tour of England, Brown's successor, a Mr. G. F. Richings, avoided controversy and stressed achievements rather than obstacles in his lectures. According to one Englishwoman, the new consensus abroad was that "Miss Wells Discouraged, Mr. Richings Encourages."[181] Catherine Impey finally resigned from the SRBM in early 1895, citing faction fights and disputes over tactics.[182] Albion Tourgée publicly cheered but privately doubted the practical impact of the Society on either the course of empire in the British colonies or the persistence of scientific racism and lynching in the United States. "The battle, which though slight and indeterminate," he wrote to T. Thomas Fortune, "was a poem of truth in an age of greed."[183]

Lynching did not stop, but Ida B. Wells successfully made antilynching into news. Northern press compendiums like the *Literary Digest* and *Public Opinion* reproduced British newspaper coverage, giving Wells's message an even wider audience.[184] Well-established, reform-minded journals like *The Independent* of New York credited Wells with a "masterly flank movement" of publicity from abroad, though it remained editorially inconsistent on the causes of and remedies against lynching.[185] Most commentators, however, insisted that American practices were of no outsider's concern—least of all that of English meddlers who had their own colonial "race problem." The British were generally denounced as gullible busybodies.[186]

An important note sounded among the few sympathetic white northern commentators of the time: the idea that African Americans should work toward an end of lynching, effectively shifting responsibility to black activists. "Alone Miss Ida Wells may not be able to accomplish much," remarked a white Indianapolis editor, "but hers is a move in the right direction, and she will undoubtedly be followed by others of her color working in the same cause."[187] George Chandler

Holt's paper before the American Social Science Association in September of 1894 praised Wells as an "intelligent and eloquent black woman" but left the burden on "the colored citizens" to "agitate thoroughly" in order to secure the "ultimate abandonment" of mob action.[188] Even more troubling was the reaction of white commentators who condemned the lawlessness of lynching but failed to challenge the assumption that lynching was a natural response to black-on-white rape. Distancing himself from the "impulsive" tactics of Wells and her British followers, former antislavery supporter Thomas Wentworth Higginson argued that a "condemnation of lynching . . . was in no way impaired by linking with it the condemnation of another offense closely connected with it in the public mind as often affording the occasion for lynching, and always its argumentative excuse."[189] By contrast, African American supporters picked up on the abolitionist fervor that Wells sought to rekindle in the fight against lynching. "Whether we endorse all Miss Wells has to say or not, the fact remains that nothing should be done to hinder her work," affirmed the AME *Zion Church Quarterly*. "She is only doing what Garrison and Phillips did sixty years ago in denunciation of the institution of slavery."[190] Outraged at a lynching in Urbana, Ohio, black writer Charles H. Williams proclaimed that the demand to end lynching "MUST ORIGINATE WITH THE PEOPLE OF THE NORTH."[191]

Temperance, Again

Given Wells's moral claim on the legacy of antislavery and the "Christian forces" of the nation, she again pressed for a response to lynching from the American temperance movement. Wells decided to attend the WCTU's twentieth anniversary convention, held in Cleveland in November 1894. The convention's key resolution persisted in linking lynching with the rape of white women and children. It described "unspeakable outrages" and "atrocities worse than death" (rape) committed against "childhood, maidenhood, and womanhood" which provoked "lawlessness" (lynching).[192] In her presidential address, Willard criticized Wells personally, expressing repugnance at the idea of voluntary sexual liaisons between black men and white women: "It is my firm belief that in the statements made by Miss Wells concerning white women having taken the initiative in nameless acts between the races she has put an imputation upon half the white race in this country that is unjust, and, save in the rarest exceptional instances, wholly without foundation."[193] The disagreement between Wells and Willard turned on their respective definitions of rape. Frances Willard rejected the idea that white women acted on desire for black men; even the mere *suggestion* of such sexual initiative defamed every white woman in America ("half the white race"). Willard's racial chauvinism and her investment in the notion of the inherent sexual passivity of white women allowed her to define any such sexual contact as rape.[194]

As in the debate over tactics at the World's Fair, the reaction to Wells among African American WCTU delegates was mixed. The AME Church's Rev. Reverdy C. Ransom and his wife, Emma Ransom, helped lobby the delegates to pass a resolution condemning lynching and expressed dismay at Willard's comments.[195] Boston club woman Josephine St. Pierre Ruffin already considered Willard an "apologist" for lynching.[196] But others were reluctant to publicly criticize the WCTU leader. According to Reverdy Ransom, one "colored delegate" at Cleveland "went about cackling" that Wells "had zeal without knowledge," apparently eager to prevent a rupture between black and white conventioneers.[197] Black delegates valued participation in such national gatherings and were reluctant to disturb the decorum of interracial settings, all too aware that whites were predisposed to blame black women for provoking tension and prejudice.[198] In the midst of Wells's protest, a group of "Afro-American ladies" from Cleveland's clubs and churches wanted to present a welcoming bouquet of flowers to Willard in a gesture of mutual respect and recognition. They hoped that shared religious and class assumptions would create space for them and their issues in a mixed-race association of women, and they resented Wells's threat to the bridges they had painstakingly built. Rev. Ransom decried the club women's demonstration as a "back-handed 'blow in the face' for Miss Wells [and] a rank insult to every Afro-American lady in the city."[199]

For her part, Frances Willard did not understand Wells's critique, and she personalized their differences. She explained to Albion Tourgée that she found Wells's personality to be "percussive" as compared to the "good" Frederick Douglass. Willard did not engage Wells's ideas but opined that Wells lacked "the balance and steadiness that are requisite in a successful reformer." In this patronizing vein, Willard concluded: "I do not mention this as her fault but as her misfortune," hinting at an inherent defect.[200] According to historian Frances Bordin, "problems with black constituents" over the lynching issue "proved the thorniest problem and the most persistent cause of trouble" in the last years of Willard's presidency of the WCTU.[201] Tourgée defended Wells's stance on the temperance organization in his column in the *Inter-Ocean*, giving her a publicity boost.[202] Her protest, like Fannie Barrier Williams's effort against racist exclusion in the General Federation of Women's

Clubs that same year, highlighted the pitfalls of the politics of genteel Christian womanhood for African American women.[203] White women simply could not fathom black women's opposition to racial exclusion nor comprehend their urgent need to discuss the racial politics of rape.

A Red Record

Wells's struggles before American audiences, white and black, prompted her to revise and restate her antilynching arguments in another pamphlet, *A Red Record*, in 1895. Its dedication was grand and goading: "Respectfully submitted to the Nineteenth Century civilization in 'the Land of the Free and the Home of the Brave.'" Like the social science surveys produced by the women of Hull-House in Chicago or by Du Bois in Philadelphia during these same years, *A Red Record* addressed "the student of American sociology" and was subtitled "Tabulated Statistics."[204] Beyond the facts and figures, Wells grimly mocked not just the hypocrisy of "Southern honor," as in her first pamphlet, but all of "white man's civilization." Her conclusion advised readers:

> Think and act on independent lines . . . remembering that after all, it is the white man's civilization and the white man's government which are on trial. This crusade will determine whether that civilization can maintain itself by itself, or whether anarchy shall prevail; whether this Nation shall write itself down a success at self government, or in deepest humiliation admit its failure complete; whether the precepts and theories of Christianity are professed and practiced by American white people as Golden Rules of thought and action, or adopted as a system of morals to be preached to heathen until they attain the intelligence which needs the system of Lynch Law.[205]

If lynching was a product of "white man's civilization," then that civilization was perverse, destined to corrupt the integrity of so-called heathens across the globe. Wells stressed the corruption of language and meaning involved in the rape charge and thereby exposed the mob to be worse than an "uncivilized" race. Any "red Indians" or "cannibals," she argued, were guilty only of living by their precepts. The white South professed Christianity and the "majesty of law," defied both, then lied about their actions.[206]

This scathing indictment of "white civilization" in *A Red Record* occurred alongside a shift in Wells's antilynching arguments—away from "race" and toward universalistic arguments for the health of the republic, the integrity of the constitution, and freedom for all citizens. In *A Red Record*, she argued "not for the colored people alone, but for all victims of the terrible injustice which puts men and women to death without form of law."[207] Where *Southern Horrors* criticized the white South and vindicated Afro-American manhood, *A Red Record* stressed not racial but archetypal victims of lynching, like prisoners, the insane, and children. Whole chapters document the singling out of defenseless and outnumbered prisoners and "imbeciles" by lynch mobs.[208] The identification of prisoners, the insane, and children as lynching victims called up compassion outside the rubric of race. This shift reflected Wells's bitter recognition that "our color stands as a synonym for weakness, poverty and ignorance" and the dismal reality that stressing race did not make for the strongest humanitarian suit in the 1890s.[209] The more general appeal for the strong to protect the weak reworked humanitarian narratives of victimization derived from the antislavery tradition and applied them to antilynching.[210] In an "age of greed," however, the problem was not sentiment but money, for the "white man's dollar is his god," and many whites exhibited indifference or overt sadism toward black suffering.[211]

Gender also figured rather differently in *A Red Record* than in *Southern Horrors*. As in the earlier work, *A Red Record* refuted the rape charge against black men with an argument about gender, offering a defense of "good name of the manhood of my race," as Wells put it. The later pamphlet documented consensual relations by black men and white women who "fell in love."[212] In these tellings, African American men were full historical subjects who exercised agency, virtue, and even desire. Yet these descriptions of true black manhood coexisted with examples of African Americans as a "weak people" and of black men as the meekest of victims.[213] This tension between images of black men as "true men" and needy individuals identified the political dilemma posed by lynching in an age of scientific racism. Black men's status as physical victims could undercut their claim to manly independence, a core attribute of nineteenth-century citizenship and civic worth. More frighteningly, if only the strong survived, "the Negro," like "the Indian," seemed destined for extinction.[214] Wells's political analysis was richer and more complex than Darwinian logic. She understood that black people—indeed, all people—needed both freedom *and* protection in violent times. But in an age increasingly committed to "black and white" views of social reality, some audiences did not want to see shades of gray—or even the evidence. In England, pictures of lynched men were censored in the press and in the United States were viewed as suspiciously "salacious."[215] Insisting that people look again, *A Red Record* backed its facts and figures with several cuts and photographs of lynched men (see Figure 10).

FIGURE 10. "The Lynching of C. J. Miller, 1893" illustration from Ida B. Wells, *A Red Record* (1895), in *Selected Writings of Ida B. Wells-Barnett*, edited by Trudier Harris (New York: Oxford, 1991), 179

As representation of the interests of black male victims became increasingly fraught, those of black women twisted into obscurity. Images—including photographs—of physically abused slave women were a staple of antislavery fiction and reportage. Open discussion of rape, however, exceeded the bounds of the politically possible in the 1890s, and a picture was out of the question. By using newspaper copy as evidence, however, Wells documented cases of sexual assault and rape against black females. Five of the six she selected for *A Red Record* were girls, like "a little Afro-American girl," "eight-year-old Maggie Reese," and "an Afro-American child."[216] The child, of course, is the ultimate object of sentimental charity. *A Red Record*'s stress on the black girl-child victim suggests how little moral claim adult black women had on American society by the 1890s, a marked break with antislavery arguments, which frequently portrayed the downtrodden slave mother as deserving universal pity. Wells's attempt to fully disclose black victimization was marked by the need to call attention to yet shield the bodies of African Americans, especially of women, the complete exposure of which would either play into negative racist stereotypes or perhaps cause shame or embarrassment for her African American readers.

To obtain a fair hearing for these issues around race, sex, and place,

Wells relied on African American women. Her agitation set in motion a wave of hope and possibility among black women even as she inadvertently touched off a new round of attacks by racists. Early on Wells faced individual attack; now an entire "race" was assailed. In March 1895, a white Missouri newspaper editor named Jacks wrote a public letter designed to impugn the antilynching movement through a libel on all African Americans, including the charge that "the women are prostitutes and all are natural liars and thieves."[217] At a meeting called in Boston in July 1895, the First National Conference of the Colored Women of America took collective action for self-defense.[218]

Wells's antilynching initiative both inspired and cautioned these organized black women, who eventually took as their name the National Association of Colored Women (NACW). The initial meeting in 1895 gave Wells their "unanimous endorsement," yet at the same time many participants recommended prudence. Even the usually bold Josephine Ruffin modulated her tone at the Boston convention. She encouraged African American women to break the "mortified silence" induced by Jacks's "humiliating . . . charges" not by "noisy protestations of what we are not" but through a "dignified showing of what we are and hope to become."[219] In contrast to Wells's penchant for exposé, many in Boston concluded that Jacks's letter was "too indecent for publication," and they counseled restraint, advising women to "use it carefully."[220] Already ignored or harassed by the dominant culture and struggling to protect scant resources, club women agreed to the principle of resisting lynching and self-defense, but there was less than a consensus about tactics.[221] To be safe, they shunned "boisterous denials of accusations," controversy, or notoriety. Like Julia Coston, some rejected the likes of Ida Wells, identifying "fierce denunciation[s]" made by " 'mercurial persons' of the race" as outside the proper tone and direction of their work. AME Church women from New York insisted that only "truly representative women" and "conservative workers" could lay "true foundations" for reform."[222] Independent spirit Wells, like Maria Stewart before her, affirmed the freedom to engage fully in public life where the interest of African Americans was concerned. In so doing, however, she scrambled and defied the gender roles and racial categories of a society obsessed with labels.

Conditions only got worse. Particularly heinous, spectacular outbursts of violence took place in 1898: a race riot at Wilmington, North Carolina, and a lynching of Postmaster Frazier Baker and his family in Lake City, South Carolina. Both incidents had the explicit purpose of crushing the Republican Party and black political power in each state. In March 1898, Wells-Barnett (now married) traveled to Washington, D.C., with a petition to the president for redress of the Baker injustice.[223] At the same time, black military service in the Cuban and Philippine arenas of the Spanish-American War gave fresh accent to the political meanings of gender and manhood. Booker T. Washington gave pride of place to the "Superb Heroism and Daring Deeds of the Negro Soldier" in Cuba in his volume *A New Negro for a New Century* (1900), and several other laudatory volumes on black soldiers appeared in these years.[224] Although women often moved into otherwise proscribed areas of social activity in wartime, the so-called "splendid little war" squelched social innovation and reform.

The spike in conservatism at the turn of the century provided the context for Wells-Barnett's shifting location in organizational life. The NACW leadership, already ambivalent about Wells-Barnett's boldness in the public sphere, became further divided over loyalty to Booker T. Washington and squeezed her out during the Chicago convention of 1899.[225] It was as a member of the Afro-American Council, a mixed-sex but mostly male-led organization, that she achieved official, national leadership of antilynching protest. This achievement had its own gender entanglements. Wells-Barnett had initially been nominated financial secretary of the Council, but this move elicited criticisms from those who thought her better placed in "an assignment more in keeping with the popular idea of women's work." Instead, Wells-Barnett became head of a newly created Anti-Lynching Bureau. "She is a woman of unusual mental powers," admitted one observer, "but the financial secretary of the Afro-American Council should be a man."[226]

In the summer of 1899, the antilynching movement faced another crisis. The torture, dismemberment, and burning of Sam Hose before a crowd of thousands near Palmetto, Georgia, enraged and grieved black communities across the nation. It was especially demoralizing to African Americans who had served and sacrificed in the war. Tempers flared in Boston, where cries went up for armed self-defense against mobs.[227] On his way to the *Atlanta Constitution*'s editorial office with an article of protest, a despondent W. E. B. Du Bois heavily retraced his steps back to his study at Atlanta University, repulsed by the prospect of seeing pieces of Hose's body on display in a downtown shop window.[228] Black Chicagoans, led by Wells-Barnett and Reverdy Ransom (recently located to the city from Ohio), hired a detective to establish the facts surrounding the Hose lynching, which Wells-Barnett compiled and published as a pamphlet.[229] In her prefatory remarks to the investigation's results, *Lynch Law in Georgia*, she offered a bleak assessment of southern conditions: "The real purpose of these savage demonstrations is to teach the Negro that in the South he has no rights that the law will enforce . . . that no matter what a white man does," black victims "must not resist."[230]

A growing sense of alarm in the face of slaughter pervaded Wells-Barnett's writing in 1900. Continuing to stress national themes, Wells-Barnett's article in Boston's *Arena* magazine, "Lynch Law in America," argued that lynching seriously threatened the nation's moral fiber and political institutions. Her claim that "our country's national crime is *lynching*" implicated all citizens in law breaking and murder. This article projected an intense scrambling for frameworks to press the case against mob rule. It cited constitutional "consistency," self-interested "economy," patriotic "love of country," and even the "honor of Anglo-Saxon civilization" to argue that lynching concerned the "entire nation," not just African Americans.[231] This scramble reflected a dismal ideological moment in which Wells-Barnett drew on an amalgam of new and old arguments to inspire resistance to the mob. Wells-Barnett gloomily concluded that the "silence and seeming condonation" of lynching "grow more marked as the years go by."[232] *A Red Record* provocatively indicted "white civilization" at the bar of public opinion; the article "Lynch Law" still demanded justice at court but would have settled for mercy.

Wells-Barnett did not stop there. Written in her capacity as head of the Afro-American Council's Anti-Lynching Bureau, her pamphlet *Mob Rule in New Orleans* (1900) revisited ideas about gender, the use of force, and Christianity as they might figure in a reinvigorated project of black resistance. She published the piece at her own expense, noting in her introduction that the Council's Anti-Lynching Bureau had "no funds and is entirely dependent upon contributions from friends and members for carrying on the work."[233] *Mob Rule* marked an even sharper break with her earlier, comprehensive treatments of race and sex and the situation of black women in southern society. Events in New Orleans now posed the question of manhood in its starkest terms. Through the image of the honorable Christian soldier, *Mob Rule* revisioned true black manhood to meet the burden of the new century's urban, sometimes police-led violence against African Americans.[234]

The events of the riot were set in motion when two white police officers arrested two African Americans, a man named Robert Charles and a youth, Leonard Pierce. Charles resisted arrest, shot one officer, escaped, and was ordered to be shot on sight. He evaded the police for five days, during which time the city erupted in white-on-black violence that left eight people dead and hundreds injured.[235] *Mob Rule* vindicated Robert Charles as "the hero of New Orleans" through an account of his courage and marksmanship, his intimidation of the police, and his dra-

matic death while facing the mob. Charles was not only a brave individual but a Christian martyr. His work for the AME Church's publication,
the *Voice of Missions*, as well as testimonial letters from upstanding
church workers, reproduced in the pamphlet, testified to Charles's sterling character. Wells-Barnett's point was that even the best Christian
saint needed a gun for self-defense.

Mob Rule in New Orleans updated the antebellum image of the black
man as an idealized, cheek-turning Christian, the image popularized by
Stowe, with a dose of the turn-of-the-century's new ideal of martial
masculinity and respect for brute force. Such advice from a woman was
unusual, though, and distinguished Wells-Barnett from the materialistic, politically conservative Booker T. Washington and the high-culture,
protest-oriented approach taking shape in the writings of W. E. B. Du
Bois.[236] Instead, *Mob Rule in New Orleans* echoed Sojourner Truth's
famous query, reminding her readers that "God is not dead" and encouraging the work of resistance at the grassroots.[237] Nor did Wells-
Barnett fit comfortably in the NACW, now led by Mary Church Terrell,
whose watchword was "Homes, more homes, better homes, purer
homes."[238] Wells-Barnett continued to address the nation, even if the
Council was broke and no one seemed to be listening: "Men and
women of America, are you proud of this record which the Anglo-
Saxon race has made for itself?" she asked in her classic style in *Mob
Rule*. "Only by earnest, active, united endeavor to arouse public sentiment can we hope to put a stop to these demonstrations of American
barbarism."[239]

Conclusion

During the antilynching crusade of the 1890s, Ida B. Wells pushed the
bounds of heroic possibility for African American womanhood to the
breakpoint. She was described as unsexed and supersexed, unladylike
and too feminine, a paragon and a prostitute, a "black" woman and a
"mulattress," a martyr and a savior. Uncomfortable with the message,
most opponents criticized the messenger. Black women stepped up to
the opportunities she created, but because Wells-Barnett's work proved
as provocative as it was empowering, the NACW sought to mediate and
channel her impact. The combination of Wells-Barnett's boldness and
vulnerability mobilized African American women to band together for
mutual support and draw more tightly defined, reliable standards of
feminine behavior under the rubric of racial uplift, middle-class respectability, and dignified ladyhood. If, as historian Evelyn Brooks Higginbotham argues, the NACW remained "locked within hegemonic artic-

ulations of race, class and gender," it was not without struggle and tension, and in the 1890s Ida B. Wells was at its center.[240]

With a major intellectual intervention in the discourse on race, sex, and social place in her day, Ida B. Wells-Barnett debunked the racist assumptions and media misrepresentations surrounding lynching. Her argument that white women were complicit in mob violence and engaged in consensual sex across the color line infuriated both southern white supremacists and northern white reformers, because it undermined a shared ideological pillar of their worldview: female moral purity for whites only. Given this bedrock assumption, Wells-Barnett's effort to place racism and black victimization at the center of her analysis of power relations made little headway. Furthermore, the marginalization of real rape and black women's issues in antilynching paralleled the hostility to the point of violence that Ida B. Wells-Barnett faced as an actor in the public sphere. To meet these challenges, the NACW rewrote the script for feminine politics and edged Wells-Barnett out of her leading role. Combined with the general weakness of the Afro-American Council, the ascendancy of the conservative Booker T. Washington, and the stress of war, the result was the continuing political exile of Ida B. Wells-Barnett.

By the turn of the century, the most searching questions Wells-Barnett raised about the United States—namely, what does "civilization" mean if it is racially construed?—were literally taken over by others, particularly W. E. B. Du Bois. He took on the topic in his landmark essay "The Conservation of Races," written for the American Negro Academy, a new forum to foster black intellectual life begun in 1895 by Alexander Crummell.[241] The American Negro Academy excluded women; female aspiration was now contained in substantially domestic if still political terms within the NACW. On the literary front, poet Katherine Davis Tillman and short story writer Pauline Hopkins found patronage with significant publishing powers, the AME Church and the Washington, D.C.–based *Colored American Magazine*, respectively. No well-established church press or ambitious journal of culture supported Wells-Barnett. Her pamphlets *A Red Record*, *Lynch Law in Georgia*, and *Mob Rule in New Orleans* were all published privately, at her own expense.

Though she experienced antilynching as a kind of political exile, Wells-Barnett was not alone in articulating the distorted content and damaging uses of sexual ideologies in American culture. This vision created a number—some would say a generation—of intellectual exiles in the 1890s.[242] White writers like southerner Kate Chopin and midwesterner Theodore Dreiser also treated the social and political origins of social degradation and vice and similarly attributed them to human

choice or lack of choice, rather than to "biological" or "racial" imperatives. They, too, suffered marginality and neglect for their views. In
penning *Mob Rule in New Orleans* in 1900, Wells-Barnett, at age thirty-
eight, should have been coming into her full intellectual powers, but
there is little evidence that anyone read this pamphlet. Instead, like
Dreiser's *Sister Carrie* (1900) and Chopin's *The Awakening* (1899), Wells-
Barnett's work met initially with public criticism and then a deafening
silence.

It could be said that Ida B. Wells—rather like the populists, or even
Anna Julia Cooper—simply peaked early. Like Cooper, Wells-Barnett's
best writing was behind her. Like Dreiser, she still had another book in
her, the autobiography. Wells-Barnett experienced some of the opportunities but more of the cruelty meted out to creative, oppositional
Americans in the turbulent 1890s. The conspicuous successes of that
decade, Jane Addams of Hull-House and Booker T. Washington of
Tuskegee Institute, were of particularly flexible, conciliating tempera-
ments; their access to deep financial pockets in private philanthropy
underwrote their successful institution building in an era typified by
mergers, monopolies, and corporate domination. Addams later wrote
that the "decade of economic discussion" at Hull-House during the
1890s yielded a reconciliation between "abstract" and "concrete"
minds, each in the end seeing the other's point of view and which she
likened to the "changing of swords in Hamlet."[243] Characteristically,
Addams viewed all oppositions as resolving into ultimate harmony, but
Wells-Barnett surely would have disagreed. She knew her Shakespeare
as well as the fullness of human tragedy: when Hamlet and Laertes
exchanged swords in their duel, both died. As we shall see, Ida B. Wells-
Barnett never relinquished her weapon.

CHAPTER FOUR

Progress against Itself

Emerging slowly from a demoralized state at the turn of the century, advocates for racial justice seized new potential for a legislative end to lynching in the aftermath of World War I. Unlike the 1890s, however, this phase of protest took shape without Ida B. Wells-Barnett. The death of Booker T. Washington in 1915 created a breakpoint in leadership akin to that following Frederick Douglass's passing in 1895. A black women's literary and activist renaissance crested to meet that opening in the mid-1890s, but in this later period, men and manhood moved to the center of civil rights discourse. With the advent of black military service during World War I, the vision articulated by Wells-Barnett, Cooper, and the NACW—that African American women's particular needs and struggles were central to race progress and that womanhood might represent "the race" in the public sphere—went into partial eclipse.[1]

After World War I, a gender division of labor emerged in antilynching protest. This pattern was particularly visible at the level of national organizations and found vivid expression in activist efforts to pass the Dyer Antilynching Bill that came before Congress in 1921. The bill was designed to activate the Fourteenth Amendment's due process clause in order to hold mobs liable to prosecution in federal court. The National Association for the Advancement of Colored People (NAACP), founded in 1909, lobbied federal legislators in Washington, D.C., an effort led by Walter F. White and James Weldon Johnson. African American women, organized as the "Anti-Lynching Crusaders," worked under the aegis of the NAACP, carrying out the feminine vocations of prayer, networking, and fundraising among women across the country. The NAACP's *Crisis* magazine trumpeted the women's work in deeply religious terms, referring to it as "The Ninth Crusade." Marking the distance from Wells-Barnett's call to arms in the early 1890s, these crusaders engaged in a "moral battle" aimed at fostering a "new sense of personal responsibility" among American citizens on the lynching question.[2] Despite these combined efforts, a Senate filibuster killed the Dyer bill, and later versions presented in the 1930s and 1940s never passed.[3]

Ida B. Wells-Barnett was of, but not in, this effort against lynching, even though her legacy was everywhere in evidence. Instead, the NAACP's nascent expert on lynching, Walter White, walked in her footsteps. In 1921, White made a pilgrimage to England to mobilize British public opinion on behalf of racial justice in the United States.[4] The women Anti-Lynching Crusaders mobilized the religious energy and grassroots appeal that Wells-Barnett had tapped in her own earlier "crusade." But Wells-Barnett herself was mostly absent from the effort to pass the Dyer bill, and almost no journalistic or academic treatments of lynching in this period credited her work in any way.[5] Some officials within the NAACP felt that her exposés in the 1890s had succeeded only in hardening southern defensiveness about lynching, making a new approach necessary.[6]

Wells-Barnett made lynching a legitimate focus of American reform, amenable to the signal social remedies of the Progressive era: education and protective legislation. In becoming such, however, antilynching at the elite, national level shed its association with heroic black womanhood and deflected much of the searching treatment of racism and sexism pioneered by her in the 1890s. Taking cues from the obstacles Wells-Barnett faced, the NAACP represented a commitment to progress and social harmony rather than radical social critique or armed resistance. Comprised of lawyers, writers, teachers, and social work professionals, NAACP advocates, like other "new radicals" in this period, marketed an ameliorative, mostly upbeat vision of legislative reform to burgeoning elites in business, government, and philanthropy, sectors that themselves consolidated unprecedented wealth and prestige in this period.[7] The institutionalization and professionalization of reform—

the creation of social settlements, specialized schools, and national advocacy organizations and publications—deeply implicated race and gender.[8] Over time, and not without struggle, these dynamics marginalized Ida B. Wells-Barnett.

To be sure, Wells-Barnett did her best to build her own social settlement, launch her own publications, and court elites in this period, but she was effective only in Illinois and even there with limited results. After departing from the Afro-American Council in 1903, Wells-Barnett worked against racial violence without reliable institutional support or financial backing. She retained her appeal as a trusted community organizer through local agitation and interventions rather than through academic credentials or a professional affiliation. She still met with prisoners and presidents, sometimes risking jail herself, and kept on writing and organizing for racial justice, often at her own expense. Yet antilynching was able to get a rational hearing among white Americans only when framed as a matter of one group of men controverting the law vis-à-vis another group of men. Wells-Barnett tried to tell a broader, more demanding story in the 1890s and was rejected. Progressive-era efforts to stop the wanton murder of African Americans for any or no reason in the United States required a narrow, legalistic focus and entailed the marginalization of Ida B. Wells-Barnett from the national reform scene.

New Talk about Lynching

Elements of a gendered turn in antilynching were well expressed at the opening of the twentieth century by Mary Church Terrell. In her 1904 article "Lynching from a Negro's Point of View," published in the *North American Review*, Terrell offered an eloquent and comprehensive treatment. In the tradition of Wells-Barnett, she cited figures against the validity of the rape charge and explained lynching as a product of both race hatred and lawlessness. Terrell's statement, "Everybody who is well informed on the subject of lynching knows . . ." implied a body of popular knowledge that had to include Wells-Barnett's work. She clearly had read Wells-Barnett's pamphlet *Lynch Law In Georgia* on the Sam Hose murder because her article cited the action of black Chicagoans who hired a detective to investigate in Atlanta and drew on the report for details. Terrell also echoed Wells-Barnett's insistence that lynching and stopping it was white peoples' problem and condemned both the "white women who apply flaming torches to . . . oil-soaked bodies" and the complicity of white clergy, courts, and press in mob activity. She further noted the injustice of how "young colored girls" were still regarded as the "rightful [sexual] prey of white gentlemen in the South." Learning from the negative reaction to Wells-Barnett, however, Terrell made no mention of consensual sexual contact across the color line. Instead, she counseled white women, playing up both their victimization and their presumed natural piety. Lynching distorted women's true nature, argued Terrell, charging that its "barbarism . . . converts hundreds of white women and children into savages every year." "But what a tremendous influence for law and order, and what a mighty foe to mob violence Southern white women might be," she exclaimed, "if they would arise in their purity and power of their womanhood to implore their fathers, husbands and sons no longer to stain their hands with the black man's blood!"[9]

By not mentioning by name her colleague from Memphis, Terrell muted a fact acknowledged by African American communities across the country, namely, as the *Colored American Magazine* put it in 1902, that Wells-Barnett was "without doubt the first authority among Afro-Americans on lynching and mob violence."[10] Wells-Barnett's imprint pervaded the antilynching pamphlet and periodical literature produced between 1899 and 1919, although, like Terrell, few writers acknowledged her work. Most treatments echoed her argument that racism, not rape, caused lynching and marshaled statistics to prove it.[11] Even the great conciliator Booker T. Washington held the line against the rape charge.[12] The otherwise temperate Howard University professor Kelly Miller refuted the notion that blacks were peculiarly afflicted with "sexual infirmity" and, like Wells-Barnett in *Southern Horrors*, stressed that the "womanhood of the negro race has been the immemorial victim of the white man's lasciviousness and lust."[13] Elements of her muckraking style—even friendly cribbing from it—were all around. The title of journalist John E. Bruce's 1901 pamphlet, *The Blood Red Record*, echoed *A Red Record* and similarly reproduced lists of victims by name, though Bruce referred only in passing to the falseness of the rape charge and to the sexual abuse of black women under slavery.[14] In general, the explosive issue of sexual relations between black men and white women was handled infrequently and gingerly, since in Wells-Barnett's experience it proved damaging to the cause.[15] Extensive commentary on consensual sex across the color line even dropped out of her own treatments of lynching in these years. And beyond Terrell's early effort, African American women seldom sought national white audiences in print or at the podium on the lynching question.

Except for Wells-Barnett. She consistently engaged prominent individuals and publications to spread her message. Like Frances Willard before her, settlement founder Jane Addams talked past the falseness of the rape issue when she examined the lynching question in 1901. In New York's *The Independent*, Addams considered lynching to be primarily an example of class conflict and a gruesome instance of white women's subordination as the "possession of man." She gave "Southern [white] citizens the full benefit of [their] position" on the charge of black-on-white rape to "avoid confusing the main issue," which in her mind was law and order. Addams's counter to the mob's "ablest defenders"—namely, that law enforcement, not lynching, could stop rape—became the classic progressive position against mob rule.[16]

Responding in the same journal, Wells-Barnett appreciated Addams's "helpful" protest against lynching but believed she had done a "serious, tho' doubtless unintentional" injury to her case by allowing the assumption that lynching was a response to a "certain class of crime" (black-on-white rape). Wells-Barnett declared that it was "this assumption, this absolutely unwarrantable assumption, that vitiates every suggestion which it inspires Miss Addams to make." In her rebuttal, Wells-Barnett offered statistics to show the low correlation between allegations of rape and lynching and concluded that not rape but "contempt for law and race prejudice constitute the real cause of all lynching." "It is strange that an intelligent, law abiding and fair-minded people should so persistently shut their eyes to the facts in the discussion of what the civilized world now concedes to be America's national crime," she testily concluded.[17]

Steeped in Yankee-style prejudice that tended to view blacks as criminally inclined and unable to examine rape critically, white reformers like Addams resisted Wells-Barnett's arguments about lynching's deep causes. Jane Addams believed that class conflict and sexism—woman as "the possession of man"—explained lynching. For Wells-Barnett, racism and lawlessness, sanctioned by white women, posed the greater threat to African Americans. For most white reformers, rape was simply a fact; its reality inhered in assumptions about, as Addams put it, the "bestial in man." For Wells-Barnett, rape, in the context of lynching, was an idea surrounded by race-coded assumptions that defined black men as violators of white women. Most opinion shapers in the North were simply unable to focus on black victims, male or female. When journalist Ray Stannard Baker addressed himself briefly to "The Relation of Lynching to the 'Usual Crime' " in a pair of essays in *McClure's* in 1905, he sympathized with white southerners, plagued as he felt they were by a legitimate "fear of the criminal negro." Baker failed to unlink lynching from sexual crime, encouraging readers to "go to the heart of the matter and stop lynching for rape" and remaining all the while deeply pessimistic about changing the behavior of mobs.[18]

Abetted by Booker T. Washington's self-help mantra and by newly popular deterministic thinking about human "racial" development, mainstream northern opinion echoed Baker's doubts about ending lynching. At best, commentators shifted the work to African Americans. Classic in tone was social gospel advocate Washington Gladden's address to the Eighth Atlanta Negro Conference, a series organized by Du Bois, whose theme in 1903 was "The Negro Church and the Moral and Religious Condition of the Negro." Touching on the subject of disenfranchisement in the South, Gladden suggested to a mostly African American audience that the "more strenuously men oppose your participation in political affairs the more zealous and diligent ought you to be in qualifying yourselves to take part in them."[19] This smug, passive, burden-shifting stance so typical of the turn of the century infuriated Wells-Barnett.

She responded in print to a similar refrain concerning lynching. In one of its periodic editorials on the subject, *The Independent* posted the rather contradictory advice to African American leaders to "tell their people to defend the laws and rights even to blood, but never, never take guilty participation in lynching white men or black." Wells-Barnett offered a bristling rebuttal. "Theoretically the advice is alright," she wrote, "but viewed in the light of circumstances and conditions it seems like giving a stone when we ask for bread." "For twenty years past the negro has done nothing else but defend the law and appeal to public sentiment for defense *by* the law," but to no avail. The problem, as she saw it, was that whites simply did not care if black people were killed. "When the negro has appealed to the Christian and moral forces of the country . . . that demand has been met with general indifference or entirely ignored." She continued, "Where this is not true he has been told that these same forces upon which he confidently depends refuse to make the demand for justice, because they believe the story of the mob that negroes are lynched because they commit unspeakable crimes against white women. For this reason the Christian and moral forces are silent in the presence of the horrible barbarities alleged to be done in the name of woman."[20] Here Wells-Barnett identified the perfectly hypocritical double bind facing opponents of lynching. Yes, stated popular opinion, lynching is wrong, but so is rape. By refusing to unlink the two, whites did nothing about either. This ideological block prevented a critical examination of lynching, race, and sex. As a result of this block, many critics shifted away from analyzing racism and sexism to a more instrumental, legalistic focus—punish extralegal murder—and simplified the argument in the interest of the cause's survival.[21]

The changing geography and character of racial violence created further incentives for a shift in emphasis. The number of lynchings declined around the turn of the century, but the fall off in the 1899–1903 period was primarily among white victims, from 230 to 88 (62 percent), rather than black, from 544 to 455 (16 percent), making lynching an even more starkly racial crime.[22] As violence met black migrants in northern towns and cities, commentators could no longer project the lynching problem onto a singularly defective South. New York City newspaper headlines fretted over "Bad Negroes Coming North," and white southerners clucked their tongues at how the "lynching contagion" now infected the whole country.[23] The year 1900 witnessed a brutal lynching in Akron, Ohio, and a race riot in New York City, marking both the heartland and the metropolis as home to the mob.[24]

In 1903, two northern lynchings received especially widespread attention. The first was defiantly done by a white mob while facing fire from state militia in Evansville, in southwestern Indiana, a melee that left the black victim and seven whites dead as well as twenty others wounded.[25] Then in Wilmington, Delaware, a black man was publicly burned to death on the accusation of raping a white woman. These killings brought condemnations from many quarters, including a warning from philosopher William James. James observed in the press that unless "special legislation *ad hoc* is speedily enacted" against lynching and "unless many 'leading citizens' are hung," he feared "we shall have negro burning in a very few years on Cambridge common and the Boston public garden," and thus a betrayal of America's revolutionary and antislavery legacies.[26] James's note about "special legislation" caught the drift of progressive reform, but in the mouth of an African American such words about hanging "leading citizens" could cost that person his or her life.[27]

In the wake of Evansville, President Roosevelt finally started talking. As usual, TR's pithy broadcast was a bellwether. Roosevelt denounced mob action in a public letter to Indiana's governor, but his condemnation of lynching also put the presidential seal on the politics of rape that Wells-Barnett opposed. "The feeling of all good citizens that such a hideous crime shall not be hideously punished by mob violence is due not in the least to sympathy for the criminal, but to a lively sense of the train of dreadful consequences which follow the course taken by the mob in exacting inhuman vengeance for an inhuman wrong," stated the president. "The slightest lack of vigor either in denunciation of the crime [of rape] or in bringing the criminal to justice is itself unpardonable."[28] TR became a supporter of quick and severe legal prosecution for people accused of rape—not lynching. A trend toward speedy trials and court-ordered executions for those accused of rape grew up with the twentieth century, forming a general pattern of "legal lynching" characteristic of racial justice in the pre-Scottsboro era.[29]

Gender and the Shaping of Black Resistance

African American women and men continued their resistance to lynching, but their approaches changed. Under Robert Moton's leadership as director of publicity and research, Tuskegee Institute began keeping extensive press clipping files on lynching in 1899 and published their statistics annually in the press, eventually including such information in a reference volume, *The Negro Yearbook*, begun in 1914. By 1919, the NAACP had available a mail-order library of nearly a dozen antilynching pamphlets, many based on original research and reporting.[30] The practice of establishing antilynching groups and defense committees on an ongoing or ad hoc basis, as advocated by Wells-Barnett in the 1890s, entered the everyday protest vocabulary of local activists, who were often led by women and clergy. Women organizing together against lynching at the grassroots—in groups like the Women Stop Lynching Committee of New York City—became a stock in trade of agitation.[31] It was these women, inspired by Wells-Barnett's example and educated through women's club or church work, whom NACW leader Mary B. Talbert called upon to form a ready-made phalanx of Crusaders to help pass the Dyer bill. It was on this sex-differentiated basis that antilynching became women's work.[32]

If there was a gendered turn in antilynching work at the elite level, the situation in the Midwest was far too urgent for Wells-Barnett to pay it much heed. Racist outbreaks converged in Illinois as black southerners made their way north through the center of the country. There were lynchings in Belleville (1903), Danville (1903), and Cairo (1909), as well as riots in Springfield (1908), East St. Louis (1917), and Chicago (1919)—this last being one of over two dozen race riots that shook the United States in the "red summer" of 1919. Wells-Barnett continued to take the lead at all levels: writing, publicity, organizing, and agitation that endorsed armed self-defense against attack.

In 1901, Wells-Barnett investigated a charge of rape against a black man in downtown Chicago, a wrongful accusation that nearly precipitated a lynching. Her news article headline announced: "City Papers Lied About a Negro Outraging a Little White Girl." Citing her authority as chair of the Afro-American Council's Anti-Lynching Bureau, Wells-Barnett decried the press's "reckless disregard for the truth," insisting it was a "grave injury to a defenseless man and to the good name of the city for the press to rouse the spirit of lawlessness."[33] In

1903, the lynching of David S. Wyatt, a black schoolteacher at Belleville, Illinois, (near St. Louis) brought African Americans into condemnation meetings in Chicago. A group assembled at Quinn Chapel AME Church raised funds for Wyatt's widow, who traveled to Chicago to meet with protesters, and militants gathered around Wells-Barnett. In contrast to Mary Church Terrell's emphatic but restrained tone at this time, the press reported that "Mrs. Ida B. Wells-Barnett told the men that they must organize to fight their own battles, as the whites would not fight for the negroes until the latter had shown themselves capable of fighting for themselves." When a local newspaper, the *Broad-Ax*, worried out loud that "some things were said by the speakers which would have been much better unsaid," the editor probably referred to the call for armed self-defense that went up at the meeting.[34]

This kind of discontent stirred across the country and, as several scholars have pointed out, the events of 1903 led to a strategic turning point in national forums for black protest, with conservative forces, led by Tuskegee, receiving a damaging blow.[35] The Afro-American Council's July meeting in Louisville, only 100 miles from the outrage at Evansville a few weeks earlier, nearly broke up over the admission of delegates from the National Negro Suffrage League and the placing of a picture of Booker T. Washington on the dais amid ingratiating speeches. Militants felt antagonized. When Fannie Barrier Williams, a supporter of Washington, was elected secretary of the Council, Wells-Barnett withdrew from the organization.[36] Ten years earlier, Wells-Barnett and Council leader T. Thomas Fortune had clasped hands in the work of agitation against lynching. Now dependent on Tuskegee for financing his newspaper, the *Age*, Fortune informed Washington he was "glad" Wells-Barnett had left the Council.[37] Few came to her defense. The redoubtable John Mitchell Jr., editor of the *Richmond (Va.) Planet* and a strong opponent of lynching, lamented Wells-Barnett's resignation from the Council as "the worst blow of all" to the organization, noting that she stood "first and foremost among the agitators against lynching in this country."[38]

As with Du Bois, Wells-Barnett's opposition to Washington served, in the short term, to distinguish her point of view and afford her some currency in popular debate. But a sea change was underway, one that deeply implicated gender in the reshaping of African American leadership. Whereas antebellum critics often stressed universalistic Christian imperatives about human equality to oppose slavery, turn-of-the-century advocates of racial justice tended to rely on secular concepts, gender norms prominent among them, to advance their political strategies. This shift was evident in a discussion on "The Negro Problem from the Negro Point of View" that appeared in the *World Today* magazine of New York City in 1904. Booker T. Washington, Kelly Miller, Jesse Lawson, Wells-Barnett, and Du Bois were each identified by affiliations after their name—Tuskegee, Howard, and the National Sociological Society for the first three, respectively; "Chairman of the Anti-Lynching League" (probably a Chicago group) for Wells-Barnett; and "Author of *The Souls of Black Folk*" for Du Bois. It was the first and last time that Du Bois and Wells-Barnett received equal billing in a national public forum. Clergy were conspicuous by their absence.

Each article relied on gender to make the case for solving "the Negro problem," which in this discussion focused on education. The conservatives, Washington and Miller, cited out-of-kilter female behavior to prove their points about industrial education and "the city negro" respectively. The principal example of higher education gone wrong in Washington's essay was that of a female graduate of a "Negro 'university' in the South" who studied Shakespeare, Latin, Greek, and trigonometry but still "saddened" him by her lack of skills in "cooking and sewing and housekeeping and nursing and gardening." These domestic skills, he argued, should rightly be expended in service of "her father's cabin" and "the many little girls she will teach" rather than mere self-improvement. Miller's essay sought to make sense of the new urban environment facing black migrants. "Most striking" in these new populations, he explained, was the "predominance of the female element." Labor market segmentation in cities pulled black women into domestic service, while industry remained closed to both black men and women. "The scale is being upset where nature intended a balance," observed Miller of these new dynamics. He puzzled over how the "physical and moral robustness of the Negro race" fostered by the healthful countryside could be brought into right relationship in the city, especially since urban centers contained dangerous "effeminating" (his word) powers from vice and excess women.[39]

Wells-Barnett and Du Bois relied on different gender norms in their essays: a shared understanding of "the race's manhood." She bitterly noted that the image of "the educated, Christian negro gentleman" was as rare a character in Washington's famous dinnertime speeches and jokes as in mainstream American literature. Wells-Barnett blamed Washington personally for circulating negative stereotypes of black people to whites—especially those of the chicken thief and the layabout, uneducated "darky" preacher. These stereotypes fed assumptions about black criminality and moral deviance and traveled all too quickly to a supposed inclination to rape. She tweaked Washington with her classic sarcasm: "Mr. Washington knows . . . that lynching is not invoked to punish crime but color, and not even industrial education will change that." Du Bois, too, took as his ideal "the great principle of free, self-respecting manhood for black folk," an ideal severely threatened by Jim Crow strictures on education, suffrage, and civil rights.[40]

The assumptions about gender relied upon by Wells-Barnett and Du Bois in this discussion drew in part from the association of political equality with "full manhood," a cultural link forged in the Jacksonian era.[41] In many usages, including Wells-Barnett's and Du Bois's, the call to manhood summoned the common humanity of all African Americans, much as the concept of the brotherhood of man invoked the ungendered dignity of all members of the human family. But at the turn of the century, lynching and disfranchisement often singled out men and seemed literally to demand a manly response. At the same time, cultural trends increasingly tied masculinity—full citizenship, respectability, and Christian culture—to "race."[42] This new configuration of prejudices inclined some critics to accent gender ideals in their arguments. For example, John E. Bruce indicted white Americans for failing to live up to their own presumably valuable, if wrongly race-typed, gender ideals. "If the American white man has the courage and the manliness to live up to his rule of conduct and right-living he will have made good his boast of being the 'superior race,'" wrote Bruce, "and we shall hear less of lynching and all the other iniquities which disgrace his civilization and belittle his manhood and his humanity."[43]

Faced with deadly indifference to lynching, debate sharpened over resistance strategies at the elite level, and gender was a flash point in the discussion. Booker T. Washington celebrated the black soldier in his volume *A New Negro for a New Century*. He and his followers ridiculed militants' demand for equal rights as "'manhood!' hysteria" and argued that economic self-sufficiency and attention to moral duties demonstrated the true "manhood first" necessary to earn political rights in the future.[44] For his part, Du Bois founded a short-lived organization in 1905, the Niagara Movement, which, among other things, challenged the racialized masculine ideal taking shape in American society. The platform of the "Niagara men" demanded "Manhood Suffrage" and regarded Jim Crow as "a crucifixion of manhood."[45] Du Bois placed political rights at the center of his notion of restored black manhood. "First, we would vote; with the right to vote goes everything, freedom, manhood, the honor of your wives, the chastity of your daughters, the right to work and the chance to rise."[46] White supremacists resisted both visions, of course, seeing in Washington a Trojan horse of racial subversion and, later, in Du Bois's NAACP an incitement of the "red-blooded manhood" of African Americans, with overtones of confrontation and violence.[47]

Du Bois was not inventing from whole cloth; the concept of gender protection that he described was already well developed within racial uplift discourse. However, as Ida Wells-Barnett learned in Memphis, in journalism, and on the lecture circuit, if women endorsed such an order, they would also occupy a lesser position relative to men or else take a "man's share" and potentially forfeit protection. Women officially received adjunct status within the Niagara organization; they joined a "ladies auxiliary." Niagara cofounder, William Monroe Trotter, editor of the *Boston Guardian*, actually preferred that women be excluded altogether; it was Du Bois who organized the auxiliary in 1906.[48]

Gender, Family, and Politics

These percolating tensions continued to shape organizational life. Back in 1892, when Wells-Barnett and T. Thomas Fortune exchanged toasts at an Afro-American Press Association banquet, he toasted "The Ladies" and she "The Gentlemen," gestures of gender complementarity, even equality, in journalism. A shift was evident in the Niagara years, as demonstrated at the group's Chicago gathering in 1907. After a speech by Reverdy Ransom on "The Constitutional Rights of the Afro-American," Wells-Barnett offered a toast to "The Ideal Negro Manhood" but no one offered one to womanhood. Other toasts saluted "The Niagara Movement" and "Negro Enterprises," but space for an appreciation of womanhood vanished for the moment.[49]

This shift did not strictly entail less space for women; Wells-Barnett still went to meetings. Since the 1890s, she had defended black manhood in order to oppose racism and to create a role for women as critics; many people supported this aspect of her work. The *Chicago Conservator* declared: "God grant the race a few more Lady Macbeths like Ida Barnett to pump self respect into our loud-mouthed Negro leaders." The image of Lady Macbeth marks the distance from the biblical heroines that underwrote black women's initiatives for racial justice in the 1890s. In the play, Lady Macbeth conjures the spirits and unsexes herself in the interest of Macbeth's ascent to power. That she loses her mind and her husband loses his life and kingdom sounds a tragic note indeed for black protest. As the *Conservator* caustically concluded its advice to readers: "Negro men who would fear to die for their homes and their women and little ones are unfit for American citizenship, and should have never been born."[50]

This harshness had many sources. Its life-or-death tone and male-centeredness reflected the influence of social Darwinism and the martial ideal of modern masculinity. The anguish and spirit of sacrifice dated back in print to Stewart's *Meditations* and Walker's *Appeal*. As Stewart put it in the 1830s, "we shall but die" in the fight for freedom.[51] As for the Niagara Movement, its gendered structure and manhood rhetoric highlights a well-documented tendency in modern institution building in which the social prestige of a group rises in proportion to which low-status members of society—like women or other dependents—are excluded. Finally, the accent on secular rather than biblical archetypes for women also caught the modernizing trend in protest, a trend that stressed hard science and high culture rather than scripture in social thought.

Like Stewart before them, organized African American women retained a vital connection to religious inspiration, but their pronouncements in the early twentieth century stressed the domestic, not the heroic. In 1907, NACW leader Josephine Silone Yates praised Jesus' mother as a model for women, but she did not hold up heroines, religious or otherwise, as models for black children, as Kate Tillman had celebrated Wells-Barnett back in 1895. "The father, however, and not the mother," insisted Yates, "provides the boy's idea of the manly greatness to which he someday hopes to attain; his mother stands for love, goodness, kindness, sweetness, perhaps, but not for manly greatness."[52]

Though herself a conservative, Yates was in the mainstream of NACW women who reflected on their roles in the "uplift of the race" in the opening decade of the twentieth century in journals, newspapers, and club notes across the county. A central theme of these writings was motherhood.[53] This emphasis established a civic, even political role for women while retaining an ideological commitment to marriage, family, and a vision of domesticity that, among other things, spoke to the class aspirations of a generation distancing themselves from the deprivations of slavery times. As the one editor put it: "In the days of slavery we had mammies, in the day of freedom we must have mothers."[54] Club women rooted their maternalism in religion. Christianity, they contended, was the "medium by which woman had been exalted to her legitimate sphere in the world."[55] Like Yates and Wells-Barnett in Memphis days, black women looked to the image of the biblical Mary for inspiration. As the "Christ-Mother," Mary was the humble source for the redemption of the world. Since the redemption of mankind came through a woman and motherhood, so the redemption of African Americans would come through women and mothers.[56] Women were the deliverers of nations; the black mother's job was "race-making" and "race-building."[57] The home and family were the defining arenas for these achievements, entailing significant civic and political ramifications.

In the context of southern disenfranchisement, educated African American women framed their power as primarily moral and as linked to men's. When club leader Addie Hunton argued that "[w]hile we [women] may not be permitted to directly deal with the world's movements, the strength or weakness of our influence is the strength or weakness of our manhood," she referred to both the "race's manhood" and to black men.[58] The idea of interdependence, however, only partly resolved the question of gender roles, especially since women could be held responsible for male behavior, as in the notion that "men are what women make them."[59] This view gave rise to inspiring phrases, as in "Negro women should be the best, the holiest and the most chaste of all women," but such formulations looked past the ways in which men were the arbiters of female status and respectability.[60] Establishing women as the moral guardians of men only inverted the notion that black men's morals were somehow black women's fault. As she had in Memphis, Wells-Barnett tried to point a way out of this gender binary through a politics of solidarity, activist pressure on government, unity among "Christian forces," and armed self-defense. These tactics were difficult to sustain, however, as the assault against African Americans by whites continued.

The Atlanta riot of 1906, brazenly abetted by newspaper headlines screaming about a "rape epidemic" in the city; the discharge without honor that same year of 167 black soldiers who were wrongly charged with shooting up the town of Brownsville, Texas, after a rumor of black-on-white rape was circulated; and a race riot in 1908 at Springfield, Illinois, in the shadow of Abraham Lincoln's grave—all were gestures seemingly determined to crush African American resistance.[61] Wells-Barnett's response to this deteriorating situation occurred in church.

After pensively wending her way to teach Sunday school at Grace Presbyterian a few days after the Springfield riot, Wells arrived in class and gave "vent to a passionate denunciation of the apathy of our people," one that transported her with feeling. After she, as she put it, "came to myself," she convinced a handful of students to join her at her home to continue the discussion, a group that took as its name the Negro Fellowship League.[62] During the coming year, Wells-Barnett also served as one of two African Americans on a committee headed by Jane Addams to direct the Lincoln Centenary in Chicago planned for February 1909. The centenary was the date on which appeared "The Call," a circular that set in motion the meetings that eventually led to the formation of the National Association for the Advancement of Colored People (NAACP). Given the racial violence in Illinois and Wells-Barnett's redoubled efforts at building local resistance among young people, her signature on the Call was both promising and logical.

Toward the NAACP

From its inception, the NAACP offered an elite, reformist challenge to the conservative political bossism of Booker T. Washington and a self-conscious embrace of the legacy of antislavery in the North, applied to modern conditions.[63] In addition to a commitment to public protest and to securing civil rights for African Americans, its members valued new criteria for leadership, especially college degrees, professional credentials, and formal relationships to official constituencies. Wells-Barnett no longer led any well-recognized group, and this probably weakened her initial claim to high standing in the association. Gender also figured in the shaping of the new politics. Wells-Barnett overrode ambivalence about female initiative in the 1890s with quick and successful action that earned her praise as a "modern Joan" or a "Queen Esther." Now religious rhetoric lost some of its cachet, and rescues by women were looked at askance. Black protest newly accented masculinity (or motherhood), and Du Bois and others were on record as committed to a manly response to racism. In this setting, women like Mary Church Terrell and Maria Baldwin of Boston fit more comfortably in the NAACP than Wells-Barnett.

Wells-Barnett was the only African American from Chicago present at the NAACP's organizing meetings, held in New York in April 1909. She had hoped the organization would take up the fight against lynching and said so in a strong speech at the conference entitled "Lynching: Our National Crime." In this address she hammered home her now decades-old arguments. First, lynching was "color line murder." Second, "crimes against women" were the excuse for, not the cause of, mob murder. Third, lynching was a "national crime" that demanded a "national remedy." "Various remedies have been suggested to abolish the lynching infamy," she pointed out, but to no avail. "The only certain remedy is an appeal to law," she argued. "Federal protection of American citizenship is the remedy for lynching." Noting that several proposals to investigate lynching were presently before Congress, Wells-Barnett encouraged the conference to establish a bureau to do its own research and investigations in order to aid the work of legislators and influence public opinion through the media. These suggestions were not fully followed up by the NAACP for over six years; when the leadership finally addressed lynching systematically, it did so without her help.[64]

The third day of the organizing conference culminated in the selection of a "Committee of Forty" charged with defining the program and structure of the new organization. It is not clear whether Wells-Barnett formally reviewed the list of committee candidates or just managed a glance at it before it was read. According to her autobiography, she felt confident that her own name plus those of "others who were known be to opposed to . . . Mr. Washington's industrial ideas" were on it. When Du Bois took the podium and read the list, however, "bedlam broke loose," because neither she nor any of the militants, like William Monroe Trotter, were named. Wells-Barnett was "surprised" but claimed in her autobiography to have put "the best face possible on the matter" and, rather dramatically, left the meeting.[65] Wells-Barnett had turned on her heel back in 1894 when Philadelphia's AME clergy hesitated to endorse her antilynching work. Then as now, Wells-Barnett determined to "carry on just as I had done," content that "there was going to be a committee which would try to do something in a united and systematic way, because the work was far too large for any one person."[66] As she walked out, New York philanthropist John Milholland (who was white) stopped her in the aisle to say that the list he had seen included her name, suggesting last-minute tinkering. Wells-Barnett and Trotter departed. New York social worker and Du Bois ally Mary White Ovington (who was white) later noted that "their anger as they went out was perhaps justified."[67] Outside on the sidewalk, May Childs Nearny, the meeting's secretary, flagged them down and asked Wells-Barnett to return. Trotter counseled against it but then agreed to see what they wanted. Wells-Barnett's autobiography reports that as she waited outside, Ovington "swept by" her with "an air of triumph and a very pleased look on her face."[68]

Though Wells-Barnett felt antagonized by Ovington, Du Bois was apparently behind the changes. He immediately approached her upon her return and explained his actions. Rev. Celia Parker Woolley would represent Chicago's interracial settlement, the Frederick Douglass Center, to the NAACP. According to Wells-Barnett's version of events, Du Bois "took the liberty" of "substituting" for her name that of Charles Bentley, a respected dentist and personal friend of Du Bois, as the other Chicago delegate. Du Bois wanted Bentley to represent the Niagara Movement, even though the group had been nearly defunct since 1907 and Bentley himself was not even present at the New York meeting. Du Bois may have seen in Wells-Barnett a rival or a disruptive presence who insisted on the primacy of the fight against lynching, about which she was still the most published expert in the country. Or perhaps Du Bois understood some aspects of antilynching to be "women's work" and devalued her contribution to agitation.[69] He likely felt pressure to defer to or perhaps even agreed with individuals like Ovington, who regarded Trotter and Wells-Barnett as "powerful personalities . . . but perhaps not fitted to accept the restraint of organization."[70]

In her autobiography, Wells-Barnett admitted her "anger" at the situation and even her "foolish" reaction to it in walking out. But she was "furiously indignant" with Du Bois and maintained that he "deliberately" intended to "ignore" her and her work.[71] Since key white allies Milholland, Oswald Garrison Villard (grandson of William Lloyd Garrison), and Ovington were strongly motivated to create a national venue for Du Bois, Wells-Barnett's own powerful voice potentially created competition among a core group of colleagues already comfortable assembling together in New York. Milholland tried but failed to persuade Villard to add her name to the Committee of Forty. In a phone call to Wells-Barnett he offered to resign in protest but backed down at her insistence.[72] Apparently Celia Woolley also lobbied Villard on Wells-Barnett's behalf. Ovington understood that Wells-Barnett complained directly to chairman Charles Edward Russell about the omission and that it was he who "quite illegally, but wisely" finally placed her name on the Committee of Forty.[73]

Of course, any gender division of labor in antilynching protest was neither fixed nor absolute. African American women across the country were active members of the Afro-American Council, and now the NAACP, as they were later members in the Universal Negro Improvement Association and the Urban League. At the local level, opinion shapers remained welcoming to female initiative in a variety of spheres, praising both the genteel accomplishments of literary and artistic women as well as the "iconoclastic agitation" of figures like Sojourner Truth and Ida B. Wells-Barnett in the "active world."[74] But elite, East Coast groups like the American Negro Academy and the Niagara Movement excluded women or assigned them to an auxiliary position, reserving high intellectual and political leadership for men.[75] Apart from female-only organizations, formal positions of African American leadership were the province of men; local activism was the province of women. Furthermore, men could claim primacy in both provinces, if they chose, without losing caste. Wells-Barnett's situation suggests that women "unsexed" themselves if they moved out of their proper place. "The hour had come, where was the man?" asked the *Freeman* back in 1894. "Unfortunately, the man was not forth coming—but Miss Wells was!"[76] "We regret we have not a hundred more Ida B. Wells [*sic*] to proclaim and defend the truth," stated the *Christian Recorder* during the early antilynching crusade. "But where, oh where are our leading men?"[77]

While the lines of protest leadership consolidated at the national level, gender distinctions in black resistance often crumbled and dissolved at the grassroots. Day-to-day community life afforded women much more leeway for initiative than did Capitol Hill or the pages of nationally circulated journals of opinion. Since the 1890s, Wells-Barnett had sought to develop the ability of local communities—women, men, and youth—to resist lynching, rather than develop a national antilynching organization under a single leader. In womanist tradition, her approach blended vanguard leadership and grassroots organizing into a flexible style that defied easy categorization.[78] In keeping with traditions of religiously inspired activism by black women, Wells-Barnett's work found its deep purpose in relationship to community. She affirmed her commitment to that relationship every time she went to the scene of a lynching to collect facts, lobby, or protest, as she did at Cairo, Illinois, in the autumn of 1909.

Cairo

"Girl Murdered; Body Mutilated . . . Bloodhounds Capture Four Negroes," announced the *Chicago Tribune* on November 10, 1909. The accompanying article described an Illinois lynching scripted from the Southern archetype. A white woman named Anna Pelley was found murdered in an alley in Cairo, a small town at the southernmost tip of the state, an area settled mostly by white southerners in the nineteenth century. Four African Americans—Arthur Alexander, William "Frog" James, Will Thomas, and "a Negress named Green"—were arrested on suspicion of murder.[79] That night, James was taken from the jail by a mob, and after "confessing" to the crime, he was hanged, his body shot up with bullets, then cut down. His heart was cut from his body, sliced in pieces, and handed out as souvenirs. His body was burned. The mob then removed from the jail one Harry Salzner (who was white) and hanged him. The mob's attempt to remove Alexander, one of James's alleged accomplices, failed. The lynch mob assembled on the steps of the sheriff's office in order to get their man, white women participated in the lynching ("Five Hundred Women Pull Rope"), and federal troops did nothing to quell the disturbance until martial law was declared three days after the killing of James. Preachers in Cairo's white churches that Sunday proclaimed the lynching "necessary."[80]

When the news broke in Chicago, meetings were immediately called and a telegram sent to Republican governor Charles S. Deneen with protest resolutions. In accordance with the Illinois Mob Violence Act of 1905, petitioners requested that Deneen remove Sheriff Frank E. Davis of Alexander County for failing to protect a prisoner in his custody. This was done, but any sheriff so removed had the right to a hearing before the governor to plead for reinstatement. Black activists mobilized to block Davis. Ferdinand Barnett approached his fellow members of Chicago's Appomattox Club (the core black political club that helped elect African American assemblyman Edward Green and draft the anti-mob law) to support the fight against Davis at Cairo.[81] Two Appomattox members had been on a hunting trip in the area during the outbreak and visited Cairo themselves. Apparently they witnessed the usual demoralizing scenes that followed lynchings: scattered clumps of the mob still roving the streets, white people pawing over the corpse for "souvenirs," occasional shots ringing out, armed soldiers on patrol. According to Wells-Barnett, these men despaired over an anticipated "whitewash" of the case and refused her husband's request to testify at the hearing.[82] Another strategy was needed.

In her autobiography, Wells-Barnett cast her family members—and God working through them—in the role of legitimizing her intervention at Cairo, a portrait consonant with club women's commitment to family and faith as politics. Though, as she put it, "some of our men" accused her of "jumping in ahead of them and doing work without giving them a chance," in this particular scenario her husband and even her own child insisted that she do her "duty" and take on the "work that others refuse." After explaining that the investigation was at a dead end in Chicago, Ferdinand directed his wife to Cairo: "And your train leaves at eight o'clock." Here Wells-Barnett "objected very strongly," citing personal inconvenience as well as the sniping that sometimes followed her initiatives. In a rare glimpse into their marriage, the narrative portrays a standoff at the Barnett dinner table over the Cairo strategy, with Ferdinand huffily drawn up behind his newspaper and Ida marching upstairs to put their youngest child to bed. Their eldest, Charles Aked, literally awakened his mother to her duty after she fell asleep with little Alfreda: "Mother," he said, "if you don't go nobody else will." At this point in the account, Wells-Barnett recalled "that passage of Scripture which tells of the wisdom from the mouths of babes and sucklings." She referred here either to Psalms 8:2–3 or to Matthew 21:16, both of which describe "praise" and "glory" to God as springing intuitively from the young. As in her theologizing of the Beatitudes, Wells-Barnett found in this scripture another source of "wisdom" to meet her political situation. The next day her family escorted her to the train station. "They were intensely interested and for the first time were willing to see me leave home," she wrote, justifying her controversial behavior with both familial and scriptural approval, an example of visionary pragmatism in action.[83]

Religion informed Wells-Barnett's subsequent account of events at Cairo. The autobiography describes how she converted the African American community there from a dark state of economic and political dependence to the light of resistance. The city's leading AME minister, Rev. T. A. Head, met Wells-Barnett at the station and took her to his evening service. To Wells-Barnett's surprise, Head's congregation believed that the lynched man, Frog James, was guilty of rape-murder, and the minister had already written to the governor supporting Sheriff Davis's reinstatement. James was an outsider and a drifter; he was neither an ideal hero nor, perhaps, someone the community felt compelled to take risks for. Moreover, some black Republican Party faithfuls in Cairo held coveted patronage posts in Sheriff Davis's office, and they hoped his reinstatement would maintain their political relationships.

Wells-Barnett thus had two tasks: to convince Cairo's black community that a stand against lynching served their long-term political interests and to convince officials that she represented both the truth about Frog James's murder and the genuine sentiments of the local community in opposing Sheriff Davis. To achieve these tasks she abandoned Rev. Head, who did not see things her way, and joined forces with a local businessman, a druggist named Will Taylor, formerly of Chicago. At a quickly assembled meeting, Wells-Barnett described her intention to become the community's "mouthpiece," but it took two hours of discussion to persuade her listeners to oppose Davis. For their part, the pro-Davis forces had circulated petitions favoring his reinstatement in the black community before Wells-Barnett's arrival. She recalled going around to barbershops—typically male provinces—and giving "the most blistering talk that I could lay my tongue to" in order to prevent more individuals from signing. She also conducted interviews and investigations to establish her case for James's innocence. In an echo of her success in Memphis among restive Baptist ministers as opposed to the more staid AME clergy, Wells-Barnett finally convinced Cairo's Baptist churchmen to repudiate their pro-Davis stance and instead sign her petition, a reversal described in the autobiography like a conversion scene. The moderator of the Baptists' meeting proclaimed his new view of the situation thanks to the words of "the sister," and in a tearful confession he offered his support for her case, winning over the assembly to the anti-Davis position.[84]

The autobiography highlights Wells-Barnett's outstanding verbal skills in the male domains of preaching, barbershop debate, and legal advocacy. Using the research that his wife sent up to Chicago, Ferdinand Barnett prepared a brief on James's behalf for the hearing and sent it ahead to Springfield for her to read at the hearing. There Wells-Barnett also had moral support from an African American attorney, A. M. Williams, who sat with her during the hearing and took her into his home. After the first day of hearings, her opponents (who were white) shook hands and complemented Wells-Barnett on her fine arguments and speech. On the last day, these men "swept off [their] hats" at her approach up the courthouse steps. Another conversion had taken place; they recognized Wells-Barnett's womanly dignity and her intelligence, no mean feat in an era in which whites did not extend social courtesies to any black woman. The two sides finally agreed to stipulate the facts and submit a single version to the governor for a decision. The Barnetts had a friend at court in the governor, having worked closely with Deneen's faction of the Republican Party for over a decade.[85] On 6 December, Deneen handed down his decision not to reinstate Davis. The governor agreed that the sheriff had failed to carry out his duty to protect his prisoners. He affirmed Wells-Barnett's argument that a reinstatement would legitimate mob violence and pave the way for more lynching and riots in Illinois.[86]

Like her antilynching crusade in the 1890s, Wells-Barnett's terrific success at Cairo produced a flutter of reactions shot through with gender significance. A Springfield paper described her as "assuming the position of mother protector" in the case.[87] Some African American editors waxed romantic. "Why wouldn't the race be proud of such a woman?" asked the *Freeman*. "She is fit to be a queen."[88] But a sour note was also sounded. Wells-Barnett's initiative still potentially put men in an unflattering light. The *Chicago Defender* exclaimed: "If we only had a few men with the backbone of Mrs. Barnett, lynching would soon come to a halt in America." Here the *Defender* expressed the kind of sentiment that, in a less generous moment, could feed the backlash against women who "jumped in ahead" of men. In a show of appreciation, however, black Chicagoans took up a collection to defray some of Wells-Barnett's expenses incurred in the fight at Cairo.[89]

More Political Meanings

The leadership of the fledgling NAACP was, according to Wells-Barnett, chagrined by her success at Cairo. Her autobiography noted a rather sheepish letter from John Milholland admitting that her victory at Cairo was "the most outstanding thing done for the race during the year."[90] He wanted her to come to New York to address the Committee in March 1910. She agreed only after the organization consented to pay her expenses. At this second annual meeting, Wells-Barnett functioned as a guest speaker rather than an insider, even though her name still appeared on the roster of the Committee of Forty and on official stationery.[91]

Her address in New York described the Cairo fight as a textbook on how to end lynching and mob violence. Her remarks, "How Enfranchisement Stops Lynching," showcased the importance of black political power and the broad principle of self-defense. She made this case without relying on the rhetoric of "manhood" that she and Du Bois had shared a few years earlier. Instead, she stressed practical politics: African Americans had elected a black legislator, Edward Green, to the Illinois state house in 1904; had helped draft the mob violence act of 1905 and lobbied for its passage; and had then created the pressure to have the law enforced at Cairo. Her prediction that the effective enforcement of the law in Illinois had "given lynching its death blow in this State" unfortunately was far too sanguine.[92]

So were Wells-Barnett's hopes that the NAACP would support her local work against lynching. Less than a year after Cairo, New York officials failed to contribute to or publicly credit her efforts to aid a black refugee from Arkansas named Steve Green, who had fled the country to avoid a lynch mob.[93] In April 1911, Wells-Barnett was left out of a Chicago NAACP branch planning meeting. "Both Mr. Villard and Prof. Du Bois gave me the impression they rather feared some interference from me in the Chicago arrangements," she wrote to a sympathetic Joel Spingarn, professor at Columbia University and member of the Committee of Forty. Wells-Barnett felt that "the exclusive academic few" on the executive committee preferred to "bask in the light" of famous figures like Jane Addams rather than to do the difficult and unglamorous work of advocacy in the backwoods and barbershops of the nation. "Of course I am not very popular with the exclusive few," she concluded, "and I can not say that I look with equanimity upon their patronizing assumptions."[94] Wells-Barnett also complained about Mary Ovington's personality and the intellectual snobbery of the New York crowd. Ovington revealed a grating attitude in her comments on black club women: "Negro women enjoy organization. They are ambitious for power, often jealous, very sensitive. But they get things done."[95] Wells-Barnett felt that Ovington "made little effort to know the soul of the black woman" which prevented her from "helping a race which has suffered as no white woman has ever been called upon to suffer or to understand."[96]

As ties to the NAACP frayed and broke, Wells-Barnett cast about for ways to maintain support for her work. In March 1910, she affiliated with another interracial New York group, the short-lived Original Rights Society. She may have been approached by her former pastor at Chicago's Bethel AME Church, Reverdy Ransom, recently relocated to the East and now a Society member, for help in setting up a branch of the organization. The "original rights" to which the Society directed itself were the basic civil rights possessed by each citizen, rights that were now underserved and lacking protection by a trained leadership. The Society's official statement of aims urged that "those gifted with intelligence and will power and character should be trained along the lines of political morality and in social sciences into statesmen" and lamented, "The lack of statesmanship is now the bane of American society."[97] This focus probably attracted figures like Ransom and Wells-Barnett, talented individuals who lacked a firm institutional base or constituency. It is likely, too, that Wells-Barnett appreciated the openly political stance of the group as opposed to that of the officially nonpartisan NAACP: "We are in politics," stated the Society, "in the ideal and to a purpose." She wrote a long letter to the *Defender* soliciting members. In a clear dig at the NAACP, she wrote: "This is the only fair and square invitation the Negro has had from any white organization to join them on equal terms, and I repeat, that for this reason if for no others, we should accept."[98] In June, the Society published Wells-Barnett's NAACP speech "How Enfranchisement Stops Lynching" in their new *Original Rights Magazine*.

In the pages of this journal Wells-Barnett also offered an assessment of African American women's status in the North, perhaps seeking to reestablish ties and credibility with organized black women in the region. Her essay "The Northern Negro Woman's Social and Moral Condition," published in April 1910, was a somber appraisal. She stressed how racial proscription and "caste influences" injured both middle- and working-class black women by denying them access to decent jobs, housing, and education, as well as to outlets for culture and recreation. Rather than sound an alarm over the predominance of black women in urban employments, as did Kelly Miller, Wells-Barnett echoed club women's writing, praising the "mother-love" that motivated their paid and unpaid work. Women with advantages helped build institutions like orphanages or Old Folks' Homes. Women without advantages also labored hard, and Wells-Barnett noted that "it is the toil of the women which keeps the family together after the men have grown discouraged." "If slavery could not crush mother-love out of the hearts of Negro women," she insisted, "the race prejudice of the present cannot do it." Finally, Wells-Barnett addressed the prevalent negative stereotypes of black women. She criticized those who "like the naturalist" observing insects, generalized about African American women from a single negative example. "Such logic confounds itself with all fair-minded persons," she wearily concluded.[99]

At least one northern club woman responded. Elizabeth C. Carter of Massachusetts, president of the NACW, invited Wells-Barnett to the club women's biennial convention in Louisville that summer. Carter, also an NAACP member, asked Wells-Barnett to update the NACW on the new organization. It was Wells-Barnett's first appearance at a biennial convention since 1899, when tensions between Chicago and Washington, D.C., women resulted in her exclusion from the proceedings.[100] Wells-Barnett went to Louisville as an official delegate representing the Ideal Woman's Club of Chicago, a group she cofounded in 1908. She sat with the Illinois delegation and was assigned to the resolutions committee of the convention.[101]

The event was plagued by hot weather as well as the unwieldy size of the sessions. The NACW was outgrowing its original structure and format. Time was spent reading reports from clubs and departments rather than discussing policy and conducting business. The tone of the group had also changed. The NACW was somewhat less adventuresome in supporting advanced political positions or controversial causes. In the first decade of the twentieth century, the issues of antilynching, the convict-lease system, and suffrage were muted in its agenda.[102] Some critics pointed out that even the uncontroversial goal of funding kindergartens for black children had not been met and that the most talented, educated women were no longer leaders or participants. Wells-Barnett walked into a group that for the moment was as disinclined as it was divided over politics.[103]

As usual, her skillful address generated excitement; she was swamped with requests for NAACP literature. Near the end of the conference, a particularly vigorous report was read regarding *The National Notes*, the NACW's publication, which pointed out problems with accounting for the journal's funds, spotty publication, and the unaccountability of its appointed editor. Inspired by the positive reception of the club women and fresh from discussions in New York about the NAACP's new journal, *The Crisis*, Wells-Barnett could not resist intervening. She stepped on dangerous ground. *National Notes* had been run for fourteen years by Margaret Murray Washington, wife of Booker. In the resolutions committee, Wells-Barnett proposed more rigorous and independent reporting, expanded and consistent distribution, and the election of its editor by the NACW membership. She moved that the report be adopted for action. The motion passed. Then President Carter ruled Wells-Barnett out of order, since reports were to be dealt with in the upcoming year by officers, rather than by the convention itself. Wells-Barnett objected to the ruling and asked for an appeal. Here the convention seems to have lost patience—temperance leader Lucy Thurman, in particular—and Wells-Barnett was booed from the floor. "Upon my head rained a storm of disapproval," Wells-Barnett remarked in her autobiography, and embarrassing headlines—"Hisses for Mrs. Barnett"—ran in the press. Totally humiliated, she went home to bed, skipping the banquet that was the social highlight of the biennial.[104]

In the 1890s, Wells-Barnett successfully played upon her status as a cultural insider/outsider, her southernness and exile, in order to gain an international hearing. Now she was left out both among the college-educated, socially connected male professionals whose star rose with progressivism as well as among the distaff side of reform, the women's club movement. While Wells-Barnett earned praise as a "race woman" for putting the interests of the community ahead of all other considerations in her work, she still earned criticism for pushing herself forward to make that case. In their pioneer sociological study of black Chicago, completed in 1940, St. Clair Drake and Horace R. Cayton point out in a telling footnote that African Americans tended to "be more trustful of the Race Woman," because she "can't capitalize on her activities like a Race Man."[105] This standard of selflessness could be a burden, if not a contradiction, and in a context that celebrated male forcefulness and deprived women of economic and political power, assertive female behavior could be easily dismissed as tedious or overreaching.

Men much more easily than women cast themselves as either brave and rebellious or simply objective and disinterested. Du Bois translated opposition to Booker T. Washington into a professional career in literature and reform at *The Crisis*. For Wells-Barnett, such opposition proved disastrous. When she publicly criticized Tuskegee back in 1900, Washington (oddly using her unmarried name) smugly reported that "Miss Wells" was "fast making herself so ridiculous that every body is getting tired of her."[106] Former supporter Monroe Majors, now, by 1909, in Washington's camp, offered a disingenuous critique: "Mrs. Barnett is not fair," he stated in the press. "She goes forth to battle with only a loud cry. She has neither argument, logic nor sober sense to conduct her through the labyrinth of the difficulties she would move in the twinkling of an eye."[107] Even the facts, long the backbone of her antilynching arguments, no longer delivered much political punch. T. Thomas Fortune rolled his eyes in the *Age*: "Mrs. Ida Wells-Barnett is always full of lynchings and the figures thereof, which never lie and never grow fewer in number" but which somehow never added up to much.[108] The assimilation of Wells-Barnett's antilynching facts to social science discourse blunted the need for a special spokesperson on lynching, especially a black woman.

After her frustrations with the NAACP and NACW, Wells-Barnett had perhaps little to lose in directly opening fire on Booker T. Washington. In a Chicago press interview discussing the NACW biennial that summer of 1910, she made a blistering indictment of Washington, dubbing his "doctrine of non-resistance" as the "most dangerous menace to the race today."[109] Wells-Barnett's anger was a source of personal strength as well as a political liability, since it rankled decorous notions of ladyhood valued by many of her colleagues as well as potentially provoked hostile whites.[110] It certainly set her apart from Booker T. Washington, who, his biographer notes, conspicuously lacked "the capacity for righteous public anger against injustice."[111] Her anger also distanced her from progressives, who generally recoiled at violence and whose sensibilities tended toward pacifism and antimilitarism, as in the case of Du Bois, Addams, and Terrell.[112] "Death may be at your doors," Wells-Barnett warned a Chicago audience in 1906. "Go ready for a fight. Fight when the time comes. . . . Guard your colored women and if need be die for them."[113] In a period of gender retrenchment in elite reform circles, Wells-Barnett's anger made her vulnerable to being ridiculed as unfeminine or being dismissed as a naïve "bull in a China shop."[114]

If Wells-Barnett underestimated Tuskegee's power to divide and conquer through political and financial patronage, she certainly tried to compete with the new professional experts and social scientists who now shaped protest at the national level. In her comments at the founding NAACP sessions, she pointedly distinguished between "our people" who were unable to see "things from a scientific standpoint" and those who had the "training necessary to see abstract things," clearly aligning herself with the latter.[115] She did so by claiming specialized local knowledge, much as did "Exiled" or the "southern girl, born and bred." "I hope you will not think me egotistic when I tell you I know the Negro in New York as well as I know him in Chicago," she wrote to Joel Spingarn, "because it has been my good province to work among and with them for the past 18 years. This knowledge and experience, I am always glad to offer to any one whom I believe to be sincerely interested in the race's welfare."[116] Wells-Barnett's claim to expertise was out of date, as academic credentials now trumped experience and wisdom gained in the school of life.

As she had in the 1890s, Wells-Barnett tried to work her social marginality to an advantage for the cause and to maintain her foothold as a nationally recognized authority on lynching. The arguments in her 1913 article in *The Survey*, a national organ of professional social work, were as up-to-date as any the NAACP produced in the coming decade.[117] Although the overall number of lynchings had dropped from a high of 241 in 1892 to 65 in 1912, the justification of lynching as punishment for rape still gripped the public's imagination. In "Our Country's Lynching Record," Wells-Barnett pointed out the appalling fact that the lynching-for-rape excuse could be heard from the mouths of brazenly racist elected officials like Governor Cole Blease of Georgia. She offered a statistical analysis to show that the percentage of rape charges in recorded lynchings had dropped even further, from one-third to one-sixth, yet the facts hardly seemed to matter now. Anticipating the fiftieth anniversary of the Emancipation Proclamation, Wells-Barnett posed one of her classic questions to the reader at the end of the *Survey* article: "Does it seem too much to ask white civilization, Christianity and Democracy to be true to themselves on this as all other questions?"[118]

The answer continued to be yes. Moreover, it seemed that white America did not want to hear. They barely noticed, and then dismissed, Moton's *Negro Yearbook*. "It is an effective way Tuskegee has of putting out the lynching statistics, with absolutely no comment," sighed a patronizing *Harper's Weekly* in 1916. "How much more effective these facts are than any talk about them can be."[119] This attitude made a horrendous situation all the more galling given the many, many spoken and written words of Wells-Barnett and others on the subject of lynching since the 1890s. In July 1917, African Americans staged an eloquent response to the feigned deafness of the United States with a silent protest parade against lynching and race riots down Fifth Avenue in New York City.[120]

As the pageantry of the protest parade suggests, World War I created openings for new forms of resistance against lynching. African Americans' successful military service and the spread of woman suffrage at the state level also offered activists new leverage for political change. The migration of a half million southern African Americans to northern cities tipped electoral demographics in places like New York, Philadelphia, and Chicago. Booker T. Washington's death silenced a powerful conservative voice and shifted the Tuskegee political machine into neutral. The war effort and military service especially heightened expectations of respect and equality at home among African Americans. As Du Bois famously put it: "*We return. We return from fighting. We return fighting.*"[121]

In this period, too, however, manhood became further entrenched in the symbolics of black protest. Gender and manhood had been prominent elements in antilynching discourse before 1917, but as the United

FIGURE 11. "Loyalty."
Richmond (Va.) Planet, 16
June 1917

States entered the war, the black soldier literally moved to the front and center of the discussion, as the image from the *Richmond Planet* suggests (see Figure 11). As legitimate wielders of force in the nation's service, black soldiers protected both the black community and American society, exhibiting both the manly restraint of Victorian constructions of manhood as well as more modern martial masculinity. Echoing Wells-Barnett's pamphlets as well as the "Niagara men's" rhetoric of manhood, the *Planet* represented manly sacrifice through images of battlefield triumph and Christ-like martyrdom (see Figure 12). But unlike Wells-Barnett's early work, the *Planet* left black women on the sidelines or out of the picture altogether. In 1916, the year the NAACP officially launched its own antilynching crusade, the NAACP pamphlet *The Waco Horror*, describing the horrific burning a sixteen-year-old black boy in Texas, appended a brief table entitled "Colored Men Lynched by Years."[122]

This accent on men and manhood in national antilynching discourse obscured the more complex situation at the grassroots level, where women continued to act and resist attack. "Men have failed," stated one reporter in the *Chicago Defender* in 1915. "It is up to the women to protect their homes, as the sons and fathers and brothers refuse to do it."[123] When a mob searched out a boy in a black neighborhood for a

FIGURE 12. "Not Kultur But Americans Passed This Way." *Richmond (Va.) Planet*, 22 November 1919

lynching in Louisiana in 1916, the paper noted that "several girls and women of the Race saw the mob coming and they hid the children till things cooled down. They jeered the mob and refused to run. The men were at the mills working."[124] When human life was at stake, African Americans resisted by any means necessary. In the aftermath of lynchings, however, and particularly when community prestige was at stake (as in the scenarios of war and patriotism), gender expectations structured ideal responses. The *Defender* lamented the rarity of black men's forcible resistance to mobs, which required fighting unto death. "Since there are no men, women come to the front; protect the weaklings that still wear the pants from the lynch mobs."[125] Black women were expected to be strong, even giants, for the race (see Figures 13 and 14) even as war put the spotlight on men. Nowhere were the unsettled dynamics of black resistance to violence more visible than in two major urban race riots of the period, both of which occurred in Illinois.

Illinois Race Riots

To Wells-Barnett, the events at East St. Louis combined some of the worst racist elements of conflicts in which black self-defense was defined as criminal and punished. At the center of the East St. Louis case was Dr. Leroy Bundy, described by Wells-Barnett as a "high-spirited young professional man" who combined the enterprising bent of Tom

FIGURE 13. "East St. Louis Riot." The caption for this cartoon asked, "Mr. President, why not make America safe for democracy?" Though women in Illinois could vote for president, the black mother here is portrayed as a kneeling supplicant. Cartoon by Morris, in *New York Evening Mail*, 1917; reprinted in *Current Opinion* 63, no. 2 (August 1917): 77

FIGURE 14. "Woman to the Rescue!" was the title of this cartoon, which portrayed the African American woman as a giant and defender of the race, armed with the political rights of the federal constitution. *The Crisis* (May 1916): 43

Moss with the fearlessness of Robert Charles.[126] On the night of 2 July 1917, a car full of plainclothes police cruised the African American neighborhood of East St. Louis and began shooting into homes. When a group organized for self-defense shot back and killed a white officer, an attack on the black community ensued. In three days of rioting, 39 African Americans were killed and at least 100 injured. It was a bloody climax to a season of intense labor strife and mounting racial tensions in the area. A protest memorial against the violence at East St. Louis, drafted in Chicago and sent by Wells-Barnett to state officials, captured the dilemma of African Americans in war time: "As American Citizens our lives are subjected to the Nation's call, and at no call have we faltered or failed. As American citizens we call to the Nation to save our lives; to that call will the Nation falter or fail?"[127]

Wells-Barnett took an active, if little noted, role in the three phases of response to the terrible events at East St. Louis. She mobilized public opinion in Illinois, demanding from officials a full investigation and fair prosecution of the guilty.[128] Through publicity and fundraising, she also aided the Bundy defense effort during his trial as a ringleader of the so-called negro rioters who were convicted and sentenced after the outbreak. Finally, Wells-Barnett added her voice to the call for federal investigation and publicity about the horrors of the riot (see Figure 15).[129] She made two trips to East St. Louis, one immediately after the riot, in company with Mrs. Delores Johnson Farrow (a nurse from Chicago) and one in November to meet with Bundy in jail. The latter visit revealed to her that the NAACP and Bundy were at loggerheads over his defense. Wells-Barnett's reports in the *Defender* exemplified the widespread grassroots support for Bundy as the "hero" of East St. Louis, fanning skepticism toward the NAACP's more measured and critical approach to his case.[130]

Her investigations resulted in a pamphlet, *The East St. Louis Massacre: The Greatest Outrage of the Century*, whose title stated the proportions of the crime in no uncertain terms. Grisly details from the scene, testimony from survivors, and newspaper clips in the pamphlet drove home the gruesome fact that "a black skin was a death warrant" during the riot. The "saddest part" of the story for Wells-Barnett was the passive complicity of law enforcement and military personnel, who let the mob tear around at will. She led a committee of Chicago protesters to Governor Lowden of Illinois with her findings and was met by the patronizing, burden-shifting attitude that so infuriated her. After the interview, the committee was given parting advice "against incendiary talk." In the pamphlet's telling, Lowden was treated to vintage Wells-Barnett: "The writer told him that if he had seen women whose husbands had been beaten to death, whose children had been thrown into the flames and in the river, whose women had been burned to death, he would not say it was incendiary talk to denounce such outrages."[131] The federal government went one better than the state of Illinois. Military intelligence picked up on Wells-Barnett's investigative work and, citing the pam-

FIGURE 15. "1917." In this cartoon, the grief and redemptive hope of African American people are represented by the female figure "Ethiopia." Her posture and classical garb evoke the biblical promise, "Ethiopia shall again stretch forth her hands unto God." Behind Ethiopia and the tomb of the nation's lynching victims, a buried but still live investigation of mob activity lies beneath a weeping willow tree, symbolizing the unreleased report produced by the federal government on the race riot in East St. Louis. In the background, a weak sun rises over the capitol dome, the dawn of 1918. *Washington Bee*, 22 June 1918

phlet as "being used to stir up a great deal of inter-racial antagonism," put her under surveillance.[132]

Given the national attention focused on this racial clash, a victory for Leroy Bundy would have enhanced the status and legitimacy of one of several elements within the ranks of black protest: the NAACP, Bundy himself, Wells-Barnett and her Chicago Citizens Committee, or Trotter's Equal Rights League, which also weighed in on the defense effort. Of these, Bundy came out best, but just barely. As fearful for his life as he was headstrong in his determination to win and live, Bundy was found guilty of conspiracy in March 1919, a decision eventually reversed by the Illinois Supreme Court and not retried.[133] The NAACP had withdrawn from the case six months earlier, having been unable to come to terms with Bundy over his political mistakes (like a partial jailhouse confession to the state's attorney) and his desire to retain independence in fundraising.[134] Through public appearances and personal appeals, Bundy raised most of the money for his defense, testimony to the effectiveness of the grassroots approach. He survived his ordeal to reopen his dental practice in Cleveland. The lessons of East St. Louis were clear to Wells-Barnett, who celebrated the strength of local initiative and publicity. "[W]hether or not [Bundy] appreciates the work done by the Chicago *Defender* in his behalf," she later wrote, "the wide publicity which was given to his case by the *Defender* is the largest cause of his being a free man today."[135] She was far less disappointed with Bundy than with state's attorney Edward Brundage, whom she never forgave for prosecuting the so-called black conspirators more severely than the whites, who overwhelmingly did most of the killing at East St. Louis.[136]

East St. Louis was at best a neutral and at worst a lost opportunity for the NAACP's new antilynching campaign just underway as of 1916. The Chicago branch never entered the fray. Wells-Barnett remained ambivalent about the NAACP and distant from the Chicago branch, whose thin ranks were perennially thick with Tuskegee supporters.[137] Local officers, including attorney Edward Osgood Brown (who was white), felt remote from doings in the southern part of the state and seemed eager to kick the case up to the federal level.[138] Several scholars have puzzled over the NAACP's weakness in Chicago, citing reasons ranging from elitism and inertia to ideological differences.[139] While these factors no doubt played their part, several other important issues are hinted at by Wells-Barnett's intervention at East St. Louis. Black Chicagoans had two major institutions at their disposal to accomplish the work of publicity and legal intervention promised by the NAACP. First was the *Defender*, the premier African American newspaper of the era whose circulation surpassed that of *The Crisis* by at least 40 percent. The *Defender's* credibility, especially among working-class black readers North and South, was far greater than that of *The Crisis*, which had a somewhat more elite and racially mixed subscriber base.[140]

Second was the Cook County Bar Association (CCBA), founded in 1915 and comprised of black attorneys in the city. The CCBA functioned both as a legal defense arm for African American citizens and as a political launchpad for ambitious office seekers, welcoming its first female member in 1920.[141] With the trusted Wells-Barnett leading the way, the *Defender* and the CCBA could deliver national publicity, legal talent, and political patronage directly to black Chicago, neither of which the nonpartisan NAACP could rival in 1917.[142] Black Chicago's own resources made a rescue squad from New York at the very least redundant, if not insulting. As a result of Wells-Barnett's interview with Bundy while he was in prison, for example, her husband became one of his attorneys.[143] As they had during the Cairo fight, Ida and Ferdinand, himself an early and active member of the CCBA, regularly worked as a team in such cases, with the *Defender* tracking and trumpeting their successes.[144] Politically minded attorneys Barnett and S. Laing Williams, as well as Edward H. Wright and Edward Green, all achieved appointive or elective political office before 1910 through local networks and institutions; women like Wells-Barnett also found a powerful voice. New black women voters put another lawyer, Oscar DePriest, on the Chicago City Council in 1915 and eventually sent him to Congress in 1928, the first African American elected to that office from any region since the nineteenth century.[145] In these years, the *Defender*'s editor Robert S. Abbott broadcast the notion that Chicago and "The World's Greatest Weekly" could teach the world a thing or two. African Americans across the nation listened and agreed. One southern migrant testified about the city and Abbott's paper: "Everything is just like they say, if not better."[146]

For these reasons, the Chicago race riot of 1919 was especially devastating. To be sure, conditions had been deteriorating for years. Inadequate housing, schools, and recreational facilities for southern migrants, labor unrest, and crackdowns against radicals all fed an atmosphere of suspicion and violence in the city. Wells-Barnett wrote prophetically in early July of scattered beatings, killings, and bombings by white hoodlums and "sporting clubs" designed to intimidate blacks. "It was just such a situation as this which led up to the East St. Louis riot two years ago," she warned in a letter to the *Chicago Tribune*. "Will the legal, moral, and civic forces of this town stand idly by and take no notice here of these preliminary outbreaks? I implore Chicago to set the wheels of justice in motion before it is too late, and Chicago be disgraced by some of the bloody outrages that have disgraced East St. Louis."[147] But on 27 July 1919, police stood idly by when a black youth was stoned and drowned at the Twenty-fifth Street beach, touching off four days of violence that left 23 blacks and 15 whites dead, over 500 people injured, and many homeless.[148]

Hand-to-hand combat between blacks and whites using stones, knives, bats, and guns marked the Chicago riot as a turning point in U.S. race relations. As in East St. Louis, whites did most of the murder and did it on the offensive, traveling by car into black neighborhoods on the South Side looking for people to hurt and kill. But also as in East St. Louis, African Americans resisted forcibly and did some serious damage as well. For her part, Wells-Barnett was "out on the streets every day" during the riot.[149] Her daughter Alfreda recalled the Chicago riot this way: "My mother went out every day looking for trouble sites and never did get into one. But she went out every day." Alfreda slyly intimates here that her mother, at age fifty-seven, was still the fearless investigator.[150] "She kept a pistol available in the house," the daughter later wrote, "and dared anyone to cross her threshold to harm her or any member of her family."[151] This evidence, plus the fact that the Barnetts aided and counseled riot victims in their home at 3624 Grand Street near the thick of the violence, suggests that Wells-Barnett probably packed protection on the street.

In the riot's aftermath, Wells-Barnett put her investigative skills to work, taking testimony from victims and then herself appearing before a grand jury.[152] Again black women met the challenge of resistance. They did so through a Women's Committee organized by Wells-Barnett to collect funds for the legal defense of African Americans involved in the riot, and they joined the local Peace and Protective Association.[153] As discussed in Chapter 1, Wells-Barnett's departure from the Protective Association in protest over the service of Edward Brundage in the state's investigation suggests the clergy's unwelcoming stance toward women in political matters traditionally reserved for men. Secular leaders initially anticipated that woman suffrage would redound to the advantage of clergy in politics, but the ministers knew better than to rely on reflexive female support. They seem to have closed ranks, breaking with Wells-Barnett as a way to head off open or protracted conflict.[154]

In her autobiography, Wells-Barnett indicates that the Protective Association's rejection wounded her, but her willingness to challenge clergy was neither new nor unusual. Her decision to leave the organization might also point to opportunities to affiliate with other promising political associations. Specifically, these were the Boston-based Equal Rights League (ERL) and Marcus Garvey's Universal Negro Improvement Association (UNIA). The ERL was mainly Monroe Trotter's bully pulpit, but he and the organization were consistently militant and vocal throughout this period in a way that Wells-Barnett appreciated.[155] She was also optimistic about Garvey's abilities. When he visited the United States in 1918, Garvey's stop in Chicago included a visit to Ferdinand's law office and dinner at the Barnett home.[156] In December 1918, Wells-Barnett traveled to Baltimore to address the UNIA, again drawing the attention of military intelligence monitoring "Negro Subversion." The spy noted "[n]othing of interest" in her address, remarking only that Wells-Barnett's reputation was better established and more radical than the Jamaican's. She was, he reported, a "far more dangerous agitator than Marcus Garvey." The military advised caution in granting her a passport.[157] Both the UNIA and ERL nominated Wells-Barnett as a delegate to the Peace Conference in Versailles. The ERL even agreed to fund her trip and that of another female delegate, Madame C. J. Walker, but Wells-Barnett noted that "President Wilson forbade" them to leave the country.[158]

When black soldiers detained in the wake of a riot in Houston, Texas, were convicted, sentenced, and thirteen secretly hung by a military court in late 1917, Wells-Barnett was outraged. Chicago clergy, probably leery of the taint of disloyalty in wartime, declined her appeal to hold a memorial service for the dead men. Instead, Wells-Barnett distributed buttons commemorating the "martyred Negro soldiers" through the Negro Fellowship League (see Figure 16). Either looking for a story or encouraged by authorities to report suspicious activities (or both), a local reporter came poking around Wells-Barnett's settlement house, asking questions about the buttons. Soon after leaving, agents from a "secret service bureau" appeared at the door with the reporter in tow. The agents tried to rattle Wells-Barnett with accusations of "treason," at which she bridled. Seizing the moment to be heard in the press, *Crusade for Justice* recorded the following declaration to the assembled: "I'd rather go down in history as one lone Negro who dared to tell the government that it had done a dastardly thing than to save my skin by taking back what I have said. I would consider it an honor to spend whatever years are necessary in prison as the one member of the race who protested, rather than to be with all the 11,999,999 Negroes who didn't have to go to prison because they kept their mouths shut." She closed the scene with a theatrical flourish: "Lay on, Macduff, and damn'd be him that first cries 'Hold enough!'"[159] Here Wells-Barnett claims for herself not Lady Macbeth's role but the Duke's own doomed ambition to fight to the end. While the autobiography played up personal sacrifice, the contemporary press account of this incident stressed the soldiers' martyr status as well as white fears of retaliation for the executions from black military personnel. The *Chicago Herald* reporter received a tour of Christmas boxes destined for black soldiers in training at Illinois's Camp Rockford, which were being stored at the Negro Fellowship League. He also was treated to a classic interrogatory from

Memorial Button To Negro Rioters

Reproduction of button prepared for sale by Mrs. Ida Wells Barnett.

FIGURE 16. "Memoriam: Martyred Negro Soldiers." *Chicago Sunday Herald*, 23 December 1917

Wells-Barnett: "Does it look to you as if I would go out and offer seditious literature and propaganda to others of my race to kill their own soldiers?" Here she apparently stressed her sex and the gifts as evidence of caregiving and patriotism rather than violent or treasonous intent. "No," she concluded, "it is just a feeling I have that I think something ought to be done for our race."[160]

The problem with such media appearances—as well as with the Equal Rights League and Garvey—was that Wells-Barnett's expertise on the lynching question was going to waste. Antilynching was not the main focus of either the ERL or the UNIA. As the outcomes after East St. Louis and Houston demonstrated, however, the new dynamics of lynching and racial violence made time-honored propaganda efforts seem woefully inadequate. Antilynching now involved challenging government dispensations of justice, including the use of the death penalty, and moved even more firmly into the technical areas of law, politics, and bureaucratic administration. Aided by her husband, Wells-Barnett successfully intervened in these spheres locally in Illinois, exemplified by the fight at Cairo in 1909. But by the decade's end, the scale of lawlessness, rioting, and legal lynchings moved beyond the individual's reach, stretching all the way to the nation's capital. The scope, complexity, and high symbolic stakes involved in executions by the state came together in the case of another unlucky group of black captives: a group of twelve farmers from Arkansas sentenced to die in the electric chair in October 1919. The denouement to their case—the NAACP triumphant and Wells-Barnett ignored—capped a decade of struggle over resistance to mob rule that finally gave the edge to mostly male, elite professionals in New York.

Arkansas

Late on the night of 1 October 1919, a motor car containing the sheriff and several trusties pulled up at a black church near the rural village of Hoop Spur in Phillips County, eastern Arkansas. A meeting of the Progressive Farmers and Householders Union was in session with about 100 African American men, women, and children inside. After months of searching for an opportunity to break up rural organizing in Phillips County, the sheriff was looking for a fight. He created one, but he got one, too. Armed guards posted outside the church returned the shots fired, killing one of the sheriff's men. The posse then opened fire, and as many as twenty people were killed inside the church, which was burned the next day to destroy evidence of the slaughter. Upon the report of violence in Hoop Spur and of related arrests in the town of Ratio, the governor ordered black citizens disarmed and called for federal troops. The disarming of Phillips County became a spree of violence, aided at points by the Third Division of the U.S. Army. Scores of people were chased from their homes and farms, which were then looted of goods and crops. People hiding in the swamps and woods were hunted down and shot. Over 200 African Americans were jailed, including several women.[161] An official report written by a committee handpicked by the governor dubbed the original meeting at the Hoop Spur church a black conspiracy to kill whites. At a trial that made a farce of due process (the jury deliberated only a few minutes), twelve black men were found guilty of murder and were sentenced to die. Seventy-six others received sentences ranging from one to twenty-one years at hard labor.[162]

The defense of the Arkansas farmers marked a major turning point in the history of antilynching protest in the United States. Unlike in the Bundy defense, this time a black Arkansas group, the Citizens' Defense Fund Commission (CDFC), and the NAACP successfully partnered to supply the funds and legal talent—attorneys Scipio Africanus Jones (who was black) and Moorefield Storey (who was white)—to secure the release of the condemned men. The fight cost thousands of dollars, took three years, and ended in the Supreme Court. This major victory against lynching stabilized the reputation and fundraising ability of the NAACP and definitively launched the career of Walter F. White as the country's new premier authority on lynching. This historical juncture in antilynching produced neither a contest nor a ceremonial mantle passing between Wells-Barnett and White. It was a blind eclipse.

In 1919, White was a 24-year-old recent graduate of Atlanta University, who left a brief stint in the insurance business to throw himself into the work of the NAACP, first in Georgia and then in New York. After the Arkansas case, he wrote numerous articles and pamphlets on lynching, including a novel, *Fire in the Flint* (1924), and *Rope and Faggot: A Biography of Judge Lynch* (1929), the latter completed with a Guggenheim Fellowship and considered a landmark monograph on the subject.[163] By contrast, Arkansas was Wells-Barnett's swan song. Her 62-page pamphlet, *The Arkansas Race Riot* (1920), was printed at her own expense and did not circulate widely. She never again turned her pen to a sustained treatment of racial violence until she wrote her autobiography. Wells-Barnett and White nearly crossed paths in Arkansas when they went undercover as journalists to get the Phillips County story. Had they met on the streets of Little Rock or Helena, however, neither would have recognized the other. Even if they had, they could not have let on. Each was passing—White for a Caucasian and Wells-Barnett for an inconspicuous country woman.

With the help of Chicago NAACP officer Charles Bentley, White secured correspondent status with the *Chicago Daily News* to pursue the story in Arkansas. The light-skinned, blue-eyed Walter White obtained interviews with Governor Charles Brough and other influential Arkansas whites. Though he fooled the governor and others for a couple of days, a black man in Helena alerted White that his identity had been discovered and that a mob was assembling to take his life. White immediately fled by train, but he had gotten his story. His article came out in the *Daily News* on 18 October, was picked up by other papers, and transmitted across the country. *The Nation* magazine's version was reprinted as a pamphlet, and the NAACP distributed more than 1,000 copies.[164]

At the heart of White's exposé was the information he received from the governor and a local white attorney named U.S. Bratton. Bratton's firm had been retained by black farmers and croppers who sought aid in avoiding local landowners and merchants in order to sell their cotton independently, and thus more profitably, in the boom market that year. In addition to the background provided by Bratton, White also reported on the torture of black prisoners in Helena—beatings, electric shocks, and the use of burning inhalants—to extract confessions about "murder" and "conspiracy" against white people. White told of the murder of at least twenty-five blacks in the county sweep by white deputies after the initial shooting at Hoop Spur. Later revelations included the assassination of the four Johnson boys, brothers and independent businessmen who were apprehended while on a fishing trip during the sweep, taken to the woods, and shot. The total number of people killed, injured, robbed, or harmed in the riot grew to around 200, with depredations committed mostly by posses of whites who came from all over the state to join in the sweep of the area, but some few by federal troops as well.[165]

The NAACP's initial publicity succeeded, but assembling the legal defense was more difficult and had to be kept silent. Secrecy was maintained for about a year due to widespread prejudice against the organization among southern whites and to prevent the destabilizing effect of outsiders on the efforts of the CDFC, whose efforts were essential to securing a fair trial in Arkansas. The initial slowness and secrecy of the defense likely prompted Wells-Barnett to write a public letter in mid-December 1919 in the *Defender* urging a national fundraising initiative for the incarcerated men. "The principle at stake involves every one of us—the right to organize for our own protection!" exclaimed Wells-Barnett. "The man or woman who does not see that does not deserve the liberty he or she enjoys."[166] In response to her statements, one of the Arkansas prisoners wrote her a personal letter of gratitude. "So I thank God that thro you, our Negroes are looking into this trouble, and thank the city of Chicago for what it did to start things and hope to hear from you all soon."[167]

Wells-Barnett then teamed up with Oscar DePriest and his local political club, The People's Movement, as well as local members of the ERL and her settlement, to pledge active support to Arkansas migrants who were arriving in Chicago in the aftermath of the riot. Her autobiography credits the petition sent by her group in support of migration to Chicago with motivating the Arkansas governor to convene a local conference of white and black citizens to investigate the riots more thoroughly. "Our pledge in it was one that he could not very well ignore," she stated.[168] That Governor Brough tried to suppress distribution of the *Defender* and *The Crisis* in mid-October 1918 suggests he was well aware of the influence of advice from northerners in Arkansas.[169]

Few cheered Wells-Barnett's initiative, however. Her partnership with DePriest actually antagonized her Chicago colleagues in the ERL, which promptly moved to restrict such collaborations by members through changes in their by-laws. Complaining that the ERL had done nothing about Arkansas and bridling at their censure of her work, Wells-Barnett then "walked out" of the group and, according to her narrative, she "never attempted to do any work through the means of the Equal Rights League." Then the NAACP objected to her independent fundraising, going on in the pages of the *Defender*. Smaller groups like the ERL had their own reasons to resent any defection or independence by members that could dilute their local talent and credibility. For its part, the NAACP was content to ignore Wells-Barnett until she interfered with their fundraising. In the end, she secured the "consent" of her local contributors to use the money already collected for her own investigation.[170] After almost thirty years of "exile" from the South, she traveled to Arkansas to assess the situation.

Wells-Barnett, like Walter White, engaged in an ingenious bit of political theater to get her story. Upon arriving in Little Rock, she encountered some of the wives and mothers of the incarcerated men. The autobiography describes her making herself "look as inconspicuous as possible"—perhaps exchanging her city-wise jacket and hat for a country shawl—and joining the group of women. Posing with what the guard took to be "a group of insignificant looking colored women who had been there many times before," Wells-Barnett passed into the Arkansas jail. The autobiography invites the reader to imagine the stage whisper of one Mrs. Frank Moore, "the leading spirit among the wives," who introduced Wells-Barnett to the men behind bars as her own "'cousin . . . from St. Louis.'" Then, in the privacy of the visitors' huddle outside the cell, Moore presented Wells-Barnett's real identity: "This is Mrs. Barnett from Chicago." "An expression of joy spread over their faces," later wrote Wells-Barnett, "but I put my fingers to my lips and cautioned them not to let on, and immediately a mask seemed to drop over the features of each one."[171] Her contemporary rendering of this encounter in the pamphlet captures this same shock of recognition, though Mrs. Moore is not mentioned. "I wish everyone whose contribution enabled me to make this investigation could have seen the light which came on the faces of these men when I told them who I was!"[172]

Wells-Barnett and Walter White blamed peonage and economic exploitation of black sharecroppers as the cause of the conflict in Phillips County. Unlike in White's account, however, the voices and experiences of African Americans are at the center of Wells-Barnett's telling. She spoke not with powerful whites but with the black prisoners, survivors, and witnesses of the riots. Her pamphlet printed the defendants' court testimony, material from jailhouse interviews, tallies of lost and stolen property, and even the hymns the prisoners sang in prison. This material links *The Arkansas Race Riot* with Wells-Barnett's writings from the 1890s, catching the emotional core and southern accent of those early investigations. The tone of the pamphlet's chapter "What White Folks Got from the Riot" echoes the pique and sarcasm of "The Black and White of It" from *Southern Horrors* and draws a similar conclusion: the perpetrators of the violence were motivated by economic envy as much as race hatred. "It seems not too high as an estimate to say that these twelve men alone had $100,000 worth of cotton, corn and cattle stolen from them by the mob which stole their liberty and are in a fair way to steal their lives unless the nation intervenes!" wrote Wells-Barnett.[173]

Most striking, especially in comparison with other contemporary and historical treatments of the Arkansas case, is Wells-Barnett's attention to African American women. Her autobiography noted that she "spent nearly all night writing down the experiences of the women who were also put in prison."[174] Wells-Barnett documented the importance of black women's field labor, home production, and personal resourcefulness in the political economy of sharecropping, aspects of southern history only recently gaining the attention of scholars. *The Arkansas Race Riot* demonstrates that, contrary to the images current then and now, neither the lynching victim nor the southern peon was exclusively male.[175]

The Arkansas Race Riot amplified themes that Wells-Barnett identified back in the 1890s, especially African American economic competence and self-possession on the one hand and the cowardly penchant of white mobs for singling out the weakest individuals for attack on the other. For example, among the first four black croppers who resisted the landowners' monopoly on pricing cotton in the spring of 1919 was a woman named Daisy Frazier. "These [four] worked and stood together, determined to stay and gather their crops, ignored the insults and threat of [the landowners] and were careful to give no offense."[176] When Frank Moore, another of the four, was taken ill, his wife stepped in and "hired help and laid by the crop first of all on the farm." After the riot, Mrs. Moore confronted the landlord with their confiscation of her crop and was then jailed for speaking up. Moore, along with "fifteen other colored women," was imprisoned in Helena and forced to work eighteen hours a day for eight days before being released. Others were imprisoned at "hard labor" for a month.[177] Another woman, Lula Black, "worked a farm" with her four children and was attacked at her home for belonging to the Farmer's Union. "[T]hey knocked her down, beat her over the head with their pistols, kicked her all over her body," reported Wells-Barnett; they "almost killed her." "The same mob," she continued, "went to [another] house and killed Frances Hall, a crazy old woman housekeeper," stripping her naked and leaving her body publicly exposed. The final insult after the beatings, confiscations, and jailings was that the women were charged a dollar each by the warden to visit their kin in prison.[178]

With a nod to Du Bois's *The Souls of Black Folk*, the first chapter of *The Arkansas Race Riot* includes the text of a "heart-breaking" hymn written and sung by the jailed men, whose chorus was "And I just stand and wring my hands and cry." "This they sang in the most mournful tones ever heard," Wells-Barnett explained.[179] Du Bois sifted the "Sorrow Songs" from slavery and found a breath of hope, a "faith in the ultimate justice of things" even if achieved only in death, the final equalizer of human existence.[180] Wells-Barnett never reconciled herself to the ultimate justice of death. She was fierce about living life, and she encouraged the imprisoned men to focus on life, not death. Both the pamphlet and her autobiography record her advice to the men to not sing about dying but to pray for freedom in this world. "But why don't you pray to live and ask to be freed?" she recalled asking. "Pray to live and believe you are going to get out."[181] *Crusade for Justice* works this exchange into a kind of prophesy and conversion experience for the men and their cause. The chapter on the Arkansas riot, probably written in 1929 or 1930, concludes with an encounter between Wells-Barnett and one of the released men, who one day visits her Chicago home unannounced. The man testifies to her family that after "Mrs. Barnett told us to quit talking about dying," the men "did as she told us, and now every last one of us is out and enjoying his freedom."[182]

In contrast to the narrative's self-vindicating parable, *The Arkansas Race Riot* ends with a chapter entitled "Summary and Contrast," a damning comparison between the United Mine Workers and the Arkansas Farmers Union. These two organizations of working people, "seeking through peaceful appeal to win better wage and working conditions," met starkly different fates. The coal strike, though it cut off needed services to citizens, got the attention of the president and achieved at least some of its objectives.[183] The farmers hurt no one, but their union activity cost many of them their lives. The miners' union was "rewarded by the President of the United States with a patient hearing and final success, the other . . . suffer[ed] massacre at the hands of the mob and the death penalty in courts of law."[184] In a sarcastic dig at Woodrow Wilson, whom she no doubt still resented for his action against black soldiers at Houston, the Arkansas case disclosed "to thinking people a phase of democracy not safe for the world or any part of it." The chapter ends with one of Wells-Barnett's classic, steely questions posed to the reader: "If this is democracy, what is bolshevism?"[185]

The events of 1919 crushed both labor militants' vision of industrial democracy and black leaders' hope for racial justice. The 1920s brought, if not a complete end to progressive reform, a decade of labor quiescence and a new Ku Klux Klan, a period of "peace without justice."[186] Like many Americans in the 1920s, New York literati like Du Bois put an accent on culture and the arts. Wells-Barnett put an accent on faith. *The Arkansas Race Riot* closed with the following advice to the incarcerated men: "I said they should pray daily that God would give the authorities the wisdom to realize the wrong that had been done, and the courage to right that wrong. I earnestly believe such prayers will strengthen the hands of the white people of the state who want to do the right thing."[187]

Conclusion

Wells-Barnett's conviction about both prayer and help from white Americans indicated the drift of women's antilynching protest after the war. At the heart of the Anti-Lynching Crusaders' appeal to pass the Dyer Antilynching Bill was also a prayer. This prayer circulated in newspapers and magazines across the country, designed to touch and rally women under the slogan "A Million Women United to Stop Lynching."[188] In addition, the Crusaders produced a circular in support of Dyer, *The Shame of America*. Run as a full-page ad in the *New York Times*, the Crusaders' statement compressed many of Wells-Barnett's insights about lynching along with the NAACP's legal remedy in a package designed to draw women's attention. In addition to pointing out that by 1920, fewer than 17 percent of lynchings involved the rape charge, the Crusaders placed in bold type the fact that some eighty-three women from both sides of the color line had been lynched since the 1880s. It also carried photographs and sketches highlighting mothers' agony. Though the Crusaders fell far short of their goal of a million dollars raised and one million women petitioners united against lynching, *The Crisis* noted that *The Shame of America* reached thousands of readers, some for the "first time," presenting a new generation of Americans with a critical perspective on lynching.[189] Even if Du Bois exaggerated here, *The Shame of America* reached many more readers than Wells-Barnett's pamphlet, *The Arkansas Race Riot*.

Nor was Wells-Barnett active among the Crusaders. Even in her hometown of Chicago, it was Mrs. James Weldon Johnson who interviewed Robert Abbott and enlisted the *Defender* in the cause of the Dyer bill.[190] Still, Wells-Barnett may have taken inspiration from the women's efforts, and in 1922 she reconnected with the NACW, attending the biennial convention held in Richmond that August.[191] During the NACW's meeting, a delegation was formed to appear before President Harding concerning Dyer. Although neither the minutes of the meeting nor the official history mentions this delegation, Jessie Fausett, reporting for *The Crisis*, picked up the story and printed a photo of its members (see Figure 17). Wells-Barnett was part of this delegation; only two of these fifteen women were officers of the Anti-Lynching Crusaders. Speaking "in the name of the NACW and behalf of all the colored women in the country," the petitioners highlighted their status as "women," "citizens," and "voters," pointedly requesting that the Republican Party make good on its public statements against lynching. The delegation stressed politics rather than prayer, and accountability of elected officials rather than moral idealism.[192] *The Shame of America* had a different emphasis. The Crusaders argued that the "remedy" for lynching was the Dyer Bill, passage of which would quell social "unrest" as well as halt harm to "agriculture" and the "productiveness of labor." They cast its litany of benefits not in partisan terms but in the interest of "100 per cent Americanism," crediting the NAACP with supporting this ideal "for all the people, white or black, all of the time."[193]

It is difficult to imagine Wells-Barnett subscribing to "100 per cent Americanism," given the censorious and ethnocentric connotations of that phrase after the war. As a fully enfranchised citizen after the passage of the Nineteenth Amendment, she felt not just willing but entitled to criticize the government that overlooked and sometimes perpetrated racial injustice. Like the Crusaders, Wells-Barnett preserved faith in the human heart, personal conscience, and the power of prayer. Rather than express 100 percent–style patriotism, however, *The Arkansas Race Riot* hinted at another avenue for social justice. The pamphlet concluded with a clear statement of outreach directed to liberal white southerners. "Believing that under normal conditions with the black man's rights guaranteed him and the protection of the law for his life, liberty and property, the South is the best section of our country for the Negro, the writer (a native of the South) will be only too glad to cooperate with the progressive elements of the white South in bringing about such a desideratum."[194]

Rejected by a consolidating, northern, urban elite in professional reform, Wells-Barnett turned southward. She probably referred in the above passage to opportunities presented by the newly formed Commission for Interracial Cooperation (CIC). The CIC was founded in 1919 in Atlanta by clergy, social workers, and educators to foster understanding among blacks and whites through conferences, education, and publicity. Perhaps, too, Wells-Barnett's statement reflects a dim view of life

FIGURE 17. "Anti-Lynching Delegation to President Harding, August 14,
1922." The original caption identified the delegates as follows: (first row, left to
right) Mrs. Ida Brown, New Jersey; Miss Mary B. Jackson, Rhode Island; Mrs.
Ida W. Barnett, Illinois; Mrs. Mary Parrish, Kentucky; Miss Hallie Q. Brown,
Ohio; Mrs. Minnie Scott, Ohio; Mrs. Cora Horne, New York; Mrs. Estelle
Davis, Ohio; Mrs. E. G. Rose, Delaware; (second row) Mrs. Lethia Fleming,
Ohio; Mrs. Ida Posties, Michigan; Mrs. Pearl Winters, California; Mrs. Myrtle F.
Cook, Missouri; Mrs. C. Chiles, Kansas; Mrs. Ruth Bennett, Pennsylvania. *The
Crisis* (October 1922): 260

in northern cities after the hideous bloodshed in Illinois of 1917–1919,
prompting her to identify herself as a "native of the South" rather than
as an expert on the "Northern Negro," as she had argued to Joel Spingarn a decade earlier.

The transformation of antilynching protest and the gendered dimensions of African American organizational life between 1900 and 1920
had many sources and uneven results. Wells-Barnett could not sustain
her momentum and the visibility she enjoyed in the 1890s. The controversial nature of her references to and revelations about sex across
the color line tainted Wells-Barnett as disreputable among conservatives and as a radical among many other reformers, black or white.
Black women faced their own challenges. Faced with libel and attack,
the NACW closed ranks around the politics of home and respectability,
joining national-level protest against lynching in partnership with the
NAACP in the 1920s. Northern white reformers failed to engage the issue
of rape and its racial entanglements. As a result, Wells-Barnett's ideas

and the credibility of lynching as an object of reform were taken over by others—mostly, but not exclusively, professional male intellectuals. This was especially true in the case of W. E. B. Du Bois and Walter White, men of talent, credentials, and connections, who managed to eclipse both the conservative Washington and the rebellious Wells-Barnett in these years.

It would be a mistake to overdraw the gendered dimensions of African American resistance to lynching. After all, women's prayer groups took on new meaning when they were backed by the vote in the 1920s, and male activists, clergy or not, engaged in their own share of prayer and moral suasion. Wells-Barnett herself moved through multiple public venues in which her freedom to act varied depending on the local, regional, and national context. That she was viewed as a heroine at Cairo but as a heel in New York must have made a personally taxing situation supremely frustrating. To mediate some of these tensions, there emerged at the elite level a gender division of labor, which assigned political and intellectual leadership to men while entrusting to women a parallel role of prayer, education, and fundraising in female networks. When the Anti-Lynching Crusaders revived the issues of rape and the abuse of black women in the 1920s, they enriched the legal, sociological, and psychological discourses around lynching and paid tribute to Wells-Barnett's legacy. If Wells-Barnett lost standing in civil rights work at the national level, she gained it at the local level through her work in Chicago. With the failure of the Dyer bill in 1922, Ida B. Wells-Barnett's exile in antilynching was finally over.

CHAPTER FIVE

Settlements, Suffrage, Setbacks

An anecdote from Ida B. Wells-Barnett's autobiography describes her settlement, the Negro Fellowship League, as an expression of godly black womanhood's leavening role in the community. Located at 2830 State Street—"a very questionable section," in her words, of the central boulevard on Chicago's South Side—the League opened on a warm Sunday in May 1910. As worship service began, noise in the alley disrupted those gathered. Wells-Barnett sent the janitor to investigate, who reported that a "bunch of drunken men . . . were out in the next yard shooting craps and paid no attention to him when he asked them to be quiet." He recommended that someone go for the police, but Wells-Barnett objected, stating, "Oh, no, we have come over here to be friends to these people," and then she went into the alley. The men did not hear her approach over their dice game, so she called to them. They responded to the presence of a lady: "Instantly every one of them got up except one man who was too drunk to do so," quickly making assurances that "they would make less noise" or leave. "I would rather you would come into the meeting," explained Wells-Barnett. "We have come over here to be your neighbors and we will hold meetings every Sunday. Do come in." The men declined with protestations about their dirty appearance and again offered to go away. "They answered too readily that they would," stated Wells-Barnett, who then tried to persuade them to come the next week: "I said, 'will you shake hands on it?' and I stretched my hand through the fence. They all said that they didn't want to dirty my white gloves by shaking hands but reiterated that they would go away and also repeated their promise to come next Sunday." Though readers never learn whether these men eventually came to a meeting, Wells-Barnett concludes the account by affirming that the Negro Fellowship League stayed on State Street ten years and was "never again disturbed or molested in all that time."[1] The story is more than a self-serving gloss on Wells-Barnett's work in community betterment.[2] The men's polite rejection of the gloved hand of fellowship is an instance of resistance by working-class and immigrant urbanites to "uplift" by Christian ladies and gentlemen, a response well-documented by historians.[3] The scene at the NFL also evokes the black club women's motto "Lifting As We Climb" in action, but Wells-Barnett's particular story ends in disappointment. The League's closure due to lack of funds leaves her a very frustrated Christian witness, one unable to completely fulfill her mission.

The Negro Fellowship League was one of a handful of social settlements that emerged in the early twentieth century to serve the growing population of African Americans in Chicago. Its relative longevity and the multiple roles it played in politics and social service delivery mark it as outstanding among independent, start-up settlements.[4] The League's constant scramble for funds and the continued controversy over Wells-Barnett's leadership point to the struggles facing African Americans, particularly black women, to affirm their place in the city. The story of the Negro Fellowship League demands a close reckoning in light of the fact that Chicago institutions built by white women—the Woman's Building of the 1893 World's Fair, the WCTU's Woman's Temple, and, most famously, Jane Addams's Hull-House—were internationally recognized models of female achievement in this period. Wells-Barnett was known as "the Jane Addams among the Negroes," but the origins, shape, and destiny of these two women's work were quite different.[5]

Like its leader, the Negro Fellowship League does not fit the usual categories that historians apply to female institution-building in this period. The League was not primarily a "community of women reformers," as Hull-House has been described, though it often facilitated connections among women. It was not a mission through official religious affiliation or stated evangelical purpose, but Christian worship, outreach, and moral instruction figured prominently in its program. Nor was it simply a political club, a mere platform for or against any candidate or faction of the major parties, though the League partici-pated intensely in the electoral life of the surrounding ward before, during, and after the achievement of woman suffrage. Jane Addams supported woman suffrage but carefully stressed women's participation in the public sphere as an extension of their historic role in the care of children and the home.[6] By contrast, the Negro Fellowship League announced itself as the "first social work for men and boys" in black Chicago, a point of pride from the settlement's opening until the end of Wells-Barnett's life.[7]

The League's roots were in southern black women's traditions of faith and community work, transplanted by Wells-Barnett to the North. Unlike the schools and neighborhood houses established by North Carolina's Charlotte Hawkins Brown or Atlanta's Lugenia Burns Hope, however, Wells-Barnett did not adopt an ambassadorial role to whites in a context of black male disfranchisement.[8] Different, too, from suc-cessful black women's institutions in the urban North—especially the "colored" YWCAs and the Phillis Wheatley Homes—Wells-Barnett's set-tlement did not especially hold itself out as a protector or champion of women and children. By focusing on men as objects of uplift, the NFL shifted attention away from black women, who were so often blamed by whites for the failings of men and "the race."[9] The credo of the Illinois Federation of Colored Women's Clubs was "Loyalty to Women, Justice to Children."[10] The Negro Fellowship League's organ, the *Fel-lowship Herald*, proclaimed its own perfectly innocuous, utterly sweeping credo: "We Worship God by Serving Man."[11] This cagey and ambitious charge aptly expressed Wells-Barnett's visionary pragmatism and al-lowed her to lay claim to the toughest of city streets and urban poli-tics as means of self-affirmation and service to God and Man, broadly put. This vision led the Negro Fellowship League into partisan poli-tics more quickly and directly than either the white women reformers around Hull-House or the African American women educators and social service professionals on the South Side. Wells-Barnett's work at the League exemplified the ways in which she declined to settle on a singular definition of womanhood or women's roles, but rather took on the world and its woes according to how she and her God saw fit.

Locating the Vision

Some scholars have puzzled over or outright denied an interest in government action among African American leaders at the turn of the century, inadvertently segregating black activists' work from progres-sive social thought about the welfare responsibilities of an expanded state.[12] A closer look at figures like Wells-Barnett reveals a keen and ongoing interest in both political opportunity and government responsibility in social welfare. This interest was neither idealistic nor ideological, but pragmatic and instrumental. Wells-Barnett herself was critical of American politics, testifying before World War I to a queasy, "unsettled feeling about the whole of our vaunted democratic scheme of government."[13] Nevertheless, state and party were among the most viable spheres for social engagement for African American women in the urban North. Like their immigrant and white working-class neighbors, black women had a complex relationship to party machinery, and they determined, lacking many practical alternatives, to make it go for their own purposes.[14] In this context, even before full female enfranchisement, Wells-Barnett functioned as a key political player and trusted community organizer in a manner very different from the white women of Hull-House before World War I. Addams and her colleagues in reform did not really find a political home until the Progressive Party formed in 1912, and that home was for whites only.[15]

Wells-Barnett's social vision reflects more than a lack of opportunity born of the strange fruits of Jim Crow in the urban North. Though she wrote little general social commentary in this period, the assumptions evident in her press reporting did not have much in common with either organized labor's demand for power sharing through "industrial democracy" or white progressive reformers' goal of fairness through "social democracy." Wells-Barnett had neither the time nor the temperament to seek out a middle ground in "the Negro problem" in the way Addams appealed to a natural harmony of interests in her discussions of "the labor question."[16] Wells-Barnett's idea of "serving God by serving Man" resonated more with the worldview of southern black and white women educators and religious workers who championed "Christian democracy" and whose efforts to realize a moral order paved the way for civil rights initiatives in that region. Since her Memphis days, however, Wells-Barnett had been somewhat less ideologically invested in the feminine gender constructs, especially motherhood, which offered the fundamental vehicle for southern women's activism in this period.[17]

Wells-Barnett's dual impulse to faith and politics instead found expression in her description of the ballot as sacred. The concept of the ballot as sacred caught an essence of the American experiment with democracy whose heart was the Reconstruction Amendments and whose soul was the legacy of slavery in the United States, in particular its heritage of religious faith. "With no sacredness of the ballot there can be no sacredness of human life itself," argued Wells-Barnett, "for if the strong can take the weak man's ballot when it suits his purpose to do so, he will take his life also."[18] African Americans had a "sacred duty," according to Wells-Barnett, to "use their political strength" against segregation and racial injustice.[19] The formulation "rights equals life" dramatizes Wells-Barnett's commitment to politics as a means to insure the safety and survival of African Americans. As a strategy of resistance to lynching and racism, the idea of the ballot as sacred supported the dual truths that black people were each and all individuals worthy of respect and that as a group, they merited recognition in the body politic. Wells-Barnett's thinking went deeper than the commonsense arguments popular among many suffragists that votes for women was consistent with a "Golden Rule" level of Christian sentiment. Its depth lay in the essential link between political rights and the historic struggle of black people against slavery and oppression, a struggle inseparable from faith.[20]

As she had traced out in articles written in Memphis, Wells-Barnett tried to make real in Chicago the idea that political rights dignified an individual's humanity and offered a practical means for groups to secure economic opportunity and social justice. "What material benefit is a 'leader' if he does not, to some extent, direct his time, talent and wealth to the alleviation of the poverty, misery and elevation of his people?" asked Wells-Barnett back in 1885.[21] Rather than mock southern honor or "Nineteenth Century civilization" as she had in the early 1890s, Wells-Barnett's activities after 1900 continued these other, earlier reflections on politics. In Chicago, she advocated a rights-centered activism that enabled participation in interest group tactics then emerging in electoral politics, civic affairs, and the shaping of public opinion. By stressing the religious value of voting, Wells-Barnett also smuggled in a claim for women in public life without highlighting sex difference, a ubiquitous feature of the discourse surrounding race, rights, and civilization at the turn of the century.[22] Wells-Barnett's concept of the ballot as sacred fixed moral duty in the official political realm equally for men and women across the color line.[23]

The concept of the ballot as sacred was visionary in its appeal to things holy, pragmatic in its use of earthly tools near at hand.[24] The concept updated and recombined mid-nineteenth-century republican and evangelical ideals to answer the materialism and racism of the turn of the century. Wells-Barnett's sympathy with both Henry McNeal Turner and Marcus Garvey allied her more with the "civilizationist" thread of nineteenth-century black nationalism than with the more modernist sensibility of W. E. B. Du Bois. Du Bois was interested in questions of cultural hybridity and pluralism as well as in the concept of the "folk"; Wells-Barnett's thinking about power and race was mainly strategic.[25] Though she had been deeply "touched for Africa" while listening to missionary preaching back in Memphis, she supported migration and related schemes in instrumental rather than "racially" ideological terms. African migration was a natural right, a way to avoid violence, and a means to financial security.[26] Whether she envisioned the United States, Christianity, or "civilization" as "black," "white," some pluralist composite, or a multiethnic blend, Wells-Barnett never fully explained. Certainly her social vision was less bound by our contemporary polarity between racially driven social remedies and so-called colorblind meritocracy. Antilynching taught Wells-Barnett that U.S. citizens needed both freedom and protection—the latter sometimes by the state, sometimes from the state, depending on the circumstances. Similarly, she valued integration and race consciousness, because one was not really possible without the other. In Chicago, she rarely reflected on "the black and white of it" in American life, as she had in *Southern Horrors*. Between 1895 and 1920, Ida B. Wells-Barnett wrote little about "race" per se and instead taught and worked and organized as if the ballot were sacred. That she articulated but never fully worked out this idea on paper or made it perfectly transparent in social organization points to both her creativity and the limits of her historical moment.

Husband, Family, and Home

Wells-Barnett was not only a lonely political prophet or missionary for God on State Street, though at moments she felt herself to be just that. Chicago was also home. By organizing among women during the World's Fair, writing for local papers like the *Conservator* and *Inter-Ocean*, and agitating against lynching, Wells-Barnett created special ties to the city. The press reported that "cheer after cheer" greeted her return at a welcome celebration at Quinn Chapel AME Church in July 1894 (organized by the Ida B. Wells Club) and that she was "repeatedly compelled to rise and acknowledge the appreciation of the enthusiastic reception tendered her on behalf of the colored citizens of Chicago."[27] This splendid homecoming capped a pleasant ship's passage back to the United States during which she enjoyed the company of Mr. and Mrs. Moncure Conway, ex-patriots from Virginia and former abolitionists.[28] By comparison, W. E. B. Du Bois's return from his studies in Germany that same summer was, his biographer notes, "vintage huddled masses." The broke but high-minded graduate student rode steerage with immigrant travelers and arrived home not to fanfare but to a job search for a teaching post from his mother's home in the Berkshires.[29]

Life in Chicago dramatically transformed the existence of a woman who had constructed an international identity as an "exile" and "orphan." Her marriage to Ferdinand Lee Barnett in June 1895, and the birth of four children, Charles (1896), Herman (1897), Ida Jr. (1901), and Alfreda (1904) freighted Wells-Barnett's first decade in Chicago with intensive family commitments. Wells-Barnett claimed in her autobiography to have officially given up "all . . . public work" and retired "to the privacy of my home to give my attention to the training of my children" in these years. Yet the narrative scarcely describes any retirement. By making a fine match and by purchasing the *Conservator* newspaper from Barnett, she achieved a constructive move in the work of agitation.[30] As the mother of one-year-old Charles, she lectured across Illinois during the McKinley campaign on behalf of the Republican Women's State Central Committee.[31] The following summer, while pregnant with Herman, she investigated and reported on the horrific lynching of a young black hotel worker falsely charged with rape in Urbana, Ohio.[32] In her adopted home, Wells-Barnett remained active in protest and social organizing, often in concert with her politically active and reform-minded husband.

The union of Ida B. Wells and Ferdinand L. Barnett exemplified the ways that marriage enmeshed rather than isolated women in tightly knit African American communities. The wedding itself was a major social event for black Chicago, putting everyone on a "tip toe of eagerness."[33] The pending marriage initially highlighted the ways in which orphanhood and celebrity distanced Wells-Barnett from kin and community. The autobiography recounts concern over securing a proper church wedding and festivities, since, in Wells's words, the bride had "no relative, either to give me away or to tender me a reception." Like the women of Brooklyn, however, Chicago women embraced her. She was "very glad" to accept the proposal of the Ida B. Wells Club to give her a wedding reception and they managed the "whole affair."[34] Amid numerous offers from local women, sisters Lily and Annie Wells came from California to act as bridesmaids.

The couple hoped that Rev. Charles Aked would marry them, but the British minister's trip to the United States did not come off in time, and Reverend D. A. Graham of Bethel AME Church performed the ceremony instead. Ferdinand's coeditor at the *Conservator*, R. P. Bird, and his friend S. J. Evans stood up for him. On 25 June, Bethel church was filled to overflowing. Wells-Barnett remembered that the streets were "so packed with humanity" that the bridal party was barely able to enter the church door. They considered it "a very great honor" that a number of white guests attended the service in evening dress, a demonstration of social respect apparently unusual in Chicago. These guests included members of the Republican Women's State Central Committee as well as newspaper colleagues from the *Inter-Ocean*. Dressed in a satin gown and carrying orange blossoms, fashionable yet understated attire, the bride was not given away but walked herself down the aisle, a fitting gesture for someone who had struggled to stake out social autonomy.[35] By hyphenating her married name to Wells-Barnett, she avoided completely, as her daughter put it, "los[ing] the identity of Ida B. Wells," through which she had earned a living and become so well known.[36]

Ferdinand Barnett remains rather more in the background of the historical record of Wells-Barnett's career than does Frederick Douglass, but his presence was significant. In the 1890s, he contributed to the World's Fair pamphlet, offered counsel on the intended libel suit against the *Memphis Commercial*, petitioned congressional leaders on behalf of the antilynching crusade, and gave an address at the Quinn Chapel welcome celebration.[37] According to daughter Alfreda, the courtship began in earnest in 1894 during her mother's tour of the United States: "Wherever she stopped there would be a letter from my father. And so they had a long distance correspondence courtship and I understand—I never saw one—but I understand my father could write a beautiful love letter."[38] Perhaps Barnett's quiet consistency and trusted competence in big-city Chicago proved attractive for the fiery itinerant lecturer from the South. The autobiography is nearly silent on the emotional dimensions of the courtship, not at all surprising given the heavy, negative scrutiny to which Wells-Barnett's sexuality had been subjected as an unmarried public figure.[39]

The Wells-Barnett partnership is notable because many accomplished black women of this generation—Anna Julia Cooper, Victoria Earle Mathews, Alice Dunbar Nelson, and Madame C. J. Walker—made their names in the worlds of writing, business, and reform after early widowhood freed them from the duties of marriage and domesticity. Others married only briefly, like Charlotte Hawkins Brown, or not at all, like Nannie Helen Burroughs. Black women writers stressed that marriage ideally was compatible with efforts on behalf of race uplift, yet the Wells-Barnett partnership still stands out.[40] They literally "met in the work" of journalism and agitation. Alfreda recalled that the two "had like interests . . . [and] their journalist career[s] were intertwined." She noted that her mother's "public and private life were all one"; as for her father, she remembered, "our house was his extended office." "And my father and mother always went places and did things together," she explained, "but there wasn't too much time for intimate family life in the home, since it was almost a business."[41] This consecrated, activist partnership averted Wells-Barnett's worst fears about female subordination and domestic confinement in marriage, as expressed in her Memphis diary.

Information about Ferdinand Barnett is sketchy. Most sources place his birth at 1859 in Nashville. His father was a skilled slave, a blacksmith, who purchased his freedom and married a free woman. During the Civil War, the family left for Canada, a popular destination among Tennessee and Kentucky runaway slaves and freedpeople. In 1869, the Barnetts moved to Chicago with a stop in Detroit.[42] From there, Ferdinand's father made his living as a steamboat cook on Lake Superior, and his son accompanied him often enough to learn to be "a very good cook." Because of this talent, he later "did much of the cooking" at home, providing another asset for Wells-Barnett, who did not enjoy food preparation.[43] After high school, Ferdinand taught school for two years and later graduated from law school at Northwestern University around 1878.

Ferdinand Barnett married his first wife, Mary H. Graham, a native of Ontario, Canada, in 1882. Graham was also a high achiever, an accomplished musician and the first black woman to graduate from the University of Michigan, where she earned a bachelor's degree in philosophy in 1880. The two probably met in Michigan and, after marrying, moved to Chicago, where Graham assisted her husband on the staff of the *Conservator*.[44] Upon Graham's death in 1890, Ferdinand's mother moved in with her son and presumably took major responsibility for Ferdinand Jr. and Alfred, two young sons named for family on the Barnett side. How much pressure Barnett felt to remarry can only be surmised. Alfreda noted that her father had been "looking for a certain type of woman who would mean something meaningful to his life and his career. And evidently Mama fit that pattern. He pursued and married her."

Barnett's status as a widower with children may have offered his second wife some potential relief from childbearing, especially since she claimed to have no particular "longing for children" upon entering marriage. The autobiography notes, however, that she was "glad" she had not been "swayed by advice given me on the night of my marriage which had for its object to teach me how to keep from having a baby." Wells-Barnett "reveled" in the "wonderful discovery" of the importance and power of motherhood in her life, perceiving that God gave woman "a joint share in the work of creation."[45] After their wedding, the couple held a customary "at home" reception at the residence that Ferdinand and Mary had established. Not long after the new bride moved in, however, mother-in-law and stepsons moved out. "You know," explained Alfreda, "it's hard for two ladies to be in one household, especially one with as positive and direct a character as my mother."[46] In 1901, the Barnetts moved their growing family to a spacious and elegant residence at 3234 Rhodes Avenue, the family's home for the next twenty-five years.

Church and Politics

Chicago, a rising "second city" in the United States, was an excellent place for an ambitious, talented couple like the Barnetts to make their mark in the world. Like Memphis and Brooklyn, Chicago was home to a vital and well-organized African American community. As a lawyer, agitator, founder of a newspaper, and longtime resident of the city, Ferdinand Barnett was an established member of the local elite. At the turn of the century, this group was made up of mostly freeborn, educated professionals who asserted cultural and political leadership in a black community of approximately 20,000 people. By 1920, that community had grown to over 100,000 people. In these years, black Chicagoans developed a valiant if vulnerable business sector that included two banks. Provident Hospital, founded in 1891, and a Home for the Aged and Infirm were most prominent among about a dozen other social service institutions. Soldiers and veterans of the Illinois Eighth Regiment comprised a well-organized sector of the community and the local Republican political establishment. Several newspapers, including the nationally renowned *Chicago Defender*, and a burgeoning entertainment scene in theater, music, and sports rounded out the realms of commercial media, arts, and leisure. Before 1920, however, the churches stood out as a point of special pride, constituting, in the opinion of one contemporary observer, the "one institution that shows the Negro in the light concerning which he does not have to make excuses."[47] According to sociologists Drake and Cayton, Chicago churches were "the most powerful single institution in terms of wealth and mass support." Before the Great Migration of black southerners, that wealth and support resided with the Methodist denominations—African Methodist Episcopal (AME), Methodist Episcopal (ME), and Colored Methodist Episcopal (CME)—which together outnumbered the Baptists, with thirteen to nine major congregations.[48]

A significant number of black Chicago's leading families were members of two AME congregations. The first was "Mother" Bethel, founded in the 1850s and located in the heart of the emerging "black belt" of African American homes at 30th and Dearborn. The other was Quinn

Chapel, founded in 1847, and situated nearer the edge of concentrated black residences at 24th and Wabash (Figure 18).[49] Two talented men occupied these pulpits at the turn of the century. One was freeborn Ohioan Reverdy C. Ransom, who came to Bethel AME after training at Oberlin College and Wilberforce University and pastoring in towns in his home state. According to Wells-Barnett, Ransom arrived without fanfare, "a tall, spare stranger" with "a musical voice, a pleasant smile and a winning manner" that quickly made him "the best known preacher Chicago has ever had."[50] These comments reflected Ransom's widely acknowledged ability (he became a bishop before World War I and served as editor of the scholarly AME *Church Review*) as well as Wells-Barnett's personal respect. *Crusade for Justice* does not much discuss her association with Ransom, but it does hint at her bitterness toward his chief rival in town, Archibald J. Carey of Quinn Chapel. The son of former slaves from Georgia, Carey was born in 1868 and educated at Atlanta University. After taking over at Quinn in 1898, Carey became an AME bishop in 1920, securing along the way a number of prominent appointed political offices. In the process, the outspoken and socialist-inclined Ransom was sacrificed to both Carey's ambition and the political conservatism of the AME hierarchy in the Illinois conference.[51] Before leaving Chicago for New England in 1904, however, Ransom preached to standing-room-only crowds, enjoyed a yeasty collaboration with leading figures in reform, and innovated the delivery of education and social services to the community through his Institutional Church and Social Settlement, founded in 1900. In all of this, Ida B. Wells-Barnett was his ally.

The connection between Ransom and Wells-Barnett began in 1894, during the early antilynching crusade, when the young minister defended her stand against Frances Willard's racism in the WCTU. Like Bishop Turner, Ransom was willing to push the gender boundaries of female initiative and leadership proscribed by the church. In a major address before the Ida B. Wells Woman's Club in 1897, Ransom identified Wells-Barnett's antilynching work as an exemplary model of service, likening her to the biblical heroines Deborah and Jael. He praised women's club work as a courageous "new departure" through which womanhood would take its place "side by side with our manhood in the field of action in the greatest and largest questions of our day and time."[52] To meet these questions, women's roles had to expand, and so did the church's. Ransom felt keenly the new demands on urban African Americans and insisted that the church "be built so that it may serve as the center of the life of the people, and in that center the people may be

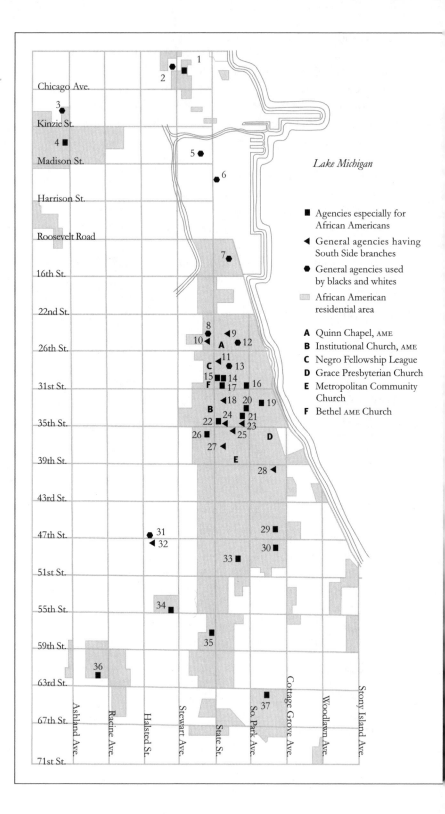

Chicago Ave.

Kinzie St.

Madison St.

Harrison St.

Roosevelt Road

16th St.

22nd St.

26th St.

31st St.

35th St.

39th St.

43rd St.

47th St.

51st St.

55th St.

59th St.

63rd St.

67th St.

71st St.

Lake Michigan

■ Agencies especially for
   African Americans

◄ General agencies having
   South Side branches

● General agencies used
   by blacks and whites

▨ African American
   residential area

A Quinn Chapel, AME
B Institutional Church, AME
C Negro Fellowship League
D Grace Presbyterian Church
E Metropolitan Community
   Church
F Bethel AME Church

Ashland Ave.
Racine Ave.
Halsted St.
Stewart Ave.
State St.
So. Park Ave.
Cottage Grove Ave.
Woodlawn Ave.
Stony Island Ave.

educated and uplifted instead of in the saloons and the drinking halls."[53]
Publicly returning the praise, Wells-Barnett wrote in the AME *Christian Recorder* that Ransom successfully turned Bethel Church into a "storm center for all matters affecting the race as well as spiritual interests."[54]

Wells-Barnett likely had a hand in pushing Ransom's thinking toward social issues when she appealed to him in the mid-1890s for space in his church for a kindergarten for neighborhood children. Amid fears of self-segregation voiced by the congregation, Ransom "strongly supported" the kindergarten, which was run by the Ida B. Wells Club.[55] The kindergarten was part of the rapid growth in "auxiliary movements" at Bethel during the Ransom years. According to Wells-Barnett, Ransom "brought a new gospel to the city which was to the effect that whatever was of moral or racial or educational value to the community; whatever was of an elevating or intellectual character; should be fostered and encouraged and established by the church."[56] Encouraged by the example of his congregants as well as by social innovation around the city, Ransom helped shepherd Bethel's expanding social functions, which soon evolved under a single roof. The new Institutional Church combined welfare, employment, and educational services with a library, a

---

MAP LEGEND
1. Butler Social Settlement
2. United Charities
3. United Charities
4. Wendell Phillips Settlement
5. Dependent Children's Department of the Juvenile Court
6. Illinois Children's Home and Aid Society
7. St. Luke's Hospital
8. Post Graduate Hospital
9. Moseley Dental Clinic
10. South Side Dental Dispensary
11. Soldier's Bureau
12. Mary Thompson Hospital for Women and Children
13. United Charities
14. Chicago Urban League
15. Frederick Douglass Center
16. Olivet Baptist Church Day Nursery
17. Unity Club
18. South Side Soldiers and Sailors Club
19. Phillis Wheatley Home
20. Day Nursery, Equal Rights & Protective Association
21. Jane Ridley Home
22. National Association for the Advancement of Colored People
23. Illinois Free Employment Bureau
24. American Red Cross
25. YWCA
26. Provident Hospital and Dispensary
27. YMCA
28. Abraham Lincoln Center
29. Elaine Home for Working Girls
30. Julia Johnson Home for Colored Girls
31. United Charities Dental Clinic
32. Children's South Side Free Dispensary
33. Illinois Technical School for Colored Girls
34. Home for Aged and Infirm Colored People
35. Baptist Missionary Women's Home
36. Louise Training School for Colored Boys
37. Woodlawn Community Center

FIGURE 18. Social agencies and churches serving the black community in Chicago during the first two decades of the twentieth century. Based on map titled "Social Agencies Used by Negroes," in Chicago Commission on Race Relations, *The Negro in Chicago: A Study of Race Relations and a Race Riot in 1919* (Chicago, 1922; reprint, New York: Arno, 1968), facing page 148

day nursery, music and business classes, and an auditorium for community forums and church services. "With the fire of youthful enthusiasm warm in my heart and my brain," recalled Ransom in his autobiography's chapter on Chicago, "these were for me glorious days."[57]

Politics and Institution Building, 1900–1906

Wells-Barnett and Ransom's collaboration unfolded on one level according to their shared faith and ideas and, on another, according to their disparate access to patronage and finances. Like New South Memphis, Progressive-era Chicago was shot through with intense competition over resources in the black community, conditions that sharply raised the stakes for denominationalism in church life. This was as true for individual clergy as it was for their heavily female congregations, especially activists like Wells-Barnett, who stretched the bounds and categories of women's church roles. The results in her case were tragic. The church nurtured her vision, but when Ransom left Chicago in 1904, Wells-Barnett lost her patron and was left to play the harsh game of politics largely on her own.

Initially, however, the two inhabited the "storm center" of agitation and reform together. After organizing the Sam Hose lynching investigation in the summer of 1899, Ransom and Wells-Barnett hosted the Afro-American Council's annual convention. He officially "welcomed" visiting guests and she, in her old role from Memphis days, "presided as toastmaster" at the culminating banquet.[58] Wells-Barnett was especially proud of that meeting, the historic occasion on which for the first time "colored women had partaken of a dinner in one of the Loop hotels" in downtown Chicago.[59] Ill-disposed toward temporizing over Booker T. Washington's or President McKinley's silence on southern outrages, Ransom became frustrated when Washington sought to influence the Council by private meetings with the leadership in his hotel rather than in open session at the convention. Not unlike his spirited friend Wells-Barnett, the minister lost his temper and handled both the Wizard and the president "without gloves" in his remarks during Council debate. Heading into an election year, the local press seized on Ransom's words as potentially destabilizing to Republican power at the polls, and this fear circulated in the northern papers. Members of the Council—in particular an articulate first-time visitor to its proceedings, W. E. B. Du Bois—quickly poured oil on the troubled waters, assuring the *Chicago Tribune* that the group stood with Washington and McKinley and adding a dig at Ransom's comments as "foolish and ill-timed."[60] With black electoral politics this volatile, Ransom felt it necessary to make amends with the Republicans via the press and to patch things up with Washington by letter.[61]

Ransom's inclination to repair breaks with Washington and his ability to turn from politics back to the church for support sharply separates his Chicago career from that of Wells-Barnett and her husband. Ransom's patron in the church, Bishop Henry Y. Arnett (another ally of the McKinley administration) channeled funds from his post at Wilberforce to Chicago in order to start the Institutional Church and boost Ransom's career. Ransom became full-time pastor there in 1901.[62] The Barnetts lacked such a patron outside party politics. Less dependent on Republican patronage than the Barnetts, Ransom's relationship to Tuskegee was also less loaded, though Washington still tried to block Ransom's elevation to bishop in 1911. Ransom kept up his own political interests, entailing other risks closer to home.

The risk was tangling with Archibald Carey, who had his own ambitions to tend. Ransom's Bethel Church became home to the Equal Opportunity League, comprised of Charles Bentley, Edward Morris, and others known as politically minded militants, who, along with the Barnetts, would wend their way with Ransom to the Niagara Movement and then to the NAACP.[63] By contrast, Carey's Quinn Chapel regularly hosted Washington's conservative Negro Business League and came out strongly pro-Tuskegee.[64] Carey managed to extend his Chicago influence with aid from local Bishop Abram Grant (another close ally of Tuskegee) by getting Ransom barred from preaching on Sunday mornings and thereby eliminating competition with his own sermons. When rumors circulated that Bishop Grant intended to remove him from Chicago altogether, Ransom abandoned Illinois for Massachusetts in the summer of 1904, securing a pastorate in New Bedford through Arnett's help.[65]

The Barnetts were not as mobile as their friend and ally Reverdy Ransom. Amid Tuskegee's machinations of 1900, they remained with the Republican Party and recommitted themselves to the McKinley campaign. Ferdinand headed the Republicans' "Negro Bureau" and now his wife stumped the state among "Negro voters."[66] In 1903, when Wells-Barnett left the Afro-American Council in opposition to Booker T. Washington's influence—the same year that Monroe Trotter's noisy "riot" of protest against Tuskegee in Boston landed him in jail—no patron looked after her interests or funneled her cash to start her own organization.[67] She and her husband had enemies. While Ransom engineered an exit from Chicago, Washington sought to "block Barnett and his wife" in Republican politics and local leadership. By spying and working behind the scenes to undermine the Barnetts' standing in the party in 1904, Washington meddled with Ferdinand's job security at an especially tender moment, as Ida gave birth to their fourth child, Alfreda, that summer.[68] Ferdinand stayed at the helm of the party's western "Negro Bureau" for the next campaign, but his name was bandied about in the local press in scurrilous reports designed to hurt him politically. These reports (probably planted by Tuskegee) concerned a purported jail sentence for contempt of court, charges of stealing from Civil War pensioners, and later a rumor that he aspired to the position of foreign minister to Haiti, implying that he vainly fancied himself another Fred Douglass.[69] In the context of a general economic downturn and bitter labor conflict involving black workers in Chicago, these tensions marked 1904 as a turning point.[70]

Turbulent political conditions and the pressing need for new allies in community work may have made Wells-Barnett receptive to an idea brought to her during the winter of 1904–5 by a white Unitarian minister, Rev. Celia Parker Woolley. Wells-Barnett had been acquainted with Woolley through events at Hull-House and at the influential Chicago Woman's Club, which Woolley led at the turn of the century. Counting the Barnetts among her few African American acquaintances in town, Woolley called at their home to confer about a new project. Appalled by the violence directed at black workers employed as strikebreakers during the summer's stockyard strike, Woolley announced a plan to establish what she called the "Frederick Douglass Center," a settlement-like organization where "white and colored persons could meet and get to know each other better." Opened in 1905, the Douglass Center would be Woolley and her husband's full-time residence for thirteen years, until her death in 1918.[71]

With Tuskegee sniping around the Barnetts political efforts in Chicago, Woolley likely appeared to be a welcome political neutral and well-connected potential patron. In becoming the Douglass Center's "militant champions," however, the Barnetts took a political gamble that yielded very mixed results. The first was bad press. The women organizers endured reports that mocked their initial meeting as a "Black Social Tea" comprised of "White Women and Negresses" plotting in an "astounding attempt to force social equality."[72] Then there were program problems. Though the Center stood admirably first and alone in the city with its interracial agenda, it fell far short of community hopes for practical problem solving and leadership opportunities for black women.[73] Finally, as the Douglass Center's "most ardent supporters," the Barnetts provoked the ire of Rev. Carey, who jealously contended for the support and loyalty of leading families; Wells-Barnett later described clergy as "naturally opposed" to such an undertaking as the

Center.[74] Ironically it was Ferdinand, a teacher and board member at the Douglass Center, who paid the short-term political price for affiliating with Woolley.

The opening for an attack by Rev. Carey came in April 1906, when the local papers announced a plan for a fundraiser for the Douglass Center at Bob Motts's Pekin Theatre, a local entertainment hall.[75] Wells-Barnett, a theater bug and race-conscious leader, was impressed with Motts's "little gem" of a theater, home to an all-black stock company, orchestra, and employees. When the Douglass Center women's club started a subscription for the event, beginning with one hundred local "patronesses," Rev. Carey moved to squelch the campaign. Carey, who by now had moved over to Bethel AME in the wake of Ransom's departure, took the opportunity of the fundraiser to denounce Motts's Pekin—and by extension the Center and its supporters—for its supposed low morals.[76] Perhaps having anticipated the minister's negative public response, Wells-Barnett sarcastically informed the church women who complained to her that Carey was "serving splendidly as a press agent for the benefit" by circulating his condemning remarks to "every Negro newspaper on the South Side."[77] For good measure, Ferdinand Barnett was prepared to initiate a lawsuit against any newspaper that libeled the Center. Then Carey shrewdly held out the olive branch to Celia Woolley, offering to take up a church collection on the Center's behalf rather than give aid and comfort to his declared enemy and whipping boy, Motts. Woolley, backed by her own Unitarian Church and Woman's Club networks, declined the gesture.[78]

Carey's denunciation, however, found its mark in the black community. A South Side theater school canceled its participation in the fundraiser, citing the Pekin's reputation and its adverse effect on the school's students who were "young ladies . . . from the best families of the city." Wells-Barnett held the line, later admitting that her biting response to this situation was "not very diplomatic." Throughout her life she and, more immediately, the Douglass Center women, braved public scorn to breech the color line and reject slander concerning black women's moral reputations. Wells-Barnett informed the theater school that the "young ladies could not have a very secure hold on their reputations if giving one night's performance would cause them to lose them."[79] This fence was not mended but replaced. Woolley and Wells-Barnett had addressed a Hull-House audience on their work at the Douglass Center the previous month. Jane Addams now came to their aid, offering performers from her settlement's School of Dramatic Art.[80] The press trumpeted the women's success. When thanks were delivered at the evening's close, Wells-Barnett reportedly "took a fall or two out of our local ministers, whom she said had opposed the movement upon purely selfish or personal grounds. . . . Many of the listeners gave significant nods as if they understood and approved of the rebuke, and knew the principal minister referred to."[81]

In *Crusade for Justice*, Wells-Barnett blamed Rev. Carey and his Ministers' Alliance for later failing to adequately support Ferdinand's bid for judge of Chicago's Municipal Court in the fall of 1906, just months after the Douglass Center brouhaha. Carey charged Barnett with implicitly encouraging people to visit the Pekin "saloon," no doubt angry about Barnett's willingness to interfere with his public relations campaign against Motts and his attempt to draw independent support around the Douglass Center.[82] The moment must have been a supremely ironic one for Barnett, who himself was a strict teetotaler and whose daughter recalled that no alcohol ever was served at home because her father "didn't want anyone to say that they took their first drink at our house."[83] According to Wells-Barnett, her husband firmly placed responsibility for proving negative claims about the Pekin on Carey, noting that "he was quite sure that his wife would not have given her time and effort to support a movement of such degraded character."[84] A community newspaper, the *Broad-Ax*, strongly backed Barnett's candidacy for judge, but he lost narrowly, by a few hundred votes.[85] That this defeat took place without loyal support of black voters violated a closely held principle of Ida B. Wells-Barnett's: that the ballot and its use in the interest of racial justice and community betterment was sacred.

Launching the Negro Fellowship League, 1908–1910

Since Memphis days, Wells-Barnett had advocated solidarity at the voting booth and voting with one's feet in matters of church and community influence. Her tangle with Carey expressed her long-standing belief that clergy and church women should work together to advance a community agenda, as in her own work with Taylor Nightingale or Reverdy Ransom, and that women need not submit to a minister with whom they had an honest, principled disagreement. Her own institutional loose ends in the period 1903–4 may have motivated Wells-Barnett to take on the powerful Rev. Carey. As tensions between Ransom and Carey peaked, the moral turpitude of one Rev. A. L. Murray, assistant pastor at Bethel AME, pushed Wells-Barnett's patience to the break point. When Murray's sexual indiscretions became public, the Barnetts withdrew from the church. "I had a family of growing children," Wells-Barnett explained in her autobiography, "and all my teachings would be null and void if I continued in a church with a man who had become so notoriously immoral."[86] It was after leaving Bethel AME, around 1904, that the Barnetts linked up with the Douglass Center and began to more actively support Amanda Smith's Industrial Home for orphans.[87] In a move that must have tweaked the local AME organization, Ida joined the Presbyterians and Ferdinand the Baptists.[88]

Though "not a Presbyterian by doctrine," Wells-Barnett later explained, "since all Christian denominations agreed on a standard of conduct and right living it seemed to me to matter very little what name we bore." This "confession of faith" apparently satisfied Rev. Moses H. Jackson, the founding pastor of Grace Presbyterian Church, who likely considered Wells-Barnett's membership a feather in the cap of his congregation.[89] Daughters Alfreda and Ida Jr. went through a more traditional passage to church membership. They were baptized and "Publicly Acknowledged" by Grace in 1915, and both later served as teachers in the Sunday school program, following in their mother's footsteps.[90] The Presbyterian church was not Wells-Barnett's final religious home in Chicago, but she found at Grace the support denied her at Carey's Bethel AME, and it was from Grace that she launched her community-building work through 1920.

Grace was a middle-class congregation, one of the few churches prosperous enough at the turn of the twentieth century to own its building. The impetus for its founding in 1888 came from two southern women, a Mrs. Dyson and a Mrs. Crutcher from Kentucky, who initially joined Quinn Chapel, biding their time to establish a "Presbyterian Church of the colored race in Chicago."[91] Soon after her arrival at Grace, Wells-Barnett was asked to teach the "men's Bible class by the members themselves." "Every Sunday we discussed the Bible lessons in a plain common-sense way," she later wrote, "and tried to make application of their truths to our daily lives."[92] This class and its "lively discussions" were remembered fondly by participants in later years; Wells-Barnett herself recalled her decade of teaching as "one of the most delightful periods of my life in Chicago."[93] Wells-Barnett offered the church her seasoned leadership, lecturing the "teachers and officers of the Sunday School" and addressing the church's annual business meeting.[94] Grace surrounded its youth with special pride. "The flower of our young womanhood and manhood, just from the cradle of the church, homeward bound, faultless in deportment and correct and immaculate in dress, is an inspiration to everyone," waxed J. Hockley Smiley in the *Defender* one fine June day in 1912. "There is no grander sight on a Sunday than 'when Grace lets out.'"[95]

Wells-Barnett's settlement efforts grew out of her commitment to education through the church, a commitment forged in the South. After the Springfield riot of 1908, a group of motivated Grace Sunday School students joined Wells-Barnett at her home for meetings and discussions, as mentioned earlier, taking the name Negro Fellowship League (NFL). The Barnett daughters also joined in ("mother always kept something going for the young people" at home, Alfreda recalled), and their mother noted that the "young men became interested and it gradually came to be quite the thing to bring their young lady friends to my home on a Sunday afternoon." "Here we discussed matters affecting the race and invited prominent persons who might be in the city to address us."[96] Among the many issues discussed were events at Springfield and even closer to home, the fate of African Americans imprisoned at the nearby Joliet and Bridewell facilities, information likely gleaned from Ferdinand Barnett's legal work. This focus was consistent with both the "friendly visiting" of women's traditional church work as well as the investigative journalism and sociological surveys that Wells-Barnett pioneered among African Americans and which were going on in Chicago in these same years.

From its inception, the Negro Fellowship League expressed a social vision quite different from that of the Douglass Center or Hull-House. "Negro" identified racial solidarity rather than interracialism; "Fellowship" highlighted a religious core; and "League" accented social action. Wells-Barnett described its purpose as "developing loyalty to and fellowship within the race: to labor for the elevation of the moral, civic and social standards of the race, especially of the young men."[97] She described men as both agents and clients of uplift. "Most of my young men had come from good families and other sections of the country," she noted. "Many of them were well educated. Some were taking courses in law and medicine while they earned their daily bread by night work in the post office."[98] On the client side, Wells-Barnett responded to a generally acknowledged "boy problem" in urban America as well as to the particular needs in Chicago's black community, itself undergoing generational and regional adjustments. As club woman Irene Lewis argued in an article on "Our Young Boys" in the *Defender*: "the Sunday Schools do not reach the youth we want to reach, not the young men we want to reach," those who would become the next generation's "Douglass . . . Bruce . . . [or] Dunbar."[99]

Beyond the "boy problem," Wells-Barnett claimed that the need for the Negro Fellowship League was exacerbated by African Americans' exclusion from Christian fellowship and uplift organizations across the city. White-run settlements in Chicago generally upheld the color line;

ironically, racist exclusion offered an argument for philanthropic support of the League.[100] When in 1909 Wells-Barnett addressed Chicago's Congregational Union, she informed the audience that African Americans were the "most neglected group" in the city, denied access to settlements, YMCAS, YWCAS, and "every other movement for uplift." After this meeting, YMCA supporters Mr. and Mrs. Victor F. Lawson became aware of and interested in remedying this discrimination. "I did not think that our Christian forces should leave State Street to the devil," Wells-Barnett recalled arguing to the Lawsons. "If we could have a modern, up-to-date reading room set down there in the midst of all those temptations . . . it would be a splendid beginning in the way of having something that would help the young men who came to the city."[101] Victor Lawson agreed.

With wealth gained from decades of publishing the *Chicago Daily News*, Lawson was a force in local philanthropy. Among many things, he helped put the city's YMCA on sure financial footing, and in 1911 he agreed to fund the reading room Wells-Barnett outlined. The term of support was one year or until a YMCA opened on the South Side, at which point the Negro Fellowship League would be absorbed into that organization.[102] Lawson contributed some $9,000 to the support of the Negro Fellowship League and went on to serve on the city's Race Relations Commission, which was charged with investigating the violence of 1919, and to support the Urban League in the 1920s.[103] Wells-Barnett recalled being "lifted to the seventh heaven" at the prospect before her and "cheerfully" established the library and furnishings for the reading room, whose doors she opened in a "blaze of glory."[104]

Lawson's largesse allowed Wells-Barnett the kind of bankroll that she and her peers rarely experienced in settlement and uplift work. The financial resources available to the wealthy Jane Addams or the well-connected Celia Woolley were hard to come by for northern, urban black women around the turn of the century. The Hull-House annual budget was over $20,000 in 1900; in flush times the Negro Fellowship League's was about $6,000. Louise DeKoven Bowen contributed nearly three-quarters of a million dollars of her personal fortune to Hull-House. When the South Side's Phillis Wheatley Home came into $10,000 through a bequest in 1928, president Elizabeth Lindsay Davis reported to the NACW, "We are all so excited about it that we can hardly talk sanely."[105] Addams worked at fundraising, but she neither desired nor feared that her institution would need to exchange its autonomy in order to secure financial support from the city or other public or private agencies. Her claim that Hull-House "always held its activities lightly, ready to hand them over to whosoever would carry them on properly" was sincere, but it did not extend to the settlement itself.[106] By contrast, adoption of African American start-up institutions by states and municipalities was a regular and even sought-after way to stabilize the delivery of services to black communities that would otherwise be completely neglected.[107] Further complicating matters, handing over black community work to white-dominated social agencies was often fraught with fears of racism. Underwritten by independent wealth, Addams could afford to premise the constructive force of her settlement upon its freedom from both compromising political debts and religious dogma, comparing the work of Hull-House favorably to either the corrupt local party machine, which lined its pockets and left the trash piled up, or to church missions interested in mere "souls." The contrast with the politicized, race-conscious, and strongly religious context of Wells-Barnett's settlement work could not be more striking.[108]

Program and Prospects of the Negro Fellowship League, 1910–1912

Settlements like the Negro Fellowship League and other start-up institutions in black communities were difficult to incorporate into the "mixed economy" of early public welfare, education, and social service modeled by Hull-House.[109] African American agencies were usually small programs functioning in racially hostile cities, a less than inviting context for securing a government contract or long-term foundation support. Black self-help institutions also usually delivered de facto segregated services. The progressive ideal, however, was nondiscrimination, even racial integration, in service delivery, and the bias in newly professional social service was away from the institutionalized care of dependents that was favored in African American communities.[110] Catholic and Jewish social agencies were often wealthy enough to ward off these trends; African American institutions usually were not. As a result, institutions adopted by government or other agencies often lost community control and support. Finally, suspicion toward black peoples' ability to exercise leadership or properly handle money pervaded the attitudes of new white professionals in social service and undermined collaborative work across the color line.[111] Even Victor Lawson's letters to Wells-Barnett were peppered with sharp instructions concerning the proper management of a trust. These instructions questioned not her arithmetic but her willingness to move into areas of expenditure unapproved by him.[112] Wells-Barnett resisted the racist drift in social welfare work and "struggled along" as best she could alone.[113]

She had her own ideas, besides. In describing the Negro Fellowship

League, Wells-Barnett interchangeably used the terms "social work" and "missionary work." These uses point to the religious grounding of the project and to Wells-Barnett's distance from the academic debates that were making fine distinctions between settlement work and church work in these years.[114] Yet very much like Hull-House and the other Chicago college and religious settlements, clubs were at the heart of the League's operation. The core members of the League were the young men and women Wells-Barnett led from Sunday school to social service and who met weekly for religious worship, lectures, and discussions. Beyond this core group, a raft of weekly meetings also gathered in the League's rooms. A Men's Civic Club was inaugurated by Ferdinand Barnett, and a Negro Fellowship League orchestra and chorus were assembled to provide the music that was a staple of club, church, and association life in black Chicago. Women also expressed their interests and social concerns through the League. A number of women's clubs associated with the NFL, an in-house group called the Woman's Alliance, for example, along with the affiliated Ideal Woman's Club (which hosted the NFL's opening) and a new Women's Second Ward Republican Club. The political club was a group designed much like the NFL, as a mediator and facilitator to "assist the men in getting better laws for the race and having representation in everything which tends to the uplift of the city and its government."[115] As in Wells-Barnett's Sunday school work, her focus remained practical and applied. For a $1.00 membership fee, the NFL promised to "make a special effort to keep you at work as long as you keep your dues paid."[116]

Despite the early accolades, gender and class concerns tagged close behind the League's eclectic bustle of activity.[117] In May 1911, Wells-Barnett began publishing a small newspaper called the *Fellowship Herald*, and these issues surfaced in print. Editorials echoed the dilemmas of female initiative that had dogged Wells-Barnett since the 1890s. She felt pressed to respond to criticism about "the leadership of a woman" at the League. Referring to herself in the third person, Wells-Barnett explained that "the President" of the organization would be "very glad to retire" at that point when the "League develops a leader among men who will look after the race's affairs." Though the settlement's appeal was directed at "women, too," the NFL (like antilynching) accented men's needs—the needs of "every aspiring, ambitious young man of the race"—in its mission.[118] No less than in the 1890s, the dilemmas of gender and leadership remained unresolved.

But the stakes had changed. In 1912–13, the woman suffrage fight and victory in Illinois pointedly raised the question of female political power. Concerned League members needed only to look as far as the women's Republican club that met in their own rooms to have a glimpse at what mobilized female voters might mean. Most African American institutions in Chicago, from churches to the Old Folks' Home to the Urban League, relied on affiliated women's clubs to contribute fundraising, donations in kind, and other support.[119] Though officially designed to meet the needs of men and boys, League membership was open to both men and women, and sometimes catered to the latter. The League sponsored "Ladies' Day" events and mothers' meetings. The *Fellowship Herald* produced a "Women's Edition" during its first summer of operation and did a stint of double duty as the "organ of the Negro Fellowship League and the State and City Federations of Colored Women's Clubs."[120] Few, if any, black institutions survived without women's support, but female leadership at the NFL, with its broad vision of community development, drew fire. People simply did not know what to make of Wells-Barnett. After she stumped for Taft in 1912, for example, the *Defender* mangled metaphors and trivialized her work with references to age (she was now fifty): "Were it not for her gentle sex, we would like to call Mrs. Ida B. Wells-Barnett the 'Old Roman' of racial endeavor and accomplishment within the range of femininity. But how dare we say 'old' in speaking of such a delightful lady. . . . Mrs. Barnett is truly a veteran, but in doing things she has the spirit of a debutante with the wisdom of a chaperon."[121] Gone was the anchor of godly imperative for black women's public work that Reverdy Ransom invoked in the 1890s. The mixed symbols of battlefield and courtship suggest that Wells-Barnett was as hard as ever to pin down.

Nipping at the heels of her disclaimer to official leadership at the Negro Fellowship League were the end of Lawson's funding and a need for a fresh source of support. The League's next phase stressed another of her personal strengths: teaching. Alongside social settlements, this period witnessed the flowering of numerous new bible colleges and religious training institutes in Chicago, whose certificates qualified graduates to take on paraprofessional and lay-ministerial responsibilities within churches and religious organizations.[122] Dwight Moody's Institute was among the best known of these schools, and a young Mary McLeod among the most famous of its African American graduates. The YMCA and YWCA and, later, the Urban League, similarly evolved an array of seminars, fellowships, and institutes, sometimes affiliated with colleges and universities, to train professional staff. The Negro Fellowship League tried to provide an internship for Grace Sunday School students, likely taking cues from the new Chicago schools as well as from successful programs in youth training that were historically strong among black churches, especially the Southern Baptists' Young People's Union movement.[123] Faced with the end of philanthropic support in early 1912, Wells-Barnett approached the church for aid.

She had in mind a school, "a place for practical training of young men and women who wanted to do social service work," she explained in her autobiography. "I knew the church had the money. They knew I had the vision." The church seemed willing as long as they could install a male ministerial student at the helm, a prospect which "very much grieved" Wells-Barnett but to which she agreed after a "sleepless night." When she felt that the chairman of the committee responsible for assessing the NFL's viability both looked down upon her work and seemed distrustful of her ability to handle the check he gave her to cover back rent payments, she responded with vehemence: "I lost control of myself and told him that I wouldn't go on with the deal."[124] Wells-Barnett found herself at a classic juncture documented by many scholars of independent social service delivery in African American communities. As a black woman, she found herself personally devalued and her abilities condescendingly second-guessed. The survival of NFL's program entailed the institution's absorption by a larger entity, potentially eroding its grassroots mission and constituency of support, especially among women.[125] Like Amanda Smith, who invested her life savings from missionary work in an orphanage for black children in nearby Harvey, Illinois, Wells-Barnett could not get the church to support an independent community institution run by a black woman.[126]

Amidst the funding crises, a number of other contradictions in the work of the NFL also emerged. Attracting the support of prosperous black families and encouraging their children to serve the down-and-out proved difficult. The genteel young people from Grace were "averse to visiting the poolrooms, saloons, and street corners in order to find and invite young men and distribute cards." At the same time, Wells-Barnett became aware of the interlocking needs for jobs, housing, and recreation in the neighborhood. Her operation soon moved beyond the reading room to include broader offerings, including an employment service and a flophouse in rooms upstairs. Though she later noted with pride that "[s]everal men who are now prosperous practicing physicians in this town took advantage of several occasions to rent a bed at twenty-five cents a night" courtesy of the League, sometimes the white glove of fellowship was simply rejected or ignored.[127] Finally, the NFL's initial premise as a stopgap until the coming of the YMCA to the South Side contained the seeds of its own destruction. Yet the work also gathered its own momentum, raising the hopes of Wells-Barnett and her neighbors for self-directed success in mutual aid and political development.

Adult Probation and a New Phase for the League, 1913–1915

Facing a financial crisis, Wells-Barnett revamped her settlement and turned to politics. The League moved to a smaller space, a storefront at 3005 State Street, and eliminated the flophouse. Members also had their dues raised to $12 per year and only those paying had the privileges of events, clubs, the reading room, job placement, or participation in the popular Fellowship Chorus. These changes reconfigured the cross-class character of the League, shifting its emphasis from uplift to achievement. In order to raise funds, Wells-Barnett had to deliver and market success. In February 1913, the Fellowship Chorus performed to great acclaim inside Chicago's downtown Loop at the fiftieth anniversary celebration of the Emancipation Proclamation. The performance garnered Wells-Barnett much-needed press visibility and registered a clear victory against racial segregation to her neighbors.[128] Cut off from philanthropy and church support, it was but a short step to official politics. The League involved itself both in the fight for woman suffrage at the state and national levels and in Republican Party work at the local level. The recognition Wells-Barnett needed came from this new mix of initiatives. In the spring of 1913, she received a patronage appointment as adult probation officer in the Domestic Relations Department of the Chicago Municipal Court from Chief Judge Harry Olson, a job she received, in her words, "on a silver salver" and which breathed new life into the NFL.[129]

Chartered by the Illinois legislature in 1905, the Chicago Municipal Court was a pioneer experiment with socialized law in criminal adjudication, widely replicated by cities across the country.[130] The major preoccupations of the Chicago Municipal Court—youth behavior, poor peoples' access to resources, and lower-class sexuality and family life—were also the obsessions of social progressivism and came together in especially concentrated form under the rubric of Domestic Relations. The cases in this division involved mainly claims of nonsupport by working-class and lower-middle-class wives and female relatives against husbands and fathers. Probation officers in Domestic Relations oversaw the compliance of mostly male laborers and clerks with the terms of their "sentence," usually a mandate to financially contribute to the support of their wives and children. As described by the presiding judge of Domestic Relations, Joseph Z. Uhlir, the probation officer "sees that the order of the court to pay for support of the family is obeyed; if probationer is out of work, obtains a job for him; settles quarrels between husband and wife; in cases of necessity, procures charitable help; and generally acts as the good samaritan."[131] It was uphill work. "In many of these cases there is an exceedingly bitter feeling between husband and wife, and between husband and the wife's relatives," explained Chief Probation Officer John Houston. "The defendant usually leaves the Court swearing that he never will make the payments ordered; and it is like drawing teeth to get the money out of him."[132] Domestic Relations achieved the lowest percentage of "improved" probationers in the entire criminal division. Contributing to the dependency of a minor consistently ranked third highest after larceny and disorderly conduct in the Court's annual crime statistics.[133] "It is clearly evident, after several years of experience," concluded Houston, "that the domestic cases are the hardest ones to handle."[134]

Such was Ida B. Wells-Barnett's task as the first African American adult probation officer for the Municipal Court of Chicago.[135] She was well-prepared for the assignment. Cases from the city's socialized courts were already being sent to the Negro Fellowship League. The Juvenile Court's pioneer woman judge Mary Bartelmae (who was white) sent black youths to the League, as did the judge and officers of the Boy's Court.[136] Wells-Barnett helped direct a local Woman's Protective Association, which sent attaches to the Court to oversee the treatment of women and supported the court's growth when it expanded to include a Morals Division, whose goal was curbing prostitution and vice in the city.[137] Wells-Barnett's autobiography recounts her successful intervention in the case of one young man, a teenager named George Thomas, who had "beaten his way" alone from Georgia to Chicago and who got caught in the court system. Through her personal connections to Judge Swanson and staff at the Boy's Court, to the YMCA, and to a series of local employers, Wells-Barnett shepherded Thomas through a rocky period of homelessness, unemployment, and police brutality, finally setting him on a path to becoming a "respected citizen of Chicago."[138] By the time she was tapped by Judge Olson, Wells-Barnett was already well-known and respected at the Municipal Court. The growth of Adult Probation and the bulging caseload from the Court of Domestic Relations created new needs for staff that resulted in her appointment in May 1913.

Before the Great Migration, the idea that black clients needed black supervisors in social service received support among black leaders in Chicago.[139] When Mrs. Alberta Moore Smith and Mrs. Jessie Thomas earned appointments as probation officers in the Juvenile Court, they proved, according to the *Defender*, "that merit counts, no matter what the color of the skin."[140] The *Defender*'s pride in black achievement and colorblind meritocracy belied underlying trends, however. As the paper admitted in Wells-Barnett's case a few years later, it was Olson's idea to appoint a probation officer "who by identity of race interest and relationship would be best fitted to help probationers in their efforts to regain the 'straight and narrow path.'"[141] The politics of race skittered around in South Siders' arguments for equity and fairness in city employment in this period. By the 1920s, however, any kind of job mongering—especially positions that smacked of racial tokenism or that created segregated (and sometimes unequal) delivery of services— would be heatedly opposed by the *Defender* as damaging to community interests.

Wells-Barnett, the visionary pragmatist, did not quibble over such matters. People like George Thomas needed help, and she could provide it. While her settlement experience made probation work a logical fit, the prospect of paid employment made the job compelling. Judge Olson indicated that she "could carry on the work in connection with the social center," that is, at the League's office. "I accepted this understanding," wrote Wells-Barnett later, "because I could see how the $150 a month would help me meet the current expenses of the place."[142] The difficulty with compliance in Domestic Relations created incentives to investigate a probationer's home and work environment before placement in the program. Short staffing and growing caseloads made such investigations difficult, but Wells-Barnett's South Side location could facilitate personal inquiries, especially if she was kept to mostly black probationers.

According to the available records of cases, Wells-Barnett received exclusively African American probationers from Domestic Relations. Of seventeen cases identified, all concerned either family abandonment or contributing to the dependency of a child, sixteen in the case of fathers and one in the case of a mother.[143] Nearly all probationers worked in menial or service sector jobs, mostly as laborers or porters. Her caseload seems to be a representative sample. Unemployment was a major contributing factor to noncompliance with orders for family maintenance, so much so that the Municipal Court found it necessary to open an employment bureau of its own.[144] Another factor in noncompliance was the pervasive sentiment of probationers that they were wrongly charged. Individuals invariably plead "not guilty," and the man involved usually felt he had "not violated any law and his quarrel is with his wife, or with his wife's relative, and he resents being arrested and brought into court."[145] These conditions also characterized Wells-

Barnett's sample of cases, and as far as her terse notations indicate, many failed to satisfy their terms of probation.

Though the Municipal Court was founded on the idea that people's behavior could be changed, men's failure to support their families violated deeply held common sense about gender norms. "The failure of so many men to support their families, no matter what the cause, is a very bad condition of affairs," concluded one annual probation report. The unrepentant derelict father, like the brazen "erring daughter" who dabbled in the fast life of "treating" and light prostitution, led officials to diagnose such individuals as mentally deficient or otherwise diseased, with alcoholism ranking high among the diseases.[146] "Some are subnormal and some defective—some are the victims of environment," noted one report, "but a great deal of the criminality is caused by the low moral tone of this community."[147] While the court had an interest in playing up "the powerful arm of the law" in stemming the tide of "Domestic Slackers," officials also admitted that probationers struggled with "all kinds of trouble."[148] Wells-Barnett's relationship to these kinds of diagnoses is not entirely clear, nor is it clear whether she became an advocate for the wives involved, some of whom testified to severe domestic violence and even to living in fear of their lives.[149]

Though she was capable of stern teaching within her community, the available evidence suggests that Wells-Barnett became an ally for those with whom she dealt in her official capacity. "My probationers reported to me there and many an evening found me at nine and ten o'clock at night still wrestling with their problems," she recalled in her autobiography.[150] She told Joel Spingarn of the NAACP that she found the work "most gratifying" and was proud of providing a place "where adult humans come with their woes for adjustment."[151] But it was the system, not the people caught in it, that needed adjusting. Likely viewing her probation work as an extension of her antilynching activities and of her husband's work at the bar, Wells-Barnett focused on abuses in the criminal justice system. She used the press to bring attention to the ill treatment of black prisoners (such as solitary confinement), and the Negro Fellowship League eventually appointed its own "jail visitors" who met with inmates at the Joliet and Bridewell facilities.[152] Wells-Barnett also educated South Side women about her work, addressing the Ida B. Wells Club on the subject of the "Court of Domestic Relations."[153] Finally, she put her badge to creative and characteristically theatrical use on behalf of petitioners who came directly to her for aid.

One such case involved the virtual incarceration of a "colored girl" as a domestic servant in the home of a white woman. The girl was isolated from the black community—even from church—and worked for this mistress without pay for thirteen years. A disagreement broke out when the white woman "found the girl talking to a colored man who did odd jobs in the neighborhood." "When she attempted to beat the girl for this," recalled Wells-Barnett in her autobiography, "she left the house and feared to go back because she believed the woman could have her arrested, although she was twenty-three years old." When presented with this situation, Wells-Barnett telephoned the employer and, taking the young woman along to the house, confronted her with her "star as an adult probation officer in addition to being president of the Negro Fellowship League." The white woman's opposition collapsed upon being threatened with legal action, and she gave her former servant back pay and her clothing after what Wells-Barnett slyly termed "a very pleasant interview, all things considered." *Crusade for Justice* offered a telling conclusion: "The poor girl was dumbfounded because she hadn't dreamed it was possible for a colored woman to succeed in getting justice for her."[154]

Woman Suffrage, Race Politics, and the Fate of the NFL

It was no longer merely a dream for African American women to get justice for themselves. To one who had long held the ballot sacred, the coming of woman suffrage to Illinois in 1913 added force to that dream. Out of principle and necessity, Ida B. Wells-Barnett placed her hopes in politics, but politics proved to be the undoing rather than the salvation of her settlement work.[155] As historian Wanda Hendricks has noted, where the ballot was concerned, "female justice equaled community justice."[156] Woman suffrage promised the integration of black women into the decision-making and distributive power of the state in the interest of the community of which the NFL was a part. As in the 1890s, however, deep ambivalence over women's roles in public life frustrated Wells-Barnett's hope for a reliable avenue for empowerment.

She began with great enthusiasm, inspired no doubt by Chicago black women's jubilation at enfranchisement. "Tell the world I am of voting age!" crowed a Miss Annette Troutman to a *Defender* reporter during her birthday celebration in the winter of 1914.[157] The vehicle for Wells-Barnett's ambition was the Alpha Suffrage Club for black women, founded in January 1913. The Alphas embraced several tactics designed to negotiate the uncertainties of electoral politics. The first was nonpartisanship for women, a compelling framework but one that failed to hold in a system fueled by fierce partisanship. Another approach was interest group lobbying and the public presence of black women in the halls of power. Finally, the Alphas pooled their resources with the League and other clubs into a new group that Wells-Barnett called the Federated Organizations, an umbrella political arm for the black community. The result was a significant expansion of black women's activist repertoire in community life but one not able to deliver the dollars and support needed to sustain the Negro Fellowship League and its developing political agenda.

Nonpartisanship was the initial keynote of the Alpha Suffrage Club, touted as "the only woman suffrage club of the race in the Second ward" and which held its weekly meetings at the NFL.[158] "The women are studying politics, getting all the necessary points on voting," explained Wells-Barnett in the press. "The women on the whole are nonpartisan. What they do hope to do is to become strong enough to help elect some conscientious race man as alderman. We are not looking for his politics, but we hope to elect a good man. But women as well as men must stand together as one if we hope to be successful." "By so doing," she concluded, "the colored women of Chicago can demand recognition just as other nationalities."[159] With the grumblings over female leadership at the League echoing in her ears, Wells-Barnett stressed that access to suffrage by black women promised a better reckoning between the black community—"women as well as men"—and local government, to be mediated by a male leader, a "race man." Her focus on "race" in politics was instrumental, analogized to the ethnic status of any of the "other nationalities" in polyglot Chicago.[160] Beyond the race issue, the gendered aspect of official nonpartisanship—support for a "good man" and not "his politics"—could defuse anxiety about female challenges to official leadership. Nonpartisanship also gave women credibility untainted by the supposed wheeling and dealing of men's smoke-filled back rooms. As Fannie Barrier Williams put it, women brought to voting "not partisanship but patriotism, not the spirit of office seeking but of law enforcing."[161] Such talk created consensus by bracketing a closer reckoning about policy setting and power sharing.[162]

With political equality and electoral influence also came the pressing need, long insisted upon by Wells-Barnett, that African American women be respectfully seen and heard in the public sphere. Since black women could not compete financially with the establishment, Wells-Barnett moved decisively into the ritual and symbolic aspects of politics, ventures fraught with rather more risk than white women's exploits with street theater, on picket lines, and in open-air meetings in the early twentieth century.[163] Her participation in panels, dinners, canvassing, parades, and speech-making all intensified in 1912–14. So did resistance. Black women's voter registration efforts on the South Side were jeered in the streets and mocked in the press.[164] Wells-Barnett later noted that the activities of the women "surprised . . . our men politicians . . . [and] even our ministers," none of whom had "said one word to influence women to take advantage of the suffrage opportunity Illinois had given to her daughters."[165] As in the antilynching campaign, Wells-Barnett shrewdly shifted tactics, avoiding confrontation with community men by launching an attack on racial segregation among white women.

In an event that showcased her media instincts, Wells-Barnett protested the jim-crowing of African American women to the back of a major pro-woman-suffrage parade held in Washington, D.C., in March 1913. The parade was a national event that drew thousands of women from across the country. Several white women from the Illinois suffrage delegation supported Wells-Barnett's antisegregation position at the parade. During the women's confrontation with parade organizers, a reporter caught Wells-Barnett talking through tears. The *Chicago Tribune* described a "Plea by Mrs. Barnett" in which her voice "trembled with emotion and two large tears coursed their way down her cheeks before she could raise her veil and wipe them away."[166] The Illinois women lost their protest, but Wells-Barnett, ever the astute judge of a political and theatrical moment, devised another plan. On parade day, she stepped from the sidelines to join the Illinois delegation at the head of the procession. This dramatic gesture required not just confidence in her colleagues' support (the Illinois women did not know of her plan ahead of time) but also personal courage. The paraders faced rowdy crowds of male antisuffrage hecklers throughout the day and finished their march only with the protection of cavalry troops from nearby Fort Myer.

After returning to Chicago, Wells-Barnett thanked a white Illinois suffrage leader, Catherine Waugh McCullough, for supporting her bold action at the parade. Her confession to McCullough—"I have not yet seen the newspapers, I do not know a thing about what they have been saying [about the incident]"—is almost laughable given Wells-Barnett's experience with the press as an antilynching agitator.[167] A veteran publicist, she would scarcely have bothered stealing the show at the suffrage parade without the assurance that she would make the papers and her point—which, cruelly enough, the hostilities against the marchers guaranteed. As McCullough herself well knew, the parade was a carefully orchestrated pageant, replete with allegorical tableaux, elaborate costuming, and signage. The entire event was shot through with staged and spontaneous political theater, including several competing dramas about race and gender, placing Wells-Barnett in a superb context for her action.[168] "Again the glorious traditions of Anglo-Saxon manhood have been upheld!" exclaimed W. E. B. Du Bois in a wicked send up of the suffrage hecklers in *The Crisis*. "Again the chivalry of American white men has been magnificently vindicated."[169] Characteristically, Du Bois ignored Wells-Barnett's intervention against Jim Crow on behalf of black women. But the *Chicago Defender* cheered her on its front page as "The Modern Joan [of] Arc," praising her stand against racism with a paean to her sex: "Mrs. Barnett represents the highest type of womanhood in Illinois."[170] Neither of these accounts by African Americans noted her tears, but she skillfully made her point.

Wells-Barnett's successful theatrics at the parade was only one in a series of new public ventures for Chicago black women. *Crusade for Justice* highlights an unprecedented massing of African American women to lobby legislators at the Illinois state capitol in April 1913. At issue was a series of racist measures proposed in that legislative session, including a Jim Crow public accommodations bill and a bill making miscegenation a punishable offense.[171] In the previous election, the Progressive Party vote in Illinois had siphoned support from Republicans, giving the Democrats the governorship as well as a majority in the legislature. "A meeting was called in Springfield which was attended by representative groups of club women from different parts of the state to protest [the two bills]," recalled Wells-Barnett, and as the club women "visited committee rooms," she served as "spokesman for the women on this momentous occasion." Keen as ever on political theater, Wells-Barnett afterward proclaimed that "the winding through the capitol building of two or three hundred colored women was itself a sight that had never been witnessed before." "The legislature got the impression that the Negro womanhood of the state was aroused," she explained, "and the visible massing of hundreds of them did as much even as the arguments presented to impress the members of the legislature with the seriousness of the situation."[172] The concerted effort by African Americans from across the state defeated the targeted measures. The *Defender* lauded the action at Springfield, giving special praise to Wells-Barnett on its "roll of honor." "The name of Mrs. Barnett stands out alone because that constant and fearless champion of equal rights was on the firing line all the time. Her eloquent pleas in private conferences with the legislators and in open session were eloquent and forcible. Ida B. Wells-Barnett has again endeared herself to the world."[173]

These events underscored the salience of interest group methods— mass demonstrations and voting blocs—for black women in politics. In such a context, however, the rhetoric of nonpartisanship could not long hold as an anti-ideological center. Like the *Defender*'s ambivalence about merit- versus race-based access to civil service, claims about female nonpartisanship coexisted uneasily with black women's need for public recognition, funds, and jobs. Though the Alpha Suffrage Club's rhetoric was nonpartisan, a significant selling point for the club's legitimacy and practical worth was its ability to deliver votes and patronage. "This club is the only one which has been able to secure any political appointments for its members so far," wrote Wells-Barnett at the end of 1914. "As its membership grows, it will be able to do more." The Alphas also secured patronage as election workers and sent their first delegate to the state Republican convention in 1914.[174] As a political club president, Wells-Barnett was expected to deliver both votes and jobs. In the spring of that year, she wrote to Judge Harry Olson urging the appointment of the NFL's secretary, Mr. O. B. Payne, as bailiff in the Municipal Court. This interest sprang from the difficulty of meeting Payne's $75 monthly salary in the absence of Victor Lawson's subsidy, the strain of supervising her heavy probationers' caseload, and the influence that would no doubt follow such a successful placement.[175]

Initially unencumbered by political debts in the community, the Alpha Suffrage Club provided a fresh venue for political gatherings, as it did in the 1914 campaigns for county commissioner, municipal judge, and in the mayor's race.[176] "Great interest is being manifested and the club is accomplishing splendid results in teaching the women their duties in affairs of government," commended the *Defender*.[177] The definition of those duties did not stand still, however. In some instances, women's nonpartisanship reflected race consciousness, the idea, expressed in the *Alpha Suffrage Record*, that Chicago's "colored men are colored men first—Republicans, Progressives and Democrats afterward."[178] "As the Club is non-partisan, it has not taken a stand for any special candidate," explained Wells-Barnett. "It sincerely hopes, however, that one will be elected to represent the Negro in the City Council."[179] Overwhelmingly, the idea of a black male candidate created the most consensus, but even that idea raised as many questions as it answered. In the case of the 1915 aldermanic race, it meant choosing which black male candidate, because three were running in a crowded field.

Like the passage of woman suffrage, the "aldermanic situation in the second ward" of 1915 created as many questions as it solved for political empowerment. On the intensely factionalized South Side, pressure centered on the Alphas, who sponsored the only meetings in which all the candidates participated. Club president Wells-Barnett exerted her own brand of political discipline with a tactic honed in public life in Memphis. "A motion unanimously prevailed that any member of the club known to be working for the white alderman candidates should be expelled and the names of those who are not members published in the weekly press."[180] Like everyone else, black women were hardly in lock step. The Alphas were divided enough to sponsor their own internal primary in February, resulting in a victory for candidate DePriest.[181] Another black women's club more friendly to the machine's candidate, Louis B. Anderson, emerged with the cleverly confusing name of the "Aloha" Club. Their leader, Bertha Montgomery, would rival Wells-Barnett as a highly skilled leader of African American women in the electoral realm through the 1920s.[182] The Alphas registered a major first success when their votes lifted DePriest into the city council to represent the second ward.[183] In 1917, however, DePriest declined to run when a scandal touched him, and the seat went to Anderson, who maintained a lock on the Republican regulars that allowed him to remain in office for eight consecutive two-year terms.

Wells-Barnett was among a cohort of activist Chicago women who strategized around the party machinery in the interest of reform before World War I. Women of every ideological stripe had great difficulty in avoiding or defeating entrenched interests in the political wards and in the business sector.[184] In their efforts to improve sanitation and safety in housing, the white women of Hull-House tried in vain to dislodge the machine and its ties to local landlords in the Halstead Street district's Nineteenth Ward. When they failed, their multiple sources of support and deep pockets permitted them to simply change tactics, turning from electoral strategies to legal action in the courts.[185] When business and political interests forced white activist Florence Kelley out of her factory inspection job, Hull-House supported her and her three children through several years of on-and-off unemployment until she secured the chairmanship of the National Consumers League and moved to New York in 1900.[186] Few if any black women had such resources at their disposal. And while they had little choice but to cooperate with the Republican Party, African American women did not simply accommodate themselves to business and politics as usual, because both were in rapid transition.[187] Their neighborhood was fought over precinct by precinct, vote by vote, by an array of individuals and groups, among them older elites like Ferdinand Barnett, that teetotaling stalwart of Republican virtues, ambitious new young men like Oscar DePriest, and a crazy quilt of European immigrants who also located their homes and businesses on the South Side.

In this churning environment, Wells-Barnett sought to stabilize and expand her influence through consolidation. All too aware that plans for empowering women sometimes stirred controversy, she assembled an agenda of "race interests" through the Federated Organizations, a consortium of her settlement, the Alphas, a sprinkling of other clubs, and the Chicago chapter of Monroe Trotter's Equal Rights League (ERL).[188] A keystone of her agenda involved an antisegregation fight at Wendell Phillips High School, long valued in the community as a racially integrated public school. In 1915, Wells-Barnett coordinated a meeting between school personnel, parents, and public officials which was, according to the *Defender*, "perhaps, the first of its kind held in Chicago, and claimed among its eager and heterogeneous audience, some of Chicago's best citizens of both races."[189] Picking up where the Mutual Protective Association in Memphis left off, the Federated Organizations created new links and spaces for social engagement, and their activities merged into political action.[190] Women's shared interests—like a mother's meeting featuring an address by Judge Mary Bartelmae—and ties of affection also figured in this consolidating trend at the NFL.[191] As the Ida B. Wells Club had thrown their president a welcome reception and a wedding party back in the 1890s, the Alphas now honored Ida and Ferdinand's twentieth wedding anniversary in a celebration at the Barnett home in June 1915.[192]

Though it is difficult to trace, the Federated Organizations met in conference during 1915 and firmed up its leadership during the following year.[193] Wells-Barnett herself was not among the elected leaders. Men served as president (and chaplain), but the other officers were women, and the board of trustees was of mixed sex. Accenting racial solidarity rather than women's newfound political clout, the Federated Organizations was made up of representatives of clubs and social organizations and sought to extend race consciousness into the political and economic realms.[194] As part of the Federated Organizations, the Negro Fellowship League's social action philosophy found full expression. "Opposed to prejudice, it has diligently used every means in its power to defeat it," declared Wells-Barnett in 1916.[195] The Federated Organizations joined the League's ongoing community education project, cosponsoring the annual Lincoln Celebration and Douglas Day events that same year.[196]

In an attempt to defuse yet strengthen black women's claim to political influence by spotlighting race, the Federated Organizations nonetheless drew new criticisms that would plague Wells-Barnett into the 1920s. In early 1916, the charge was raised that her efforts to build resistance to Jim Crow on the South Side somehow smacked of unacceptably separatist, race-based organizing. Wells-Barnett "stoutly denied that she was endeavoring to establish segregation in the effort to have the colored children discuss conditions affecting their welfare" in the public schools.[197] There was also a cryptic notice in the press that the Alpha Suffrage Club heard a "report of the insult offered to its president at the women's civic meeting held at the Institutional Church," a congregation now presided over by Rev. Archibald J. Carey.[198] When South Side women's support was sought by the Municipal Voters League, a nonpartisan group associated with white progressives in the city, Carey stepped in to intervene. He objected to any endorsement of Oscar DePriest as a candidate, since DePriest was battling charges that he, though not a drinking man, consorted with Bob Motts and other elements of the saloon and cabaret scene. Carey proclaimed that "it was not the policy of the Race to uphold" such men, especially since the "present alderman was in the field because of his color."[199] Carey's attack—a direct affront to Wells-Barnett's leadership where DePriest was concerned—grew out of the flux over defining "the Race's interests" and women's political roles as well as from tensions over creeping segregation at Wendell Phillips, tensions that became a political football when the mayor appointed a new school board the next year.[200]

Carey was on the offensive for good reason. During the 1915 elections, it was Wells-Barnett whom the supporters of mayoral candidate William Thompson initially approached as one "who the masses of colored people accepted as a leader" to help organize the black vote. Though Thompson and Carey had a long-standing political friendship, Carey had sided with the winning Democrats in recent years. The Thompson campaign dangled before Wells-Barnett the prospect of an "orphanage for colored girls" (Amanda Smith had passed away earlier that year), and though suspicious of such tactics, she was willing to hear out a proposal. When she and Ferdinand met with the politicians, Wells-Barnett informed those gathered that "it would be impossible for [her] to make any pledge" until she knew "what Mr. Thompson's program was with reference to colored people." She was, she wrote, "tired of having white men come out in the Second Ward just before or on election day and buy up the votes of Negroes who had no higher conception of the ballot than to make it a question of barter and sale." As a leading spirit behind the Federated Organizations, Wells-Barnett tentatively outlined an agenda. The city, she wrote, must show the black community "greater interest . . . in our welfare," a "better chance for employment in the city work," and especially "representation [must] be given us commensurate with our voting strength." Securing Thompson's support, Wells-Barnett signed on to the campaign, possibly holding in the back of her mind the hope of securing a Municipal Court judgeship for Ferdinand, a prospect Oscar DePriest entertained when he needed the Alphas and then promptly forgot upon his election to office.[201]

Twenty thousand pledge cards later, Wells-Barnett was proud of her work for Thompson, which she claimed to have achieved "without machine organization and without newspaper assistance." Cheek by jowl with this disclaimer about high-minded independence was patronage politics. "It was understood," she later wrote, "that if Mr. Thompson won, our reading room and social center was to be made an auxiliary of the city, and through our employment agency, colored men were to be given street-cleaning jobs and work in other departments" of city government. The Alpha Suffrage Club was the "very first organization" to endorse Thompson for mayor, but this initiative came to nothing. Early into the campaign, Wells-Barnett's political fortunes collapsed. Judge Harry Olson announced for mayor, backed by the city's well-organized progressive reformers, many of whom had a direct stake in the success of the Municipal Court. Out of personal loyalty to Olson, Wells-Barnett ceased her efforts for Thompson, suggesting that attorney Edward Wright pick up the reins. Joined now by Rev. Carey and Louis Anderson, Wright relaunched his own stymied political career. Carey was motivated to get back into the good graces of local Republicans since he aimed to achieve the regional bishopric. For coming back around to his old friend Thompson, Carey received a patronage appointment as assistant corporation counsel to the city, enhancing a résumé already studded with political gems. With Thompson's victory, Carey and Anderson secured access to the inner circles of the mayor's colorful and long-lived administration.[202] Wells-Barnett resented Carey's political machinations, as did many on the South Side, and she used her talent for exposé against him. She sent a letter to the AME Church's annual conference at Philadelphia complaining about the political funding and crass campaign tactics Carey had used in his quest to become bishop, a letter that she later claimed "turned the trick" against him at the meeting.[203]

After losing the mayor's race, Olson was unable to keep Wells-Barnett at the Municipal Court, and she was out in six months. Once the darling of reformers, the court was itself becoming part of the machine, the vaunted "peoples' court" increasingly staffed by "deputies . . . selected by the managers of the political parties."[204] Because Wells-Barnett had not stayed with Thompson "until the end" of the campaign, the administration took the liberty of ignoring her for patronage. She recalled, "I have been told that when some suggestion was made about keeping a promise to put me on the school board, our men told the mayor that 'he didn't owe Mrs. Barnett anything because she did not go with them to the end.' "[205] Rather than complain of betrayal by "our men" or the political establishment, however, Wells-Barnett chided herself for "foolishness" in not sticking with the Thompson forces. Like her regret over not turning her antilynching fame into a profitable lecturing career, Wells-Barnett realized that personal scruples put political access out of reach. While obviously capable of simple party discipline, the more complex questions of personal loyalty and political purpose created new conflicts and dilemmas for African American women. Like the men, they sought to honor ties of friendship and reciprocity in public life, but because their institutional connections were more tenuous than black men's and more constricted than white women's, they had limited negotiating room. Unlike well-connected churchmen who played both sides of the aisle and well-heeled white female reformers who did not need official politics for jobs and cash, black women had nowhere else to go if the party turned on them. The coming of war only raised the stakes for political survival in this fraught and competitive environment.

Settlement Work in War Time, 1916–1919

World War I prospered organizations that were officially allied with the war effort: the YWCA, the YMCA, the Urban League, the Red Cross, and, at least briefly, labor unions. It all but killed the Negro Fellowship League. The South Side's own new YMCA (1912) and YWCA (1914) achieved a critical financial foothold through official war work in the federally sponsored War Camp Community Service. The newly formed Urban League (1915), by virtue of its national stature and apolitical, academic credentials, captured Red Cross and U.S. Employment Service functions during wartime and gained major funding and prestige.[206] As faithful allies of the state, war work brought the "Ys" and the Urban League resources and visibility that completely bypassed Wells-Barnett and the Negro Fellowship League. Politically inclined independents like the League met with government suspicion, surveillance, and stigma. Moreover, the war released a tide of racial violence that claimed the conscience and energy of Wells-Barnett, diverting her attention from the bureaucratic politics that proved so critical to institutional success in these years.

The Negro Fellowship League certainly rose to meet the new stresses and demands created by migration and war. A committee was appointed in March 1917 to foster cooperation among local organizations to meet southern black migrants' needs; at a Ladies' Day program at the NFL, Wells-Barnett spoke on "Lessons from the War," and military personnel visited to discuss the subject of "Colored Officers in the United States Army."[207] The joint committee of the NFL and the City Federation of Colored Women's Clubs raised funds for "soldiers' comfort kits" and sent 900 pounds of goods to men training at Camp Grant that first Christmas of the war.[208] In a Fourth of July speech to Fulton Street ME Church, Wells-Barnett's subject was history: "Negro Women in the Wars of Our Country."[209] Through the Negro Fellowship League, Wells-Barnett made inquiries concerning discrimination against black women in employment in Chicago, both in the private sector and in war industries.[210] The League continued its focus on politics, however, holding meetings concerning the Cook County Republican Convention, labor organizing, and "political conditions" in the ward. With the drumbeat of preparedness sounding loudly, the NFL debated, "Why Should the Negro Fight for This Country?"[211]

The calculus of patriotism was not simple for Wells-Barnett. War mobilization and the migration northward of southern African Americans resulted in racial clashes that piqued her intense anger, especially after East St. Louis. The riot, coupled with a horrific burning of a black man in Memphis that same summer of 1917 preoccupied the NFL.[212] These outbreaks roughly coincided with a low point in Wells-Barnett's local political fortunes (the loss of her patronage post) and perhaps motivated her to reclaim some of her former influence as a leader of resistance to racial violence. To this end, Wells-Barnett activated the Equal Rights League's local operation, tracking the Bundy defense and planning for the ERL's national meeting in Chicago.[213] "Colored America, on to Chicago!" pitched Wells-Barnett in the *Defender*. "This organization, as you doubtless know, is the only one of national strength organized and officered by men and women of our own Race."[214] As the Alpha Suffrage Club embraced a more moderate new president, Dr. Fannie Emmanuel, and the Federated Organizations faded in the flurry of wartime activity, Wells-Barnett hoped that the historically militant ERL would rise to meet the challenge of black resistance to violence and injustice.[215] Unfortunately, these efforts found Wells-Barnett overextended, politically exposed, and alone.

While Wells-Barnett made the case for Leroy Bundy, and the Alphas managed without her, black women's patriotic war work proceeded apace on the South Side. Club leader Carrie Lee Hamilton rallied the women with the hope that "the promise of the newest freedom of all since 1865 is about to be fulfilled."[216] Black women gathered into the War Camp Community Service as well as into independent groups, like the Young Women's Patriotic Club of Bethel Church. In December 1917, a "women's patriotic rally" was held at St. Mary's Church, presided over by prominent club women and elected officials.[217] A committee of white women from the National Board of Defense judged an essay contest on the theme "The Woman in the War," coordinated by the new South Side YWCA's industrial secretary, Irene McCoy Gaines.[218] The Second Ward branch of the Woman's Committee of the Council of National Defense, under the leadership of Elizabeth Lindsay Davis, met at the Douglass Center.[219] Dr. Mary Fitzhugh Waring—African American physician, club woman, and affiliate of the Juvenile Protective Association—coordinated the Red Cross efforts that were also operating out of the Douglass Center.[220] In early 1918, some 14,000 African Americans jammed the Chicago coliseum to see Robert Abbott present the colors to the 365th Regiment in a ceremony held under the auspices of the National Security League of Chicago.[221] Eight weeks after Wells-Barnett was harassed by federal agents at the Negro Fellowship League, Fannie Emmanuel was elected president of the YWCA.[222] From her office at the Douglass Center, Elizabeth Lindsay Davis took charge of a yet another women's group, soliciting subscriptions to the new Chicago Urban League, which moved into the building space vacated by Celia Woolley's death in early 1918.[223]

More like her distant neighbor Jane Addams, who came out for peace during the war, Wells-Barnett suffered political and institutional setbacks for her own critical, if not pacifist, views of the government in wartime from which it took many years to recover.[224] In an unexpected career convergence, Addams and Wells-Barnett each paid dearly for their political independence in wartime. Like thousands of women across the United States, Wells-Barnett sold Liberty Bonds at home and supported the boys abroad.[225] But her association with the ERL and Monroe Trotter, who was considered by some to be tainted with treason for supposedly insulting President Wilson back in 1916 during a testy White House interview concerning Jim Crow in the capitol, possibly undermined her credibility among those African Americans who, like Du Bois, "closed ranks" for the duration.[226] True to form, Addams tried to split the difference, coming out for peace while making Hull-House available as a military recruitment center. Wells-Barnett was more consistent in her demand for racial fairness in the armed forces, sending aid to military men at Camp Grant while protesting the execution of black soldiers in 1917. Unlike Hull-House, however, the Negro Fellowship League had no financial cushion or social safety net to wage the political fights then central to its identity and survival, fights now more urgent than ever.

The Equal Rights League generated heat but no light. Trotter's attempt to participate at Versailles failed as badly as had Henry Ford's "Peace Ship" mission to bring the boys home by Christmas. Trotter stowed away on the SS *Yarmouth* and all but missed the deliberations in

France.[227] Wells-Barnett's effort to secure justice after East St. Louis was visible enough in the press but not much appreciated by either Bundy or the NAACP.[228] She and Ferdinand faced other disappointments. Their efforts to free a local black prisoner, "Chicken Joe" Campbell, sentenced to hang for the rape-murder of a woman prison official at Joliet, was rejected by the Illinois Supreme Court in early 1918.[229] After three years of fundraising and legal work, Barnett made one last scramble and finally secured from the governor a commutation to life imprisonment. "The struggle has been long, and at times, discouraging," Barnett wrote to the *Defender* in May 1918, "but success comes at last, and a human life has been saved instead of sacrificed upon the behest of race prejudice."[230] The Barnetts had hoped for more.[231]

With the political chips down and wartime stress all around, Wells-Barnett and her husband's focus on the criminal justice system and legal action to resist violent racism met a pressing need in the community. Barnett ran advertisements in the *Defender*—"NEW COMER, ATTENTION!"—offering his services for legal aid against police harassment.[232] Unfortunately, their work did not deliver the money, public credibility, or social advancement needed to jumpstart a political career or sustain a social service agency. Wells-Barnett's autobiography lamented the drain of the Campbell case on their family resources: "Only the recording angel knows what the Barnett family lost in helping to save one poor devil's neck from the noose."[233] Her own intervention in 1918 on behalf of John Cloures, another black prisoner at Joliet, points up both her skill at finding political pressure points and her limited opportunity to translate that skill into a workable career track or movement for reform. With his client found guilty of murdering an inmate and sentenced to hang, Cloures's court-appointed lawyer, David Field, appealed the verdict to the Illinois Supreme Court. Perhaps having learned her name and reputation from insiders at Joliet, Cloures also wrote to Wells-Barnett for help. They met at the jail and she agreed to do what she could. In the meantime, the conviction and death sentence were upheld on appeal at Springfield. When Cloures's lawyer raced over to the capitol, he learned that "Mrs. Barnett," aided by a "Mr. Whitman" (probably an attorney), had already successfully petitioned the governor for a reprieve that morning. Field then traveled to Chicago where he met with Wells-Barnett and continued the fight for Cloures's life, but they failed to save him.[234] The scene lends poignancy to Alfreda Duster's recollection that her mother "always wanted to be a lawyer" and that she encouraged her daughters to pursue that career path. They did not.[235]

By 1919, the Negro Fellowship League was financially on its knees. Just up the street, the Urban League was flooded with funds, having cashed in on the bureaucratization and political conservatism churned up by waging war. The Urban League ran a branch of the U.S. Employment Service through its offices, work that expanded so quickly that a second branch soon opened on the South Side to help place people in jobs.[236] Stepped-up government intervention in the economy only hurt the Negro Fellowship League. The League's job placement efforts could scarcely compete with the federal government's offerings, and the annual licensing fee the League paid to the state of Illinois taxed its limited resources without delivering increased access to patrons or clients.[237] Under the leadership of Robert Park of the University of Chicago (a white sociologist and former secretary to Booker T. Washington), the Urban League initially kept to a strictly research function, establishing itself as an authority on conditions among African Americans in part through the work of African American graduate student interns E. Franklin Frazier, Charles H. Johnson, and others. The Negro Fellowship League could barely afford one secretary. "We were so busy doing the work that we kept no record of the number of persons who were aided," Wells-Barnett later explained, "and we would have had no money with which to print such a record if we had preserved it." Even the NFL's attempt to assist black migrants at the Illinois Central Station was rebuffed by the Travelers Aid Society, which testily guarded its turf, and Wells-Barnett's effort to have a League member hired by that organization came to nothing.[238]

When the race riot broke out in Chicago in July 1919, the city looked for expertise and guidance not to its resident expert on lynching and racial violence, Ida B. Wells-Barnett, but to the academic, professional, and political newcomer, the Urban League. Having established itself as a neutral broker and go-between, the Urban League lent itself to the perceived need for mediation brought on by the crisis. For example, the organization made available its Douglass Center offices to distribute pay packets to black workers who then would not be forced to cross into danger zones during the riot. The Urban League also placed its research files and college-trained investigators at the disposal of the city's Commission on Race Relations.[239] Ignored by the Urban League and the city's Commission, scoffed at by the local clergy's Protective Association, it is no wonder that Wells-Barnett looked southward and boarded a train for Arkansas when the black farmers of Phillips County needed help in October.

In retrospect, it seemed to Wells-Barnett that "the Urban League was brought to Chicago to supplant the activities of the Negro Fellowship League,"[240] but that was neither the plan nor, exactly, the impact of the Urban League. Reflecting the strand of reform invested in facts and information as means to problem solving, the League self-consciously cultivated an apolitical research agenda and a mediating social role, most notably as a clearinghouse for jobs.[241] The result was not so much the supplanting of NFL-style advocacy but its marginalization and neglect, even its avoidance. It was not the substance of the Urban League's work—most of its early research had been on cases outside Illinois—but rather its access to government funds, corporate allies, and academic prestige that eclipsed start-up, politically wired operations like the Negro Fellowship League. Wells-Barnett concluded in her autobiography:

> All I can say of that ten years I spent on State Street is that no human being ever came inside the doors asking for food who was not given a card to the restaurant across the way. No one sought a night's lodging in vain, for after his case was investigated, a card to the Douglass Hotel was given him. And nobody who applied for a job was ever turned away. Very few had the price to pay for the job, but they always promised to come back. I am sorry to say that very few of them came back, and so we took what satisfaction we could out of the fact that we had helped a human being at the hour of his greatest need and that the race would get the benefit of our action if we did not.[242]

As a spiritual autobiography, *Crusade for Justice* foregrounds the self-sacrificing mission of the Negro Fellowship League. The historical record reveals this quality and more, namely the strong self-help and advocacy focus of the work, which was so glaringly absent from that of either the Douglass Center or the Urban League. With its forthright engagement in social and political contestation on the streets, at the polls, and in the state's and nation's capitals, the NFL offered African Americans—especially women—a place to gather and test their strength in new ways that inspired, confounded, and sometimes irritated the plethora of individuals and groups competing for power on Chicago's South Side in the World War I era.

Conclusion

Ida B. Wells-Barnett's settlement work drew on southern black women's church traditions of home missions as well as on club women's impulse to uplift. In competition for support in a northern, urban, industrial setting, Wells-Barnett embraced racial solidarity and political action over more conservative bureaucratic strategies of institution building. The explicit goal of empowerment for African Americans and the value it placed on the ballot as "sacred" set the League apart from the mainstream settlement movement, whose signal characteristic, according to its leadership, was an "absence of programme."[243] To a much greater extent than most black women's schools, settlements, and rescue homes built in the North in this same period, Wells-Barnett embraced social and political action rather than the sheltering of women and children. Given these ambitions, the NFL's decade of existence is impressive because, as historian Thomas Philpott and others have shown, most black settlements and self-help institutions in Chicago led much shorter and even more precarious lives.[244] The NFL's aggressive social agenda shaped and was shaped by an extremely volatile economic and political context. This volatility inspired creativity and high hopes in Wells-Barnett and her associates even as it made survival difficult.

Wells-Barnett was unable to secure consistent support from either church, party, or state for her community work, despite the fact that all of these institutions relied on her skills and dedication to meet the expanding needs of African American youth and adults. Jane Addams preserved her autonomy from church and party with the financial and moral support of middle- and upper-class white club women, some of whom were millionaires. South Side agencies like the Phillis Wheatley Home and the YWCA flourished in part because they, like the Urban League, enjoyed ties to national organizations that offered financial and institutional support when hard times hit at the local level. In addition, the Phillis Wheatley Home and the YWCA had much more self-effacing, feminine profiles in the community. Start-up organizations, especially overtly political ones like the Negro Fellowship League, led by charismatic and independent-minded—indeed, famous—black women like Wells-Barnett or Amanda Smith struggled along, contending as best they could on a grossly unequal playing field.

Crusade for Justice stresses the devastation of 1919–20, which left Wells-Barnett's health wrecked, her neighbors murdered, her neighborhood bombed, and her settlement shuttered. These were grave setbacks that made her much less well-positioned to lead her community in 1920 than she was in 1910. Yet in a surviving letter from October 1920, just before she took sick, we glimpse not despair but personal vitality, joy in her daughters, firmness of purpose, and a sustaining faith in God.

As she did so often, Wells-Barnett sat down and wrote a letter home while traveling, addressing "My Dear Folks." She was in Springfield attending the Conference of Charities and Corrections, a trip that also entailed visits to the State Hospital for the Insane and the State School for the Blind, as well as addresses to local black churches. She regretted not being able to return to Chicago in order to "help my girls celebrate Halloween." The connections between women's organizational networks and their bonds of affection were evident in Wells-Barnett's reminder to her daughters to stick close with their friends and their friends' parents during their outing, which included a stop at the YWCA. Wells-Barnett closed her letter with words of love and guidance. "You know all that is in my heart to say to you, so I will not need say it." She continued, "Whenever I think of my dear girls, which is all the time, such a feeling of confidence comes over me. I know my girls are true to me, to themselves and their God wherever they are, and my heart is content. I have had many troubles and much disappointment in life, but I feel that in you I have an abiding joy. I feel that whatever others may do, my girls are now and will be shining examples of noble true womanhood, and so mother's heart is glad & happy when she thinks of her daughters, for she knows that wherever they are & whatever they are doing they are striving to please her and reach the ideal of true womanhood." She signed the letter, "With all the love in the world, Mother."[245] Loyalty and honor to a girl's mother was a strong theme from Wells-Barnett's slave heritage. Here that legacy is passed to the next generation in the same breath as love of God and self-respect. True womanhood concerned one's own mother's heart, religious faith, and personal integrity, not submissiveness or domesticity. During the 1920s, Wells-Barnett would be honored by African American women as the "Mother of Clubs" in Chicago. The meaning of this gesture in the history of black women's social thought, politics, and institution-building needs further exploration.

CHAPTER SIX

For Women, of Women, by Women

My greatest interest during the 35 years of residence in Chicago has been the welfare of the Race and especially of our women," stated Wells-Barnett in the *Defender* in 1930. Her remarks stood out tellingly among the press profiles of women celebrated for "Doing Their Parts Well in Upbuilding" the community. Wells-Barnett's biography appeared first in the group, the only one written in the subject's own words. After a synopsis of her life from Memphis days, she listed proud firsts achieved in the North: "[M]y friends point with pride to my record as the first organizer of women's clubs, in 1893; of the first Race orchestra, in 1895; of the first kindergarten of our children, 1896; the first social work for men and boys, 1910; the first suffrage and political club among our women which put the first Colored man in the City council, 1913; the first 100-voice chorus in the Loop, 1909; and last but not least, the first woman of the Race to run for state senator." Wells-Barnett was justifiably proud—and far from alone—in her accomplishments. The *Defender*'s article congratulated more than a dozen women, especially praising those who had broken the color line in the public sphere. A few women had built South Side institutions—notably Elizabeth Lindsay Davis, president of the Phillis

Wheatley Home, and Elizabeth Barnett-Lewis, proprietor of the Vincennes Hotel.[1] All the women except Wells-Barnett had achieved distinction through long-term affiliation with other major entities—like the Republican Party, city government, hospitals, fraternal orders, or the YWCA—underscoring the centrality of institutions to African American women's postwar community work. This pattern among Chicago black women—and Wells-Barnett's more fractured trajectory—offers a map for rereading the 1920s, a period long viewed as racist, prosperous but corrupt, and marked by antifeminist backlash.[2]

Wells-Barnett prepared her profile for the *Defender* at a high point of female achievement, especially political achievement, in Illinois. Capped by the U.S. Senate bid of Republican "congressman" Ruth Hanna McCormick (who was white), a large number of women campaigned for elective office in the 1930 campaign cycle. In and around Chicago, five African American women ran for office.[3] That they all lost their races raises questions still puzzled over by historians and political scientists: to what extent did sex remain a viable basis for female solidarity in politics after the full enfranchisement of women citizens? In what ways did black women candidates rely on ideologies of sex and race to shape their agendas and mobilize electoral support? How did African American women's vision of female equality and racial uplift play out in Chicago, one of the nation's centers of male-dominated machine politics? How does Wells-Barnett's work illuminate the promise and frustration of party politics for black women, and what can be made of her self-identification as someone "especially" dedicated to "our women"?

The 1920s, like the 1890s, was a pivotal decade in which Ida B. Wells-Barnett seized opportunities to expand her own and other black women's role in the political life of her community and state. Political life in the North entailed rather different tactics than those of stealth, anonymity, and ambassadorship—those cultivated by southern African American women in a context of disfranchisement.[4] Lead by Wells-Barnett, black women in Chicago pressed ahead into the electoral realm, literally putting their names, faces, and agendas before the public (see Figure 19). In a sharp break with the approach of the Alpha Suffrage Club, however, Wells-Barnett and her colleagues joined official politics in the 1920s not on behalf of male candidates but with the goal of electing women to office. Far from being an isolated figure, Wells-Barnett was firmly grounded in the burgeoning ranks of politicized black women's clubs among African Americans in the city and nation. When she joined the National League of Republican Colored Women's Clubs (NLRCWC) in 1927, she united with thousands of women working on electoral politics across the country. The motto of the Third Ward

Hat in Ring	Candidate	Mrs. Barnett Runs for State Senator

—P. & A. Photo.

MRS. MARY C. CLARK
Prominent Republican politician and president of the Illinois Women's Republican league, who has announced her intention of making a run for the Illinois legislature at the next election. Mrs. Clark hopes to be elected from the Fifth district to fill the vacancy created by the death of Mrs. Flora Cheyney (white) last year.

—Defender Photo.

ATTY. GEORGIA JONES-ELLIS
Who is a candidate for the general assembly from the Fifth senatorial district. If elected, she will be the first woman of our Race to be sent to a state legislature. Attorney Ellis charges that she has been double-crossed by Deneen workers. The mark fails to appear before her name on the sample ballots being distributed in the Third ward.

MRS. IDA B. WELLS-BARNETT
To the Voters of the Third District: In response to letters of indorsement, I hereby announce my candidacy for the office of State Senator in the Illinois Legislature, and pledge myself if elected to work as hard for the benefit of my Race and my district as I have done for the past 37 years I have lived in Chicago. If every registered voter in the Third Senatorial district who believes this will go to the polls on April 8 and vote for me in the primary election I know I will be elected.

FIGURE 19. Candidates for office, 1930. From *Chicago Defender*: "Hat in Ring," 16 November 1929; "Candidate," 4 April 1930; "Mrs. Barnett Runs for State Senator," 8 March 1930

Women's Political Club she founded that year, "For Women, of Women, by Women," invoked the "new birth of freedom" promised by Lincoln's Gettysburg Address and linked black women's modern politics to the historic struggle against slavery.[5] The 1890s commenced a "woman's era" of female service to the cause of racial advancement; the 1920s accented a woman-centered approach to community development. Wells-Barnett's previous initiatives in uplift, reform, and agitation had implied female equality; those in the twenties insisted upon it.[6]

New demographics, new prosperity, and new political opportunities underwrote the potency of Wells-Barnett and other Chicago club women in the 1920s. Like the 1830s and 1890s, the twentieth century's second decade was another "age of association" for American women, the largest and perhaps most far-reaching of all such eras in U.S. history.[7] Club growth was outstanding in Chicago. Between 1900 and 1925, the number of black women's clubs affiliated with the Chicago and Northern District federations grew from fifteen to seventy-two and included some 10,000 women.[8] The overall number of African American clubs in Chicago at least doubled between 1920 and 1930, resulting in some 400 organizations.[9] Most clubs among white, native-born women tended toward a more secular orientation in these years, but African American women's clubs retained a strong religious dimension. Christianity shaped the vocabulary, ritual, organizational base, and identity of black club women. Nearly all activist and club women were church women, although not all church women were activists. As Elizabeth Lindsay Davis wryly noted in a press biography, she had "occupied every position in the church except that of a licensed minister."[10]

As association life expanded, South Side women recast and updated their work in a number of directions. The National Association of Colored Women (NACW) was never stronger in terms of numbers, but it ceased to be the sole mediator of African American women's social agenda, political voice, or public image in these years. After the war, a multiplicity of local and national organizations vied for women's loyalty and support in the urban North. Marcus Garvey's Universal Negro Improvement Association (UNIA), churches and fraternal orders, and women's unaffiliated social clubs boomed in Chicago after the Great Migration. Upwardly mobile young people joined Greek societies and college alumni groups. Organizations like the Brotherhood of Sleeping Car Porters, the NAACP, and the Urban League were gender-inclusive or offered women their own branch or auxiliary.[11] Women's institutions like the Phillis Wheatley Home and the YWCA came into maturity. Wells-Barnett herself reflected rather skeptically on the phenomenal growth of institutional life on the South Side in this period. It was all too easy, she claimed in her autobiography, to "point to our wonderful institutions with complacence and draw the salaries connected therewith" rather than exercise the "vigilance" she deemed necessary for "the preservations of our rights."[12]

This comment surely reflects the marginalization Wells-Barnett experienced during the war years. Her day-to-day engagement with the institutionalizing trends of the twenties is difficult to trace due to scant records. Indeed, compared to the well-documented events of the 1890s, the 1920s figure in most popular and scholarly treatments of her life as a mumbled coda of isolation, a declension narrative abetted by the fact that her autobiography effectively ends in 1919.[13] Haunting the period is Wells-Barnett's provocative autobiographical statement during her illness in 1920–21: "All at once the realization came to me that I had nothing to show for all those years of toil and labor. It seemed to me that I should now begin to make some preparation of a personal nature for the future, and this I set about to accomplish."[14] This ambition was a far cry from either the pedestal of chilvaric protection offered to women by the Garvey movement or the bourgeois femininity now accented within the NACW, and Wells-Barnett was hardly alone in her thinking on the South Side of Chicago.[15]

Views to the Twenties

The above portrait of Wells-Barnett builds on the work of historians Evelyn Brooks Higginbotham and Rosalyn Terborg-Penn on African American women's concerted and effective political activism in the 1920s.[16] In contrast to their findings, other scholars tend to emphasize black women's marginalization in official politics due to racism, citing low rates of election to public office and their absence from major welfare policy conferences and government institutions during the Progressive Era and New Deal.[17] Some theorists take this position even further, as in Eileen Boris's contention that black women regarded "the state" as a "negative force" or "enemy" of social betterment in their communities, a position that leaves her puzzling over their "avid" suffragism.[18] Social science treatments of African Americans in party politics before World War II mostly overlook women, focusing on high-profile men and male-dominated networks and institutions.[19] Finally, discussions of civil rights and related initiatives in the 1920s generally point to the waning influence of the NACW and emphasize how black men and women worked together more often than separately on such issues.[20]

As the preceding chapter tried to suggest, however, Wells-Barnett and her peers worked in a complex universe of political constraints and possibilities. In examining the twenties, a finer distinction needs to be made between the politics of "the state" and those of the political parties, especially since the relationship between the two changed markedly in this period. The distribution of resources shifted from parties to the state, a shift that culminated during the New Deal. Further complicating matters, the distinction between state and party also could blur or break down at the local level, particularly in the proliferation of jobs in expanding government agencies and bureaus. During the twenties, the federal government, states, and municipalities continued to regulate and institutionalize the zone between public and private life that historically served as a point of political entrée for women. One expression of this trend was the Sheppard-Towner Infancy and Maternity Act of

1921, a program of federal grants to states that funded visiting nurses, public health clinics, and data collection about the nation's mothers and babies and which was largely staffed by women. As public schools, civil service, health care, recreation, and the penal system expanded under government aegis in the postsuffrage period, women's participation in these sectors took on new political meanings.

Elizabeth Lindsay Davis pointedly observed this change in Chicago. The African American club women who had volunteered in the court and prison systems for years were now "an important factor in the political world" as evidenced by the new "eagerness with which the wily politicians of all parties seek to win favor with them."[21] At the same time, paid employment and community welfare work were more likely to be one and the same thing. Historian Stephanie Shaw recently outlined educated black women's patterns of employment and professionalism in the twenties, especially noting jobs in the "race relations" field in and around government.[22] Organized women applauded these trends at the time. The executive committee of the NACW reported at their general session in 1922: "Clubs are doing much along the lines of social work in connection with the social agencies. We have learned the fact that the day for the individual alone to accomplish much is past and that through co-operation with others may they hope to attain."[23] Paying positions in uplift were also a source of pride. Davis bragged to NACW leadership when an Illinois woman was tapped by the National Recreational Association to "take over the recreational activities in Springfield for our group."[24]

Women's uplift work was also increasingly political in the sense of connection to the electoral fortunes and partisan loyalties of the community. The *Chicago Defender* understood a government clerkship or agency appointment in highly political terms, as either advancing the race, striking a blow against Jim Crow, or getting a fair share for black people from the state. In pink- and white-collar sectors, African American women often broke the color line before men, as did attorney Georgia Jones-Ellis, the "first and only" African American member of the state board of pardons and paroles; or Mrs. Charlotte Jackson, head clerk in the Juvenile Court; or Hattie Simmons Goode, the "first Race woman to be employed in the social service department of the state attorney's office in Cook County."[25] In an era of notable government regulation of the economy, it was almost impossible to avoid official politics or the state. For example, in 1929, when a group of African American women wanted to open a hot dog stand on the South Side, they appealed for a permit to their local alderman. Despite opposition from a local property owners' association, the alderman agreed to the permit, persuaded perhaps as much by the voting power the women represented as by their argument that the stand would "be used as a community center for the children in the neighborhood."[26] African American women's traditional "other-mothering"—care and protection of people outside immediate kin[27]—was increasingly caught up with wage-earning and voting power, all of which rolled into a volatile new politics of racial tokenism and segregation in public life.

This confluence of issues leads to a key argument about female partisanship in the postsuffrage era. Despite the history of cordial relations across the color line in the Illinois woman suffrage movement, black and white women had different investments in partisanship. These investments derived from the distinctive ideological traditions and practical contexts of their work, momentarily suppressed in the heat of the fight for the Nineteenth Amendment but becoming starkly evident after its passage. The white woman busily tending a "female dominion" in reform at Hull-House, the Chicago School of Social Work, and the U.S. Department of Labor supported the development of an administrative state run by experts to battle poverty and meet social needs. This vision, partly the result of the failure to dislodge local politicians and monied interests in urban wards, was also underwritten by assumptions about sexual difference and "natural" gender roles, assumptions that found political expression in female nonpartisanship (see Figure 20).[28] The ideology of disinterestedness, of women as "beyond" or "above" party politics, created a wedge between black and white Republican women in Illinois. In 1924, for example, the newly formed Illinois division of the National League of Republican Colored Women's Clubs sought to affiliate with the Illinois Republican Club, a white women's group. The white women rebuffed the black women on the grounds that the black women were all "paid workers" of the Republican Party.[29] African American women could not afford the politics of "disinterestedness."

As the Alpha Suffrage Club had demonstrated in the preceding decade, Chicago black women developed their own ideas about nonpartisanship and disinterestedness in politics, a trend that was evident nationally. In 1920 the NACW announced its hope that "club women shall purify not merely increase the volume of the stream of politics."[30] Whether "disinterested" or not, however, black women's politics were often premised on a religious ethos rather than on gender ideology alone. They also avoided the sex antagonism that figured in white women's critiques of political corruption, as in discussions of the saloon and the machine.[31] When Elizabeth Lindsay Davis affirmed that in politics, "no one party can say that it owns colored women body and soul," she

FIGURE 20. "The Old Ringmaster" cartoon captured one view of women's nonpartisanship, ca. 1912. Reprinted in Adade M. Wheeler and Marlene Stein Wortman, *The Roads They Made: Women in Illinois History* (Chicago: Charles H. Kerr, 1977): 134; photo courtesy of the Newberry Library, Chicago

appealed to African American women's particular relationship to the history of slavery and freedom in the United States, a history that could not be collapsed into a statement solely about gender.[32] When Wells-Barnett urged her female audiences to "do their Christian duty and vote for Race women" during her state senate race, she similarly drew on a distinct sensibility among black women that linked religious and political values.[33]

These expressions by Davis and Wells-Barnett, however rich and constructive in most applications, faced tough going in the official electoral realm. Cynical observers scratched their heads and shrugged—or scoffed. An article in the *Defender* in 1924 noted that female delegates to a state party convention were proudly going in "uninstructed" and, in the words of one woman, would only "heed . . . those [instructions] prompted by my own conscience," to which the reporter editorialized, "so there!" This woman hoped that male delegates already pledged to a candidate on the first ballot would switch on the second ballot under influence of new female delegates like herself. "Where is the man who would wager on just how these delegates will switch," the reporter mused, adding sarcastically: "Bring on the wise ones who say they understand women."[34]

African American women thus faced a dilemma. On the one hand, the male-dominated political world was disinclined to reward or even recognize appeals like Wells-Barnett's or that of the "uninstructed" female delegate. On the other hand, new white women political players dismissed black women because of their "interested" position as committed partisans, supposedly beholden to the corrupt ways of men. For white women, disinterestedness gained them credibility with white men. For black women, partisanship was the main path to politics, but that path was strewn with its own obstacles.

Race, Gender, and Progress in the New Era

Ida B. Wells-Barnett traced a path to politics as the very ground beneath her heaved with ideological controversy and contradiction. On the South Side, a major ground shift in the definition of race progress erupted between the *Defender*'s ardent colorblind integrationism and Marcus Garvey's black nationalism and separatism.[35] African American women like Wells-Barnett historically worked in the strategic, pragmatic middle ground. In the twenties, however, that middle ground no longer was neutral female territory carefully cultivated by local activists. Aggressive new men in Chicago politics, especially business leaders, made decisive bids to lead and reorder the African American community's agenda.

The *Chicago Defender* promulgated a clear program to meet the decade's cynicism, racism, and apathy: break the color line. The paper's editor-publisher and founder Robert S. Abbott argued that Jim Crow institutions were wrong and unacceptable. Black Chicagoans were encouraged to not rent apartments in buildings with obnoxious "for colored renters" signs on them and to oppose the creation of new public agencies in the neighborhood, like a fire house or hospital, if they were going to be de facto "black" institutions.[36] Segregation, he argued, undermined true Americanism and material progress, cultural values characteristic of the twenties but applied by the *Defender* to the interests of "the Race." From Abbott's point of view, financial independence led to political independence, which in turn would lead to equality. A self-made millionaire and admirer of Booker T. Washington, Abbott was especially harsh on so-called job-seekers and career politicians. "A few of these gentlemen, whose future depends upon small political jobs" in the Republican organization "have a false impression of their importance," complained Abbott in 1920.[37] The editor also criticized individuals who supported segregation (or failed to challenge it) from what he called selfish interests, like teachers who argued that "their children advance faster in their own schools and that their sons and daughters could get jobs teaching only in Jim Crow schools."[38] "Half a loaf is better than no loaf," declared Abbott. "It is better that we die of neglect as we did 60 years ago than that we barter our souls and our self respect for another segregated institution—better, far better, that we perish!"[39]

The spirit of self-sacrifice evident in Abbott's declaration echoed back through generations of black protest in the United States. In the immediate context of the twenties, the *Defender*'s politics also took important cues from assumptions about gender. Ideally, duly appointed men, especially in the business realm, advanced African American interests through stringent adherence to integration. When those initiatives failed or were blocked, women and the churches should step in to tide the community over. Churches and women's groups were assigned responsibility for meeting the gap in social services and resources denied to the community by racism. When conditions deteriorated—for example, when girls brought in to the Morals Court were released to the streets without money or jobs—the *Defender* headlines clearly assigned responsibility: "Club Women and Ministers Asleep."[40] Abbott, heir to Tuskegee's legacy of business success and secular-mindedness, firmly located clergy and the churches on the distaff side of community advancement precisely when the achievement of woman suffrage poised both ministers and their heavily female congregations to lay definitive political claim to community leadership.[41] Conflict was in the offing, and the *Defender* sought to shape the terms.

Gender in the Vision

If "100 percent Americanism" during the 1920s diluted the political purchase of appeals to color, race, or "hyphens," so too did the achievement of woman suffrage potentially undermine the ability of voting women to mobilize around sex. The *Defender*'s war on the color line shows, however, that gender scarcely dissolved as an organizing category in social and political life. To be sure, the paper was quite advanced on women's rights issues. Editors supported woman suffrage, equal pay for equal work, and even endorsed the "radical" National Woman's Party—if the group would extend fair treatment to black women. But Robert Abbott still regarded as "open to question" whether women should fill judgeships, sit on juries, perform military service, and hold "important executive offices" or other unspecified "official positions."[42] Most commentators understood female political participation along gender lines, noting, for example, that the "feminine touch in politics" would be felt because "be it ever so gentle, maternal instinct is in every woman as she hopes, plans, pursues, and suffers in terms of her children's future."[43] In general, the *Defender* featured conventional if positive images of women. Mother's Day garnered plenty of ink, especially from ministers. Mother's love was "divine," her sacrifices "saintly," her praises to be sung in hymns as praise to God.[44] The paper celebrated feminine charms and attractiveness through publicity of hair contests, beauty pageants, and fashion shows.[45] Women's distinctive roles, interests, and concerns found outlets in the paper's Woman's Page, society column, and household economy section.

The paper especially promoted female activities that meshed with its assumptions about gender and race progress. Classic was its support for women police officers. Reports argued that black women should have parity with white women's access to positions on the force and that women qua women could "break vice." "If more women were placed in the field there would be fewer vice dens."[46] This position successfully preserved the gender stereotype of woman as natural moral force and neatly sidestepped the matter of equality with men. Similarly, the paper advocated the development of South Side women's institutions, especially the YWCA and the Phillis Wheatley Home. By caring for dislocated girls and women, these organizations performed the "other mothering" historically done by black women, work that dovetailed with the *Defender*'s special charge to women and clergy in the work of upbuilding.

As a religiously based, pro-woman but not strongly feminist, "interracial" organization, the YWCA perfectly fit the *Defender*'s ideological ideal in the 1920s.[47] The YWCA's publicity drew on the late-Victorian notion of men not rising above the moral level of women, a concept developed so well by the NACW. As industrial secretary Irene McCoy Gaines put it in 1920: "As the Colored girl lives, plays, works, dreams, thinks, and acts, so does her Race. The Colored man cannot rise above her standards."[48] The *Defender* agreed: "it is infinitely more important that our young women be properly housed and directed than our young men."[49] Editors were proud of African American representation on national and state YWCA boards and advocated the additional "inspiration from one of our own number" among the national secretaries.[50] The *Defender* never referred to the local YWCA in the parlance of the day, as a "colored" branch, highlighting instead its openness to all girls regardless of race or nationality.[51] Ever alert to the business interests of the community, the *Defender* also appreciated the YWCA's focus on labor and employment issues.[52]

Not everyone was impressed, however. Wells-Barnett did not much take part in YWCA activities, as her investment in "interracial" organizing was minimal after the Chicago race riot. "Thot [*sic*] annual YWCA meeting amateurish for a sixty yr celebration," she sniffed in her diary in 1930, grumbling that "Colored girls appeared only as 'industrials.'"[53] Where labor was concerned, Wells-Barnett briefly put her imprimatur on the Brotherhood of Sleeping Car Porters (founded in 1925) and sponsored the first Chicago meetings for the group in her own home. Wells-Barnett's new congregation, the Metropolitan Community Church, was the first public institution to offer a Chicago podium to the Brotherhood's leader, the socialist A. Philip Randolph, whom some considered a radical figure.[54] In the coming years, however, Wells-Barnett put her faith in organized women rather than organized labor.

A highly visible index to female potential in Chicago was the annual Woman's World's Fair, begun in 1925. Updating to modern ends the widely successful handcraft fairs and church bazaars of the nineteenth century, the Woman's World's Fair sponsored booths, exhibits, and demonstrations that showcased women's achievements, skills, talents, and history. Familiar in form and usually uncontroversial in content, the Woman's World's Fair expressed the postwar hope for female solidarity and cooperation around themes like peace and domestic science. It also caught the gender ambivalence of the period in its theme for 1926: "Woman's Place—Where is it—What is it?" The Fair movement grew to a large and greatly anticipated yearly event in Chicago that drew Illinois club women together across the lines of color and ethnicity. It eventually included representatives of forty countries, boasted 280 booths and exhibits, and netted profits of $160,000 per year.[55] It was a darling event of the *Defender*'s, catching the inclusive and entrepreneurial spirit Robert Abbott so cherished.

The solid record of social betterment achieved by the YWCA and women's clubs notwithstanding, several assumptions made the *Defender*'s division of labor in the war against Jim Crow unworkable. First was the expectation that churches and women's groups could meet the needs of a growing community on a voluntary or private basis. Churches and women's groups could not address the requirements of a population that more than doubled, from 100,000 to 230,000, between 1920 and 1930. Second, racism and residential segregation were at the root of many of the community's sorest needs—neglected social services, poor schools, inadequate parks, and biased policing. Jim Crow in housing and development was complained about bitterly but not halted by the press or anyone else. *Defender* editors also branded honest people who genuinely disagreed with zero-sum integrationism as sellouts and traitors to the race, thereby polarizing debate.[56] Finally, the *Defender* itself realized that the colorblind stance was ultimately untenable within the imperatives of "racial" advancement. In 1928, the editors urged voters to "forget every loyalty" except race at election time in order to put Oscar DePriest in the U.S. Congress.[57] "The idea is not advanced that we should be clannish on this question," explained political commentator A. N. Fields, "but that we should exercise race consciousness in seeing to it that we continue the unbroken line in the elevation of members of our group with the distinct idea in mind that in so doing we elevate ourselves."[58] Ida B. Wells-Barnett had long known that it was impossible to fight exclusion and inequality without some degree of racial consciousness and solidarity. Yet the new interconnectedness of black women's community work and official politics in the 1920s made negotiating gender expectations and the war on Jim Crow like trying to stand on a spinning top.

Case in Point: Geneva

These contradictions reached the breakpoint in Ida B. Wells-Barnett's work in the penal system. In early 1930, she reported in the *Defender* about the outrage of parents at Cater Practice School. A fifteen-year-old schoolgirl named Frances Jordan had been arrested when the "yard man" at Cater told a police officer that she had struck one of the school's personnel. Upon Jordan's apprehension, police threatened to "shoot her legs off if she attempted to run." With no notice to her parents, she was "locked up for two days" and examined for venereal disease (and charged three dollars) before her mother and father could raise the funds to bail her out. By marshalling the support of neighbors through community meetings, securing the legal counsel of Ferdinand Barnett, and obtaining Judge Mary Bartelmae's "fair and impartial" treatment at the Juvenile Court, Wells-Barnett led the fight for justice in the case. Without prompt community interventions and reliable political contacts, however, she warned in her article in the *Defender* that Frances Jordan would have been "headed for Geneva."[59]

"Geneva" was shorthand for the State Training School for Girls, the primary facility for youthful female offenders in Illinois, located thirty miles west of Chicago in the town of Geneva. Founded around the turn of the century, Geneva historically admitted girls regardless of color or religion. By the early 1920s, however, the facility played multiple roles, including as a home for incorrigibles and even as an orphanage. Like women's penal facilities in other metropolitan areas in the North, Geneva filled up rapidly after the war, and segregation emerged to manage a newly diverse prison population. By 1928, African American inmates at Geneva were housed in separate cottages, reportedly performed "'servant's work' while the whites [were] given easier tasks," and suffered dangerous overcrowding. Other black female offenders were being either released to the streets or sent to the county jail with "hardened criminals."[60]

Ida and Ferdinand Barnett had made fairness to African Americans in the justice system central to their work in Chicago for decades.[61] Worsening conditions at Geneva and elsewhere became immune to the individual approach after World War I. Population growth in the context of segregation taxed children's services—schools, parks, beaches, and the Ys—to the limit. For example, the student population at Wendell Phillips Junior High School doubled from 700 to 1,400 between 1921 and 1925; the white policeman stationed on campus to keep order served only to "break down the morale" of the students.[62] Beyond sheer numbers, racism became more deeply entrenched in social and institutional life. Bias in policing included rank political retaliation through targeted raids and arrests around election time.[63] Major problems included crackdowns on black peoples' use of public space and police abuse of youth.[64] Women, if "known prostitutes," could "not even go to a neighborhood store and return to their homes without being arrested if seen by certain policemen," reported the *Defender*.[65] In addition to taxing the Barnetts' time and abilities, these conditions politicized African American women's relationship to schools and the penal system through their roles as employees in civil service, as voters, as teachers, and as mothers and "other mothers" in the community. These roles, in turn, were increasingly scrutinized by male community gatekeepers in the new political era.

Since the turn of the century, Illinois club women had made the protection of women and children central to their work. Postwar developments pushed that work into official politics. Club women tracked conditions in the courts, monitored schools and neighborhoods, raised money, and, in 1925, opened their own Home for "problem girls" in Chicago. The Home was coordinated by the "Friendly Big Sisters," an NACW affiliate. The Big Sisters adapted the friendly visiting tradition of nineteenth-century church women to modern conditions. The Chicago group was led by attorney Violette Anderson, the first black woman admitted to the Illinois bar in 1920 and a highly visible figure through her weekly "Legal Hints to Women" column in a local paper, the *Chicago Whip*.[66] The Home was a product not of simple volunteerism, but of the political power, professional skills, and the employment needs of black women.[67] Suffrage played its part, especially in the election of judges. The well-regarded Mary Bartelmae of the Juvenile Court made a difference for black women's access to the court system and to political influence. For example, Bartelmae brokered the meeting between African American leaders and the governor to protest conditions at Geneva in 1928.[68] The mixed-sex and partisan composition of the protest delegation illustrated the new political stakes involved for black women in uplift and protective work. The delegation included women's club leaders, representatives of the Urban League and the NAACP, Robert Abbott, elected male officials, new female politicos like Susie Meyers of the Illinois Republican Colored Women's Clubs, Lulu Lawson of the YWCA, and former probation officer Ida B. Wells-Barnett. The protesters presented a united front, arguing that the problem at Geneva was Jim Crow. Governor Len Small promised to investigate, correct conditions, and expand facilities.[69]

While the *Defender* usually advocated for policewomen and matrons in the court system, in the case of Geneva the paper was highly critical. Reports roundly criticized the so-called job seekers who had argued a few years back that "a 'Colored woman' was needed on the staff to look after girls of her Race who would not [get] the proper attention and instructions from white matrons." The terrible conditions at Geneva, according to the *Defender*, "proved . . . correct" the prediction that such an appointment would lead to institutionalized inequality for black inmates.[70] There was little ideological difference between the demand for women police officers in the city and the job that Mrs. C. H. Mercer performed as "matron over our girls" at Geneva.[71] The line between inclusion and tokenism proved slippery, however, and an appointment that was cheered before the war now created political problems that demanded political solutions. The urgency and frustration surrounding these issues perhaps inspired Wells-Barnett to announce her candidacy for public office just one week after Frances Jordan was arrested.

The Road to Geneva

Wells-Barnett traveled a bumpy road of community initiatives before weighing in on Geneva and running for the state senate in 1930. Little record of that work would exist today without her continued journalistic access to the *Chicago Defender*. That access was briefly in jeopardy early in the twenties when she and Robert Abbott had an ideological falling out over the status of Wendell Phillips High School, which was fast becoming a de facto "black" institution.[72] Wells-Barnett's proud endorsement of "race leadership" in "institutions established for race benefit" before the war likely clashed with Abbott's increasingly staunch opposition to anything resembling a Jim Crow organization in the twenties.[73] Given the public grousing about "segregated" politics at the Negro Fellowship League, conflict between Wells-Barnett and Abbott seems likely but apparently did not make the papers. There was hardly a moratorium on her work in the pages of the *Defender*.

The complete loss of access to the *Defender* would have been tragic for Wells-Barnett. Without the ability to exercise her skills as a journalist and publicist, her choices during the first half of the 1920s might have disqualified her from public life altogether. Early on she took sides in a conflict at Bethel AME Church. One of the ministers there, Rev. W. D. Cook, became embroiled in a conflict with fellow clergy and bolted from the congregation. Wells-Barnett joined Cook and his hundreds of followers from Bethel at his new independent organization, the Metropolitan Community Center and People's Church, which was built on institutional church lines.[74] This move was apparently liberating, but she then backed a couple of dead-end causes.

The first was an attempt to rebuild the Equal Rights League and reconnect with this historically militant organization. The effort to pass the Dyer antilynching bill sparked the ERL back to life, and an organizer came to Chicago to restart a local branch and make plans for a national meeting to be held in that city.[75] Putting aside her anger from the Bundy defense entanglements, Wells-Barnett joined up, heading the League's Publicity and Promotion Committee. In articles in the *Defender*, Wells-Barnett hoped the League would promote black enterprise, support Dyer, end peonage and convict labor in the South, support the needs of southern migrants in northern cities, fight the Klan, and end Jim Crow in the trade union movement. "Let the world see you can organize for your rights just as well as for taking care of the sick and burying the dead," she charged her readers. "Get busy!" The new energy brought new friction. A reported "complete lack of sympathy between the powerful Chicago branch and the national organization" broke up the convention that summer. Some "suspicion on both sides" over monies, offices, and membership ended the meeting in limbo. When the ERL righted itself a year later, Wells-Barnett steered clear.[76]

Also in the summer of 1921, Wells-Barnett joined a local women's committee organized to raise $100,000 for the Fort Dearborn Hospital and Training School for Nurses. The campaign seems to have been a rallying point for political outsiders. The committee was heavily populated with politicians, mostly Democrats or marginal Republicans, leaders of the oppositional press, and businessmen (especially insurance brokers). As was true of Provident Hospital, women's volunteer efforts were essential to the functioning of local health care institutions, even after Fort Dearborn became a city agency. A woman's auxiliary monitored child welfare, ran a milk station and a nurses' home, provided linens, and did community visiting. The other public facility, Cook County Hospital, discriminated in nursing hires, vesting the Fort Dearborn effort with expectations of better working conditions and more jobs for black women.[77] Unfortunately, the women's campaign was too late. Early in 1922, with only a handful of patients and $10,000 in debt, the hospital went into receivership, its management and finances in "deplorable and chaotic condition." Somehow attorneys managed to put off creditors and lawsuits until the facility closed.[78]

The Equal Rights League flop, the closure of Fort Dearborn Hospital, and the defeat of the Dyer Bill were leavened by the achievements of the NACW early in the decade and prompted Wells-Barnett to turn her attention back to federated club work. In August 1922, she packed up her youngest daughter Alfreda and a friend and motored east for a three-week trip. She attended NACW's biennial meeting in Richmond as well as the dedication of the Frederick Douglass Memorial Home in Anacostia, Maryland, a project that association leader Mary Talbert shepherded to completion with great fanfare.[79] In addition to attending official meetings and programs, Wells-Barnett was "royally entertained by friends, especially in Washington, D.C., with dinner, teas, motor rides," and a "brilliant reception." When she returned to Chicago, she was elected editor of the Illinois Federation of Colored Women's Clubs' journal, the *Woman's Forum*.[80]

Over the next two years, however, the Illinois and Chicago federations reported no new initiatives. Wells-Barnett addressed Grace Church's lyceum with "echoes" from the Richmond biennial; helped entertain Charlotte Hawkins Brown when she was in town on a fundraising tour for her school, the Palmer Memorial Institute; attended a local convention of the National League of Women Voters (LOWV); and gave lectures as far away as Kansas City.[81] The press reported no noteworthy activity on the club women's part until plans began for the 1924 Chicago biennial.[82] Finances may have been a factor in the low level of club activity. Prosperity was slow in reaching the South Side after the war and then spread itself only thinly. Wells-Barnett had borrowed money against the *Woman's Forum* in order to travel to Richmond in 1922 and was unable to publish the journal for the next six months.[83] The Barnett family also sold their home and moved to an apartment around 1925, perhaps adding personal or financial turmoil to the mix of constraints on their activism.[84]

After this pause, new energy in the club world sprang to life at the NACW's Chicago meeting. The convention was, by all reports, constructive, congenial, and dramatic.[85] "Pandemonium" broke out when the Illinois and Ohio delegations paraded with their prizes for most money raised for the education fund. Tears flowed during testimonials for the recently deceased Mary Talbert. The election of officers generated special excitement. Wells-Barnett, backed by the Chicago delegates, placed her name on the presidential ticket. She withdrew after the first ballot, losing to Mary McLeod Bethune, founder of Bethune-Cookman College in Daytona, Florida. Her withdrawal was a moment of intense political theater, the kind never passed up by the former stage star from Memphis. "No greater scene was enacted than when Mrs. Ida B. Wells-Barnett walked to the center of the platform and put her arms around Mrs. Bethune," waxed *Defender* reporter Nettie George Speedy of this would-be torch-passing. "It was that harmony that prevailed throughout the sessions." Another Chicago club leader, Dr. Mary Waring, "heavily backed by her home town folks," also lost a bid for vice president.[86] Though the aspirations of Chicago club women were still not given their due in the NACW, new opportunities for social engagement and political leadership clearly emerged during the meeting.[87] In this presidential election year, political party operatives aggressively lobbied the club women. Just a few weeks after the biennial, NACW leaders clustering in Washington, D.C., formed the National League of Republican Colored Women Clubs, an organization that functioned as an arm of the Republican National Committee.[88]

The size of the Chicago convention, the attention of the political parties, and the NACW's prominent new president, Bethune, garnered the women media praise. Black women were successful "because they are never aggressive, but always ready quietly to walk into the way of opportunity when it is presented," stated Jane Addams in the *Chicago Daily News*. "They are not boastful or self-assertive: they are modest, but they are untiring."[89] Addams's perception that African American women filled in the cracks, picked up the pieces, and patiently waited their turn was typically condescending sentiment in white liberal circles, although such a view hardly could have squared with her encounters with Well-Barnett over the years. A highly publicized reception for the NACW leadership given by the Chicago Woman's Club, during which black and white women reportedly "talked to each other straight out from the shoulder," raised hopes for progress in interracial work.[90] Still, a *Defender* editorial griped that "all the [women's] talk seem to be about the candidates for office for the coming year" and blithely wished that they would raise "a half million or million dollars" for a solid business or educational enterprise.[91] African American club women impressed everyone with their new numbers, proven ability, and political potential. In what direction would they move?

The Promise of Club Life

Whether it was a hot dog stand or the Geneva training school, a hospital or a scholarship fund, black women's club work in the twenties touched and sometimes meshed with party politics. Club life, however, was never reducible to politics. The NACW biennial in Chicago contained the tears, exultation, prayers, reports, songs, debates, and ceremony that constituted federated club life for two generations. Bonds of friendship and love, family and kin, history and Christian sisterhood preceded and profoundly shaped black club women's political encounters in the new era. This was especially true of the clubs that founded the Illinois State Federation in 1899—the "magic seven"—which adopted self-conscious leadership, catalyst, or mentoring roles in the community, and among whom Wells-Barnett was regarded as a founding "mother."[92]

Outstanding among this group was the Ida B. Wells (IBW) Woman's Club, founded in 1893. From its "helpful programs, race unity and parliamentary drills"—all hallmarks of Wells-Barnett's—this club was credited with having brought forth "all the other clubs of Chicago and the state." Education in citizenship and the teaching of history were consistent features of the club's work. Its annual Douglass Day and Emancipation Day celebrations were always open to the public and often enough turned into organizing meetings around current events.[93] Blending religious and political impulses, IBW supported ministers, teachers, writers, and political leaders who shared its vision of "moral and civic betterment of our group and the city as well."[94] Music was almost always featured at meetings. The club helped sponsor the first "race orchestra," of which Wells-Barnett was so proud, and occasional musicales and guest performances at meetings were especially enjoyed events.[95] Over the years, Wells-Barnett served as club president, programming coordinator, and civics chair. She also represented the club in the community, lecturing on black history for general audiences, on modern banking for women, and on the value of "Club Life" to young people.[96] In 1929, Wells-Barnett's sister, Mrs. Annie Wells Fitts, became IBW Club president.[97] In her history of the Illinois Federation of Colored Women's Clubs, Elizabeth Lindsay Davis underscored the unique role of this club: "From the ranks of its members have come many of our club presidents, our leading business women and our leading church and social service workers."[98]

The work of organizations like IBW was at a premium in the twenties, when women's clubs competed with movies, jazz, and other urban amusements for young people's attention. Though pleasure clubs far and away dominated community life in terms of numbers, the ethos of Christian service and sisterhood at the heart of club work successfully bridged generational and institutional boundaries. For example, the I.Q. Social Club, founded in 1925, had the "purpose of associating young women in personal loyalty to one another" and promoting "a growth in social character and service through physical and mental training." The club motto was "Be A Friend Always," the creed was "Loyalty," and the "uplift" of the club was "Civility." "The success of the club has been due to the interest and close friendship each individual has for one another," reported the *Defender*, "with the united patience of their president, sponsor and adviser, Mrs. Mabel Washington." Washington was an AME Church and YWCA stalwart who taught young people the importance of women's commitment to one another and to the community.[99]

The Christian tradition of women teaching other women and girls also took on professional overtones, as befitting the thoroughly modern twenties. The Xenias was formed in 1929 by Nettie George Speedy, "dean of women journalists" and outstanding reporter for the *Defender*. The club's motto was "Finer Womanhood," and it was Speedy's goal to "assist young women, giving them the advantage of her experience and knowledge" in newspaper work. The club had a closed membership of twelve and functioned as a tutorial in reporting.[100] This work was an outgrowth of Speedy's leadership at the *Defender*, where she made coverage of women a more visible, inclusive, and outreach-oriented feature of the paper. After thirteen years as a successful court and police reporter, Speedy initiated a "Scrapbook of Doers" column in 1925 in order to publicize female achievement to Chicago and the nation. She felt that the time was over for women to "hide behind a screen which they christen modesty," yet her column was no mere brag sheet. Under the caption "Let's Get Acquainted," Speedy stressed community building and the sharing of information.[101] Soon she edited a new and impressive Woman's Page (usually three pages) with the goal of making "the Woman's Page of the Chicago *Defender* the greatest ever."[102]

Fed by these new and old traditions, women's practice of Christian outreach and upbuilding spilled over into official politics. "A new awakening in politics has come to our women," announced the NACW's *National Notes* in 1924. "Expect great things from the middle west."[103] Women's political clubs were among the more striking innovations in Chicago club life during the 1920s. The Illinois division of the National

League of Republican Colored Women's Clubs, organized in 1924 by Irene Goins, reflected, according to the *Defender*, "the valuable part women are playing in the Republican Party and the need that the party feels for the feminine interest and cooperation."[104] Goins came to Chicago in the 1890s, became active in the Women's Trade Union League and YWCA, the National Council of Defense during the war, and then joined the LOWV.[105] The *Defender* approvingly reported that a "large number of women's political organizations" were on hand to hear state legislator Catherine Hancock Goode (who was white) at the annual gathering of the Illinois division of the NLRCWC in early 1927.[106] Whether the average white woman noticed or not, the conventions sponsored by the NLRCWC primed black women voters for a bid for recognition in the Republican Party.[107]

In this context, new women in club life aspired to recognition and influence. In 1927, a South Side resident named Mrs. Susie Meyers founded the Women's Republican Council within the Illinois NLRCWC and quickly connected with elected officials and candidates through the classic gesture of the period: a testimonial. Through the ritual speech-making, shared meals, toasts, endorsements, and gift exchanges (usually a "loving cup" or flowers) at these events, individuals and groups negotiated for leadership standing and solidified their constituencies in the community. Meyers staged two major testimonials in the mid-1920s: a luncheon for political aspirant Ruth Hanna McCormick and a dinner for editor Robert S. Abbott. As we shall see, these events successfully put Meyers and her women's group on the political map.[108] Plotting a successful course to elective office for black women, however, proved much more challenging.

More Political Moves

Ruth Hanna McCormick strongly advocated that Illinois women get on the political map—but she wanted to steer. A supremely well-connected and wealthy Republican, McCormick urged women to "discard the time-wasting trivialities attributed to their club activities" and turn instead to "important political issues."[109] Born in 1880, McCormick was the daughter of Mark Hanna, Ohio governor and leading Republican Party kingmaker. She grew up in high politics and high society. At age twenty-three she married Joseph Medill McCormick, heir to the McCormick reaper fortune and, as Joseph Medill's grandson, in line to become publisher of the *Chicago Tribune*. In addition to working for woman suffrage in Illinois, Ruth greatly assisted her husband in politics. Medill McCormick was elected to the state legislature in 1912 and then to the U.S. Senate. In 1924 he lost his seat and suddenly died, with alcohol largely to blame. At that point, Ruth Hanna McCormick was politically experienced, independently wealthy, and had her three children in boarding school. She was Illinois national Republican "committeeman" and angling for office herself. After briefly considering the governor's race in 1926, party managers settled on Congress. In 1928, McCormick was elected "congressman-at-large" for Illinois.[110]

Because of Medill McCormick's blue-chip Republican credentials and his support of the Dyer Bill, Chicago black voters supported him and now gave Ruth a fair hearing. McCormick might have especially appealed to African American women because of her forthright commitment to party politics. She was publicly critical of the nonpartisan LOWV, insisting that women commit to "good parties" and get involved with the electoral process. Her complaints about the "rigidity of the non-partisan minds" likely resonated with party loyalists among South Side women.[111] Yet this shrewd politician also appealed to white women's "above politics" sensibility. She consistently positioned herself against the machine as an "independent Republican," determined to win and serve "without obligating myself to any particular faction . . . or giving pledges to any organization." McCormick's independence was underwritten by her personal fortune, on which she drew extravagantly in her campaigns (and came under a congressional investigation for so doing).[112] Where black voters were concerned, she essentially coattailed on her late husband's record. The *Defender* surely stretched her reputation when it likened McCormick to "another Harriet Beecher Stowe" as a "friend to the Race."[113] To African American women, Ruth Hanna McCormick presented a simple, upbeat, and uncontroversial message, one they had implicitly shared for many years. "We are going to distribute our life's service on three things—home, church, government," she stated. "It is your responsibility and mine to make our government what we want it to be." When Susie Meyers hosted a luncheon for South Side women in 1925, she praised McCormick as the "best informed woman in the Republican Party and the daughter of one of the truest friends we have ever had."[114]

While McCormick angled for federal office, Wells-Barnett was also on her way to the center of official politics. In 1926, the Ida B. Wells Club sharpened its meeting agendas with Wells-Barnett serving as "organizer and parliamentarian."[115] She took strong public positions on partisan matters in the press, like the Senate's refusal to seat Illinois's senator-elect Frank L. Smith. In the *Defender*, Wells-Barnett charged Democratic leaders with rank hypocrisy for denying Smith his seat on the basis of "moral turpitude" after they effectively stole elections through black disfranchisement in the South. With her characteristic sarcasm, Wells-Barnett decried the Democrats for criticizing a man for needing money for politics—"fast becoming a rich man's game"—in a section where "one needs no money in election campaigns because there are no campaigns."[116]

Though Wells-Barnett made a peace offering to southern liberals after the war in *The Arkansas Race Riot*, she regained a strong public voice later in the decade through a critique of southern racism and the planter elite in the press. Nature gave her an unexpected opening. In May 1927, the greatest flood in U.S. history displaced 120,000 people in the Mississippi-Yazoo delta region, the former home of many black Chicagoans. After white victims were ferried out of the worst zones around Greenville, Mississippi, black sharecropping families remained behind at the behest of local planters, who forced them to live in the mud, labor on the levee at gunpoint under a pass system, and endure police roundups for stints at hard labor, one instance of which resulted in the murder of a black man. Wells-Barnett's letters to Herbert Hoover, who directed federal flood relief as secretary of commerce, her series of articles in the *Defender* documenting and condemning the conditions of black refugees, and the way in which everyday people turned to her in this crisis heightened her political profile on the local and national level.[117] Southern whites blamed the *Defender* for unfair "vilification" of local elites during the flood, but Wells-Barnett earned praise in Chicago as "an uncompromising fighter for [our] rights."[118]

Wells-Barnett was not alone among African American women in gaining expanded media attention in the late 1920s. Mary McLeod Bethune made the well-known white journalist Ida Tarbell's "most prominent women in America" lists in 1929 and 1930.[119] Mary Church Terrell's "Up To Date" column reached hundreds of thousands of *Defender* readers every week, and in 1928 Terrell became the only African American woman to have her name inscribed on a plaque unveiled at a national commemoration of the life of Susan B. Anthony.[120] Prominent club and church women like Nannie Burroughs, Hallie Q. Brown, and Mrs. George S. Williams worked as national organizers of African American women in the Republican Party.

Back in Chicago, South Siders' political fortunes were on the rise as well. In 1926, attorney Edward H. Wright's star rose briefly as he testified before the Illinois Commerce Commission in a highly publicized graft investigation, which inspired talk about a possible congressional bid by Wright.[121] That same year, Rev. Carey scored a major high point when Mayor Thompson appointed him to the city's Civil Service Commission.[122] Then Susie Meyers, with help from Republican alderman

Berthold Cronson (who was white), threw a love feast for Robert Abbott in 1927. A full complement of elected officials and politicos appeared, including Ruth McCormick, whose remarks emphasized the friendship between Abbott and her late husband. Comments were offered by Lulu Lawson of the YWCA, Nannie Reed of the Illinois Federation of Colored Women's Clubs, and Dr. Lillian S. Dove, a local physician and club woman. Wells-Barnett offered a spontaneous vote of thanks to Mrs. Meyers, and the event received a splashy front-page treatment in the *Defender*, courtesy of Nettie Speedy. "Mrs. Meyers wields an unquestioned influence in public affairs," affirmed Speedy, since she had "established valuable contacts and friendship with the most important figures in the country" through her political work.[123] Chicago black women were ready to make a move.

By way of preparation, they turned to Wells-Barnett. In May 1927, the Ida B. Wells Woman's Club held a testimonial dinner for their founder. In February, Wells-Barnett had referred to the IBW Club as the "mother club" in her letter about Frank Smith's senate seat. At a Bethune luncheon in early April, club woman and friend Sadie Adams in turn dubbed Wells-Barnett herself the "mother of our clubs," and this refrain provided the theme for the testimonial. The committee intended for club women to honor their "mother" and, through the pages of the *Defender*, welcomed "all those from every walk of life who have benefited by Mrs. Barnett's work in civic and social service." Organizers aimed high, inviting both Bethune and Jane Addams, though neither attended (Addams claimed an illness). At the dinner, Major John R. Lynch of the Eighth Illinois Regiment gave the main address, celebrating Wells-Barnett as an "internationally known champion of the rights of her people."[124] The next week, yet another dinner was given honoring both Ida and Ferdinand together. "Chicago owes more to the two Barnetts for the improvement of racial conditions than any other two people," reported the *Defender*.[125] Whether or not the South Side would vote like it still remained an open question.

Black Women in the Political Game

The IBW Club testimonial dinner was more than just a nice party. Honor to women within the club movement had its own logic of feeling and social purpose, of course, but this event surely had larger political import, since public testimonials were a major venue for establishing leaders and constituencies in the community. The Wells-Barnett testimonial occurred just as political hopes were riding high among black Chicagoans. Six months after the event, Wells-Barnett started the Third

Ward Women's Political Club. Her founding address identified the need for "women uniting politically and supporting women for office."[126] By not naming the club "Republican," the group distanced itself from the local machine. Rather than simply support candidates picked for them by the party or court powerful establishment figures, the Third Ward Women's Political Club trained women to run for office. They invited female elected officials to give talks and instruction and received encouragement from Susie Meyers, who "strongly urged [the club] to put women in the field to run for office, especially the state legislature."[127]

Although starting a brand new club suggests an independent perspective, Wells-Barnett worked closely with Bertha Montgomery, president of the Women's Cook County Permanent Republican Club (WC-CPRC), in her programming and educational efforts. The WCCPRC was the regular or loyal Republican group for black women in the county encompassing Chicago. Montgomery had started the group in 1916. She owed her job at the County Board of Assessors Office to her "tireless political energy in behalf of GOP candidates and principles," explained the *Defender*. "Through her contact with powerful politicians, she has been able to pave the way for many others by securing lucrative positions for them." Montgomery's wartime work with the Red Cross gave her standing among nurses and veterans, both highly visible and well-organized constituencies on the South Side. Not simply derivative of the Republican Party, however, the WCCPRC was a member of the NACW and supplied mutual benefit to its members.[128] Montgomery's group in turn contrasted with the Ladies' Auxiliary to the Fifth Ward Republican Club. As its name suggests, this group had a more traditionally feminine focus, performing the "women's work" so essential to political life, especially cooking food for receptions, dinners, and fundraisers. The Ladies' Auxiliary supported "wholesome community activities" for "all citizens of the ward" and aspired toward "better and more harmonious race relations." The Auxiliary also provided mutual benefit to members and, again highlighting the connection between party politics and community betterment work, supported charitable institutions.[129]

While shoring up her local base through the testimonial and club work, Wells-Barnett also reconnected with Republican Party structures. In 1928, she was made "National Organizer of Colored Women of Illinois" for the Hoover campaign.[130] At age sixty-six, she traveled across the state registering Republican black women to vote. She wrote a pro-Hoover pamphlet and urged his support, tersely praising his flood relief work as "efficient." Wells-Barnett claimed—with the aid of three assistants—to have raised black women's registration "nearly 50 percent" in Illinois.[131] Though she was disappointed with stingy Republican campaign spending in the southern part of the state, Wells-Barnett insisted that black women were eager to support the party and Hoover. She wrote confidently to Claude A. Barnett of the Associated Negro Press that "a large number who are today indifferent or hostile will listen to an expression from me and be guided by it."[132] This comment suggests that Wells-Barnett was as attuned to her own pull with voters as she was to Hoover's. With this campaign, Wells-Barnett's and black women's presence in politics, historically strong in Illinois, moved to new heights.

And with good reason. Republicans sent Oscar DePriest and Ruth Hanna McCormick to Congress with the 1928 election. Wells-Barnett's response to these victories does not survive in the record, but she probably agreed with Elizabeth Lindsay Davis. With McCormick's win, Davis felt that "the stock of women in Politics has risen immensely" in Illinois.[133] What also emerges in the record is Wells-Barnett's own continuing high visibility in the press in 1929–30 compared to the early part of the decade. She was a featured guest in a new series of women's meetings at the YWCA celebrating female achievement.[134] For her work in "public affairs," Wells-Barnett was one of five local African American women who proudly appeared in a Woman's Pageant organized by Jane Addams at the University of Chicago in the spring of 1929.[135] In September 1929, the *Defender*'s caption "Who is she?" above a photo of Wells-Barnett (this one had Nettie Speedy's hand all over it) neatly captured her situation: she was still famous enough to warrant a front page photo in the "World's Greatest Weekly," yet the quiz format suggested that there might be many who would be stumped by a picture of her face.[136] By mid-1929, Ida B. Wells-Barnett and Ruth Hanna McCormick each achieved a high point of name recognition in their respective careers. This was, of course, the second time around for Wells-Barnett; McCormick's second time would come in 1940, when she was picked to head Thomas Dewey's presidential election campaign, the first woman ever to fill that job for one of the major parties.

Also in September 1929, midway through her congressional term, McCormick announced her candidacy for the U.S. Senate. As in her previous race, McCormick again pledged disinterestedness in her campaign, vowing to keep herself "free from any direct or indirect obligation."[137] In establishing her campaign's presence in Chicago's black community, she brought in Mary Church Terrell of Washington, D.C., to head her committee. The two had become friends in the capital, where they moved in overlapping Republican circles. Terrell's appointment in Chicago was greeted warmly by elected men on the South Side, and the *Defender* duly noted that McCormick's well-funded campaign meant jobs and patronage. "Mrs. Terrell will be able to help the colored women of the state materially in the coming campaign." Echoing McCormick's own rhetorical diffidence about political factions and loyalties, Terrell described her role in Chicago as that of a salutary "outsider" whose "viewpoint is entirely impersonal" and who, as a disinterested political operative, could "render a service free from bias."[138] Terrell's public pronouncements tried to assuage fears that she intended to "usurp" or "dictate" to local women, a critical matter because existing patronage debts and votes hung in the balance. For example, Terrell openly stated in the press that since Susie Meyers's husband had received an appointment in the postal service through the offices of McCormick's father and the personal support of Ruth, Meyers would be expected to deliver the votes of the Illinois NLRCWC to McCormick.[139] She soon learned otherwise.

Terrell's appointment created great turmoil among activist Republican women on the South Side. According to Elizabeth Lindsay Davis, local women "rose in their might" and sent "letters galore" to McCormick protesting Terrell.[140] Wells-Barnett, Bertha Montgomery, and four other local women leaders met and rallied their supporters in a special meeting, but not before dismissing the *Defender* reporter from the room in order to work in private. They expressed their resentment of "the slight thus put upon the Negro women of Illinois" by the appointment of Terrell, a situation that touched on the old rivalry between Chicago and Washington, D.C., club women.[141] Wells-Barnett and Montgomery succeeded in pressuring McCormick to appoint Irene McCoy Gaines to head her committee, displacing Terrell to the role of state speaker, a job that took her mostly out of Chicago (see Figure 21).[142] Terrell's autobiography noted that local women threatened pointedly to withdraw their votes from McCormick if Terrell was not removed.[143]

No doubt discouraged by squabbling over posts in other people's campaigns, Wells-Barnett and her colleagues soon turned away from McCormick to focus on their own candidate for state legislature. Back in June, the Third Ward Women's Political Club endorsed Mrs. Mary C. Clark, now head of Meyers's Women's Republican League. The club proudly announced that they were "first in the field with a Race woman candidate for the legislature" to fill a seat vacated by the death of a white woman officer holder in the Fifth District. As it turned out, however, another African American woman, attorney Georgia Jones-Ellis, was also running for the same legislature seat as Clark. According to the *Defender*, Jones-Ellis had the regular Republican men as well as the Northern District and state federations of club women behind her.[144] The paper not very helpfully stated that the women's efforts created "much disturbance in an already muddled situation."[145]

FIGURE 21. South Side women's political luncheon, 1929. *Chicago Sunday Bee*, 10 November 1929; copy courtesy of Chicago Historical Society

Then in early March, scarcely a month before the primary and in the middle of the Frances Jordan trial, Wells-Barnett announced for the Third District's state senate seat. "In response to letters of endorsement," she pledged to "work as hard for the benefit of my race as I have done for the past 37 years I have lived in Chicago." "If every registered voter in the Third senatorial district who believes this will go to the polls . . . and vote for me in the primary election I know I will be elected."[146] None of the women's campaigns created much heat in the press. The *Defender* ran Wells-Barnett's picture and campaign plug several times in the coming weeks, but Georgia Jones-Ellis and Mary Clark were mostly invisible. On election day, Wells-Barnett ran a poor fourth to winner Adelbert Roberts, a black career politician with ties to Mayor Thompson and, ironically enough, the holder of a decades-plus sinecure as a clerk in the Municipal Court.[147] No woman would be elected to the Illinois state senate until 1950.[148]

Both Wells-Barnett and Jones-Ellis felt "double crossed" during their campaigns. Jones-Ellis expected the regular Republican organization's endorsement, but sample ballots distributed on election day did not have her name marked with an "X" as promised.[149] In her diary, Wells-Barnett noted that clubs flip-flopped late in the race. For example, the Abraham Lincoln Republican Club regularly had her in to speak to their weekly meetings but withdrew their support on voting day.[150] That the *Defender* ran Du Bois's poem "God Give Us Men"—a lament over leadership dating from Niagara days—in the middle of the primary race could not have helped the five black women candidates.[151] A former IBW Club officer, Florence Kibble, testily commented on the poem's appearance as the paper's lead editorial: "Now Mr. Editor of the World's Greatest Weekly . . . will you please tell us just what in the name of high heaven do you mean?" Kibble objected to such old-fashioned breast beating over leadership. She stated that club women "firmly believe that our race has leaders who can measure up to the standard, and we believe that we have men who daily pray for divine guidance to help them live above the fog."[152] Club women rallied at a post-primary dinner honoring the efforts of Wells-Barnett and the others. Despite their losses, observers felt the women had "good reasons for congratulating themselves."[153]

The election results and the surrounding political culture suggest the dilemmas of official politics for African American women. Black women's candidacies meant different things to different people, just as female equality and race progress did. To skilled and confident black women activists, running for office meant many things, among them breaking away from the tutelage and condescension of white women. But such bids could appear as confusion or naïveté to the local male establishment. As far as the "regular" Republicans were concerned, female independence potentially upset the balance of political debts in relationships already tilted against the African American community. Longtime political operatives also could safely ignore female candidates because women did not command the resources to extract party discipline. Wells-Barnett encouraged "women voters to do their Christian duty and vote for Race women," but she did so painfully aware that the "independent vote is weak, unorganized and its workers purchasable."[154]

As in the 1890s, female initiative in leadership and politics during the twenties revived the old chiding, more or less good-natured, about whether women would "excel the men in effective organizations, far-sightedness, general ability and the back-bone to ask for what they want and Get It!"[155] Wells-Barnett bluntly noted in her diary that experienced political men like Edward H. Wright were simply "still stubborn about helping women."[156] Though she did not campaign as the "Mother of Clubs," female solidarity was as difficult to muster in black Chicago as it was elsewhere. The NACW may have been 100,000 strong, but it hardly had a lock on the votes of African American women, especially in diverse and contentious centers like Chicago. Despite Ida B. Wells-Barnett's high hopes and hard work for election victory, she confessed to her diary: "Few women responded as I had hoped."[157]

Conclusion

As African American women exercised their constructive abilities and political ambitions in the late 1920s, the resurgence of lurid, racialized sexism in the media must have angered them in a way that Florence Kibble's frustrated letter to the editor only hinted at. In sharp contrast to the early decade's adulation of feminine beauty and paeans to motherhood, negative images of black women stood out sharply in the press on the eve of the Great Depression. In 1927, a torrent of letters in the *Defender* claimed that a female student at nearby Crane Junior College named Marian Burton had "betrayed her race" by criticizing sexism in the community in a short story she published in the school newspaper.[158] A spate of vicious images of black women followed. Reports in early spring of 1929 claimed that an "ape-woman"—purportedly the offspring of a black African woman and a gorilla—had been "captured" in the jungle and was due to arrive in the United States as a sideshow attraction.[159] This obvious hoax did not come to pass, but another, perpetrated through the movies, did. A film entitled *Ingagi* featured a similar coupling. Ida B. Wells-Barnett led the film committee of the women's division of the Urban League to oppose the showing of this film in 1929.[160]

Readers on the South Side were shocked that the *Defender* deigned to publish a cruel letter libeling black women just after the 1930 elections. The editors apparently hoped to stage a dialogue and framed the letter with the provocative headline: "Are Our Women As Bad As This?" The letter was from one J. Wilson of Oakland, California, who ostensibly wrote to refute the *Defender*'s long-standing editorial position that white men had "poured their blood into Colored veins" by sexually abusing African American women. Wilson's letter instead argued that such outcomes were "halfway invited or altogether invited" by black women themselves. He then denounced all " 'Nigger' women" as "easy," condemning "[e]ven these so called respectable Colored women (there isn't no such animal)." His advice to "all Colored men" was to "get anything but a 'nigger' woman, for they will take your money and love a white man [for] free in their home in broad daylight, let alone at night."[161] Wilson's rambling and ungrammatical letter combined several of the sharpest barbs of racialized sexism—namely, black woman as traitor to the race and black woman as morally loose—as well as the canard that victims of rape asked for it. Such a litany must have galled women like Wells-Barnett who constructed their ideal of womanhood on the memory of their slave mothers' resistance to sexual and physical abuse. In the coming weeks, *Defender* readers ably rebutted Wilson, making it clear that his words showed only disrespect to his own mother, himself, and all African Americans.[162] In a final twist, however, one Mrs. M. W. Simpson of Cincinnati revived a version of the double standard: black women needed a higher standard of morality than white women because of the disadvantages facing her and her group. "The Negro woman who is bad is ethically worse than her Nordic sister," she argued. "Mr. Wilson, in my opinion, is right." This old Victorian chestnut that black women had to be the best of all women was thus recycled and circulated among a new generation of modern *Defender* readers.[163]

This backlash exhibited an ill temper fanned by the economic hardship of the Great Depression, which hit African American communities early, and it turned the tide of political thinking. Just after the war, those still invested in the idea that "true" (if not heroic) women could lead black progress might have carried the day. Typical of this enthusiasm was reporter Roscoe Simmons's view that in "matters of ethics, high ideals and morals we are dependent upon our women folk to set the standard." "If Colored women make up their minds to do it," Simmons argued, "they can free their Race in fifty years."[164] Robert Abbott also agreed that "women are still leading the advance" of human progress.[165] But by decade's end, as historian Deborah Gray White has argued, this vision unraveled.[166] A *Defender* editorial on "The Weaker Sex" now speculated that the implications of the Nineteenth Amendment could make any man "apprehensive."[167]

Over the course of the 1920s, it proved difficult to assimilate women into the *Defender*'s war on Jim Crow because the achievement of woman suffrage blurred the gendered line between public and private in the work of "upbuilding." Female equality also potentially disrupted conventions of gender, especially the ideology of protection, which charged men with defending and providing for women and other dependents. In addition, a new generation of successful business and professional men embraced patriarchal gender ideals and prided themselves according to new, colorblind criteria—in E. Franklin Frazier's words, on leadership "not dependent for status upon the Colored group but . . . upon the intrinsic worth of its achievements."[168] Even if women kept to their roles of "other mothering" and moral leadership, it was impossible to steer completely clear of paid employment or the world of elections, patronage, and appointments, all of which touched partisan nerves and the government purse. When women moved directly into official politics as candidates, they met with a chilly indifference or self-serving manipulation.

For their part, politically minded white women ignored or exploited African American women's partisanship for their own purposes. Ruth McCormick tried to have it both ways, playing the ideologically disinterested (gender) card among whites while using her personal fortune to buy media access and campaign support via jobs and patronage in the black community. With few social or financial reserves behind them, African American women entered the political game at a great disadvantage, though they played it valiantly. Despite Ida B. Wells-Barnett's belief in the ballot as sacred, the unforgiving and high-stakes game of party politics in the 1920s quickly transformed her hopes for empowerment into new questions and challenges for the next generation.

It was not death she feared. It was misunderstanding.

—Zora Neale Hurston, *Their Eyes Were Watching God* (1937)

Conclusion

The years 1930–31 devastated the ranks of Chicago's black leadership. In a 1930 address to the National DeSaible Memorial Society (a group establishing the legacy of Jean Baptiste DeSaible, a Chicago pioneer of African descent), a reporter noted that Wells-Barnett "deplored the lack of unity within the Race, and declared that it has need of a greater number of followers rather than of more leaders."[1] Had she lived a year, she might have changed her view. Veteran club women Carrie Hamilton and Irene Goins, Dr. George Cleveland Hall of Provident Hospital, and attorney Edward Wright all died in 1930. So did Rev. W. D. Cook, founder of the Metropolitan Community Church.[2] In March 1931, Archibald Carey and Wells-Barnett passed away within days of each other. As in life, their deaths competed for space on the *Defender*'s front page.[3] On the day Ida B. Wells-Barnett died, Wednesday, 25 March 1931, a dozen black men and boys were arrested from a boxcar outside of Scottsboro, Alabama. Her passing marked the beginning and end of an era.

Wells-Barnett did not leave the world easily, enduring two days of "intense suffering" before dying in hospital. After shopping downtown on Saturday afternoon, she felt ill and spent the next day resting. According to Alfreda, within twenty-four hours she was "incoherent" and slipped into a coma from which she never recovered. Upon her death, press and private accounts all noted people's "shock," "surprise," and "stunned" reaction; Ferdinand was "pretty much broken up" by his loss. Rumor had it that Wells-Barnett exerted herself to the end. The *Defender* reported that her "indefatigable labors were kept up to within a few hours of her death."[4] Even if apocryphal, the rumor evokes a credible sense of her work as unfinished. The press's assertion also places Wells-Barnett within a folk tradition of venerating women who, like Mary Talbert, worked themselves to death for the race.[5]

It is difficult indeed to separate fact from fiction at the mythic moment of death. For example, youngest son Herman K. Barnett asserted to historian Herbert Aptheker many years later that his mother directed her sisters from her deathbed to deliver the draft of her autobiography to him for safekeeping.[6] As it happened, Herman worried his mother grievously in the year before she died. He skipped town to escape some gambling debts, leaving his parents with "the bag to hold" financially and potentially disgracing them by his possible disbarment from the law. Yet Wells-Barnett had a soft spot for her son. "Charles always felt that Herman pulled the wool over mother's eyes," recalled Alfreda. "He could do something and then get out of it very easily."[7] Charles, Ida Jr., and, to some extent, Alfreda appear in the record as rather self-effacing souls. As an aspiring lawyer and brash politico, Herman may have seemed the most likely among the children to carry on the family tradition of agitation.[8] Entrusting that legacy directly to Herman might have been Wells-Barnett's way of directing her son to a constructive role. Part of the autobiography's original draft was handwritten on the back of mass-circulated letters carrying her son's signature for the "First Precinct Neighborhood Club" of the Third Ward Republican organization. But it was Alfreda who shepherded the manuscript to publication some forty years after her mother's death.[9]

The theme of inspiring the next generation emerges strongly from the scant public record of Wells-Barnett's passing. She literally bequeathed her story and example to her children; the preface of *Crusade for Justice* contained a dedication to "our youth." Outstanding Chicago club woman, Irene McCoy Gaines, gave a moving tribute to Wells-Barnett just a few days after her death, probably to a gathering of women. Gaines called Wells-Barnett a "pioneer" whose "faithful service to club work and the general welfare of the women of this city" left an important legacy. Wells-Barnett's "last official act," according to Gaines, was a circular she sent out to women's clubs soliciting the purchase of "books by N. [Negro] authors" to benefit the YWCA.[10] Club women produced the most knowing and heartfelt tributes. "Ida B. Wells-Barnett was a woman of strong character, forceful personality, and unflinching courage," stated the memoriam in the NACW's *National Notes*. "She was often criticized, misjudged and misunderstood because she fought for justice and civil righteousness both in America and Europe as God gave her vision to see the RIGHT."[11]

Rather more terse reflection marked other obituaries. The perfunctory notice in the *Tribune* was perhaps to be expected. That the *Pittsburgh Courier* got Ferdinand's name wrong (identifying the husband as "Herman K. Barnett") suggests the dim memory of the *Conservator* and the bright spot of Herman's renown in the press. The faint praise of *The Crisis* was less forgivable. "More than an ordinary obituary" was called for in Wells-Barnett's case, Du Bois acknowledged, yet in a mere handful of sentences he concluded that the work of this "pioneer" in antilynching "has been easily forgotten because it was afterward taken up on a much larger scale by the NAACP and carried to greater success."[12] Fortunately, more wholesome understatement characterized her funeral.

The ceremony at Metropolitan Community Church was one of "simple dignity," according to the *Defender*. While hundreds thronged the streets at Archibald Carey's funeral at Bethel AME that week, Wells-Barnett's farewell entailed no "fanfare or trumpets, no undue shouting, no flowery oratory—just plain, earnest, sincere words from the mouths of those to whom their grief was real." The lighter touch was in keeping with the "simple lives led by members of the Barnett family since it became a force in Chicago public life nearly 38 years ago" (Figure 22). In addition to remarks from clergy and the singing of several hymns, two testimonials were given, both by women. An unnamed representative of the "Colored Women's Clubs" praised Wells-Barnett's work in journalism, and Mrs. Mary C. Clark saluted her recent efforts in electoral politics. "Others there were who came to bow their heads in grief at the passing of Mrs. Barnett," noted the reporter, "but, for the most part, they bowed their heads in silence."[13] Known for her powerful words and political theater, Ida B. Wells-Barnett was a hard act to follow.

Ida B. Wells-Barnett's life and work offers several new perspectives on the Age of Reform in the United States. In the 1890s, African American women exercised their religious mandate for uplift, education, and community building in ways that took them well beyond the walls of home and church. The mobility and achievements of the "female talented tenth" in this decade took almost everyone aback. Of this

FIGURE 22. "Noted Clubwoman Buried." The original caption read in full: "Funeral of Mrs. Ida B. Wells-Barnett Monday afternoon from the Metropolitan Community Church. She passed away last week after a short illness on the eve of her 63d birthday. Mrs. Barnett was perhaps one of the best known clubwomen in the United States and was called 'the mother of clubwomen.'" *Chicago Defender*, 4 April 1931

group Wells-Barnett went the farthest politically, but she was hardly alone either in the New South or on the international stage of Anglo-American reform. By the turn of the century, however, significant backlash from both white racists and conservative voices within the African American community resulted in gender retrenchment in organizational and political life. The American Negro Academy, the Negro Business League, the Niagara Movement, the NAACP, and, of course, the NACW each expressed elements of a gender division of labor in activism, a division designed to contain and mediate tensions around women's roles. Black women retained greater latitude for influence and initiative at the local rather than at the national or elite level, and Wells-Barnett's persistence in Chicago allowed her to move decisively into politics, especially after the coming of woman suffrage to Illinois in 1913. Unfortunately, party politics suffered from the same consolidating, corporate trends as reform; indeed, the latter helped to create the former. For African American women, progressive reform, in the end, favored professional experts, well-funded national organizations, and men. Neither a civic-minded "maternalist" à la the NACW nor a "church woman" in a strictly denominational sense, Ida B. Wells-Barnett burst the gender roles held out to black women of her generation. Her talents and bravery notwithstanding, she struggled to negotiate a landscape of reform pitted by war, big money, bureaucratic politics, and violent racism.

Throughout the period, black women's choices in the public sphere were considerably more circumscribed than those of white women. Poverty and racism account for much of their disadvantage, but there is an equally important story about ideology and social commitment. In the North by 1930, white women tended toward professionalism and somewhat away from grassroots constituencies in politics and reform. Ruth Hanna McCormick ran as a Republican, neither "as a woman" nor as a standard bearer of any particular movement or interest group. McCormick also distanced herself from the "female dominion in reform," which offered influence to less politically driven women like Jane Addams and the members of the popular Illinois League of Women Voters. By contrast, Ida B. Wells-Barnett ran as a "Race woman" who invoked Christian duty before a heavily female constituency. A keynote for white women in the 1920s was "drop the sex line in politics," but no such tocsin sounded for black women.[14]

As in the 1890s, when southern black men experienced disfranchisement, African American women in the 1920s moved ahead in public life for themselves and for "the race," with God's help. In both instances, however, the power plays of official politics denied them equity. The ambitions of bossy, careerist white women and the defensive, low-risk strategizing of black male leaders together undermined Wells-Barnett's initiatives in antilynching, institution building, and electoral politics. She and her female colleagues made heroic efforts in the realms of agitation and social service delivery, and their work touched and improved many, many lives. Despite these successes, however, church, party, and state all failed to consistently support Wells-Barnett's vision and work. Independents like the Negro Fellowship League settlement and Amanda Smith's Industrial Home faced especially difficult conditions for survival. Those who worked under the aegis of national institutions—like the NAACP, NACW, YWCA, and Urban League—fared considerably better in a world that at best ignored black women.

Although hemmed on many sides, Wells-Barnett's writings, lectures, and community work enabled African American women to imagine and act in creative, even daring ways in matters of survival and social change throughout the period. Like evangelists Sojourner Truth and Maria Stewart before her, Wells-Barnett carved out essentially but not exclusively religious space to engage in resistance work, and in so doing she rewrote the narrow scripts of race, sex, and place of her day. Of particular note is her identification as "Exiled," a persona that expressed political status in a religious idiom, rather than through the gender or racial categories that tended to denigrate and confine black women. As both cultural insider and outsider, Exiled "slipped the yoke," as Ralph Ellison once put it, of the dichotomous labels of Victorianism, gaining for Wells-Barnett a rich if unstable (because liminal) terrain from which to work. A provocateur on principle, Wells-Barnett consistently defied categorization. Her life's principle was best expressed in her idea of the ballot as sacred, a concept that the captured the dual impulse to faith and politics that she derived from African American Christianity and the legacy of Reconstruction in the South.

Stewart, Truth, and Wells-Barnett comprise a radical tradition of African American women's resistance work that was sharply political, female-centered, and religiously inspired. Wells-Barnett's work moves any discussion of the history of African American civil rights strategies in the United States at the turn of the century beyond the binary model of Du Bois integrationism versus Washington accommodationism. Her willingness to speak plainly about sexuality, her frank religious commitments in a skeptical and materialistic age, and her instrumental rather than ideological deployment of race consciousness in politics distinguish Wells-Barnett as a visionary pragmatist working in black feminist and womanist theological modes. Wells-Barnett's visionary pragmatism allowed her to advocate pride in African American institutions *and* insist on equal citizenship rights and full participation for black people in U.S. society. In so doing, she propounded a flexible yet militant perspective that complicates the spectrum of black nationalisms offered in the 1920s by Du Bois's Pan-Africanism and Garvey's separatism.

Finally, Wells-Barnett pioneered a brand of political theater that would eventually figure prominently in the southern civil rights movement of the 1960s, especially staging racial dramas in a media context. Her shrewd experiments in this sphere have affinity with the "weapons of the weak" used all over the globe by disempowered groups angling for survival and political advantage on an unequal playing field.[15] In her willingness to "talk back" to power and dramatize her opposition to racism, the courageous Wells-Barnett displayed not a defective personality, as Frances Willard and even some contemporary scholars[16] would have it, but rather suffered the pitfalls of politics for the disempowered. Walking out of a meeting, boycotting an event, or bolting a church congregation are resistance strategies used by everyday people and disadvantaged groups. Such strategies carry large symbolic and practical political potential, especially when used collectively. Ida B. Wells-Barnett's penchant for drama in public life reflects her severe disempowerment vis-à-vis the dominant order as much as it does her gift for theater and her keen political instincts. During her lifetime, lynching, rape, un-checked mobs, and police brutality confronted African Americans who contemplated a move out of their "place" in the U.S. social hierarchy. That Ida B. Wells-Barnett accomplished as much as she did should impress us all the more when we remember that white supremacists wanted her dead and could have killed her with impunity.

Ida B. Wells-Barnett began her career in public life with a protest against lynching that vindicated African American males as "true men" and exposed the deforming effects of the ideology of ladyhood for all women, especially its racist justification for the murder of so-called black rapists. She ended her career in 1930 with an affirmation that African American women merited a place of their own in the official political life of their communities, state, and nation. Despite many obstacles and much indifference, her writing and teaching enriched American discussions of race, power, and sexuality well into our own time. Clarence Thomas's ability to describe his Supreme Court confir-mation process as a "high tech lynching" in 1991 was possible in part because Wells-Barnett forged a credible cultural narrative of victimiza-tion out of the lurid lynching stories told by white Americans nearly a century earlier. That Anita Hill was so quickly labeled disreputable, even mentally unstable, during the hearings points to the persistent cultural habit among whites of projecting their deepest fears of social and moral disorder onto black women.

On a personal level, Wells-Barnett's status as an orphan, a self-supporting woman, and a godly crusader for justice allowed her to demand unusual amounts of both support and autonomy for activism in a time when most American women were expected to consecrate themselves to family, home, and "race" primarily, if not exclusively, through marriage, motherhood, and domesticity. In the volatile con-texts of New South Memphis, fin-de-siècle London, and Progressive-era and Jazz Age Chicago, Ida B. Wells-Barnett experimented with making herself heard and understood in the service of God and Man in the broadest sense, efforts that sometimes required packing a gun and talking through tears. The results of her work—"Iola," "Exiled," "a modern Joan of the race," and the "Mother of Clubs"—comprise a powerful and peculiarly American blend of religion, theater, and poli-tics and a remarkable chapter in the history of modern lives in the United States.

Abbreviations

The following abbreviations are used in the notes.

AT Papers	Albion Tourgée Papers, Chautauqua Historical Society, May-ville, N.Y.
BTW Papers	Booker T. Washington Papers, Library of Congress, Washington, D.C.
CD	*Chicago Defender* newspaper
CF Papers	Church Family Papers, Mississippi Valley Historical Collection, Memphis State University, Memphis, Tenn.
FD Papers	Frederick Douglass Papers, Library of Congress, Washington, D.C.
IMG Papers	Irene McCoy Gaines Papers, Chicago Historical Society, Chicago, Ill.
JES Papers	Joel E. Spingarn Papers, Moorland-Spingarn Research Center, Howard University, Washington, D.C.
MC Papers	Municipal Court Papers, Chicago Historical Society, Chicago, Ill.
MCT-LOC	Mary Church Terrell Papers, Library of Congress, Washington, D.C.
NAACP Papers	National Association for the Advancement of Colored People Papers, Library of Congress, Washington, D.C.
NACW Papers	*Records of the National Association of Colored Women's Clubs, 1895–1992.* Bethesda, Md.: University Publications of America, 1994. Microform edition.
WEA Papers	William E. Axon Papers, John Rylands Library, Manchester, England

Introduction

1. Lynching refers to the extralegal murder of individuals and groups of people by a mob of two or more persons. In the United States, lynching was primarily a means to "intimidate, degrade, and control black people throughout the southern and border states from Reconstruction to the mid-twentieth century." Between 1882 and 1930, 4,561 people lost their lives through lynchings, 74 percent of whom were black. Zangrando, *NAACP Crusade Against Lynching*, 3, 6–7.

2. M. H. Washington, "Teaching *Black-Eyed Susans*," 212–13.

3. hooks, *Talking Back*, 5–9; Henderson, "Speaking in Tongues"; Painter, "Representing Truth"; Tate, *Domestic Allegories*, 124–49.

4. Peterson, *"Doers of the Word"*, 3–23.

5. E. B. Brown, "To Catch the Vision of Freedom," 86.

6. James and Busia, *Theorizing Black Feminisms*, especially p. 3 of the introduction; Collins, *Black Feminist Thought*, 1–67, 251–71; Braxton, *Black Women Writing Autobiography*, 15–79; Lee, *For Freedom's Sake*, 1–22; D. G. White, *Ar'n't I a Woman*; West, *American Evasion of Philosophy*, 211–39; and West, *Prophetic Fragments*, 45–46. See also W. James, *Pragmatism and Other Essays*, 5–132; Kloppenberg, "Pragmatism"; Diggins, *Promise of Pragmatism*, 108–57; Seigfried, *Pragmatism and Feminism*, 174–201.

7. See D. S. Williams, *Sisters in the Wilderness*; and Townes, *Womanist Justice, Womanist Hope*.

8. Shaw, *What a Woman Ought to Be and to Do*; Higginbotham, *Righteous Discontent*; E. B. Brown, "Womanist Consciousness"; Moldow, *Women Doctors in Gilded Age Washington*; Wolcott, " 'Bible, Bath and Broom' "; Hine, *Black Women in White*.

9. On black women in the South, see Rouse, *Lugenia Burns Hope*; Neverdon-Morton, *Afro-American Women of the South*; and Gilmore, *Gender and Jim Crow*. On black women in the North, see Weisenfeld, *African American Women and Christian Activism*; and Knupfer, *Toward a Tenderer Humanity and a Nobler Womanhood*. For a general overview, see Salem, *To Better Our World*. Works focused specifically on racial politics in reform include Lasch-Quinn, *Black Neighbors*; and L. Gordon, "Black and White Visions of Welfare." Treatments reflecting the secular and mostly white-dominated aspects of reform include M. Carson, *Settlement Folk*; Muncy, *Creating a Female Dominion in American Reform*; and Sklar, "Hull-House in the 1890s." The following works analyze racism and attempt to integrate black women into their interpretations: Goodwin, *Gender and the Politics of Welfare Reform*; L. Gordon, *Women, the State, and Welfare*; Frankel and Dye, *Gender, Class, Race, and Reform in the Progressive Era*; A. F. Scott, *Natural Allies*; and Turner, *Women, Culture, and Community*. See also essays in Kerber, Kessler-Harris, and Sklar, *U.S. History as Women's History*; Hewitt and Lebsock, *Visible Women*; Koven and Michel, *Mothers of a New World*; and Mjagkij and Spratt, *Men and Women Adrift*.

Chapter One

1. Ida B. Wells Diary, 18 February 1886, IBW Papers.

2. Carby, *Reconstructing Womanhood*, chaps. 4 and 6.

3. Ida B. Wells-Barnett Diary, 13 January 1930, IBW Papers. Woodson's text first appeared in 1922 and was reprinted and enlarged many times; Wells proba-

bly was referring to the 1928 edition. See Woodson and Wesley, *The Negro in Our History*, 11th ed. (1966); *that* edition still did not mention Wells.

4. See T. Holt, "Lonely Warrior"; Townes, *Womanist Justice, Womanist Hope*; Giddings, *When and Where I Enter*, chap. 1; Thompson, *Ida B. Wells-Barnett*; Schechter, "Unsettled Business." For treatments focusing on language, discourse, and ideology, see Bederman, *Manliness and Civilization*, chap. 2; Royster, "'To Call a Thing by Its Name': The Rhetoric of Ida B. Wells"; and S. Davis, "The 'Weak Race' and the Winchester." On rape and relations between white and black women, see A. Walker, "Advancing Luna—And Ida B. Wells"; McKay, "Alice Walker's 'Advancing Luna—And Ida B. Wells': A Struggle Toward Sisterhood"; Aptheker, *Woman's Legacy*, 53–76.

5. Tayleur, "The Negro Woman," 267.

6. Gagnier, *Subjectivities*, 14. See also V. Smith, *Self-Discovery and Authority in Afro-American Narrative*; Cheryl Walker, "Persona Criticism and the Death of the Author"; R. Wilson, "Producing American Selves"; T. Davis, "Separating Self from Self-Created Fiction"; Decker, "Reconstructing Enterprise"; and Painter, "Writing Biographies of Women." Also very helpful is Ryan, *Women in Public*.

7. Wells-Barnett Diary, 9 January 1930.

8. Wells-Barnett, *Crusade for Justice*, 419. See typescript drafts in IBW Papers. Correspondence in the archives sketches out the publication history of the autobiography. In 1940, at the urging of organized black women in Chicago, a federal housing project was named in honor of Ida B. Wells. In response to a sharp demand from the public for more information about her mother, daughter Alfreda Duster attempted to research and publish her mother's memoir from a typed manuscript left in her aunts' care. Letters exchanged with publishing houses, academic scholars, and independent black researchers suggest that Alfreda and her husband hoped to generate an "immediate best seller." Though "weighed down with family responsibilities" for most of four decades after her mother's death, Alfreda's literary ambition was stimulated. She tried her hand at a biography of her mother and even unsuccessfully entered the George Washington Carver Memorial Contest for a book prize offered by Doubleday in 1945. The project remained stymied until early 1966, the year of John Hope Franklin's appointment at the University of Chicago and the creation of the Negro American Autobiographies series at the university's press. Within six months of the initial contact between Franklin and Duster, the contract for publication was signed. Alfreda painstakingly annotated portions of the text, and the Dusters received their first advance in royalties in mid-1967. See Ben Duster to Mr. William Hard, 18 May 1940; Alfreda M. Duster to Doubleday and Doran, 7 November 1945; Herman K. Barnett to Herbert Aptheker, 21 April 1948; Alfreda M. Duster to Miss Bucklin, 13 November 1958; John Hope Franklin to Alfreda M. Duster, 15 February, 17 August 1966; Alfreda M. Duster to Mrs. Morris Phillipson, 15 June 1967, all in IBW Papers.

9. Butterfield, *Black American Autobiography*, 201; and Franklin, *Living Our Stories, Telling Our Truths*. Braxton, *Black Women Writing Autobiography*, 102–38, emphasizes Wells's text as historical memoir. In *Witnessing Slavery*, 152, Frances Smith Foster points out that most narratives about breaking away from slavery in the South tend to draw on religious sensibilities about freedom, especially God's calling, as opposed to stories of breaking into northern society, where success was measured by secular (intellectual, political, or financial) achievements. For

examples of Christian conversion narratives, see A. Smith, *Autobiography*; and Houchins, *Spiritual Narratives*, which includes the following narrators: Maria Stewart, Jarena Lee, Julia A. Foote, and Virginia W. Broughton. On finding one's mother after slavery, see especially Frances Ellen Watkins Harper's *Iola Leroy, or, Shadows Uplifted* (1892).

10. Wells-Barnett, *Crusade for Justice*, 4–5.

11. Spillers, "Permanent Obliquity."

12. Foster, *Written by Herself*, 117–30. Wells-Barnett's *Crusade for Justice* does not fit the two predominant modes of postbellum African American autobiography, those focusing on childhoods spent in slavery or those telling "black success stories" in freedom. See narratives on childhood slavery by Lucy A. Delaney (1891), Kate Drumgoold (1898), and Annie L. Burton (1909) in Andrews, *Six Women's Slave Narratives*. A classic black success story is Booker T. Washington's *Up From Slavery* (1901). See also Blackburn, "In Search of the Black Female Self"; Townes, *Womanist Justice, Womanist Hope*, 17–39; and M. H. Washington, "Teaching *Black-Eyed Susans*."

13. Wells-Barnett, *Crusade for Justice*, 7–15. The baby Stanley died of the fever, and Eddie died before the outbreak.

14. Ibid., 10, 16.

15. Montgomery, *Under Their Own Vine and Fig Tree*, 13–19; and Raboteau, *Slave Religion*.

16. "Shaw University," in Simpson, *Cyclopedia of Methodism*, 795–96.

17. Wells-Barnett, *Crusade for Justice*, 9.

18. "In Her Own Defense," *Indianapolis Freeman*, 27 April 1895. I am indebted to Linda McMurry for this citation. See her *To Keep the Waters Troubled*, 11.

19. E. B. Brown, "Negotiating and Transforming the Public Sphere." See also S. A. Holt, "Making Freedom Pay." For treatments that stress a shrinking of black women's role in the public sphere after slavery and reconstruction, see Mann, "Slavery, Sharecropping, and Sexual Inequality"; and J. Jones, *Labor of Love, Labor of Sorrow*, chaps. 2 and 3.

20. Townes, *Womanist Justice, Womanist Hope*; D. S. Williams, *Sisters in the Wilderness*; Connor, *Conversions and Visions in the Writings of African American Women*, chap. 1; and Cannon, "Moral Wisdom in the Black Women's Literary Tradition," 281–92. See also Townes, "Black Women"; Townes, *In a Blaze of Glory*, chap. 1; Weems, *Just A Sister Away*; J. Grant, *White Women's Christ, Black Women's Jesus*; and Madsen, "A God of One's Own."

21. See related impulses documented in E. B. Brown, "Womanist Consciousness." See also Lorde, *Sister/Outsider*; Collins, *Black Feminist Thought*, 21–43; and Higginbotham, *Righteous Discontent*.

22. Wells Diary, 6 July 1887.

23. Ibid., 4 September 1886.

24. Ibid., 16 July 1887.

25. Matthew 5:5, 6.

26. Wells Diary, 1 March 1886.

27. Lorde, "The Uses of Anger: Women Responding to Racism," 127–29, and "Eye to Eye: Black Women, Hatred, and Anger," both in *Sister/Outsider*. See also Jaggar, "Love and Knowledge"; Harrison, "Power of Anger in the Work of Love"; and Ransby, "Righteous Rage." For biblical models, see Isaiah 10:1–11 and 40:1–31 and Jeremiah 2:1–37 and 22:13–30.

28. Wells-Barnett, *Crusade for Justice*, 286. Glenda Gilmore observed that Wells "earned a right to her temper." Personal communication in author's possession.

29. Wells, *Southern Horrors*, 45.

30. *Indianapolis Freeman*, 30 April 1892.

31. Wells Diary, 28 January 1886.

32. Stearns and Stearns, *Anger*, chap. 4: Schechter, " 'All the Intensity of My Nature.' "

33. Majors, *Noted Negro Women*, 188; Fortune, "Ida B. Wells, A.M.," 33.

34. Wells-Barnett, *Crusade for Justice*, 9.

35. Ibid., 10.

36. Ibid., 42–45.

37. Recent scholarship demonstrates how Southern freedwomen and their daughters used the courts, schools, the press, and other institutions to shape new conditions and identities for themselves after slavery. See E. B. Brown, "Negotiating and Transforming the Public Sphere"; and L. F. Edwards, "Sexual Violence, Gender, Reconstruction and the Extension of Patriarchy in Granville, N.C."

38. Wells-Barnett, *Crusade for Justice*, 45.

39. Francesca Sawaya brought my attention to the significance of this scene and its placement in the autobiography.

40. Wells-Barnett, *Crusade for Justice*, 17.

41. Wells Diary, 18 August 1886; 29 December 1885.

42. Ibid., 13 July 1886 (emphasis added).

43. Ward, *Sensible Etiquette of the Best Society*, 114.

44. hooks, *Talking Back*, 5–10.

45. Wells Diary, 29 December 1885. Her clenched fists present a vivid image of the repressed rage of many black women, echoed by Mary McLeod Bethune who, in a memoir, recalled her reaction to poor treatment of a student of hers at a Florida hospital: "Even my toes clenched with rage." Bethune, "Faith That Moved a Dump Heap," 142.

46. Williams explains that suffering, forgetting, and self-sacrifice are theologically ill-suited for African American women's historic survival. D. S. Williams, *Sisters in the Wilderness*, 159–69.

47. Wells-Barnett, *Crusade for Justice*, 31.

48. Mossell, *Work of the Afro-American Woman*, 99; hooks, *Talking Back*, 160–66.

49. T. Thomas Fortune, quoted in *Crusade for Justice*, 33.

50. Wells Diary, 9 August 1886.

51. Ibid., 29 December 1885.

52. Wells-Barnett, *Crusade for Justice*, 4.

53. Ibid., 47.

54. Goldman wrote of her conversion-like experience: "I had a distinct sensation that something new and wonderful had been born in my soul. A great ideal, a burning faith, a determination to dedicate myself to the memory of my martyred comrades, to make their cause my own, to make known to the world their beautiful lives and heroic deaths." Goldman, *Living My Life*, 10. Ironically, Wells was not very sympathetic to the actual Haymarket anarchists. The men had been hanged for supposedly "inciting" the bomb-throwing in Chicago. "Pity that the same law cannot be carried into force in Georgia!" she wrote bitterly after the

press incited the lynching of Sam Hose there in 1899. Wells-Barnett, *Lynch Law in Georgia*, 8.

55. Wells-Barnett, *Crusade for Justice*, 64.

56. On black southerners' response to white violence, see Painter, *Exodusters*; and Shapiro, *White Violence and Black Response*.

57. C. Taylor, *Black Churches of Brooklyn*, 18–20. Lyons documented and celebrated the achievements of her sister workers in New York (as well as those of several other prominent New England women) in Hallie Q. Brown's *Homespun Heroines and other Women of Distinction*. See especially sketches of New Yorkers Sarah J. S. Garnet, Susan S. McK. Steward, and Henrietta C. Ray.

58. Wells-Barnett, *Crusade for Justice*, 79.

59. Wells, *Southern Horrors*, 15.

60. Wells-Barnett, *Crusade for Justice*, 80. *Detroit Plaindealer*, 21 and 28 October 1892.

61. Wells-Barnett, *Crusade for Justice*, 79–80 (emphasis added).

62. Wells Diary, 25 February 1886; *Washington Bee* quoted in the *New York Freeman*, 12 December 1885.

63. *Washington Bee*, 29 October 1892.

64. *New York Age*, 12 July 1894 (courtesy of Paul Lee).

65. Wells combined two famous passages from the New Testament. The first is Ephesians 3:19, in which Paul prays that those to whom he preaches may "know the love of Christ which surpasses knowledge, that you may be filled with all the fullness of God." The second is Philippians 4:7, another of Paul's prayers: "And the peace of God, which passes all understanding, will keep your hearts and your minds in Christ Jesus."

66. Wells-Barnett, *Crusade for Justice*, 86.

67. Ibid., 231.

68. Quoted in Wells, *Southern Horrors*, 15.

69. Ida B. Wells to Frederick Douglass, 3 June 1894, FD Papers.

70. Ellen Richardson to Frederick Douglass, 29 May 1894, FD Papers.

71. Ida B. Wells to Frederick Douglass, 3 June, 6 May 1894; Frederick Douglass to Reverend Aked, 22 May 1894; all in FD Papers.

72. Ida B. Wells to Mrs. [Florida Ruffin] Ridley, 30 May 1894, reprinted in *Woman's Era* (July 1894): 4. Hallie Quinn Brown defended Wells's right to full disclosure of the horrible details of lynching in a public letter printed in *Fraternity* in September 1894.

73. Frederick Douglass to Rev. Dr. Clifford, 22 May 1894, reprinted in the *New York Age*, 5 July 1894 (courtesy of Paul Lee).

74. *Daily Chronicle*, 28 April 1894.

75. *New York Sun*, 1 August 1894.

76. Wells-Barnett, *Crusade for Justice*, 232; for Douglass's death scene, see 74–75. Wells was far from alone in her treatment of Douglass. Writing about his life, work, and death became a cultural convention among aspiring black leaders and writers of Wells's generation. See, for example, Terrell, *A Colored Woman in a White World*, and Booker T. Washington's ghostwritten biography of Douglass, *Frederick Douglass* (1907).

77. *Indianapolis Freeman*, 30 March 1895.

78. Wells-Barnett, *Crusade for Justice*, 159, 174.

79. Wells, *Red Record*, 150.

80. Ibid., 140, 138.

81. For a related treatment of Hagar and the "wilderness" experience, see D. S. Williams, *Sisters in the Wilderness*, 159–60.

82. Raboteau, "African Americans, Exodus, and the American Israel."

83. Painter, "Difference, Slavery, and Memory"; and Painter, "Representing Truth."

84. The phrase "androgyne critic" is from Kappeler, *Pornography of Representation*, 155–57.

85. Stanton, "Speech to the Anniversary of the American Anti-Slavery Society," 83.

86. Antebellum black women Sojourner Truth, Harriet Tubman, and Jarena Lee all encountered the charge from incredulous whites that they were not really women, but men dressed as women. See O. Gilbert, *Sojourner Truth's Narrative and Book of Life*, 138. On Tubman, see Allen, *Reluctant Reformers*, 136; on Lee, Jarena Lee, *Religious Experience of Mrs. Jarena Lee* [1849] in Houchins, *Spiritual Narratives*, 23. See general discussion in Painter, *Sojourner Truth: A Life, A Symbol*, 138–42.

87. Frances Ellen Watkins Harper also was called "painted" by whites who did not believe her competence possible in a "real" black woman. See Harper, "Almost Constantly Either Travelling or Speaking," 126–27. For a founding theoretical perspective, see Fields, "Slavery, Race, and Ideology in the United States of America"; and Fields, "Ideology and Race in American History." The title of Frederick Douglass's second autobiography, *My Bondage and My Freedom* (1855), neatly summarized the antebellum association between authentic blackness and slavery. The cultural demotion of Douglass from heroic slave to merely clever mulatto caught the postwar drift. See J. C. Nott, M.D. to O. O. Howard, 25 November 1865, printed in *Washington National Intelligencer*, 8 February 1866. See also Stone, *Studies in the American Race Problem*, 423–42.

88. Wells-Barnett, *Crusade for Justice*, 214–15.

89. Ibid., 212.

90. *Christian World*, 15 March 1894; Aked, "A Blot on a Free Republic," 97. See also *Daily Chronicle*, 28 April 1894.

91. *Westminster Gazette*, 10 May 1894 (emphasis in original).

92. At one point Wells agreed to assist a British physician who was researching "the relative mortality from tuberculosis between [among] those of mixed blood." *New York Age*, 21 June 1894 (courtesy of Paul Lee).

93. Lorimer, *Colour, Class and the Victorians*, 82–91; S. Anderson, *Race and Rapprochement*.

94. Marshall, *Actresses on the Victorian Stage*.

95. Catherine Impey to Albion Tourgée, 24 June 1893, AT Papers.

96. *Manchester Guardian*, 30 March 1894.

97. *Chicago Inter-Ocean*, 9 April 1894; and *Manchester Guardian*, 9 May 1894.

98. *Christian Register*, 12 April 1894.

99. Wells-Barnett, *Crusade for Justice*, 156.

100. Luke 4:24.

101. Wells-Barnett, *Crusade for Justice*, 357–58.

102. D. S. Williams, *Sisters in the Wilderness*, 165–67.

103. Wells-Barnett, *Crusade for Justice*, 415. See Psalms 127:1: "Unless the Lord guards the city, The watchman keeps awake in vain."

104. Wells-Barnett, *Crusade for Justice*, 294–95. Wells echoed Psalms 137:56: "If

I forget you, O Jerusalem, May my right hand forget her skill. May my tongue cleave to the roof of my mouth, If I do not remember you, If I do not exalt Jerusalem above my chief joy."

105. Booker, *Techniques of Subversion in Modern Literature*, 1–19.

106. Painter, "Hill, Thomas, and the Use of Racial Stereotype."

107. Wells-Barnett, *Crusade for Justice*, 222–23.

108. Foster, *Written By Herself*, 181; Schechter, "'All the Intensity of My Nature,'" 58–59, 61.

109. Wells-Barnett, *Crusade for Justice*, 223.

110. Ibid., 238.

111. Ida B. Wells to Mrs. Douglass, 26 April 1894, FD Papers.

112. Wells-Barnett, *Crusade for Justice*, 238.

113. Exodus 17:8–16.

114. Wells-Barnett, *Crusade for Justice*, 241. For positive examples, see the *Indianapolis Freeman*, 13 July 1895, which applauds Wells's accession to the *Conservator*.

115. Fannie Barrier Williams, "Illinois," *Woman's Era* (June 1895): 5; "Ida Wells Married," *New York Times*, 28 June 1895; "Miss Ida B. Wells Married," *New York Tribune*, 28 June 1895. For a related example, see Foster's discussion of Elizabeth Keckley in *Written By Herself*, 117–30.

116. Wells-Barnett, *Crusade for Justice*, 255.

117. See especially D. G. White, "Cost of Club Work, Price of Black Feminism."

118. Wells-Barnett, *Crusade for Justice*, 256.

119. "Committee Appointed," *CD*, 30 August 1919.

120. Wells-Barnett, *Crusade for Justice*, 406–8.

121. Ibid., 408.

122. Ibid., 413–14.

123. *CD*, 21 September 1929.

124. "Pay Tribute to Mrs. Ida Wells Barnett," *CD*, 8 May 1927; "200 Chicagoans Honor Two Distinguished Residents," *CD*, 14 May 1927.

125. Wells-Barnett Diary, 9 January 1930.

126. *National Baptist World* quoted in Higginbotham, *Righteous Discontent*, 143; Ransom, *Deborah and Jael*.

127. Wells-Barnett, *Crusade for Justice*, 3. Sojourner Truth's memory endured a similar twist at her death in 1883. People knew her name but not the words or deeds behind it. See Painter, *Sojourner Truth*, 261.

128. Wells-Barnett, *Crusade for Justice*, 4.

129. Here I differ somewhat with the conclusion that Wells was deficient in the pastoral side of her work, a view found in Townes, *Womanist Justice, Womanist Hope*, 203–5.

130. Gagnier, *Subjectivities*, 15.

131. Quoted in Tucker, "Miss Ida B. Wells and Memphis Lynching," 120.

132. Wells-Barnett, *Crusade for Justice*, 284–85.

133. As Audre Lorde put it in nearer our own time: "Black women are expected to use our anger only in the service of other people's salvation or learning." Lorde, "Uses of Anger," in *Sister/Outsider*, 132.

134. Cooper, *Voice from the South*, 31 (emphasis in original).

135. *Memphis Evening Scimitar*, quoted in Wells, *Southern Horrors*, 18.

Chapter Two

1. "Among the People," *New York Freeman*, 12 December 1885.

2. Du Bois, *Souls of Black Folk*, 121, 136.

3. Higginbotham, *Righteous Discontent*, 19–46 (quote on 19); Carby, *Reconstructing Womanhood*, 7.

4. Moses, *Alexander Crummell*, 207.

5. Cooper, *Voice from the South*, 144.

6. Frederick Douglass to Monroe A. Majors, 26 August 1892, in Sterling, *We Are Your Sisters*, 436.

7. Majors, *Noted Negro Women*, viii–ix.

8. Higginbotham, *Righteous Discontent*, 185–229; D. G. White, "Cost of Club Work, Price of Black Feminism"; Wolcott, "'Bible, Bath and Broom'"; Shaw, "Black Club Women"; Higginbotham, "African American Women's History and the Metalanguage of Race"; Gaines, *Uplifting the Race*. On the antebellum period, see Horton, "Freedom's Yoke."

9. Cooper, *Voice from the South*, 135.

10. "Editorial," *AME Zion Church Quarterly* 3 (April 1893): 416.

11. Kletzing and Crogman, *Progress of a Race*, 198.

12. Painter, "'Social Equality,' Miscegenation, and the Maintenance of Power"; Hall, "The Mind that Burns in Each Body"; Hall, *Revolt Against Chivalry*; MacLean, *Behind the Mask of Chivalry*. In general, see Ayers, *Promise of the New South*.

13. *Memphis Appeal-Avalanche*, 8 September 1891.

14. Ellis, "Disease and the Destiny of a City," 75–89; Humphreys, *Yellow Fever and the South*, 101–7.

15. Cartwright, *Triumph of Jim Crow*, 223.

16. Roitman, "Race Relations in Memphis, Tennessee," 66–68; Young, *Standard History of Memphis*, 172, 213, 223; Berkeley, "*Like a Plague of Locusts*".

17. Young, *Standard History of Memphis*, 186–87.

18. Wrenn, "Commission Government in The Gilded Age," 221.

19. "Iola's Letter," *Living Way*, 5 October 1885, clipping in IBW Papers.

20. Hart, *Redeemers, Bourbons and Populists*, chap. 1; Cartwright, *Triumph of Jim Crow*, 31, 83; Lovett, "Memphis Riot." Two whites and forty-six blacks died in the 1866 riot.

21. Editorial, "Race Relations in Memphis," *Memphis Appeal*, 21 December 1886.

22. *Sholes' Memphis Directory for 1885*, 16–19, puts the total number of "colored" churches at twenty-eight. The military organizations were the Tennessee Rifles, the McClellan Guards, and the Zouave Guards. On African American society and Robert R. Church's wedding to Miss Annie Wright, see "Memphis," *Cleveland Gazette*, 10 January 1885.

23. Church and Church, *The Robert R. Churches of Memphis*, 5–6; A. A. Taylor, *The Negro in Tennessee*, chaps. 10–13. See also Qualls, "Beginnings and Early History of Le Moyne School at Memphis"; A. L. Robinson, "'Plans Dat Comed From God'"; E. Lewis, "Connecting Memory, Self, and the Power of Place."

24. "The New South: Memphis and Its Afro-American Population," *Indianapolis Freeman*, 5 April 1890.

25. Wedell, *Elite Women*, 73; and Young, *Standard History of Memphis*, 236. In

general, see Sims, *Power of Femininity in the New South*; and A. F. Scott, *Southern Lady*, 135–36.

26. Wedell, *Elite Women*, 37, 46, 19; "White Ribbon Hall," *Memphis Appeal*, 19 December 1886. White women also ran a Women's Christian Association, a Children's Home, and a Women's Exchange for the "reception and sale of women's handiwork." *Dow's City Directory of Memphis for 1892*, 59.

27. "Willard an Honest Woman," *Memphis Appeal*, 2 July 1881; Wedell, *Elite Women*, 55–76; Willard, *Woman and Temperance*, 540–57.

28. Prescott, "Woman Suffrage Movement in Memphis"; Wedell, *Elite Women*, 73–74; A. F. Scott, *Southern Lady*, 173–74; Kirkley, " 'This Work Is God's Cause.' "

29. Wells Diary, 28 December 1886, IBW Papers.

30. "Odds and Ends," *New York Freeman*, 15 January 1887.

31. A. F. Scott, *Southern Lady*, 173.

32. Cartwright, *Triumph of Jim Crow*, 188.

33. *Memphis Daily Appeal*, 13 and 16 March 1881; Church and Walter, *Nineteenth-Century Memphis Families of Color*, 43, 35; Lewis and Kremer, *Angel of Beale Street*, 234–35.

34. Broughton, *Twenty Year's Experience of a Missionary*, 38; Higginbotham, *Righteous Discontent*, 69–72. Broughton later helped found and lead the Woman's Convention of the National Baptist Convention, established in 1900.

35. Wells Diary, 13 July 1887; Terrell, *Colored Woman in a White World*, 234–35. See also Berkeley, " 'Colored Ladies Also Contributed,' " 192. Berkeley calculates that during Reconstruction, African American women in Memphis "assumed leadership positions in roughly one-third of the black associations" developed for mutual aid and benefit.

36. In the second incident, the trainman refused to take Wells's first-class ticket and pushed her back when she tried to enter the ladies' car. Wells refused to sit in the smoking car and was again put off the train, this time by a "colored porter" who "politely assisted" her to alight. See *Ida Wells v. C.O. & S.W. R.R. Co.*, 4 November 1884, p. 11 in Manuscript Court Records, Tennessee State Supreme Court, Tennessee State Library and Archives, Nashville; *New York Globe*, 24 May 1884; Wells-Barnett, *Crusade for Justice*, 18–19; "Civil Rights," *Memphis Appeal-Avalanche*, 1 January 1885. See also "A Darky Damsel," *Memphis Appeal-Avalanche*, 25 December 1884, clipping in IBW Papers.

37. Wells-Barnett, *Crusade for Justice*, 19–21; *The Chesapeake, Ohio, and Southwestern Railroad Company v. Ida Wells*, 31 March 1885, p. 21 in Manuscript Court Records, Circuit Court of Shelby County, Tennessee State Library and Archives, Nashville.

38. Wells-Barnett, *Crusade for Justice*, 21.

39. Ibid., 23–24; Penn, *Afro-American Press*, 407.

40. It seems to have taken Wells until 1884–85 to secure a teaching position in the Memphis schools. She first appears listed as a teacher in *Dow's City Directory of Memphis for 1885*, 687. I agree with DeCosta-Willis that it is unlikely that she clerked in a downtown department store in 1883 or 1884, as the listing of a "Miss Ida Wells" in a city directory for 1884 indicates. DeCosta-Willis, *Memphis Diary of Ida B. Wells*, 47.

41. Berkeley, "Politics of Black Education in Memphis," 202–11.

42. Wells Diary, 7 November 1886.

43. *Eleventh Decennial Census of the U.S., 1890*; G. P. Hamilton, *Bright Side of Memphis*, 40. Nationally, black women achieved parity with men in teaching by 1890. Collier-Thomas, "Impact of Black Women in Education."

44. Berkeley, *"Like a Plague of Locusts"*, 172–78; Wedell, *Elite Women*, 23–24.

45. For the North Carolina case, see Durrill, "New Schooling for a New South."

46. Mossell, *Work of the Afro-American Woman*, 98.

47. *Detroit Plaindealer*, 26 February 1892; Sampson, "American People to the Common Law." Sampson was part of a local Republican convention (along with Ed Shaw and Robert Church) that weighed in on the state debt and tax questions plaguing Tennessee politics in the late 1870s and early 1880s. See "Resolutions and Delegates," *Memphis Appeal*, 4 April 1882.

48. Shaw, *What a Woman Ought to Be and to Do*, chap. 3.

49. Wells Diary, 12 June 1886.

50. Ibid.

51. Ibid., 29 December 1885; 11 March, 28 November, 4 December 1886; 14 February, 11 April, 17 June, 29 July 1887; 1886.

52. See, for example, 28 January and 11 March 1886.

53. Wells-Barnett, *Crusade for Justice*, 21, 23.

54. Wells Diary, 31 October 1886; Wells-Barnett, *Crusade for Justice*, 23.

55. *Washington Bee*, 12 December 1885.

56. *New York Age*, 25 July 1891. It should be noted that although the Philadelphia-born Quaker Anna Dickinson (1842–1932) was talented and very well-known for her antislavery speeches and later for her Republican Party campaigning during 1864, she was also controversial and mocked in the press as an outrageous, even slightly disreputable woman in Wells's own time. See R. Edwards, *Angels in the Machinery*, 71.

57. *Cleveland Gazette*, 17 January 1885.

58. Wells Diary, 18 January 1887. Delegates to a press convention in 1892 were "entertained by Miss I. B. Wells at dinner," according to the *Kansas City American Citizen*, 29 January 1892. "Miss I. B. Wells entertained quite a number of ladies and gentlemen a few evenings ago," noted another press report. See "Memphis," *Cleveland Gazette*, 31 October 1885.

59. Wells Diary, 4 July 1886.

60. Ibid., 6 May 1886. "The Cynthia Poems," written by a lesser Roman poet, Propertius, were witty, graceful poems reflecting on love, marriage, and women's roles. The Cynthia cycle ends tragically, with Cynthia deserted by her lover Claudius.

61. Wells Diary, 20 March 1887, 13 July 1886; Iola [Ida B. Wells], "The Minister in the Pulpit," *Christian Index*, ca. March 1888, (courtesy of Paul Lee).

62. Wells Diary, 5 January 1886.

63. Quoted in "Some Seasonable Suggestions," *Indianapolis Freeman*, 28 June 1890.

64. Wells Diary, 24 January 1886.

65. Ibid., 21 January 1886; Levine, *Highbrow/Lowbrow*, 13–81.

66. Wells Diary, 14 March, 24 April, 2 and 3 May 1887.

67. Ibid., 20 February 1887. After seeing a show, Wells wrote that she felt "like a guilty thing for breaking my word," noting in her diary, "Already I've had it thrown at me for so doing, & I regret having yielded." Ibid., 18 January 1887.

68. Wells Diary, 28 January 1886; Ayers, *Promise of the New South*, 373–408.

69. Wells Diary, 26 August 1886.

70. Ibid., 5 January 1886.

71. Ibid., 4 September 1886.

72. Ibid., 5 January 1886. Robert Church also advanced her money against her monthly paycheck at least once. Ida B. Wells to Robert R. Church, 29 January 1891, CF Papers.

73. Wells Diary, 17 June 1887.

74. Ibid., 5 May, 17 June 1887.

75. Ibid., 8 February 1886.

76. Ibid., 28 December 1886.

77. Ibid., 3 January 1887.

78. Ibid., 4 December, 19 May 1886; 3 January 1887.

79. Ibid., 7 June 1886.

80. "Memphis: A Grievous Insult to a Young Colored Lady," *Cleveland Gazette*, 8 August 1885.

81. Wells Diary, 21 January 1886.

82. Angell, "Controversy Over Women's Ministry in the African Methodist Episcopal Church in the 1880s"; Angell, *Bishop Henry McNeal Turner*, 182–84.

83. Tate, *Domestic Allegories*; Carby, *Reconstructing Womanhood*.

84. Crummell, "The Black Woman of the South," in *Africa and America*, 61–82; Moses, *Alexander Crummell*, 222–43.

85. Cooper, *Voice from the South*, 9–47, quotes on 24–25, 42–43. Frances Harper also agreed that "education of the intellect and the training of the morals should go hand-in-hand." See F. E. W. Harper, "A Factor in Human Progress," 276.

86. Iola, "Woman's Mission," *New York Freeman*, 26 December 1885.

87. Ibid.

88. Iola, "A Story of 1900," reprinted in DeCosta-Willis, *Memphis Diary of Ida B. Wells*, 182–84.

89. Iola, "Our Women," *New York Freeman*, 1 January 1887.

90. Iola, "The Model Woman: A Pen Picture of the Typical Southern Girl," *New York Freeman*, 18 February 1888.

91. S. A. Holt, "Making Freedom Pay."

92. Meyerowitz, *Women Adrift*; Janiewski, *Sisterhood Denied*; MacLean, "Leo Frank Case Reconsidered." Shaw, *What a Woman Ought to Be and to Do*, emphasizes not so much conflict over wage labor itself as work's impact on gender ideology and domesticity in a somewhat later period. B. W. Jones, "Race, Sex, and Class," 446, notes that families and fathers "controlled daughters' wages."

93. Wedell, *Elite Women*, 135–39. The process of destigmatizing "spinsterhood" for white women began in the antebellum period. See M. Fuller, "The Great Lawsuit." On visions of female community and mothering without men, see Charlotte Perkins Gilman's novella *Herland* (1915); Sklar, "Hull-House in the 1890s"; and Pascoe, *Relations of Rescue*, 32–69.

94. Wells Diary, 1 February 1887. Of the twenty-two black teachers listed as elected to the Memphis public schools in 1881, eleven were men (no marital status given), five were "misses," and six were married women. *Memphis Watchman*, 21 July 1888, clipping in CF Papers. In 1859, antislavery lecturer Frances Ellen Watkins felt socially self-conscious in her work as an unmarried woman;

she confessed to feeling like "an old maid going about the country meddling in with the slaveholders' business." Quoted in Collier-Thomas, "Frances Ellen Watkins Harper," 47.

95. Wells Diary, 15 June 1886.

96. Ibid., 28 June 1886.

97. Wells-Barnett, *Crusade for Justice*, 7. Applications from African Americans for marriage licenses were publicly announced in the newspapers, one of the few instances of equitable reporting in the local white press; see, for example, *Memphis Appeal*, 20 January 1881. According to one scholar of postbellum black society, "[the] progressive development in Negro social life was further reflected by the dignified [white] press reports of weddings held among the Negro elite." A. A. Taylor, *The Negro in Tennessee*, 243. See also Herman, "Loving Courtship or the Marriage Market?"

98. Kantrowitz, " 'No Middle Ground': Gender Protection and the Wilmington Riot of 1898"; Whites, "Rebecca Latimer Felton and the Problem of 'Protection' in the New South."

99. Wells Diary, 23 March, 9 May 1886.

100. Ibid., 30 January 1886.

101. Carolivia Herron, "Introduction," in A. W. Grimké, *Selected Works*; and Yezierska, *Bread Givers*, 186.

102. Wells Diary, 14 September 1886. Since Wells referred to Lutie elsewhere as "Mrs. Rice who has a little girl," perhaps she was a self-supporting widow. Ibid., 20 March 1887.

103. Ibid., 18 September 1887; 4 December 1886.

104. DeCosta-Willis, *Memphis Diary of Ida B. Wells*, 30–31, 155. A Colored Orphan Home was founded in 1878, and the Canfield Orphan Asylum was listed as a "colored" institution in the city directory of 1885. See *Sholes' Memphis Directory for 1885*, 13. A later chronicler explained, however, that the Home "at no time received that healthy response and cheerful co-operation which its worthy character deserved . . . and the result was that the project was very slow of realization." As late as 1908, this African American publicist for Memphis could only note: "We do not say that our people have done their whole duty in [charity work], but they might have done a great deal worse." G. P. Hamilton, *Bright Side of Memphis*, 20–21.

105. DeCosta-Willis, *Memphis Diary of Ida B. Wells*, 7; Alfreda M. Duster, "Biography I Wrote," unpublished typescript, 2, in IBW Papers.

106. Wells-Barnett, *Crusade for Justice*, 9; Stanton, *Eighty Years and More*, 20–34.

107. Wells, "Two Christmas Days," 132.

108. Literary black women wrote about similar ideas at the turn of the century. See especially Tate, *Domestic Allegories*, 124–79; and D. E. McDowell, "The Changing Same," 34–57.

109. Wells Diary, 4 September 1886.

110. Ibid., 15 June, 8 February 1886.

111. Ibid., 28 June 1886.

112. Ibid., 13 January 1886.

113. Ibid., 30 January 1886.

114. Ibid., 2 October 1886. Another example of male manipulation concerned a Prof. H. T. J. Johnson. Johnson made requests of Wells (probably in her capacity as officeholder in the lyceum) to secure him speaking venues in town

and to edit a manuscript. At one point he also "proposed that [she] join with him in the edition of a book & outlined his plan." Johnson was apparently willing to apply some unspecified pressure to secure her commitment. When Wells equivocated and "gave him no satisfactory answer" about the project, Johnson "grew warm enough to express himself as to what he would do in case [she] did not." Wells was "surprised" at this outburst and addressed Johnson "coldly." After this exchange, Johnson informed B. K. Sampson that he would be leaving town forthwith, without acknowledging Wells, which she felt officially severed their relationship. Sampson may have functioned as a mediator in this case. The diary notes that Sampson possessed a letter, perhaps clearing up any misunderstanding or potential threats, of which he advised Wells but would not let her see. Ibid., 26 November, 4 December 1886; 18 January 1887.

115. Ibid., 30 January, 3 April 1886.

116. Wells-Barnett, *Crusade for Justice*, 40.

117. Wells Diary, 14 September 1886.

118. Ibid.; Wells-Barnett, *Crusade for Justice*, 24–31.

119. Penn, *Afro-American Press*, 367–427, included portraits of more than a dozen black women journalists. Mossell also offered women plenty of how-to in *Work of the Afro-American Woman*, 98–103. The movement of white women into journalism dated from the antebellum period. The origins of the General Federation of Women's Clubs (GFWC) had its roots in a journalists' group, Sorosis, founded in New York City in 1868 when female journalists were excluded from a press banquet in honor of the visiting Charles Dickens. Sorosis's founder, Jane Cunningham Croly, went on to found the GFWC in 1890.

120. Penn, *Afro-American Press*, 120; T. O. Fuller, *Negro Baptists of Tennessee*, 144–62. Under Bishop Turner's leadership, the AME Church built several educational institutions in the region at this time, including the short-lived Turner College in Hernando, Mississippi, ten miles to the south of Memphis. After five years, the school reopened in Shelbyville, Tennessee, around 1887. Angell, *Bishop Henry McNeal Turner*, 160–61.

121. Higginbotham, *Righteous Discontent*, 64. See also Streitmatter, "African American Women Journalists and Their Male Editors"; and Streitmatter, "Economic Conditions Surrounding Nineteenth-Century African American Women Journalists."

122. Quoted in Penn, *Afro-American Press*, 381.

123. Mossell, *Work of the Afro-American Woman*, 10.

124. *Washington Bee*, 2, 16, and 23 April 1887.

125. Kletzing and Crogman, *Progress of a Race*, 199.

126. Wells-Barnett, *Crusade for Justice*, 41, 32; *New York Age*, 11 August 1888; *Indianapolis Freeman*, 20 July 1889; and Penn, *Afro-American Press*, 408.

127. Wells Diary, 13 July 1887.

128. Wells-Barnett, *Crusade for Justice*, 31–32.

129. Wells Diary, 28 January 1886; "'Iola' Newspapers and Magazines," *Washington Bee*, 13 January 1886.

130. Wells Diary, 28 January 1886.

131. *Memphis Watchman*, 9 February 1889, clipping in CF Papers.

132. *Cleveland Gazette*, 26 March 1887.

133. Wells Diary, 12 August 1887.

134. Quoted in Tucker, "Miss Ida B. Wells and Memphis Lynching," 113.

135. *Indianapolis Freeman*, 24 August 1889.

136. Fortune, "Ida B. Wells, A.M.," 33–39. Fortune credited Wells with an honorary degree from Rust College that I have been unable to verify.

137. *Indianapolis Freeman*, 10 May, 19 April 1890.

138. "'Iola' v. 'Grace Ermine,'" *The American Baptist* (Louisville), 27 January 1888 (courtesy of Paul Lee).

139. Quoted in *Indianapolis Freeman*, 17 May 1890.

140. Blanchard, "Boundaries and the Victorian Body."

141. Wells Diary, 12 August 1887.

142. Wells, "Requirements of Southern Journalism," 191.

143. Iola, "Race Pride," originally published 5 March 1887, reprinted in *The American Baptist*, 17 February 1989 (courtesy of Paul Lee). See also E. B. Brown, "To Catch the Vision of Freedom." For related examples, see Higginbotham, *Righteous Discontent*, 17, which warns against falsely opposing secular and religious efforts in "uplift." Connor, *Conversions and Visions in the Writings of African American Women*, shows how black women's religious experiences and writings do not sharply distinguish the sacred and the profane, the religious and the political; see especially 1–42, 268–74.

144. On competition, bolting, and schisms in southern church life, see Montgomery, *Under Their Own Vine and Fig Tree*, esp. chap. 3; Dvorak, *African American Exodus*; "Our Southern Field," *Methodist Quarterly Review*; and Bennett, "Religion, Race, and Region: Churches and the Rise of Jim Crow in New Orleans."

145. Iola, "The Minister in the Pulpit," part 1, ca. March 1888; "The Minister in the Pulpit," part 2, ca. April 1888; "The Minister Out of the Pulpit," part 3, ca. May 1888, *Christian Index* (courtesy of Paul Lee).

146. Gilkes, "The Politics of 'Silence'"; Higginbotham, *Righteous Discontent*, 67–80. See also Cooper, *Voice from the South*, 75–79.

147. F. B. Williams, "Religious Duty to the Negro," 269.

148. Iola, "The Minister in the Pulpit," parts 1 and 2.

149. Wells Diary, 1 February 1886.

150. Ida B. Wells to Booker T. Washington, 30 November 1890, in Harlan, *Booker T. Washington Papers*, 3:108–9.

151. Wells-Barnett, *Crusade for Justice*, 41.

152. Washington, Wood, and Williams, *New Negro for a New Century*. The chapter "Fathers of the Race" treats Frederick Douglass, Toussaint Louverture, Phillis Wheatley, and Sojourner Truth; Truth is the only religious figure featured. Williams's essay was entitled "The Club Movement among the Colored Women of America."

153. Wells Diary, 26 August 1886.

154. Ibid., 7 June, 23 February 1886.

155. Ibid., 24 April 1887.

156. Ibid., 18 January 1887. My research has been inconclusive as to what church, or series of churches, Wells may have actually joined during her Memphis years. Linda O. McMurry argues that Wells joined Vance Street Christian Church, led by an independent-minded Rev. D. R. Wilkins in these years. McMurry, *To Keep the Waters Troubled*, 69–70, 350 n. 66. DeCosta-Willis is more persuaded that Wells regularly attended Beale Street Baptist, where Rev. Taylor Nightingale presided. DeCosta-Willis, *Memphis Diary of Ida B. Wells*, 143. My sense is that they are both likely right, but a lack of evidence prevents me from

substantiating the sequence or precise nature of Wells's connection to either congregation. That Wells nowhere specifies which church she belonged to in Memphis and that she changed congregations probably six times in her lifetime are facts more salient to my argument about mobility, competition, and leverage in African American women's religious lives.

157. The limits on Harper's effectiveness in the WCTU derived from resistance on the part of clergy who, according to Harper biographer Bettye Collier-Thomas, "sometimes gave tacit support but were unwilling to turn their members and money over to any long-term cause they did not control." Collier-Thomas, "Frances Ellen Watkins Harper," 61.

158. Harper did attend to economic issues in black women's lives. See her essay "Coloured Women of America," first published in England in 1878. During her travels in Mississippi, Harper noted the competence of freedwomen in the economic realm, calling them "models of executiveness" who bore up well in sometimes turbulent marriages or else made their way alone.

159. Harper, Wells, et al., "Symposium—Temperance." See also Harper, "The WCTU and the Colored Woman."

160. Tucker, *Black Pastors and Leaders*, 21–22.

161. Iola, "The Minister in the Pulpit," part 1.

162. M. W. Taylor, *Life, Travels, Labors and Helpers of Mrs. Amanda Smith.*

163. A. Smith, *Autobiography*, 138, chaps. 11 and 12. See also Israel, *Amanda Berry Smith*, 118.

164. DeCosta-Willis, *Memphis Diary of Ida B. Wells*, 5, 61.

165. Wells Diary, 3 January 1887.

166. Ibid., 25 April 1886.

167. Ibid., 28 June 1886.

168. Ibid., 11 April 1886; 18 January 1887; 18 March 1886; 1 March 1887; 20 April, 3 June 1886.

169. Wells-Barnett, *Crusade for Justice*, 22.

170. "Notes by the Wayside," *Christian Index*, ca. August 1888 (courtesy of Paul Lee).

171. *Eleventh Census, 1890*. Baptist Church assets from its less well-off members amounted to $31,200. The AME, with only half the number of members, reported accounts of $45,050.

172. A. A. Taylor, *Negro in Tennessee*, 220.

173. Tucker, *Black Pastors and Leaders*, 34; Tucker, "Black Politics in Memphis, 1865–75"; Montgomery, *Under Their Own Vine and Fig Tree*, 97–141. See also Clarence Walker, *Rock in a Weary Land.*

174. *Memphis Avalanche & Appeal*, [2 January 1885?], clipping in CF Papers.

175. Higginbotham, *Righteous Discontent*, 70; Tucker, *Black Pastors and Leaders*, 38–39; T. O. Fuller, *Negro Baptists of Tennessee*, 147.

176. "Flying for Life," 5 August 1885; and "The Countee Can-Can," 7 August 1885, both in *Memphis Appeal*. See also *Cleveland Gazette*, 31 October, 14 November 1885, which notes death threats against Countee.

177. Wells-Barnett, *Crusade for Justice*, 35, 66–67; *Indianapolis Freeman*, 29 June 1889.

178. Iola, "Race Pride."

179. Wells Diary, 18 April 1887; Cartwright, *Triumph of Jim Crow*, 195.

180. F. B. Williams, "The Club Movement among the Colored Women of America," 383.

181. Tucker, *Black Pastors and Leaders*, 44–46. See also "Voice of the People," 8 September 1891; "Down on Nightingale," 10 September 1891; "Deacons and Trustees," 11 September 1891, all in *Memphis Appeal-Avalanche*.

182. Wells-Barnett, *Crusade for Justice*, 39–40.

183. Quoted in Tucker, "Miss Ida B. Wells and Memphis Lynching," 114.

184. Cartwright, *Triumph of Jim Crow*, 140–47; Rabinowitz, "Continuity and Change," 120.

185. Wells Diary, 13 January 1886; and Wrenn, "School Board Reorganization in Memphis, 1883," 337.

186. Quoted in Cartwright, *Triumph of Jim Crow*, 49.

187. *Memphis Appeal*, 28 July 1885; Cartwright, *Triumph of Jim Crow*, 49–51; Wells Diary, 18 February 1886. For similar treatment of another black political leader, Thomas Cassells, see Cartwright, *Triumph of Jim Crow*, 115.

188. Shannon, *Cases Argued and Determined in the Supreme Court of Tennessee*, 615, copy in Manuscript Court Records, Tennessee State Library and Archives, Nashville.

189. Wells Diary, 11 April 1887.

190. Brief of Greer & Adams for Defendant in Error, *Chesapeake, Ohio & S.W. Railroad v. Ida Wells*, 5–6, copy in Manuscript Court Records, Tennessee State Library and Archives, Nashville.

191. Wells Diary, 2 October 1886; Berkeley, "Politics of Black Education in Memphis," 212; DeCosta-Willis, *Memphis Diary of Ida B. Wells*, 33.

192. *Detroit Plaindealer*, 12 June 1891; Wells-Barnett, *Crusade for Justice*, 36–37. There is a silence where Hattie's suicide should be in Lewis and Kremer's *Angel of Beale Street*, 253–72.

193. Wells-Barnett, *Crusade for Justice*, 36.

194. Ibid., 36–37; *Indianapolis Freeman*, 19 September 1891. Wells was not listed among black Memphis teachers that fall. See "The Teacher's Roster," *Memphis Appeal-Avalanche*, 12 September 1891.

195. Wells-Barnett, *Crusade for Justice*, 31; Wells Diary, 30 January 1886.

196. *Indianapolis Freeman*, 12 July 1890.

197. Wells-Barnett, *Crusade for Justice*, 37.

198. Ibid., 37–39; "Senator Bruce and the Race," "Senator Bruce's Postoffice," and "Senator Bruce," in, respectively, 8, 15 August and 12 September 1891, *New York Age*. On African American women critical of male leadership, see Gaines, *Uplifting the Race*, 42–43.

199. Holmes, "Arkansas Cotton Pickers Strike of 1891." A city directory for 1892 (printed at the close of 1891) listed a "Benjamin Patterson, c[olored]" as a resident. *Dow's City Directory of Memphis for 1892*, 836. See also Gaither, "Negro Alliance Movement in Tennessee, 1888–1891."

200. *Memphis Commercial*, 3 March 1892, 4 July 1891.

201. Wells, *The Reason Why The Colored American Is Not in the Columbian Exposition*, 78. Only Louisiana had more lynchings, with twenty-nine that year.

202. *Memphis Commercial*, 1 August 1891.

203. Ibid., 14 August 1891.

204. *Memphis Appeal-Avalanche*, 23 and 25 August, 8 September 1891.

205. "Let Him Steal Big," *Indianapolis Freeman*, 7 November 1891.

206. *Memphis Commercial*, 6 and 8 March 1892.

207. *Memphis Commercial*, 6 March 1892; Wells-Barnett, *Crusade for Justice*, 48.

208. *Memphis Commercial*, 8 March 1892; Wells-Barnett, *Crusade for Justice*, 48.

209. *Memphis Commercial*, 8 and 9 March 1892.

210. *Memphis Watchman*, 9 February 1889, clipping in CF Papers.

211. Wells-Barnett, *Crusade for Justice*, 48; *Memphis Commercial*, 10 March 1892.

212. *Memphis Commercial*, 6 March 1892.

213. Ibid., 7 and 9 March 1892.

214. Ibid., 10 March 1892. The *Free Speech* reported that by the end of March the company had completely disbanded, turning the rest of their equipment over to the National Guard of Tennessee. *Detroit Plaindealer*, 1 April 1892.

215. *Memphis Commercial*, 10 March 1892.

216. *Detroit Plaindealer*, 18 March, 15 April 1892.

217. *Memphis Commercial*, 4 and 5 June 1892; *Memphis Appeal-Avalanche*, 5 June 1892.

218. *Free Speech* quoted in *Detroit Plaindealer*, 15 April 1892; Wells-Barnett, *Crusade for Justice*, 51.

219. *Memphis Commercial*, 20 March 1892; *Detroit Plaindealer*, 25 March, 1 and 15 April 1892; *Indianapolis Freeman*, 7 May 1892; Wells-Barnett, *Crusade for Justice*, 58.

220. *Detroit Plaindealer*, 6, 13, and 27 May 1892; Wells-Barnett, *Crusade for Justice*, 55.

221. Wells-Barnett, *Crusade for Justice*, 62, 64.

222. Wells, "Requirements of Southern Journalism," 191.

223. *Memphis Commercial*, 11 March 1892.

224. *Detroit Plaindealer*, 1 April 1892.

225. Ibid., 23 September 1892.

226. Wells-Barnett, *Crusade for Justice*, 58.

227. Ibid., 39.

228. Ibid., 65–66. See also Tucker, "Miss Ida B. Wells and Memphis Lynching," 117.

229. Wells-Barnett, *Crusade for Justice*, 62.

230. Wells describes her knowledge of Duke's situation in *Southern Horrors*, 5–6. Also see note on Duke in Harlan et al., *Booker T. Washington Papers*, 2:325–26. Duke and Wells worked together briefly in the winter before the Curve incident in a short-lived organization called the Southern Press Association. See *Detroit Plaindealer*, 5 February 1892; and *Kansas City American Citizen*, 29 January 1892.

231. Wells, "Requirements of Southern Journalism," 191.

232. Wells-Barnett, *Crusade for Justice*, 61–62.

233. *Detroit Plaindealer*, 17 June 1892.

234. Wells-Barnett, *Crusade for Justice*, 69–71.

Chapter Three

1. Douglass, "Lynch Law in the South."

2. *New York Age*, 20 February 1892; *Indianapolis Freeman*, 19 March 1892. There is evidence that this whole discussion of leadership was begun by Wells's provocative critique of black Senator Blanche Bruce's patronage practices in Mississippi, which she discovered on an extended visit there in July 1891. Her reports

started a "war on paper." See *New York Age*, 27 June, 8 and 15 August, 12 September 1891; 30 January 1892.

3. McFeely, *Frederick Douglass*, 359–74; Meier, *Negro Thought in America*, 80–82.

4. Cooper, *Voice from the South*, 134.

5. Ayers, *Promise of the New South*; Bellamy, *Looking Backward, 2000–1887*; Addams, *Twenty Years at Hull-House*, chap. 9, quote on 142; Painter, *Standing at Armageddon*.

6. Berthoff, "Conventional Mentality." A number of resolutions were broached at the time, mainly in law: Native Americans were reduced to wards of the state; other citizens of the male sex were constitutionally established as full citizens through the Fourteenth and Fifteenth Amendments; Chinese immigrants were excluded from entering the United States by the congressional Exclusion Act of 1882; all women citizens were denied the vote; and the legal fiction of "corporate personality" was raised in 1886. In *Ex parte Crow Dog* (1883), the Court ruled that Native Americans were not eligible for citizenship. In *Minor v. Happersett* (1875) the Court denied women citizens suffrage rights. DuBois, "'Taking the Law into Our Own Hands,'" 19–41. On "corporate personality" and the Supreme Court case *Santa Clara v. Southern Pacific Railroad* (1886), see Horwitz, *Transformation of American Law*, 65–107.

7. Douglass made these comments at the World's Congress of Representative Women in Chicago, 1893. Sewell, *World's Congress of Representative Women*, 117–18. Lynching soured even Douglass before his death. In 1895, he confessed to the view that "the New South is but a slightly revised edition of the Old South," a new jail built on an old jail site, incarcerating the same "prisoners." Douglass, "Letter from the Late Hon. Fred. Douglass," 61.

8. Quoted in Wells, *Southern Horrors*, 31. See also Hall, "'The Mind That Burns in Each Body'"; and Hale, *Making Whiteness*, chap. 5.

9. Painter, "'Social Equality,' Miscegenation, Labor, and the Maintenance of Power," 54; Weigman, "Anatomy of Lynching"; Weigman, *American Anatomies*, 2–42; Bederman, "'Civilization,' the Decline of Middle-Class Manliness, and Ida B. Wells's Anti-Lynching Campaign," 5–30; MacLean, "Leo Frank Case Reconsidered." For a contemporary treatment in law, see Roberts, *Killing the Black Body*; in philosophy, Butler, *Bodies that Matter*.

10. Here I disagree with the rather static model presented in Alexander, "'We Must Be about Our Father's Business,'" 338. Because body/identity politics were highly contested at this moment, any self-authorization and social analysis by Wells required significant political effort, much more than simply "writing [the] body into the text" of an argument, as Alexander suggests. Useful treatments can be found in Sanchez-Eppler, "Bodily Bonds"; and Samuels, "Identity of Slavery."

11. Wells, *Southern Horrors*, 42; Wells-Barnett, *Crusade for Justice*, 62. Wells indicated to a New York reporter in 1894 that although she did "not fear personal injury," she had "not failed to provide herself with means with which to protect her life." Interview in *New York Sun*, 1 August 1894. On southern civil rights traditions of arms bearing, see Tyson, "Robert F. Williams"; and Tyson, *Radio-Free Dixie*, 4–25.

12. Wells-Barnett, *Crusade for Justice*, 59.

13. Aptheker, *Lynching and Rape*, 1–33; Aptheker, *Woman's Legacy*, 53–76; Terborg-Penn, "African American Women's Networks in the Anti-Lynching

Crusade"; Moses, *Golden Age of Black Nationalism*, 103–31. See also Carby, *Reconstructing Womanhood*, 108–16; and J. James, *Transcending the Talented Tenth*, chaps. 2 and 3.

14. Painter, *Sojourner Truth*, 220–33.

15. Before Hall's *The Revolt Against Chivalry* was published in 1976, the most often cited American authorities on lynching were W. White, *Rope and Faggot* (1929), Raper, *The Tragedy of Lynching* (1933), Cutler, *Lynch-Law* (1905), and National Association for the Advancement of Colored People, *Thirty Years of Lynching in the United States, 1889–1918* (1919).

16. Wells, *Southern Horrors*, 30. The most comprehensive recent survey of lynching data in ten southern states also concludes that alleged sexual crimes accounted for approximately 30 percent of all lynchings. Tolnay and Beck, *Festival of Violence*, chap. 4. These authors cite Wells's early pamphlets in their bibliography.

17. Wells, *Southern Horrors*, 14.

18. Tom Paine's legacy benefited from a revival at the hands of former abolitionist and southerner Moncure Conway, who, back in the United States during the 1890s, brought out a biography, *The Life of Thomas Paine* (1892), and *The Writings of Thomas Paine*, the latter in four volumes (1894–96). Wells and Conway shared a platform in England and may have shared ideas. See "Mr. Moncure D. Conway on Mob-Murder in America," *The Echo*, 23 May 1894. Conway also signed on to the London antilynching committee. See *Christian World*, 2 August 1894; Wells-Barnett, *Crusade for Justice*, 217.

19. Wells, *Southern Horrors*, 29, 19.

20. Henderson, "Speaking in Tongues."

21. Wells, *Southern Horrors*, 23, 43.

22. Hodes, "Sexualization of Reconstruction Politics."

23. Wells, *Southern Horrors*, 19.

24. *Christian World*, 3 May 1894.

25. Wells, *Southern Horrors*, 19; Wells, *Red Record*, 147.

26. Hofstadter, *Social Darwinism*; Bederman, *Manliness and Civilization*; and Frederickson, *Black Image*.

27. Ryan, *Women in Public*, 3–18. The phrase "people's peoplehood" is Elizabeth Lunbeck's.

28. Wells, *Southern Horrors*, 37.

29. Ibid., 30.

30. Ibid., 26.

31. *Christian World*, 3 May 1894 (emphasis in original); Wells, *Southern Horrors*, 26.

32. Joan Scott, "Gender: A Useful Category of Historical Analysis." For a related but distinct view, see Carby, *Reconstructing Womanhood*, 113–15. See also E. B. Brown, "Imaging Lynching"; E. B. Brown, "Negotiating and Transforming the Public Sphere"; Pateman, "Feminist Critiques of the Public/Private Dichotomy"; P. Baker, "The Domestication of Politics"; and introduction and essays in Helly and Reverby, *Gendered Domains*.

33. Cooper, *Voice from the South*, 29–33, 55–56.

34. Douglass, "Lynch Law in the South."

35. Wells, *Southern Horrors*, 22–23, 25, 44.

36. *Memphis Commercial*, 27 May 1893.

37. *Detroit Plaindealer*, 5, 12 (quote), and 19 August 1892; *Indianapolis Freeman*,

20 August 1892; *Memphis Appeal-Avalanche*, 12 and 30 June 1892. Wells soon softened her view of the response of black Memphis. She noted before a Boston audience that Rev. Taylor Nightingale had been abused by a "committee" that forced him at "pistol point" to "sign a letter which was written by them, in which he denied all knowledge of the [*Free Speech*] editorial, denounced and condemned it as a slander on white women." Wells refrained from censuring Nightingale, explaining, "because, having never been at the pistol's point myself, I do not feel that I am competent to sit in judgement on him, or say what I would do under such circumstances." Wells, "Lynch Law in All Its Phases," 179.

38. *Washington Bee*, 22 and 29 October 1892; Wells-Barnett, *Crusade for Justice*, 82.

39. Ida B. Wells to Frederick Douglass, 17 October 1892, 24 February 1893, FD Papers; Wells-Barnett, *Crusade for Justice*, 81; *Indianapolis Freeman*, 25 February 1893.

40. Wells-Barnett, *Crusade for Justice*, 83; *Washington Bee*, 28 January 1893.

41. Mary Church Terrell, "Introducing Ida Wells Barnett—to Deliver an Address on Lynching, ca. 1893," handwritten manuscript, MCT-LOC.

42. Wells-Barnett, *Crusade for Justice*, 83.

43. Ibid., 84–85.

44. Ibid., 86. In April 1893 a meeting of southern governors declined to receive an African American delegation petitioning for redress of lynching. See *Baltimore Afro-American*, 29 April 1893.

45. *Memphis Commercial*, 15 December 1892.

46. Before 1896, women were plaintiffs in an overwhelming majority of libel and slander suits involving "imputation[s] of unchastity or immorality," according to cases listed in the *American Digest*, 32:1933–2014. The nineteenth century's Anglo-American law of defamation turned on causing the victim "major social disgrace." This standard was solidified in England's Slander of Woman Act of 1891, which held that "any words spoken or published which impute unchastity or adultery to any woman or girl" were actionable without proof of damages. American legal decisions and state laws generally followed English precedents. See Prosser et al., *Prosser and Keeton on the Law of Torts*, 789, 793; *Encyclopedia of the Laws of England*, 14:184; *Tennessee Code*, 5:432.

47. Ida B. Wells to Albion Tourgée, 22 February 1893, AT Papers.

48. Albion Tourgée to Ida B. Wells (emphasis in original), undated draft, AT Papers. Wells approached Tourgée because she felt that the leading black lawyers in Memphis held a "personal grudge" against her. She was disappointed at Tourgée's rejection and his "conservative" views of the value or promise of her case. Ida B. Wells to Albion Tourgée, 10 February 1893; Ferdinand Barnett to Albion Tourgée, 23 February and 4 March 1893, AT Papers.

49. Ferdinand L. Barnett to Albion Tourgée, 4 March 1893, AT Papers. When the *Commercial* attacked her again in 1894, Wells simply let it go. See "Miss Wells's Reply to the *Memphis Commercial*," Liverpool *Daily Post*, 18 June 1894. "There is no court in the State in which the editor would be punished for these gross libels [as they are] directed against a negro," she stated. The *Memphis Commercial* later made a bizarre statement concerning this libel in 1894. The paper claimed to have learned of Wells's supposed misconduct with Nightingale from black Memphis newspaper editor J. Thomas Turner of the *Watchman*. The *Commercial* eventually sought to clear Turner's role in the accusation, announcing: "This is a

mistake. The information was obtained from another source. This correction is made in justice to Editor Turner, who knows nothing about the character of Ida B. Wells." See "Wanted to Make Trouble," *Memphis Commercial*, 27 May 1894.

50. Ware, *Beyond the Pale*, 189.

51. *Detroit Plaindealer*, 14 October 1892; Catherine Impey to William Axon, 9 June 1990 (emphasis in original), WEA Papers.

52. *New York Age*, 5 July 1890.

53. Wells-Barnett, *Crusade for Justice*, 82.

54. *Topeka Weekly Call*, 15 April 1893.

55. Wells-Barnett, *Crusade for Justice*, 82–85.

56. *Detroit Plaindealer*, 14 and 22 April 1893.

57. Catherine Impey to Frederick Douglass, 4 September 1889. See also Impey to Douglass, 4 July 1887, 13 April 1889, and 12 March 1890, all in FD Papers. See also "Launched, Full Steam Ahead!" *Fraternity* (August 1893): 1; and "What We Think: How the S.R.B.M. Originated," *Fraternity* (1 December 1894): 17. See also Catherine Impey to William Axon 4 June 1889, WEA Papers.

58. Catherine Impey to Frederick Douglass, 4 September 1889, FD Papers. Accusations of personal profiteering also plagued Douglass while abroad in Britain in the 1840s. See the following letters in Clare Taylor, *British and American Abolitionists*, 258–60 and 277–78: Douglass to Maria Weston Chapman, 29 March and 18 August 1846; and R. D. Webb to Maria Weston Chapman, 16 May 1846.

59. Wells-Barnett, *Crusade for Justice*, 109–10.

60. Catherine Impey to Frederick Douglass, 13 April 1889, FD Papers.

61. Wells-Barnett, *Crusade for Justice*, 104; Ware, *Beyond the Pale*, 190–97; Catherine Impey to Mrs. Tourgée, 23 June 1893, AT Papers. In another letter, Impey described Ferdinands as "half Indian by race." See Catherine Impey to William Axon, 9 November 1894, WEA Papers.

62. Catherine Impey to Frederick Douglass, 13 April 1889, FD Papers; Wells-Barnett, *Crusade for Justice*, 104.

63. Ginzberg, *Women and the Work of Benevolence*, 28; Wells-Barnett, *Crusade for Justice*, 105, 100. In her narrative, Wells claimed to have "hesitate[d] long" before relating the full story of Impey's "indiscreet letter," such was its impropriety.

64. Wells-Barnett, *Crusade for Justice*, 212.

65. E. Grant, " 'Room Enough' "; and A. Smith, *Autobiography*, xxxvii.

66. Wells-Barnett, *Crusade for Justice*, 110–11, 103–5, 72–75.

67. *Ida B. Wells in England*, 2 (emphasis in original), copy in AT Papers.

68. Rydell, *All the World's A Fair*; Trachtenberg, *Incorporation of America*, 211, 220. See also Massa, "Black Women in the 'White City' "; Rudwick and Meier, "Black Man in the 'White City' "; Weimann, *Fair Women*, chap. 6.

69. F. L. Barnett, "The Reason Why," in Wells, *The Reason Why the Colored American Is Not in the World's Columbian Exposition*, 134–35, 126.

70. *Detroit Plaindealer*, 28 April 1893; *Indianapolis Freeman*, 24 June 1893; Baltimore *Afro-American*, 29 April 1893; *Detroit Plaindealer*, 24 February, 24 March 1893; *Indianapolis Freeman*, 25 March, 8 July 1893.

71. F. J. Loudin to Albion Tourgée, 13 March 1893, AT Papers; Wells-Barnett, *Crusade for Justice*, 115.

72. In Boston, an all-female "Colored Jubilee Day" Committee advocated a

special day for blacks at the Fair—not unlike the special days already set aside for various nations and nationalities. *Indianapolis Freeman*, 4 March 1893.

73. Ferdinand Lee Barnett to Mrs. Potter Palmer, 20 December 1891; Bertha Potter Palmer to Mrs. Wilkins, 20 October 1891; Mrs. Logan to Mrs. Palmer, 16 October 1891; Fannie Barrier Williams to Mrs. Potter Palmer, 1 July, 16 August, 5 October 1893; and Mrs. Potter Palmer to Mrs. [F. B.] Williams, 21 October 1891, all in Chicago World's Columbian Exposition Papers, Chicago Historical Society, Chicago, Ill. Hale G. Parker, an African American man from Missouri, was finally designated an alternate commissioner.

74. *Cleveland Gazette*, 15 July 1893; Wells-Barnett, *Crusade for Justice*, 117.

75. *Indianapolis Freeman*, 8 July 1893.

76. On the pamphlet controversy, see *Detroit Plaindealer*, 28 April 1893; *Indianapolis Freeman*, 25 March, 1 April, 24 June, 8 July 1893.

77. *Cleveland Gazette*, 15 and 23 July 1893.

78. *Topeka Weekly Call*, 15 July 1893.

79. *Denver Statesman* quoted in *Indianapolis Freeman*, 1 April 1893.

80. *Kansas City American Citizen*, 14 July 1893.

81. Other proposals for black participation in the Fair stressed men's role in leadership positions. Leading AME clergy recommended that the state solicitor "should be a man," but for county solicitors "male or female would suffice." Henry Y. Arnett to Bertha Potter Palmer, 27 March 1892, Chicago World's Columbian Exposition Papers, Chicago Historical Society, Chicago, Ill.

82. *Indianapolis Freeman*, 4 March 1893; *New York Age*, 18 February 1893, clipping in IBW Papers.

83. Wells-Barnett, *Crusade for Justice*, 120–22.

84. Ida B. Wells's letter in the *New York Age*, reprinted in *Cleveland Gazette*, 16 September 1893.

85. Cooper, *Voice from the South*, 90–91.

86. Wells-Barnett, *Crusade for Justice*, 120.

87. *Cleveland Gazette*, 22 and 15 July 1893; *Topeka Weekly Call*, 15 July 1893.

88. McFeely, *Frederick Douglass*, 369–70.

89. Wells-Barnett, *Crusade for Justice*, 118–19.

90. *Kansas City American Citizen*, 15 December 1893.

91. Ida B. Wells to Frederick Douglass, 20 December 1893; C. H. J. Taylor to Frederick Douglass, 16 and 19 April, 14 and 24 May 1895, FD Papers.

92. *Indianapolis Freeman*, 6, 13, 20, and 27 January 1894.

93. Wells-Barnett, *Crusade for Justice*, 125.

94. Ida B. Wells to Frederick Douglass, 13 March 1894, FD Papers.

95. "Letter Box," *Fraternity* (July 1894): 15.

96. C. F. Aked to Ida B. Wells, 12 September 1893; Ida B. Wells to Frederick Douglass, 13 March, 6 April, 6 May 1894, FD Papers.

97. "Miss Wells's Second English Trip," *Fraternity* (August 1894): 4.

98. Charles R. Hand, "History of Edgehill," handwritten manuscript (1916), 72–76; Quill, "Liverpool's 'Pembroke' May Become Barracks of 'Blood and Fire,'" undated clipping; I. Sellers, "Salute to Pembroke, 1838–1931," typescript (1960), all in the Liverpool Public Library; Rev. C. F. Aked, "Five Years in Liverpool," *Liverpool Pulpit* (22 September 1895): 112–15.

99. Waller, *Democracy and Sectarianism*, 135–52; Murdoch, "From Militancy to Social Mission"; and Bohstedt, "More than One Working Class."

100. Aked, "Race Problem in America"; and Aked, "Blot on a Free Republic," 97. See also two articles by Aked in the *Liverpool Pulpit*—"Lynch Law in the United States" (April 1894): 49–51; and "More Lynch Law" (May 1894): 64–65—and the series "A Nineteenth Century Pilgrim: The Gospel of the Second Emancipation of the Coloured Race," published in the *Liverpool Review*, 24 and 31 March; 7, 14, and 28 April; 5 and 26 May; 9 June 1894. Aked made trips to the United States in 1894 and again in 1904. During the second trip, he gained the patronage of none other than John D. Rockefeller and served as pastor of Rockefeller's Fifth Avenue Baptist Church in New York City between 1907 and 1911. After settling in California, he ministered to a series of congregations around Los Angeles while keeping a hand in reform efforts, notably woman suffrage and Henry Ford's "Peace Ship" mission. Norman Vincent Peale eulogized Aked upon his death in 1941. See clippings in Liverpool Public Library: "Mr. Aked's Holiday," n.d., n.p.; "Famous on Two Continents as Preacher," *The Liverpolitan* (February 1937): 11; and "Death Takes Dr. C. F. Aked," *Los Angeles Times*, 13 August 1941. Additional source: M. V. Blatchley to Patricia Schechter, 18 September 1990, personal communication in author's possession.

101. *Christian World*, 19 July 1894.

102. Ida B. Wells to Mr. and Mrs. W. E. A. Axon, 11 May 1894, WEA Papers.

103. See clippings from the *Birmingham Daily Post* and the *Manchester Guardian* (n.d.) in IBW Papers. Also see coverage of meetings in London, like that held at a "Democratic Club" (*Sun*, 31 May 1894) and another at the South Place Chapel's Ethical Society (*Echo*, 23 May 1894).

104. "Miss Wells's Second English Trip"; Aked, "One Woman's Work," *Christian World*, 19 July 1894.

105. *Daily Chronicle*, 14 May 1894.

106. *Christian World*, 19 July 1894.

107. *Fraternity* (14 July 1894): 1; see also *Fraternity* (15 April 1894): 16; and (15 June 1894): 14–15.

108. Wells-Barnett, *Crusade for Justice*, 190.

109. *Liverpool Daily Post*, 14 April 1894; *Liverpool Pulpit* (May 1894): 1; *Manchester Guardian*, 14 April 1894; *Inquirer*, April 28, 5 May 1894.

110. Ida B. Wells to Mr. Axon, [April 1894?], WEA Papers.

111. Wells-Barnett, *Crusade for Justice*, 111, 161–63. Wells described how her lectures were received in England: "As I imagine *Uncle Tom's Cabin* was first received," she stated in an interview. A member of her audience had "said as much" at a London lecture. See interview in the *Christian World*, 19 July 1894. "Nothing since the days of 'Uncle Tom's Cabin' had taken such a hold in England as the Anti-Lynching Committee," was the comment of the Reverend Dr. Clifford of London, as reported by the *New York Tribune*, 30 July 1894.

112. Wells, "Liverpool Slave Traditions and Present Practices."

113. Wells-Barnett, *Crusade for Justice*, 214, 217.

114. Stange, *British Unitarians against American Slavery*; and Stange, *Patterns of Antislavery among American Unitarians*. See also Clare Taylor, *British and American Abolitionists*, 1–16.

115. Florida Ruffin Ridley to Mrs. Ormistan Chant, *Manchester Guardian*, 19 June 1894; Wells-Barnett, *Crusade for Justice*, 197–200.

116. Brooke Hereford to W. Axon, 8 May 1894, WEA Papers.

117. Tyrrell, *Woman's World/Woman's Empire*, 1–2, 62–63. The WWCTU

reached its height in 1927 with 766,000 dues-paying members and "a following of more than a million women." Bordin, *Woman and Temperance*, 194.

118. "Mr. Moody and Miss Willard," *Fraternity* (15 May 1894): 15–16. The original article can be found in Frances E. Willard, "The Race Problem," *New York Voice*, 23 October 1890.

119. "Interview with Miss Willard," clipping in FD Papers. See endorsement of Wells by the BWTA in *Christian World*, 10 May 1894. See also *Fraternity* (15 May 1894): 16.

120. Lady Henry Somerset to Frederick Douglass, 22 May 1894, FD Papers.

121. Wells-Barnett, *Crusade for Justice*, 210. See "Miss Willard and Race Prejudice," *The Word of Brotherhood* (June 1895); "A Blot on the W.C.T.U.," *Christian World* (August 1895); and "The Lynching Question," *Anti-Caste* (n.d.), clippings in Temperance and Prohibition Papers (microfilm collection).

122. Ida B. Wells to Frederick Douglass 3 June 1894, FD Papers.

123. Frederick Douglass to Ida B. Wells, 27 March 1894, FD Papers.

124. Ida B. Wells to Frederick Douglass, 6 April 1894, FD Papers.

125. Ida B. Wells to Frederick Douglass, 6 May 1894, FD Papers.

126. Frederick Douglass to C. F. Aked, 22 May 1894; Frederick Douglass to R. A. Armstrong, 22 May 1894, FD Papers. An antilynching resolution passed the "British and Foreign Unitarian Association." See *Manchester Guardian*, 16 May 1894; *Christian World*, 17 May 1894; *London Daily Chronicle*, 16 May 1894.

127. Ida B. Wells to Frederick Douglass, 3 June 1894, FD Papers.

128. Mossell, *Work of the Afro-American Woman*, 32–45; Wells-Barnett, *Crusade for Justice*, 215.

129. Wells-Barnett, *Crusade for Justice*, 211–12.

130. *Philadelphia Christian Recorder*, 2 August 1894.

131. *Kansas City American Citizen*, 13 July 1894.

132. "Great Britain's Compliment to American Colored Women," *Woman's Era* (August 1894): 1.

133. *Philadelphia Christian Recorder*, 5 July 1894. Wells inspired verse from admirers all over the country. See "Poetry" by J. T. Williams of Texas in the *Philadelphia Christian Recorder*, 6 December 1894.

134. *Indianapolis Freeman*, 10 and 24 June 1893.

135. *Topeka Weekly Call*, 7 July 1894, 8 January 1893.

136. *Indianapolis Freeman*, 15 December 1894.

137. *Indianapolis Freeman*, 9 June 1894.

138. *Methodist Times*, 24 May 1894.

139. *New York Sun*, 30 July 1894. Wells quoted Henry Highland Garnet. Garnet, "An Address to the Slaves of the United States of America."

140. This is best sketched in Wells, *Red Record*, 246–52.

141. New Orleans dateline, carried by Associated Press in the *New York Sun*, 3 August 1894. See also a letter to the editor highly critical of Wells's antilynching argument: "Some Facts about the Lynching of Black men for Assaults upon White women," *New York Sun*, 29 July 1894.

142. Reprinted in *Public Opinion* (9 August 1894): 440. This argument is echoed in "A Georgian on Lynching," *New York Sun*, 5 August 1894.

143. Reprinted in *Literary Digest* (11 August 1894): 421. To squelch the spirit of protest and discredit Wells among southern blacks, enterprising white southerners fabricated an interview with prominent black lawyer John Mercer Lang-

ston of Detroit that was critical of the antilynching crusade. See *Indianapolis Freeman*, 16 and 30 June 1894.

144. *New York Sun*, 25 July 1894.

145. *Memphis Commercial*, 17 June 1894; and *New York Sun*, 25 July 1894. At meetings in more southern areas, like St. Louis, Wells would offer to leave her name off resolutions against lynching because of the controversy and risk involved. See Wells-Barnett, *Crusade for Justice*, 236–37.

146. *Memphis Appeal*, 12 June, 29 May 1894.

147. *Memphis Appeal-Avalanche*, 29 May 1894.

148. Ibid.; *Memphis Commercial*, 15 December 1892; *Memphis Commercial*, 26 May 1894. Sapphira is a New Testament character associated with lying and the betrayal of the early church. Acts 5:1.

149. *Memphis Commercial*, 15 December 1892; *New York Times*, 2 August 1894.

150. *New York Times*, 30 July, 29 April, 2 August 1894.

151. *New York Tribune*, 19 November 1894. See O'Malley, "Specie and Species"; Painter, "Thinking about the Languages of Money and Race"; and O'Malley, "Response to Nell Irvin Painter." In "Thinking About the Languages of Money and Race," Painter notes that the ideological connection between "the market" and "the real" has a long history in the West and contains particularly charged associations in the United States through the history of slavery, gendered reproduction, and sexuality. According to Painter, nineteenth-century conservatives such as these critics of Wells traveled ideologically from "color to race-mixing to corruption to blackness to dirt, and from there . . . to money" (399).

152. "Ida B. Wells's Crusade Against Lynching," *Public Opinion* (9 August 1894): 439; "How Miss Wells' Crusade is Regarded," *Literary Digest* (28 July 1894): 366.

153. On economic conspiracies behind antilynching, see *Indianapolis Freeman*, 7 July 1894; *New York Sun*, 26 July 1894; "Ida B. Wells's Crusade Against Lynching," *Public Opinion* (9 August 1894): 439; "An Anti-Lynching Crusade," *Literary Digest* (11 August 1894): 421. Wells was received cordially in the labor press in England, but no significant immigration of workers was coming from England at the time. See interview in *Labour Leader*, 12 May 1894.

154. "Thirteen Lynchers Indicted," *New York Times*, 16 September 1894. Governor Jones of Alabama condemned lynching in that state; see "English Committee to Investigate," *Public Opinion* (20 September 1894): 589–90. See also "A Bad Week for the Lynchers," *The Independent* (13 September 1894): 1187.

155. "We had considerable hope of good resulting to our race from the Populist party . . . but I am disgusted with the development which the movement has now taken," reported Wells in *Labour Leader*, 12 May 1894. See also Watson, "The Negro Question in the South"; Woodward, *Tom Watson*, 220–21, 238–39, 432.

156. The following states passed antilynching legislation: North Carolina and Georgia in 1893, Ohio and South Carolina in 1896, Texas and Kentucky in 1897. Georgia's antilynching laws were introduced by Democratic legislators to defuse the Populists's appeal to blacks. D. L. Grant, *Anti-Lynching Movement*, 68–70. See also Floyd Crawford, "Ida B. Wells: Some American Reactions to Her Anti-Lynching Crusades in Britain," (1963) and "Ida B. Wells: Her Anti-Lynching

Crusades in Britain and Repercussions from Them in the United States" (1958), unpublished articles in IBW Papers.

157. *Christian Recorder*, 12 July 1894.

158. *Indianapolis Freeman*, 28 April 1894. See also Fleming's bitterness and charges of "ungratitude" directed at Wells in *Indianapolis Freeman*, 21 and 28 July 1894.

159. *Christian Recorder*, 14 June 1894; and *Indianapolis Freeman*, 25 August 1894.

160. *New York Times*, 4 September 1894; *New York Sun*, 13 August 1894; *Indianapolis Freeman*, 25 August 1894.

161. Wells-Barnett, *Crusade for Justice*, 220.

162. J. W. Mans and John S. Durham, letter to the editor, *New York Times*, 30 May 1894.

163. Quoted in *Washington Post*, [n.d. 1894] (courtesy of Paul Lee).

164. Ibid.

165. Quoted in Majors, *Noted Negro Women*, 253–54.

166. *Indianapolis Freeman*, 25 August 1894.

167. Majors, *Noted Negro Women*, 188 (emphasis in original).

168. *Indianapolis Freeman*, 8 September 1894.

169. Ibid., 25 August 1894.

170. Ibid., 1 September 1894.

171. Wells-Barnett, *Crusade for Justice*, 226–27.

172. Wells addressed the Anti-Lynching Society, as reported in the *New York Times*, 11 December 1894. According to the *New York Tribune*, she also addressed the Church of the Divine Paternity on 19 November 1894 and the Methodist Book Concern on 11 December 1894.

173. *Indianapolis Freeman*, 4 August 1894.

174. *Rochester Union and Advertiser*, 29 March 1895.

175. *Indianapolis Freeman*, 8 June 1895.

176. See, for example, the following articles from *Woman's Era*: "How to Stop Lynching" (May 1894): 7; "Apologists for Lynching" (June 1894): 14; and "Lynching in the United States" (August 1895): 17.

177. Moses, *Golden Age of Black Nationalism*, 123.

178. *Indianapolis Freeman*, 30 November 1895.

179. Ibid., 4 January 1896.

180. *New York Times*, 10 and 11 September, 7 and 15 October, 23 November 1894; and *The Times* (London), 6 October, 9 November 1894.

181. In a letter published in *Fraternity* (September 1894): 7–8, Brown defended Wells and offered her own services to the SRBM. On Brown's own trip abroad, see *Indianapolis Freeman*, 17 November and 8 December 1894, 2 and 9 February 1895; and *Philadelphia Christian Recorder*, 1 November 1894 and 17 January 1895.

182. Catherine Impey to the Hon. Sec. of the Society for the Recognition of the Brotherhood of Man, 12 February 1895, copy in AT Papers.

183. Albion Tourgée to T. Thomas Fortune, "personal," n.d., AT Papers. "The agitation of the question of lynch law is beginning to bear fruit," wrote Tourgée in his "Bystander" column, reprinted in *Topeka Weekly Call*, 8 December 1894.

184. In *Public Opinion*, see "Ida B. Wells's Crusade Against Lynching" (9 August 1894): 439–40, and "An English Committee to Investigate Lynching" (20 September 1894): 589. In *Literary Digest*, see "How Miss Wells's Crusade Is Regarded in America" (28 July 1894): 366–67; "An Anti-Lynching Crusade in

America Begun" (11 August 1894): 421–22; and "The Anti-Lynching Crusade" (8 September 1894): 544–45. See also "Straight from the Shoulder and the Heart," *The Independent* (4 October 1894): 1280–81; and "Public Sentiment Against Lynching," *New York Times*, 8 December 1895.

185. *The Independent* (3 May 1894): 560. See also ibid. (28 June 1894): 828.

186. "Lessons for Busybodies," *New York Times*, 15 October 1894; "Gov. Fishback [of Arkansas] Replies," *New York Times*, 23 November 1894; "Southern Governors on English Critics," *Literary Digest* (22 September 1894): 601–2. For a positive assessment of British influence, see T. Thomas Fortune, "The English View of It," reprinted in *Topeka Weekly Call*, 22 September 1894.

187. "Ida B. Wells's Crusade Against Lynching," 440.

188. G. C. Holt, *Lynching and Mobs*, 15. See also Cutler, *Lynch Law*, 229–30, 273.

189. Quoted in the pamphlet *Lady Henry's Statement* (n.p., 1895), 7; copy in FD Papers.

190. "Brave Little Woman."

191. C. H. Williams, *The Race Problem*, pamphlet in Schomburg Center for Research in Black Culture, New York. See also Ida B. Wells-Barnett "Story of a Lynching," *Chicago Inter-Ocean*, 17 July 1897.

192. The WCTU's *Union Signal*, quoted in Wells, *Red Record*, 236.

193. *Chicago Inter-Ocean*, 17 November 1894.

194. My discussion here follows that found in Giddings, *When and Where I Enter*, 90–91. See also Aptheker, *Woman's Legacy*, 53–76.

195. *Cleveland Gazette*, 24 November 1894.

196. "Apologists for Lynching," *Woman's Era* (June 1894): 14; "Miss Willard and the Colored People," *Woman's Era* (July 1895): 12, 16.

197. Rev. Reverdy C. Ransom, "Two Great Women at Variance," *Philadelphia Christian Recorder*, 6 December 1894.

198. Catherine Impey described the situation as follows: "Having allowed their coloured sisters to be defrauded of fellowship under local jurisdiction, the WCTU seems to hope to salve this over by 'freely and gladly accepting the coloured women as officers and delegates' to their great annual national conventions—monster assemblies where a few timid black faces are not so very conspicuous." Catherine Impey, editorial, *Anti-Caste*, March 1895, clipping in Temperance and Prohibition Papers.

199. *Cleveland Gazette*, 24 November 1894.

200. Frances E. Willard to Albion Tourgée, 21 December 1894, AT Papers. Continuing her public relations efforts, Willard arranged a meeting with Frederick Douglass just before his death, the result of which was a circular endorsing the Cleveland resolutions and restating a firm faith in Willard, signed by Douglass, former abolitionists, and others. This circular was reprinted in the black press (see, for example, *Indianapolis Freeman*, 27 April 1895) and created more controversy. Florence Balgarnie, secretary of the BWTA and a Wells supporter, thought that the signers were not fully aware of the content of the objectionable Cleveland resolution. Balgarnie attempted to publicize this fact, since she felt that the reputations of famous abolitionists, especially that of Frederick Douglass, were being manipulated. See the appendix to *Lady Henry's Statement*, "In Vindication of the Honoured Name of the Late Frederick Douglass, June 17, 1895," by Florence Balgarnie, pamphlet in Temperance and Prohibition Papers. See also Mary A. Marks, "The Lynching Question and the Women's [*sic*] Chris-

tian Temperance Union," undated clipping from *Fraternity*, in Temperance and Prohibition Papers.

201. Bordin, *Frances Willard*, 216, 224; "The W.C.T.U. and Lynching," *Christian World*, 8 August 1895. Under increasing pressure to close the issue, the *Union Signal*, the WCTU's organ, printed an oblique retraction of Willard's public statements in December 1894, pleading that she had been "misunderstood" in a "literal interpretation" of her words. Quoted in Wells, *Red Record*, 238.

202. Ida B. Wells to Albion Tourgée, 27 November 1894, AT Papers.

203. "The Chicago Woman's Club Reject Mrs. Williams," *Woman's Era* (December 1894): 20.

204. Residents of Hull-House, *Hull-House Maps and Papers*; and W. E. B. Du Bois, *Philadelphia Negro*.

205. Wells, *Red Record*, 249.

206. Ibid., 248; and Wells-Barnett, "Lynch Law in America."

207. Wells, *Red Record*, 149–50.

208. Ibid., 157–71.

209. Harper, Wells, et al., "Symposium—Temperance," 380.

210. Clark, " 'The Sacred Rights of the Weak' "; Laqueur, "Bodies, Details, and the Humanitarian Narrative"; Halttunen, "Humanitarianism and the Pornography of Pain in Anglo-American Culture." This interpretation differs slightly from that found in Bederman, *Manliness and Civilization*, 38–71, which stresses the gender focus of Wells's argument.

211. Wells, *Southern Horrors*, 40.

212. Wells, *Red Record*, 173, 205, 209.

213. This usage is present but in much more muted form in her earlier pamphlet, in which Wells refers only once in her introduction to African Americans as a "weak race." Wells, *Southern Horrors*, 15. For an alternate interpretation, see S. Davis, "The 'Weak Race' and the Winchester."

214. Frederickson, *Black Image in the White Mind*, 256–83.

215. The *Liverpool Daily Post* refused to publish the images, stating that "such pictures were demoralizing and should not be drawn and published." Quoted in the *New York Sun*, 26 July 1894. See also *Daily Chronicle*, 9 June 1894.

216. In Wells, *Red Record*, 212–14, eight of nine black female victims are described as girls, some as young as eight, ten, or twelve years old. Of eight white female victims of "rape," three are described as "girls," but one of these was seventeen years old and another was sexually mature, since she gave birth to a child after the alleged incident of rape.

217. Jno. W. Jacks to Florence Balgarnie, 19 March 1895, Mary Church Terrell Papers, Moorland-Spingarn Research Center, Howard University, Washington, D.C.

218. Giddings, *When and Where I Enter*, chap. 5; Hine and Thompson, *Shining Thread of Hope*, 189; D. G. White, *Too Heavy A Load*, 22–23, 52.

219. *Historical Records of the Conventions, 1895–96*, 32. On club women's endorsements of Wells's antilynching work, see ibid., 9, 50; and Wells-Barnett, *Crusade for Justice*, 242.

220. *Historical Records of the Conventions, 1895–96*, 4–5. See also Editorial, "Be Bold, Be Bold, But Not Too Bold," *Woman's Era* (July 1895): 12.

221. D. G. White, "The Cost of Club Work" and *Too Heavy a Load*.

222. *Historical Records of the Conventions, 1895–96*, 19.

223. *New York Tribune*, 22 March 1898; *Indianapolis Freeman* 26 March 1898; Wells-Barnett, *Crusade for Justice*, 252–53.

224. Washington, Wood, and Williams, *New Negro for a New Century*; Lynk, *Black Troopers*; Steward, *Colored Regulars in the U.S. Army*; J. T. Wilson, *Black Phalanx*.

225. Giddings, *When and Where I Enter*, 106–8. See reports in *Chicago Tribune*, 15, 16, and 17 August 1899.

226. Quoted in Giddings, *When and Where I Enter*, 111; *Washington Colored American*, 21 January 1899.

227. Harlan et al., *Booker T. Washington Papers*, 2:93–94; D. L. Grant, *Anti-Lynching Movement*, 51–53.

228. Du Bois, "A Pageant in Seven Decades," in *W. E. B. Du Bois Speaks*, 39.

229. *Indianapolis Freeman*, 10 June 1899; *Philadelphia Christian Recorder*, 6 July 1899.

230. Wells-Barnett, *Lynch Law in Georgia*, preface.

231. Wells-Barnett, "Lynch Law in America."

232. Ibid., 24.

233. Wells-Barnett, *Mob Rule in New Orleans*, 256.

234. Bederman, *Manliness and Civilization*; Cullen, " 'I's a Man Now' "; and Bair, "True Women, Real Men."

235. Hair, *Carnival of Fury*, 206. Hair agrees with Wells that the New Orleans police department was embarrassed that Charles eluded them for five days and that Charles was "basically a decent black workingman who had simply tried to protect his sense of dignity, and his life."

236. In *White Violence and Black Response*, Shapiro emphasizes Wells's approach to antilynching as a "moral struggle" (58). Outbreaks of racial violence, like the lynching of Postmaster Baker, the Wilmington Riot, or the New Orleans riot brought forth calls to arms from black commentators. Wells's old supporter Maritcha Lyons of Brooklyn spoke out at the turn of the century: "Let every negro get a permit to carry a revolver. You are not supposed to be a walking arsenal, but don't you get caught again. Have your houses made ready to afford protection from the fury of the mob, and remembering that your home is your castle and that no police officer has right to enter it, unless he complies with the usage of the law, see that he does not." Quoted in Shapiro, *White Violence and Black Response*, 485 n. 3. New Yorker David Fulton penned the following advice after the New Orleans riot: "The child should be taught that self-defense is as essential, as obligatory as self-respect, and the use of the rifle as the alphabet." Fulton, *Eagle Clippings by Jack Thorne*, 71, copy in Brooklyn Historical Society, New York. Also significant is journalist John E. Bruce's 1889 speech made in Washington, D.C., in which he argued that blacks should "meet force with force, everywhere it is offered." Bruce, "Application of Force," 32. Interestingly, Bruce made no comment about forcible resistance in his antilynching pamphlet *The Blood Red Record*, published just two years later in 1901.

237. Wells-Barnett, *Mob Rule in New Orleans*, 255.

238. Terrell, *Progress of Colored Women*, 10.

239. Wells-Barnett, *Mob Rule in New Orleans*, 319–20.

240. Higginbotham, "African American Women's History and the Metalanguage of Race," 271.

241. Du Bois, "The Conservation of Races," in *W. E. B. Du Bois Speaks*, 73–85; Moss, *American Negro Academy*.

242. Ziff, *American 1890s*, esp. chaps. 13 and 15.

243. Addams, *Twenty Years at Hull-House*, 143. I am indebted to Larzar Ziff for reminding me of this passage.

Chapter Four

1. Deborah Gray White identifies another intense phase of this "masculinizing" shift in the 1920s. See D. G. White, *Too Heavy a Load*, chap. 4.

2. "The Anti-Lynching Crusaders," *Crisis* (November 1922): 8; "The Ninth Crusade," *Crisis* (March 1923): 213–17; "The Shame of America," *Crisis* (October 1923): 167–69.

3. See Ferrell, *Nightmare and Dream*; D. L. Grant, *Anti-Lynching Movement*; Zangrando, *NAACP Crusade Against Lynching*; Waskow, *From Race Riot to Sit-in*, 12, 304–7; Hall, *Revolt Against Chivalry*.

4. Report to Board by Walter F. White on English Committee on Lynching, 17 October 1921, JES Papers.

5. None of the following works mentioned Wells-Barnett's contributions: W. White, *Rope and Faggot* (1929); Raper, *Tragedy of Lynching* (1933); Chadbourn, *Lynching and the Law* (1933); and Commission on Interracial Cooperation, *Lynchings and What They Mean* (ca. 1930). Exceptions are Cutler, *Lynch Law* (1905), as mentioned in Chapter 3, and Shay, *Judge Lynch: His First Hundred Years* (1938).

6. Roy Nash, "Memorandum for Mr. Phillip G. Peabody on Lynch-Law and the Practicability of a Successful Attack Thereon," 22 May 1916, NAACP Papers.

7. Lasch, *New Radicalism in America*.

8. On black women and the politics of race and gender in the professions and reform, see Moldow, *Women Doctors in Gilded Age Washington*, 134–61; Shaw, *What a Woman Ought to Be and to Do*, 164–210; and Gilmore, *Gender and Jim Crow*, 31–59.

9. Terrell, "Lynching from a Negro's Point of View."

10. "Editorial," *Colored American Magazine* 4 (1902): 279.

11. See L. J. Brown, "Philosophy of Lynching"; Stemmons, "Unmentionable Crime"; Tyler, "Does Lynching Thrive Under Democracy?"

12. B. T. Washington, *The Future of the Negro Race* (1899), in Harlan et al., *Booker T. Washington Papers*, 4:371; *Booker T. Washington Gives Facts and Condemns Lynchings in a Statement Telegraphed to the New York World* (1908) and *An Open Letter by Booker T. Washington of Tuskegee Alabama upon Lynchings in the South* (1899), copies in Rare Books Collection, Schomburg Center for Research in Black Culture, New York. Kellogg, *NAACP*, 211; Zangrando, *NAACP Crusade Against Lynching*, 13–14; and D. L. Grant, *Anti-Lynching Movement*, 37–29, all concur that Washington's views on lynching improved over time. His most troubling statements on lynching appeared in an interview in the *Indianapolis Freeman*, 28 August 1897, and in a statement to the *Birmingham Age-Herald*, 25 April 1899, which implied an acceptance of the rape charge against black men. See Harlan et al., *Booker T. Washington Papers*, 4:323–24 and 5:90–91. Edward H. Morris, Chicago attorney and close colleague of the Barnetts, was so enraged by Washington's early positions that he

laid the blame for two Illinois lynchings in 1903 at his feet in a newspaper inter-view in the *Chicago Inter-Ocean*. See Harlan, *Booker T. Washington Papers*, 7:226–27.

13. Kelly Miller, "Attitude of the Intelligent Negro Toward Lynching."

14. J. E. Bruce, *Blood Red Record*, 3, 7–11, 15.

15. Murray, "Educated Colored Men and White Women," 93–95. Another notable exception was Archibald Grimké's 1915 essay "The Sex Question and Race Segregation," in which he examined the sexual double standard. Racism created "upper" (white) and "under" (black) racial "worlds," Grimké contended, with seduction, rape, adultery, and concubinage relegated to the "under" world. Grimké concluded that the "double moral standard" must be abandoned "as quickly as possible, applicable alike to the men and women of both races." A. H. Grimké, "The Sex Question and Race Segregation." An unusually outspoken white southerner, Rev. W. D. Weatherford, included a condemnation of sexual abuse of black women by white men in his pamphlet of 1916: "We of the white race must brand every white man who seduces a colored girl as a fiend of the same stripe as the Negro who rapes a white woman." Weatherford, *Lynching*, 8.

16. Addams's article is reprinted in Aptheker, *Lynching and Rape*, 23–27. See also Addams, "Has the Emancipation Act Been Nullified by National Indif-ference?"

17. Wells-Barnett, "Lynching and the Excuse for It." On the idea that black women's resistance to lynching made rape a political issue, see Aptheker, *Woman's Legacy*, 63.

18. Shapiro, "Muckrakers and Negroes." R. S. Baker, "What Is a Lynching?" and "Lynching in the South." Baker's chapter "Lynching South and North" in *Following the Color Line: The State of the Negro Citizen in the American Democracy* (1908) mainly reproduced these two articles.

19. "Eighth Atlanta Negro Conference," *Colored American Magazine* 6 (1903): 534–36.

20. Wells-Barnett, "Negro's Case in Equity," 246.

21. For a similar shift toward instrumental arguments among white feminists, see Kraditor, *Ideas of the Woman Suffrage Movement*. On the black elite's generally temperate if consistent opposition to lynching, see Gaines, *Uplifting the Race*, 85–88.

22. Figures calculated from table in Hall, *Revolt Against Chivalry*, 134.

23. *New York Sun*, 27 June 1903; *Memphis Commercial Advertiser*, 9 July 1903; and "The North's Negro Problem," *New York Sun*, 6 June 1903, clippings in Schom-burg Scrapbooks, Schomburg Center for Research in Black Culture, New York. In 1904, activist Kelly Miller noted, "Already the cry has been raised that the large cities of the country are threatened with a black deluge." Miller, "Problems of the City Negro."

24. "The Moral of Akron," 25 August 1900, untitled clipping in Schomburg Scrapbooks; Shapiro, *White Violence and Black Response*, 93–95.

25. "Seven Killed in Mob Fight with Militia," *New York Times*, 7 July 1903.

26. William James to the editor, *Springfield Daily Republican*, 23 July 1903.

27. Among whites, despair and passivity alternated with stern calls for law and order. See, for example, the following articles in the *Literary Digest*: "Pro-posed Remedies for Lynching" (25 July 1903): 94–95; "How Can Lynching Be Stopped?" (8 August 1903): 156–57; "Critics of the President's Letter on Lynch-

ing" (22 August 1903): 213–14; and "Religious Views of the Lynching Problem" (29 August 1903): 259.

28. Theodore Roosevelt to Governor Durbin, 6 August 1903, Tuskegee Institute News Clippings File, Series 2 (microfilm collection; hereafter Tuskegee Clippings File). Southern white supremacists set the parameters of debate. "While the sentimentalists resolve on lynch law, the mob acts on rape," declared Atlanta's John Temple Graves, also in 1903, with "rape" here signifying black-on-white rape. "Let them orate less on lynchings and act more earnestly and practically for the suppression of rape," he counseled. *Literary Digest* (22 August 1903): 214. For more on Graves, see "He Defends Lynch Law," *New York Times*, 12 August 1903; and responses in the *New York Times* from Rev. Dr. Babbitt on 13 August 1903 and from "A Southerner" and Arthur A. Schomburg on 16 August 1903. See also Kelly Miller, *An Appeal to Reason on the Race Problem: An Open Letter to John Templeton Graves* (1906).

29. On "legal lynchings," see Shapiro, *White Violence and Black Response*, 206–7, 290. Roosevelt argued, "Each community should provide that rape be treated as a capital crime, and that legislation be enacted permitting the instant assembling of a grand and petty jury, and the immediate trial of the criminal, and his immediate execution if convicted." Roosevelt, "Lynching and the Miscarriage of Justice," *Outlook* (25 November 1911): 706–7. Similar sentiments can be found in Gibbons, "Lynch Law." On Roosevelt and race relations, see Miller, *Roosevelt and the Negro*; and Scheiner, "President Theodore Roosevelt and the Negro."

30. The most frequently cited NAACP pamphlets are *Thirty Years of Lynching in the U.S., 1889–1918* (1919); *The Fight Against Lynching* (1919); *Notes on Lynching in the United States* (1912); and *Burning at the Stake in the U.S.* (1919). Pamphlets and articles by African American men include Pickens, *Lynching and Debt Slavery* (1921); Grimké, *The Lynching of Negroes in the South* (1899); Kelly Miller, *The Disgrace of Democracy* (1917); Work, *The Law and the Mob* (1925); and Moton, "The South and the Lynching Evil" (1919).

31. On "The Women Stop Lynching League" and the "Citizen's Lynching Protest Parade Committee," see Mrs. Elenora Johnson to My Dear Mrs. Terrell, 20 April 1928; and Walter H. Brooks to "Dear Friend," 16 July 1922, both in MCT-LOC. The League also met in Chicago. See "Women Unite in Crusade Against Lynching," *CD*, 8 May 1927.

32. Terborg-Penn, "African American Women's Networks in the Anti-Lynching Crusade"; E. B. Brown, "Imaging Lynching."

33. *Chicago Herald*, 21 November 1901, Tuskegee Clippings File.

34. *Chicago Tribune*, 9 June 1903, and *Chicago Herald*, 24 June 1903, both clippings in Schomburg Scrapbooks; *Chicago Broad-Ax*, 27 June 1903. The anger of Chicago African Americans was fanned by the refusal of the Illinois state attorney general to press for a full investigation of the situation, leaving the case in the hands of local St. Clair County officials. See "State Will Not Act at Belleville," *Chicago Inter-Ocean*, 9 June 1903. One minister felt pressure to restate his position, softening but not retracting his view that "self-preservation is the first law of nature" and that black people should be prepared to defend themselves from attack. See "Minister Advises His Race to Act," *Chicago Herald*, 28 June 1903, clipping in Schomburg Scrapbooks.

35. Meier, *Negro Thought*, 174–78; Harlan, *Booker T. Washington: Wizard of Tuskegee*, 40; S. R. Fox, *Guardian of Boston*, 49–54.

36. *Chicago Broad-Ax*, 11 July 1903.

37. T. Thomas Fortune to Booker T. Washington, 20 April 1903, BTW Papers; Thornbrough, *T. Thomas Fortune*, 229, 246–47.

38. Mitchell, "Shall the Wheels of Race Agitation Be Stopped?"; Brundage, " 'To Howl Loudly.' "

39. B. T. Washington, "Tuskegee Idea"; and Kelly Miller, "Problems of the City Negro."

40. Wells-Barnett, "Booker T. Washington and His Critics"; and Du Bois, "Parting of the Ways."

41. Roediger, *Wages of Whiteness*; Dailey, "Race, Sex, and Citizenship"; Saxton, *Rise and Fall of the White Republic*. On Douglass, see Yarborough, "Race, Violence, and Manhood."

42. Bederman, *Manliness and Civilization*; Bederman, " 'Civilization,' the Decline of Middle-Class Manliness, and Ida B. Wells's Anti-lynching Campaign (1892–4)," 7.

43. J. E. Bruce, *Blood Red Record*, 27. One planter's son had another view: "Only the white man writes volumes to establish on paper the fact of a superiority which is either self-evident and not in need of demonstration . . . or is not a fact and is not demonstrable." Stone, *Studies in the American Race Problem*, 214.

44. S. Laing Williams to Booker T. Washington, 24 October 1904, BTW Papers.

45. Quoted in Rudwick, "Niagara Movement," 179. For comparison of Bookerites and Niagara members, see *Outlook* (1 September 1906): 3–4, and (8 September 1906): 54–55.

46. Du Bois, "We Claim Our Rights," in *W. E. B. Du Bois Speaks*, 171.

47. Harlan, "Booker T. Washington and the Politics of Accommodation," 16; Barry C. Smith to Julius Rosenwald, 6 October 1920, Negro Notebooks, Julius Rosenwald Papers, Reggenstein Library, University of Chicago.

48. Rudwick, "Niagara Movement," 177–200; Salem, *To Better Our World*, 147; S. R. Fox, *Guardian of Boston*, 103.

49. *Indianapolis Freeman*, 8 October 1892; *Chicago Broad-Ax*, 14 December 1907. See related issues outlined in E. F. White, "Africa on My Mind"; and Bair, "True Women, Real Men."

50. *Chicago Conservator*, 21 April 1906, clipping in BTW Papers.

51. M. W. Stewart, "Lecture," 51.

52. Yates, "Parental Obligation."

53. Yates, "Kindergartens and Mothers' Clubs"; Yates, "Woman as a Factor in the Solution of Race Problems"; Johnson, "Home Life"; F. B. Williams, "Colored Girl"; Burroughs, "Not Color But Character."

54. "The NACW" (editorial), *Voice of the Negro* (July 1904): 310–11.

55. Mrs. Rosa D. Bowser, "What Role Is the Educated Woman to Play in the Uplifting of Her Race?" in Culp, *Twentieth Century Negro Literature*, 178.

56. Hunton, "Negro Womanhood Defended"; Tillman, "Afro-American Women and Their Work."

57. Graves, "Motherhood," 495. See also D. G. White, *Too Heavy A Load*.

58. Hunton, "Deeper Reverence for Home Times," 59.

59. Mrs. Rosa D. Bowser, "What Role Is the Educated Woman to Play in the Uplifting of Her Race," in Culp, *Twentieth Century Negro Literature*, 182. See also Mrs. C. C. [Sarah Dudley] Pettey, in Culp, *Twentieth Century Negro Literature*, 183:

"If the mother be good all the vices and shortcomings of father will fail to lead the children astray; but if mother is not what she should be all of the holy influences of angels can not save the children." See also Mrs. E. F. Stewart, "Woman's Responsibility."

60. Rush, "Bend the Tree While It Is Young," 53.

61. Shapiro, *White Violence and Black Response*, 96–103; Tinsley, "Roosevelt, Foraker, and the Brownsville Affray."

62. Wells-Barnett, *Crusade for Justice*, 299.

63. Kellogg, *NAACP*, 13–14.

64. Wells-Barnett, "Lynching: Our National Crime." The establishment of a fund of $10,000 in 1916 underwrote the official start of antilynching work by the NAACP. See Zangrando, *NAACP Fight Against Lynching*, 28.

65. Wells-Barnett, *Crusade for Justice*, 323–24.

66. Ibid., 325.

67. Ovington, *Walls Came Tumbling Down*, 106.

68. Wells-Barnett, *Crusade for Justice*, 325; Wedin, *Inheritors of the Spirit*, 110, 314 n. 23.

69. See Terborg-Penn, "African American Women's Networks." For a related view, see Sklar, "Hull-House Maps and Papers."

70. Ovington, *Walls Came Tumbling Down*, 106.

71. Wells-Barnett, *Crusade for Justice*, 325–26. David Levering Lewis gives basic credence to Wells-Barnett's version of events and raises the issue, parenthetically, of some "possible sexism" at work in Du Bois's "calculations" for "balancing" the committee to the satisfaction of the group. See D. L. Lewis, *W. E. B. Du Bois*, 397.

72. Wells-Barnett, *Crusade for Justice*, 326.

73. Ovington, *Walls Came Tumbling Down*, 106.

74. "The Negro Woman," *Champion Magazine* (December 1916): 171–72.

75. Moss, *American Negro Academy*, 41; Allen, *Reluctant Reformers*, 111–12. The black Baptist church provided "men with full manhood rights, while offering women a separate and unequal status." Higginbotham, *Righteous Discontent*, 3.

76. *Indianapolis Freeman*, 29 September 1894.

77. *Philadelphia Christian Recorder*, 9 August 1894.

78. E. B. Brown, "Womanist Consciousness." Other helpful treatments, which are less attentive to gender, include Childs, *Leadership, Conflict, and Cooperation in Afro-American Social Thought*, 5; Cornel West, *Prophetic Fragments*, 45–46; and Walzer, *Company of Critics*, 22. Childs distinguishes between "vanguard" leadership, which emphasizes individual initiative and ideas, and "mutual" styles of protest, which are more communally based and organized. Walzer's notion of "antagonistic connection" also resonates with Wells-Barnett's approach.

79. *Chicago Tribune*, 10 November 1909.

80. *Chicago Tribune*, 10, 12, and 13 November 1909; and *St. Louis Republic*, 13 and 15 November 1909. Wells-Barnett described Frog James as a "shiftless, penniless colored man . . . unable to give a good account of himself." Wells-Barnett, *Crusade for Justice*, 309. See also *New York Age*, 16 November 1909.

81. *New York Age*, 25 November 1909; Wells-Barnett, *Crusade for Justice*, 310.

82. *St. Louis Republic*, 13 November 1909; *New York Age*, 18 November 1909; Wells-Barnett, *Crusade for Justice*, 311.

83. Wells-Barnett, *Crusade for Justice*, 311–12; *New York Age*, 9 December 1909.

84. Wells-Barnett, *Crusade for Justice*, 314–16.

85. Gosnell, *Negro Politicians*, 37–38, 206; Wells-Barnett, *Crusade for Justice*, xxix.

86. Ibid., 318–19; *Illinois State Journal*, 7 December 1909; *Illinois State Register*, 2 and 7 December 1909; *New York Age*, 16 December 1909. Wells-Barnett's fears about Illinois's alarming proclivity toward racial violence was borne out only six weeks later. On 17 February 1910, another Cairo mob attempted to break into the prison for the purpose of "stringing up . . . a Negro purse snatcher." The lynchers were successfully repulsed by Davis's successor, Sheriff Nellis, who shot into the crowd, killing one and injuring several. But members of the mob were later acquitted of the charge of "attack on the county jail," and in November Nellis was voted out of office. See *Crisis* (November 1910): 6, and untitled newspaper clipping dated 22 July 1910 in NAACP Papers.

87. *Illinois State Journal*, 2 December 1909.

88. *Indianapolis Freeman*, 18 December 1909.

89. *CD*, 1 January 1910.

90. Wells-Barnett, *Crusade for Justice*, 326.

91. Kellogg, *NAACP*, 303–4.

92. Wells-Barnett, "How Enfranchisement Stops Lynching."

93. Wells-Barnett must have been very satisfied, however, that the individual who apprehended Green and sent him to up Chicago (instead of back to Arkansas) for help was none other than Sheriff Nellis of Cairo, who had replaced Sheriff Davis. Wells-Barnett, *Crusade for Justice*, 335–37; Kellogg, *NAACP*, 63, n. 731; "The Steve Green Case," *Crisis* (November 1910): 14. It seems that the NAACP resisted sending funds to Chicago because lawyer Edward Wright was trying to collect attorney's fees for the case after Green was thought to be already successfully on his way to Canada, thanks to money collected by Wells-Barnett. Edward H. Wright to Prof. J. E. Spingarn, 17 October 1910; and Oswald Garrison Villard to Prof. J. E. Spingarn, 19 October 1910, both in JES Papers.

94. Ida B. Wells-Barnett to Prof. J. E. Spingarn, 21 April 1911, JES Papers.

95. Ovington, *Walls Came Tumbling Down*, 124.

96. Wells-Barnett, *Crusade for Justice*, 328. Ovington's haughtiness is evident in her warning to William Pickens after he publicly complained of racism in northern universities: "The North is bad enough," she admitted, "but if its people are told [this] too often . . . we shall 'jim crow' . . . and then you will not have the chance to find out how bad the Northerner is!" See Ovington, "Disagrees with Pickens"; and Pickens, "Pickens' Reply to Miss Ovington."

97. See "Our Aims" and "Program of the Original Rights Society," *Original Rights Magazine* (April 1910): 3–6, 61–64.

98. *CD*, 19 March 1910.

99. Wells-Barnett, "The Northern Negro Woman's Social and Moral Condition."

100. Wells-Barnett, *Crusade for Justice*, 328, 258–60; Giddings, *When and Where I Enter*, 106.

101. *Chicago Broad-Ax*, 7 August 1910.

102. E. L. Davis, *Lifting as They Climb*, 42–51. See also D. G. White, *Too Heavy a Load*, 84–85.

103. *Chicago Broad-Ax*, 30 July 1910; Hunton, "National Association of Col-

ored Women"; Williams, "Work Attempted and Missed in Organized Club Work"; Giddings, *When and Where I Enter*, 108.

104. Wells-Barnett, *Crusade for Justice*, 328–29; *Chicago Broad-Ax*, 30 July, 7 August 1910; *New York Age*, 28 July 1910. The controversy did not appear in official reports of the convention. Elizabeth Lindsay Davis wrote that at Louisville, Wells-Barnett chaired the Committee on Resolutions and that "her committee presented a strong and very timely set, which was heartily endorsed," E. L. Davis, *Lifting As They Climb*, 52.

105. Drake and Cayton, *Black Metropolis*, 394–95; Gaines, *Uplifting the Race*, 162–69, 171–78.

106. Booker T. Washington to Emmett J. Scott, 21 July 1900, in Harlan et al., *Booker T. Washington Papers*, 5:589.

107. *Indianapolis Freeman*, 26 June 1909.

108. *New York Age*, 10 June 1909.

109. *Chicago Broad-Ax*, 7 August 1910.

110. Schechter, "'All the Intensity of My Nature.'"

111. Harlan, *Booker T. Washington: Wizard of Tuskegee*, 308, 322.

112. Mary Church Terrell joined the Women's International League for Peace and Freedom that Addams helped found. However, Terrell broke with the group over a petition requesting the removal of black troops stationed in Germany after World War I on charges of assaults on German women. See Mary Church Terrell to My dear Miss Addams, 18 March 1921, MCT-LOC. See also B. W. Jones, *Quest for Equality*; and Terrell, *Colored Woman in A White World*.

113. *Chicago Conservator*, 21 April 1906, clipping in BTW Papers.

114. T. Thomas Fortune to Booker T. Washington, 25 September 1899, BTW Papers. By this point, Fortune was on Tuskegee's payroll, and he had abandoned his former ally Wells-Barnett.

115. Quoted in *Proceedings of the National Negro Conference, 1909*, 118.

116. Ida B. Wells-Barnett to Prof. J. E. Spingarn, 21 April 1911, JES Papers.

117. Later there was an overlay of psychological theory, which informed Walter White's *Rope and Faggot*, and detailed constitutional analyses, found in Chadbourn, *Lynching and the Law* (1933).

118. Wells-Barnett, "Our Country's Lynching Record."

119. *Harper's Weekly*, 29 January 1916, Tuskegee Clippings File; *Negro Yearbook*, 28–29.

120. *Crisis* (September 1917): 241.

121. Quoted in Rudwick, "W. E. B. Du Bois," 76 (emphasis in original). See also Shapiro, *White Violence and Black Response*, 107–11; Barbeau and Henri, *Unknown Soldiers*.

122. *The Waco Horror*, supplement to *Crisis* (July 1916): 8; Zangrando, *NAACP Crusade Against Lynching*, 28.

123. *CD*, 30 October 1915.

124. "Mob Dispersed by Women," *CD*, 2 December 1916, Tuskegee Clippings File.

125. *CD*, 4 September 1915, Tuskegee Clippings File. See also editorial "The Women Have Entered the Fight," *CD*, 18 November 1922: "In consequence of the political subjection of our group . . . our men are powerless to protect their own women from the greedy lust of the degraded element of Southern white men."

126. Wells-Barnett, *Crusade for Justice*, 392.

127. "To the Congress of the United States, Washington, D.C." from the Chicago Citizens Committee and "Citizens Committee Report," by Ida B. Wells-Barnett et al., 20 July 1917; both in Lawrence Y. Sherman Papers, State Library of Illinois, Springfield.

128. *CD*, 2 March 1918.

129. Ida B. Wells-Barnett to Senator Lawrence Y. Sherman, 21 February 1918; and "Resolutions Passed by the Negro Fellowship League," in Lawrence Y. Sherman Papers.

130. Wells-Barnett, *Crusade for Justice*, 384–90; *CD*, 15 September, 3 November 1917; Rudwick, *Race Riot at East St. Louis*, 120–21; "Side Lights or Shadows on the Recent Race Riots at East St. Louis, Illinois," *Chicago Broad-Ax*, 28 July 1917, clipping in IBW Papers.

131. Wells-Barnett, *East St. Louis Massacre*, 8–10, 14, copy in Military Intelligence Division File, RG 165, National Archives, Washington, D.C. I am indebted to Linda McMurry for this citation. See McMurry, *To Keep the Waters Troubled*, 315, 384 n. 33.

132. Ralph A. Hayes to Inspector General, 24 November 1917, Military Intelligence Division File, RG 165.

133. Rudwick, *Race Riot at East St. Louis*, 119–32.

134. At issue was a confession that Bundy gave the state's attorney to the effect that he was "one of the tools and go-betweens who herded and bought Negro votes by the wholesale" in the party machinations of East St. Louis. Bundy's confession—made without consultation with his NAACP lawyers—as well as his unwillingness to route all funds raised for his defense through the Association's accounts explains the break between him and the NAACP defense effort. W. E. B. Du Bois, "Leroy Bundy," *Crisis* (November 1922): 16–21.

135. Wells-Barnett, *Crusade for Justice*, 395. Bundy acknowledged the support of midwesterners in Missouri and Illinois in a letter to the NAACP that was published in the *CD*. See "Bundy Reply to NAACP Attack," *CD*, 17 August 1918.

136. Rudwick, *Race Riot at East St. Louis*, 390; Wells-Barnett, *Crusade for Justice*, 406.

137. Meier, *Negro Thought*, 184.

138. W. E. B. Du Bois to Edward Osgood Brown, 19 July 1917; W. E. B. Du Bois to Mr. Arthur Spingarn, 13 July 1917; Edward Osgood Brown to Joel Spingarn, 19 and 26 July 1917, NAACP Papers. Du Bois also investigated at East St. Louis. See "The Massacre at East St. Louis," *Crisis* (September 1917): 219–38.

139. A recent scholar stresses that elitism and inertia take the blame more than ideological conflict or conservatism; see Reed, *Chicago NAACP*, chaps. 1–3. See also Reed, "Organized Racial Reform in Chicago during the Progressive Era"; and Spear, *Black Chicago*, 87–89.

140. Grossman, *Land of Hope*, 80. Walter White admitted that the *Defender* probably reached 300,000 people in 1920 as compared to the 125,000 on the *Crisis* subscriber list.

141. Gosnell, *Negro Politicians*, 108–9; "Cook County Bar Association Outlines Its Work," *CD*, 16 August 1924.

142. According to the *Defender*, "[The NAACP] should defend Bundy in spite of any personal matters of which it does not approve. That is exactly what the people are paying their money into it for." *CD*, 14 September 1918.

143. *CD*, 26 April 1919; Wells-Barnett, *Crusade for Justice*, 395.

144. The Barnetts also collaborated in the case of Joseph "Chicken Joe" Campbell, who was accused of a jailhouse murder and sentenced to hang in 1915. See Wells-Barnett, *Crusade for Justice*, 337–42; and *CD*, 17 July, 21 August, 30 October, 6 and 20 November, and 25 December 1915.

145. Wells-Barnett, *Crusade for Justice*, 348; Gosnell, *Negro Politicians*, 163–95; Hendricks, *Gender, Race, and Politics in the Midwest*, 105–11.

146. Quoted in Grossman, *Land of Hope*, 89.

147. Wells-Barnett, "The Race Problem in Chicago," letter to the editor, *Chicago Tribune*, 17 July 1919.

148. Tuttle, *Race Riot*, chaps. 1 and 2.

149. Wells-Barnett, *Crusade for Justice*, 405–6. She had done likewise two years earlier. Though she "saw not another colored person" when she arrived in East St. Louis after the violence, Wells-Barnett "sauntered up the main street just as if everything was alright." Ibid., 385. Her pamphlet noted that the militia had things under control by the time she arrived. "No one molested me in my walk from the station to the City Hall, although I did not see a single colored person until I reached the City Hall building." Wells-Barnett, *East St. Louis Massacre*, 3.

150. Alfreda M. Duster interview, 6–7, in Black Women Oral History Project Interviews, Schlesinger Library, Radcliffe Institute for Advanced Study, Harvard University, Cambridge, Mass. Duster noted, however, that her mother did not cross the so-called "von Hindenberg line" at State Street, beyond which blacks dared not cross, because "whoever got caught on the wrong side was severely beaten." Ten women were injured during the riot, most of whom, William Tuttle maintains, were hurt incidentally rather than being specific targets of violence. Yet the rape charge against black men as well as a rumor of a vengeful murder of a black mother and infant nosed its way into the press and fanned feelings of revenge on both sides of the color line. See Tuttle, *Race Riot*, 48–49.

151. Wells-Barnett, *Crusade for Justice*, xxv.

152. Ibid., 406.

153. "Women's Committee to Receive Funds to Aid in the Defense of Those Charged with Rioting," *Chicago Broad-Ax*, 23 August 1919; "National Equal Rights League Annual Meeting," *CD*, 6 September 1919. The paper noted that the discussion of the topic "Chicago Riots and the Negro" was led by Wells-Barnett. A "Colored Citizens Committee" that approached the mayor with grievances was "mostly composed of prominent preachers," according to the *Chicago Broad-Ax*, 2 August 1919.

154. Gosnell, *Negro Politicians*, 95–100. See also Chapter 6.

155. Wells-Barnett, *Crusade for Justice*, 375–80; S. R. Fox, *Guardian of Boston*, 140–41.

156. Wells-Barnett, *Crusade for Justice*, 380–82.

157. Maj. Wrisley Brown to Lt. Col. H. A. Parkenham, 21 December 1918; and "Meeting of the Baltimore Branch of the Universal Negro Improvement Association and African Communities League," 18 December 1918, in Hill, *Marcus Garvey and Universal Negro Improvement Association Papers*, 1:334, 329.

158. Wells-Barnett, *Crusade for Justice*, 379; S. R. Fox, *Guardian of Boston*, 223–24.

159. Wells-Barnett, *Crusade for Justice*, 367–70.

160. "Assure Christmas Kits," 15 December 1917; and "Negro Rioters Called Martyrs," 23 December 1917, *Chicago Herald*.

161. *New York Times*, 4 October 1919.

162. Waskow, *From Race Riot to Sit-In*, 123–26; Cortner, *Mob Intent on Death*, 5–23.

163. See Roy Wilkins's preface to W. White, *Rope and Faggot*.

164. Cortner, *Mob Intent on Death*, 24–38.

165. W. White, "Race Conflict in Arkansas," 233–34; "Lay Riots to Cotton Row," *New York Times*, 13 October 1919; W. White, *A Man Called White*, 47–51.

166. Wells-Barnett, "Condemned Arkansas Rioters," *CD*, 13 December 1919.

167. Quoted in Wells-Barnett, *Arkansas Race Riot*, 5.

168. Wells-Barnett, *Crusade for Justice*, 399.

169. Cortner, *Mob Intent on Death*, 32.

170. Wells-Barnett, *Crusade for Justice*, 400–402. Despite this caveat in her autobiography, as late as February 1920 Wells-Barnett approached the Gary, Indiana, NAACP branch with an appeal for funds in the name of the Equal Rights League. Her appeal, in turn, was complained about to NAACP headquarters in New York. A critic in Gary understood that "members of the Equal Rights League here, boast that they will supplant the N.A.A.C.P.," suggesting significant local controversy over leadership in civil rights initiatives. See L. Campbell to Miss M. W. Ovington, 25 February 1920, NAACP Papers. Rev. Archibald J. Carey fanned his reputation as an outstanding leader of African Americans and was received as "one of the next bishops of the AME Church" when he spoke about the riots to "a great ovation" in Helena in January 1920, as was reported glowingly in the *CD*, 3 January 1920. Wells-Barnett did reconnect with the Equal Rights League in the early 1920s; see Chapter 6.

171. Wells-Barnett, *Crusade for Justice*, 401–2.

172. Wells-Barnett, *Arkansas Race Riot*, 5.

173. Ibid., 22.

174. Wells-Barnett, *Crusade for Justice*, 403.

175. S. A. Holt, "Making Freedom Pay." Holt's treatment revises historians' view that black women largely withdrew from field work after emancipation. J. Jones, *Labor of Love*, 44–78; and Mann, "Slavery, Sharecropping, and Sexual Inequality." See also Schwalm, " 'Sweet Dreams of Freedom' "; and Schwalm, *A Hard Fight for We*, esp. chap. 7. On black women as lynching victims, see A. W. Grimké, "Goldie" (1920) in *Selected Works*. See also Tate, *Domestic Allegories*, 209–28. The story of "Goldie" was probably inspired by widely circulated reports in 1918 of the lynching of Mary Turner in Georgia. Turner was eight months pregnant when she threatened to reveal to local authorities the identities of those who lynched her husband. She herself was lynched and burned, her infant cut from her womb and crushed. John Shillady to Senator Knute Nelson, 20 November 1918, NAACP Papers. See also Shapiro, *White Violence and Black Response*, 146.

176. Wells-Barnett, *Arkansas Race Riot*, 19.

177. Ibid., 20.

178. Ibid., 19–22.

179. Ibid., 6.

180. Du Bois, *Souls of Black Folk*, 274.

181. Wells-Barnett, *Crusade for Justice*, 403; Wells-Barnett, *Arkansas Race Riot*, 6.

182. Wells-Barnett, *Crusade for Justice*, 404.

183. Wells-Barnett probably referred here to Theodore Roosevelt's interven-

tion with the United Mine Workers' strike in Pennsylvania in 1902, in which he brokered some concessions for the union short of official recognition. The miners' more recent experience with Woodrow Wilson, in November 1919, was a disaster; that strike was broken by government-ordered injunction.

184. Wells-Barnett, *Arkansas Race Riot*, 52.

185. Ibid., 55.

186. Shapiro, *White Violence and Black Response*, 159.

187. Wells-Barnett, *Arkansas Race Riot*, 6.

188. "The Anti-Lynching Crusaders," *Crisis* (November 1922): 8.

189. "The Shame of America," *Crisis* (October 1923): 167–69; "The Ninth Crusade," *Crisis* (March 1923): 213. Ovington noted that the women's fundraising "made possible our spectacular page in the *New York Times* headed 'The Shame of America.'" Ovington, *Black and White Sat Down Together*, 96.

190. *CD*, 4 and 18 November 1922.

191. *CD*, 9 September 1922.

192. Jessie Fausett, "Thirteenth Biennial of the NACW," *Crisis* (October 1922): 260; *Minutes of the Thirteenth Biennial Session* (1922), copy in NACW Papers; E. L. Davis, *Lifting as They Climb*, 65–67.

193. "The Shame of America," 167.

194. Wells-Barnett, *Arkansas Race Riot*, 58.

Chapter Five

1. Wells-Barnett, *Crusade for Justice*, 305–6.

2. A later, related anecdote in the autobiography reinforces the theme of godly womanhood as exemplar to the community. A woman who lives near the League is "mortified" to meet Wells-Barnett on the street while carrying a pail of beer. This woman testifies that the League's "very presence" on State Street was so much of a "reproach" to the conscience of another neighbor, it shamed her into closing the "good time house" she ran. Ibid., 330.

3. Gaines, *Uplifting the Race*. Shaw emphasizes the successes of cross-class work in *What a Woman Ought to Be and to Do*, 59–60. Wolcott, "'Bible, Bath and Broom,'" 88–110, stresses the consensus across class about—and the working-class origins of—the ideology of "uplift." On working-class forms of resistance to racism, see Kelley, "We Are Not What We Seem," in *Race Rebels*. Knupfer, *Toward a Tenderer Humanity and a Nobler Womanhood*, notes status differences as well as sites of exchange across class in black women's club work. On cross-class work by mostly white reformers, see May, "'Problem of Duty'"; L. Gordon, *Heroes of Their Own Lives*; Odem, *Delinquent Daughters*; Boyer, *Urban Masses and Moral Order in America*; Stansell, *City of Women*.

4. By "independent, start-up settlements," I mean those not affiliated with any national organization, such as the YWCA or a government bureau or agency. The major African American social settlements on the South Side before 1920 included the Emmanuel Settlement, founded by Dr. Fannie Emmanuel, a local podiatrist, who ran mostly child-centered programs between 1908 and 1910; the Frederick Douglass Center, 1905–1918; the Institutional (AME) Church and Social Settlement, 1900–1920; and Wells-Barnett's Negro Fellowship League, 1910–1920. P. Jackson, "Black Charity in Progressive Era Chicago"; Diner, "Chi-

cago Social Workers and Blacks in the Progressive Era"; Philpott, *The Slum and the Ghetto*; L. DeK. Bowen, *Colored People of Chicago*.

5. *CD*, 17 April 1914. Wells-Barnett favorably compared her work to that of Hull-House in *Crusade for Justice*, 356. See also *CD*, 18 May 1912.

6. A. F. Davis, *American Heroine*, 92–109; V. B. Brown, "Jane Addams, Progressivism, and Woman Suffrage"; Sklar, "Hull-House in the 1890s"; Muncy, *Creating a Female Dominion in America Reform*, 3–37.

7. "Doing Their Part in Upbuilding," *CD*, 3 May 1930.

8. Gilmore, *Gender and Jim Crow*, 177–202; Rouse, *Lugenia Burns Hope*; Neverdon-Morton, *Afro-American Women of the South*.

9. Weisenfeld, *African American Women and Christian Activism*; and Salem, *To Better Our World*. See also Ladd-Taylor, "Toward Defining Maternalism in U.S. History." I am indebted to Kevin Gaines for this last point.

10. E. L. Davis, *Story of the Illinois Federation of Colored Women's Clubs*, frontispiece; Knupfer, *Toward a Tenderer Humanity and a Nobler Womanhood*, chaps. 4 and 5.

11. *Fellowship Herald*, 22 June 1911 (courtesy of Paul Lee).

12. Boris, "Power of Motherhood"; Stovall, "Chicago *Defender* in the Progressive Era"; L. Gordon, "Black and White Visions of Welfare: Women's Welfare Activism, 1890–1945." Lasch-Quinn, *Black Neighbors*, attends mostly to religious versus social scientific conceptions of settlement work among intellectuals. Goodwin, *Gender and the Politics of Welfare Reform*, attributes the marginalization of black women in welfare activism to racism among whites. See also E. L. Ross, *Black Heritage in Social Welfare, 1860–1930*, and essays in Frankel and Dye, *Gender, Class, Race, and Reform in the Progressive Era*.

13. Wells-Barnett, "Northern Negro Woman's Social and Moral Condition," 33.

14. Hall, "O. Delight Smith's Progressive Era"; Czitrom, "Underworlds and Underdogs"; Harzig, "Ethnic Female Public Sphere."

15. Painter, *Standing at Armageddon*, 268–69. Gustafson, "Partisan Women," chap. 3, emphasizes Addams's seriousness about suffrage and political power for women. See also chap. 5, her discussion of racial politics in the Progressive Party. Chicago black leader Dr. Charles Bentley wrote a long letter to the *Defender* sympathizing with Addams's limited ability to budge Roosevelt from his prejudiced and "unscrupulous" resistance to black suffrage as a plank in the Progressive platform. See "Important Conference on the Negro," *CD*, 17 August 1912.

16. Addams, *Twenty Years at Hull-House*, 148–68; "The Settlement as a Factor in the Labor Movement," in Residents of Hull-House, *Hull-House Maps and Papers*, 183–204.

17. See sources in note 12; Gilmore, *Gender and Jim Crow*; Lasch-Quinn, *Black Neighbors*, chaps. 3 and 4; Roydhouse, "Bridging Chasms"; Sims, *Power of Femininity in the New South*; and Turner, *Women, Culture, and Community*.

18. Wells-Barnett, "How Enfranchisement Stops Lynching."

19. Wells-Barnett, "National Equal Rights Congress Comes to an End," *CD*, 14 October 1916.

20. E. B. Brown, "To Catch the Vision of Freedom." Since at least the mid-nineteenth century, African Americans had drawn on religious rhetoric and Christian history to bolster their claims to political equality, though according to Rosalyn Terborg-Penn's recent study, such arguments were not the most promi-

nent. Terborg-Penn, *African American Women in the Struggle for the Vote, 1850–1920*. In a discussion by black leaders in *The Crisis* in 1915, neither clergy nor activist women gave particularly theological arguments for woman suffrage. Typical was the position of Miss M. E. Jackson, president of the Rhode Island Association of Colored Women's Clubs: "Looked at from a sane point of view, all objections to the ballot for women are but protests against progress, civilization, and good sense." "Votes for Women," *Crisis* (August 1915): 187.

The use of religious language in discussions of political rights among white women also dates from the antebellum period. For example, the Declaration of Sentiments (1848) refers to the "sacred rights" of citizenship. Kraditor argues that despite Elizabeth Cady Stanton's iconoclastic criticism of the Bible in the 1890s, by the early twentieth century many white suffragists made a comfortable, uncontroversial connection between Christianity and votes for women suffrage via the "Golden Rule," rather than strict theology. Kraditor, *Ideas of the Woman Suffrage Movement*, 75–95. See also Jane Addams, "Communion of the Ballot." On white women in the South, see Kirkley, " 'This Work Is God's Cause.' "

21. Iola, "Functions of Leadership," *New York Freeman*, 8 August 1885. See also Iola, "Freedom of Political Action," *New York Freeman*, 7 November 1885. Before the advent of woman suffrage, Wells-Barnett was less of a partisan, arguing in 1885 that voters should put the "interest of the race" before "party favors or interests." See Iola, "Stick to the Race," *New York Freeman*, 7 February 1885. When pressed, she explained: "I am a Republican, but I was an Afro-American before I was a Republican." *New York Age*, 19 November 1893, clipping in IBW Papers.

22. Bederman, *Manliness and Civilization*; and Gaines, *Uplifting the Race*.

23. For similar positions by black women, see E. B. Brown, "To Catch the Vision of Freedom" and "Womanist Consciousness." See also J. James, *Transcending the Talented Tenth*, chaps. 2 and 3. James points out that Wells-Barnett's emphasis on race and black women does not qualify or undermine her credibility as a "feminist." First, as an antilynching crusader, Wells-Barnett connected the abuse of black women to racism, sexism, and patterns of political and economic oppression. Second, James points out that omission of race analysis—or the advocacy of white supremacy, for that matter—historically has not jeopardized white women's feminist credentials; in fact, it often established them. For examples, see Bederman on Charlotte Perkins Gilman in *Manliness and Civilization*; and Lebsock, "Woman Suffrage and White Supremacy."

24. See James and Busia, *Theorizing Black Feminisms*.

25. Moses, *Golden Age of Black Nationalism*, pt. 2; Gaines, *Uplifting the Race*, chap. 4: Rampersad, *Art and Imagination of W. E. B. Du Bois*, chaps. 4–6.

26. Ida B. Wells Diary, 4 December 1886, IBW Papers; Ida B. Wells, "Afro-Americans and Africa." In an 1893 survey of over a dozen opinion-shapers on African migration, Wells was the only woman commentator and, as she did all her life, "most emphatically advocated immigration to Africa for all those who wish and are able to go." See "Judicious Immigration," *Indianapolis Freeman*, 25 November 1893.

27. *Chicago Inter-Ocean*, 8 August 1894, clipping in IBW Papers; E. L. Davis, *Story of the Illinois Federation*, 22; *Kansas City American Citizen*, 24 August 1894.

28. Wells-Barnett, *Crusade for Justice*, 217–18.

29. D. L. Lewis, *W. E. B. Du Bois*, 147–52.

30. Respectful, congratulatory press notices can be found in the *New York Times*, 28 June 1895, 1; *New York Tribune*, 28 June 1895; *Indianapolis Freeman*, 22 June, 13 July 1895.

31. Wells-Barnett, *Crusade for Justice*, 250, 243–45.

32. Wells-Barnett's article appeared in the *Chicago Inter-Ocean*, 17 July 1897.

33. *The Woman's Era* (July 1895): 5.

34. Wells-Barnett, *Crusade for Justice*, 241.

35. Ibid., 239–40.

36. Alfreda M. Duster interview, 16–17, in Black Women Oral History Project Interviews, Schlesinger Library, Radcliffe Institute for Advanced Study, Harvard University, Cambridge, Mass.

37. On Barnett's antilynching work in the 1890s, see Ferdinand L. Barnett to William E. Chandler, 8 May 1894; and Ida B. Wells to William E. Chandler, 10 May 1894, both in William E. Chandler Papers; *Chicago Inter-Ocean*, 8 August 1894, clipping in IBW Papers.

38. Alfreda M. Duster interview, 11.

39. Hine, "Rape and the Inner Lives of Black Women in the Middle West," 294.

40. Tate, *Domestic Allegories*; duCille, *Coupling Convention*.

41. Alfreda M. Duster interview, 10–11, 49, 6–7.

42. Krieling, "Making of Racial Identities in the Black Press," 125; Spear, *Black Chicago*, 158–61; *Chicago Broad-Ax*, 10 November 1906; "Chicago's Liberality," *Voice of the Negro* (November 1906): 467; Krieling, "Rise of the Black Press in Chicago," 132–36.

43. Alfreda M. Duster interview, 3.

44. "Barnett-Graham," *Chicago Conservator*, 18 November 1882; Necrology File on Mary H. Graham, Bentley Historical Library, University of Michigan, Ann Arbor.

45. Wells-Barnett, *Crusade for Justice*, 251–52.

46. "Alfred M. Duster Interview," 11, 57; Wells & Barnett wedding invitation (courtesy of Paul Lee).

47. Phelps, "Negro Life in Chicago"; Spear, *Black Chicago*, 51–70.

48. Drake and Cayton, *Black Metropolis*, 398; Drake, *Churches and Voluntary Associations*, 148. By 1919, Baptist congregations outnumbered Methodist nearly 2.5 to 1.

49. Withers, "Bethel Church"; "Quinn Chapel, AME," in Wright, *Centennial Encyclopedia of the AME Church*, 301.

50. Ida B. Wells-Barnett, "Rev. R. C. Ransom, D.D.," *Philadelphia Christian Recorder*, 26 January 1900.

51. Wills, "Reverdy C. Ransom," 197; Logsdon, "The Rev. Archibald J. Carey," 13–33; "Rev. A. J. Carey, D.D.," in Wright, *Centennial Encyclopedia of the AME Church*, 60.

52. Ransom, *Deborah and Jael*, 4–5, copy in Reverdy Ransom Papers.

53. Ransom, *Pilgrimage*, 99. See also Ransom, *Industrial and Social Conditions of the Negro*, 6, copy in Reverdy Ransom Papers. Ransom was first exposed to mission/settlement work during an early pastorate at Allegheny City, Pennsylvania, in the 1880s. Morris, *Reverdy C. Ransom*, 103.

54. Wells-Barnett, "Rev. R. C. Ransom, D.D."

55. Wells-Barnett, *Crusade for Justice*, 250; E. L. Davis, *Story of the Illinois Federation*, 27.

56. Wells-Barnett, "Rev. R. C. Ransom, D.D."

57. Ransom, *Pilgrimage*, 87. See also Bishop A. Grant, "Institutional Church"; and "Northern Social Settlements for Negroes." On Provident Hospital, see Buckler, *Daniel Hale Williams*, 67–84.

58. *Chicago Tribune*, 20 August 1899.

59. Wells-Barnett, *Crusade for Justice*, 261. This achievement was savored all the more since the NACW's Washington, D.C., leadership had frozen Wells-Barnett out of their Chicago convention that same weekend.

60. "Closes in Tumult," untitled clipping, 20 August 1899, Tuskegee Clippings File; *Chicago Tribune*, 18, 19, and 20 August 1899; Harlan, *Booker T. Washington: Making of a Black Leader*, 264–65.

61. *Indianapolis Freeman*, 2 September 1899. See also *Chicago Broad-Ax*, 26 August 1899; *Cleveland Gazette*, 26 August 1899; Wills, "Reverdy C. Ransom," 200.

62. Wills, "Reverdy C. Ransom," 196.

63. Meier, *Negro Thought in America*, 229; Ransom, "Boston's Inheritance"; and Ransom, "Spirit of John Brown."

64. "Booker T. Washington Orated at Quinn Chapel," *Chicago Broad-Ax*, 9 April 1904. See also S. Laing Williams to Booker T. Washington, 24 October, 9 and 17 November 1903; Emmett J. Scott to S. Laing Williams, 23 March 1904. The Institutional Church also hosted Washington in 1904. See S. Laing Williams to Emmett J. Scott, 16 May 1904, all in BTW Papers

65. Ransom, *Pilgrimage*, 84; Wills, "Reverdy C. Ransom," 202.

66. Wells-Barnett, *Crusade for Justice*, 163–64; Harlan, *Booker T. Washington: Wizard of Tuskegee*, 27–28.

67. S. R. Fox, *Guardian of Boston*, 49–57.

68. Emmett J. Scott to Booker T. Washington, 12 July 1904, in Harlan, *Booker T. Washington Papers*, 8:16; and Booker T. Washington to Charles William Anderson, 16 June 1904, in ibid., 7:533. See also S. Laing Williams to Emmett J. Scott, 14 October, 17 November 1903, 15 August 1904; Booker T. Washington to S. Laing Williams, 3 September 1904; S. Laing Williams to Emmett J. Scott, 8 July, 15 August, 26 September, 28 November 1904; S. Laing Williams to Booker T. Washington, 23 March 1905, 6 June 1908, all in BTW Papers.

69. *Chicago Broad-Ax*, 22 August, 5 September 1903; 29 October 1904; 4 March 1905.

70. On the Chicago stockyards strike, see Tuttle, *Race Riot*, 115–21; and Herbst, *The Negro in the Slaughtering and Meat Packing Industry in Chicago*, 24–27.

71. Wells-Barnett, *Crusade for Justice*, 279; "Report of Memorial Service," *Unity Magazine* (18 April 1918): 115.

72. F. B. Williams, "Frederick Douglass Centre," *Voice of the Negro*, 601; Davis's tribute in "Report of Memorial Service," 120. Even the *Colored American Magazine*, shaded by Tuskegee's influence, mocked the Chicago women's gatherings as being "Organized for Social Equality" during which "Colored and white ladies" meet on "absolute equality, discuss the progress of the work in hand, dine together, chat, talk, and we presume gossip, and depart, each member feeling perfectly herself, and no one feeling she has lowered herself on the one hand, or that she had been graciously lifted on the other." See "Organized for Social

Equality." When in 1903 Fannie Barrier Williams lunched at the Evanston home of Catherine Waugh McCullough, the state's leading white suffragist, the press report in the *Inter-Ocean* was bumpered with an allusion to Booker T. Washington's controversial meal at Theodore Roosevelt's White House. "Colored Woman Honored Guest," *Chicago Inter-Ocean*, 1 June 1903.

73. Elizabeth Lindsay Davis cited only the Douglass Center and the rather tepid welcome of the Illinois Federation of Woman's Clubs and Woman's City Club of Chicago as meriting mention under "Inter-racial Co-operation" in her *Story of the Illinois Federation*, 36–40. Another Unitarian outpost, the Abraham Lincoln Center, was conducted under Rev. Jenkin Lloyd Jones of All Soul's Church and attempted to minister across the color line on a rather more "churchy" basis, explicitly on the ideal of "interracial fellowship." See Philpott, *The Slum and the Ghetto*, 338–39. For positive appraisals of the Douglass Center, see F. B. Williams, "Frederick Douglass Center," *Southern Workman*; Woolley, "Frederick Douglass Center, Chicago"; and F. B. Williams, "New Method for Dealing with the Race Problem." On elitism and social snobbery at the Douglass Center, see *Chicago Broad-Ax*, 29 April 1905, 23 and 30 June 1906. On the Center in general, see Philpott, *The Slum and the Ghetto*, 316–19.

74. Wells-Barnett, *Crusade for Justice*, 280–81. Leading club woman Elizabeth Lindsay Davis also commented that "no group of officials were more antagonistic at the outset of [women's club work] than the ministers" but added that they soon came around. Davis, *Story of the Illinois Federation*, 4.

75. *Chicago Broad-Ax*, 28 April 1906.

76. Wells-Barnett, *Crusade for Justice*, 290.

77. Ibid., 291; *Chicago Broad-Ax*, 5 May 1906.

78. Wells-Barnett, *Crusade for Justice*, 292. Wells-Barnett noted that Woolley reminded Carey and his colleagues that their own churches were in debt. It should be borne in mind that a key proving ground for clergy was getting their churches on firm financial footing, which usually meant paying off the building mortgage. This Carey successfully achieved at both Quinn and Bethel. See "Rev. A. J. Carey, D.D.," in Wright, *Centennial Encyclopedia of the AME Church*, 60.

79. Wells-Barnett, *Crusade for Justice*, 293.

80. *Hull-House Bulletin* 7, no. 1 (1905–6): 10, in Department of Special Collections, University of Illinois at Chicago Circle; *Chicago Broad-Ax*, 12 May 1906.

81. *Chicago Broad-Ax*, 12 May 1906.

82. Wells-Barnett, *Crusade for Justice*, 294.

83. Alfreda M. Duster interview, 12.

84. Wells-Barnett, *Crusade for Justice*, 294.

85. See *Chicago Broad-Ax*, 27 October, 3 and 10 November, 22 December 1906; Gosnell, *Negro Politicians*, 85; Drake and Cayton, *Black Metropolis*, 246. See also S. Laing Williams to Booker T. Washington, 16 and 26 November 1906, in BTW Papers.

86. Wells-Barnett, *Crusade for Justice*, 297–98; *Chicago Broad-Ax*, 5 December 1903, 5 November and 17 December 1904.

87. On Wells-Barnett's support of Amanda Smith, see Wells-Barnett, *Crusade for Justice*, 373–74; "Amanda Smith's 13th Anniversary," *Fellowship Herald*, 22 June 1911 (courtesy of Paul Lee); *CD*, 6 March 1915. Ferdinand served on the board of Amanda Smith's Home beginning around 1911.

88. It is not clear exactly when Ferdinand joined Pilgrim Baptist Church on

Indiana Avenue, but by the mid-1920s he was well ensconced in its leadership at the executive and lay ministerial levels. See F. L. Barnett and I. W. Brown to "Dear Friend," 7 May 1926 on Pilgrim Baptist Laymen's League stationery, IBW Papers.

89. Wells-Barnett, *Crusade for Justice*, 298.

90. Dr. Clementine McConico Skinner to Patricia Schechter, 3 March 1990, personal communication in author's possession.

91. Drake, *Churches and Voluntary Associations*, 106; Grace Presbyterian Church, "Fifty-Seventh Anniversary Tea," 13 May 1945, pamphlet in Vivian G. Harsh Collection, Carter G. Woodson Public Library, Chicago.

92. Wells-Barnett, *Crusade for Justice*, 299.

93. "Rev. Jackson to Speak of Forty Years Work: Recalls Early History of Grace Church," *CD*, 23 June 1928; Wells-Barnett, *Crusade for Justice*, 298.

94. *CD*, 20 April 1912, 4 and 11 October 1913.

95. *CD*, 8 June 1912. Grace also sponsored a Christian Endeavor Society, a Men's Club, a "Helping Hand" society, a Wednesday prayer meeting, a baseball team, an Altar Guild, a Women's Home Missionary Society, and a very popular and well-supported Young People's Lyceum. See *CD*, 23 June 1928.

96. Alfreda M. Duster interview, 17–18; Wells-Barnett, *Crusade for Justice*, 300.

97. *CD*, 20 September 1913.

98. Wells-Barnett, *Crusade for Justice*, 304.

99. *Chicago Broad-Ax*, 30 April 1910. For related points, see L. DeK. Bowen, *Colored People of Chicago*.

100. Lasch-Quinn, *Black Neighbors*; McCarthy, *Noblesse Oblige*; Kusmer, "Functions of Organized Charity in the Progressive Era."

101. Wells-Barnett, *Crusade for Justice*, 301–3.

102. Strickland, *Chicago Urban League*, 77; Sawyers, "Victor Lawson," in *Chicago Portraits*, 153–54; "Contributions, 1900–1916," in Victor F. Lawson Papers, Newberry Library, Chicago. See also Dennis, *Victor Lawson*.

103. The figure $9,000 is from Wells-Barnett, *Crusade for Justice*, 332. The figure may have been closer to $6,000. See Victor F. Lawson to Ida B. Wells-Barnett, 10 June, 7 September 1910; 3 and 9 January, 16 August, 18 November 1911, in Victor F. Lawson Papers.

104. Wells-Barnett, *Crusade for Justice*, 304.

105. Elizabeth Lindsay Davis to My Dear President, 10 October 1928, in NACW Papers. These monies brought the Home within striking range of retiring its mortgage. "Interesting Facts about the Phyllis [*sic*] Wheatley Home—Origin," *The National Notes* (July 1924): 9. See also "The Phyllis [*sic*] Wheatley Home for Girls," pamphlet in Department of Special Collections, University of Illinois at Chicago Circle. See also Sklar, "Who Funded Hull-House?"

106. Addams, *Twenty Years at Hull-House*, 221.

107. Shaw, *What a Woman Ought to Be and to Do*, 171–75.

108. Addams, *Twenty Years at Hull-House*, 25. See also Sklar, "Hull-House in the 1890s"; and Quinn, *Black Neighbors*, chaps. 1–2. For a recent treatment that stresses the spiritual dimension of white women's settlement commitment, see Stebner, *Women of Hull-House*.

109. A classic example of the difference between Hull-House and South Side community development strategies is how each neighborhood came to sponsor the "first" public playground for children in Chicago. Hull-House women cob-

bled together a mix of private and public sources that included a local landlord who offered a lot rent-free; Hull-House, which paid the costs of fixing up the lot; and a local public school, which gave equipment for the playground that opened in 1895. Residents of Hull-House, *Hull-House Maps and Papers*, 224. Mayor William Thompson claimed to have opened the "first municipal playground for kiddies in the world" during his first term on the city council between 1900 and 1902 when he obtained $1,200 from the city to build a park right across from his friend Archibald Carey's church on the South Side. Logsdon, "Rev. Archibald J. Carey," 38. Another example is how when neighborhood women around Hull-House clamored for a public washing and bathing facility in the late 1890s, Addams and the local ward's Improvement Club petitioned the Chicago City Council for funds, and the thing was done. Residents of Hull-House, *Hull-House Maps and Papers*, 219. See also McCree and Davis, *One Hundred Years at Hull-House*, 18; A. F. Davis, *American Heroine*, 107–8.

110. L. Gordon, "Black and White Visions of Welfare"; Ladd-Taylor, "Toward Defining Maternalism"; and Goodwin, *Gender and Politics of Welfare Reform*.

111. On Woolley's condescension toward black women, see "Afro-American Women 'Jim-Crowed'," *Chicago Broad-Ax*, 7 July 1906; and Wells-Barnett, *Crusade for Justice*, 281–88.

112. Victor F. Lawson to Ida B. Wells-Barnett, 7 September 1910, and esp. 16 August and 18 November 1911, Victor F. Lawson Papers.

113. Wells-Barnett, *Crusade for Justice*, 358.

114. Stebner, *Women of Hull-House*, 27–48; and esp. Lasch-Quinn, *Black Neighbors*, chap. 2. On black activists' blended approach, see Nelson, "Settlement Work for Negroes."

115. *Chicago Broad-Ax*, 23 July 1910; *CD*, 30 April 1910; Knupfer, *Toward a Tenderer Humanity and a Nobler Womanhood*, 52.

116. *Fellowship Herald*, 22 June 1911 (courtesy of Paul Lee).

117. Praise for the work of the League can be found in *Chicago Broad-Ax*, 7 May 1910; and *CD*, 27 January 1912, 20 September 1913, 14 August 1915.

118. *Fellowship Herald*, 31 August 1911, copy in W. E. B. Du Bois Papers, University of Massachusetts, Amherst.

119. See *CD*, 30 April 1910. On women's support of the Urban League, see Strickland, *Chicago Urban League*, 206–7. On the Old Folks' Home, see E. L. Davis, *Story of the Illinois Federation*, 4, 14–15, 28.

120. *Fellowship Herald*, 21 December 1911, clipping in IMG Papers.

121. "Shooting of T.R. No Significance," *CD*, 18 October 1912.

122. On strategies for training and leadership of black women within their churches, see Jualynne E. Dodson, "Introduction," in A. Smith, *Autobiography*, xxvii–xlii; Angell, "Controversy Over Women's Ministry"; Higginbotham, *Righteous Discontent*. For another local start-up in the Chicago black community, see "South Side Religious School," *CD*, 28 April 1928. On white women's training and involvement in the ministry, see Hassey, *No Time for Silence*.

123. It is likely that Wells-Barnett was familiar with the Baptist Young People's Union (BYPU) movement and program from her days in Memphis. The BYPU started in the Upper South and Midwest in the 1880s. T. O. Fuller, *History of the Negro Baptists of Tennessee*, chap. 6.

124. *Crusade for Justice*, 355–58. She approached the Methodist Episcopal Church for this aid.

125. O'Donnell, "Care of Dependent African American Children in Chicago"; Stehno, "Public Responsibility for Dependent Black Children"; Lide, "National Conference on Social Welfare and the Black Historical Perspective."

126. Smith appealed to the AME Church. "Amanda Smith's Life Work Ends," *CD*, 6 March 1915. On Smith, see Knupfer, *Toward a Tenderer Humanity and a Nobler Womanhood*, 77–81; Dodson, "Introduction," in A. Smith, *Autobiography*; "Amanda Smith, 1837–1915," in H. Q. Brown, *Homespun Heroines*, 128–32. See also "Amanda Smith's 13th Anniversary," *Fellowship Herald*, 22 June 1911 (courtesy of Paul Lee). The orphanage did receive a state license around 1903, but state officials admitted continuing the certified status of the Home as "a matter of tolerance," because no other facility for "colored girls" existed in Illinois. From scattered reports, it appears that public money did not find its way to Smith until sometime after 1913, and, even then, donations were still vital to the solvency of the Home. County funds were held up in 1916 due to political controversy over sectarian organizations' eligibility for public funds. Ferdinand Barnett, who served on Smith's board of directors, also came in for a hard time with state officials, who accused him of overcounting black inmates and overcharging the county $100 in 1915. See "Departments," report on Amanda Smith Home [ca. 1918]; Charles Virden, State Agent, "Condensed Report of the Amanda Smith Industrial School for Girls," 18 June 1915; Esther W. S. Brophy to Julius Rosenwald, 7 December 1915; Adah M. Waters to Mr. William C. Graves, 20 December 1917; Charles Virden to Mr. Graves, 30 June 1915; Edward C. Wentworth to Mr. Graves, 1 April 1916; all in Julius Rosenwald Papers, Reggenstein Library, University of Chicago.

127. Wells-Barnett, *Crusade for Justice*, 330.

128. Ibid., 332; *Chicago Broad-Ax*, 8 February 1913; *CD*, 15 February, 1 March 1913. See also George Washington Ellis to Madam Ida B. W. Barnett, 13 February 1913, George Washington Ellis Papers. Wells-Barnett claimed to have first broken the color barrier in the Loop when the chorus performed at the Lincoln Centenary in 1909. See *CD*, 5 May 1930.

129. Wells-Barnett, *Crusade for Justice*, 352.

130. Willrich, "City of Courts"; Clapp, *Mothers of All Children*, chap. 6.

131. Quoted in Houston, *Annual Report of the Adult Probation Office of Cook County, Illinois*, 2:14 (1913).

132. Ibid., 2:24–25.

133. Houston, *Annual Report of the Adult Probation Office*, 3:16 (1914).

134. Houston, *Annual Report of the Adult Probation Office*, 4:5 (1915).

135. There were nine men and six women who served during her first term. Houston, *Annual Report of the Adult Probation Office*, 2:20 (1913).

136. *CD*, 5 June, 14 August 1915.

137. Fundraising letter on Woman's Protective Association stationery, [ca. 1912?]; clipping from *Chicago Record-Herald*, 2 April 1913, both in MC Papers.

138. Wells-Barnett, *Crusade for Justice*, 410–13.

139. Of course, this thinking was not at all unique to African Americans. Many Chicago groups sought to have "one of their own" in the evolving bureaucratic and policing institutions of the city. Mrs. Minnie Jacobs Berlin was a probation officer for the Jewish Aid Society and held multiple positions in and around government during the decade of 1910–20. She served the particular needs and interests of "Jewish inmates of the Joliet Prison and . . . the paroled men of that

race." She also held a position in the National Conference of Charities and Corrections, to which she was appointed by the governor, as well as serving in the Juvenile Court. "An Interview with Mrs. Minnie Jacobs Berlin," *The Joliet Prison Post* (1 July 1915): 69. On antiblack racism at Joliet, see other *Joliet Prison Post* articles: "Our Annual Minstrels" (15 October 1916): 63; "No Brute" (1 July 1915): 89; "Little Zeke Visits the Honor Farm" (1 September 1914): 468–69; and "Zeke Goes Hunting on the Joliet Honor Farm" (1 October 1914): 528–29.

140. "Splendid Work of Probation Officers," *CD*, 20 March 1915.

141. *CD*, 9 December 1915.

142. Wells-Barnett, *Crusade for Justice*, 333.

143. Case No. 121523, *People v. Ralph Thomas*; No. 105699, *People v. William Rhodes*; No. 121610, *People v. Peter Hayes*; No. 121379, *People v. Robert Barnett*; No. 129902, *People v. Augusta Starks*; No. 120828, *People v. James Howard*; No. 120594, *People v. Charles Cocolough*; No. 120572, *People v. Roger Haddiman*; No. 120312, *People v. George Bonner*; No. 120163, *People v. William Foster*; No. 112049, *People v. Samuel Davis*; No. 108814, *People v. Marshall Davis*; No. 108740, *People v. William Hill*; No. 108572, *People v. Albert Partlow*; No. 105784, *People v. John Wooten*; No. 105630, *People v. Willie Scott*; No. 105696, *People v. Richard Henderson*, all in Criminal Court Records, 1913–1914, Municipal Court of Chicago Criminal Court Records, Daley Center Archives, Chicago.

144. Houston, *Annual Report of the Adult Probation Office*, 5:4–5 (1916).

145. Houston, *Annual Report of the Adult Probation Office*, 4:12 (1915).

146. Houston, *Annual Report of the Adult Probation Office*, 5:22 (1916), 3:16 (1914). See also Peiss, " 'Charity Girls' and City Pleasures"; and May, "The Problem of 'Duty.' "

147. Houston, *Annual Report of the Adult Probation Office*, 2:25 (1913).

148. Houston, *Annual Report of the Adult Probation Office*, 3:16 (1914), 6:6 (1917). Houston complained of exaggeration and bragging about success on the part of his probation officers, implying they were overzealous missionaries.

149. Cases Nos. 120828, 121523, and 121379 from note 143.

150. Wells-Barnett, *Crusade for Justice*, 333.

151. Ida B. Wells-Barnett to Joel E. Spingarn, 29 July 1913, IBW Papers.

152. "The Ordeal of the 'Solitary': Mrs. Barnett Protests," *CD*, 26 June 1915; and *CD*, 25 May 1918. See also "Women's Club Visits Jail," *CD*, 29 May 1915.

153. *CD*, 13 March 1915.

154. Wells-Barnett, *Crusade for Justice*, 409–10. The autobiography places this event in 1919, but a *Defender* report of the Negro Fellowship League's activities describes a very similar case in 1915. See *CD*, 14 August 1915. The earlier date makes sense, since Wells-Barnett actually was an officer of the court at that time. While Wells-Barnett's theatrical abilities may have enabled her to hoodwink a gullible white woman at any given point, I doubt she would have risked flashing her badge when no longer an officer of the court in 1919.

155. A similar observation has been made about organized labor's politicking through the New Deal. See Dubofsky, *State and Labor in Modern America*.

156. The phrase is from Hendricks "The Politics of Race: Black Women in Illinois," 136. See also Hendricks, *Gender, Race, and Politics in the Midwest*; and P. Baker, "Domestication of Politics," 620–48.

157. *CD*, 14 February 1914.

158. *Alpha Suffrage Record*, 18 March 1914, in IBW Papers. The Alphas hosted a

reception honoring R. R. Jackson, who supported the suffrage legislation and invited white women suffragists Antoinette Funk and Catherine Waugh McCullough and Senator Medill McCormick to help celebrate (see *CD*, 19 July 1913). Fifty people attended the Alphas' anniversary dinner in November ("Alpha Suffrage Club Banquet," *CD*, 22 November 1913). A white woman, Mrs. K. L. Wolf, lectured at the NFL on suffrage (*CD*, 30 March 1912). Wells-Barnett joined a city federation meeting on suffrage (*CD*, 8 March 1913). She addressed the literary society of Bethesda Baptist Church regarding votes for women (*CD*, 2 November 1912). On the woman suffrage fight in Illinois in general, see Buechler, *Transformation of the Woman Suffrage Movement*.

159. *CD*, 23 August 1913. Elizabeth Lindsay Davis made a similar point in 1915: "The highest and most successfully developed philanthropical work depends absolutely on the control of political influence by the best American citizenship, men and women working in unity and cooperation at the polls." "Votes for Philanthropy," *Crisis* (August 1915): 191.

160. This interest-group/ethnic-group model is also implicit in Gosnell's pioneering study of Chicago, *Negro Politicians*.

161. "Our Women," *CD*, 12 July 1913.

162. Gustafson, "Partisan Women in the Progressive Era"; DuBois, *Harriot Stanton Blatch*, 122–26.

163. DuBois, "Working Women, Class Relations, and Suffrage Militance." Chicago black women, with Wells-Barnett in the lead, confronted prejudice in hotel and department store service. See "La Salle Hotel," *CD*, 5 April 1913; and "Marshall Field & Co.," *CD*, 20 June 1914. Wells-Barnett also protested the use of racist language by the *Tribune*; see letter reprinted in *CD*, 9 May 1914. She was extremely critical of the treatment of black patrons by a local Greek restaurant on the South Side. One establishment, the scene of repeated shootings, came to the attention of the NFL, and Wells-Barnett tried to encourage better police investigation of perpetrators of violence and a black boycott of the restaurant. See "Race Trades with Foreigners," *CD*, 25 July 1914.

164. Wells-Barnett, *Crusade for Justice*, 346; "Women Voted with Intelligence," *CD*, 7 February 1914. This article razzed women for vainly falsifying their ages during voter registration.

165. Wells-Barnett, *Crusade for Justice*, 346.

166. "Illinois Women Feature Parade," *Chicago Daily Tribune*, 4 March 1913.

167. Ida B. Wells-Barnett to Catherine Waugh McCullough, 15 March 1913. See also Ida B. Wells-Barnett to Catherine Waugh McCullough, [ca. 1906], both in Catherine Waugh McCullough Papers, Schlesinger Library, Radcliffe Institute for Advanced Study, Harvard University, Cambridge.

168. Moore, "Making a Spectacle of Suffrage."

169. "Hail Columbia!" *Crisis* (April 1913): 289–90.

170. "Marches Despite Protests," *CD*, 8 March 1913.

171. *CD*, 19 April 1913; Logsdon, "Rev. Archibald J. Carey," 16; Illinois General Assembly, *Journal of the House of Representatives of the 48th General Assembly*, 819, 865.

172. Wells-Barnett, *Crusade for Justice*, 360; Illinois General Assembly, *Journal of the House*, 9 and 11 April 1913.

173. *CD*, 19 April 1913. The women subsequently held a reception praising representative Martin Madden for his "splendid defense of Negro womanhood"

in opposing the antimiscegenation bill. See *Alpha Suffrage Record*, 18 March 1914. In order to make amends with black voters in the state, the legislature appropriated funds toward a celebration of Emancipation's fiftieth anniversary. Wells-Barnett made sure that when there was an opportunity, a black woman was appointed to serve on the anniversary commission. That woman was Dr. Mary Waring of Chicago, who eventually became president of the National Association of Colored Women in 1933. Wells-Barnett, *Crusade for Justice*, 361–65. See also "Our Mary," *CD*, 18 May 1929; E. L. Davis, *Story of the Illinois Federation*, 62–63.

174. *CD*, 26 December 1914; K. E. Williams, "Alpha Suffrage Club."

175. Ida B. Wells-Barnett to Judge Olson, 23 April 1914, MC Papers.

176. *CD*, 22 September 1914; 3, 10, 24, and 31 October 1914; 7 November 1914.

177. *CD*, 21 November 1914. The NFL's regular meetings experienced multiplying political questions, including the viability of a municipal dance hall in the Second Ward and the distribution of mothers' pensions to black women, themes that were also taken up by the Alphas. *CD*, 12 and 19 December 1914, 3 July 1915.

178. *Alpha Suffrage Record*, 18 March 1914.

179. *CD*, 28 November 1914.

180. *CD*, 6 February 1915.

181. *CD*, 13 February 1915. The club endorsed DePriest. See *CD*, 13 March 1915.

182. "Women Favor L. B. Anderson," *CD*, 16 January 1915. On Montgomery, see Chapter 6 and "Second Ward Voters Throw Off Political Yoke," *CD*, 12 December 1914.

183. Edward H. Wright ran unsuccessfully for alderman in 1910 and 1912. See Hendricks, "Ida B. Wells-Barnett and the Alpha Suffrage Club of Chicago." See also Hendricks, "'Vote for the Advantage of Ourselves and Our Race'"; Gosnell, *Negro Politicians*, 73–75; and Wells-Barnett, *Crusade for Justice*, 348.

184. Tax, *Rising of the Women*, 73. The Chicago Labor and Trades Association struggled with the fact that factory inspectors "inevitably became part of the political machine that ran the city."

185. Addams, *Twenty Years at Hull-House*, 202–11. Rather than tackle the machine directly, Hull-House advocates sued private individuals for noncompliance with city codes. My interpretation here differs from that emphasized in Gustafson, "Partisan Women," 130–40.

186. Sklar, *Florence Kelley*, chaps. 11 and 12.

187. Gosnell's main point was that black politics were comprised of competing centers of power among an array of individuals and institutions, all of which were in a shifting relationship to parties and machines. See Gosnell, *Negro Politicians*. A recent scholar agrees; see Pinderhughes, *Race and Ethnicity in Chicago Politics*.

188. Wells-Barnett aided Trotter in pressuring Woodrow Wilson to curb segregation occurring in federal employment in Washington by traveling to the White House and making a personal appeal. After being snubbed by the president in a subsequent meeting, Trotter took his case to black communities across the country, and Wells-Barnett welcomed him at the NFL when he came to Chicago. On Trotter, see "Chicago People Organize," *CD*, 9 January 1915. Wells-Barnett

personally fought off mischief makers in the press who tried to impugn Trotter's integrity with Chicago's Irish Fellowship Club. Scurrilous reports were circulated, clearly designed to raise the specter of social equality and stir resentments between Irish and blacks in the city. See "Trotter, the Press, and the Irish," *CD*, 16 January 1915; Wells-Barnett, *Crusade for Justice*, 375–77; S. R. Fox, *Guardian of Boston*, 175–85. On protests against limiting immigration from Africa to the United States, see "Illinois Defeats Reed Proposal," *CD*, 9 January 1915. Wells-Barnett also mobilized the ERL on behalf of an antimiscegenation act for the District of Columbia; see "Equal Rights League Opposes Marriage Act," *CD*, 9 January 1915.

189. *CD*, 16 and 23 January 1915. An unfortunate compromise was reached: no social functions at all were to be held at the school. See *CD*, 17 April 1915; Hormel, *Down from Equality*, 12–17.

190. *CD*, 24 April, 15, 22, and 29 May 1915.

191. *CD*, 12 June 1915.

192. *CD*, 26 June 1915.

193. *CD*, 3 July, 23 October, 20 November 1915.

194. *CD*, 12 February 1916.

195. *CD*, 15 January 1916.

196. *CD*, 19 February 1916.

197. *CD*, 8 April 1916.

198. *CD*, 15 April 1916.

199. Ibid.; Gosnell, *Negro Politicians*, 172.

200. Hormel, *Down from Equality*, 19–20.

201. Wells-Barnett, *Crusade for Justice*, 349–50, 348. Carey had teamed up with Democratic Governor Dunne in the preceding year and may have temporarily been on the "outs" with Chicago Republicans. See Logsdon, "Rev. Archibald J. Carey," chap. 2. On DePriest's debt to Chicago women voters, see Hon. Oscar DePriest, "Chicago and Woman Suffrage," *Crisis* (August 1915): 179.

202. Gosnell, *Negro Politicians*, 49–51, 170–74; Wells-Barnett, *Crusade for Justice*, 350–51.

203. Wells-Barnett, *Crusade for Justice*, 393. Joseph Logsdon credits southern control of the AME church convention with blocking Carey's ambitions in 1916. Wells-Barnett was far from alone in resenting Carey's monopolization of patronage before the war. When Democratic Governor Dunne appointed Carey to chair the state's Emancipation Celebration committee in 1913, placing him in charge of a considerable number of jobs and largesse, a "shout of opposition" rose up from religious and secular leaders in Chicago. Logsdon, "Rev. Archibald J. Carey," 25–30, 56–60.

204. H. T. Gilbert, *Municipal Court of Chicago*, 102, 105. The *Defender* complained about the politics that squeezed Wells-Barnett out of the court. See "Probation Officers Denied the Race," *CD*, 9 December 1915.

205. Wells-Barnett, *Crusade for Justice*, 353.

206. Strickland, *Chicago Urban League*, 25–55; "War Stimulated YWCA," *CD*, 24 October 1925. On black women and war work, see E. L. Davis, *Story of the Illinois Federation*, 35, 63.

207. *CD*, 24 March, 28 April, 26 May 1917.

208. *CD*, 29 December 1917.

209. *CD*, 6 July 1918.

210. *CD*, 22 and 29 June 1918.

211. *CD*, 15, 23, and 29 July 1916.

212. *CD*, 9 June 1917; see Chapter 4.

213. *CD*, 15 and 29 September 1917; 3, 10, and 17 November 1917; 24 August 1918.

214. *CD*, 7 and 14 September 1918.

215. On Fannie Emmanuel and the Alphas, see *CD*, 25 November, 2 and 23 December 1916; 27 January, 3 and 10 February, 3 March 1917; 4 May 1918. The Alphas ceased to meet at the League and instead moved over to the Institutional Church.

216. C. L. Hamilton, "Women and the War"; and Farrar, "War Work Among Colored Women."

217. *CD*, 15 December 1917.

218. Ibid. See "Organization of Community Forces," [ca. 1918], War Camp Community Service document in IMG Papers.

219. *CD*, 26 January 1918.

220. E. L. Davis, *Story of the Illinois Federation*, 63.

221. *CD*, 16 February 1918.

222. *CD*, 23 February 1918.

223. *CD*, 2 March 1918.

224. A. F. Davis, *American Heroine*, chaps. 12 and 13.

225. At least one report stated that the "Ida B. Wells-Barnett Club of Chicago" raised the largest amount in Liberty Bonds among any woman's club in the state, $22,500 worth. See "Women's Club Notes." See also *CD*, 5 October 1918.

226. Du Bois very nearly accepted a commission in the Military Intelligence Bureau in an assignment monitoring "Negro Subversion" and was reported in the press to be busy with research for his next book on the Negro soldier in wartime. *CD*, 5 October 1918; Wells-Barnett, *Crusade for Justice*, 377; D. L. Lewis, *W. E. B. Du Bois*, 535–60.

227. S. R. Fox, *Guardian of Boston*, 222–28. Wells-Barnett produced a handbill at the League giving advice to African American men interested in finding labor in France at good wages. See "To The Young Men Who Want to Go to France," IBW Papers.

228. Bundy stated his appreciation to the "friendly spirits" of Illinois and Missouri for help in his defense in the press. *CD*, 17 August 1918.

229. *CD*, 2 March 1918.

230. *CD*, 13 and 20 April, 11 May 1918.

231. Wells-Barnett, *Crusade for Justice*, 337–42. Because of the "vicious" campaign against Campbell by prison personnel, Wells-Barnett felt Campbell deserved his freedom. See " 'Joe' Campbell Declares He Is Innocent," *CD*, 17 July 1915.

232. *CD*, 23 June 1917.

233. Wells-Barnett, *Crusade for Justice*, 341.

234. *CD*, 8, 22, and 29 June 1918. See also "Negro Notebooks," Notes on John Cloures, May–June 1918, Julius Rosenwald Papers.

235. Alfreda M. Duster interview, 6.

236. Strickland, *Chicago Urban League*, 25–55.

237. Wells-Barnett, *Crusade for Justice*, 330.

238. Ibid., 333, 372.

239. Strickland, *Chicago Urban League*, 56–62. Charles Johnson served as associate executive secretary of the Chicago Race Commission, and several Urban Leaguers and Park graduate students worked on the staff. Chicago Commission on Race Relations, *The Negro in Chicago*, 652–55.

240. Wells-Barnett, *Crusade for Justice*, 372.

241. E. K. Jones, "Reconstruction Program for the Negro."

242. Wells-Barnett, *Crusade for Justice*, 333.

243. Quoted in Lasch-Quinn, *Black Neighbors*, 50–51.

244. Philpott, *The Slum and the Ghetto*, chaps. 13 and 14.

245. Ida B. Wells-Barnett to My Dear Folks, 30 October 1920, IBW Papers.

Chapter Six

1. "Playing Their Parts Well in Upbuilding," *CD*, 3 May 1930. Elizabeth Lindsay Davis was an extremely popular and influential club woman. A native of Peoria and a high school graduate with a lifelong love of learning, she is perhaps best remembered through her published histories of the club movement, *Lifting as They Climb* (1933) and *The Story of the Illinois Federation of Colored Women's Clubs* (1922). Married to William H. Davis in 1885, she was a long-standing member and Sabbath School teacher at St. Mark's Methodist Episcopal Church as well as a charter member of both the NACW in 1896 and the Illinois Federation in 1899. Though she joined and led many service, charity, and study clubs, Davis made her principal mark in Chicago as president of the local Phillis Wheatley Club and Home, founded in 1896, where she presided for more than thirty years. She and her husband were childless, but Davis was known as an "intense lover of all girls," and, wrote one admirer, "hundreds claim her as their adopted 'mother.'" Nettie George Speedy, "My Scrapbook of Doers: We Offer Our Sincere Thanks for Knowing and Having a Friend like Elizabeth Lindsay Davis," *CD*, 28 November 1925.

2. Terborg-Penn, "Discontented Black Feminists"; Higginbotham, "In Politics to Stay"; and Higginbotham, "Club Women and Electoral Politics." See also Dumenil, *A Modern Temper*; Cott, *Grounding of Modern Feminism*; D. M. Brown, *Setting a Course*; Kristi Anderson, *After Suffrage*.

3. The candidates were Mrs. Ida B. Wells-Barnett for state senate; attorney Georgia Jones-Ellis and Mrs. Mary C. Clark for state legislature; and Mrs. Eola Richardson and Elizabeth Russell for precinct committeewomen in Evanston. "Irene M. Gaines Again Heads Republican Women," *CD*, 26 April 1930. In 1921, a Mrs. Lulu Sims filed for the alderman's race in the Fourteenth Ward on the West Side. *Chicago Whip*, 5 February 1921.

4. Gilmore, *Gender and Jim Crow*.

5. *CD*, 8 May, 26 November 1927.

6. The 1920s retained the connection between "female justice" and "community justice," as outlined by Wanda Hendricks, but shifted the emphasis to women's agency with the vote and elective office. See Hendricks, *Gender, Race, and Politics in the Midwest*, xvii. See also D. G. White, *Too Heavy a Load*, 120. I agree with White that the eclipse of the NACW eroded the assumption that African American progress could be measured or led by the progress of black women. But in Chicago, where black men never "lost" the vote as they did in the South, men's

and women's public culture, institutions, and networks grew up together in the nineteenth century and coexisted in the twentieth. For Wells-Barnett, woman suffrage offered the possibility of marshaling them together in the community's interest.

7. Cott, *Grounding of Modern Feminism*, 85–114. See also A. F. Scott, *Natural Allies*, chap. 7.

8. *CD*, 31 October 1925.

9. A typical list from 1921 contained 16 clubs in the *Defender's* weekly club reporting (see 22 October). A listing from 14 February 1925 noted 52 clubs; from 21 January 1928, 82 clubs; and 1 February 1930, 102 clubs. Knupfer identifies over 200 clubs among mostly black women at the turn of the century. Knupfer, *Toward a Tenderer Humanity and a Nobler Womanhood*, appendix.

10. Speedy, "My Scrapbook of Doers," *CD*, 28 November 1925.

11. Bates, "The Brotherhood"; and Chateauvert, *Marching Together*. See also Cronon, *Black Moses*; and Strickland, *Chicago Urban League*. The Cook County Bar Association also had a very active Ladies' Auxiliary in which Wells-Barnett participated. See *CD*, 10 November 1928.

12. Wells-Barnett, *Crusade for Justice*, 415.

13. "Ida B. Wells: A Passion for Justice," a film by William Greaves, aired on *The American Experience*, December 1989; T. Holt, "Lonely Warrior"; McMurry, *To Keep the Waters Troubled*, 331–39; Townes, *Womanist Justice, Womanist Hope*, 174–212; Thompson, *Ida B. Wells-Barnett*. Paula Giddings, in *When and Where I Enter*, 180–81, stresses the continuity of Wells-Barnett's activism during the twenties. See also Hine and Thompson, *Shining Thread of Hope*, 213–39.

14. Wells-Barnett, *Crusade for Justice*, 414.

15. D. G. White, *Too Heavy a Burden*, 130–32.

16. Terborg-Penn, "Discontented Black Feminists"; and Higginbotham, "In Politics to Stay" and "Club Women and Electoral Politics."

17. L. Gordon, "Black and White Visions of Welfare"; Goodwin, *Gender and the Politics of Welfare Reform*; Ladd-Taylor, "Toward Defining Maternalism in U.S. History"; P. Jackson, "Black Charity in Progressive Era Chicago"; Diner, "Chicago Social Workers and Blacks in the Progressive Era"; Lide, "National Conference on Social Welfare and the Black Historical Perspective"; Kusmer, "Functions of Organized Charity in the Progressive Era." On the later period, see Mink, *Wages of Motherhood*; Sullivan, *Days of Hope*; B. J. Ross, "Mary McLeod Bethune."

18. Boris, "Power of Motherhood," 215, 232.

19. Gosnell, *Negro Politicians*; Lisio, *Hoover, Blacks, and Lily-Whites*; Gurin, Hatchett, and Jackson, *Hope and Independence*; Pinderhughes, *Race and Ethnicity in Chicago Politics*.

20. Giddings, *When and Where I Enter*, 171–215; D. G. White, *Too Heavy a Load*, chap. 4.

21. E. L. Davis, *Story of the Illinois Federation*, 4.

22. Shaw, *What a Woman Ought to Be and to Do*, 164–210.

23. NACW, *Minutes of the Biennial* (n.p., 1922), 22, copy in NACW Papers.

24. Elizabeth Lindsay Davis to Sallie Stewart, 22 December 1930, NACW Papers.

25. "Atty. Georgia Ellis Honored at Banquet," *CD*, 9 November 1929; "Doing Their Work Well in Upbuilding," *CD*, 3 May 1930. Jones-Ellis was a Deneen

appointee to the Municipal Court in 1925; see Gosnell, *Negro Politicians*, 203–4. Black women also worked as census enumerators; see *CD*, 24 January 1920.

26. *CD*, 11 May 1929.

27. Collins, "Shifting the Center."

28. Higginbotham, "In Politics to Stay"; Gustafson, "Partisan Women in the Progressive Era"; Gustafson, "Partisan Women," chaps. 1, 2, 5. Jane Addams tried to nudge white women into the political fray to protect institutions like the juvenile court. See Addams, "Pragmatism in Politics." On white women's nonpartisanship in the early twentieth century, see DuBois, *Harriot Stanton Blatch*, 122–26; and R. Edwards, *Angels in the Machinery*, 150–66. On white women and politics generally in Illinois, see Tax, *Rising of the Women*, pt. 2; and Beuchler, *Transformation of the Woman Suffrage Movement*. On reform and white women's relationship to ideas and politics, see Muncy, *Creating a Female Dominion in American Reform*; Lasch-Quinn, *Black Neighbors*; Goodwin, *Gender and the Politics of Welfare Reform*, chap. 3.

29. *CD*, 6 July 1929.

30. NACW, *Minutes of the Biennial* (n.p., 1920), 40, copy in NACW Papers.

31. Schechter, " 'All the Intensity of My Nature' "; P. Baker, "Domestication of Politics," 620–47. See also Epstein, *Politics of Domesticity*; and Ginzberg, *Women and the Work of Benevolence*.

32. E. L. Davis, *Story of the Illinois Federation*, 4. See also Fannie Barrier Williams, "Home Life Improved," *CD*, 10 October 1914.

33. Ida B. Wells-Barnett Diary, ca. 19 May 1930, IBW Papers.

34. *CD*, 19 April 1924.

35. Ottley, *Lonely Warrior*, 212–18; Gaines, *Uplifting the Race*, 234–60; Moses, *Golden Age of Black Nationalism*, chaps. 11 and 12; Meier, *Negro Thought in America*, chap. 13.

36. "Jim Crow Signs," *CD*, 17 October 1925; "Get Rid of Jim Crow Jails," *CD*, 12 March 1927; "Blot Out Segregation," *CD*, 19 March 1927. See related themes in *CD*, 7 and 14 August 1926.

37. "Political Pot," *CD*, 7 February 1920.

38. *CD*, 12 February 1927. See also Abbott, "We Must Cease Segregating Ourselves," *CD*, 15 January 1927.

39. *CD*, 28 April 1928.

40. *CD*, 12 May 1917. Many women actively embraced this role, especially as moral arbiter. A "Women's Auxiliary Union" drew up resolutions concerning those individuals who put themselves and the community at risk by breaking prohibition and thereby drawing the fire of untrustworthy police. The women felt that such an individual was "not worthy of a place among good citizens" and, for good measure, added an admonition to clergy to make sure that young parishioners were in church and not at the movies on Sunday nights. See *CD*, 10 April 1920.

41. Throughout the twenties, the *Defender* advocated strong separation between church work and official politics. Most arguments assumed an economics of scarcity, the idea that churches drained capital rather than created jobs and resources. See *Defender* articles "Church losing influence. . . . Problems Costly," 9 October 1926; "Is the Race Overchurched?" 25 June 1927; and Editorial, "Time to Call a Halt to Church Buying," 10 May 1930. Plenty of letters to the editor came in on this topic. Most people supported the churches. See "Put Reli-

gion First," 27 November 1927; "Too Much Religion," 12 March 1927; "Buying Churches," 19 March 1927; "Not Too Many Churches," 26 March 1927; "The solution of the race problem," 4 June 1927; "Pulpit Politics," 8 May 1927; "Religion vs. Politics," 23 February 1929.

The paper offered many different opinions about religion in this period. For example, the *Defender* envisioned the uniting of all "Race Methodists" by combining the AME, CME, and AME Zion churches. See "Widen Scope of AME Church," *CD*, 15 May 1920. Editors also condemned what they termed "primitive forms of religious conduct," like mass public baptisms. See "Sunday Circus in Lake Michigan," *CD*, 26 July 1924. The *Defender* also criticized selfishness or corruption among clergy, as in a searing cartoon portraying the "Anything for a Dollar Minister," *CD*, 12 April 1924. For a clergyman's critical view of the church's intellectual lag in modern times, see Rev. Dr. Duncan C. Milner's articles in the *Defender*, "Preachers and Churches," 16 August 1924; "The Church and Young Men," 30 August 1924; and "Church Services," 13 September 1924.

Abbott also took cues from secular-minded thinkers like Du Bois and Kelly Miller, who shared a modernizing, high cultural perspective in the twenties. In 1926, he approvingly quoted Du Bois: "Members of the Race are not particularly religious and Race churches are in the main great social institutions where you may hear religious phrases but won't be particularly bothered by religion. . . . [O]ur most significant advance will be a social and economic progress, rather than one taking its rise in the church," *CD*, 27 February 1926. See also Kelly Miller, "The Preacher in Politics," *CD*, 14 May 1927. The paper advocated a moral and educational role for the church, epitomized by the *Defender*'s invention of "Race Relations Sunday." In observance of Lincoln's birthday, clergy were encouraged to engage in pulpit exchanges and to sponsor religious fellowship across the color line. See George E. Haynes, "The Church as Avenue of Racial Peace," 10 February 1923; "Church Relations," 3 March 1923; "Real Religion," 23 February 1924. For reports on Race Relations Sunday, see *CD* articles on 14 February 1925; 20 February 1926; 12 February 1927; and 11 February 1928.

42. *CD*, 15 April 1922.

43. *CD*, 19 April 1924.

44. "Hungry, Unemployed Men Sing Praises in Church," 18 June 1921; "Mother's Day," 7 May 1921; "The Divine Comfort That Mothers Give," 20 May 1922; "Mother's Day," 10 May 1924, all in *CD*. Mother's Day became an official holiday in 1914. See Rice, *Mother's Day*.

45. Competition for best bobbed hair was a regular feature of *Defender* coverage in 1922 and 1923. See "Hair Galore!" 9 December 1922; "In the Wake of Clippers," 16 December 1922; "More Hair," 23 December 1922; and "Oodles of Hair," 13 January 23. Beauty contests sometimes included men and babies: "Prettiest Girl Contest," 23 May 1925; "Miss Defender Contest," 11 August 1928; and "Most Handsome Man Contest," 22 June 1929. On images of "mammy" and opposition to the proposed Mammy Memorial Institute, see "Mammy Statue Not Race Issue Say Dixieites," 24 February, 21 April, 14 July 1923. The first Miss America pageant took place in 1920 at Atlantic City, New Jersey. See Banner, *Women in Modern America*, 163.

46. "Women Would Break Vice," *CD*, 25 August 1928; "Policewoman," *CD*, 24 January 1920; "Must Have More Race Policewomen on Force," *CD*, 29 Octo-

ber 1927; "Use Pulpits to Wipe Out Segregation," *CD*, 5 November 1927; "Reason for Policewomen," *CD*, 21 April 1928.

47. Spratt, "To Be Separate or One."

48. *CD*, 28 February 1920.

49. *CD*, 29 April 1922.

50. "YWCA Gives Working Facts," *CD*, 29 December 1928.

51. "No Color Line at Girls' Party," *CD*, 29 September 1928; Weisenfeld, *African American Women and Christian Activism*, 111, 174. Weisenfeld notes that in New York, by contrast to Chicago, the African American YWCA proudly announced its racial identification and mission during fundraising campaigns. Other Chicago programs included mothers' study groups, "the result of a request from the church women's race relations committee of the Chicago Church Federation and the ministers' wives group of the YWCA who expressed a desire for such a training class in parent education." *CD*, 3 November 1928. The Chicago branch's executive secretary, Mrs. Lulu E. Lawson, was a Howard University graduate who during World War I served as a field worker with the American Red Cross, responsible for housing for soldiers. In 1929, she left the YWCA for a new appointment as social worker for the Michigan Boulevard Garden Apartments, a housing project financed by Julius Rosenwald, where she supervised a nursery school and helped with tenant selection. "Playing Their Parts Well in Upbuilding," *CD*, 3 May 1930.

52. For example, the Women's Trade Union League held a forum on the eight-hour law and "the group's responsibility to it." *CD*, 1 October 1927. See also "Girls in 'Y. W.' Drive Tell of Their Hardships," *CD*, 28 May 1921; "Blasting Prejudice from Path of Women Workers," *CD*, 13 May 1922; "How YWCA Serves Chicago Girls" and "YW Girls Ask Aid of Chicagoans," *CD*, 12 May 1923.

53. Wells-Barnett was on hand for the YWCA's opening and Christmas week events in 1920 but was scarcely visible otherwise, according to press coverage. See *CD*, 10 January 1920; Wells-Barnett Diary, 24 January 1930, IBW Papers.

54. *CD*, 21 January 1928; Bates, "The Brotherhood," 10.

55. Kristie Miller, *Ruth Hanna McCormick*, 154; "Complete Plans for Woman's World's Fair," *CD*, 17 April 1926; "Open World's Fair with a Pageant," *CD*, 24 April 1926. The Woman's World's Fair included participation from the General Federation of Women's Clubs, the Illinois Federation of Colored Women's Clubs, and the National Council of Jewish Women. See "Woman's World's Fair Planned in Chicago," *CD*, 19 March 1927; "Club Women Stage Pageant at Coliseum," *CD*, 21 May 1927; "Women of all Nations in Booths at Big World's Fair," *CD*, 28 May 1927; "Close Woman's World's Fair," *CD*, 26 May 1928.

56. For two eloquent rebuttals to the stifling charge of "self segregation," see "Why Not Correct These Evils?" George F. McCray to the Editor, 18 May 1929; and "For Separate Beaches," Mrs. L. R. F. to the Editor, 10 August 1929, both in *CD*.

57. "Shall Our Leadership Be Destroyed?" *CD*, 20 October 1928.

58. "Official Count May Put Judge George in the Court," *CD*, 26 April 1930.

59. Ida B. Wells-Barnett, "Club Woman Tells of Rotten Conditions in Chicago's Public Schools," *CD*, 1 March 1930; "Jam Court to Hear School Girl's Case," *CD*, 15 March 1930. Two months later, Wells-Barnett noted in her diary that Frances Jordan's case dragged on a bit: "May 19th—the Jordan girl was again

in Juvenile Court but case was continued." Wells-Barnett Diary, 19 May 1930, IBW Papers.

60. Breckinridge, *Delinquent Child and the Home*, 217. See also Chicago Commission on Race Relations, *The Negro in Chicago*, 18; pamphlet by the Illinois Youth Commission, *Illinois State Training School for Girls, Geneva, Illinois*; "Governor to Investigate State School," *CD*, 7 April 1928; "Club Women Take Facts to Governor," *CD*, 31 March 1928. The segregated facilities held 104 girls in two cottages originally designed for 32. See also Freedman, *Their Sisters' Keepers*, 139–41, 148.

61. Barnett defended three black teenagers in trouble during 1920. "Boys Freed on Murder Charge," *CD*, 17 January 1920. He also defended the family of 29-year-old George Brooks, an Illinois Steel Works employee and father of five, who was shot at point-blank range and killed by a white police officer in 1927. "Officer to Face Court in Shooting," *CD*, 22 October 1927. Wells-Barnett lobbied officials on behalf of a mentally deficient young black man found guilty of murdering a white woman, saving him from the death penalty. "Shanks Case Again in Supreme Court, Springfield," *CD*, 6 April 1929; and "Shanks, Two Others Miss Execution," *CD*, 13 April 1929.

62. "Citizens Fire First Gun at Phillips Junior High," *CD*, 23 May 1925.

63. Gosnell, *Negro Politicians*, 59, 245, 270; "Police Run Riot in South Side Raids," *CD*, 5 March 1927; and "Council Urged to Halt Terrorism in South Side Wards," *CD*, 12 March 1927.

64. Judge Helander of the Morals Court "discharged a number of cases, criticizing the police officers for making arrests without sufficient evidence against the defendants," 90 percent of whom were "colored." "South Side Hit Hardest in Raids, Judge Admits," *CD*, 31 October 1925. See also "West Side Goes Wild Again," *CD*, 18 September 1926.

65. The *Defender* noted the need for arrest warrants and checks on police as well as for a new system of "protection for women who are not prostitutes when they are arrested" in order to avoid the mandatory internal examinations and general rough treatment prostitutes received. "Citizens Meet With Judge to Discuss Moral Issues," *CD*, 24 November 1928.

66. *CD*, 5 June 1920. See "President's Annual Report," 1 January 1927, by Anderson to the Friendly Big Sisters, copy in IMG Papers. For Anderson's "Legal Hints to Women" column, see weekly editions of the *Chicago Whip*, October 1920–November 1921.

67. *CD*, 1 September 1923; "Big Sisters Open Home for Problem Girls," *CD*, 10 and 17 October 1925. The home was still struggling with mortgage payments in late 1927; *CD*, 29 October 1927. White women also worked to extend control over the care of women in the penal system. Spearheaded by Mary McDowell, the League of Women Voters undertook a major project in the mid-1920s, the creation of a "Woman's Detention Home" to replace the old Moral's Court downtown. They formed a committee, wrote the legislation, raised part of the funds, and in 1931 a state-run "Woman's Reformatory" was opened at Dexter, Illinois. Irene Goins was a long-standing member of the LOWV, but the status of black women in the Dwight project is unclear from scattered records. See report by Edith Rockwood, "Court Visiting, Woman's Detention Home, Woman's Reformatory" (1926); Mary McDowell et al., circular letter from "Joint Committee for the Care and Training of Women Offenders" (20 June 1925); "By-Laws of

Illinois Committee for a State Reformatory for Women" (March 1926); and Charlotte S. Butler, "The Woman Recidivist in Illinois," *The Clubwoman* (March 1925); all clippings in the Illinois League of Women Voters Papers.

68. "Club Women Take Facts to the Governor," *CD*, 31 March 1928.

69. "Governor to Investigate State School," *CD*, 7 April 1928.

70. Ibid.

71. I have found no information on Mrs. Mercer, but the career of her colleague Mrs. Grace Wilson is instructive. Wilson served as "house mother" at the Geneva State Training School for Girls, resigning in 1918 to accept a position as policewoman for the City of Chicago. Active as an investigator for the Union Charity Club and Wells-Barnett's Negro Fellowship League, Wilson also received training at the Chicago School of Civics and Philanthropy. Her high score on the civil service exam earned her a place on the force; she had been the first "woman of the Race" to pass the civil service exam for the initial job at Geneva. In 1920, Wilson was asked to return to Geneva to "organize the cottages for girls." Wilson also taught Sunday school at the Institutional Church and was active in the Improved Benevolent Protective Order of Elks of the World (IBPOEW). "A Scrapbook for Women in Public Life: Mrs. Grace Wilson of Police Force Scores," *CD*, 21 September 1929; "Playing Their Parts Well in Upbuilding," *CD*, 3 May 1930.

72. For evidence of their cordiality, see Ida B. Wells-Barnett, "Thanks to the Editor," *CD*, 5 March 1927. Ottley, *Lonely Warrior*, 241–42, makes a point of their parting of ways. *Crusade for Justice* describes only Abbott and Wells-Barnett's shared opposition to segregation in a group called the American Citizenship Association, a postwar patriotic organization. Wells-Barnett, *Crusade for Justice*, 417–18. See also Hormel, *Down from Equality*, chap. 1.

73. Wells-Barnett was extremely proud of institutions like the Eighth Illinois Regiment and Provident Hospital. See her letter to the editor, *CD*, 17 October 1914.

74. Wells-Barnett organized the Women's Forum, a women's group that did weekly programming at the Community Center. See *Chicago Whip*, 12, 19, and 26 November, 3 December 1921; Wells-Barnett, *Crusade for Justice*, xxx. Of Metropolitan Community Church, the *Defender* noted: "In 1920 [Cook] resigned from the AME connection and founded the People's Church movement, which has blossomed forth as the real religion of tomorrow. This church has for its chief motivating power 'Welcome for all,' removing the emphasis from sects and placing it on Christianity." "W. D. Cook Laid to Rest," *CD*, 12 July 1930.

75. *CD*, 9 and 16 July 1921.

76. "Equal Rights League Urges Racial Uplift," 6 August 1921; "Equal Rights League Opens War on Klan," 3 September 1921; and "National Equal Rights League is Tottering," 24 September 1921, all in *CD*, the first two probably written by Wells-Barnett. See also Wells-Barnett, *Crusade for Justice*, 375–80.

77. "Women Get in Fight Against Hospital Evil," *CD*, 5 August 1922.

78. "Women to Start Fort Dearborn Hospital Drive," 13 August 1921; "Thomas Carey to Help Fort Dearborn Plan," 27 August 1921; "Fort Dearborn Hospital Now a City Institution," 22 October 1921; "Fort Dearborn Hospital in Receivership," 25 February 1922, all in *CD*. See also "Women's Auxiliary Meets," *Chicago Whip*, 17 December 1921; and "Hospital Tangle in New Twist," *Chicago Whip*, 4 March 1922.

79. In addition to promoting the Douglass Memorial and heading up the Anti-Lynching Crusaders, NACW leader Mary Talbert "represented the Race women of America" at the International Council of Women in Norway in 1920. "Mary Talbert Wins Spingarn Medal," *CD*, 17 June 1922. See also "Mary Burnett Talbert," in H. Q. Brown, *Homespun Heroines*, 217–19.

80. "Women's Club at Quinn," 29 July 1922; "Leaves for Richmond," 5 August 1922; "Mrs. Barnett Returns," 9 September 1922, all in *CD*. I have not been able to locate copies of the *Woman's Forum*.

81. "Mrs. Ida B. Wells-Barnett Opens Grace Lyceum Season," 23 September 1922; 11 November 1922; 5 May 1923; 28 February 1925, all in *CD*.

82. "Women's Clubs to Meet," 7 June 1924; "Women Arrive for Great Convention," 26 July 1924, both in *CD*.

83. "Motor to East St. Louis" and "Women Close Big Club Meet in St. Louis," *CD*, 1 September 1923.

84. Alfreda Duster indicated that the Barnetts moved to an apartment on East Garfield Street in 1925, since by then most of the children were grown and married. She also refers to a fire in the Barnett home that may have figured in the decision to move. See Wells-Barnett, *Crusade for Justice*, xxx, xxvii.

85. Hallie Q. Brown, "Our Woman's Crusade," *National Notes* (December 1924): 7; E. L. Davis, *Lifting As They Climb*, 67–69; *Minutes of the Fourteenth Biennial Convention of the National Association of Colored Women* (n.p., 1924), copy in NACW Papers.

86. Nettie George Speedy, "Mrs. Mary Bethune of Florida Elected Next National President," *CD*, 9 August 1924.

87. Circular letter by Elizabeth Lindsay Davis, "Reasons Why Illinois Wants the Presidency of the National Association of Colored Women . . ." [ca. 1931], copy in NACW Papers.

88. Higginbotham, "In Politics to Stay."

89. Quotation from *Chicago Daily News*, reprinted in *CD*, 16 August 1924.

90. "The Chicago Woman's Club," *CD*, 23 August 1924; "City Club Entertains Women's Federation," *CD*, 30 August 1924.

91. A. L. Jackson, "Women's Clubs," *CD*, 16 August 1924.

92. The founding clubs included the Ida B. Wells Woman's Club, the Phillis Wheatley Home, the Civic League, the Progressive Circle of King's Daughters, the Ideal Women's Club, the GOP Elephant Club, and the Julia Gaston Club. E. L. Davis, *Story of the Illinois Federation*, 2.

93. See *CD*, 5 March 1927; 16 and 23 February, 2 March, 10 August 1929. See also E. L. Davis, *Story of the Illinois Federation*, 26–28; and Chapter 5 of this study.

94. *CD*, 29 May, 24 July 1926.

95. See report in *CD*, 3 December 1927. The club's musicales often featured female performers; see *CD*, 13 April, 3 August 1929. The club also hosted a reception for the black performers from *Showboat* at the Barnett residence; see *CD*, 25 January 1930. The "Ida B. Wells Club 36th Anniversary" celebration reportedly featured "some of the best literary and musical talent in the city" as well as a commemoration of women's "contributions to the civic life of the city, state, and nation," *CD*, 5 October 1929. Club members shared their New Year's resolutions and quotations; *CD*, 28 December 1929.

96. Wells-Barnett installed officers of the DeSaible Club and gave a lecture on the black founder of Chicago. The club's object was to secure a monument in

DeSaible's honor. See *CD*, 20 April 1929; "Federation Women Visit S. Park National Bank," *CD*, 14 September 1929; "Mrs. Ida Wells-Barnett Addresses Girls Club," *CD*, 15 February 1930.

97. *CD*, 26 January 1929.

98. E. L. Davis, *Story of the Illinois Federation*, 28.

99. "Short History of the IQSC," *CD*, 6 July 1929.

100. *CD*, 16 March 1929.

101. "Let's Get Acquainted," *CD*, 7 February 1925. The following week Speedy's column expanded to include men. See "Let's Get Acquainted," *CD*, 14 February 1925. "The appeal this week extends to the men," stated Speedy. "We want to know each other."

102. "Hark, Attention! Women and Girls," *CD*, 3 December 1927; and 17 March 1928.

103. Lillian I. Browder, "Ward and Precinct Work in Chicago," *National Notes* (December 1924): 14.

104. *CD*, 8 January 1927, 27 April 1929.

105. "City Mourns Death of Mrs. Irene Goins," *CD*, 16 March 1929.

106. "Women's Political Club Meets," *CD*, 8 January 1927. Illinois League of Women Voters literature from 1922 listed Goins as a member of the board of directors. The Illinois LOWV's "Pledge for Conscientious Citizens" ended with a decidedly Christian appeal for women to help create "the Kingdom of Heaven on earth." See "Illinois League of Women Voters" pamphlet in IMG Papers.

107. "Club Leaders Give Platform in Convention: Send Resolutions on Vital Issues," *CD*, 6 July 1929. See also *CD*, 15 and 29 June 1929.

108. "Mrs. M'Cormick Is Guest at Luncheon," *CD*, 21 November 1925. See also "Noted Woman Speaker at Convention," *CD*, 3 December 1927.

109. "Mrs. M'Cormick Is Guest at Luncheon," *CD*, 21 November 1925.

110. Kristie Miller, *Ruth Hanna McCormick*, chaps. 1, 5, 6.

111. *CD*, 3 December 1927.

112. Kristie Miller, *Ruth Hanna McCormick*, 159, 224–29. McCormick spent just over a quarter of a million dollars in her race (not the first to do so), and the investigation was a purely political if not merely partisan attack, which ended up casting aspersions on the already disliked Gerald Nye of South Dakota.

113. *CD*, 7 April 1928. In addition to supporting Dyer, Medill McCormick's record was notable for his defense of a black political appointee in New Orleans against a politically inspired ouster by southern Democrats, thus demonstrating his willingness to defend black access to political power and patronage. He was on record, however, for endorsing the Progressive Party as a "white man's party." Quoted in Gustafson, "Partisan Women," 213.

114. "Mrs. M'Cormick Is Guest at Luncheon," *CD*, 21 November 1925.

115. *CD*, 9 and 16 October 1926.

116. "Voters Should Protest Senate Disfranchisement of Illinois," *CD*, 5 February 1927. Smith accepted campaign money from public utilities while sitting on the Illinois Commerce Commission. Gosnell, *Negro Politicians*, 159, 182. Wells-Barnett also praised the NAACP and Senator Charles Deneen, the Barnett's patron, for helping to defeat the appointment of Judge Parker of North Carolina to the Supreme Court. See "Judge Parker's Defeat," *CD*, 10 May 1930.

117. See "City Nurses Return from Flood Area," 28 May 1927; "Compare Notes on Mississippi Flood," 2 July 1927; Ida B. Wells-Barnett, "South Backs

Down After Probe Looms," 25 June 1927; Ida B. Wells-Barnett, "Flood Report Found Untrue to Conditions," 9 July 1927; Ida B. Wells-Barnett, "Flood Refugees Are Held as Slaves in Mississippi Camp," 16 July 1927, all in *CD*. See also Barry, *Rising Tide*, 291–336.

118. Percy, *Lanterns on the Levee*, chap. 20, esp. 263–64; "The Week," *CD*, 23 July 1927.

119. "Mrs. Bethune Named Among Fifty Leaders," *CD*, 20 September 1930.

120. "Mary Church Terrell Gets Signal Honor," *CD*, 25 February 1928.

121. *CD*, 31 July 1926, 12 November 1927; Gosnell, *Negro Politicians*, 153–62.

122. "Bishop Carey Given Civil Service Post," 16 April 1927; and "Friends Do Honor to Archibald J. Carey," 2 July 1927, both in *CD*.

123. Nettie George Speedy, "Chicago Pays Tribute to Robert S. Abbott," *CD*, 10 December 1927, and other articles in same issue.

124. "Plan Testimonial Dinner," 16 April 1927; "Plan Testimonial Dinner to Honor Mrs. Ida B. Wells-Barnett," 23 April 1927; "To Be Honored," 30 April 1927; "Pay Tribute to Mrs. Ida Wells-Barnett in Testimonial Dinner," 8 May 1927, all in *CD*.

125. Nettie George Speedy, "Two Hundred Chicagoans Honor Two Distinguished Residents," *CD*, 14 May 1927.

126. *CD*, 26 November 1927.

127. *CD*, 10 December 1927.

128. *CD*, 3 May 1930; 1 June 1929. See also NACW, *Minutes of the Biennial* (1924), 4, copy in NACW Papers.

129. "Club Notes," 2 and 9 February; 23 March 1929, *CD*.

130. See "National Organizer," *CD*, 15 September 1928, which reported: "Mrs. Ida B. Wells-Barnett has been appointed national organizer for Illinois for women. Mrs. Barnett is a noted lecturer, educator, and club woman." Irene McCoy Gaines was appointed chairman for Illinois's first congressional district's campaign for Hoover, arguably a more critically situated post within the state party organization. See "Women Perfect Campaign Drive," untitled clipping dated 19 September 1928, in IMG Papers. See also Ida B. Wells-Barnett to Illinois Negro Women Voters, 11 September 1928, in Claude A. Barnett Papers, Chicago Historical Society, Chicago, Ill.

131. It is impossible to substantiate Wells-Barnett's claims on a statewide basis, since counties were neither required to keep registration rolls nor to file them with the state. However, her contention does have some basis, given available evidence for trends in Chicago. Over the course of the 1920s, rates of women's voter registration improved in the general population as well as in the heavily African American second ward (see Table 1).

132. Ida B. Wells-Barnett to Claude A. Barnett, 19 and 21 October 1928; "Why I Am for Hoover" (pamphlet), September 1928, Claude A. Barnett Papers, Chicago Historical Society.

133. Elizabeth Lindsay Davis to My Dear Prez [Sallie Stewart], 10 April 1930, NACW Papers.

134. *CD*, 1 June 1929.

135. "Distinctive Women To Be in Featured Processional," *CD*, 6 April 1929; "Women of All Races Honored at University of Chicago," *CD*, 13 April 1929. Chicago black women in attendance included Wells-Barnett, Elizabeth

Table 1. Voter Registration in Chicago by Sex, 1914–1929

A. Registered Voters in Chicago

Year	Women	Men	Total	Female:Male Ratio
1914	217,614	455,283	672,897	1:2.0
1915	282,291	486,815	769,106	1:1.7
1919	236,102	438,907	675,009	1:2.0
1923	313,381	539,063	852,444	1:1.7
1927	440,919	705,489	1,146,408	1:1.6
1929	583,735	756,994	1,340,729	1:1.3
% change				+65%

B. Registered Voters in Second Ward of Chicago

Year	Women	Men	Total	Female:Male Ratio
1914	7,290	16,327	23,617	1:2.3
1915	10,099	18,282	28,381	1:1.8
1919	8,233	15,265	23,498	1:1.8
1923	7,458	13,880	21,338	1:2.0
1927	13,262	20,575	33,837	1:1.6
1929	9,351	13,170	23,471	1:1.4
% change				+60%

Sources: *The Chicago Daily News Almanac and Year-Book* (Chicago: Chicago Daily News Company, 1914–1930): *1914* yearbook (published 1915), 632; *1915* (1916), 560, 584; *1919* (1920), 845; *1923* (1924), 728; *1927* (1928), 760; *1929* (1930), 738.

Lindsay Davis, LuLu Lawson, settlement worker Ada McKinley, and pianist Hazel Harrison.

136. *CD*, 21 September 1929.

137. Quoted in Kristie Miller, *Ruth Hanna McCormick*, 203; "Victory Seen for Mrs. Ruth H. M'Cormick," *CD*, 7 April 1928.

138. Major R. R. Jackson to Mrs. Ruth Hanna McCormick, 18 September 1929; Louis B. Anderson to Mrs. Ruth Hanna McCormick, 20 September 1929; Mary Church Terrell to Hon. Oscar DePriest, 26 February 1930, all in MCT-LOC. "Mrs. Terrell Here to Head Senate Drive," *CD*, 28 September 1929.

139. Meyers tried to backpedal and credit another local official, Arthur C. Lueder, for her husband's job. Terrell in turn published Ruth Hanna McCormick's letters in the *Defender* to confirm her original view. See "Mrs. McCormick Has Record of Fairness," 12 October 1929; "Mrs. Meyers Answers Mary Church Terrell," 19 October 1929; "Refutes Statement of Mrs. Susie Meyers," 26 October 1929, all in *CD*.

140. Elizabeth Lindsay Davis to Sallie Stewart, 1 November 1929. See also

Davis to Stewart, 24 November, 24 December 1929; 13 January 1930, all in NACW Papers.

141. "Women Open War on Mrs. Ruth McCormick," *CD*, 19 October 1929. Wells-Barnett also complained that members of McCormick's staff were unskilled sycophants instead of knowledgeable political workers and faithful Republicans. "Mrs. McCormick Has Record of Fairness," "Women Voters Oust Defender Reporter," and "Apology Demanded from Mrs. Barnett," all in *CD*, 12 October 1929.

142. There is some indication that Terrell was not performing to the satisfaction of McCormick's Washington office. See LeRoy M. Hardin to Mrs. Mary Church Terrell, 4 February 1930; and Mary Church Terrell to Mr. James Snyder, 5 February 1930, both in MCT-LOC. See also copies of reports filed by Irene McCoy Gaines in her position as "Chairman [of] State Work Among Colored Women" for McCormick, dated 16 and 30 November 1929, in IMG Papers. Gaines also noted that black women doing campaign work pressed her for "definite instructions re compensation for services rendered." "Report of Irene M. Gaines," 22 March 1930, IMG Papers.

143. Terrell, *Colored Woman in a White World*, 356.

144. "Women's Republican League First Dinner" and "Attny. Georgia Ellis Honored at Banquet," *CD*, 9 November 1929; "Hat in Ring," *CD*, 16 November 1929.

145. "Women Voters Oust Defender Reporter," *CD*, 12 October 1929.

146. "Mrs. Barnett Runs for State Senator," *CD*, 8 March 1930. Wells-Barnett perhaps had a double incentive, since McCormick was running against Charles Deneen in the primary. Further complicating matters, Oscar DePriest came out for McCormick, since she had interceded in his behalf when political shenanigans almost prevented his seating in Congress in 1928. See Gosnell, *Negro Politicians*, 44–45, 183–84.

147. Gosnell, *Negro Politicians*, 68–70, 202–3.

148. The victor was Lottie Holman O'Neill (1878–1967), a career politician who was first elected to the legislature in 1922. A staunchly conservative white Republican, she supported the death penalty for convicted rapists only and later allied herself with Senator Joseph McCarthy during his charges of communism in the Eisenhower administration. Interestingly, O'Neill also accused Ruth McCormick of high-handedness in politics during her U.S. senate race. "Woman Politician Accuses Mrs. McCormick of Bossism," *CD*, 2 February 1929. See articles on her retirement in the *Chicago Tribune*, 8 January 1962, and the *Illinois American*, 8 January 1962; and her obituary in the *Chicago Tribune*, 18 February 1967, all in Chicago Historical Society vertical file on O'Neill.

149. *CD*, 5 April 1930.

150. Wells-Barnett Diary, 19 May 1930, IBW Papers.

151. *CD*, 29 March 1930.

152. *CD*, 5 April 1930.

153. "Mrs. Irene M. Gaines Again Heads Republican Women," *CD*, 26 April 1930.

154. Wells-Barnett Diary, ca. 19 May 1930, IBW Papers.

155. Editorial, *Chicago Competitor* 3 (January–February 1921): 23.

156. Wells-Barnett Dairy, 27 January 1930, IBW Papers.

157. Ibid., ca. 19 May 1930.

158. "Crane College Students in Near Riot over Girl's Article," *CD*, 2 November 1929; "Opinions Evenly Divided on Crane Student's Article," *CD*, 9 November 1929; "Final Letters Come in on Marian Burton," *CD*, 23 November 1929.

159. "Ape Woman on Way to U.S. from Africa," *CD*, 20 April 1929; and "Stop this Ape-Woman," letter to the editor from Rev. G. W. Taylor, *CD*, 4 May 1929.

160. "Mrs. George Presides for Committee," 26 July 1930; "From 'Ingagi' Himself," and "Urban League Women Hold Lawn Meet," 19 July 1930, both in *CD*.

161. "Are Our Women as Bad as This?" *CD*, 24 May 1930.

162. "Why Indeed" and "In Defense of Women," 7 June 1930; "This Ought to Make Mr. Wilson's Ears Burn," "They're OK With This War Veteran," "A Woman Speaks," "Not So Good," and "A Reason," 14 June 1930; "True in Some Cases," 28 June 1930; "Final Letter," 16 August 1930, all in *CD*.

163. "And Still They Come," *CD*, 26 July 1930.

164. "Womanhood," *CD*, 13 August 1921; *CD*, 24 June 1922.

165. "Achievement Week Celebration," *CD*, 10 October 1925. On Woman's Night during the Achievement Week celebration, Robert Abbott told a packed house: "Until the manhood of the Race arises as it should and asserts itself as it someday must we still look to you, women of the Race, to continue leading us on, to continue pointing the way to that great destiny that God has marked out for this Race in America!"

166. D. G. White, *Too Heavy A Load*, 110–41.

167. "The Weaker Sex," *CD*, 10 August 1929. The *Defender* supported equal pay for equal work, but ambivalence tagged alongside these positions. A debate over "married women and teaching" in 1927 marked the distance between Wells-Barnett's experience in Memphis, when African American women routinely taught school and were praised for so doing. *CD*, 18 June 1927. Such concerns only made sense, perhaps, in light of a program at Wendell Phillips High School called "Girls' Week." The week culminated in a successful day of role playing by female students, who filled every position of responsibility at the school from principal on down. *CD*, 27 March 1926. By decade's end, the *Defender* carried articles sounding the era's backlash against married women's wage work, reporting on sociological studies that proclaimed "old maids" the "ablest workers" and on scientific proof that women were too emotional to properly serve on juries. See "Says Old Maids Ablest Workers," *CD*, 1 May 1926; and "Women Not Best Jurors, Doctor Says," *CD*, 18 January 1930. Women's competence in traditionally male spheres, like the handling of guns, also attracted attention in the 1920s. See "Women Are Good Shots," *CD*, 25 November 1922; and "Women Win Rifle Meet," *CD*, 21 April 1923.

168. Frazier, "The American Negro's New Leaders," 59. On the elitist and patriarchal trends in civil rights leadership, see Reed, *Chicago NAACP*, chaps. 1–5.

Conclusion

1. "Well-Known Person Talks to DeSaibles," *CD*, 7 June 1930.

2. "E. H. Wright Is Dead," 9 August 1930; "Bury Attorney," 16 August 1930; "Carrie Lee Hamilton Dies," 14 June 1930; "George Cleveland Hall Dead," 21

June 1930; "W. D. Cook Laid to Rest," 12 July 1930; "City Mourns Death of Mrs. Irene Goins," 16 March 1929, all in *CD*.

3. "Ida B. Wells-Barnett, Noted Club Woman, Dies Suddenly" and "Mourn Bishop Carey," both in *CD*, 28 March 1931.

4. Elizabeth Lindsay Davis, "Ida B. Wells-Barnett," *National Notes* (May 1931): 17; Alfreda M. Duster quoted in "Afterword" by Dorothy Sterling, in DeCosta-Willis, *Memphis Diary of Ida B. Wells*, 199; "Dies Suddenly," *CD*, 28 March 1931.

5. The word among club women was that Talbert practically worked herself to death. See "The Cost of Leadership," *National Notes* (December 1923): 3

6. Herman K. Barnett to Dr. Herbert Aptheker, 8 April 1948, IBW Papers.

7. Alfreda M. Duster interview, 15, in Black Women Oral History Project Interviews, Schlesinger Library, Radcliffe Institute for Advanced Study, Harvard University, Cambridge, Mass.; Ida B. Wells-Barnett Diary, May 1930, IBW Papers.

8. Alfreda, as she put it, "continued the same line of things that [her mother] did" in her own outstanding career of community service in Chicago. She worked professionally in juvenile delinquency prevention, and in addition to recognition by the National Council of Negro Women and the University of Chicago for her service, she was locally named "Mother of the Year" in 1950 and 1970. Alfreda M. Duster interview, iv–v, 2.

9. Dear Friend from Herman K. Barnett, 30 March 1926, IBW Papers; Wells-Barnett, *Crusade for Justice*, xxx.

10. Irene McCoy Gaines, "Tribute" (handwritten manuscript), 30 March 1931, IMG Papers.

11. "In Memoriam: Ida B. Wells-Barnett," *National Notes* (May 1931): 17.

12. "Mrs. Ida B. Wells-Barnett, Colored Leader, 62, Dies Suddenly," *Chicago Tribune*, 25 March 1931; "Mrs. Ida Wells Barnett Dies," *Pittsburgh Courier*, 28 March 1931; "Ida Wells Barnett: Postscript by W. E. B. Du Bois," *Crisis* (June 1931): 207.

13. "Hold Last Rites for Ida B. Wells-Barnett," *CD*, 4 April 1931.

14. Blair, "Why I Am Discouraged about Women in Politics," 332.

15. J. W. Scott, *Weapons of the Weak*.

16. A commentator recently asserted that Wells-Barnett "had personality traits that limited her effectiveness" in reform as much as did historical constraints. See Adam Fairclough's review of Brundage, *Under Sentence of Death: Lynching in the South* (1997) in the *Journal of Southern History* 64, no. 3 (1998): 574.

Primary Sources

MANUSCRIPTS
Amherst, Mass.
  University of Massachusetts Library
    W. E. B. Du Bois Papers
Ann Arbor, Mich.
  Bentley Historical Library, University of Michigan
    Necrology Files
Brooklyn, N.Y.
  Brooklyn Historical Society
Cambridge, Mass.
  Schlesinger Library, Radcliffe Institute for Advanced Study, Harvard
    University
    Black Women Oral History Project Interviews
      Alfreda M. Duster
    Catherine Waugh McCullough Papers
Chicago, Ill.
  Carter G. Woodson Public Library
    Vivian G. Harsh Collection
  Chicago Historical Society
    Claude A. Barnett Papers
    Chicago World's Columbian Exposition Papers
    George Washington Ellis Papers
    Illinois League of Women Voters Papers
    Irene McCoy Gaines Papers

Lottie Holman O'Neill Vertical File
Municipal Court Papers
Daley Center Archives
Municipal Court of Chicago Criminal Court Records
Newberry Library
Victor F. Lawson Papers
Reggenstein Library, University of Chicago
Julius Rosenwald Papers
Ida B. Wells Papers
University of Illinois at Chicago Circle
Department of Special Collections
Liverpool, England
Liverpool Public Library
Charles F. Aked Clipping Files
Manchester, England
John Rylands Library
William E. Axon Papers
Mayville, N.Y.
Chautauqua Historical Society
Albion Tourgée Papers
Memphis, Tenn.
Mississippi Valley Historical Collection, Memphis State University
Church Family Papers
Nashville, Tenn.
Tennessee State Library and Archives
Manuscript Court Records
New York, N.Y.
Schomburg Center for Research in Black Culture
Arthur A. Schomburg Scrapbooks
Springfield, Ill.
State Library of Illinois
Lawrence Y. Sherman Papers
Washington, D.C.
Library of Congress
William E. Chandler Papers
Frederick Douglass Papers
Ruth Hanna McCormick Papers
National Association for the Advancement of Colored People Papers
Albert Barnett Spingarn Papers
Mary Church Terrell Papers
Booker T. Washington Papers
Moorland-Spingarn Research Center, Howard University
Joel E. Spingarn Papers
Mary Church Terrell Papers
National Archives of the United States
Military Intelligence Division, Record Group 165
Wilberforce, Ohio
Wilberforce University
Reverdy C. Ransom Papers

COLLECTIONS ON MICROFILM

Records of the National Association of Colored Women's Clubs, 1895–1992. Bethesda, Md.: University Publications of America, 1994.

Temperance and Prohibition Papers, 1977 microform edition. Ohio Historical Society, Columbus, Ohio.

Tuskegee Institute News Clippings File, Series 2, 1899–1966. Tuskegee Institute, Tuskegee, Ala.

U.S. NEWSPAPERS AND PERIODICALS

Alabama
  The National Notes
District of Columbia
  Colored American Magazine
  Washington Bee
  Washington Colored American
  Washington National Intelligencer
Georgia
  The Voice of the Negro
Illinois
  The Champion Magazine
  Chicago Broad-Ax
  Chicago Conservator
  Chicago Inter-Ocean
  Chicago Record-Herald
  Chicago Tribune
  Chicago Whip
  The Commons
  The Competitor Magazine
  Half-Century Magazine
  Illinois State Journal
  Illinois Republican
  The Joliet Prison Post
Indiana
  Indianapolis Freeman
Kansas
  Topeka Weekly Call
Maryland
  Baltimore Colored American
Massachusetts
  The Arena
  North American Review
  Springfield Republican
  The Woman's Era
Michigan
  Detroit Plaindealer
Missouri
  Kansas City American Citizen
  St. Louis Republican

New York
  The Crisis
  The Independent
  The Literary Digest
  New York Age
  New York Freeman
  New York Globe
  New York Sun
  New York Times
  New York Tribune
  New York World
  The Outlook
  Public Opinion
  Rochester Union and Advertiser
  The Survey
  The Voice
  World Today
North Carolina
  A.M.E. Zion Church Quarterly
  South Atlantic Quarterly
Ohio
  Cleveland Gazette
Pennsylvania
  A.M.E. Church Review
  Philadelphia Christian Recorder
  Pittsburgh Courier
Tennessee
  Memphis Appeal
  Memphis Appeal-Avalanche
  Memphis Commercial

BRITISH NEWSPAPERS

Anti-Caste (Street, Somersetshire, England)
Birmingham Daily Post
Christian Register (London)
The Christian World (London)
The Daily Chronicle (London)
The Echo (London)
Fraternity (London)
The Inquirer (London)
Labour Leader (London)
Liverpool Daily Post
The Liverpool Pulpit
The Liverpool Review
Review of the Churches
The Sun (London)
The Times (London)
Manchester Guardian
Westminster Gazette

PUBLISHED WORKS

"A Brave Little Woman." *AME Zion Church Quarterly* 4 (July 1894): 406.

Addams, Jane. "The Communion of the Ballot." *Woman's Journal* 14 (December 1912).

———. *Democracy and Social Ethics*. Cambridge: Harvard University Press, 1964. Originally published 1902.

———. "Has the Emancipation Act Been Nullified by National Indifference?" *The Survey* (1 February 1913): 565–66.

———. "Pragmatism in Politics." *The Survey* (5 October 1912): 11–12.

———. *Twenty Years at Hull-House*. New York: Signet, 1981. Originally published 1910.

Aked, C. F. "A Blot on a Free Republic." *Review of the Churches* 9 (May–October 1894): 96–98.

———. *Eternal Punishment: Two Lectures*. London: Clarke & Co., 1891.

———. "The Race Problem in America." *The Contemporary Review* 65 (June 1894): 818–27.

American Digest. A Complete Digest of All Reported American Cases from the Earliest Times to 1896. Vol. 32. St. Paul, Minn.: West Publishing Co., 1902.

Andrews, William L., ed. *Six Women's Slave Narratives*. New York: Oxford University Press, 1988.

Baker, Ray Stannard. *Following the Color Line: The State of the Negro Citizen in the American Democracy*. New York: Harper Torchbooks, 1964. Originally published 1908.

———. "Lynching in the South." *McClure's* 25 (February 1905): 422–30.

———. "What Is a Lynching?" *McClure's* 25 (January 1905): 299–313.

Barber, J. Max. "The Niagara Movement." *Voice of the Negro* (September 1906): 671.

———. "The Niagara Movement at Harper's Ferry." *Voice of the Negro* (October 1906): 405.

Bartelmae, Mary M. "Opportunity for Women in Court Administration." *Annals of the American Academy* 52 (March 1914): 188–90.

Bellamy, Edward. *Looking Backward, 2000–1887*. New York: St. Martin's, 1995.

Bethune, Mary McLeod. "Faith that Moved a Dump Heap." In *Black Women in White America: A Documentary History*, edited by Gerda Lerner, 134–43. New York: Vintage, 1974.

Blair, Emily Newell. "Why I Am Discouraged about Women in Politics." In *Major Problems in American Women's History*, edited by Mary Beth Norton and Ruth M. Alexander, 331–33. Lexington, Mass.: D. C. Heath, 1996.

Bowen, Cornelia. "The Nation's Nursery." *Voice of the Negro* (March 1904): 113–15.

———. "Woman's Part in the Uplift of Our Race." *Colored American Magazine* 12, no. 3 (1907): 222–23.

Bowen, Louise DeKoven. *The Colored People of Chicago: An Investigation Made for the Juvenile Protective Association*. Chicago, 1913.

Bradford, Mrs. B. E. "Woman." *Colored American Magazine* 17 (1909): 103–4.

Breckinridge, Sophonisba. *The Delinquent Child and the Home*. New York: Charities Publications Committee, 1912.

Broughton, V. W. *Twenty Year's Experience of a Missionary*. Chicago: Pony Press Publishers, 1907.

Brown, Hallie Q. *Homespun Heroines and Other Women of Distinction*. New York: Oxford University Press, 1988. Originally published 1926.

Brown, L. J. "Philosophy of Lynching." *Voice of the Negro* (November 1904): 554–59.

Bruce, John E. "The Application of Force." In *The Selected Writings of J. E. Bruce: Militant Black Journalist*, edited by Peter Gilbert, 229–32. New York: Arno, 1971.

——. *The Blood Red Record*. Albany, N.Y.: Argus Co., 1901.

Bruce, Mrs. Josephine B. "The Afterglow of the Women's Convention." *Voice of the Negro* (November 1904): 541–43.

——. "What Has Education Done for Colored Women." *Voice of the Negro* (July 1904): 294–98.

Burroughs, Nannie Helen. "Not Color But Character." *Voice of the Negro* (July 1904): 283–87.

Chicago Commission on Race Relations. *The Negro in Chicago: A Study of Race Relations and a Race Riot in 1919*. New York: Arno, 1968. Originally published 1922.

The Chicago Daily News Almanac and Year-Book. Chicago: The Chicago Daily News Company, 1914–1930.

"Chicago's Liberality." *Voice of the Negro* (November 1906): 467.

Commission on Interracial Cooperation. *Lynchings and What They Mean*. Atlanta, Ga.: The Commission, n.d. [ca. 1930].

Cooper, Anna Julia. *A Voice from the South*. Edited by Mary Helen Washington. New York: Oxford University Press, 1988. Originally published 1892.

Crummell, Alexander. *Africa and America: Addresses and Discourses*. Springfield, Mass.: Wiley & Co., 1891.

Culp, D. W., ed. *Twentieth Century Negro Literature*. New York: Arno, 1969. Originally published 1902.

Cutler, James Elbert. *Lynch-Law: An Investigation into the History of Lynching in the United States*. New York: New Universities Press, 1905.

Davis, Elizabeth Lindsay. *Lifting as They Climb*. New York: G. K. Hall, 1996. Originally published 1933.

——. *The Story of the Illinois Federation of Colored Women's Clubs*. Chicago, 1922.

DeCosta-Willis, Miriam, ed. *The Memphis Diary of Ida B. Wells: An Intimate Portrait of the Activist as a Young Woman*. Boston: Beacon, 1995.

Douglass, Frederick. *The Lessons of the Hour*. Boston: Thomas & Evans, 1894.

——. "A Letter from the Late Hon. Fred. Douglass." *AME Zion Quarterly Review* 3, no. 1 (April 1895): 61.

——. "Lynch Law in the South." *North American Review* 155 (July 1892): 17–24.

Dow's City Directory of Memphis for 1885. Memphis, Tenn.: Harlow Dow, 1884.

Dow's City Directory of Memphis for 1890. Memphis, Tenn.: Harlow Dow, 1889.

Dow's City Directory of Memphis for 1892. Memphis, Tenn.: Harlow Dow, 1891.

Du Bois, W. E. B. *Darkwater: Voices from Within the Veil*. New York: Schocken, 1969. Originally published 1920.

——. *Efforts of American Negroes at Social Betterment*. Atlanta, Ga.: Atlanta University Press, 1898.

——. "The Niagara Movement." *Voice of the Negro* 2 (September 1905): 62.

———. "The Parting of the Ways." *World Today* 6 (1904): 521–23.

———. *The Philadelphia Negro*. New York: Shocken, 1967. Originally published 1899.

———. *The Souls of Black Folk*. New York: Signet, 1982. Originally published 1903.

———. *W. E. B. Du Bois Speaks*. Edited by Philip Foner. New York: Pathfinder, 1970.

"Editorial." *AME Zion Church Quarterly* 3 (April 1893): 416.

"Editorial." *Chicago Competitor* 3 (January 1921): 23.

"Editorial." *Colored American Magazine* 4 (1902): 279.

"Eighth Atlanta Negro Conference." *Colored American Magazine* 6, no. 8 (1903): 534–36.

Encyclopedia of the Laws of England, Vol. 14. London, 1898.

Farrar, Addie. "War Work Among Colored Women." *Half-Century Magazine* (November 1918): 9.

Fortune, T. Thomas. "Ida B. Wells, A.M." In *Women of Distinction: Remarkable in Works and Invincible in Character*, edited by Lawson V. Scruggs, 33–39. Raleigh, N.C.: Lawson V. Scruggs, 1893.

Frazier, E. Franklin. "The American Negro's New Leaders." *Current History* 28 (April 1928): 56–59.

Fuller, Margaret. "The Great Lawsuit." In *The Feminist Papers: From Adams to de Beauvoir*, edited by Alice Rossi, 176–82. Boston: Northeastern University Press, 1973.

[Fulton, David]. *Eagle Clippings by Jack Thorne*. N.p., n.d.

Garnet, Henry Highland. "An Address to the Slaves of the United States of America." In *Walker's Appeal in Four Articles and An Address to the Slaves of the United States of America*, edited by William Loren Katz, 144–66. New York: Arno, 1969.

Gibbons, Cardinal. "Lynch Law: Its Causes and Remedy." *North American Review* (October 1905): 502–9.

Gilbert, Hiram T. *The Municipal Court of Chicago*. Chicago: Hiram T. Gilbert, 1928.

Gilbert, Olive. *Sojourner Truth's Narrative and Book of Life*. New York: Arno, 1968. Originally published 1878.

Gilman, Charlotte Perkins. *Herland*. New York: Pantheon, 1979.

Goldman, Emma. *Living My Life*. New York: New American Library, 1977. Originally published 1931.

Grant, Bishop A., D.D. "The Institutional Church." *Colored American Magazine* 15 (1908): 632–35.

Graves, Mrs. "Motherhood." *Colored American Magazine* 14 (1908): 495.

Grimké, Angelina Weld. *Selected Works of Angelina Weld Grimké*. Edited by Carolivia Herron. New York: Oxford, 1991.

Grimké, Archibald H. "The Sex Question and Race Segregation." In *American Negro Academy Occasional Papers*, 1–22, 5–24. New York: Arno, 1970.

Grimké, Rev. Francis J., D.D. *The Lynching of Negroes in the South: Three Sermons*. Washington, D.C.: 1899.

———. *The Roosevelt-Washington Episode or Race Prejudice*. Washington, D.C.: Hayworth Publishing House, 1901.

Hamilton, Carrie Lee. "Women and the War." *Half-Century Magazine* (January 1918): 12.

Hamilton, G. P. *The Bright Side of Memphis*. Memphis, Tenn.: G. P. Hamilton, 1908.

Harlan, Louis R., et al., eds. *The Booker T. Washington Papers*. 10 vols. Urbana, Ill.: University of Illinois Press, 1972–1981.

Harper, Mrs. F. E. W. "Almost Constantly Either Traveling or Speaking." In *A Brighter Coming Day: A Frances Ellen Watkins Harper Reader*, edited by Frances Smith Foster, 126–27. New York: Feminist Press, 1990.

———. "Coloured Women of America." In *A Brighter Coming Day: A Frances Ellen Watkins Harper Reader*, edited by Frances Smith Foster, 271–75. New York: Feminist Press, 1990.

———. "A Factor in Human Progress." In *A Brighter Coming Day: A Frances Ellen Watkins Harper Reader*, edited by Frances Smith Foster, 275–80. New York: Feminist Press, 1990.

———. *Iola, or Shadows Uplifted*. New York: Oxford, 1988. Originally published 1892.

———. "The Woman's Christian Temperance Union and the Colored Woman." *AME Church Review* 4 (1888): 316–18.

———. "Woman's Political Future." In *Black Women in Nineteenth-Century American Life: Their Words, Their Thoughts, Their Feelings*, edited by Burt Loewenberg and Ruth Bogin, 244–47. University Park: Pennsylvania University Press, 1976.

Harper, Mrs. F. E. W., Ida B. Wells, et al. "Symposium—Temperance." *AME Church Review* (April 1891): 375–81.

Hill, Robert A., ed. *The Marcus Garvey and Universal Negro Improvement Association Papers*. 10 vols. Berkeley: University of California Press, 1983.

Historical Records of the Conventions of 1895–96 of the Colored Women of America. N.p., 1902.

Holt, George Chandler. *Lynching and Mobs*. Elizabeth, N.J., 1894.

Houchins, Sue E., ed. *Spiritual Narratives*. New York: Oxford University Press, 1988.

Houston, John W. *Annual Report of the Adult Probation Office of Cook County, Illinois*. Vols. 1–6. Chicago, 1912–1917.

Hunton, Mrs. Addie W. "A Deeper Reverence for Home Ties." *Colored American Magazine* 12 (1907): 58–59.

———. "The National Association of Colored Women: Its Real Significance." *Colored American Magazine* 14 (1908): 417.

———. "Negro Womanhood Defended." *Voice of the Negro* (July 1904): 280–82.

Hurston, Zora Neale. *Their Eyes Were Watching God*. New York: Perennial, 1979. Originally published 1935.

Ida B. Wells in England. St. Paul, Minn.: The Appeal, 1894.

Illinois General Assembly. *Journal of the House of Representatives of the 48th General Assembly of the State of Illinois*. N.p., 1913.

James, William. *Pragmatism and Other Essays*. New York: Washington Square, 1963.

Johnson, Alice. "Home Life." *Colored American Magazine* 12 (1907): 136.

Jones, Eugene Kinkle. "A Reconstruction Program for the Negro." *The Survey* (2 August 1919): 679.

Kletzing, H. F., and W. H. Crogman. *Progress of a Race; or, the Remarkable Advancement of the Afro-American*. New York: Arno, 1969. Originally published 1897.

Lynk, Miles V., M.D. *The Black Troopers: or, The Daring Heroics of the Negro Soldier in the Spanish American War.* New York: AMS, 1971. Originally published 1899.

Majors, Monroe A. *Noted Negro Women: Their Triumphs and Activities.* Chicago: Donohue & Henneberry, 1893.

Marks, George P., III, ed. *The Black Press Views American Imperialism, 1898–1900.* New York: Arno, 1971.

Miller, Kelly. *An Appeal to Reason on the Race Problem: An Open Letter to John Templeton Graves.* Washington, D.C.: Hayworth Publishing House, 1906.

——. "The Attitude of the Intelligent Negro Toward Lynching." *Voice of the Negro* 2 (1905): 307–12.

——. *The Disgrace of Democracy.* Washington, D.C., 1917.

——. "Problems of the City Negro." *World Today* 6 (1904): 514–16.

——. *Roosevelt and the Negro.* N.p., n.d.

Mitchell, John, Jr. "Shall the Wheels of Race Agitation Be Stopped?" *Colored American Magazine* 5 (1903): 386.

Moody, Anne. *Coming of Age in Mississippi.* New York: Vintage, 1968.

Mossell, Mrs. N. F. [Gertrude]. *The Work of the Afro-American Woman.* New York: Oxford University Press, 1988. Originally published 1894.

Moton, Robert R. "The South and the Lynching Evil." *South Atlantic Quarterly* 18, no. 3 (July 1919): 191–96.

Murray, George Henry. "Educated Colored Men and White Women." *Colored American Magazine* 8 (1904): 93–95.

"The NACW" (editorial). *Voice of the Negro* (July 1904): 310–11.

National Association for the Advancement of Colored People (NAACP). *Burning at the Stake in the U.S.* New York, 1919.

——. *The Fight Against Lynching.* New York, 1919.

——. *Notes on Lynching in the United States.* New York, 1912.

——. *Thirty Years of Lynching in the United States, 1889–1918.* New York, 1919.

National Negro Conference: Proceedings. New York, 1909.

"The Negro Woman." *The Champion Magazine* (December 1916): 171–72.

The Negro Yearbook. Tuskegee, Ala., 1914.

Nelson, Waterloo S., A.M. "Settlement Work for Negroes." *Colored American Magazine* 13, no. 3 (1907): 223–25.

"The Niagara Movement." *Voice of the Negro* (September 1906): 671.

"Northern Social Settlements for Negroes." *AME Church Review* (April 1906): 353–56.

"Organized for Social Equality." *Colored American Magazine* 7, no. 12 (1904): 704.

"Our Southern Field." *Methodist Quarterly Review* 60 (1878): 219–38.

Ovington, Mary White. *Black and White Sat Down Together: The Reminiscences of an NAACP Founder.* New York: Feminist Press, 1995.

——. "Disagrees with Pickens." *Voice of the Negro* (July 1905): 469.

——. *The Walls Came Tumbling Down.* New York: Schocken, 1970.

Penn, I. Garland. *The Afro-American Press and Its Editors.* New York: Arno, 1969. Originally published 1891.

Phelps, Howard A. "Negro Life in Chicago." *Half-Century Magazine* (May 1919): 12.

Pickens, William. *Lynching and Debt Slavery.* New York: American Civil Liberties Union, 1921.

———. "Pickens' Reply to Miss Ovington." *Voice of the Negro* (August 1905): 559–60.

Proceedings of the National Negro Conference, 1909. New York: Arno, 1969.

Ransom, Rev. Reverdy C. "Boston's Inheritance." *Voice of the Negro* (June 1906): 497–501.

———. *Deborah and Jael: Sermon to the I.B.W. Woman's Club.* Chicago: Bethel A.M.E. Church, 1897.

———. *The Industrial and Social Conditions of the Negro: A Thanksgiving Sermon.* Chicago: Bethel A.M.E. Church, 1896.

———. *The Pilgrimage of Harriet Ransom's Son.* Nashville, Tenn.: Sunday School Union, 1949.

———. "A Programme For the Negro." *AME Church Review* (April 1900): 430.

———. "The Spirit of John Brown." *Voice of the Negro* (October 1906): 412–17.

Raper, Arthur F. *The Tragedy of Lynching.* Chapel Hill: University of North Carolina Press, 1933.

"Report of the Memorial Service." *Unity Magazine* (18 April 1918): 115–22.

Residents of Hull-House. *Hull-House Maps and Papers.* New York: Arno, 1970. Originally published 1895.

Roosevelt, Theodore. "Lynching and the Miscarriage of Justice." *The Outlook* (25 November 1911): 706–7.

Rush, Mrs. "Bend the Tree While It Is Young." *Colored American Magazine* 12, no. 2 (1907): 53–54.

Sampson, Prof. B. K. "The American People to the Common Law." *AME Church Review* 1 (January 1885): 252–56.

Scruggs, Lawson V. *Women of Distinction; Remarkable in Works and Invincible in Character.* Raleigh, N.C.: Lawson V. Scruggs, 1893.

Sewell, May Wright, ed. *The World's Congress of Representative Women.* Chicago: Rand, McNally, 1894.

Shannon, Robert T. *Reports of Cases Argued and Determined in the Supreme Court of Tennessee,* Vol. 85. Louisville, Ky.: Fetter Law Book Co., 1902.

Sherwood, Mrs. John. *Manners and Social Usages.* New York: Harper & Brothers Publishers, 1897.

Sholes' Memphis Directory for 1885. Memphis, Tenn.: A. E. Sholes, 1884.

"The Significance of the Niagara Movement." *Voice of the Negro* (September 1905): 603.

Simmons, William. J. *Men of Mark: Eminent, Progressive and Rising.* New York: Arno Reprints, 1968. Originally published 1887.

Simpson, Mathew. *Cyclopedia of Methodism.* Philadelphia: Louis H. Everts, 1882.

Smith, Mrs. Amanda. *An Autobiography: The Story of the Lord's Dealings with Mrs. Amanda Smith, the Colored Evangelist.* Edited by Jualynne E. Dodson. New York: Oxford University Press, 1988. Originally published 1893.

Stanton, Elizabeth Cady. *Eighty Years and More: Reminiscences, 1815–1897.* New York: Shocken, 1971.

———. "Speech to the Anniversary of the American Anti-Slavery Society" [1860]. In *Elizabeth Cady Stanton / Susan B. Anthony: Correspondence, Writings, Speeches,* edited by Ellen Carol DuBois, 78–85. New York: Shocken, 1981.

Stemmons, James Samuel. "The Unmentionable Crime." *Colored American Magazine* 6 (1903): 636–41.

Sterling, Dorothy, ed. *We Are Your Sisters: Black Women in the Nineteenth Century.* New York: W. W. Norton, 1984.

Steward, T. G. *The Colored Regulars in the United States Army.* New York: Arno, 1969.

Stewart, Mrs. E. F. "Woman's Responsibility." *Colored American Magazine* 12 (1907): 60.

Stewart, Maria W. "A Lecture." In *Spiritual Narratives*, edited by Sue E. Houchins, 51–56. New York: Oxford University Press, 1988.

———. *Maria W. Stewart, America's First Black Woman Political Writer: Essays and Speeches.* Edited by Marilyn Richardson. Bloomington: Indiana University Press, 1987.

Stone, Alfred Holt. *Studies in the American Race Problem.* New York: Doubleday, Page, & Co., 1908.

Tayleur, Eleanor. "The Negro Woman—Social and Moral Decadence." *The Outlook* 76 (30 January 1904): 266–74.

Taylor, Alrutheus Ambush. *The Negro in Tennessee, 1865–1880.* Washington, D.C.: Associated Publishers, 1941.

Taylor, Clare, ed. *British and American Abolitionists: An Episode in Transatlantic Understanding.* Chicago: Aldine, 1974.

Taylor, Marshall W., D.D. *The Life, Travels, Labors, and Helpers of Mrs. Amanda Smith, the Famous Negro Missionary.* Cincinnati, Ohio: Cranston and Stowe, 1887.

Tennessee Code, Vol. 5. Charlottesville, Va.: Michie, 1980.

Terrell, Mary Church. *A Colored Woman in a White World.* Washington, D.C.: Ransdell, 1940.

———. "The Duty of the NACW to the Race." *AME Church Review* (July 1896): 219–25.

———. "Lynching from a Negro's Point of View." *North American Review* 178 (June 1904): 853–68.

———. *The Progress of Colored Women.* Washington, D.C.: Smith Brothers, Printers, 1898.

Tillman, K. D. "Afro-American Women and Their Work." *AME Church Review* (October 1894): 477–99.

Tyler, Ralph W. "Does Lynching Thrive Under Democracy?" *Colored American Magazine* 14 (1908): 477–79.

United States Census Office. *Eleventh Census of the United States, 1890: Population.* Washington, D.C.: GPO, 1895–1897.

Ward, Mrs. H. O. *Sensible Etiquette of the Best Society: Customs, Manners, Moral and Home Culture.* Philadelphia: Porter & Coates, 1878.

Washington, Booker T. *Booker T. Washington Gives Facts and Condemns Lynchings in a Statement Telegraphed to the New York World.* Baltimore, Md., 1908.

———. *Frederick Douglass.* Philadelphia: G. W. Jacobs & Co., 1907.

———. *An Open Letter by Booker T. Washington of Tuskegee Alabama upon Lynchings in the South.* Tuskegee, Ala., 1901.

———. "The Tuskegee Idea." *World Today* 6 (1904): 511–14.

———. *Up From Slavery.* New York: Penguin, 1986. Originally published 1900.

Washington, Booker T., N. B. Wood, and Fannie Barrier Williams. *A New Negro for a New Century.* Chicago: American Publishing House, 1900.

Washington, Margaret Murray. "The Advancement of Colored Women." *Colored American Magazine* 8, no. 4 (1904): 183–89.

———. "Club Work as a Factor in the Advance of Colored Women." *Colored American Magazine* 11, no. 2 (1906): 83–90.

———. "The Social Improvement of the Plantation Woman." *Voice of the Negro* (July 1904): 288–90.

Watson, Thomas E. "The Negro Question in the South." *The Arena* (October 1892): 540–50.

Weatherford, W. D. *Lynching: Removing Its Causes.* New Orleans, La., 1916.

Wells, Ida B. "Afro-Americans and Africa." *AME Church Review* (July 1892): 40–44.

———. "Liverpool Slave Traditions and Present Practices." *The Independent* 46 (19 May 1894): 617.

———. "Lynch Law in All Its Phases." In *Ida B. Wells-Barnett: An Exploratory Study of an American Black Woman, 1893–1930*, edited by Mildred I. Thompson, 171–87. Brooklyn, N.Y.: Carlson, 1990.

———. *The Reason Why the Colored American Is Not in the World's Columbian Exposition.* In *Selected Works of Ida B. Wells-Barnett*, compiled by Trudier Harris, 46–137. New York: Oxford University Press, 1991.

———. *A Red Record: Tabulated Statistics and Alleged Causes of Lynchings in the United States, 1892–3–4.* In *Selected Works of Ida B. Wells-Barnett*, compiled by Trudier Harris, 138–252. New York: Oxford University Press, 1991.

———. "The Requirements of Southern Journalism." *AME Zion Church Quarterly* (April 1892): 189–96.

———. *Southern Horrors: Lynch Law in All Its Phases.* In *Selected Works of Ida B. Wells-Barnett*, compiled by Trudier Harris, 14–45. New York: Oxford University Press, 1991.

———. "A Story of 1900." In *The Memphis Diary of Ida B. Wells*, edited by Miriam DeCosta-Willis, 182–84. Boston: Beacon, 1995.

———. "Two Christmas Days. A Holiday Story." *AME Zion Church Quarterly* 4 (January 1894): 129–40.

———. *United States Atrocities: Lynch Law.* London: Lux Publishing, 1894.

Wells-Barnett, Ida B. *The Arkansas Race Riot.* Chicago: Ida B. Wells-Barnett, 1920.

———. "Booker T. Washington and His Critics." *World Today* 6 (1904): 518–21.

———. *Crusade for Justice: The Autobiography of Ida B. Wells.* Edited by Alfreda M. Duster. Chicago: University of Chicago Press, 1970.

———. *The East St. Louis Massacre: The Greatest Outrage of the Century.* Chicago: The Negro Fellowship Herald Press, 1917.

———. "How Enfranchisement Stops Lynching." *Original Rights Magazine* (June 1910): 42–53.

———. "Lynch Law in America." *The Arena* 24 (January 1900): 16–24.

———. *Lynch Law in Georgia.* Chicago: Ida B. Wells-Barnett, 1899.

———. "Lynching and the Excuse for It." *The Independent* 53 (May 1901): 1133–36.

———. "Lynching: Our National Crime." In *National Negro Conference: Proceedings*, 174–79. New York, 1909.

———. *Mob Rule in New Orleans: Robert Charles and His Fight to the Death.* In *Selected*

Works of Ida B. Wells-Barnett, compiled by Trudier Harris, 253–322. New York: Oxford University Press, 1991.

———. "The National Afro-American Council." *Howard's American Magazine* 6, no. 10 (1901): 413–16.

———. "The Negro's Case in Equity." In *Ida B. Wells-Barnett: An Exploratory Study of an American Black Woman*, edited by Mildred I. Thompson, 245–46. Brooklyn, N.Y.: Carlson, 1990.

———. "The Northern Negro Woman's Social and Moral Condition." *Original Rights Magazine* (April 1910): 33–37.

———. "Our Country's Lynching Record." *The Survey* (1 February 1913): 573–74.

White, Walter. *A Man Called White: The Autobiography of Walter White*. New York: Viking, 1948.

———. "The Race Conflict in Arkansas." *The Survey* (13 December 1919): 233–34.

———. *Rope and Faggot: A Biography of Judge Lynch*. New York: Arno, 1969. Originally published 1929.

Willard, Frances E. *Woman and Temperance, or. The Work and Workers of the Woman's Christian Temperance Union*. Hartford, Conn.: Park Publishing Co., 1883.

Williams, Charles H. *The Race Problem*. N.p., 1897.

Williams, Fannie Barrier. "The Awakening of Women." *AME Church Review* (April 1897): 392–98.

———. "The Club Movement among the Colored Women of America." In *A New Negro for a New Century*, edited by Booker T. Washington, N. B. Wood, and Fannie Barrier Williams, 378–428. Chicago: American Publishing House, 1900.

———. "The Colored Girl." *Voice of the Negro* (June 1905): 400–403.

———. "Do We Need Another Name?" *Southern Workman* (January 1904): 33–36.

———. "An Extension of the Conference Spirit." *The Voice of the Negro* (July 1904): 300–303.

———. "The Frederick Douglass Center." *Southern Workman* (June 1906): 334–36.

———. "The Frederick Douglass Centre: A Question of Social Betterment, and Not of Social Equality." *Voice of the Negro* (December 1904): 601–4.

———. "The Intellectual Progress of the Colored Women of the United States since the Emancipation Proclamation." In *The World's Congress of Representative Women*, edited by May Wright Sewell, 696–729. Chicago: Rand, McNally, 1894.

———. "The Negro and Public Opinion." *Voice of the Negro* (January 1904): 31–32.

———. "A New Method for Dealing with the Race Problem." *Voice of the Negro* (July 1906): 502–5.

———. "Religious Duty to the Negro." In *Black Women in Nineteenth-Century American Life: Their Words, Their Thoughts, Their Feelings*, edited by Burt Loewenberg and Ruth Bogin, 265–70. Philadelphia: Pennsylvania State University Press, 1976.

———. "The Smaller Economies." *Voice of the Negro* (May 1904): 184–85.

———. "The Woman's Part in a Man's Business." *Voice of the Negro* (November 1904): 543–47.

———. "Work Attempted and Missed in Organized Club Work." *Colored American Magazine* 14 (1908): 281–85.

Williams, Katherine E. "The Alpha Suffrage Club." *Half-Century Magazine* (September 1916): 12.

Wilson, Joseph T. *The Black Phalanx: A History of the Negro Soldier of the United States in the Wars of 1775–1812, 1861–65*. Hartford, Conn.: American Publishing Co., 1890.

Withers, Z. "Bethel Church." *Half-Century Magazine* (July 1918): 8.

"Women's Club Notes." *Half-Century Magazine* (September–October 1918): 11.

Woolley, Celia Parker. "The Frederick Douglass Center, Chicago." *The Commons* 5 (July 1904): 328–29.

Work, Monroe N. *The Law and the Mob*. N.p., 1925.

Wright, Richard R. *Centennial Encyclopedia of the AME Church*. Philadelphia, 1916.

Yates, Josephine Silone. "Kindergartens and Mothers' Clubs." *Colored American Magazine* 12 (1904): 304–11.

———. "The National Association of Colored Women." *Voice of the Negro* (July 1904): 283–87.

———. "Parental Obligation." *Colored American Magazine* 12 (1907): 285–90.

———. "Woman as a Factor in the Solution of Race Problems." *Colored American Magazine* 12 (1907): 126–35.

Yezierska, Anzia. *Bread Givers*. New York: Doubleday, 1925.

Young, J. P. *Standard History of Memphis, Tennessee*. Knoxville, Tenn.: H. W. Crew & Co., 1912.

Secondary Sources

Alexander, Elizabeth. "'We Must Be about Our Father's Business': Anna Julia Cooper and the In-Corporation of the Nineteenth Century African-American Woman Intellectual." *Signs* 90 (Winter 1995): 330–42.

Allen, Robert. *Reluctant Reformers: Racism and Social Reform Movements in the United States*. Washington, D.C.: Howard University Press, 1974.

Alpern, Sara, Joyce Antler, Ingrid Scobie, and Elizabeth Israels Perry, eds. *The Challenge of Feminist Biography: Writing the Lives of Modern American Women*. Urbana: University of Illinois Press, 1992.

Anderson, James D. *The Education of Blacks in the South, 1865–1925*. Chapel Hill: University of North Carolina Press, 1988.

Anderson, Kathryn. "Practicing Feminist Politics: Emily Newell Blair and U.S. Women's Political Choices in the Early Twentieth Century." *Journal of Women's History* 9 (Autumn 1997): 50–72.

Anderson, Kristi. *After Suffrage: Women in Partisan and Electoral Politics Before the New Deal*. Chicago: University of Chicago Press, 1996.

Anderson, Stuart. *Race and Rapprochement: Anglo-Saxonism in Anglo-American Relations*. Rutherford, N.J.: Fairleigh Dickinson University Press, 1981.

Angell, Stephen Ward. *Bishop Henry McNeal Turner and African-American Religion in the South*. Knoxville: Tennessee University Press, 1992.

———. "The Controversy Over Women's Ministry in the African Methodist Episcopal Church in the 1880s: The Case of Sarah Ann Hughes." In *This Far by Faith: Readings in African-American Women's Religious Biography*, edited by

Judith Weisenfeld and Richard Newman, 94–109. New York: Routledge, 1996.

Aptheker, Bettina. *Lynching and Rape: An Exchange of Views*. Occasional Paper No. 25. San Jose, Calif.: American Institute for Marxist Studies, 1977.

———. *Woman's Legacy: Essays on Race, Sex, and Class in American History*. Amherst: University of Massachusetts Press, 1982.

Asbaugh, Carolyn. *Lucy Parsons: American Revolutionary*. Chicago: Charles H. Kerr, 1976.

Ayers, Edward L. *The Promise of the New South: Life After Reconstruction*. New York: Oxford University Press, 1992.

Bair, Barbara. "True Women, Real Men: Gender, Ideology and Social Roles in the Garvey Movement." In *Gendered Domains: Rethinking Public and Private in Women's History*, edited by Dorothy O. Helly and Susan M. Reverby, 154–66. Ithaca, N.Y.: Cornell University Press, 1992.

Baker, Paula. "The Domestication of Politics: Women and American Political Society, 1780–1920." *American Historical Review* 89 (June 1984): 620–47.

Banner, Lois W., *Women in Modern America: A Brief History*. 3d ed. New York: Harcourt Brace, 1995.

Barbeau, Arthur Edward, and Florette Henri. *The Unknown Soldiers: Black American Troops in World War I*. Philadelphia: Temple University Press, 1974.

Barry, John M. *Rising Tide: The Great Mississippi Flood of 1927 and How it Changed America*. New York: Simon and Schuster, 1997.

Bates, Beth Tompkins. "The Brotherhood." *Chicago History* (Fall 1996): 4–23.

Bederman, Gail. " 'Civilization,' the Decline of Middle-Class Manliness, and Ida B. Wells's Anti-lynching Campaign (1892–4)." *Radical History Review* 52 (Winter 1992): 1–30.

———. *Manliness and Civilization: A Cultural History of Gender and Race in the United States, 1880–1917*. Chicago: University of Chicago Press, 1996.

Bell, Bernard W., Emily Grosholz, and James B. Stewart, eds. *W. E. B. Du Bois on Race and Culture: Philosophy, Politics, and Poetics*. New York: Routledge, 1996.

Bender, Thomas, ed. *The Antislavery Debate: Capitalism and Abolitionism as a Problem in Historical Interpretation*. Berkeley: University of California Press, 1992.

Bennett, James B. "Religion, Race, and Region: Churches and the Rise of Jim Crow in New Orleans." Unpublished paper in author's possession, 1998.

Berkeley, Kathleen C. " 'Colored Ladies Also Contributed': Black Women's Activities from Benevolence to Social Welfare." In *Black Women in United States History: From Colonial Times to the Nineteenth-Century*, edited by Darlene Clark Hine, 1:61–83. Brooklyn, N.Y.: Carlson, 1990.

———. *"Like a Plague of Locusts": From An Antebellum Town to a New South City, Memphis, Tennessee, 1850–1880*. New York: Garland, 1991.

———. "The Politics of Black Education in Memphis, Tennessee, 1868–1881." In *Southern Cities, Southern Schools: Public Education in the Urban South*, edited by Rick Ginsberg and David N. Plank, 199–231. Westport, Conn.: Greenwood, 1990.

Berry, Mary Frances, and John W. Blassingame. *Long Memory: The Black Experience in America*. New York: Oxford University Press, 1982.

Berthoff, Rowland. "Conventional Mentality: Free Blacks, Women, and

Business Corporations as Unequal Persons, 1820–1870." *Journal of American History* 76, no. 3 (1989): 753–84.

Blackburn, Regina. "In Search of the Black Female Self: African American Women's Autobiographies and Ethnicity." In *Women's Autobiography: Essays in Criticism*, edited by Estelle Jelinek, 133–48. Bloomington: Indiana University Press, 1990.

Blanchard, Mary W. "Boundaries and the Victorian Body: Aesthetic Fashion in Gilded Age America." *American Historical Review* 100 (February 1995): 21–50.

Bohstedt, John. "More than One Working Class: Protestant-Catholic Riots in Edwardian Liverpool." In *Popular Politics, Riot and Labour: Essays in Liverpool History, 1790–1940*, edited by John Belcham, 172–216. Liverpool, England: Liverpool University Press, 1992.

Booker, M. Keith. *Techniques of Subversion in Modern Literature: Transgression, Abjection, and the Carnivalesque*. Gainesville: University of Florida, 1991.

Bordin, Ruth. *Frances Willard: A Biography*. Chapel Hill: University of North Carolina Press, 1986.

———. *Woman and Temperance: The Quest for Power and Liberty*. New Brunswick, N.J.: Rutgers University Press, 1981.

Boris, Eileen. "The Power of Motherhood: Black and White Activist Women Redefine the 'Political.' " In *Mothers of a New World: Maternalist Politics and the Origins of Welfare States*, edited by Seth Koven and Sonya Michel, 213–45. New York: Routledge, 1993.

Boyer, Paul. *Urban Masses and Moral Order in America, 1820–1920*. Cambridge: Harvard University Press, 1978.

Braxton, Joanne M. *Black Women Writing Autobiography: A Tradition within a Tradition*. Philadelphia: Temple University Press, 1989.

Brekus, Catherine A. *Strangers and Pilgrims: Female Preaching in America, 1740–1845*. Chapel Hill: University of North Carolina Press, 1998.

Brown, Dorothy M. *Setting a Course: American Women in the 1920s*. Boston: Twayne, 1987.

Brown, Elsa Barkley. "Imaging Lynching: African American Women: Communities of Struggle, and Collective Memory." In *African American Women Speak Out on Anita Hill–Clarence Thomas*, edited by Geneva Smitherman, 100–124. Detroit, Mich.: Wayne State University Press, 1995.

———. "Negotiating and Transforming the Public Sphere: African American Political Life in the Transition from Slavery to Freedom." *Public Culture* 7 (Fall 1994): 107–46.

———. "To Catch the Vision of Freedom: African American Women's Political History, 1865–1880." In *African American Women and the Vote, 1837–1965*, edited by Ann D. Gordon, Bettye Collier-Thomas, John H. Bracey, Arlene Voski Avakian, and Joyce Avrech Berkman, 66–99. Amherst: University of Massachusetts Press, 1997.

———. " 'What Has Happened Here': The Politics of Difference in Women's and Feminist Politics." *Feminist Studies* 18 (Summer 1992): 295–313.

———. "Womanist Consciousness: Maggie Lena Walker and the Independent Order of Saint Luke." *Signs* 14 (1989) 3: 610–33.

Brown, Victoria Bissell. "Jane Addams, Progressivism, and Woman Suffrage: An Introduction to 'Why Women Should Vote.' " In *One Woman, One Vote:*

Rediscovering the Woman Suffrage Movement, edited by Marjorie Spruill Wheeler, 179–202. Troutdale, Ore.: New Sage, 1995.

Brownell, Blaine A., and David R. Goldfield, eds. *The City in Southern History: The Growth of Urban Civilization in the South*. Port Washington, N.Y.: Kennikat Press, 1977.

Brundage, W. Fitzhugh. *Lynching in the New South: Georgia and Virginia, 1880–1930*. Urbana: University of Illinois, 1993.

———. " 'To Howl Loudly': John Mitchell, Jr., and His Campaign Against Lynching in Virginia." *Canadian Review of American Studies* 22 (Winter 1991): 325–41.

———, ed. *Under Sentence of Death: Lynching in the South*. Chapel Hill: University of North Carolina Press, 1997.

Buckler, Helen. *Daniel Hale Williams, Negro Surgeon*. New York: Pitman, 1970.

Buechler, Steven M. *The Transformation of the Woman Suffrage Movement: The Case of Illinois, 1850–1920*. New Brunswick, N.J.: Rutgers University Press, 1986.

Bullock, Penelope L. *The Afro-American Periodical Press, 1838–1909*. Baton Rouge, La.: Louisiana State University Press, 1981.

Butler, Judith. *Bodies that Matter: On the Discursive Limits of "Sex."* New York: Routledge, 1993.

Butterfield, Stephen. *Black American Autobiography*. Amherst: University of Massachusetts, 1974.

Bynam, Victoria. *Unruly Women: The Politics of Social and Sexual Control in the Old South*. Chapel Hill: University of North Carolina Press, 1992.

Cannon, Katie Geneva. "Moral Wisdom in the Black Women's Literary Tradition." In *Weaving the Visions: New Patterns in Feminist Spirituality*, edited by Judith Plaskow and Carol P. Christ, 281–92. San Francisco: Harper Collins, 1989.

Caraway, Nancie. *Segregated Sisterhood: Racism and the Politics of American Feminism*. Knoxville: University of Tennessee Press, 1991.

Carby, Hazel V. *Reconstructing Womanhood: The Emergence of the Afro-American Woman Novelist*. Cambridge: Harvard University Press, 1987.

Carnes, Mark C., and Clyde Griffen, eds. *Meanings for Manhood: Constructions of Masculinity in Victorian America*. Chicago: University of Chicago Press, 1990.

Carson, Clayborne. *In Struggle: SNCC and the Black Awakening in the 1960s*. New York: Cambridge University Press, 1991.

Carson, Mina. *Settlement Folk: Social Thought and the American Settlement Movement, 1885–1930*. Chicago: University of Chicago Press, 1990.

Cartwright, Joel. *The Triumph of Jim Crow: Race Relations in Tennessee, 1865–1880*. Knoxville: University of Tennessee Press, 1985.

Chadbourn, James Harmon. *Lynching and the Law*. Chapel Hill: University of North Carolina Press, 1933.

Chateauvert, Melinda. *Marching Together: The Women of the Brotherhood of Sleeping Car Porters*. Urbana: University of Illinois Press, 1998.

Childs, John Brown. *Leadership, Conflict, and Cooperation in Afro-American Social Thought*. Philadelphia: Temple University Press, 1989.

Church, Annette E., and Roberta Church. *The Robert R. Churches of Memphis*. Ann Arbor, Mich.: Edwards Brothers, 1974.

Church, Robert, and Ronald Walter. *Nineteenth-Century Memphis Families of Color, 1850–1900*. Memphis, Tenn.: Church-Walter, 1987.

Clapp, Elizabeth L. *Mothers of All Children: Women Reformers and the Rise of Juvenile Courts in Progressive-Era America*. University Park: Pennsylvania State University Press, 1998.

Clark, Elizabeth B. " 'The Sacred Rights of the Weak': Pain, Sympathy, and the Culture of Individual Rights in Antebellum America." *Journal of American History* 82 (September 1995): 463–93.

Coleman, Willi. "Black Women and Segregated Public Transportation: Ninety Years of Resistance." In *Black Women in United States History: The Twentieth Century*, edited by Darlene Clark Hine, 1:295–302. Brooklyn, N.Y.: Carlson, 1990.

Collier-Thomas, Bettye. "Frances Ellen Watkins Harper, Abolitionist and Feminist Reformer." In *African American Women and the Vote, 1837–1965*, edited by Ann D. Gordon, Bettye Collier-Thomas, John H. Bracey, Arlene Voski Avakian, and Joyce Avrech Berkman, 41–65. Amherst: University of Massachusetts Press, 1997.

———. "The Impact of Black Women in Education: An Historical Overview." *Journal of Negro History* 51, no. 3 (1982): 173–80.

Collins, Patricia Hill. *Black Feminist Thought: Knowledge, Consciousness, and the Politics of Empowerment*. 2d ed. New York: Routledge, 2000.

———. "Shifting the Center: Race, Class, and Feminist Theorizing About Motherhood." In *Mothering: Ideology, Experience, and Agency*, edited by Evelyn Nakano Glenn, Grace Chang, and Linda Rennie Forcey, 45–66. New York: Routledge, 1994.

Connor, Kimberly Rae. *Conversions and Visions in the Writings of African-American Women*. Knoxville: University of Tennessee, 1994.

Cortner, Richard C. *A Mob Intent on Death: The NAACP and the Arkansas Riot Cases*. Middletown, Conn.: Wesleyan University Press, 1988.

Coston, Lela B. *Two Sisters for Social Reform: Grace and Edith Abbott*. Urbana: University of Illinois Press, 1983.

Cott, Nancy F. *The Grounding of Modern Feminism*. New Haven, Conn.: Yale University Press, 1987.

Cronon, Edmund David. *Black Moses: The Story of Marcus Garvey and the University Negro Improvement Association*. Madison: University of Wisconsin Press, 1966.

Crunden, Robert M. *Ministers of Reform: The Progressives' Achievement in American Civilization, 1889–1920*. New York: Basic, 1982.

Cullen, Jim. " 'I's a Man Now': Gender and African American Men." In *Divided Houses: Gender and the Civil War*, edited by Catherine Clinton and Nina Silber, 76–96. New York: Oxford University Press, 1992.

Curry, Richard O., ed. *Radicalism, Racism, and Party Realignment*. Baltimore, Md.: Johns Hopkins University Press, 1970.

Czitrom, Daniel J. "Underworlds and Underdogs: Big Tim Sullivan and Metropolitan Politics in New York, 1889–1913." *Journal of American History* 78, no. 2 (1991): 536–58.

Dailey, Jane. "Race, Sex, and Citizenship: Biracial Democracy in Readjuster Virginia, 1879–1883." Ph.D. diss., Princeton University, 1994.

Dann, Martin E. *The Black Press, 1827–1890: The Quest for National Identity*. New York: G. P. Putnam's Sons, 1971.

Davies, Margery. "Woman's Place Is at the Typewriter: The Feminization of the Clerical Labor Force." In *Capitalist Patriarchy and the Case for Socialist Feminism*, edited by Zillah Eisenstein, 248–66. New York: Monthly Review Press, 1979.

Davis, Allen F. *American Heroine: The Life and Legend of Jane Addams*. New York: Oxford University Press, 1973.

Davis, Angela. *Women, Race, and Class*. New York: Random House, 1981.

Davis, Simone. "The 'Weak Race' and the Winchester: Political Voices in the Pamphlets of Ida B. Wells-Barnett." *Legacy* 12, no. 2 (1995): 77–97.

Davis, Thadious. "Separating Self from Self-Created Fiction." In *The Challenge of Writing Black Biography*. New York: Hatch-Billops Collection, 1986.

Dearborn, Mary. *Pocahontas's Daughters: Gender and Ethnicity in American Culture*. New York: Oxford University Press, 1986.

DeBoer, Clara Merritt. *His Truth Is Marching On: African Americans Who Taught the Freedmen for the American Missionary Association, 1861–1877*. New York: Garland, 1995.

Decker, Jeffrey Louis. "Reconstructing Enterprise: Madam Walker, Black Womanhood, and the Transformation of the American Culture of Success." In *The Seduction of Biography*, edited by Mary Rhiel and David Suchoff, 99–112. New York: Routledge, 1996.

D'Emilio, John, and Estelle B. Freedman. *Intimate Matters: A History of Sexuality in America*. New York: Harper & Row, 1988.

Dennis, Charles H. *Victor Lawson: His Time and His Work*. N.p., 1935.

Diggins, John Patrick. *The Promise of Pragmatism: Modernism and the Crisis of Knowledge and Authority*. Chicago: University of Chicago Press, 1994.

Dill, Bonnie Thornton. "Dialectics of Black Womanhood." *Signs* 4 (1979): 43–55.

———. "Race, Class, and Gender: Prospects for an All-Inclusive Sisterhood." *Feminist Studies* 9 (Spring 1983): 131–50.

Diner, Steven J. "Chicago Social Workers and Blacks in the Progressive Era." *Social Service Review* 44 (December 1970): 393–410.

Dittmer, John. *Local People: The Struggle for Civil Rights in Mississippi*. Urbana: University of Illinois Press, 1994.

Doyle, Don H. *New Men, New Cities, New South: Atlanta, Nashville, Charleston, Mobile, 1860–1910*. Chapel Hill: University of North Carolina Press, 1990.

Drake, St. Clair. *Churches and Voluntary Associations in the Chicago Negro Community* (report of official project). Chicago: Works Project Administration, 1940.

Drake, St. Clair, and Horace R. Cayton. *Black Metropolis: A Study of Negro Life in a Northern City*. New York: Harcourt Brace, 1945.

Dubofsky, Melvyn. *The State and Labor in Modern America*. Chapel Hill: University of North Carolina Press, 1994.

DuBois, Ellen. *Feminism and Suffrage: The Emergence of an Independent Women's Movement in America, 1848–1969*. Ithaca, N.Y.: Cornell University Press, 1978.

———. *Harriot Stanton Blatch and the Winning of Woman Suffrage*. New Haven, Conn.: Yale University Press, 1997.

———. "'Taking the Law into Our Own Hands': Bradwell, Minor, and Suffrage Militancy in the 1870s." In *Visible Women: New Essays in American Activism*, edited by Nancy A. Hewitt and Suzanne Lebsock, 19–40. Urbana: University of Illinois Press, 1993.

———. "Working Women, Class Relations, and Suffrage Militance: Harriot Stanton Blatch and the New York Woman Suffrage Movement, 1894–1909."

In *Unequal Sisters: A Multicultural Reader in U.S. Women's History*, edited by Ellen Carol DuBois and Vicki L. Ruiz, 228–48. New York: Routledge, 1990.

DuBois, Ellen Carol, and Linda Gordon. "Seeking Ecstasy on the Battlefield: Danger and Pleasure in Nineteenth-Century Feminist Sexual Thought." In *Pleasure and Danger: Exploring Female Sexuality*, edited by Carol Vance, 31–49. New York: Pandora's/Harper Collins, 1989.

DuCille, Ann. *The Coupling Convention: Sex, Text, and Tradition in Black Women's Fiction*. New York: Oxford University Press, 1993.

———. "The Occult of True Black Womanhood: Critical Demeanor and Black Feminist Studies." *Signs* 19 (1994): 591–629.

Dumenil, Lynn. *A Modern Temper: American Culture and Society in the 1920s*. New York: Hill and Wang, 1995.

Durrill, Wayne K. "New Schooling for a New South: A Community Study of Education and Social Change, 1875–1885." *Journal of Social History* (Fall 1997): 155–81.

Dvorak, Katharine L. *An African American Exodus: The Segregation of Southern Churches*. Brooklyn, N.Y.: Carlson, 1991.

Edwards, Laura F. *Gendered Strife and Confusion: The Political Culture of Reconstruction*. Urbana: University of Illinois Press, 1997.

———. "Sexual Violence, Gender, Reconstruction and the Extension of Patriarchy in Granville, N.C." *North Carolina Historical Review* 68 (July 1991): 237–60.

Edwards, Rebecca. *Angels in the Machinery: Gender in American Party Politics from the Civil War to the Progressive Era*. New York: Oxford University Press, 1997.

Ellis, John H. "Disease and the Destiny of a City: The 1878 Yellow Fever Epidemic in Memphis." *West Tennessee Historical Society Papers* 28 (1974): 75–89.

———. "Memphis' Sanitary Revolution." *Tennessee Historical Quarterly* 23 (March 1964): 59–72.

Ellison, Ralph. *Shadow and Act*. New York: Random House, 1953.

Epstein, Barbara Leslie. *The Politics of Domesticity: Women, Evangelism, and Temperance in Nineteenth-Century America*. Middletown, Conn.: Wesleyan University Press, 1981.

Evans, Sara M. "Women's History and Political Theory: Toward a Feminist Approach to Public Life." In *Visible Women: New Essays in American Activism*, edited by Nancy Hewitt and Suzanne Lebsock, 119–39. Urbana: University of Illinois Press, 1993.

Ferrell, Claudine. *Nightmare and Dream: Antilynching in Congress*. New York: Garland, 1986.

Fields, Barbara Jeanne. "Ideology and Race in American History." In *Region, Race, and Reconstruction: Essays in Honor of C. Vann Woodward*, edited by J. Morgan Kousser and James McPherson, 143–77. New York: Oxford University Press, 1982.

———. "Slavery, Race, and Ideology in the United States of America." *New Left Review* 181 (May/June 1990): 95–118.

Fitzpatrick, Ellen, *Endless Crusade: Women Social Scientists and Progressive Reform*. New York: Oxford University Press, 1990.

Flanagan, Maureen A. "Gender and Urban Political Reform: The City Club and the Woman's City Club of Chicago in the Progressive Era." *Journal of American History* 95 (October 1990): 1032–50.

Fleming, Cynthia Griggs. "'More than a Lady': Ruby Doris Smith Robinson and Black Women's Leadership in the Student Nonviolent Coordinating Committee." In *Hidden Histories of Women in the New South*, edited by Virginia Bernhard, Elizabeth Hayes Turner, and Betty Brandon, 204–23. Columbia: University of Missouri Press, 1994.

Foster, Frances Smith, ed. *A Brighter Coming Day: A Frances Ellen Watkins Harper Reader*. New York: Feminist Press, 1990.

———. *Witnessing Slavery: The Development of the Antebellum Slave Narrative*. Westport, Conn.: Greenwood, 1979.

———. *Written By Herself: Literary Production by African American Women, 1746–1892*. Bloomington: Indiana University Press, 1993.

Fox, Richard Wightman. "The Culture of Liberal Protestant Progressivism, 1875–1925." *Journal of Interdisciplinary History* 23 (Winter 1993): 639–60.

Fox, Stephen R. *The Guardian of Boston: William Monroe Trotter*. New York: Atheneum, 1971.

Frankenberg, Ruth. *White Women, Race Matters: The Social Construction of Whiteness*. Minneapolis: University of Minnesota Press, 1993.

Frankel, Noralee, and Nancy S. Dye, eds. *Gender, Class, Race, and Reform in the Progressive Era*. Lexington: University Press of Kentucky, 1991.

Franklin, V. P. *Living Our Stories, Telling Our Truths: Autobiography and the Making of the African-American Intellectual Tradition*. New York: Scribner, 1995.

Frederickson, George. *The Black Image in the White Mind: The Debate on Afro-American Character and Destiny, 1817–1914*. Middletown, Conn.: Wesleyan University Press, 1971.

Freedman, Estelle B. "Separatism as Strategy: Female Institution Building and American Feminism, 1870–1930." *Feminist Studies* 5 (Fall 1979): 512–29.

———. *Their Sisters' Keepers: Women's Prison Reform in America, 1880–1930*. Ann Arbor: University of Michigan Press, 1981.

Fuller, T. O. *History of the Negro Baptists of Tennessee*. Memphis, Tenn.: Roger Williams-Howe College, 1936.

Gagnier, Regenia. *Subjectivities: A History of Self-Representation in Britain, 1832–1920*. New York: Oxford University Press, 1991.

Gaines, Kevin K. *Uplifting the Race: Black Leadership, Politics, and Culture in the Twentieth Century*. Chapel Hill: University of North Carolina Press, 1996.

Gaither, Gerald H. "The Negro Alliance Movement in Tennessee, 1888–1891." *West Tennessee Historical Society Papers* 27 (1973): 50–62

Garrison, Dee. "The Tender Technicians: The Feminization of Public Librarianship, 1876–1905." *Journal of Social History* 6 (1972–73): 131–59.

Gates, Henry Louis, Jr. "The Trope of the 'New Negro' and the Reconstruction of the Image of the Black." *Representations* 24 (Fall 1988): 129–55.

Gatewood, Willard B., Jr. *Black Americans and the White Man's Burden, 1898–1903*. Urbana: University of Illinois Press, 1975.

Giddings, Paula. *When and Where I Enter: The Impact of Black Women on Race and Sex in America*. New York: Bantam, 1984.

Gilkes, Cheryl Townsend. "The Politics of 'Silence': Dual-Sex Political Systems and Women's Tradition of Conflict in African-American Religion." In

African American Christianity, edited by Paul E. Johnson, 80–110. Berkeley: University of California Press, 1994.

Gilman, Sander. *Difference and Pathology: Stereotypes of Sexuality, Race and Madness.* Ithaca, N.Y.: Cornell University Press, 1985.

Gilmore, Glenda Elizabeth. *Gender and Jim Crow: Women and the Politics of White Supremacy in North Carolina, 1896–1920.* Chapel Hill: University of North Carolina Press, 1996.

———. "'A Melting Time': Black Women, White Women, and the WCTU in North Carolina, 1880–1900." In *Hidden Histories of Women in the New South*, edited by Virginia Bernhard, Elizabeth Hayes Turner, and Betty Brandon, 153–72. Columbia: University of Missouri Press, 1994.

Gilroy, Paul. *The Black Atlantic: Modernity and Double Consciousness.* Cambridge: Harvard University Press, 1993.

Ginzberg, Lori D. *Women and the Work of Benevolence: Morality, Politics, and Class in the Nineteenth-Century United States.* New Haven, Conn.: Yale University Press, 1990.

Glazer, Penina Migdal, and Miriam Slater. *Unequal Colleagues: The Entrance of Women into the Professions, 1890–1940.* New Brunswick, N.J.: Rutgers University Press, 1987.

Goodwin, Joanne L. *Gender and the Politics of Welfare Reform: The Mothers' Pension in Chicago, 1911–1929.* Chicago: University of Chicago Press, 1997.

Gordon, Ann D., Bettye Collier-Thomas, John H. Bracey, Arlene Voski Avakian, and Joyce Avrech Berkman, eds. *African American Women and the Vote, 1837–1965.* Amherst: University of Massachusetts Press, 1997.

Gordon, Linda. "Black and White Visions of Welfare: Women's Welfare Activism, 1890–1945." *Journal of American History* 78 (September 1991): 559–90.

———. *Heroes of Their Own Lives: The Politics and History of Family Violence, 1880–1930.* New York: Penguin, 1988.

———. "Putting Children First: Women, Maternalism, and Welfare in the Early Twentieth Century." In *U.S. History as Women's History: New Feminist Essays*, edited by Linda K. Kerber, Alice Kessler-Harris, and Kathryn Kish Sklar, 63–86. Chapel Hill: University of North Carolina Press, 1995.

———, ed. *Women, the State, and Welfare.* Madison: University of Wisconsin Press, 1990.

Gosnell, Howard F. *Negro Politicians: The Rise of Negro Politics in Chicago.* Chicago: Chicago University Press, 1935.

Gould, Stephen Jay. *The Mismeasure of Man.* Rev. ed. New York: W. W. Norton, 1996.

Grant, Donald L. *The Anti-Lynching Movement, 1883–1932.* San Francisco: R and E Research Associates, 1975.

Grant, Eric. "'Room Enough': The Fisk Jubilee Singers, 1870–71." Unpublished paper in author's possession, 1998.

Grant, Jacquelyn. *White Women's Christ, Black Women's Jesus: Feminist Christology and Womanist Response.* Atlanta, Ga.: Scholars Press, 1988.

Grantham, Dewey. *Southern Progressivism: The Reconciliation of Progress and Tradition.* Knoxville: University of Tennessee Press, 1983.

Grossman, James R. *Land of Hope: Chicago, Black Southerners, and the Great Migration.* Chicago: University of Chicago Press, 1989.

Gustafson, Melanie. "Partisan Women: Gender and the Politics of the Progressive Party, 1912." Ph.D. diss., New York University, 1993.

——. "Partisan Women in the Progressive Era: The Struggle for Inclusion in American Political Parties." *Journal of Women's History* 9 (Summer 1997): 8–29.

Gurin, Patricia, Shirley Hatchett, James S. Jackson, eds. *Hope and Independence: Blacks' Response to Electoral and Party Politics.* New York: Russell Sage, 1989.

Guy-Sheftall, Beverly. *"Daughters of Sorrow": Attitudes toward Black Women, 1880–1920.* Brooklyn, N.Y.: Carlson, 1990.

Haber, Samuel. *Efficiency and Uplift: Scientific Management in the Progressive Era, 1890–1920.* Chicago: University of Chicago Press, 1964.

——. *The Quest for Authority and Honor in the American Professions, 1750–1900.* Chicago: University of Chicago Press, 1991.

Hair, William Ivy. *Carnival of Fury: Robert Charles and the New Orleans Race Riot of 1900.* Baton Rouge: Louisiana State University Press, 1976.

Hale, Grace Elizabeth. *Making Whiteness: The Culture of Segregation in the South, 1890–1940.* New York: Vintage, 1999.

Hall, Jacquelyn Dowd. " 'The Mind that Burns in Each Body': Women, Rape, and Racial Violence." In *Powers of Desire: The Politics of Sexuality*, edited by Sharon Thompson, Anne Snitow, and Christine Stansell, 328–49. New York: Monthly Review Press, 1983.

——. "O. Delight Smith's Progressive Era: Labor, Feminism, and Reform in the Urban South." In *Visible Women: New Essays in American Activism*, edited by Nancy A. Hewitt and Suzanne Lebsock, 166–98. Urbana: University of Illinois Press, 1993.

——. *The Revolt Against Chivalry: Jessie Daniel Ames and the Women's Campaign Against Lynching.* Rev. ed. New York: Columbia University Press, 1992.

——. " 'You Must Remember This': Autobiography as Social Critique." *Journal of American History* 85 (September 1998): 439–65.

Halttunen, Karen. *Confidence Men and Painted Women: A Study of Middle-class Culture in America, 1830–1870.* New Haven, Conn.: Yale University Press, 1982.

——. "Humanitarianism and the Pornography of Pain in Anglo-American Culture." *American Historical Review* 100 (April 1995): 303–34.

Haraway, Donna. *Primate Visions: Gender, Race, and Nature in the World of Modern Science.* New York: Routledge, 1989.

Harlan, Louis R. *Booker T. Washington: The Making of a Black Leader, 1856–1901.* New York: Oxford University Press, 1975.

——. *Booker T. Washington: The Wizard of Tuskegee, 1901–1915.* New York: Oxford University Press, 1983.

——. "Booker T. Washington and the Politics of Accommodation." In *Black Leaders of the Twentieth Century*, edited by John Hope Franklin and August Meier, 1–18. Urbana: University of Illinois Press, 1982.

Harley, Sharon. "For the Good of Family and Race: Gender, Work and Domestic Roles in the Black Community, 1880–1930." *Signs* 15 (Winter 1990): 336–49.

Harris, Trudier. *Exorcising Blackness: Historical and Literary Lynching and Burning Rituals.* Bloomington: Indiana University Press, 1984.

——, comp. *Selected Works of Ida B. Wells-Barnett.* New York: Oxford University Press, 1991.

Harrison, Beverly Wildung. "The Power of Anger in the Work of Love." In *Weaving the Visions: New Patterns in Feminist Spirituality*, edited by Judith Plaskow and Carol P. Christ, 211–25. San Francisco: Harper Collins, 1989.

Hart, Roger L. *Redeemers, Bourbons and Populists: Tennessee, 1870–1896*. Baton Rouge: Louisiana State University Press, 1975.

Harzig, Christine. "The Ethnic Female Public Sphere: German-American Women in Turn-of-the-Century Chicago." In *Midwestern Women: Work, Community, and Leadership at the Crossroads*, edited by Lucy Eldersveld Murphy and Wendy Hammand Venet, 141–57. Bloomington: Indiana University Press, 1997.

Haskell, Thomas, ed. *The Authority of Experts: Studies in History and Theory*. Bloomington: Indiana University Press, 1984.

Hassey, Janette. *No Time For Silence: Evangelical Women in Public Ministry Around the Turn of the Century*. Grand Rapids, Mich.: Academie, 1986.

Helly, Dorothy O., and Susan Reverby, eds. *Gendered Domains: Rethinking Public and Private in Women's History*. Ithaca, N.Y.: Cornell University Press, 1992.

Henderson, Mae Gwendolyn. "Speaking in Tongues: Dialogics, Dialectics, and the Black Woman Writer's Literary Tradition." In *Feminists Theorize the Political*, edited by Judith Butler and Joan W. Scott, 144–66. New York: Routledge, 1992.

Hendricks, Wanda A. *Gender, Race, and Politics in the Midwest: Black Club Women in Illinois*. Bloomington: Indiana University Press, 1998.

———. "Ida B. Wells-Barnett and the Alpha Suffrage Club of Chicago." In *One Woman, One Vote: Rediscovering the Woman Suffrage Movement*, edited by Marjorie Spruill Wheeler, 263–76. Troutdale, Ore.: New Sage, 1995.

———. "The Politics of Race: Black Women in Illinois, 1890–1920." Ph.D. diss., Purdue University, 1990.

———. " 'Vote for the Advantage of Ourselves and Our Race': The Election of the First Black Alderman in Chicago." *Illinois Historical Journal* 87 (Autumn 1994): 171–84.

Herbst, Alma. *The Negro in the Slaughtering and Meat Packing Industry in Chicago*. Boston: Houghton Mifflin, 1932.

Herman, Sondra R. "Loving Courtship or the Marriage Market? The Idea and Its Critics, 1871–1911." In *Our American Sisters: Women in American Life and Thought*, edited by Jean E. Friedman, William G. Shade, and Mary Jane Capozzoli, 359–77. Lexington, Mass.: D. C. Heath, 1987.

Hewitt, Nancy A. "Compounding Differences." *Feminist Studies* 18 (Summer 1992): 313–26.

Hewitt, Nancy A., and Suzanne Lebsock, eds. *Visible Women: New Essays in American Activism*. Urbana: University of Illinois Press, 1993.

Higginbotham, Evelyn Brooks. "African American Women's History and the Metalanguage of Race." *Signs* 17 (Winter 1992): 251–76.

———. "Club Women and Electoral Politics in the 1920s." In *African American Women and the Vote, 1837–1965*, edited by Ann D. Gordon, Bettye Collier-Thomas, John H. Bracey, Arlene Voski Avakian, and Joyce Avrech Berkman, 134–55. Amherst: University of Massachusetts Press, 1997.

———. "In Politics to Stay: Black Women Leaders and Party Politics in the 1920s." In *Women, Politics, and Change*, edited by Louisa A. Tilly and Patricia Gurin, 199–220. New York: Russell Sage, 1990.

——. *Righteous Discontent: The Women's Movement in the Black Baptist Church, 1880–1920*. Cambridge: Harvard University Press, 1993.

Hine, Darlene Clark. *Black Women in White: Racial Conflict and Cooperation in the Nursing Profession, 1890–1956*. Bloomington: Indiana University Press, 1989.

——. "Rape and the Inner Lives of Black Women in the Middle West: Preliminary Notes on the Culture of Dissemblance." *Signs* 14 (Summer 1989): 912–20.

Hine, Darlene Clark, and Kathleen Thompson. *A Shining Thread of Hope: The History of Black Women in America*. New York: Broadway, 1998.

Holmes, William F. "The Arkansas Pickers' Strike of 1891 and the Demise of the Colored Farmers' Alliance." *Arkansas Historical Quarterly* 32 (Summer 1973): 107–19.

Hodes, Martha. "The Sexualization of Reconstruction Politics: White Women and Black Men in the South after the Civil War." *Journal of the History of Sexuality* 3, no. 3 (1993): 402–17.

——. *White Women, Black Men: Illicit Sex in the Nineteenth-Century South*. New Haven, Conn.: Yale University Press, 1997.

Hofstader, Richard. *The Age of Reform: From Bryan to F.D.R.* New York: Vintage, 1956.

——. *Social Darwinism in American Thought*. Rev. ed. Boston: Beacon, 1955.

Holt, Rackham. *Mary McLeod Bethune: A Biography*. Garden City, N.Y.: Doubleday, 1964.

Holt, Sharon Ann. "Making Freedom Pay: Freedpeople Working for Themselves, North Carolina, 1865–1900." *Journal of Southern History* 60 (May 1994): 229–62.

Holt, Thomas. "The Lonely Warrior: Ida B. Wells-Barnett and the Struggle for Black Leadership." In *Black Leaders of the Twentieth Century*, edited by John Hope Franklin and August Meier, 39–61. Urbana: University of Illinois Press, 1982.

hooks, bell. *Feminist Theory: From Margin to Center*. 2d ed. Boston: South End, 2000.

——. *Talking Back: Thinking Black, Thinking Feminist*. Boston: South End, 1989.

Hormel, Michael. *Down from Equality: The Segregation of Chicago Public Schools, 1920–1940*. Champaign-Urbana: University of Illinois Press, 1984.

Horton, Oliver James. "Freedom's Yoke: Gender Conventions Among Antebellum Free Blacks." *Feminist Studies* 12 (September 1986): 51–76.

Horwitz, Morton J. *The Transformation of American Law, 1870–1960: The Crisis of Legal Theory*. New York: Oxford University Press, 1992.

Humphreys, Margaret. *Yellow Fever and the South*. New Brunswick, N.J.: Rutgers University Press, 1992.

Hunter, Tera. "Domination and Resistance: The Politics of Household Labor in New South Atlanta, Georgia." *Labor History* (Spring/Summer 1993): 205–20.

Hutton, Mary M. B. "The Rhetoric of Ida B. Wells: The Genesis of the Anti-Lynch Movement." Ph.D. diss., University of Indiana, 1975.

Illinois Youth Commission. *Illinois State Training School for Girls, Geneva, Illinois*. N.p., 1963.

Israel, Adrienne M. *Amanda Berry Smith: From Washerwoman to Evangelist*. Lanham, Md.: Scarecrow, 1998.

Jackson, Kenneth T. *The Ku Klux Klan and the City, 1915–1930*. New York: Oxford University Press, 1967.

Jackson, Philip. "Black Charity in Progressive Era Chicago." *Social Service Review* 53 (September 1978): 400–417.

Jaggar, Alison M. "Love and Knowledge: Emotion and Feminist Epistemology." In *A Feminist Reconstruction of Being and Knowing*, edited by Alison M. Jaggar and Susan R. Bordo, 145–71. New Brunswick, N.J.: Rutgers University Press, 1989.

James, Joy. *Transcending the Talented Tenth: Black Leaders and American Intellectuals*. New York: Routledge, 1997.

James, Stanlie M., and Abena P. A. Busia, eds. *Theorizing Black Feminisms: The Visionary Pragmatism of Black Women*. New York: Routledge, 1993.

Janiewski, Dolores E. *Sisterhood Denied: Race, Gender and Class in a New South Community*. Philadelphia: Temple University Press, 1985.

Jones, Adrienne Lash. "Struggle Among Saints: African-American Women and the YWCA." In *Men and Women Adrift: The YMCA and the YWCA in the City*, edited by Nina Mjagkij and Margaret Spratt, 160–87. New York: New York University Press, 1997.

Jones, Beverly W. *Quest for Equality: The Life and Writings of Mary Eliza Church Terrell, 1863–1954*. Brooklyn, N.Y.: Carlson, 1990.

———. "Race, Sex, and Class: Black Female Tobacco Workers in Durham, North Carolina, 1920–1940, and the Development of Female Consciousness." *Feminist Studies* 19 (Fall 1984): 446.

Jones, Jacqueline. *Labor of Love, Labor of Sorrow: Black Women, Work, and the Family*. New York: Vintage, 1985.

Kantrowitz, Stephen. " 'No Middle Ground': Gender Protection and the Wilmington Riot of 1898." Unpublished paper in possession of the author, 1990.

Kappeler, Susanne. *The Pornography of Representation*. Minneapolis: University of Minnesota Press, 1986.

Katz, Sherry J. "A Politics of Coalition: Socialist Women and the California Suffrage Movement, 1900–11." In *One Woman, One Vote: Rediscovering the Woman Suffrage Movement*, edited by Marjorie Spruill Wheeler, 245–62. Troutdale, Ore.: New Sage, 1995.

Kelley, Robin D. G. *Race Rebels: Culture, Politics and the Black Working Class*. New York: Free Press, 1994.

Kellogg, Charles Flint. *NAACP: A History of The National Association for the Advancement of Colored People*. Baltimore, Md.: Johns Hopkins University Press, 1967.

Kennedy, David. *Over Here: The First World War and American Society*. New York: Oxford University Press, 1980.

Kerber, Linda K., Alice Kessler-Harris, and Kathryn Kish Sklar, eds. *U.S. History as Women's History: New Feminist Essays*. Chapel Hill: University of North Carolina Press, 1995.

King, Deborah K. "Multiple Jeopardy, Multiple Consciousness: The Context of a Black Feminist Ideology." *Signs* 14 (1988): 42–72.

Kirkley, Evelyn A. " 'This Work Is God's Cause': Religion in the Southern Woman Suffrage Movement, 1880–1920." *Church History* 59, no. 4 (1990) 507–22.

Kloppenberg, James T. "Pragmatism: An Old Name for Some New Ways of Thinking?" *Journal of American History* 83 (1996) 1: 100–138.

Knupfer, Anne Meis. *Toward a Tenderer Humanity and a Nobler Womanhood: African American Women's Clubs in Turn-of-the-Century Chicago*. New York: New York University Press, 1996.

Koven, Seth, and Sonya Michel, eds. *Mothers of a New World: Maternalist Politics and the Origins of Welfare States*. New York: Routledge, 1993.

Kraditor, Aileen S. *The Ideas of the Woman Suffrage Movement*. New York: Columbia University Press, 1965.

Krieling, Albert Lee. "The Making of Racial Identities in the Black Press: A Cultural Analysis of Race Journalism in Chicago, 1878–1929." Ph.D. diss., University of Illinois, Urbana-Champagne, 1973.

———. "The Rise of the Black Press in Chicago." *Journalism History* 4 (Winter 1977–78): 132–36.

Kubitschek, Missy Dehn. "Subjugated Knowledge: Toward a Feminine Exploration of Rape in Afro-American Fiction." In *Black Feminist Criticism and Critical Theory*, edited by Joe Weizmann and Houston A. Baker, 43–56. Greenwood, Fla.: Penkeville, 1988.

Kusmer, Kenneth L. "The Functions of Organized Charity in the Progressive Era: Chicago as a Case Study." *Journal of American History* 60, no. 3 (1972): 657–78.

Ladd-Taylor, Molly. "Toward Defining Maternalism in U.S. History." *Journal of Women's History* 5 (Fall 1993): 110–13.

Lane, Roger. *William Dorsey's Philadelphia and Ours: On the Past and Future of the Black City in America*. New York: Oxford University Press, 1991.

Laqueur, Thomas W. "Bodies, Details, and the Humanitarian Narrative." In *The New Cultural History*, edited by Lynn Hunt, 176–204. Berkeley: University of California Press, 1989.

Larsen, Lawrence H. *The Rise of the Urban South*. Lexington: University Press of Kentucky, 1985.

Lasch, Christopher. *The New Radicalism in America: The Intellectual as a Social Type, 1889–1963*. New York: W. W. Norton, 1965.

Lasch-Quinn, Elizabeth. *Black Neighbors: Race and the Limits of the American Settlement House Movement, 1890–1945*. Chapel Hill: University of North Carolina Press, 1993.

Lebsock, Suzanne. "Woman Suffrage and White Supremacy: A Virginia Case Study." In *Visible Women: New Essays in American Activism*, edited by Nancy A. Hewitt and Suzanne Lebsock, 62–100. Urbana: University of Illinois Press, 1993.

Lee, Chana Kai. *For Freedom's Sake: The Life of Fannie Lou Hamer*. Urbana: University of Illinois Press, 1999.

Leidenberg, George. " 'The Public Is the Labor Union': Working-Class Progressivism in Turn-of-the-Century Chicago." *Labor History* 36 (1995): 187–210.

Lemons, J. Stanley. *The Woman Citizen: Social Feminism in the 1920s*. Urbana: University of Illinois Press, 1973.

Levine, Lawrence W. *Highbrow/Lowbrow: The Emergence of Cultural Hierarchy in America*. Cambridge: Harvard University Press, 1988.

Lewis, David Levering. *W. E. B. Du Bois: Biography of a Race, 1868–1919*. New York: Henry Holt, 1993.

Lewis, Earl. "Connecting Memory, Self, and the Power of Place in African American Urban History." In *The New African American Urban History*, edited by Kenneth W. Goings and Raymond A. Mohl, 116–41. Thousands Oaks: Sage, 1996.

Lewis, Selma S., and Marjean G. Kremer. *The Angel of Beale Street: A Biography of Julia Ann Hooks*. Memphis, Tenn.: St. Luke's Press, 1986.

Lide, Pauline. "The National Conference on Social Welfare and the Black Historical Perspective." *Social Service Review* 47 (June 1973): 171–83.

Lisio, Donald J. *Hoover, Blacks, and Lily-Whites*. Chapel Hill: University of North Carolina Press, 1985.

Litwak, Leon F. *Trouble in Mind: Black Southerners in the Age of Jim Crow*. New York: Alfred A. Knopf, 1998.

Logan, Rayford W. *The Betrayal of the Negro: From Rutherford B. Hayes to Woodrow Wilson*. 2d ed. New York: Collier, 1964.

Logsdon, Joseph A. "The Rev. Archibald J. Carey and the Negro in Chicago Politics." M.A. thesis, University of Chicago, 1961.

Lorde, Audre. *Sister/Outsider: Essays and Speeches*. Freedom, Calif.: Crossing Press, 1984.

Lorimer, Douglass A. *Colour, Class and the Victorians: English Attitudes to the Negro in the Mid-Nineteenth Century*. Leicester, England: Leicester University Press, 1978.

Lovett, Bobby L. "Memphis Riots: White Reaction to Blacks in Memphis, May 1865–July 1866." *Tennessee Historical Quarterly* 38 (Spring 1979): 9–33.

Luker, Ralph E. *The Social Gospel in Black and White: American Racial Reform, 1885–1912*. Chapel Hill: University of North Carolina Press, 1991.

Lunbeck, Elizabeth. *The Psychiatric Persuasion: Knowledge, Gender, and Power in Modern America*. Princeton, N.J.: Princeton University Press, 1994.

McCarthy, Kathleen D. *Noblesse Oblige: Charity and Cultural Philanthropy in Chicago, 1849–1929*. Chicago: University of Chicago Press, 1982.

McCluskey, Audrey Thomas. " 'We Specialize in the Wholly Impossible': Black Women School Founders and Their Mission." *Signs* 22 (Winter 1997): 403–26.

McCree, Mary Lynn, and Allen F. Davis. *One Hundred Years at Hull-House*. Bloomington: Indiana University Press, 1990.

McDowell, Deborah E. *"The Changing Same": Black Women's Literature, Criticism, and Theory*. Bloomington: Indiana University Press, 1995.

McDowell, John Patrick. *The Social Gospel in the South: The Women's Home Mission Movement in the Methodist Episcopal Church, South, 1886–1939*. Baton Rouge: Louisiana State University Press, 1982.

McFeely, William S. *Frederick Douglass: A Biography*. W. W. Norton, 1991.

Mack, Kenneth W. "Law, Society, Identity and the Making of the Jim Crow South: Travel and Segregation on Tennessee Railroads, 1875–1905." *Law and Social Inquiry* 24 (Spring 1999) 2: 377–409.

McKay, Nellie. "Alice Walker's 'Advancing Luna—And Ida B. Wells': A Struggle Toward Sisterhood." In *Rape and Representation*, edited by Lynne A. Higgins and Brenda R. Silver, 248–60. New York: Columbia University Press, 1991.

MacLean, Nancy, *Behind the Mask of Chivalry: The Making of the Second Ku Klux Klan*. New York: Oxford University Press, 1994.

——. "The Leo Frank Case Reconsidered: Gender and Sexual Politics in the Making of Reactionary Populism." *Journal of American History* 78 (December 1991): 917–48.

McMurry, Linda O. *To Keep the Waters Troubled: The Life of Ida B. Wells*. New York: Oxford University Press, 1999.

Madsen, Catherine. "A God of One's Own: Recent Work by and about Women in Religion." *Signs* 19 (Winter 1994): 480–98.

Mann, Susan A., "Slavery, Sharecropping, and Sexual Inequality." In *We Specialize in the Wholly Impossible: A Reader in Black Women's History*, edited by Darlene Clark Hine, Wilma King, and Linda Reed, 281–302. Brooklyn, N.Y.: Carlson, 1995.

Marilley, Suzanna M. "Frances Willard and the Feminism of Fear." *Feminist Studies* 19 (Spring 1993): 123–46.

Marshall, Gail. *Actresses on the Victorian Stage: Feminine Performance and the Galatea Myth*. Cambridge, England: Cambridge University Press, 1998.

Massa, Ann. "Black Women in the 'White City.'" *American Studies* 8, no. 3 (1974): 319–37.

May, Martha. "The 'Problem of Duty': Family Desertion in the Progressive Era." *Social Service Review* 62 (March 1988): 40–60.

Mehaffy, Marilyn Maness. "Advertising Race/Raceing Advertising: The Feminine Consumer(-Nation), 1876–1900." *Signs* 23, no. 1 (1997): 131–74.

Meier, August. *Negro Thought in America, 1880–1915: Racial Ideology in the Age of Booker T. Washington*. Ann Arbor: University of Michigan Press, 1966.

Meyerowitz, Joanne J. *Women Adrift: Independent Wage Earners in Chicago, 1880–1930*. Chicago: University of Chicago Press, 1988.

Milkman, Ruth. "Redefining 'Women's Work': The Sexual Division of Labor in the Auto Industry during World War II." *Feminist Studies* 8 (Summer 1982): 337–72.

Miller, Kristie. *Ruth Hanna McCormick: A Life in Politics, 1880–1944*. Albuquerque: University of New Mexico Press, 1992.

Mink, Gwendolyn. *The Wages of Motherhood: Inequality in the Welfare State, 1917–1924*. Ithaca, N.Y.: Cornell University Press, 1996.

Mjagkij, Nina, and Margaret Spratt, eds. *Men and Women Adrift: The YMCA and the YWCA in the City*. New York: New York University Press, 1997.

Moldow, Gloria. *Women Doctors in Gilded Age Washington: Race, Gender, and Professionalization*. Urbana: University of Illinois, 1987.

Montgomery, William E. *Under Their Own Vine and Fig Tree: The African American Church in the South, 1865–1900*. Baton Rouge: Louisiana State University Press, 1993.

Moore, Sarah J. "Making a Spectacle of Suffrage: The National Woman Suffrage Parade, 1913." *Journal of American Culture* 20, no. 4 (1997): 89–103.

Morris, Calvin S. *Reverdy C. Ransom: Black Advocate of the Social Gospel*. New York: University Publications of America, 1990.

Morton, Patricia. *Disfigured Images: The Historical Assault on Afro-American Women*. New York: Greenwood, 1991.

Moses, Wilson Jeremiah. *Alexander Crummell: A Study of Civilization and Discontent*. New York: Oxford University Press, 1989.

———. *The Golden Age of Black Nationalism, 1850–1925*. New York: Oxford University Press, 1984.

Moss, Alfred A., Jr. *The American Negro Academy: Voice of the Talented Tenth*. Baton Rouge: Louisiana State University Press, 1982.

Muncy, Robyn. *Creating a Female Dominion in American Reform, 1890–1935*. New York: Oxford University Press, 1991.

Murdoch, Norman H. "From Militancy to Social Mission: The Salvation Army and Street Disturbances in Liverpool, 1879–1887." In *Popular Politics, Riot and Labour: Essays in Liverpool History, 1790–1940*, edited by John Belcham, 160–72. Liverpool, England: Liverpool University Press, 1992.

Murolo, Priscilla. *The Common Ground of Womanhood: Class, Gender and Working Girls' Clubs, 1884–1928*. Urbana: University of Illinois Press, 1997.

Neumann, Caryn E. "The End of Gender Solidarity: The History of the Women's Organization for National Prohibition Reform in the United States, 1929–1933." *Journal of Women's History* 9 (Summer 1997): 31–52.

Neverdon-Morton, Cynthia. *Afro-American Women of the South and the Advancement of the Race, 1895–1925*. Knoxville: University of Tennessee Press, 1989.

Odem, Mary E. *Delinquent Daughters: Protecting and Policing Adolescent Female Sexuality in the United States, 1885–1920*. Chapel Hill: University of North Carolina Press, 1995.

O'Donnell, Sandra M. "The Care of Dependent African American Children in Chicago: The Struggle Between Black Self-Help and Professionalism." *Journal of Social History* 27 (Summer 1994): 763–76.

O'Malley, Michael. "Specie and Species: Race and the Money Question in Nineteenth-Century America." *American Historical Review* 99 (April 1994): 369–95.

———. "Response to Nell Irvin Painter." *American Historical Review* 99 (April 1994): 405–8.

Ottley, Roi. *The Lonely Warrior: The Life and Times of Robert S. Abbott*. Chicago: Henry Regnery, 1955.

Painter, Nell Irvin. "Difference, Slavery, and Memory: Sojourner Truth in Feminist Abolitionism." In *The Abolitionist Sisterhood: Women's Antebellum Political Culture*, edited by Jean Fagan Yellin and John C. Van Horne, 139–58. Ithaca, N.Y.: Cornell University Press, 1994.

———. *Exodusters: Black Migration to Kansas after Reconstruction*. New York: Knopf Publishers, 1977.

———. "Hill, Thomas, and the Use of Racial Stereotype." In *Race-ing Justice, En-Gendering Power: Essays on Anita Hill, Clarence Thomas and the Construction of Social Reality*, edited by Toni Morrison, 200–214. New York: Pantheon, 1992.

———. "Representing Truth: Sojourner Truth's Knowing and Becoming Known." *Journal of American History* 81 (September 1994): 461–92.

———. " 'Social Equality,' Miscegenation, and the Maintenance of Power." In *The Evolution of Southern Culture*, edited by Numan V. Bartley, 47–67. Athens: University of Georgia Press, 1988.

———. "Sojourner Truth in Life and Memory: Writing the Biography of an American Exotic." *Gender and History* 2 (Spring 1990): 3–16.

———. *Sojourner Truth: A Life, A Symbol*. New York: W. W. Norton, 1996.

——. *Standing at Armageddon: The United States, 1877–1919.* New York: W. W. Norton, 1987.

——. "Thinking about the Languages of Money and Race: A Response to Michael O'Malley's 'Specie and Species.'" *American Historical Review* 99 (April 1994): 396–404.

——. "Writing Biographies of Women." *Journal of Women's History* 9 (Summer 1997): 154–63.

Pascoe, Peggy. *Relations of Rescue: The Search for Female Moral Authority in the America West, 1874–1939.* New York: Oxford University Press, 1990.

Pateman, Carole. "Feminist Critiques of the Public/Private Dichotomy." In *Public and Private in Social Life,* edited by S. I. Benn and G. F. Gauss, 281–306. New York: St. Martin's, 1983.

Peiss, Kathy. "'Charity Girls' and City Pleasures: Historical Notes on Working-Class Sexuality, 1880–1920." In *Powers of Desire: The Politics of Sexuality,* edited by Ann Snitow, Christine Stansell, and Sharon Thompson, 74–87. New York: Monthly Review Press, 1983.

Percy, William Alexander. *Lanterns on the Levee: Recollections of a Planter's Son.* Baton Rouge: Louisiana State University Press, 1943.

Perkins, Linda M. "The Impact of the 'Cult of True Womanhood' on the Education of Black Women." *Journal of Social Issues* 39, no. 3 (1983): 17–28.

Peterson, Carla L. *"Doers of the Word": African American Women Speakers and Writers in the North, 1830–1880.* New Brunswick, N.J.: Rutgers University Press, 1995.

Philpott, Thomas Lee. *The Slum and the Ghetto: Neighborhood Deterioration and Middle-Class Reform in Chicago, 1880–1930.* New York: Oxford University Press, 1978.

Pinderhughes, Dianne M. *Race and Ethnicity in Chicago Politics: A Reexamination of Pluralist Theory.* Urbana: University of Illinois, 1987.

Prescott, Grace Elizabeth. "The Woman Suffrage Movement in Memphis: Its Place in the State, Sectional, and National Movements." *West Tennessee Historical Society Papers* 18 (1964): 87–106.

Prosser, W. Page, et al., eds. *Prosser & Keeton on the Law Of Torts.* St. Paul, Minn.: West, 1984.

Qualls, J. Winfield. "The Beginnings and Early History of the Le Moyne School at Memphis, 1871–74." *West Tennessee Historical Society Papers* 7 (1953): 5–37.

Rabinowitz, Howard N. "Continuity and Change: Southern Urban Development, 1860–1900." In *The City in Southern History: The Growth of Urban Civilization in the South,* edited by Blaine A. Brownell and David R. Goldfield, 92–122. Port Washington, N.Y.: Kennikat, 1977.

——. "From Exclusion to Segregation: Southern Race Relations, 1865–1880." *Journal of American History* 63, no. 2 (1976): 325–50.

——. *Race Relations in the Urban South, 1865–1890.* New York: Oxford University Press, 1978.

Raboteau, Albert J. "African Americans, Exodus, and the American Israel." In *African-American Christianity: Essays in History,* edited by Paul E. Johnson, 1–17. Berkeley: University of California Press, 1994.

——. *Slave Religion: The 'Invisible Institution' in the Antebellum South.* New York: Oxford University Press, 1978.

Rampersad, Arnold. *The Art and Imagination of W. E. B. Du Bois*. New York: Schocken, 1990.

Ransby, Barbara. "A Righteous Rage and a Grassroots Mobilization." In *African American Women Speak Out on Anita Hill–Clarence Thomas*, edited by Geneva Smitherman, 42–52. Detroit, Mich.: Wayne State University Press, 1995.

Recer, Danalyn. "Patrolling the Borders of Race, Gender, and Class: The Lynching Ritual and Texas Nationalism, 1850–1994." M.A. thesis, University of Texas at Austin, 1994.

Reed, Christopher Robert. *The Chicago NAACP and the Rise of Black Professional Leadership, 1910–1966*. Bloomington: Indiana University Press, 1997.

——. "Organized Racial Reform in Chicago during the Progressive Era: The Chicago N.A.A.C.P., 1910–1920." *Michigan Historical Review* 14 (Spring 1988): 75–99.

Reverby, Susan. *Ordered to Care: The Dilemma of American Nursing, 1850–1945*. Cambridge: Cambridge University Press, 1987.

Rice, Susan Tracy. *Mother's Day: Its History, Origins, Celebration, Spirit, and Significance as Related in Prose and Verse*. New York: Dodd, Mead, 1954.

Richardson, Joe M. *Christian Reconstruction: The American Missionary Association and Southern Blacks, 1861–1890*. Athens: University of Georgia Press, 1986.

Roberts, Dorothy. *Killing the Black Body: Race, Reproduction, and the Meaning of Liberty*. New York: Pantheon, 1997.

Robinson, Armstead L. " 'Plans Dat Comed From God': Institution Building and the Emergence of Black Leadership in Reconstruction Memphis." In *Toward a New South? Studies in Post–Civil War Southern Communities*, edited by Orville Vernon Burton and Robert C. McMath Jr., 71–102. Westport, Conn.: Greenwood, 1982.

Robinson, Jo Ann Gibson. *The Montgomery Bus Boycott and the Women Who Started It: A Memoir of Jo Ann Gibson Robinson*. Edited by David J. Garrow. Knoxville: University of Tennessee Press, 1987.

Rodgers, Daniel T. "In Search of Progressivism." *Reviews in American History* 10 (December 1982): 111–32.

Roediger, David R. *The Wages of Whiteness: Race and the Making of the American Working Class*. New York: Verso, 1991.

Roitman, Joel M. "Race Relations in Memphis, Tennessee: 1886–1905." M.A. thesis, Memphis State University, 1964.

Rosen, Ruth. *The Lost Sisterhood: Prostitution in America, 1900–1918*. Baltimore, Md.: Johns Hopkins University Press, 1982.

Ross, Edyth L. *Black Heritage in Social Welfare, 1860–1930*. Metuchen, N.J.: Scarecrow, 1978.

Ross, B. Joyce. "Mary McLeod Bethune, and the National Youth Administration: A Case Study of Power Relationships in the Black Cabinet of Franklin D. Roosevelt." In *Black Leaders of the Twentieth Century*, edited by John Hope Franklin and August Meier, 191–220. Urbana: University of Illinois Press, 1982.

Rothman, David. *Conscience and Convenience: The Asylum and Its Alternatives in Progressive America*. Boston: Little, Brown, 1980.

Rouse, Jacqueline Anne. *Lugenia Burns Hope: Black Southern Reformer*. Athens: University of Georgia Press, 1989.

Roydhouse, Marion W. "Bridging Chasms: Community and the Southern

YWCA." In *Visible Women: New Essays in American Activism*, edited by Nancy A. Hewitt and Suzanne Lebsock, 270–95. Urbana: University of Illinois Press, 1993.

Royster, Jacquelyn Jones. "'To Call a Thing by Its Name': The Rhetoric of Ida B. Wells." In *Reclaiming Rhetorica: Women in the Rhetorical Tradition*, edited by Andrea A. Lunsford, 167–84. Pittsburgh: University of Pittsburgh Press, 1995.

——, ed. *Southern Horrors and Other Writings: The Anti-Lynching Campaign of Ida B. Wells, 1892–1900*. Boston: Bedford, 1997.

Rudwick, Elliott. "The Niagara Movement." *Journal of Negro History* 3 (July 1957): 177–200.

——. *Race Riot at East St. Louis, July 2, 1917*. Carbondale: Southern Illinois University Press, 1964.

——. "W. E. B. Du Bois: Protagonist of the Afro-American Protest." In *Black Leaders in the Twentieth Century*, edited by John Hope Franklin and August Meier, 63–84. Urbana: University of Illinois Press, 1982.

Rudwick, Elliott, and August Meier. "Black Man in the 'White City': Negroes and the Columbian Exposition, 1893." *Phylon* 26 (Winter 1965): 354–61.

Ryan, Mary P. *Women in Public: Between Banners and Ballots, 1825–1880*. Baltimore, Md.: Johns Hopkins University Press, 1990.

Rydell, Robert W. *All the World's a Fair: Visions of Empire at American International Expositions, 1876–1916*. Chicago: University of Chicago Press, 1984.

Salem, Dorothy. *To Better Our World: Black Women in Organized Reform*. Brooklyn, N.Y.: Carlson, 1990.

Samuels, Shirley. "The Identity of Slavery." In *The Culture of Sentiment: Race, Gender, and Sentimentality in Nineteenth-Century America*, edited by Shirley Samuels, 157–71. New York: Oxford University Press, 1992.

Sanchez-Eppler, Karen. "Bodily Bonds: The Intersecting Rhetorics of Feminism and Abolition." In *The Culture of Sentiment: Race, Gender, and Sentimentality in Nineteenth-Century America*, edited by Shirley Samuels, 92–114. New York: Oxford University Press, 1992.

Sawyers, June Skinner. *Chicago Portraits: Biographies of 250 Famous Chicagoans*. Chicago: Loyola University Press, 1991.

Saxton, Alexander. *The Rise and Fall of the White Republic: Class Politics and Mass Culture in Nineteenth-Century America*. New York: Verso, 1990.

Scary, Elaine. *The Body in Pain: The Making and Unmaking of the World*. New York: Oxford University Press, 1985.

Schechter. Patricia A. "'All the Intensity of My Nature': Ida B. Wells, Anger, and Politics." *Radical History Review* 70 (Winter 1998): 48–77.

——. "Unsettled Business: Ida B. Wells against Lynching, or, How Anti-Lynching Got Its Gender." In *Under Sentence of Death: Lynching in the South*, edited by W. Fitzhugh Brundage, 292–317. Chapel Hill: University of North Carolina Press, 1997.

Scheiner, Seth. "President Theodore Roosevelt and the Negro, 1901–1908." *Journal of Negro History* (July 1962): 169–82.

Schwalm, Leslie A. *A Hard Fight for We: Women in the Transition from Slavery to Freedom in South Carolina*. Urbana: University of Illinois Press, 1997.

——. "'Sweet Dreams of Freedom': Freedwomen's Reconstruction of Life and

Labor in Lowcountry South Carolina." *Journal of Women's History* 9 (September 1997): 9–38.

Scott, Anne Firor. *Natural Allies: Women's Associations in American History.* Urbana: University of Illinois Press, 1991.

———. *The Southern Lady: From Pedestal to Politics, 1830–1930.* Chicago: University of Chicago Press, 1970.

Scott, James W. *Weapons of the Weak: Everyday Forms of Peasant Resistance.* New Haven, Conn.: Yale University Press, 1987.

Scott, Joan. "Gender: A Useful Category of Historical Analysis." *American Historical Review* 91 (December 1986): 1053–75.

Seigfried, Charlene Haddock. *Pragmatism and Feminism: Reweaving the Social Fabric.* Chicago: University of Chicago Press, 1996.

Shapiro, Herbert. "The Muckrakers and Negroes." *Phylon* 31 (Spring 1970): 76–88.

———. *White Violence and Black Response: From Reconstruction to Montgomery.* Amherst: University of Massachusetts Press, 1988.

Shaw, Stephanie J. "Black Club Women and the Creation of the National Association of Colored Women." *Journal of Women's History* 3 (Fall 1991): 10–25.

———. *What a Woman Ought to Be and to Do: Black Professional Women Workers during the Jim Crow Era.* Chicago: University of Chicago Press, 1996.

Shay, Frank. *Judge Lynch: His First Hundred Years.* New York: Biblio and Tannen, 1968. Originally published 1938.

Sicherman, Barbara. "Working it Out: Gender, Profession, and Reform in the Career of Alice Hamilton." In *Gender, Class, Race, and Reform in the Progressive Era*, edited by Noralee Frankel and Nancy S. Dye, 127–47. Lexington: University Press of Kentucky, 1991.

Silverman, Robert Mark. "The Effects of Racism and Racial Discrimination on Minority Business Development: The Case of Black Manufacturers in Chicago's Ethnic Beauty Aids Industry." *Journal of Social History* 31 (Spring 1998): 571–97.

Sims, Anastasia. *The Power of Femininity in the New South: Women's Organizations and Politics in North Carolina, 1880–1930.* Columbia: University of South Carolina Press, 1997.

Sklar, Kathryn Kish. *Florence Kelley and the Nation's Work: The Rise of Women's Political Culture, 1830–1900.* New Haven, Conn.: Yale University Press, 1995.

———. "Hull-House Maps and Papers: Social Science as Women's Work in the 1890s." In *The Social Survey in Historical Perspective, 1880–1940*, edited by Martin Bulmer, Kevin Bales, and Kathryn Kish Sklar, 111–47. Cambridge, England: Cambridge University Press, 1991.

———. "Hull-House in the 1890s: A Community of Women Reformers." *Signs* 10, no. 4 (1985): 658–77.

———. "Who Founded Hull-House?" In *Lady Bountiful Revisited: Women, Philanthropy, and Power*, edited by Kathleen D. McCarthy, 105–10. New Brunswick, N.J.: Rutgers University Press, 1990.

Skowronek, Stephen. *Building a New American State: The Expansion of National Administrative Capacities, 1877–1920.* New York: Cambridge University Press, 1982.

Smith, Valerie. *Self-Discovery and Authority in Afro-American Narrative*. Cambridge: Harvard University Press, 1987.

———. "Split Affinities: The Case of Interracial Rape." In *Conflicts in Feminism*, edited by Marianne Hirsch and Evelyn Fox Keller, 271–87. New York: Routledge, 1990.

Spear, Allan H. *Black Chicago: The Making of a Negro Ghetto, 1890–1920*. Chicago: University of Chicago Press, 1967.

Spellman, Elizabeth V. *Inessential Woman: Problems of Exclusion in Feminist Thought*. Boston: Beacon, 1988.

Spillers, Hortense V. "Mama's Baby, Papa's Maybe: An American Grammar Book." *Diacritics* 17 (Summer 1987): 64–81.

———. "'The Permanent Obliquity of an In(pha)llibly Straight': In the Time of the Daughters and the Fathers." In *Changing Our Own Words: Essays on Criticism, Theory, and Writing by Black Women*, edited by Cheryl A. Wall, 127–49. New Brunswick, N.J.: Rutgers University Press, 1989.

Spratt, Margaret. "To Be Separate or One: The Issue of Race in the History of the Pittsburgh and Cleveland YWCAs." In *Men and Women Adrift: The YMCA and the YWCA in the City*, edited by Nina Mjagkij and Margaret Spratt, 188–205. New York: New York University Press, 1997.

Stange, Douglas Charles. *British Unitarians against American Slavery, 1833–1865*. Rutherford, N.J.: Fairleigh Dickinson University Press, 1984.

———. *Patterns of Antislavery among American Unitarians, 1831–1860*. Rutherford, N.J.: Fairleigh Dickinson University Press.

Stansell, Christine. *City of Women: Sex and Class in New York City, 1790–1860*. Urbana: University of Illinois Press, 1986.

Stearns, Peter N., and Carol Z. Stearns. *Anger: The Struggle for Emotional Control in American History*. Chicago: University of Chicago Press, 1986.

Stebner, Eleanor J. *The Women of Hull-House: A Study in Spirituality, Vocation, and Friendship*. Albany: State University of New York Press, 1997.

Stecopoulos, Harry, and Michael Uebel, eds. *Race and the Subject of Masculinities*. Durham, N.C.: Duke University Press, 1997.

Stehno, Sandra M. "Public Responsibility for Dependent Black Children: The Advocacy of Edith Abbott and Sophonisba Breckinridge." *Social Service Review* 62 (September 1988): 485–503.

Streitmatter, Rodger. "African American Women Journalists and Their Male Editors: A Tradition of Support." *Journalism Quarterly* 17 (Summer 1993): 276–86.

———. "Economic Conditions Surrounding Nineteenth-Century African American Women Journalists: Two Case Studies," *Journalism History* 18 (1992): 33–40.

———. *Raising Her Voice: African American Women Journalists Who Changed History*. Lexington: University Press of Kentucky, 1994.

Stovall, Mary E. "The Chicago *Defender* in the Progressive Era." *Illinois Historical Journal* 83 (Autumn 1990): 159–72.

Strickland, Arvarh E. *History of the Chicago Urban League*. Urbana: University of Illinois Press, 1966.

Sullivan, Patricia. *Days of Hope: Race and Democracy in the New Deal Era*. Chapel Hill: University of North Carolina Press, 1996.

Swerdlow, Amy, and Harriet Hyman Alonso. "Nobel Peace Laureates, Jane

Addams and Emily Greene Balch." *Journal of Women's History* 7 (Summer 1995): 6–26.

Tate, Claudia. *Domestic Allegories of Political Desire: The Black Heroine's Text at the Turn of the Century*. New York: Oxford University Press, 1992.

Taves, Ann. "Knowing through the Body: Dissociative Religious Experience in the African- and British-American Methodist Traditions." *Journal of Religion* 73 (1993): 200–222.

Tax, Meredith. *The Rising of the Women: Feminist Solidarity and Class Conflict, 1880–1917*. New York: Monthly Review Press, 1980.

Taylor, Clarence. *The Black Churches of Brooklyn*. New York: Columbia University Press, 1994.

Terborg-Penn, Rosalyn. *African American Women in the Struggle for the Vote, 1850–1920*. Bloomington: Indiana University Press, 1998.

———. "African American Women's Networks in the Anti-Lynching Crusade." In *Gender, Class, Race, and Reform in the Progressive Era*, edited by Noralee Frankel and Nancy S. Dye, 148–61. Lexington: University Press of Kentucky, 1991.

———. "Discontented Black Feminists: Prelude and Postscript to the Passage of the Nineteenth Amendment." In *We Specialize in the Wholly Impossible: A Reader in Black Women's History* , edited by Darlene Clark Hine, Wilma King, and Linda Reed, 487–504. Brooklyn, N.Y.: Carlson, 1995.

Thompson, Mildred I. *Ida B. Wells-Barnett: An Exploratory Study of an American Black Woman, 1893–1930*. Brooklyn, N.Y.: Carlson, 1990.

Thornbrough, Emma Lou. *T. Thomas Fortune: Militant Journalist*. Chicago: University of Chicago Press, 1972.

Tinsley, James A. "Roosevelt, Foraker, and the Brownsville Affray." *Journal of Negro History* (January 1956): 43–65.

Tolnay, Stewart E., and E. M. Beck. *A Festival of Violence: An Analysis of Southern Lynchings, 1882–1930*. Urbana: University of Illinois Press, 1995.

Townes, Emilie M. "Black Women." In *In Our Own Voices: Four Centuries of American Women's Religious Writing*, edited by Rosemary Skinner Keller and Rosemary Radford Reuther, 153–206. San Francisco: Harper Collins, 1995.

———. *In a Blaze of Glory: Womanist Spirituality as Social Witness*. Nashville, Tenn.: Abingdon, 1995.

———. *Womanist Justice, Womanist Hope*. Atlanta, Ga.: Scholars Press, 1993.

Trachtenberg, Alan. *The Incorporation of America: Culture and Society in the Gilded Age*. New York: Hill and Wang, 1982.

Tucker, David M. *Black Pastors and Leaders: Memphis, 1819–1972*. Memphis, Tenn.: Memphis State University Press, 1975.

———. "Black Politics in Memphis, 1865–1875." *West Tennessee Historical Society Papers* 26 (1972): 13–19.

———. "Miss Ida B. Wells and Memphis Lynching." *Phylon* 32 (Summer 1971): 112–22.

Turner, Elizabeth Hayes. *Women, Culture, and Community: Religion and Reform in Galveston, 1880–1920*. New York: Oxford University Press, 1997.

Tuttle, William M., Jr. *Race Riot: Chicago in the Red Summer of 1919*. New York: Atheneum, 1970.

Tyrrell, Ian. *Woman's World / Woman's Empire: The Women's Christian Temperance*

Union in International Perspective. Chapel Hill: University of North Carolina Press, 1991.

Tyson, Timothy B. "Robert F. Williams, 'Black Power,' and the Roots of the African American Freedom Struggle." *Journal of American History* 85 (September 1998): 540–70.

———. *Radio-Free Dixie: Robert F. Williams and the Roots of Black Power*. Chapel Hill: University of North Carolina Press, 1998.

Wade-Gayles, Gloria. "Black Women Journalists in the South, 1880–1905: An Approach to the Study of Black Women's History." In *Black Women in United States History: From Colonial Times to the Nineteenth Century*, edited by Darlene Clark Hine, 4:1409–23. Brooklyn, N.Y.: Carlson, 1990.

Walker, Alice. "Advancing Luna—and Ida B. Wells." In *You Can't Keep a Good Woman Down*, 85–104. New York: Harcourt Brace Jovanovich, 1981.

Walker, Cheryl. "Persona Criticism and the Death of the Author." In *Contesting the Subject: Essays in Postmodern Theory and Practice of Biography and Biographical Criticism*, edited by William H. Epstein, 109–22. West Lafayette, Ind.: Purdue University Press, 1991.

Walker, Clarence. *A Rock in a Weary Land: The African Methodist Episcopal Church during the Civil War and Reconstruction*. Baton Rouge: Louisiana State University Press, 1982.

Walkowitz, Daniel J. "The Making of a Feminine Professional Identity: Social Workers in the 1920s." *American Historical Review* 95, no. 4 (1990): 1051–75.

Wall, Cheryl A., ed. *Changing Our Own Words: Essays on Criticism, Theory, and Writing by Black Women*. New Brunswick, N.J.: Rutgers University Press, 1989.

Waller, P. J. *Democracy and Sectarianism: A Political and Social History of Liverpool, 1868–1939*. Liverpool, England: Liverpool University Press, 1981.

Walters, Ronald G. *The Anti-Slavery Appeal: American Abolitionism after 1830*. Baltimore, Md.: Johns Hopkins University Press, 1976.

Walzer, Michael. *The Company of Critics: Social Criticism and Political Commitment in the Twentieth Century*. New York: Basic, 1988.

Ware, Vron. *Beyond the Pale: White Women, Race, and History*. New York: Verso, 1992.

Washington, Mary Helen. "Plain, Black and Decently Wild: The Heroic Possibilities of Maud Martha." In *The Voyage In: Fictions of Female Development*, edited by Elizabeth Abel, Marianne Hirsch, and Elizabeth Langland, 270–86. Hanover, N.H.: Dartmouth College/University Press of New England, 1983.

———. "Teaching *Black-Eyed Susans*: An Approach to the Study of Black Women Writers." In *All the Women are White, All the Blacks are Men, But Some of Us Are Brave: Black Women's Studies*, edited by Gloria T. Hull, Patricia Bell Scott, and Barbara Smith, 208–17. Old Westbury, N.Y.: Feminist Press, 1982.

Waskow, Arthur I. *From Race Riot to Sit-in, 1919 and the 1960s*. Garden City, N.Y.: Doubleday, 1966.

Wedell, Marsha. *Elite Women and the Reform Impulse in Memphis, 1875–1915*. Knoxville: University of Tennessee Press, 1991.

Wedin, Carolyn. *Inheritors of the Spirit: Mary White Ovington and the Founding of the NAACP*. New York: John Wiley & Sons, 1998.

Weems, Renita J. *Just a Sister Away: A Womanist Vision of Women's Relationships in the Bible*. San Diego, Calif.: Luna Media, 1988.

Weibe, Robert H. *The Search for Order, 1877–1920*. New York: Hill and Wang, 1977.

Weigman, Robyn. *American Anatomies: Theorizing Race and Gender*. Durham, N.C.: Duke University Press, 1995.

———. "The Anatomy of Lynching." *Journal of the History of Sexuality* 3, no. 3 (1993): 445–67.

Weimann, Jeanne Madeline. *The Fair Women*. Chicago: Academy, 1981.

Weisenfeld, Judith. *African American Women and Christian Activism: New York's Black YWCA, 1905–1945*. Cambridge: Harvard University Press, 1997.

Welke, Barbara. "When All the Women Were White, and All the Blacks Were Men: Gender, Class, Race, and the Road to Plessy, 1855–1914." *Law and History Review* 13 (1995): 261–316.

Welter, Barbara. "The Cult of Domesticity, 1820–1860." *American Quarterly* 18 (1966): 151–74.

West, Cornel. *The American Evasion of Philosophy: A Genealogy of Pragmatism*. Madison: University of Wisconsin Press, 1989.

———. *Prophetic Fragments*. Grand Rapids, Mich: William B. Eerdmans, 1988.

Wheeler, Adade Mitchell, and Marlene Stein Wortman. *The Roads They Made: Women in Illinois History*. Chicago: Charles H. Kerr, 1977.

White, Deborah Gray. *Ar'n't I a Woman? Female Slaves in the Plantation South*. New York: W. W. Norton, 1985.

———. "The Cost of Club Work, the Price of Black Feminism." In *Visible Women: New Essays on American Activism*, edited by Nancy Hewitt and Suzanne Lebsock, 247–69. Urbana: University of Illinois Press, 1993.

———. *Too Heavy a Load: Black Women in Defense of Themselves, 1894–1994*. New York: W. W. Norton, 1999.

White, E. Frances. "Africa on My Mind: Gender, Counter Discourse, and African American Nationalism." *Journal of Women's History* 2 (Spring 1990): 73–97.

Whites, Lee Ann. "Rebecca Latimer Felton and the Problem of 'Protection' in the New South." In *Visible Women: New Essays in American Activism*, edited by Nancy A. Hewitt and Suzanne Lebsock, 41–61. Urbana: University of Illinois Press, 1993.

Williams, Delores S. *Sisters in the Wilderness: The Challenge of Womanist God-Talk*. Maryknoll, N.Y.: Orbis, 1993.

Williamson, Joel. *The Crucible of Race: Black-White Relations in the American South Since Emancipation*. New York: Oxford University Press, 1984.

Willrich, Michael. "City of Courts: Crime, Law, and Social Policy in Chicago, 1880–1920." Ph.D. diss. University of Illinois, 1997.

Wills, David. "Reverdy C. Ransom: The Making of an AME Bishop." In *Black Apostles: Afro-American Clergy Confront the Twentieth Century*, edited by Randall K. Burkett and Richard Newman, 180–212. Boston: G. K. Hall, 1978.

Wilmore, Gayraud S. *Afro-American Religious Studies: An Interdisciplinary Anthology*. Durham, N.C.: Duke University Press, 1989.

Wilson, Rob. "Producing American Selves: The Form of American Biography." In *Contesting the Subject: Essays in the Postmodern Theory and Practice of Biography and Biographical Criticism*, edited by William H. Epstein, 167–92. West Lafayette, Ind.: Purdue University Press, 1991.

Wolcott, Victoria W. " 'Bible, Bath and Broom': Nannie Helen Burrough's

National Training School and African-American Racial Uplift." *Journal of Women's History* 9 (Spring 1997): 88–110.

Woodson, Carter G., and Charles H. Wesley. *The Negro in Our History*, 11th ed. Washington, D.C.: Associated Publishers, 1966.

Woodward, C. Vann. *Tom Watson: Agrarian Rebel*. New York: Oxford University Press, 1938.

Wrenn, Lynette B. "Commission Government in The Gilded Age: The Memphis Plan." *Tennessee Historical Quarterly* 47, no. 4 (Winter 1988): 216–26.

———. "Politics of Memphis School Reform, 1883–1927." In *Southern Cities, Southern Schools: Public Education in the Urban South*, edited by Rick Ginsberg and David N. Plank, 81–107. Westport, Conn.: Greenwood, 1990.

———. "School Board Reorganization in Memphis, 1883." *Tennessee Historical Quarterly* 4 (Winter 1986): 329–41.

Yarborough, Richard. "Race, Violence, and Manhood: The Masculine Ideal in Frederick Douglass's 'The Heroic Slave.' " In *Frederick Douglass: New Literary and Historical Essays*, edited by Eric J. Sundquist, 166–88. Cambridge, England: Cambridge University Press, 1990.

Yee, Shirley. *Black Women Abolitionists: A Study in Activism, 1828–1860*. Knoxville: University of Tennessee Press, 1992.

Zangrando, Robert L. *The NAACP Crusade Against Lynching, 1909–1950*. Philadelphia: Temple University Press, 1980.

Zeiger, Susan. "Finding a Cure for War: Women's Politics and the Peace Movement in the 1920s." *Journal of Social History* 24, no. 1 (1990): 69–86

Ziff, Larzar. *The American 1890s: Life and Times of a Lost Generation*. New York: Viking, 1966.

INDEX

tion of Sarah Ann Hughes as deacon in, 51; Sunday school teaching by Wells-Barnett, 66, 67, 73, 134; Turner as bishop in, 68, 268 (n. 120); General Conference in Philadelphia in 1892, 79, 84; in Washington, D.C., 88–90; in Brooklyn, 104; and R. Charles, 118; and Tillman, 119; in Chicago, 174, 175–76, 178–81, 295 (n. 4), 312 (n. 41); wedding of Ida B. Wells and Ferdinand Barnett in, 175–76; and settlement movement, 179, 181–82, 295 (n. 4); Carey as bishop in, 179, 206, 307 (n. 203); sexual misconduct of minister of, 186–87; Cook's resignation from, 230, 315 (n. 74); and educational institutions, 268 (n. 120); financial assets of, 270 (n. 171); and race riots, 294 (n. 170)

American Citizenship Association, 315 (n. 72)

American Negro Academy, 119, 137, 250

American Social Science Association, 110

AME Zion Church, 65, 312 (n. 41)

Anderson, Louis B., 203, 206

Anderson, Violette, 228

Anger, 13–14, 16–17, 51, 58, 96, 137, 146, 208, 259 (n. 45), 262 (n. 133)

Anthony, Susan B., 28, 237

Anti-Caste, 91–92

Anti-Lynching Bureau, 116, 117, 128

Anti-Lynching Crusaders, 122, 165, 166, 168, 316 (n. 79)

Anti-Lynching League (Chicago), 130

Antilynching reform: Wells-Barnett's leadership of and impact on, 1–2, 4, 116, 124, 129, 132, 136–38, 141, 146, 179; exile as metaphor in, 3–4, 10–11, 23–26, 28, 34, 119; and *Southern Horrors* by Wells-Barnett, 4, 14, 18, 21, 37, 84–88, 90, 94, 99, 113, 124, 163, 174, 272 (n. 230); and NAACP, 4, 122–23, 135–36, 141–42, 148, 154, 165, 166, 167, 289 (n. 64), 290 (n. 93); lectures by Wells-Barnett in England, 10, 21, 22, 23–26, 86, 91–94, 97–104, 278 (nn. 103, 111); and *Free Speech*, 17,

18, 35, 69–70, 77, 78; conversion experience of Wells-Barnett, 17–18; and club women, 18–20; and black women, 18–20, 84, 108–9, 115, 116, 118, 121, 122, 128, 137–38, 148–49, 165–68, 291 (n. 125); lectures by Wells-Barnett in United States, 18–20, 88–90, 103–10, 142, 146, 281 (n. 172); and Douglass, 21–22, 81, 87, 88, 273 (n. 7); whites' dismissal and criticisms of Wells-Barnett, 33–34, 88, 91, 99–100, 101, 104–7, 111; and vindication of black manhood, 86, 107, 113, 117–18, 147–48, 253; financial contributions to, 90, 107, 108, 165, 289 (n. 64); barriers to, 90–91, 126; and Society for the Recognition of the Brotherhood of Man, 92, 93, 97, 98, 99, 102, 109, 281 (n. 181); and churches, 99–102; and temperance movement, 102, 110–12; and southern whites, 104–6, 124, 166, 275 (n. 44); and gender relations, 106–7, 121–32, 137–38, 141, 147–49, 167–68; black criticisms of, 106–9; blacks' criticisms of Wells-Barnett, 106–9, 122, 145–46; as community-based movement, 107–8; impact of British sentiment on United States, 109; blacks' responsibility for, 109–10, 126; and *Red Record* by Wells-Barnett, 112–14, 117, 119; and Du Bois, 116, 165, 168; *Lynch Law in Georgia* by Wells-Barnett, 116–17, 119, 123; and lynching as national crime, 117, 118, 125, 135; *Mob Rule in New Orleans* by Wells-Barnett, 117–18, 119, 120; concluding comments on, 118–20; laws against lynching, 121–22, 127, 128, 135, 139, 142, 165–66, 168, 230, 231, 236, 280 (n. 156); Wells-Barnett's involvement in, after World War I, 122–23, 126, 128–31, 134–47, 167–68; and Terrell, 123–24; and B. T. Washington, 124, 285–86 (n. 12); and J. Addams, 124–25; and W. James, 127; and T. Roosevelt, 127; and Cairo, Ill., lynching, 138–41, 158, 168; professional experts and social

53–55, 143–44; employment of, 55, 130, 143, 208, 220–21, 321 (n. 167); marriage and gender protection for, 55–59; and church life, 63–70; critique of the ministry by, 64–65; and temperance movement, 66, 67, 102, 111, 282 (n. 198); sexual harassment of, 72–73, 253; dual identity of, 82; rape of, 85, 87–88, 114, 123–24, 168, 244–45, 283 (n. 216), 286 (n. 15); legal rights for, 91; and World's Columbian Exposition (1893), 94–97; criticism of Wells-Barnett by, 95; and motherhood, 133–34, 135, 143, 289 (n. 59); and NAACP, 137; Ovington on, 142; status of, in the North, 143–44; standard of selflessness for, 145; as defenders of race, 148–49, 151; and race riots, 150, 156, 293 (nn. 149–50); and Arkansas case, 162, 163–64; political involvement of, 172, 191–92, 198–207, 216–23, 229, 232–46, 253, 318 (n. 130); widowhood of, 176; interracial gatherings with white women, 184, 232, 300 (n. 73); white woman's abuse of black domestic servant, 197–98; and World War I, 207–12, 308 (n. 225), 313 (n. 51); as political candidates, political officeholders, and government employees, 216–17, 220, 239, 241–44, 309 (n. 3), 311 (n. 25); "othermothering" by, 221, 225, 245; as police officers, 225, 229; and penal system for women, 227–29, 314 (n. 60); as lawyers, 228; Addams on, 232; need for higher moral standard than white women, 245; economic issues of, 270 (n. 158). See also Women's clubs; and specific individuals

Blease, Cole, 147

Blood Red Record (J. E. Bruce), 124, 284 (n. 236)

Body issues: skin color of Wells-Barnett, 24–25, 105; association of black women with the body, 33–34, 52, 84, 105; beauty and marriageability of women, 61; and lynching, 84, 85; and antislavery movement, 85;

Wells-Barnett's need to shield bodies of black women, 114; hair contests, beauty pageants, and fashion shows, 225, 312 (n. 45)

Booth, Edwin, 49

Bordin, Frances, 111

Boris, Eileen, 219

Boston, 19, 22, 90, 91, 95, 101, 111, 115–17, 132, 275 (n. 37), 276–77 (n. 72)

Bowen, Louise DeKoven, 189

Bradshaw, Fannie, 68

Bratton, U. S., 160–61

Bread Givers (Yezierska), 56

Breckinridge, Sophonisba, 3

Brinkley, Rev. W. A., 68, 77

Britain. See Great Britain

British Women's Temperance Association (BWTA), 99, 102

Britton, Hattie, 72, 78, 271 (n. 192)

Broad-Ax. See Chicago Broad-Ax

Brooklyn, N.Y., 18, 19–20, 33, 108, 178

Brooks, George, 314 (n. 61)

Brotherhood of Sleeping Car Porters, 218, 226

Brough, Charles, 160, 161

Broughton, Virginia W., 43, 44–45, 67, 69, 258 (n. 9), 264 (n. 34)

Brown, Charlotte Hawkins, 171, 176, 231

Brown, Edward Osgood, 154

Brown, Elsa Barkley, 3

Brown, Hallie Quinn, 92, 109, 237, 281 (n. 181)

Brown, Jane, 43

Brown, Louis M., 47, 57–58

Bruce, Blanche K., 73, 124, 272–73 (n. 2)

Bruce, John E., 131, 284 (n. 236)

Brundage, Edward, 29, 154, 156

Bundy, Leroy, 29, 149, 151–55, 159, 208, 210, 230, 292 (nn. 134–35, 142), 308 (n. 228)

Burroughs, Nannie Helen, 176, 237

Burton, Annie L., 258 (n. 12)

Burton, Mary, 71, 78

Butler, Fannie, 44, 56, 59

BWTA. See British Women's Temperance Association

in, 9, 10, 14–18, 23, 30; publishing history of, 9, 248, 257 (n. 8); narrative voices of, 10; Chicago work of Wells-Barnett, 10, 11, 26–33, 175, 197–98, 218; childhood and youth of Wells-Barnett, 10, 11–14; travels of Wells-Barnett in England and United States during early antilynching campaign, 10, 18–26; visionary pragmatism in, 11–14, 34; violence against slave women in, 14–15; early womanhood of Wells-Barnett in South, 14–18; reputation and character of Wells-Barnett, 15–17; journalist career of Wells-Barnett, 17; lynchings in Memphis in 1892, 17–18; Douglass in, 18, 21–23; and talking through tears, 18–23, 33; Brooklyn testimonial to Wells-Barnett, 19–20; preface of, 32–33, 248; concluding comments on, 33–35; on Wells-Barnett as "instrument" for justice, 108; Cairo, Ill., lynching in, 139–41; on military execution of black soldiers, 157–58; on Arkansas case, 162–64; on Negro Fellowship League, 169–70, 212

"Cynthia Poems" (Propertius), 265 (n. 60)

Danville, Ill., 128

Davis, Elizabeth Lindsay, 189, 209, 215–16, 218, 220–22, 233, 240, 241, 291 (n. 104), 300 (nn. 73–74), 305 (n. 159), 309 (n. 1), 318–19 (n. 135)

Davis, Frank E., 139, 140, 141

Davis, William H., 309 (n. 1)

Death penalty, 158, 159–60

Declaration of Sentiments (1848), 297 (n. 20)

DeCosta-Willis, Miriam, 264 (n. 40), 269 (n. 156)

Defamation against women, 91, 275 (n. 46)

Delaney, Lucy A., 258 (n. 12)

Delaware, 127

Democratic Party, 40, 70, 77, 106, 201, 205, 230, 236–37, 280 (n. 156), 307 (nn. 201, 203), 317 (n. 113). *See also specific Democratic politicians*

Deneen, Charles S., 138–39, 141, 310–11 (n. 25), 317 (n. 116), 320 (n. 146)

DePriest, Oscar, 155, 161, 203, 205, 227, 240, 320 (n. 146)

DeSaible, Jean Baptiste, 247

DeSaible Club, 316–17 (n. 96)

Dewey, Thomas, 240

Dickens, Charles, 268 (n. 119)

Dickinson, Anna, 48, 265 (n. 56)

Discrimination against blacks. *See* Segregation

District of Columbia. *See* Washington, D.C.

Douglass, Frederick: autobiographies of, 12, 261 (n. 87); in *Crusade for Justice*, 18, 21–23; as orator, 21–22; and antilynching reform, 21–22, 81, 87, 88, 98, 102, 103, 273 (n. 7); Wells-Barnett's relationship with, 21–23, 33, 97, 98, 102, 103; freedom purchased for, 22; death of, 22–23, 28, 33, 121; on black women's accomplishments, 38, 67; on discrimination based on race and sex, 82; and Wells-Barnett's speaking engagements, 90; and libels against Wells-Barnett, 91, 97; Impey's friendship with, 92, 93; marriage of, to white woman, 94; and World's Columbian Exposition (1893), 94, 95, 96–97; lack of reception of, in the South, 99; and Willard, 111, 282 (n. 200); writings about, 260 (n. 76), 269 (n. 152); accusations of personal profiteering against, 276 (n. 58); in Britain, 276 (n. 58)

Douglass, Helen Pitts, 28, 94

Douglass Center, 184–86, 187, 188, 209, 211, 212, 295 (n. 4), 300 (n. 73)

Douglass Day celebrations, 103, 233

Douglass Memorial Home, 231

Dove, Lillian S., 238

Drake, St. Clair, 145, 178

Dreiser, Theodore, 119–20

Drumgoold, Kate, 258 (n. 12)

Du Bois, W. E. B.: on women's status, 1, 2; and Wells-Barnett, 2, 136–37, 142, 164, 249; on "talented tenth," 37; social science surveys in Philadelphia, 112; and lynchings, 116, 165,

Manley, Hattie, 51

Marriage: of Ida B. Wells and Ferdinand Barnett, 4, 27, 28–29, 175–78; conflict between public activism and, 28–29; age of legal consent for girls, 41; and gender protection, 55–59; interracial marriage, 94

Mary (mother of Jesus), 31, 53

Mary Magdalene, 53–54

Masculinity. *See* Gender relations

Massachusetts, 144, 183. *See also* Boston

Mathews, Victoria Earle, 18, 176

Matthew, Gospel of, 139

Mayo, Isabelle Fyvie, 92, 93, 98

Memphis: social and political tensions in 1880s, 4; bias in legal system in, 7, 29, 71; Wells-Barnett as teacher in, 15, 44, 73; Wells-Barnett's move to, 16, 43, 44; newspapers in, 17, 41, 50, 69–70; lynchings in, 17–18, 20, 23, 39, 69, 75–79; destruction of *Free Speech* office in, 18, 78–79, 106; threats against Wells-Barnett in, 35; population of, 39; yellow fever epidemic in, 39–40; economic development in, 39–41; black police in, 40; schools in, 40, 41, 72–73; race relations in, 40, 41–43, 70–75; politics in, 40, 70–71; black politicians in, 40, 71; race riot and racial violence in, 40, 208; black middle class in, 40–41, 42; woman suffrage in, 41; churches in, 41, 65–69, 269–70 (n. 156); military organizations in, 41, 74, 76, 263 (n. 22), 272 (n. 214); black community organizations and institutions in, 41, 267 (n. 104); white female elite in, 41–43, 55, 264 (n. 26); segregation in, 42, 51, 70, 71–72; black women's activism in, 43; Wells-Barnett's leaving, 44; disfranchisement in, 69, 70–71; white supremacy in, 70–75; blacks' boycott of streetcars in, 77; blacks' migration from, 77–78, 88; reactions to antilynching reform in, 88, 91

Memphis Commercial, 74, 76, 88, 91, 105, 176, 275–76 (n. 49)

Mercer, C. H., 229

Meriwether, Elizabeth Avery, 41, 42, 45

Meriwether, Lide, 41

Methodist Church, 12–13, 53, 64, 178, 298 (n. 48), 312 (n. 41)

Methodist Episcopal (ME) Church, 178, 208, 302 (n. 124), 309 (n. 1)

Metropolitan Community Center and People's Church, 226, 230, 247, 315 (n. 74)

Meyers, Susie, 235–39, 241, 319 (n. 139)

Migration of blacks: to Oklahoma, 70, 77, 78; from Memphis, 70, 77–78, 88; to northern cities, 127, 128, 130, 147, 161, 207, 208, 211, 230, 286 (n. 23); to Africa, 174, 297 (n. 26)

Milholland, John, 136, 137, 141

Military service of blacks, 116, 121, 131, 134, 147, 148, 157–58, 208, 209, 291 (n. 112), 308 (n. 226)

Miller, Kelly, 107, 124, 130, 143, 286 (n. 23), 312 (n. 41)

Minor v. Happersett, 273 (n. 6)

Minstrelsy, 25

Miscegenation and anti-miscegenation laws, 86, 88, 91, 94, 105, 201, 306 (n. 173), 307 (n. 188)

Miss America pageant, 312 (n. 45)

Mississippi, 73, 237, 272–73 (n. 2). *See also* Holly Springs, Miss.; Jackson, Miss.; Vicksburg, Miss.

Mississippi-Yazoo delta flood, 237

Missouri, 292 (n. 135), 308 (n. 228)

Mitchell, John, Jr., 129

Mob Rule in New Orleans (Wells-Barnett), 117–18, 119, 120

"Model Woman" (Wells-Barnett), 52, 54–55

Montgomery, Bertha, 203, 239, 241

Montgomery, Isaiah, 73

Montgomery, Ala., 78

Moody, Dwight, 192

Moore, Frank, 163

Moore, Mrs. Frank, 162, 163

Morris, Charles, 47, 49, 50

Morris, Edward H., 183, 285–86 (n. 12)

Mosby, John, 75

Moses, Wilson, 108

Mossell, Gertrude, 38, 45, 60, 62, 268 (n. 119)

women's clubs associated with, 191;
women's activities at, 191, 192, 212;
Wells-Barnett's leadership of, 191,
193, 213; membership dues for, 191,
194; clubs associated with, 191, 194,
199; chorus of, 191, 194, 303 (n. 128);
and gender issues, 191–92, 193; education and training programs at,
192–93; housing at, 193, 194; employment service of, 193, 194, 206,
211, 308 (n. 227); from 1913 to 1915,
194; and Republican Party work, 194;
and woman suffrage, 194; and court
system, 195; and World War I, 207–
12; impact of, on neighborhood, 295
(n. 2); Wilson as investigator for, 315
(n. 71)
Negro in Our History (Woodson), 8, 256–
57 (n. 3)
Negro Mutual Protective Association,
69
Negro Yearbook, 128, 147
Nellis, Sheriff (Cairo, Ill.), 290 (nn. 86,
93)
Nelson, Alice Dunbar, 176
New Deal, 219
New Negro for a New Century (Washington, Wood, and Williams), 65,
116, 131
New Orleans, 117–18, 284 (nn. 235–
36), 317 (n. 113)
Newspapers. *See* Journalism; *Chicago
Defender; and other specific newspapers*
New York, 18, 22, 29, 79, 104, 106, 108,
127, 128, 142–43, 147, 268 (n. 119),
313 (n. 51)
New York Age, 23, 61, 79, 81, 84, 88, 90,
129, 145–46
New York Times, 105, 165, 295 (n. 189)
New York Tribune, 105
NFL. *See* Negro Fellowship League
Niagara Movement, 131, 132, 133, 136,
137, 148, 183, 243, 250
Nightingale, Rev. Taylor, 68, 69–70, 71,
73, 91, 186, 269 (n. 156), 275 (n. 37)
Nineteenth Amendment, 5, 166, 221,
245
NLRCWC. *See* National League of
Republican Colored Women's Clubs

Nonpartisanship for women, 198–99,
201–2, 221–22, 236, 251
North American Review, 81, 123
North Carolina, 115, 171, 280 (n. 156),
317 (n. 116)
Northwestern University, 177
Noted Negro Women (Majors), 38
Nye, Gerald, 317 (n. 112)

Ohio, 107, 110, 127, 175, 280 (n. 156)
Oklahoma, 70, 77, 78
Olson, Harry, 194, 195, 196, 202, 206
O'Neill, Lottie Holman, 320 (n. 148)
Original Rights Society, 143–44
"Our Women" (Wells-Barnett), 52, 54
Ovington, Mary White, 136, 137, 142,
290 (n. 96), 295 (n. 189)

Paine, Thomas, 85, 274 (n. 18)
Painter, Nell Irvin, 280 (n. 151)
Palmetto, Ga., 116
Pan-Africanism, 252
Parable telling, 9, 10, 11, 26–30
Paris, Tex., 90
Park, Robert, 211
Parker, Judge (N.C.), 317 (n. 116)
Parsons, Lucy, 105
Patterson, Benjamin, 74, 271 (n. 199)
Payne, Bishop, 84
Payne, O. B., 202
Peale, Norman Vincent, 278 (n. 100)
Pelley, Anna, 138
Pen names: of Wells-Barnett, 3, 9, 17,
19, 24, 30, 31, 34, 35, 44, 79, 82, 84,
251–52, 253; of journalists generally,
17
Penn, I. Garland, 96
Pennsylvania. *See* Philadelphia
People's Church, 226, 230, 247, 315
(n. 74)
People's Movement, 161
Philadelphia, 18, 19, 27–28, 29, 78, 79,
84, 92, 103, 106–7, 112, 147
Phillis Wheatley Home, 171, 189, 213,
215–16, 218, 225, 301 (n. 105), 309
(n. 1), 316 (n. 92)
Philpott, Thomas, 213
Pickens, William, 290 (n. 96)
Pierce, Leonard, 117

Plessy, Homère-Adolph, 82, 91
Police: black police in Memphis, 40;
failure to protect black prisoners
against lynching, 76–77, 138–40; and
stopping rape, 125, 127–28; intervention by, against lynchings, 127, 290
(n. 86); and East St. Louis race riot,
152; and Chicago race riot, 155; and
Arkansas case, 159; Barnett's work
against harassment by, 210; women
as, 225, 229, 315 (n. 71); in black
schools, 228; bias in policing in Chicago, 228, 314 (nn. 64–65); and
Mississippi-Yazoo delta flood, 237;
and violence against blacks in Chicago, 305 (n. 163), 314 (n. 61)
Political parties. See specific parties
Populism, 74
Populist Party, 82, 84, 106, 280 (n. 156),
280 (n. 155)
Pragmatism. See Visionary pragmatism
Prayers. See Religious faith
Presbyterian Church, 187–88, 193, 301
(n. 95)
Price, J. C., 81
Prisons and prisoners, 113, 188, 197,
210, 227–29, 308 (n. 231), 314
(nn. 60–61)
Probation. See Adult probation
Progressive Party, 172, 182, 201, 296
(n. 15), 317 (n. 113)
Progressivism, 122–23, 145, 146, 165,
166, 171–72, 190, 205, 206, 219
Propertius, 265 (n. 60)
Prostitutes, 228, 314 (n. 65)
Psalms, Book of, 139, 261–62 (nn. 103–
4)
Public health, 219–20

Quakers, 22, 93, 99, 265 (n. 56)

"Race Pride" (Wells-Barnett), 63, 64
Race relations: white supremacy in
Memphis, 70–75; miscegenation and
anti-miscegenation laws, 86, 88, 91,
94, 105, 201, 306 (n. 173), 307 (n. 188);
interracial marriage, 94; lynchings
caused by racism, 112, 117, 119, 124,
125, 127, 131; scientific racism, 113;

between black and white women,
184, 221, 232, 300 (n. 73); and Frederick Douglass Center, 184, 299
(n. 72); and city employment in Chicago, 195–96; Chicago Defender on, in
1910s and 1920s, 195–96, 204, 220,
223–24, 226–27, 229–30, 245; and
woman suffrage movement, 200–
201; whites' need to prove their
superiority, 288 (n. 43); racism in
northern universities, 290 (n. 96). See
also Blacks; Black women; Lynchings;
Race riots; Segregation; Whites;
White women
Race riots: in Chicago, 27, 29, 128, 155–
56, 189, 211, 213, 293 (n. 153); in
Memphis, 40; in Wilmington, N.C.,
115, 284 (n. 236); in New Orleans,
117–18; in New York City, 127, 147;
in Atlanta, 134; in Springfield, Ill.,
134, 188; in East St. Louis, 149–55,
208, 210, 292 (nn. 134–35, 142), 293
(nn. 149–50); in Arkansas, 159–65,
166, 211; Carey on, 294 (n. 170)
Racial uplift: definition of, xii; black
women as agent and symbol of, 38–
39, 118, 133–34, 225, 245, 249–51,
309 (n. 6), 321 (n. 165); and race
pride, 63, 64, 69; and churches, 64,
179, 181; and women's clubs, 69; celebrations of black pride, 74, 103, 194,
233, 306 (n. 173), 307 (n. 203); and
motherhood, 133–34, 135, 289
(n. 59); black men as agent and symbol of, 188; and political involvement
in 1920s, 220–23
Racism. See Lynchings; Race relations;
Race riots; Segregation
Railroads, 43–44, 51, 70, 71–72, 82, 264
(n. 36)
Randolph, A. Philip, 226
Ransom, Emma, 111
Ransom, Rev. Reverdy C., 111, 116, 132,
143, 179, 181–83, 185, 186, 192, 298
(n. 53)
Rape: lynching-for-rape myth, 18, 78,
83, 85–87, 90, 102, 105–6, 108, 110–
11, 113, 124, 125, 127, 135, 147, 274
(n. 16), 285 (n. 12), 287 (n. 28); of

black women and girls, 85, 87–88, 114, 123–24, 168, 244–45, 283 (n. 216), 286 (n. 15); Addams on sexism and, 125; criminal prosecution for, 125, 127–28, 210, 287 (n. 29); and Atlanta riot, 134; and black soldiers, 134

Rope and Faggot (W. White), 160, 291 (n. 117)

Reconstruction, 9, 10, 45, 252

Red Cross, 207, 209, 239, 313 (n. 51)

Red Record, A (Wells), 112–14, 117, 119

Reed, Nannie, 238

Religious faith: of Wells-Barnett, 2, 3, 12–14, 17, 21, 27–28, 34, 50–51, 53–54, 58, 59, 63–70, 72, 79, 102, 139–40, 165, 213–14; of black women, 2, 3, 34, 53, 63–70; and white Protestant women, 3; of Lizzie Wells, 12; prayers of Wells-Barnett, 13, 17, 51, 58, 59, 67, 72, 165; Memphis churches, 41, 65–69, 269–70 (n. 156); biblical women, 53–54, 132, 133, 135, 179, 280 (n. 148); and critique of the ministry by black women, 64–65; church membership of Wells-Barnett, 65–66, 186–87, 226, 230, 269–70 (n. 156); Sunday school teaching by Wells-Barnett, 66, 67, 73, 134, 187; and Social Gospel, 98, 126; churches' failure to rebuke lynching, 99–102; and sacredness of the ballot, 172–74, 246, 252; Chicago churches, 178–83, 186–88, 230; church membership of F. Barnett, 186–87, 300–301 (n. 88); and women's clubs, 218; and woman suffrage, 297 (n. 20); Du Bois on, 312 (n. 41). *See also* Bible; Visionary pragmatism; *and specific churches and ministers*

Republican Party: and Sampson, 45, 265 (n. 74); and antilynching reform, 107, 166; violent strategies against, in South, 115; in Cairo, Ill., 140; and Deneen, 141; and Wells-Barnett, 175, 183, 239–40, 242–43, 297 (n. 21); in Chicago and Illinois, 178, 182, 201, 203, 205–6, 208, 223–24, 230, 235–

36, 238–44, 307 (n. 201); and black women, 191, 192, 202, 216, 221, 229, 232, 234–36, 237, 239–42, 318 (n. 130); and Negro Fellowship League, 194; Progressive Party's impact on, 201; Abbott on, 223–24; Medill and Ruth Hanna McCormick in, 235–36, 240–41; and testimonials, 235; and Dickinson, 265 (n. 56). *See also specific Republican politicians*

Reputation of Victorian women, 15–17, 46, 78

Rhode Island Association of Colored Women's Clubs, 297 (n. 20)

Rice, Lutie, 56, 267 (n. 102)

Richardson, Ellen, 22, 101

Richardson, Eola, 309 (n. 3)

Richings, G. F., 109

Richmond (Va.) Planet, 129, 148, 149

Ridley, Florida Ruffin, 101

Roberts, Adelbert, 242

Rockefeller, John D., 278 (n. 100)

Roosevelt, Theodore, 127, 287 (n. 29), 294–95 (n. 183), 296 (n. 15), 300 (n. 72)

Rosenwald, Julius, 313 (n. 51)

Ruffin, Josephine St. Pierre, 111, 115

Rural unrest, 74, 75

Russell, Charles Edward, 137

Russell, Elizabeth, 309 (n. 3)

Rust College, 12

St. Louis, 280 (n. 145)

Salzner, Harry, 138

Sampson, Benjamin K., 45–46, 88, 265 (n. 47), 268 (n. 114)

Santa Clara v. Southern Pacific Railroad, 273 (n. 6)

Sawaya, Francesca, 259 (n. 39)

Schools for blacks. *See* Education of blacks

Scientific racism, 113

Scotland, 23, 94, 98

Scottsboro Boys, 247

Scruggs, Lawson V., 38

Segregation: in Memphis, 42, 51, 70, 71–72; of railroads, 43–44, 51, 71–72, 82, 264 (n. 36); Jim Crow laws, 72, 131, 223–24, 226–27, 230, 290

(n. 96); at World's Columbian Exposition (1893), 96; in WCTU, 102; in women's club movement, 111–12; in Chicago and Illinois, 188–89, 201, 223–24, 226–27; and woman suffrage movement, 200–201; of public accommodations, 201; of schools, 204, 205, 224, 229–30; antisegregation fight in Chicago high school, 204, 205, 229–30; criticisms of Wells-Barnett's resistance to, 204–5; in housing, 226–27; in trade unions, 230; in federal employment in Washington, D.C., 306 (n. 188). *See also* Race relations

Self-defense for blacks, 76, 77, 84, 116, 128, 129, 142, 146, 148–49, 151, 159, 273 (n. 11), 284 (n. 236), 287 (n. 34)

Settle, Josiah, 47

Settlement movement. *See* Douglass Center; Hull-House; Negro Fellowship League; Phillis Wheatley Home; *and other settlements*

Settle, Theresa, 47, 68

Sexism. *See* Gender relations

Sexual assault. *See* Rape

Shakespeare, William, 48, 49, 120, 130, 157

Shame of America (Anti-Lynching Crusaders), 165, 166

Shapiro, Herbert, 284 (n. 236)

Shaw, Edward, 40, 71, 265 (n. 47)

Shaw, Stephanie J., 220, 266 (n. 92)

Shaw University, 12, 46, 47

Sheppard-Towner Infancy and Maternity Act, 219–20

Simmons, Roscoe, 245

Simmons, Rev. William J., 60, 68

Simpson, Mrs. M. W., 245

Sims, Lulu, 309 (n. 3)

Skin color, 24–25, 105. *See also* Body issues

Slander against women, 275

Slave narratives, 10, 11, 26, 258 (n. 12)

Slavery: resistance to, 3; Wells-Barnett's parents as slaves, 10, 11, 14, 33; violence and sexual assault against slave women, 14–15, 114, 124, 245; stereotypes of slave women, 24; slave

mother as deserving of pity, 114. *See also* Antislavery movement

Small, Len, 229

Smiley, J. Hockley, 187

Smith, Alberta Moore, 195–96

Smith, Amanda, 2, 38, 67, 93, 102, 187, 193, 205, 213, 251, 300 (n. 87), 303 (n. 126)

Smith, Frank L., 236–37, 238, 317 (n. 116)

Smith, Lucy Wilmot, 60

Social Darwinism, 133

Social Gospel, 98, 126

Society for the Recognition of the Brotherhood of Man (SRBM), 92, 93, 97, 98, 99, 102, 109, 281 (n. 181)

Society of Friends, 22, 93, 99, 265 (n. 56)

Soldiers. *See* Military service of blacks

Somerset, Lady Henry, 102

Sorosis, 268 (n. 119)

Souls of Black Folk (Du Bois), 37, 130, 164

South Carolina, 115–16, 280 (n. 156)

Southern Horrors (Wells-Barnett), 4, 14, 18, 21, 37, 84–88, 90, 94, 99, 113, 124, 163, 174, 272 (n. 230)

Southern Press Association, 272 (n. 230)

Spanish-American War, 116

Speedy, Nettie George, 232, 234, 238, 240, 317 (n. 101)

Spingarn, Joel, 142, 146, 167, 197

Springfield, Ill., 26, 128, 134, 141, 188

SRBM. *See* Society for the Recognition of the Brotherhood of Man

Stanton, Elizabeth Cady, 24, 57, 297 (n. 20)

Stereotypes: of black women, 8, 9, 24, 35, 114, 142, 143–44, 232, 244–45; of black men, 130

Stewart, Henry, 75–78

Stewart, Maria, 2, 4, 28, 85, 115, 133, 251, 252, 258 (n. 9)

Still, William, 92

Storey, Moorefield, 159

"Story of 1900" (Wells-Barnett), 52, 54

Stowe, Harriet Beecher, 101, 118, 236, 278 (n. 111)

West, Cornel, 3
Wheatley, Phillis, 269 (n. 152)
White, Deborah Gray, 245, 309 (n. 6)
White, Walter F., 122, 160–61, 162, 168, 291 (n. 117), 292 (n. 140)
White Caps, 74
Whites: and Wells-Barnett's stage presence, 25–26; dismissal and criticisms of Wells-Barnett by, 33–34, 88, 91, 99–100, 101, 104–7, 111, 119; criminality of, 75, 88; consensual sex across the color line, 85, 86, 88, 93, 94, 110–11, 113, 119, 124; rape of black women by white men, 85, 87, 114, 123–24, 168; indifference of, to lynchings, 90, 113, 126, 131; and blacks' responsibility for antilynching reform, 109–10; Wells-Barnett's indictment of white civilization, 112, 117, 119, 147; lynchings of, 127, 138; white manhood, 131; and NAACP organizing meetings, 136; and Du Bois, 137; as politicians in Chicago, 205
White women: and stereotypes of black women, 9, 24, 142, 232; and lynching-for-rape myth, 18, 78, 83, 85–87, 90, 102, 105–6, 108, 110–11, 113, 124, 125, 127, 135, 147, 274 (n. 16), 285 (n. 12), 287 (n. 28); dismissal of Wells-Barnett by, 33–34; activism of, in Memphis, 41–43, 55, 264 (n. 26); as spinsters, 55, 266 (n. 93); consensual sex across the color line, 85, 86, 88, 93, 94, 110–11, 113, 119, 124; role of, in abetting mobs, 85, 138; charges of free love and sexual decadence against, 93–94; lynching and southern white women, 123, 124; lynching of, 165; and settlement movement, 170; interracial gatherings with white women, 184, 232, 300 (n. 73); abuse of black domestic servants by, 197–98; and World War I, 208–9; as political candidates and officeholders, 216, 235–36, 240–41, 246, 251, 320 (n. 148); in women's club movement, 218; and nonpartisanship, 221, 236, 251; as police officers, 225; as jour-

nalists, 237, 268 (n. 119); moral standard for, compared with black women, 245; and penal system for women, 314 (n. 67)
Wilberforce, Canon, 101
Wilberforce University, 92, 179, 183
Wilkins, Rev. D. R., 269 (n. 156)
Willard, Frances E., 41, 66, 102, 108, 110–12, 124, 179, 252, 282–83 (nn. 200–201)
Williams, A. M., 141
Williams, Charles H., 110
Williams, Delores S., 26, 259 (n. 46)
Williams, Fannie Barrier, 28, 64–65, 69, 103, 111–12, 129, 199, 300 (n. 72)
Williams, Mrs. George S., 237
Williams, L. Laing, 155
Wilmington, Del., 127
Wilmington, N.C., 115, 284 (n. 236)
Wilson, Grace, 315 (n. 71)
Wilson, J., 244–45
Wilson, Woodrow, 150, 157, 164, 209, 295 (n. 183), 306 (n. 188)
Wolf, Mrs. K. L., 305 (n. 158)
Woman's Building at 1893 World's Fair, 170
Woman's Christian Temperance Union (WCTU), 41, 66, 102, 110–12, 170, 179, 270 (n. 157), 282–83 (nn. 198, 200–201)
Woman's City Club of Chicago, 300 (n. 73)
Woman's Forum, 231
"Woman's Mission" (Wells-Barnett), 52, 53–54
Woman suffrage, 1, 5, 41, 82, 103, 171, 173, 191–92, 194, 198–203, 219, 221, 224, 235, 245, 250, 273 (n. 6), 297 (n. 20), 304–5 (n. 158), 310 (n. 6)
Woman's World Fair, 226, 313 (n. 55)
Women. *See* Black women; White women; Women's clubs; *and specific women*
Women of Distinction (Scruggs), 38
Women's Auxiliary Union, 311 (n. 40)
Women's clubs: definition of club women, xii; political involvement of, 5, 191–92, 198–207, 216–23, 232–33, 235, 238–39, 241, 243; Wells-

GENDER AND AMERICAN CULTURE

Ida B. Wells-Barnett and American Reform, 1880–1930, by Patricia A. Schechter (2001)

Taking Haiti: Military Occupation and the Culture of U.S. Imperialism, 1915–1940, by Mary A. Renda (2001)

Before Jim Crow: The Politics of Race in Postemancipation Virginia, by Jane Dailey (2000)

Captain Ahab Had a Wife: New England Women and the Whalefishery, 1720–1870, by Lisa Norling (2000)

Civilizing Capitalism: The National Consumers' League, Women's Activism, and Labor Standards in the New Deal Era, by Landon R. Y. Storrs (2000)

Rank Ladies: Gender and Cultural Hierarchy in American Vaudeville, by M. Alison Kibler (1999)

Strangers and Pilgrims: Female Preaching in America, 1740–1845, by Catherine A. Brekus (1998)

Sex and Citizenship in Antebellum America, by Nancy Isenberg (1998)

Yours in Sisterhood: Ms. Magazine and the Promise of Popular Feminism, by Amy Erdman Farrell (1998)

We Mean to Be Counted: White Women and Politics in Antebellum Virginia, by Elizabeth R. Varon (1998)

Women Against the Good War: Conscientious Objection and Gender on the American Home Front, 1941–1947, by Rachel Waltner Goossen (1997)

Toward an Intellectual History of Women: Essays by Linda K. Kerber (1997)

Gender and Jim Crow: Women and the Politics of White Supremacy in North Carolina, 1896–1920, by Glenda Elizabeth Gilmore (1996)

Delinquent Daughters: Protecting and Policing Adolescent Female Sexuality in the United States, 1885–1920, by Mary E. Odem (1995)

U.S. History as Women's History: New Feminist Essays, edited by Linda K. Kerber, Alice Kessler-Harris, and Kathryn Kish Sklar (1995)

Common Sense and a Little Fire: Women and Working-Class Politics in the United States, 1900–1965, by Annelise Orleck (1995)

How Am I to Be Heard?: Letters of Lillian Smith, edited by Margaret Rose Gladney (1993)

Entitled to Power: Farm Women and Technology, 1913–1963, by Katherine Jellison (1993)

Revising Life: Sylvia Plath's Ariel Poems, by Susan R. Van Dyne (1993)

Made From This Earth: American Women and Nature, by Vera Norwood (1993)

Unruly Women: The Politics of Social and Sexual Control in the Old South, by Victoria E. Bynum (1992)

The Work of Self-Representation: Lyric Poetry in Colonial New England, by Ivy Schweitzer (1991)

Labor and Desire: Women's Revolutionary Fiction in Depression America, by Paula Rabinowitz (1991)

Community of Suffering and Struggle: Women, Men, and the Labor Movement in Minneapolis, 1915–1945, by Elizabeth Faue (1991)

All That Hollywood Allows: Re-reading Gender in 1950s Melodrama, by Jackie Byars (1991)

Doing Literary Business: American Women Writers in the Nineteenth Century, by Susan Coultrap-McQuin (1990)

Ladies, Women, and Wenches: Choice and Constraint in Antebellum Charleston and Boston, by Jane H. Pease and William H. Pease (1990)

The Secret Eye: The Journal of Ella Gertrude Clanton Thomas, 1848–1889, edited by Virginia Ingraham Burr, with an introduction by Nell Irvin Painter (1990)

Second Stories: The Politics of Language, Form, and Gender in Early American Fictions, by Cynthia S. Jordan (1989)

Within the Plantation Household: Black and White Women of the Old South, by Elizabeth Fox-Genovese (1988)

The Limits of Sisterhood: The Beecher Sisters on Women's Rights and Woman's Sphere, by Jeanne Boydston, Mary Kelley, and Anne Margolis (1988)